COMPUTER ENGINEERING
Hardware Design

M. Morris Mano
Professor of Engineering
California State University, Los Angeles

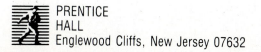
PRENTICE
HALL
Englewood Cliffs, New Jersey 07632

Library of Congress Cataloging-in-Publication Data
MANO, M. MORRIS
   Computer engineering.

   Includes bibliographies and index.
   1. Computer engineering.   I. Title.
TK7885.M27   1988   621.39   87-29282
ISBN 0-13-162926-3

Editorial/production supervision: Colleen Brosnan
Interior design: Christine Gehring-Wolf
Cover art created by GENIGRAPHICS
Manufacturing buyer: Margaret Rizzi

 © 1988 by Prentice-Hall, Inc.
A Division of Simon & Schuster
Englewood Cliffs, New Jersey 07632

Printed in the United States of America
10 9 8 7 6 5 4 3 2 1

ISBN   0-13-162926-3

Prentice-Hall International (UK) Limited, *London*
Prentice-Hall of Australia Pty. Limited, *Sydney*
Prentice-Hall Canada Inc., *Toronto*
Prentice-Hall Hispanoamericana, S.A., *Mexico*
Prentice-Hall of India Private Limited, *New Delhi*
Prentice-Hall of Japan, Inc., *Tokyo*
Simon & Schuster Asia Pte. Ltd., *Singapore*
Editora Prentice-Hall do Brasil, Ltda., *Rio de Janeiro*

CONTENTS

3 COMBINATIONAL SYSTEMS 79

4 SEQUENTIAL LOGIC 120

5 REGISTERS AND COUNTERS 152

6 MEMORY AND PROGRAMMABLE LOGIC   186

7 REGISTER TRANSFER AND COMPUTER OPERATIONS   220

8 CONTROL LOGIC DESIGN   257

9 COMPUTER INSTRUCTIONS AND ADDRESSING MODES   296

10 DESIGN OF A CENTRAL PROCESSING UNIT (CPU)   333

11 INPUT-OUTPUT AND COMMUNICATION   378

12 MEMORY MANAGEMENT   409

INDEX   427

PREFACE

Computer and Electrical Engineering programs include one or more courses that provide an understanding of the hardware design of digital systems and digital computers. Computer Science curricula introduce similar courses that deal with basic digital systems and computer organization. This book covers all aspects of computer hardware engineering from basic digital circuits to the structure of a complete computer system. It introduces the principles of computer hardware and provides the concepts needed to analyze and design digital systems.

The material covered in the book can be divided into three parts. The first four chapters deal with digital circuits from the gate and flip-flop level and present the analysis and design of combinational and sequential circuits. The next four chapters introduce digital design from the register transfer level. The various components of a computer processor unit are detailed and the design of control logic is described using the hardwire and microprogram methods. The last four chapters focus on the hardware components of the digital computer. A central processing unit (CPU) is designed using a microprogrammed control. Input and output procedures are presented together with the hardware associated with virtual memory management.

The book covers the material recommended by the IEEE Computer Society Model Program in Computer Science and Engineering subject area 6 (logic design) and subject area 7 (digital systems design). It also conforms with most of the subjects listed in course CS4, introduction to computer organization, in the ACM Curriculum Recommendations for the Undergraduate Program in Computer Science.

Often used digital components are available commercially in integrated circuits and are classified as MSI (medium scale integration) circuits. Standard graphic symbols have been developed for these components so that the user can recognize each function from the unique graphic symbol assigned to it. This standard, known as ANSI/IEEE Std. 91-1984, has been adopted by industry, government, and professional organizations. The best time to learn the standard symbols is when learning about digital systems. They are introduced throughout the book at the same time that the operation of the corresponding components are explained.

The sequence in which the material is presented provides an orderly and logical transition from the basic ideas of representing binary information to the concepts of complex computer operations. Chapter 1 presents various binary systems suitable for representing information in digital components. The binary number system is explained and binary codes are illustrated to show the representation of decimal and alphanumeric information. Chapter 2 introduces Boolean algebra and the map simplification of Boolean functions. The characteristics of digital logic gates are presented together with various possible implementations of digital logic circuits.

Chapter 3 provides procedures for the analysis and design of combinational circuits. Often used digital components such as adders, decoders, and multiplexers are analyzed and their internal construction explained. The standard graphic symbols are introduced in this chapter. However, the standard graphic symbols for components covered in subsequent chapters are shown later. Chapter 4 presents various types of flip-flops and outlines formal procedures for the analysis and design of sequential circuits.

Chapter 5 presents various sequential digital components such as registers, shift registers, and counters. These digital components are the basic building blocks from which digital computers and other digital systems are constructed. Chapter 6 deals with the memory unit and programmable logic devices such as PROM, PLA, and PAL. These components are very useful in the design and construction of complex digital circuits.

Chapter 7 introduces the register transfer method of describing digital systems. Symbols are defined for arithmetic, logic, and shift microoperations. An arithmetic logic unit is designed and a typical processor unit is developed. Chapter 8 presents methods of control logic design. Examples are given to show how the design algorithm is developed from which we proceed to show the procedure for obtaining the control subsystem. The chapter concludes with the design of a simple computer with a hardwired control unit.

Chapter 9 enumerates the most common instructions found in a typical computer together with explanations of their function. Various instruction formats are illustrated and typical addressing modes are presented in preparation for the design undertaken in the next chapter.

Chapter 10 is devoted to the design of a central processing unit (CPU). The registers of the system are defined and the computer instruction formats are specified. A microprogrammed control unit is developed together with the microinstruction formats. Some examples of microprogram routines for typical instructions with different addressing modes are presented. The chapter provides enough information for the hardware and firmware construction of the CPU.

Chapter 11 discusses the requirements of an interface between the processor and input or output devices. Various modes of transfer are explained including synchronous and asynchronous serial transfer, direct memory access, and priority interrupt. Chapter 12 introduces the concept of memory hierarchy, composed of cache, main, and auxiliary memories. The concept of memory management is introduced through the presentation of the hardware requirements for cache memory and virtual memory systems.

The book is suitable for a two-term course in basic computer engineering hardware design. Parts of the book can be used in a one-term course in a variety of ways: (1) as a first course in digital logic design using material from Chapters 1 through 8; (2) in a course on computer design with a prerequisite of basic digital circuits or switching theory, covering material from Chapters 5 through 12; or (3) in conjunction with an assembly language programming course or a computer organization course, covering the hardware aspects of computers from Chapters 9 through 12.

Each chapter includes a list of references and a set of problems. Some problems serve as exercises for the material covered in the chapter. Others are more difficult and are intended to provide some practice in solving problems associated with the area of digital computer hardware design. A solutions manual for the instructor is available from the publisher.

M. Morris Mano

1

BINARY NUMBERS AND CODES

1-1 DIGITAL COMPUTERS

Digital computers occupy a prominent place in modern society. They have contributed to many scientific, industrial, and commercial developments that would have been unattainable otherwise. Computers are used in home entertainment, medical treatment, weather prediction, space exploration, air traffic control, scientific calculations, business data processing, and numerous other fields of endeavor. The most striking property of the digital computer is its generality. It can follow a sequence of instruction, called a *program*, that operates on given data. The user can specify and change the program or the data according to specific needs. As a result of this flexibility, general purpose digital computers can perform a variety of information processing tasks that range over a wide spectrum of applications.

The general purpose digital computer is the best-known example of a digital system. Characteristic of a digital system is its manipulation of *discrete elements* of information. Discrete information is contained in any set that is restricted to a finite number of elements. Examples of discrete quantities are the 10 decimal digits, the 26 letters of the alphabet, the 52 playing cards, and the 64 squares of a chessboard. Early digital computers were used mostly for numeric computations. In this case the discrete elements used are the digits. From this application, the term *digital computer* has emerged.

Discrete elements of information are represented in a digital system by physical quantities called *signals*. Electrical signals such as voltages and currents are the most common. The signals in all present-day electronic digital systems have only two discrete values and are said to be *binary*. The digital system designer is restricted

1

to the use of binary signals because of the low reliability encountered in many-valued electronic circuits. In other words, a circuit with ten states, using one discrete voltage value for each state, can be designed, but it would possess a very low reliability of operation. In contrast, a transistor circuit that is either on or off has two possible signal values and can be constructed with extreme reliability. Because of this physical restriction of electronic components, and because human logic tends to be binary (true or false, yes or no), digital systems that are constrained to take discrete values are further constrained to take binary values.

Digital computers use the binary number system that has two digits: 0 and 1. A binary digit is called a *bit*. Information is represented in digital computers in groups of bits. By using various coding techniques, groups of bits can be made to represent not only binary numbers but also any other group of discrete symbols. By judicious use of binary arrangements to form binary codes, the group of bits are used to develop complete sets of instructions for performing computations on various types of data.

Discrete quantities of information emerge either from the nature of the process or may be purposely quantized from a continuous process. For example, a payroll schedule is an inherently discrete process that contains employee names, social security numbers, weekly salaries, income taxes, and so on. An employee's paycheck is processed using discrete data values such as letters of the alphabet (name), digits (salary), and special symbols like $. On the other hand, a research scientist may observe a process that continuously varies with time but record only specific quantities in tabular form. The scientist is thus quantizing the continuous data, making each number in the table a discrete quantity of information.

To simulate a process in a digital computer, the quantities must be quantized. When the variables of the process are presented by continuous real-time signals, the signals are quantized by an analog-to-digital conversion device. A system whose behavior may be described with mathematical equations is simulated in a digital computer by means of numerical analysis methods that formulate the mathematical equations with a series of discrete numerical quantities. When the problem to be processed is inherently discrete, as in commercial or business applications, the digital computer manipulates the variables in their original form.

A block diagram of the digital computer is shown in Figure 1-1. The memory unit stores programs as well as input, output, and intermediate data. The processor unit performs arithmetic and other data-processing operations as specified by the program. The control unit supervises the flow of information between the various units. A processor, when combined with the control unit, forms a component referred to as a *central processing unit* or CPU. A CPU enclosed in a small integrated circuit package is called a *microprocessor*.

The program and data prepared by the user are transferred into the memory unit by means of an input device such as a keyboard. An output device, such as a printer, receives the results of the computations, and the printed results are presented to the user. A digital computer can accommodate many different input and output devices. These devices are special digital systems driven by electromechanical parts and controlled by electronic digital circuits.

The control unit in the CPU retrieves the instructions, one by one, from the program stored in the memory unit. For each instruction, the control unit informs

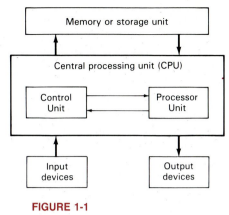

FIGURE 1-1
Block Diagram of a Digital Computer

the processor to execute the operation specified by the instruction. Both program and data are stored in memory. The control unit supervises the program instructions, and the processor unit manipulates the data as specified by the program. A digital computer is a powerful instrument. It can perform arithmetic computations as well as logical operations and can be programmed to make decisions based on internal and external conditions.

A digital computer is an interconnection of digital modules. To understand the operation of each digital module, it is necessary to have a basic knowledge of digital systems and their general behavior. The first half of the book deals with digital systems in general to provide the background necessary for their design and analysis. The second half of the book discusses the various components of the digital computer, their operation, and design. The operational characteristics of the memory unit are explained in Chapter 6. The organization and design of the processor unit are discussed in Chapter 7. Methods for designing the control unit are introduced in Chapter 8. Some typical instructions employed in digital computers are presented in Chapter 9. The organization and design of a typical central processing unit is presented in Chapter 10. The various ways that a CPU can communicate with input and output devices is discussed in Chapter 11. Memory management concepts are introduced in Chapter 12.

It has been mentioned that a digital computer manipulates discrete elements of information and that all information in the computer is represented in binary form. Operands used for calculations may be expressed in the binary number system, or in the decimal system, by means of a binary code. The letters of the alphabet are also converted into a binary code. The purpose of this chapter is to introduce the binary number system and the various binary codes as a frame of reference for further study in the succeeding chapters.

1-2 NUMBER SYSTEMS

The decimal number system is employed in everyday arithmetic to represent numbers with strings of digits. Each digit position in the string has an associated value of an integer raised to the power of 10. For example, the decimal number 724.5

is interpreted to represent 7 hundreds plus 2 tens plus 4 units plus 5 tenths. The hundreds, tens, units, and tenths are powers of 10 implied by the position of the digits. The value of the number is computed as follows:

$$724.5 = 7 \times 10^2 + 2 \times 10^1 + 4 \times 10^0 + 5 \times 10^{-1}$$

The convention is to write only the digits and deduce the corresponding powers of 10 from their positions. In general, a decimal number with a decimal point is represented by a string of coefficients:

$$\ldots A_5 A_4 A_3 A_2 A_1 A_0 . A_{-1} A_{-2} A_{-3} \ldots$$

Each A_i coefficient is one of 10 digits (0, 1, 2, 3, 4, 5, 6, 7, 8, 9). The subscript value i gives the position of the coefficient and, hence, the weight 10^i by which the coefficient must be multiplied.

The decimal number system is said to be of *base* or *radix* 10 because the coefficients are multiplied by powers of 10 and the system uses ten distinct digits. In general, a number in base r contains r digits 0, 1, 2, $\ldots$, $r-1$ and is expressed with a power series in r.

$$A_n r^n + A_{n-1} r^{n-1} + \ldots + A_1 r^1 + A_0 r^0 + A_{-1} r^{-1} + A_{-2} r^{-2} + \ldots$$

When the number is expressed in positional notation, only the coefficients and the radix point are written down:

$$A_n A_{n-1} \ldots A_1 A_0 . A_{-1} A_{-2} \ldots$$

To distinguish between numbers of different bases, it is customary to enclose the coefficients in parentheses and place a subscript after the right parenthesis to indicate the base of the number. However, when the content makes it obvious that the number is in decimal, it is not necessary to use the parentheses. The following illustrates a base 5 number and its conversion to decimal.

$$(312.4)_5 = 3 \times 5^2 + 1 \times 5^1 + 2 \times 5^0 + 4 \times 5^{-1}$$
$$= 75 + 5 + 2 + 0.8 = (82.8)_{10}$$

Note that for all the numbers not enclosed in parentheses the arithmetic is performed with decimal numbers. Also note that the base 5 system uses only 5 digits and therefore, the coefficient values in a number can be only 0, 1, 2, 3, and 4 when expressed in the base 5 system.

Three number systems are used extensively in computer work: binary, octal, and hexadecimal. They correspond to a number system of base 2, base 8, and base 16, respectively.

Binary Numbers

The binary number system is a base 2 system with two digits: 0 and 1. A binary number is expressed with a string of 1's and 0's and a possible binary point such as 11010.11. The decimal equivalent of a binary number can be found by expanding it to a power series with a base of 2. For example

$$(11010) = 1 \times 2^4 + 1 \times 2^3 + 0 \times 2^2 + 1 \times 2^1 + 0 \times 2^0 = (26)$$

TABLE 1-1
Powers of Two

n	2^n	n	2^n	n	2^n
0	1	8	256	16	65,536
1	2	9	512	17	131,072
2	4	10	1,024	18	262,144
3	8	11	2,048	19	524,288
4	16	12	4,096	20	1,048,576
5	32	13	8,192	21	2,097,152
6	64	14	16,384	22	4,194,304
7	128	15	32,768	23	8,388,608

As noted earlier, the digits in a binary number are called *bits*. When a bit is equal to 0, it does not contribute to the sum during the conversion. Therefore, the conversion to decimal can be obtained by adding the numbers with powers of two corresponding to the bits that are equal to 1. For example

$$(110101.11)_2 = 32 + 16 + 4 + 1 + 0.5 + 0.25 = (53.75)_{10}$$

The first 21 numbers obtained from 2 to the power of n are listed in Table 1-1. In computer work, 2^{10} is referred to as K (Kilo), 2^{20} as M (Mega), and 2^{30} as G (Giga). Thus $4K = 4096$ and $16M = 2^{24} = 16,777,216$.

   The conversion of a decimal number to binary can be easily achieved by a method that successively subtracts powers of two from the decimal number. To convert the decimal number N to binary, first find the greatest number from Table 1-1 that can be subtracted from N and produce a positive difference. Let the difference be designated by N_1. Find another number from Table 1-1 that can be subtracted from N_1 and produce a positive difference N_2. Continue this procedure until the difference is zero. In this way, the decimal number is converted to its powers-of-two components. The equivalent binary number is obtained from the power series that forms the sum of the components. This method is demonstrated below, by the conversion of decimal 625 to binary.

$$625 - 512 = 113 \qquad 512 = 2^9$$
$$113 - 64 = 49 \qquad 64 = 2^6$$
$$49 - 32 = 17 \qquad 32 = 2^5$$
$$17 - 16 = 1 \qquad 16 = 2^4$$
$$1 - 1 = 0 \qquad 1 = 2^0$$

$$(625)_{10} = 2^9 + 2^6 + 2^5 + 2^4 + 2^0 = (1001110001)_2$$

Note that all the subtractions can be done quickly using a calculator.

Octal and Hexadecimal Numbers

The octal number system is a base 8 system with eight digits (0, 1, 2, 3, 4, 5, 6, 7). An example of an octal number is 127.4. To determine its equivalent decimal value we expand the number in a power series with a base of 8.

$$(127.4)_8 = 1 \times 8^2 + 2 \times 8^1 + 7 \times 8^0 + 4 \times 8^{-1} = (87.5)_{10}$$

Note that the digits 8 and 9 cannot appear in an octal number.

It is customary to borrow the needed r digits for the coefficients from the decimal system when the base of the number is less than 10. The letters of the alphabet are used to supplement the digits when the base of the number is greater than 10. The hexadecimal number system is a base 16 system, with the first ten digits borrowed from the decimal system, and the letters A, B, C, D, E, and F used for digits 10, 11, 12, 13, 14, and 15, respectively. An example of a hexadecimal number is

$$(B65F)_{16} = 11 \times 16^3 + 6 \times 16^2 + 5 \times 16 + 15 = (46687)_{10}$$

The first 16 numbers in the decimal, binary, octal, and hexadecimal number systems are listed in Table 1-2. Note that the sequence of binary numbers follows a prescribed pattern: the first significant bit alternates between 0 and 1, the second significant bit alternates between two 0's and two 1's, the third significant bit alternates between four 0's and four 1's, and the fourth alternates between eight 0's and eight 1's.

As previously mentioned, all computers and digital systems use the binary representation. The octal and hexadecimal systems are useful for representing binary quantities indirectly because they possess the property that their bases are powers of two. Since $2^3 = 8$ and $2^4 = 16$, each octal digit corresponds to three binary digits and each hexadecimal digit corresponds to four binary digits. The conversion from binary to octal is easily accomplished by partitioning the binary number into groups of three digits each, starting from the binary point and proceeding to the left and to the right. The corresponding octal digit is then assigned to each group. The following example illustrates the procedure:

TABLE 1-2
Numbers with Different Bases

Decimal (base 10)	Binary (base 2)	Octal (base 8)	Hexadecimal (base 16)
00	0000	00	0
01	0001	01	1
02	0010	02	2
03	0011	03	3
04	0100	04	4
05	0101	05	5
06	0110	06	6
07	0111	07	7
08	1000	10	8
09	1001	11	9
10	1010	12	A
11	1011	13	B
12	1100	14	C
13	1101	15	D
14	1110	16	E
15	1111	17	F

$$(010\ 110\ 001\ 101\ 011.\ 111\ 100\ 000\ 110)_2 = (26153.7406)_8$$

The corresponding octal digit for each group of three bits is obtained from the first eight entries in Table 1-2. Note that 0's can be freely added to the left or right to make the total number of bits a multiple of three.

Conversion from binary to hexadecimal is similar, except that the binary number is divided into groups of four digits. The previous binary number is converted to hexadecimal as follows:

$$(0010\ 1100\ 0110\ 1011.\ 1111\ 0000\ 0110)_2 = (2C6B.F06)_{16}$$

The corresponding hexadecimal digit for each group of four bits is listed in Table 1-2.

Conversion from octal or hexadecimal to binary is done by a procedure reverse to that above. Each octal digit is converted to a three-digit binary equivalent. Similarly, each hexadecimal digit is converted to its four-digit binary equivalent. This is illustrated in the following examples:

$$(673.12)_8 = 110\ 111\ 011.\ 001\ 010 = (110111011.00101)_2$$

$$(3A6.C)_{16} = 0011\ 1010\ 0110.\ 1100 = (1110100110.11)_2$$

Most computer manuals use either octal or hexadecimal numbers to specify the binary quantities in the machine. A group of 15 bits, for example, can be represented in the octal system with only five digits in the range of 0 to 77777. A group of 16 bits can be represented in hexadecimal with four digits in the range from 0 to FFFF. The choice between octal or hexadecimal representation of binary numbers is arbitrary and is determined from the particular computer manual. During communication between people (about binary quantities in the computer) the octal or hexadecimal equivalent representation is more convenient because the numbers can be expressed more compactly with a third or fourth of the number of digits. When communicating with the computer, through console switches or by means of a machine language program, the conversion from octal or hexadecimal to binary (and vice versa) is done easily by the grouping of bits method.

1-3 ARITHMETIC OPERATIONS

Arithmetic operations with numbers in base r follow the same rules as for decimal numbers. When other than the familiar base 10 is used, one must be careful to use only r allowable digits and perform all computations with base r digits. Examples of addition, subtraction, and multiplication of two binary numbers are shown below.

Augend:	10110	Minuend:	10110	Multiplicand:	1011
Addend:	+10011	Subtrahend:	−10011	Multiplier:	× 101
Sum:	101001	Difference:	00011		1011
					0000
					1011
			Product:		110111

The sum of two binary numbers is calculated following the same rules as for decimal numbers, except that the digit of the sum in any significant position can be only 1 or 0. Any carry obtained in a given column is used by the digits in the column one significant position higher. The rules for subtraction are the same as in decimal, except that a borrow from a given column adds two to the minuend digit. (A borrow in the decimal system adds 10 to a minuend digit.) Multiplication is very simple. The multiplier digits are always 1 or 0. Therefore, the partial products are equal either to the multiplicand or to 0.

Arithmetic operations with octal, hexadecimal, or any other base r system will normally require the formulation of tables from which one obtains sums and products of two digits in base r. An easier alternative for adding two numbers in base r is to convert each pair of digits in a column to decimal, add the digits in decimal, and then convert the result to the corresponding sum and carry in the base r system. Since addition is done in decimal, we can rely on our memories for obtaining the entries from the familiar decimal addition table. The sequence of steps for adding the two hexadecimal numbers 59F and E46 is shown in Example 1-1.

Example 1-1

Perform the addition $(59F)_{16} + (E46)_{16}$.

Hexadecimal		Equivalent decimal		
			1	
5 9 F	5		9	15
E 4 6	14		4	6
1 3 E 5	19 = 16 + 3		14	21 = 16 + 5

The equivalent decimal columns show the mental reasoning that must be carried out in order to produce the hexadecimal sum. Instead of adding F + 6 in hexadecimal, we add the equivalent decimals 15 + 6 = 21. We then convert back to hexadecimal by noting that 21 = 16 + 5. This gives a sum digit of 5 and a carry to the next higher order column digits. The other two columns are added in a similar fashion. ■

The multiplication of two base r numbers can be accomplished by doing all the arithmetic operations in decimal and converting intermediate results one at a time. This is illustrated in the multiplication of two octal numbers as shown in Example 1-2.

Example 1-2

Multiply $(762)_8 \times (45)_8$.

Octal	Octal	Decimal	Octal
7 6 2	5 × 2	10 = 8 + 2	12
4 5	5 × 6 + 1	31 = 24 + 7	37
4 6 7 2	5 × 7 + 3	38 = 32 + 6	46
3 7 1 0	4 × 2	8 = 8 + 0	10
4 3 7 7 2	4 × 6 + 1	25 = 24 + 1	31
	4 × 7 + 3	31 = 24 + 7	37

The computations on the right show the mental calculations for each pair of octal digits. The octal digits 0 through 7 have the same value as their corresponding decimal digits. The multiplication of two octal digits plus a carry, if present, is done in decimal and the result then converted back to octal. The left digit of the two-digit octal result gives the carry that must be added to the next product. For example, $(5 \times 2)_8 = (12)_8$. The left digit, 1, is the carry to be added to the product $(5 \times 6)_8$, and the least significant digit, 2, is the corresponding digit of the octal partial product.

Conversion from Decimal to Other Base

The conversion of a number in base r to decimal is done by expanding the number in power series and adding all the terms as was shown previously. We now present a general procedure for the reverse operation of converting a decimal number to a number in base r. If the number includes a radix point, it is necessary to separate it into an integer part and a fraction part, since each part must be converted differently. The conversion of a decimal integer to a number in base r is done by dividing the number and all successive quotients by r and accumulating the remainders. This procedure is best explained by example.

Example 1-3

Convert decimal 153 to octal.

The conversion is to base 8. First, 153 is divided by 8 to give a quotient of 19 and a remainder of 1. Then 19 is divided by 8 to give a quotient of 2 and a remainder of 3. Finally, 2 is divided by 8 to give a quotient of 0 and a remainder of 2. The coefficients of the desired octal number are obtained from the remainders as follows:

$$153/8 = 19 + 1/8 \qquad \text{Remainder} = 1 \quad \text{Least significant digit}$$
$$19/8 = \ 2 + 3/8 \qquad\qquad\qquad\ \ = 3$$
$$2/8 = \ 0 + 2/8 \qquad\qquad\qquad\ \ = 2 \quad \text{Most significant digit}$$

Answer: $(153)_{10} = (231)_8$

Note that the first remainder gives the least significant digit of the converted number, and that the quotients are divided by r until the result is 0. We also can use this procedure to convert decimal numbers to binary. In this case, the base of the converted number is 2 and therefore, all the divisions must be done by 2.

Example 1-4

Convert decimal 41 to binary.

$$41/2 = 20 + 1/2 \qquad \text{Remainder} = 1 \quad \text{Least significant digit}$$
$$20/2 = 10 \qquad\qquad\qquad\qquad\ \ = 0$$
$$10/2 = \ 5 \qquad\qquad\qquad\qquad\ \ = 0$$
$$5/2 = \ 2 + 1/2 \qquad\qquad\qquad\ = 1$$
$$2/2 = \ 1 \qquad\qquad\qquad\qquad\ = 0$$
$$1/2 = \ 0 + 1/2 \qquad\qquad\qquad = 1 \quad \text{Most significant digit}$$

Answer: $(41)_{10} = (101001)_2$

Of course, the decimal number could be converted by the sum of powers of two.

$$(41)_{10} = 32 + 8 + 1 = (101001)_2$$

The conversion of a decimal fraction to base r is accomplished by a method similar to that used for integers, except that multiplication by r is used instead of division, and integers are accumulated instead of remainders. Again, the method is best explained by example.

Example 1-5   Convert decimal 0.6875 to binary.

First, 0.6875 is multiplied by 2 to give an integer and a fraction. The new fraction is multiplied by 2 to give a new integer and a new fraction. This process is continued until the fractional part equals 0 or until there are enough digits to give sufficient accuracy. The coefficients of the binary number are obtained from the integers as follows:

$$0.6875 \times 2 = 1.3750 \quad \text{Integer} = 1 \quad \text{Most significant digit}$$
$$0.3750 \times 2 = 0.7500 \quad\quad\quad\quad = 0$$
$$0.7500 \times 2 = 1.5000 \quad\quad\quad\quad = 1$$
$$0.5000 \times 2 = 1.0000 \quad\quad\quad\quad = 1 \quad \text{Least significant digit}$$

$$\textit{Answer:} \ (0.6875)_{10} = (0.1011)_2$$

Note that the first integer produces the first and most significant bit of the fraction. In this example, there are a finite number of digits in the converted number. The process of multiplying fractions by r does not necessarily end with zero so we must decide on how many digits of the fraction to use from the conversion. Also remember that the multiplying number is equal to r. Therefore, to convert a decimal fraction to octal, we must multiply the fractions by 8.

Example 1-6   Convert decimal 0.513 to octal.

$$0.513 \times 8 = 4.104 \quad \text{Integer} = 4 \quad \text{Most significant digit}$$
$$0.104 \times 8 = 0.832 \quad\quad\quad\quad = 0$$
$$0.832 \times 8 = 6.656 \quad\quad\quad\quad = 6$$
$$0.656 \times 8 = 5.248 \quad\quad\quad\quad = 5$$
$$0.248 \times 8 = 1.984 \quad\quad\quad\quad = 1 \quad \text{Least significant digit}$$

The answer to five significant figures is obtained from the integer digits: $(0.513)_{10} = (0.40651)_8$

The conversion of decimal numbers with both integer and fractional parts is done by converting each part separately and then combining the two answers. Using the results of Examples 1-3 and 1-6 we obtain

$$(153.513)_{10} = (231.40651)_8$$

1-4 COMPLEMENTS

Complements are used in digital computers for simplifying the subtraction operation and for logical manipulation. There are two types of complements for each base r system: 1. the radix complement and 2. the diminished radix complement. The first is referred to as the r's complement and the second as the $(r - 1)$'s complement. When the value of the base r is substituted in the name, the two types are referred to as the 2's and 1's complements for binary numbers and the 10's and 9's complements for decimal numbers.

Diminished Radix Complement

Given a number N in base r having n digits, the $(r - 1)$'s complement of N is defined as $(r^n - 1) - N$. For decimal numbers, $r = 10$ and $r - 1 = 9$; so the 9's complement of N is $(10^n - 1) - N$. Now, 10^n represents a number that consists of a single 1 followed by n 0's. $10^n - 1$ is a number represented by n 9's. For example, if $n = 4$, we have $10^4 = 10000$ and $10^4 - 1 = 9999$. It follows that the 9's complement of a decimal number is obtained by subtracting each digit from 9. Some numerical examples follow.

> The 9's complement of 546700 is $999999 - 546700 = 453299$.
>
> The 9's complement of 12389 is $99999 - 12389 = 87610$

For binary numbers, $r = 2$ and $r - 1 = 1$; so the 1's complement of N is $(2^n - 1) - N$. Again, 2^n is represented by a binary number which consists of a 1 followed by n 0's. $2^n - 1$ is a binary number represented by n 1's. For example, if $n = 4$, we have $2^4 = (10000)_2$ and $2^4 - 1 = (1111)_2$. Thus the 1's complement of a binary number is obtained by subtracting each digit from 1. However, when subtracting binary digits from 1, we can have either $1 - 0 = 1$ or $1 - 1 = 0$ which causes the bit to change from 0 to 1 or from 1 to 0. Therefore, the 1's complement of a binary number is formed by changing 1's to 0's and 0's to 1's. The following are some numerical examples.

> The 1's complement of 1011001 is 0100110
>
> The 1's complement of 0001111 is 1110000

The $(r - 1)$'s complement of octal or hexadecimal numbers are obtained by subtracting each digit from 7 or F (decimal 15) respectively.

Radix Complement

The r's complement of an n-digit number N in base r is defined as $r^n - N$ for $N \neq 0$ and 0 for $N = 0$. Comparing with the $(r - 1)$'s complement we note that the r's complement is obtained by adding 1 to the $(r - 1)$'s complement since $r^n - N = [(r^n - 1) - N] + 1$. Thus, the 10's complement of the decimal 2389 is $7610 + 1 = 7611$ and is obtained by adding 1 to the 9's complement value. The 2's complement of binary 101100 is $010011 + 1 = 010100$ and is obtained by adding 1 to the 1's complement value.

Since 10^n is a number represented by a 1 followed by n 0's, $10^n - N$, which is the 10's complement of N, also can be formed by leaving all least significant 0's unchanged, subtracting the first nonzero least significant digit from 10, and then subtracting all higher significant digits from 9. The 10's complement of 246700 is 753300 and is obtained by leaving the two zeros unchanged, subtracting 7 from 10 and subtracting the other three digits from 9. Similarly, the 2's complement can be formed by leaving all least significant 0's and the first 1 unchanged, and then replacing 1's with 0's and 0's with 1's in all other higher significant bits. The 2's complement of 1101100 is 0010100 and is obtained by leaving the two low-order 0's and the first 1 unchanged, and then replacing 1's with 0's and 0's with 1's in the other four most significant bits.

In the above definitions it was assumed that the numbers do not have a radix point. If the original number N contains a radix point, the point should be removed temporarily in order to form the r's or $(r - 1)$'s complement. The radix point is then restored to the complemented number in the same relative position. It is also worth mentioning that the complement of the complement restores the number to its original value. The r's complement of N is $r^n - N$. The complement of the complement is $r^n - (r^n - N) = N$, giving back the original number.

Subtraction with Complements

The direct method of subtraction taught in elementary schools uses the borrow concept. In this method, we borrow a 1 from a higher significant position when the minuend digit is smaller than the subtrahend digit. This seems to be easiest when people perform subtraction with paper and pencil. When subtraction is implemented with digital hardware, this method is found to be less efficient than the method that uses complements.

The subtraction of two n-digit unsigned numbers, $M - N$, in base r can be done as follows:

1. Add the minuend M to the r's complement of the subtrahend N. This performs $M + (r^n - N) = M - N + r^n$.
2. If $M \geq N$, the sum will produce an end carry, r^n, which is discarded; what is left is the result $M - N$.
3. If $M < N$, the sum does not produce an end carry and is equal to $r^n - (N - M)$ which is the r's complement of $(N - M)$. To obtain the answer in a familiar form, take the r's complement of the sum and place a negative sign in front.

The following examples illustrate the procedure.

Example 1-7   Using 10's complement, subtract $72532 - 3250$.

$$M = \qquad 72532$$
$$\text{10's complement of } N = \quad +\ \underline{96750}$$
$$\text{Sum} = \qquad 169282$$
$$\text{Discard end carry } 10^5 = \quad -\ \underline{100000}$$
$$\textit{Answer} = \qquad 69282$$

Note that M has 5 digits and N has only 4 digits. Both numbers must have the same number of digits; so we write N as 03250. Taking the 10's complement of N produces a 9 in the most significant position. The occurrence of the end carry signifies that $M > N$ and the result is positive.

Example 1-8   Using 10's complement, subtract $3250 - 72532$.

$$M = \qquad 03250$$
$$\text{10's complement of } N = \quad +\ \underline{27468}$$
$$\text{Sum} = \qquad 30718$$

There is no end carry

Answer: $-(\text{10's complement of } 30718) = -69282$ ■

Note that since $3250 < 72532$, the result is negative. Since we are dealing with unsigned numbers, there is no way to get an unsigned result for this case. When working with paper and pencil, we recognize that the answer must be changed to a signed negative number. When subtracting with complements, the negative answer is recognized by the absence of the end carry and the complemented result.

Subtraction with complements is done with binary numbers in a similar manner using the same procedure outlined above.

Example 1-9   Given the two binary numbers $X = 1010100$ and $Y = 1000011$, perform the subtraction $X - Y$ and $Y - X$ using 2's complements.

$$X = \qquad 1010100$$
$$\text{2's complement of } Y = \quad +\ \underline{0111101}$$
$$\text{Sum} = \qquad 10010001$$
$$\text{Discard end carry } 2^7 = \quad -\ \underline{10000000}$$
$$\textit{Answer: } X - Y = \qquad 0010001$$

$$Y = \qquad 1000011$$
$$\text{2's complement of } X = \quad +\ \underline{0101100}$$
$$\text{Sum} = \qquad 1101111$$

There is no end carry

Answer: $Y - X = -(\text{2's complement of } 1101111) = -0010001$ ■

Subtraction of unsigned numbers also can be done by means of the $(r - 1)$'s complement. Remember that the $(r - 1)$'s complement is one less than the r's complement. Because of this, the result of adding the minuend to the complement of the subtrahend produces a sum which is one less than the correct difference when an end carry occurs. Removing the end carry and adding one to the sum is referred to as an *end-around carry*.

Example 1-10   Repeat Example 1-9 using 1's complement.

A. $X - Y = 1010100 - 1000011$

$$
\begin{aligned}
X &= \quad 1010100 \\
\text{1's complement of } Y &= +\ \underline{0111100} \\
\text{Sum} &= \ulcorner 10010000 \\
\text{End-around carry} &\quad \llcorner\!\!\longrightarrow +\ \ 1 \\
\textit{Answer: } X - Y &= \quad 0010001
\end{aligned}
$$

B. $Y - X = 1000011 - 1010100$

$$
\begin{aligned}
Y &= \quad 1000011 \\
\text{1's complement of } X &= +\ \underline{0101011} \\
\text{Sum} &= \quad 1101110
\end{aligned}
$$

There is no end carry

Answer: $Y - X = -(\text{1's complement of } 1101110) = -0010001$

Note that the negative result is obtained by taking the 1's complement of the sum since this is the type of complement used. The procedure with end-around carry is also applicable for subtracting unsigned decimal numbers with 9's complement.

1-5   SIGNED BINARY NUMBER

Positive integers including zero can be represented as unsigned numbers. However, to represent negative integers, we need a notation for negative values. In ordinary arithmetic, a negative number is indicated by a minus sign, and a positive number by a plus sign. Because of hardware limitations, computers must represent everything with 1's and 0's, including the sign of a number. As a consequence, it is customary to represent the sign with a bit placed in the leftmost position of the number. The convention is to make the sign bit 0 for positive and 1 for negative.

It is important to realize that both signed and unsigned binary numbers consist of a string of bits when represented in a computer. The user determines whether the number is signed or unsigned. If the binary number is signed, then the leftmost bit represents the sign and the rest of the bits represent the number. If the binary number is assumed to be unsigned, then the leftmost bit is the most significant bit of the number. For example, the string of bit 01001 can be considered as 9 (unsigned binary) or a $+9$ (signed binary) because the leftmost bit is 0. The string of bits 11001 represent the binary equivalent of 25 when considered as an unsigned number or as -9 when considered as a signed number because of the 1 in the leftmost position which designates a minus and the other four bits which represent binary 9. Usually there is no confusion in identifying the bits because the type of number representation is known in advance.

The representation of the signed numbers in the last example is referred to as the *signed-magnitude* system. In this system, the number consists of a magnitude and a symbol ($+$ or $-$) or a bit (0 or 1) indicating the sign. This is the representation of signed numbers used in ordinary arithmetic. When arithmetic operations are implemented in a computer, it is more convenient to use a different system for representing negative numbers referred to as the *signed-complement* system. In this system, a negative number is indicated by its complement. While the sign and magnitude system negates a number by changing its sign, the signed-complement system negates a number by taking its complement. Since positive numbers always start with 0 (plus) in the leftmost position, the complement will always start with a 1 indicating a negative number. The signed-complement system can use either the 1's or the 2's complement, but the 2's complement is the most common.

As an example, consider the number 9 represented in binary with eight bits. +9 is represented with a sign bit of 0 in the leftmost position followed by the binary equivalent of 9 to give 00001001. Note that all eight bits must have a value and therefore, 0's are inserted between the sign bit and the first 1. Although there is only one way to represent +9, there are three different ways to represent −9 using eight bits:

In signed-magnitude representation: 10001001
In signed-1's complement representation: 11110110
In signed-2's complement representation: 11110111

In signed-magnitude, −9 is obtained from +9 by changing the sign bit in the leftmost position from 0 to 1. In signed-1's complement, −9 is obtained by complementing all the bits of +9 including the sign bit. The signed-2's complement representation of −9 is obtained by taking the 2's complement of the positive number including the sign bit.

Table 1-3 lists all possible 4-bit signed binary numbers in the three representations. The equivalent decimal number is also shown for reference. Note that the

TABLE 1-3
Signed Binary Numbers

Decimal	Signed-2's complement	Signed-1's complement	Signed-magnitude
+7	0111	0111	0111
+6	0110	0110	0110
+5	0101	0101	0101
+4	0100	0100	0100
+3	0011	0011	0011
+2	0010	0010	0010
+1	0001	0001	0001
+0	0000	0000	0000
−0	—	1111	1000
−1	1111	1110	1001
−2	1110	1101	1010
−3	1101	1100	1011
−4	1100	1011	1100
−5	1011	1010	1101
−6	1010	1001	1110
−7	1001	1000	1111
−8	1000	—	—

positive numbers in all three representations are identical and have 0 in the leftmost position. The signed-2's complement system has only one representation for 0 and is always positive. The other two systems have a positive 0 and a negative 0, which is something not encountered in ordinary arithmetic. Note that all negative numbers have a 1 in the leftmost bit position; this is the way we distinguish them from positive numbers. With four bits we can represent 16 binary numbers. In the signed-magnitude and the 1's complement representations, there are eight positive numbers and eight negative numbers, including two zeros. In the 2's complement representation, there are eight positive numbers including one zero, and eight negative numbers.

The signed-magnitude system is used in ordinary arithmetic but is awkward when employed in computer arithmetic. Therefore, the signed-complement is normally used. The 1's complement imposes difficulties because of its two representations of 0 and is seldom used for arithmetic operations except in some older computers. The 1's complement is useful as a logical operation since the change of 1 to 0 or 0 to 1 is equivalent to a logical complement operation, as will be shown in the next chapter. The following discussion of signed binary arithmetic deals exclusively with the signed-2's complement representation of negative numbers. The same procedures can be applied to the signed-1's complement system by including the end-around carry as done with unsigned numbers.

Arithmetic Addition

The addition of two numbers in the signed-magnitude system follows the rules of ordinary arithmetic: If the signs are the same, we add the two magnitudes and give the sum the common sign. If the signs are different, we subtract the smaller magnitude from the larger and give the result the sign of the larger magnitude. For example, $(+25) + (-37) = -(37 - 25) = -12$ and is done by subtracting the smaller magnitude 25 from the larger magnitude 37 and using the sign of 37 for the sign of the result. This is a process that requires the comparison of the signs and the magnitudes and then performing either addition or subtraction. The same procedure applies to binary numbers in sign and magnitude representation. In contrast, the rule for adding numbers in the signed-complement system does not require a comparison or subtraction, but only addition. The procedure is very simple and can be stated as follows for binary numbers. (Decimal numbers are considered in the next section.)

> The addition of two signed binary numbers with negative numbers represented in signed-2's complement form is obtained from the addition of the two numbers including their sign bits. A carry out of the sign bit position is discarded.

Numerical examples for addition are shown below. Note that negative numbers must be initially in 2's complement and that the sum obtained after the addition if negative, is in 2's complement form.

$+\ 6$	00000110	$-\ 6$	11111010	$+\ 6$	00000110	$-\ 6$	11111010
$+13$	00001101	$+13$	00001101	-13	11110011	-13	11110011
$+19$	00010011	$+\ 7$	00000111	$-\ 7$	11111001	-19	11101101

In each of the four cases, the operation performed is addition, including the sign bits. Any carry out of the sign bit position is discarded, and negative results are automatically in 2's complement form.

In order to obtain a correct answer, we must ensure that the result has sufficient number of bits to accommodate the sum. If we start with two n-bit numbers and the sum occupies $n + 1$ bits, we say that an overflow occurs. When one performs the addition with paper and pencil, an overflow is not a problem since we are not limited by the width of the page. We just add another 0 to a positive number and another 1 to a negative number, in the most significant position, to extend them to $n + 1$ bits and then perform the addition. Overflow is a problem in computers because the number of bits that hold a number is finite, and a result that exceeds the finite value by 1 cannot be accommodated. Computer overflow is discussed in Section 7-3.

The complement form of representing negative numbers is unfamiliar to people used to the signed-magnitude system. To determine the value of a negative number when in signed-2's complement, it is necessary to convert it to a positive number to place it in a more familiar form. For example, the signed binary number 11111001 is negative because the leftmost bit is 1. Its 2's complement is 00000111 which is the binary equivalent of +7. We therefore recognize the original number to be equal to −7.

Arithmetic Subtraction

Subtraction of two signed binary numbers when negative numbers are in 2's complement form is very simple and can be stated as follows:

Take the 2's complement of the subtrahend (including the sign bit) and add it to the minuend (including the sign bit). A carry out of the sign bit position is discarded.

This procedure stems from the fact that a subtraction operation can be changed to an addition operation if the sign of the subtrahend is changed. This is demonstrated by the following relationship:

$$(\pm A) - (+ B) = (\pm A) + (- B)$$
$$(\pm A) - (- B) = (\pm A) + (+ B)$$

But changing a positive number to a negative number is easily done by taking its 2's complement. The reverse is also true because the complement of a negative number in complement form produces the equivalent positive number. Consider the subtraction of $(-6) - (-13) = +7$. In binary with eight bits this is written as $(11111010 - 11110011)$. The subtraction is changed to addition by taking the 2's complement of the subtrahend (-13) to give $(+13)$. In binary this is 11111010 + 00001101 = 100000111. Removing the end carry we obtain the correct answer 00000111 $(+7)$.

It is worth noting that binary numbers in the signed-complement system are added and subtracted by the same basic addition and subtraction rules as unsigned numbers. Therefore, computers need only one common hardware circuit to handle both types of arithmetic. The user or programmer must interpret the results of such addition or subtraction differently depending on whether it is assumed that the numbers are signed or unsigned.

1-6 DECIMAL CODES

The binary number system is the most natural system for a computer, but people are accustomed to the decimal system. One way to resolve this difference is to convert the decimal numbers to binary, perform all arithmetic calculations in binary and then convert the binary results back to decimal. This method requires that we store the decimal numbers in the computer in a way that they can be converted to binary. Since the computer can accept only binary values, we must represent the decimal digits by a code that contains 1's and 0's. It is also possible to perform the arithmetic operations directly with decimal numbers when they are stored in the computer in coded form.

A binary code is a group of n bits that assume up to 2^n distinct combinations of 1's and 0's, with each combination representing one element of the set that is being coded. A set of four elements can be coded with two bits with each element assigned one of the following bit combinations: 00, 01, 10, 11. A set of eight elements requires a 3-bit code and a set of 16 elements requires a 4-bit code. The bit combination of an n-bit code is determined from the count in binary from 0 to $2^n - 1$. Each element must be assigned a unique binary bit combination and no two elements can have the same value; otherwise, the code assignment will be ambiguous.

A binary code will have some unassigned bit combinations if the number of elements in the set is not a power of 2. The 10 decimal digits form such a set. A binary code that distinguishes among 10 elements must contain at least four bits, but six out of the 16 possible combinations will remain unassigned. Numerous different binary codes can be obtained by arranging four bits in 10 distinct combinations. The code most commonly used for the decimal digits is the straight binary assignment as listed in Table 1-4. This is called *binary coded decimal* and is commonly referred to as BCD. Other decimal codes are possible and a few of them are presented later in this section.

Table 1-4 gives the 4-bit code for one decimal digit. A number with n decimal digits will require $4n$ bits in BCD. Decimal 396 is represented in BCD with 12 bits

TABLE 1-4
Binary Coded Decimal (BCD)

Decimal symbol	BCD digit
0	0000
1	0001
2	0010
3	0011
4	0100
5	0101
6	0110
7	0111
8	1000
9	1001

as 0011 1001 0110, with each group of 4 bits representing one decimal digit. A decimal number in BCD is the same as its equivalent binary number only when the number is between 0 and 9. A BCD number greater than 10 looks different from its equivalent binary number even though both contain 1's and 0's. Moreover, the binary combinations 1010 through 1111 are not used and have no meaning in the BCD code. Consider decimal 185 and its corresponding value in BCD and binary.

$$(185)_{10} = (0001\ 1000\ 0101)_{BCD} = (10111001)_2$$

The BCD value has 12 bits but the equivalent binary number needs only eight bits. It is obvious that a BCD number needs more bits than its equivalent binary value. However, there is an advantage in the use of decimal numbers because computer input and output data are generated by people who use the decimal system.

It is important to realize that BCD numbers are *decimal* numbers and *not* binary numbers, even though they are represented in bits. The only difference between a decimal and a BCD number is that decimals are written with the symbols 0, 1, 2, . . ., 9, and BCD numbers use the binary codes 0000, 0001, 0010, . . ., 1001 but the number value is exactly the same. Decimal 10 is represented in BCD with eight bits as 0001 0000 and decimal 15, as 0001 0101. The corresponding binary values are 1010 and 1111 and have only four bits.

BCD Addition

Consider the addition of two decimal digits in BCD, together with a possible carry from a previous less significant pair of digits. Since each digit does not exceed 9, the sum cannot be greater than $9 + 9 + 1 = 19$, the 1 being a carry. Suppose we add the BCD digits as if they were binary numbers. The binary sum will produce a result in the range from 0 to 19. In binary, this will be from 0000 to 10011 but in BCD it should be from 0000 to 1 1001; the first 1 being a carry and the next four bits being the BCD digit sum. When the binary sum is equal to or less than 1001 (without a carry), the corresponding BCD digit is correct. But when the binary sum is greater or equal to 1010, the result is an invalid BCD digit. The addition of binary 6, $(0110)_2$, to the sum converts it to the correct digit and also produces a carry as required. This is because the difference between a carry in the 2^4th position of the binary sum and a decimal carry differ by $16 - 10 = 6$. Consider the following three BCD additions:

```
   4     0100          4     0100          8     1000
 +5    +0101         +8    +1000         +9     1001
 ‾9‾    1001         ‾12‾   1100         ‾17‾  1 0001
                           +0110               + 0110
                          ‾1 0010‾             ‾1 0111‾
```

In each case, the two BCD digits are added as if they were two binary numbers. If the binary sum is greater or equal to 1010, we add 0110 to obtain the correct BCD digit sum and a carry. In the first example, the sum is equal to 9 and is the correct BCD digit sum. In the second example, the binary sum produces an invalid BCD digit. The addition of 0110 produces the correct BCD digit sum 0010 (2) and a carry. In the third example, the binary sum produces a carry. This condition occurs when the sum is greater than or equal to 16. Even though the other four bits are less than 1001, the binary sum requires a correction because of the carry. Adding 0110, we obtain the required BCD digit sum 0111 (7) and a BCD carry.

The addition of two *n*-digit unsigned BCD numbers follows the same procedure. Consider the addition of 184 + 576 = 760 in BCD.

BCD carry	1	1		
	0001	1000	0100	184
	+0101	0111	0110	+ 576
Binary sum	0111	10000	1010	
Add 6		0110	0110	
BDC sum	0111	0110	0000	760

The first, least significant pair of BCD digits produce a BCD digit sum of 0000 and a carry for the next pair of digits. The second pair of BCD digits plus a previous carry produce a digit sum of 0110 and a carry for the next pair of digits. The third pair of digits plus a carry produce a binary sum of 0111 and does not require a correction.

Decimal Arithmetic

The representation of signed decimal numbers in BCD is similar to the representation of signed numbers in binary. We can either use the familiar signed-magnitude system or the signed-complement system. The sign of a decimal number is usually represented with four bits to conform with the 4-bit code of the decimal digits. It is customary to designate a plus with four 0's and a minus with the BCD equivalent of 9 which is 1001.

The signed-magnitude system is difficult to use with computers. The signed-complement system can be either the 9's or the 10's complement, but the 10's complement is the one most often used. To obtain the 10's complement of a BCD number, we take the 9's complement and add one to the least significant digit. The 9's complement is calculated by subtracting each digit from 9.

The procedures developed for the signed-2's complement system in the previous section also apply to the signed-10's complement system for decimal numbers. Addition is done by adding all digits, including the sign digit, and discarding the end carry. Obviously, this assumes that all negative numbers are in 10's complement form. Consider the addition (+375) + (−240) = +135 done in the signed-complement system.

$$0\ 375$$
$$+\ \underline{9\ 760}$$
$$0\ 135$$

The 9 in the leftmost position of the second number represents a minus, and 9760 is the 10's complement of 0240. The two numbers are added and the end carry is discarded to obtain +135. Of course, the decimal numbers inside the computer must be in BCD including the sign digits. The addition is done with BCD digits as described previously.

The subtraction of decimal numbers either unsigned or in the signed-10's complement system is the same as in the binary system: Take the 10's complement of the subtrahend and add it to the minuend. Many computers have special hardware to perform arithmetic calculations directly with decimal numbers in BCD. The user of the computer can specify by programmed instructions that the arithmetic operation should be performed with decimal numbers without converting them to binary.

Other Decimal Codes

Binary codes for decimal digits require a minimum of four bits per digit. Numerous different codes can be formulated by arranging four bits in 10 distinct possible combinations. The BCD and three other representative codes are shown in Table 1-5. Each code uses only 10 bit combinations out of possible 16 combinations that can be arranged with four bits. The six unused combinations in each case have no meaning and should be avoided.

The BCD and the 2421 codes are examples of *weighted* codes. In a weighted code, each bit position is assigned a weighting factor in such a way that each digit can be evaluated by adding the weights of all the 1's in the coded combination. The BCD code has weights of 8, 4, 2, 1 which correspond to the power of two values of each bit. The bit assignment 0110 for example, is interpreted by the weights to represent decimal 6 because $8 \times 0 + 4 \times 1 + 2 \times 1 + 1 \times 0 = 6$. The bit combination 1101 when weighted by the respective digits 2421 gives the decimal equivalent of $2 \times 1 + 4 \times 1 + 2 \times 0 + 1 \times 1 = 7$. Note that some digits can be coded in two possible ways in the 2421 code. Decimal 4 can be assigned to bit combinations 0100 or 1010 since both combinations add up to a total weight of four, but 0100 was chosen in Table 1-5.

TABLE 1-5
Four Different Binary Codes for the Decimal Digits

Decimal digit	BCD 8421	2421	Excess-3	84-2-1
0	0000	0000	0011	0000
1	0001	0001	0100	0111
2	0010	0010	0101	0110
3	0011	0011	0110	0101
4	0100	0100	0111	0100
5	0101	1011	1000	1011
6	0110	1100	1001	1010
7	0111	1101	1010	1001
8	1000	1110	1011	1000
9	1001	1111	1100	1111
Unused bit combinations	1010	0101	0000	0001
	1011	0110	0001	0010
	1100	0111	0010	0011
	1101	1000	1101	1100
	1110	1001	1110	1101
	1111	1010	1111	1110

The 2421 and the excess-3 codes are examples of *self-complementing codes*. Such codes have the property that the 9's complement of a decimal number is obtained directly by changing 1's to 0's and 0's to 1's in the code. For example, decimal 395 is represented in the excess-3 code as 0110 1100 1000. The 9's complement (604) is represented as 1001 0011 0111 which is simply obtained by complementing each bit of the code (as with the 1's complement of binary numbers).

The excess-3 code has been used in some older computers because of its self-complementing property. It is an unweighted code where each coded combination is obtained from the corresponding binary value plus 3. Note that the BCD code is not self-complementing.

The 84-2-1 code is an example of assigning both positive and negative weights to a decimal code. In this case, the bit combination 0110 is interpreted as a decimal 2 and is calculated from $8 \times 0 + 4 \times 1 + (-2) \times 1 + (-1) \times 0 = 2$.

It is important to understand the difference between *conversion* of a decimal number to binary and the binary *coding* of a decimal number. In each case the final result is a string of bits. The bits obtained from conversion are binary digits. The bits obtained from coding are combinations of 1's and 0's arranged according to the rules of the code used. Therefore, it is extremely important to realize that a string of bits in a computer sometimes represents a binary number and at other times string of bits represents other information as specified by a given binary code.

1-7 ALPHANUMERIC CODES

Many applications of digital computers require the handling of data not only of numbers, but also of letters. For instance, an insurance company with thousands of policy holders will use a computer to process its files. To represent the names and other pertinent information, it is necessary to formulate a binary code for the letters of the alphabet. In addition, the same binary code must represent numerals and special characters like $. An alphanumeric character set is a set of elements that include the 10 decimal digits, the 26 letters of the alphabet, and a number of special characters. Such a set contains between 36 and 64 elements if only capital letters are included, or between 64 and 128 elements if both upper- and lowercase letters are included. In the first case we need a binary code of six bits, and in the second we need a binary code of seven bits.

Binary codes play an important role in digital computers. The codes must be in binary because computers can only hold 1's and 0's. It must be realized that binary codes merely change the symbols, not the meaning of the elements of information that they represent. If we inspect the bits of a computer at random, we will find that most of the time they represent some type of coded information rather than binary numbers.

ASCII Character Code

The standard binary code for the alphanumeric characters is ASCII (American Standard Code for Information Interchange). It uses seven bits to code 128 characters, as shown in Table 1-6. The seven bits of the code are designated by b_1 through b_7, with b_7 being the most significant bit. The letter A, for example, is

TABLE 1-6
American Standard Code for Information Interchange (ASCII)

$B_4B_3B_2B_1$	$B_7B_6B_5$							
	000	001	010	011	100	101	110	111
0000	NULL	DLE	SP	0	@	P		p
0001	SOH	DC1	!	1	A	Q	a	q
0010	STX	DC2	"	2	B	R	b	r
0011	ETX	DC3	#	3	C	S	c	s
0100	EOT	DC4	$	4	D	T	d	t
0101	ENQ	NAK	%	5	E	U	e	u
0110	ACK	SYN	&	6	F	V	f	v
0111	BEL	ETB	'	7	G	W	g	w
1000	BS	CAN	(	8	H	X	h	x
1001	HT	EM	)	9	I	Y	i	y
1010	LF	SUB	*	:	J	Z	j	z
1011	VT	ESC	+	;	K	[	k	{
1100	FF	FS	,	<	L	\	l	¦
1101	CR	GS	−	=	M	]	m	}
1110	SO	RS	.	>	N	^	n	~
1111	SI	US	/	?	O	_	o	DEL

Control characters:

NULL	NULL	DLE	Data link escape
SOH	Start of heading	DC1	Device control 1
STX	Start of text	DC2	Device control 2
ETX	End of text	DC3	Device control 3
EOT	End of transmission	DC4	Device control 4
ENQ	Enquiry	NAK	Negative acknowledge
ACK	Acknowledge	SYN	Synchronous idle
BEL	Bell	ETB	End of transmission block
BS	Backspace	CAN	Cancel
HT	Horizontal tab	EM	End of medium
LF	Line feed	SUB	Substitute
VT	Vertical tab	ESC	Escape
FF	Form feed	FS	File separator
CR	Carriage return	GS	Group separator
SO	Shift out	RS	Record separator
SI	Shift in	US	Unit separator
SP	Space	DEL	Delete

represented in ASCII as 1000001 (column 100, row 0001). The ASCII code contains 94 graphic characters that can be printed and 34 non-printing characters used for various control functions. The graphic characters consist of the 26 uppercase letters A through Z, the 26 lowercase letters, the 10 numerals 0 through 9, and 32 special printable characters such as %, *, and $.

The 34 control characters are designated in the ASCII table with abbreviated names. They are listed again below the table with their full functional names. The control characters are used for routing data and arranging the printed text into a prescribed format. There are three types of control characters: format effectors, information separators, and communication control characters. Format effectors are characters that control the layout of printing. They include the familiar type-writer controls such as backspace (BS), horizontal tabulation (HT), and carriage return (CR). Information separators are used to separate the data into divisions like paragraphs and pages. They include characters like record separator (RS), and file separator (FS). The communication control characters are useful during the transmission of text between remote terminals. Examples of communication control characters are STX (start of text) and ETX (end of text), which are used to frame a text message when transmitted through telephone wires.

Parity Bit

ASCII is a 7-bit code, but most computers manipulate an 8-bit quantity as a single unit called *byte*. Therefore, ASCII characters most often are stored one per byte, with the most significant bit set to 0. The extra bit is sometimes used for specific purposes, depending on the application. For example, some printers recognize an additional 128 ASCII, 8-bit characters with the most significant bit set to 1. These characters enable the printer to produce additional symbols such as the Greek alphabet or italic type font.

When used for data communication, an eighth bit is sometimes used to indicate the parity of the character. A *parity bit* is an extra bit included to make the total number of 1's either even or odd. Consider the following two characters and their even and odd parity.

	With even parity	With odd parity
ASCII A = 1000001	01000001	11000001
ASCII T = 1010100	11010100	01010100

In each case we use the extra bit in the leftmost position of the code to produce an even number of 1's in the character for even parity or an odd number of 1's in the character for odd parity. In general one parity or the other is adopted, with even parity being more common.

The parity bit is helpful in detecting errors during the transmission of information from one location to another. This is handled as follows: An even parity bit is generated in the sending end for each character; the 8-bit characters that include parity bits are transmitted to their destination; the parity of each character is then checked at the receiving end; if the parity of the received character is not even, it means that at least one bit has changed value during the transmission. This method detects one, three or any odd number of errors in each character transmitted. An even number of errors is undetected. Additional error detection codes may be needed to take care of an even number of errors.

What is done after an error is detected depends on the particular application. One possibility is to request retransmission of the message on the assumption that the error was random and will not occur again. Thus, if the receiver detects a parity error, it sends back an NAK (negative acknowledge) control character consisting of an even-parity eight bits 10010101 (Table 1-6). If no error is detected, the receiver sends back an ACK (acknowledge) control character 00000110. The sending end will respond to an NAK by transmitting the message again until the correct parity is received. If, after a number of attempts, the transmission is still in error, a message can be sent to the operator to check for malfunctions in the transmission path.

Other Alphanumeric Codes

Another alphanumeric code used in IBM equipment is the EBCDIC (Extended BCD Interchange Code). It uses eight bits for each character and a ninth bit for parity, if used. EBCDIC has the same character symbols as ASCII but the bit assignment for characters is different. As the name implies, the binary code for the letters and numerals are an extension of the BCD code. This means that the first four bits and the last four bits of the code range from 0000 through 1001 as in BCD.

When characters are used internally in a computer for data processing (not for transmission purposes), it is sometimes convenient to use a 6-bit code to represent 64 characters. A 6-bit code can specify 64 characters consisting of the 26 capital letters, the 10 numerals, and up to 28 special characters. This set of characters is usually sufficient for data processing purposes. Using fewer bits to code characters has the advantage of reducing the space needed to store large quantities of alphanumeric data.

A code developed in the early stages of Teletype transmission is the 5-bit Baudot code. Although five bits can specify only 32 characters, the Baudot code represents 58 characters by using two modes of operation. In the mode called letters, the five bits encode 26 letters of the alphabet. In the mode called figures, the five bits encode the numerals and other characters. There are two special characters that are recognized by both modes and used to shift from one mode to the other. The *letter shift* character places the reception station in the letters mode, after which all subsequent character codes are interpreted as letters. The *figure shift* character places the system in the figures mode. The shift operation is analogous to the shifting operation on a typewriter with a shift lock key.

When alphanumeric information is transferred to the computer using punch cards, the alphanumeric characters are coded with 12 bits. Programs and data in the past were prepared on punch cards using the Hollerith code. A punch card consists of 80 columns and 12 rows. Each column represents an alphanumeric character of 12 bits with holes punched in the appropriate rows. A hole is sensed as a 1 and the absence of a hole is sensed as a 0. The 12 rows are marked starting from the top, as 12, 11, 0, 1, 2, . . ., 9 punch. The first three are called the zone punch and the last nine are called the numeric punch. Decimal digits are represented by a single hole in a numeric punch. The letters of the alphabet are represented by two holes in a column, one in the zone portion and the other in the numeric punch. Special characters are represented by one, two, or three holes in a column. The 12-bit card code is inefficient in its use of bits. Consequently, most computers that receive input from a card reader convert the input 12-bit card code into an internal 6-bit code to conserve bits of storage.

REFERENCES

1. CAVANAGH, J. J., *Digital Computer Arithmetic*. New York: McGraw-Hill, 1984.
2. HWANG, K., *Computer Arithmetic*. New York: Wiley, 1979.
3. SCHMID, H., *Decimal Arithmetic*. New York: Wiley, 1974.
4. KNUTH, D. E., *The Art of Computer Programming: Seminumerical Algorithms*. Reading, MA: Addison-Wesley, 1969.
5. FLORES, I., *The Logic of Computer Arithmetic*. Englewood Cliffs: Prentice-Hall, 1963.
6. RICHARD, R. K., *Arithmetic Operations in Digital Computers*. New York: Van Nostrand, 1955.

PROBLEMS

1-1 List the binary, octal, and hexadecimal numbers from 16 to 31.

1-2 What is the exact number of bits in a system that contains (a) 32K bits; (b) 50K bits; (c) 32M bits?

1-3 What is the largest binary number that can be obtained with 16 bits? What is its decimal equivalent?

1-4 Give the binary value of a 24-bit number with the hexademical equivalent of F3A7C2. What is the octal equivalent of the binary number?

1-5 Convert the following binary numbers to decimal: 101110, 1110101.11, and 110110100.

1-6 Convert the following decimal numbers to binary: 1231, 673, 10^4, and 1998.

1-7 Convert the following numbers with the indicated bases to decimal: $(12121)_3$, $(4310)_5$, and $(198)_{12}$.

1-8 Convert the following numbers from the given base to the other three bases listed in the table.

Decimal	Binary	Octal	Hexadecimal
225.225	?	?	?
?	11010111.11	?	?
?	?	623.77	?
?	?	?	2AC5.D

1-9 Add and multiply the following numbers without converting to decimal.
(a) $(367)_8$ and $(715)_8$ (b) $(15F)_{16}$ and $(A7)_{16}$ (c) $(110110)_2$ and $(110101)_2$

1-10 Convert the following decimal numbers to the indicated bases using the methods of Examples 1-3 and 1-6.
(a) 7562.45 to octal   (b) 1938.257 to hexadecimal   (c) 175.175 to binary.

1-11 Perform the following division in binary: $11111111 \div 101$.

1-12 Obtain the 9's complement of the following 8-digit decimal numbers: 12349876, 00980100, 90009951, and 00000000.

1-13 Obtain the 10's complement of the following 6-digit decimal numbers: 123900, 090657, 100000, and 000000.

1-14 Obtain the 1's and 2's complements of the following binary numbers: 10101110, 10000001, 10000000, 00000001, and 00000000.

1-15 Perform the subtraction with the following unsigned decimal numbers by taking the 10's complement of the subtrahend.

(a) 5250 − 1321   (b) 1753 − 8640   (c) 20 − 100   (d) 1200 − 250

1-16 Perform the subtraction with the following unsigned binary numbers by taking the 2's complement of the subtrahend.

(a) 11010 − 10000   (c) 100 − 110000
(b) 11010 − 1101   (d) 1010100 − 1010100

1-17 Perform the arithmetic operations (+42) + (−13) and (−42) − (−13) in binary using signed-2's complement representation for negative numbers.

1-18 The binary numbers listed below have a sign in the leftmost position and, if negative, are in 2's complement form. Perform the arithmetic operations indicated and verify the answers.

(a) 101011 + 111000   (c) 111001 − 001010
(b) 001110 + 110010   (d) 101011 − 100110

1-19 Represent the following decimal numbers in BCD: 13597 (unsigned), + 9328, − 0120 (in 10's complement).

1-20 Represent the unsigned decimal numbers 831 and 793 in BCD and then show the steps necessary to form their sum.

1-21 Convert the following decimal numbers into signed-10's complement form: − 0950, and − 9028, then perform the following four additions with negative numbers in complement form.

(a) (+950) + (+9028)   (c) (−950) + (+9028)
(b) (+950) + (−9028)   (d) (−950) + (−9028)

1-22 Formulate a weighted binary code for the decimal digits using weights of 7, 4, 2, 1.

1-23 Represent the decimal number 8620 in (a) BCD, (b) excess-3 code (c) 2421 code, and (d) as a binary number.

1-24 Represent the decimal 3864 in the 2421 code of Table 1-5. Show that the code is self-complementing by taking the 9's complement.

1-25 Assign a binary code in some orderly manner to the 52 playing cards. Use the minimum number of bits.

1-26 Write your full name in ASCII using an eight bit code with the leftmost bit always 0. Include a space between names and a period after a middle initial.

1-27 Decode the following ASCII code: 1001010 1101111 1101000 1101110 0100000 1000100 1101111 1100101.

1-28 Show the bit configuration that represents the decimal number 295 (a) in binary, (b) in BCD, (c) in ASCII.

1-29 List the ten BCD digits with an even parity in the leftmost position. (Total of five bits per digit.) Repeat with an odd parity bit.

1-30 What bit must be complemented to change an ASCII letter from capital to lowercase, and vice versa?

1-31 How many printing characters are there in ASCII? How many of them are not letters or numerals?

DIGITAL CIRCUITS

2-1 BINARY LOGIC AND GATES

Digital circuits are hardware components that manipulate binary information. The circuits are constructed with electronics parts such as transistors, diodes, and resistors. Each circuit is referred to as a *gate*. The designer of a digital system does not have to be concerned with the internal construction of the individual gates but only with their external logical properties. Each gate performs a specific logical operation, and the output from one gate is applied to the inputs of other gates, in sequence, to form the required digital circuit.

In order to describe the operational properties of digital circuits, it is necessary to introduce a mathematical notation that specifies the operation of each gate. This mathematical system is a binary logic system known as *Boolean algebra*. The name of the algebra is in honor of the English mathematician George Boole, who in 1854 published a book introducing the mathematical theory of logic. Today Boolean algebra is used to describe the interconnection of digital gates and to transform circuit diagrams to algebraic expressions. We will first introduce the concept of binary logic and show its relationship to digital gates and binary signals. We will then present the properties of Boolean algebra together with other design methods for dealing with various aspects of digital circuits and systems.

Binary Logic

Binary logic deals with variables that take on two discrete values and with operations that assume logical meaning. The two values the variables take may be called by different names, but for our purpose it is convenient to think in terms of binary values and assign 1 and 0 to each variable. The variables are designated by letters of the alphabet such as A, B, C, X, Y, Z. There are three logical operations associated with the binary variables called AND, OR, and NOT.

1. **AND.** This operation is represented by a dot or by the absence of an operator. For example, $X \cdot Y = Z$ or $XY = Z$ is read "X AND Y is equal to Z." The logical operation AND is interpreted to mean that $Z = 1$ if and only if $X = 1$ and $Y = 1$; otherwise $Z = 0$. (Remember that X, Y, and Z are binary variables and can be equal to 1 or 0 and nothing else.)

2. **OR.** This operation is represented by a plus symbol. For example $X + Y = Z$ is read "X OR Y is equal to Z", meaning that $Z = 1$ if $X = 1$ or $Y = 1$ or if both $X = 1$ and $Y = 1$. Only if $X = 0$ and $Y = 0$, is $Z = 0$.

3. **NOT.** This operation is represented by a bar over the variable. For example, $\overline{X} = Z$ is read "X NOT is equal to Z", meaning that Z is what X is not. In other words, if $X = 1$, then $Z = 0$; but if $X = 0$, then $Z = 1$. The NOT operation is also referred to as the *complement* operation, since it changes a 1 to 0 and a 0 to 1.

Binary logic resembles binary arithmetic, and the operations AND and OR have similarities to multiplication and addition, respectively. In fact, the symbols used for AND and OR are the same as those used for multiplication and addition. However, binary logic should not be confused with binary arithmetic. One should realize that an arithmetic variable designates a number that may consist of many digits. A logic variable is always either a 1 or a 0. The possible binary values for the logical OR operation are as follows:

$$0 + 0 = 0$$

$$0 + 1 = 1$$

$$1 + 0 = 1$$

$$1 + 1 = 1$$

These resemble binary addition except for the last operation. In binary logic we have $1 + 1 = 1$ (read "one OR one is equal to one"), but in binary arithmetic we have $1 + 1 = 10$ (read "one plus one is equal to two"). To avoid ambiguity, the symbol $\vee$ is sometimes used for the OR operation instead of the $+$ symbol. But as long as arithmetic and logic operations are not mixed, each can use the $+$ symbol with its own independent meaning.

The binary values for the AND operation are

$$0 \cdot 0 = 0$$

$$0 \cdot 1 = 0$$

$$1 \cdot 0 = 0$$

$$1 \cdot 1 = 1$$

This is identical to binary multiplication provided we use only a single bit. Logical AND is sometimes referred to as *logical multiplication* and logical OR as *logical addition*.

TABLE 2-1
Truth Tables for the Three Logical Operations

AND			OR			NOT	
X	Y	X·Y	X	Y	X + Y	X	X̄
0	0	0	0	0	0	0	1
0	1	0	0	1	1	1	0
1	0	0	1	0	1		
1	1	1	1	1	1		

For each combination of the values of binary variables such as X and Y, there is a value of Z specified by the definition of the logical operation. These definitions may be listed in a compact form in a *truth table*. A truth table is a table of combinations of the binary variables showing the relationship between the values that the variables take and the result of the operation. The truth tables for the operations AND, OR, and NOT are shown in Table 2-1. The tables list all possible values for the variables and the results of the operation. These tables clearly demonstrate the definition of the three operations.

Logic Gates

Logic gates are electronic circuits which operate on one or more input signals to produce an output signal. Electrical signals such as voltages or currents exist throughout a digital system in either of two recognizable values. Voltage operated circuits respond to two separate voltage levels which represent a binary variable equal to logic-1 or logic-0. For example, a particular digital system may define logic-0 as a signal equal to 0 volts, and logic-1 as a signal equal to 4 volts. In practice, each voltage level has an acceptable range as shown in Figure 2-1. The input terminals of digital circuits accept binary signals within the allowable range and respond at the output terminals with binary signals that fall within the specified range. The intermediate region between the allowed regions is crossed only during state transition. Any desired information for computing or control can be operated upon by passing binary signals through various combinations of logic gates with each signal representing a particular binary variable.

The graphic symbols used to designate the three types of gates are shown in

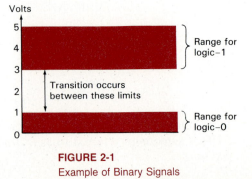

FIGURE 2-1
Example of Binary Signals

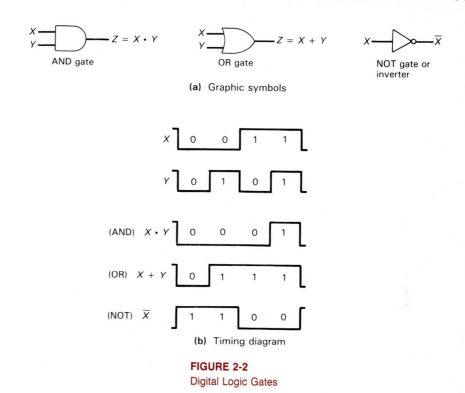

(a) Graphic symbols

(b) Timing diagram

FIGURE 2-2
Digital Logic Gates

Figure 2-2(a). The gates are blocks of hardware that produce the equivalent of logic-1 and logic-0 output signals if input logic requirements are satisfied. The input signals X and Y may exist in the AND and OR gates in one of four possible states: 00, 01, 10, or 11. These input signals are shown in Figure 2-2(b) together with the corresponding output signal for each gate. The timing diagrams illustrate the response of each gate to the four possible input signal combinations. The horizontal axis of the timing diagram represents time and the vertical axis shows the signal as it changes between the two possible voltage levels. The low level represents logic-0 and the high level represents logic-1. The AND gate responds with a logic-1 output signal when both input signals are logic-1. The OR gate responds with logic-1 output signal if any input signal is logic-1. The NOT gate is commonly referred to as an *inverter*. The reason for this name is apparent from the signal response in the timing diagram where it is shown that the output signal inverts the logic sense of the input signal.

AND and OR gates may have more than two inputs. An AND gate with three inputs and an OR gate with four inputs are shown in Figure 2-3. The three-input

(a) Three–input AND gate

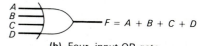

(b) Four–input OR gate

FIGURE 2-3
Gates with Multiple Inputs

AND gate responds with a logic-1 output if all three inputs are logic-1. The output produces a logic-0 if any input is logic-0. The four-input OR gate responds with a logic-1 if any input is logic-1; its output becomes a logic-0 only when all inputs are logic-0.

2-2 BOOLEAN ALGEBRA

Boolean algebra is an algebra that deals with binary variables and logic operations. The variables are designated by letters of the alphabet, and the three basic logic operations are AND, OR, and complement. A Boolean function consists of an algebraic expression formed with binary variables, the constants 0 and 1, the logic operation symbols, parentheses, and an equal sign. For a given value of the binary variables, the Boolean function can be equal to either 1 or 0. Consider as an example the following Boolean function:

$$F = X + \overline{Y}Z$$

The function F is equal to 1 if X is equal to 1 or if both $\overline{Y}$ and Z are equal to 1. Otherwise F is equal to 0. The complement operation dictates that when $\overline{Y} = 1$ then $Y = 0$. Therefore, we can say that $F = 1$ if $X = 1$ or if $Y = 0$ and $Z = 1$. A Boolean function expresses the logical relationship between binary variables. It is evaluated by determining the binary value of the expression for all possible values of the variables.

A Boolean function can be represented in a truth table. A truth table is a list of combinations of 1's and 0's assigned to the binary variables and a column that shows the value of the function for each binary combination. The number of rows in the truth table is 2^n, where n is the number of variables in the function. The binary combinations for the truth table are obtained from the binary numbers by counting from 0 through $2^n - 1$. Table 2-2 shows the truth table for the function listed above. There are eight possible binary combinations for assigning bits to the three variables X, Y, and Z. The column labeled F contains either 0 or 1 for each of these combinations. The table shows that the function is equal to 1 when $X = 1$ or when $YZ = 01$. Otherwise it is equal to 0.

A Boolean function can be transformed from an algebraic expression into a circuit diagram composed of logic gates. The logic circuit diagram for F is shown in Figure 2-4. There is an inverter for input Y to generate the complement $\overline{Y}$. There is an AND gate for the term $\overline{Y}Z$ and an OR gate that combines the two terms. In logic circuit diagrams, the variables of the function are taken as the inputs of the circuit and the binary variable F is taken as the output of the circuit.

There is only one way that a Boolean function can be represented in a truth table. However, when the function is in algebraic form, it can be expressed in a

TABLE 2-2
Truth Table for the
Function $F = X + \overline{Y}X$

X	Y	Z	F
0	0	0	0
0	0	1	1
0	1	0	0
0	1	1	0
1	0	0	1
1	0	1	1
1	1	0	1
1	1	1	1

FIGURE 2-4
Logic Circuit Diagram for $F = X + \overline{Y}Z$

variety of ways. The particular expression used to designate the function will also dictate the interconnection of gates in the logic circuit diagram. By manipulating a Boolean expression according to Boolean algebra rules, it is sometimes possible to obtain a simpler expression for the same function and thus reduce the number of gates in the circuit. To see how this is done, it is necessary first to study the basic rules of the algebra.

Basic Identities of Boolean Algebra

Table 2-3 lists the most basic identities of Boolean algebra. The notation is simplified by omitting the symbol · for the AND whenever it does not lead to confusion. The first nine identities show the relationship between a single variable X, its complement $\overline{X}$, and the binary constants 0 and 1. The next five identities, 10 through 14, are similar to ordinary algebra. The last three, 15 through 17, do not apply in ordinary algebra but are very useful in manipulating Boolean expressions.

The basic rules listed in Table 2-3 have been arranged in two columns. The two parts demonstrate the property of duality of Boolean algebra. The *dual* of an algebraic expression is obtained by interchanging OR and AND operations and replacing 1's by 0's and 0's by 1's. An equation in one column of the table can be obtained from the corresponding equation in the other column by taking the dual of the expressions on both sides of the equal sign. For example, relation 2 is the dual of relation 1 because the OR has been replaced by an AND and the 0 by 1.

The nine identities involving a single variable can be easily verified by substituting both possible values for X. For example, to show that $X + 0 = X$, let $X = 0$ to obtain $0 + 0 = 0$, and then let $X = 1$ to obtain $1 + 0 = 1$. Both equations are true according to the definition of the OR logic operation. Any expression can be substituted for the variable X in all the Boolean equations listed in the table. Thus, by identity 3 and with $X = AB + C$ we obtain

$$AB + C + 1 = 1$$

Note that equation 9 states that double complementation restores the variable to its original value. Thus if $X = 0$ then $\overline{X} = 1$ and $\overline{\overline{X}} = 0 = X$.

The commutative laws state that the order in which the variables are written will not affect the result when using the OR and AND operations. The associative laws state that the result of forming an operation among three variables is inde-

TABLE 2-3
Basic Identities of Boolean Algebra

1. $X + 0 = X$	2. $X \cdot 1 = X$	
3. $X + 1 = 1$	4. $X \cdot 0 = 0$	
5. $X + X = X$	6. $X \cdot X = X$	
7. $X + \overline{X} = 1$	8. $X \cdot \overline{X} = 0$	
9. $\overline{\overline{X}} = X$		
10. $X + Y = Y + X$	11. $XY = YX$	Commutative
12. $X + (Y + Z) = (X + Y) + Z$	13. $X(YZ) = (XY)Z$	Associative
14. $X(Y + Z) = XY + XZ$	15. $X + YZ = (X + Y)(X + Z)$	Distributive
16. $\overline{X + Y} = \overline{X} \cdot \overline{Y}$	17. $\overline{X \cdot Y} = \overline{X} + \overline{Y}$	DeMorgan

pendent of the order that is taken and therefore, the parentheses can be removed altogether.

$$X + (Y + Z) = (X + Y) + Z = X + Y + Z$$

$$X(YZ) = (XY)Z = XYZ$$

These two laws and the first distributive law are well known from ordinary algebra so they should not impose any difficulty. The second distributive law given by identity 15 is the dual of the ordinary distributive law and is very useful in manipulating Boolean functions.

$$X + YZ = (X + Y)(X + Z)$$

This equation can be used for other combination of variables. Consider the expression $(A + B)(A + CD)$. Letting $X = A$, $Y = B$, and $Z = CD$, and applying the second distributive law we obtain

$$(A + B)(A + CD) = A + BCD$$

The last two identities in Table 2-3 are referred to as DeMorgan's theorem.

$$(\overline{X + Y}) = \overline{X} \cdot \overline{Y} \quad \text{and} \quad (\overline{X \cdot Y}) = \overline{X} + \overline{Y}$$

This is a very important theorem and is used to obtain the complement of an expression. DeMorgan's theorem can be verified by means of truth tables that assign all the possible binary values to X and Y. Table 2-4 shows two truth tables that verify the first part of DeMorgan's theorem. In A, we evaluate $(\overline{X + Y})$ for all possible values of X and Y. This is done by first evaluating $X + Y$ and then taking its complement. In B, we evaluate $\overline{X}$ and $\overline{Y}$ and then AND them together. The result is the same for the four binary combinations of X and Y which verifies the identity of the equation.

Note the order in which the operations are performed when evaluating an expression. The complement over a single variable is evaluated, then the AND operation, and then the OR operation, just as we do in ordinary algebra with multiplication and addition. A complement over an expression such as $(\overline{X + Y})$ is considered as specifying NOT $(X + Y)$ so the value within the parentheses is evaluated first and then the complement of the result is taken. It is customary to exclude the parentheses when complementing an expression since a bar is drawn over the entire expression. Thus $(\overline{X + Y})$ is expressed as $\overline{X + Y}$ when designating the complement of $(X + Y)$.

TABLE 2-4
Truth Tables to Verify DeMorgan's Theorem

A.	X	Y	X + Y	$(\overline{X + Y})$	B.	X	Y	$\overline{X}$	$\overline{Y}$	$\overline{X} \cdot \overline{Y}$
	0	0	0	1		0	0	1	1	1
	0	1	1	0		0	1	1	0	0
	1	0	1	0		1	0	0	1	0
	1	1	1	0		1	1	0	0	0

DeMorgan's theorem can be extended to three or more variables. The general DeMorgan's theorem can be expressed as follows:

$$\overline{X_1 + X_2 + X_3 + \ldots + X_n} = \overline{X}_1 \overline{X}_2 \overline{X}_3 \ldots \overline{X}_n$$

$$\overline{X_1 X_2 X_3 \ldots X_n} = \overline{X}_1 + \overline{X}_2 + \overline{X}_3 + \ldots + \overline{X}_n$$

The logic operation changes from OR to AND or from AND to OR. In addition, the complement is removed from the entire expression and placed instead over each variable. For example,

$$\overline{XYZ} = \overline{X} + \overline{Y} + \overline{Z} \quad \text{and} \quad \overline{A + B + C + D} = \overline{A}\overline{B}\overline{C}\overline{D}.$$

Algebraic Manipulation

Boolean algebra is a useful tool for simplifying digital circuits. Consider for example the following Boolean function:

$$F = \overline{X}YZ + \overline{X}Y\overline{Z} + XZ$$

The implementation of this function with logic gates is shown in Figure 2-5(a). Input variables X and Z are complemented with inverters to obtain $\overline{X}$ and $\overline{Z}$. The three terms in the expression are implemented with three AND gates. The OR gate forms the logical sum of the three terms. Now consider the possible simplification of the function by applying some of the identities listed in Table 2-3.

$$
\begin{aligned}
F &= \overline{X}YZ + \overline{X}Y\overline{Z} + XZ & \\
&= \overline{X}Y(Z + \overline{Z}) + XZ & \text{by identity 14} \\
&= \overline{X}Y \cdot 1 + XZ & \text{by identity 7} \\
&= \overline{X}Y + XZ & \text{by identity 2}
\end{aligned}
$$

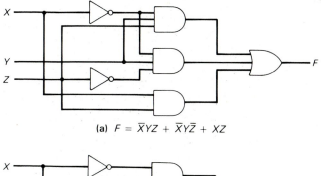

(a) $F = \overline{X}YZ + \overline{X}Y\overline{Z} + XZ$

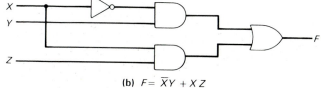

(b) $F = \overline{X}Y + XZ$

FIGURE 2-5

Implementation of Boolean Function with Gates

TABLE 2-5
Truth Table for
Boolean Function

X	Y	Z	F
0	0	0	0
0	0	1	0
0	1	0	1
0	1	1	1
1	0	0	0
1	0	1	1
1	1	0	0
1	1	1	1

The function is reduced to only two terms and can be implemented with gates as shown in Figure 2-5(b). It is obvious that the circuit in (b) is simpler than the one in (a); yet both implement the same function. It is possible to use a truth table to verify that the two expressions are equivalent, as shown in Table 2-5. The function as expressed in Figure 2-5(a) is equal to 1 when $XYZ = 011$, or when $XYZ = 010$, or when $XZ = 11$. This produces four 1's for F in the table. The function as expressed in Figure 2-5(b) is equal to 1 when $XY = 01$, or when $XZ = 11$. This produces the four 1's in the table. Since both expressions produce the same truth table, they are said to be equivalent. Therefore, the two circuits have the same output for all possible input binary combinations of the three variables. Each implements the same function but the one with fewer gates is preferable because it requires fewer components.

When a Boolean expression is implemented with logic gates, each term requires a gate and each variable within the term designates an input to the gate. We define a *literal* as a single variable within a term that may or may not be complemented. The function of Figure 2-5(a) has three terms and eight literals; the one in Figure 2-5(b) has two terms and four literals. By reducing the number of terms, the number of literals, or both, in a Boolean expression, it is sometimes possible to obtain a simpler circuit. The manipulation of Boolean algebra consists primarily of reducing an expression for the purpose of obtaining a simpler circuit. Unfortunately, there are no specific rules that guarantee a good result. The only method available is a cut-and-try procedure employing the basic relations and other manipulations that become familiar with use. The following examples illustrate a few of the possibilities.

  a. $X + XY = X(1 + Y) = X$
  b. $XY + X\overline{Y} = X(Y + \overline{Y}) = X$
  c. $X + \overline{X}Y = (X + \overline{X})(X + Y) = X + Y$

Note that the intermediate step $X = X \cdot 1$ has been omitted when X is factored out in the first equation. The relationship $1 + Y = 1$ is useful for eliminating redundant terms, as is done with the term XY in the first equation. The relation $Y + \overline{Y} = 1$ is useful for combining two terms, as is done in the second equation. The two terms to be combined must contain the same variable, but the variable must be complemented in one term and not complemented in the other. The third equation is simplified by means of the second distribution law (identity 15 in Table 2-3).

The following are three more examples of Boolean expression simplification.

  d. $X(X + Y) = X + XY = X(1 + Y) = X$
  e. $(X + Y)(X + \overline{Y}) = X + Y\overline{Y} = X$
  f. $X(\overline{X} + Y) = X\overline{X} + XY = XY$

Note that the intermediate steps $XX = X = X \cdot 1$ has been omitted during the manipulation of equation d. The expression in e is simplified by means of the second distributive law. Here again we omit the intermediate step $Y\overline{Y} = 0$ and $X + 0 = X$.

The last three equations are the dual of the first three equations. Remember that the dual of an expression is obtained by changing AND to OR and OR to AND throughout (and 1's to 0's and 0's to 1's if they appear in the expression).

The duality principle of Boolean algebra states that a Boolean equation remains valid if we take the dual of the expressions on both sides of the equal sign. Therefore, equations d, e, and f can be verified by taking the dual of equations a, b, and c, respectively.

The consensus theorem, shown below, is sometimes useful when simplifying Boolean expressions.

$$XY + \overline{X}Z + YZ = XY + \overline{X}Z$$

It shows that the third term YZ is redundant and can be eliminated. Note that Y and Z are also associated with X and $\overline{X}$ in the first two terms. The proof of the equation is obtained by first ANDing YZ with $(X + \overline{X}) = 1$.

$$XY + \overline{X}Z + YZ = XY + \overline{X}Z + YZ(X + \overline{X})$$
$$= XY + \overline{X}Z + XYZ + \overline{X}YZ$$
$$= XY + XYZ + \overline{X}Z + \overline{X}YZ$$
$$= XY(1 + Z) + \overline{X}Z(1 + Y)$$
$$= XY + \overline{X}Z$$

The dual of the consensus theorem is

$$(X + Y)(\overline{X} + Z)(Y + Z) = (X + Y)(\overline{X} + Z)$$

The following example shows how the consensus theorem can be applied when manipulating a Boolean expression.

$$(A + B)(\overline{A} + C) = A\overline{A} + AC + \overline{A}B + BC$$
$$= AC + \overline{A}B + BC$$
$$= AC + \overline{A}B$$

Note that $A\overline{A} = 0$ and $0 + AC = AC$. The redundant term here is BC.

Complement of a Function

The complement of a function, F, is obtained from an interchange of 1's to 0's and 0's to 1's in the values of F in the truth table. The complement of a function can be derived algebraically by applying DeMorgan's theorem. Remember that the generalized form of this theorem states that the complement of an expression is obtained by interchanging AND and OR operations and complementing each variable.

Example 2-1

Find the complement of the following two functions: $F_1 = \overline{X}Y\overline{Z} + \overline{X}\overline{Y}Z$ and $F_2 = X(\overline{Y}\overline{Z} + YZ)$.

Applying DeMorgan's theorem as many times as necessary the complements are obtained as follows:

$$\overline{F}_1 = \overline{\overline{X}Y\overline{Z} + \overline{X}\overline{Y}Z} = (\overline{\overline{X}Y\overline{Z}}) \cdot (\overline{\overline{X}\overline{Y}Z})$$
$$= (X + \overline{Y} + Z)(X + Y + \overline{Z})$$

$$\overline{F}_2 = \overline{X(\overline{YZ} + YZ)} = \overline{X} + \overline{(\overline{YZ} + YZ)}$$

$$= \overline{X} + (\overline{\overline{YZ}} \cdot \overline{YZ})$$

$$= \overline{X} + (Y + Z)(\overline{Y} + \overline{Z})$$

A simpler method for deriving the complement of a function is to take the dual of the function and complement each literal. This method follows from the generalized DeMorgan's theorem. Remember that the dual of an expression is obtained by interchanging AND and OR operations and 1's and 0's.

Example 2-2   Find the complement of the functions in Example 2-1 by taking their dual and complementing each literal

$$F_1 = \overline{X}Y\overline{Z} + \overline{X}\overline{Y}Z$$

The dual of F_1 $(\overline{X} + Y + \overline{Z})(\overline{X} + \overline{Y} + Z)$

Complement each literal $(X + \overline{Y} + Z)(X + Y + \overline{Z}) = \overline{F}_1$

$$F_2 = X(\overline{Y}\overline{Z} + YZ)$$

The dual of F_2 $X + (\overline{Y} + \overline{Z})(Y + Z)$

Complement each literal $\overline{X} + (Y + Z)(\overline{Y} + \overline{Z}) = \overline{F}_2$

2-3 STANDARD FORMS

A Boolean function can be written in a variety of ways when expressed algebraically. There are, however, a few algebraic expressions that are considered to be in standard form. The standard forms facilitate the simplification procedures of Boolean expressions and frequently result in a more desirable gating circuits.

The standard forms contain terms referred to as *product* terms and *sum* terms. An example of a product term is $X\overline{Y}Z$. This is a logical product consisting of an AND operation among several variables. An example of a sum term is $\overline{X} + Y + Z$. This is a logical sum consisting of an OR operation among the variables. It must be realized that the words *product* and *sum* do not imply arithmetic operations when dealing with Boolean algebra. Instead they specify *logical* operations equivalent to the Boolean operations of AND and OR, respectively.

Minterms and Maxterms

It has been shown that a truth table defines a Boolean function. An algebraic expression representing the function is derived from the table by finding the logical sum of all product terms for which the function assumes the binary value of 1. A product term in which all the variables appear exactly once either complemented or uncomplemented is called a *minterm*. Its characteristic property is that it shows

TABLE 2-6
Minterms and Maxterms for Three Variables

			Minterms		Maxterms	
X	Y	Z	Product Term	Symbol	Sum Term	Symbol
0	0	0	$\overline{X}\overline{Y}\overline{Z}$	m_0	$X + Y + Z$	M_0
0	0	1	$\overline{X}\overline{Y}Z$	m_1	$X + Y + \overline{Z}$	M_1
0	1	0	$\overline{X}Y\overline{Z}$	m_2	$X + \overline{Y} + Z$	M_2
0	1	1	$\overline{X}YZ$	m_3	$X + \overline{Y} + \overline{Z}$	M_3
1	0	0	$X\overline{Y}\overline{Z}$	m_4	$\overline{X} + Y + Z$	M_4
1	0	1	$X\overline{Y}Z$	m_5	$\overline{X} + Y + \overline{Z}$	M_5
1	1	0	$XY\overline{Z}$	m_6	$\overline{X} + \overline{Y} + Z$	M_6
1	1	1	XYZ	m_7	$\overline{X} + \overline{Y} + \overline{Z}$	M_7

exactly one combination of the binary variables in a truth table. There are 2^n distinct minterms for n variables. The four minterms for the two variables X and Y are $\overline{X}\overline{Y}$, $\overline{X}Y$, $X\overline{Y}$, and XY. The eight minterms for the three variables X, Y, and Z are listed in Table 2-6. The binary numbers from 000 to 111 are listed under the variables. Each minterm is obtained from the product term of exactly three variables with each variable being complemented if the corresponding bit of the binary number is 0 and uncomplemented if it is 1. A symbol for each minterm is also shown in the table and is of the form m_j, where the subscript j denotes the decimal equivalent of the binary number of the mintern. The list of minterms for any given n variables can be formed in a similar manner from a list of the binary numbers from 0 through $2^n - 1$.

A sum term that contains all the variables in complemented or uncomplemented form is called a *maxterm*. Again, it is possible to formulate 2^n maxterms with n variables. The eight maxterms for three variables are listed in Table 2-6. Each maxterm is obtained from the logical sum of the three variables with each variable being complemented if the corresponding bit is 1 and uncomplemented if 0. The symbol for a maxterm is M_j, where j denotes the binary number of the maxterm. Note that a minterm and maxterm with the same subscript number are the complements of each other, that is $M_j = \overline{m}_j$. For example, for $j = 3$, we have

$$\overline{m}_3 = \overline{\overline{X}YZ} = X + \overline{Y} + \overline{Z} = M_3$$

A Boolean function can be expressed algebraically from a given truth table by forming the logical sum of all the minterms which produce a 1 in the function. Consider the Boolean function F in Table 2-7(a). The function is equal to 1 for each of the following binary combinations of the variables X, Y and Z: 000, 010, 101, and 111. These combinations correspond to minterms 0, 2, 5, and 7. The function F can be expressed algebraically as the logical sum of these four minterms.

$$F = \overline{X}\overline{Y}\overline{Z} + \overline{X}Y\overline{Z} + X\overline{Y}Z + XYZ = m_0 + m_2 + m_5 + m_7$$

This can be further abbreviated by listing only the decimal subscripts of the minterms.

$$F(X, Y, Z) = \Sigma m(0, 2, 5, 7)$$

TABLE 2-7
Boolean Functions of Three Variables

(a)	X	Y	Z	F	$\overline{F}$	(b)	X	Y	Z	E
	0	0	0	1	0		0	0	0	1
	0	0	1	0	1		0	0	1	1
	0	1	0	1	0		0	1	0	1
	0	1	1	0	1		0	1	1	0
	1	0	0	0	1		1	0	0	1
	1	0	1	1	0		1	0	1	1
	1	1	0	0	1		1	1	0	0
	1	1	1	1	0		1	1	1	0

The symbol Σ stands for the logical sum (Boolean OR) of the minterms. The numbers following it are the minterms of the function. The letters in parentheses following F form a list of the variables in the order taken when the minterms are converted to product terms.

Now consider the complement of a Boolean function. The binary values of $\overline{F}$ in Table 2-7(a) are obtained by changing 1's to 0's and 0's to 1's in the values of F. Taking the logical sum of the minterms of $\overline{F}$ we obtain

$$\overline{F} = \overline{X}\overline{Y}Z + \overline{X}YZ + X\overline{Y}\overline{Z} + XY\overline{Z} = m_1 + m_3 + m_4 + m_6$$

or in abbreviated form

$$\overline{F}(X, Y, Z) = \Sigma m(1, 3, 4, 6)$$

Note that the minterm numbers for $\overline{F}$ are the ones missing from the list of the minterms of F. We now take the complement of $\overline{F}$ to obtain F.

$$F = \overline{m_1 + m_3 + m_4 + m_6} = \overline{m}_1 \cdot \overline{m}_3 \cdot \overline{m}_4 \cdot \overline{m}_6$$

$$= M_1 \cdot M_3 \cdot M_4 \cdot M_6 \qquad \text{(Since } \overline{m}_j = M_j)$$

$$= (X + Y + \overline{Z})(X + \overline{Y} + \overline{Z})(\overline{X} + Y + Z)(\overline{X} + \overline{Y} + Z)$$

This shows the procedure for expressing a Boolean function in product of maxterms. The abbreviated form for the product of maxterms form is

$$F(X, Y, Z) = \Pi M(1, 3, 4, 6)$$

The symbol Π denotes the logical product (Boolean AND) of the maxterms listed in parentheses. Note that the decimal numbers included in the product of maxterms will always be the same as the minterm list of the complemented function (1, 3, 4, 6 in the above example). Maxterms are seldom used when dealing with Boolean functions as we can always replace them with the minterm list of $\overline{F}$. The following is a summary of the most important properties of minterms:

1. There are 2^n minterms for n Boolean variables. They can be evaluated from the binary numbers from 0 to $2^n - 1$.

2. Any Boolean function can be expressed as a logical sum of minterms.

3. The complement of a function contains those minterms not included in the original function.

4. A function that included all the 2^n minterms is equal to logic-1.

A function that is not in sum of minterms can be converted to the sum of minterms form by means of a truth table, since the truth table always specifies the minterms of the function. Consider for example the Boolean function

$$E = \overline{Y} + \overline{X}\overline{Z}$$

The expression is not in sum of minterms because each term does not contain all three variables X, Y, and Z. The truth table for this function is listed in Table 2-7(b). From the truth table we obtain the minterms of the function.

$$E(X, Y, Z) = \Sigma m(0, 1, 2, 4, 5)$$

The minterms for the complement of E are

$$\overline{E}(X, Y, Z) = \Sigma m(3, 6, 7)$$

Note that the total number of minterms in E and $\overline{E}$ is equal to eight since the function has three variables and three variables can produce a total of eight minterms. With four variables, there will be a total of 16 minterms, and for two variables, there will be four minterms. An example of a function that includes all the minterms is

$$G(X, Y) = \Sigma m(0, 1, 2, 3) = 1$$

Since G is a function of two variables and contains all four minterms, it will always equal to logic-1.

Sum of Products

The sum of minterms form is a standard algebraic expression that is obtained directly from a truth table. The expression so obtained contains the maximum number of product terms and the maximum number of literals in each term. This is because, by definition, each minterm must include all the variables of the function complemented or uncomplemented. Once the sum of minterms is obtained from the truth table, the next step is to try to simplify the expression to see if it is possible to reduce the number of product terms and the number of literals in the terms. The result is a simplified expression in sum of products. The sum of products is an alternate standard form of expression that contains product terms with one, two or any number of literals. An example of a Boolean function expressed in sum of products is

$$F = \overline{Y} + \overline{X}Y\overline{Z} + XY$$

The expression has three product terms. The first term has one literal, the second has three literals, and the third has two literals.

The logic diagram of a sum of products expression consists of a group of AND gates followed by a single OR gate. This configuration pattern is shown in Figure

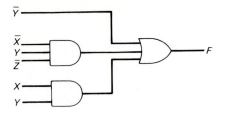

FIGURE 2-6
Sum of Products Implementation

2-6. Each product term requires an AND gate except for a term with a single literal. The logical sum is formed with an OR gate that receives its inputs from the outputs of the AND gates or the single variable. It is assumed that the input variables are directly available in their complement, so inverters are not included in the diagram. The AND gates followed by the OR gate forms a circuit configuration referred to as a *two-level* implementation.

If an expression is not in sum of products form, it can be converted to the standard form by means of the distributive laws. Consider the expression

$$F = AB + C(D + E)$$

This is not in sum of products form because the term $(D + E)$ is part of a product but is not a single variable. The expression can be converted to a sum of products by removing the parentheses.

$$F = AB + C(D + E) = AB + CD + CE$$

The implementation of this function is shown in Figure 2-7. The function is implemented in a nonstandard form in (a). This requires two AND gates and two OR gates. There are three levels of gating in this circuit. The expression is implemented in sum of products form in (b). This circuit requires three AND gates and an OR gate and uses two levels of gating. In general, a two-level implementation is preferred because it produces the least amount of delay time through the gates when the signal propagates from the inputs to the output.

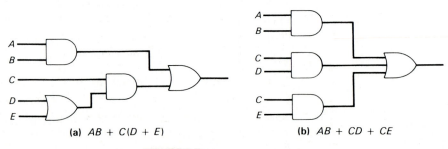

(a) $AB + C(D + E)$　　　　(b) $AB + CD + CE$

FIGURE 2-7
Three- and Two-Level Implementation

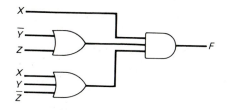

FIGURE 2-8
Product of Sums Implementation

Product of Sums

Another standard form of expressing Boolean functions algebraically is the product of sums. It is obtained by forming the logical product of sum terms. Each logical sum term may have any number of literals. An example of a function expressed in product of sums is

$$F = X(\overline{Y} + Z)(X + Y + \overline{Z})$$

This expression has three sum terms of one, two, and three literals. The sum terms perform an OR operation and the product is an AND operation.

The gate structure of the product of sums expression consists of a group of OR gates for the sum terms (except for a single literal term) followed by an AND gate. This is shown in Figure 2-8. This standard type of expression results in a two-level gating structure.

2-4   MAP SIMPLIFICATION

The complexity of the digital logic gates that implement a Boolean function is directly related to the algebraic expression from which the function is implemented. Although the truth table representation of a function is unique, when expressed algebraically, the function can appear in many different forms. Boolean expressions may be simplified by algebraic manipulation as discussed in Section 2-2. However, this procedure of simplification is awkward because it lacks specific rules to predict each succeeding step in the manipulative process and it is difficult to determine whether the simplest expression has been achieved. The map method provides a straightforward procedure for simplifying Boolean functions of up to four variables. Maps for larger number of variables can be drawn but are more cumbersome to use. The map is also known as the Karnaugh map or K-map.

The map is a diagram made up of squares with each square representing one minterm of the function. Since any Boolean function can be expressed as a sum of minterms, it follows that a Boolean function is recognized graphically in the map from the area enclosed by those squares whose minterms are included in the function. In fact, the map presents a visual diagram of all possible ways a function may be expressed in a standard form. By recognizing various patterns, the user can derive alternate algebraic expressions for the same function, from which the simplest can be selected.

The simplified expressions produced by the map are always in one of the two standard forms: either in sum of products or in product of sums. It will be assumed that the simplest algebraic expression is one with a minimum number of terms and with the fewest possible number of literals in each term. This produces a circuit logic diagram with a minimum number of gates and the minimum number of inputs to the gates. We will see subsequently that the simplest expression is not necessarily unique. It is sometimes possible to find two or more expressions that satisfy the simplification criteria. In that case, either solution would be satisfactory. This section covers only the sum of products simplification. In the next section we will show how to obtain the product of sums simplification.

Two-Variable Map

There are four minterms for a Boolean function with two variables. Hence, the two-variable map consists of four squares, one for each minterm, as shown in Figure 2-9. The map is redrawn in (b) to show the relationship between the squares and the two variables X and Y. The 0 and 1 marked on the left side and the top of the map designate the values of the variables. Variable X appears complemented in row 0 and uncomplemented in row 1. Similarly, Y appears complemented in column 0 and uncomplemented in column 1.

A function of two variables can be represented in a map by marking the squares that correspond to the minterms of the function. As an example, the function XY is shown in Figure 2-10(a). Since XY is equal to minterm m_3, a 1 is placed inside the square that belongs to m_3. Figure 2-10 (b) shows the map for the logical sum of three minterms.

$$m_1 + m_2 + m_3 = \overline{X}Y + X\overline{Y} + XY = X + Y$$

FIGURE 2-9
Two-Variable Map

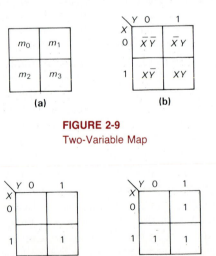

(a) XY **(b)** $X + Y$

FIGURE 2-10
Representation of Functions in the Map

The simplified expression $X + Y$ is determined from the two-square area for variable X in the second row and the two-square area for Y in the second column. Together, these two areas enclose the three squares belonging to X or Y. This simplification can be justified by algebraic manipulation.

$$\overline{X}Y + X\overline{Y} + XY = \overline{X}Y + X(\overline{Y} + Y) = (\overline{X} + X)(Y + X) = X + Y$$

The exact procedure for combining squares in the map will be clarified in the examples that follow.

Three-Variable Map

There are eight minterms for three binary variables. Therefore, a three-variable map consists of eight squares as shown in Figure 2-11. The map drawn in part (b) is marked with binary numbers in each row and each column to show the binary values of the minterms. Note that the numbers along the columns do not follow the binary count sequence. The characteristic of the listed sequence is that only one bit changes in value from one adjacent column to the next.

A minterm square can be located in the map in two ways. We can memorize the numbers listed in Figure 2-11 (a) for each minterm location, or we can refer to the binary numbers along the rows and columns. For example, the square assigned to m_5 corresponds to row 1 and column 01. When these two numbers are concatenated, they give the binary number 101, whose decimal equivalent is 5. Another way of looking at square $m_5 = X\overline{Y}Z$ is to consider it to be in the row marked X and the column belonging to $\overline{Y}Z$ (column 01). Note that there are four squares where each variable is equal to 1 and four squares where each is equal to 0. The variable appears uncomplemented in the four squares where it is equal to 1 and complemented in the four squares where it is equal to 0. For convenience, we write the variable name with the letter symbol along the four squares where it is uncomplemented.

To understand the usefulness of the map for simplifying Boolean functions, we must recognize the basic property possessed by adjacent squares. Any two adjacent squares placed horizontally or vertically (but not diagonally) correspond to minterms which differ in only a single variable. The single variable appears uncomplemented in one square and complemented in the other. For example, m_5 and m_7 lie in two adjacent squares. Variable Y is complemented in m_5 and uncomplemented

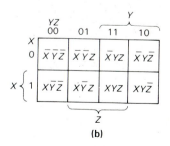

(a)

(b)

FIGURE 2-11
Three-Variable Map

in m_7, while the other two variables are the same in both squares. The logical sum of two adjacent minterms can be simplified into a single product term of two variables.

$$m_5 + m_7 = X\overline{Y}Z + XYZ = XZ(\overline{Y} + Y) = XZ$$

Here the two squares differ by variable Y, which can be removed when the logical sum (OR) of the two minterms is formed. Thus, any two minterms in adjacent squares that are ORed together produce a product term of two variables.

Example 2-3   Simplify the Boolean function

$$F(X, Y, Z) = \Sigma m(2, 3, 4, 5)$$

First, a 1 is marked in each minterm that represents the function. This is shown in Figure 2-12 where the squares for minterms 010, 011, 100, and 101 are marked with 1's. The next step is to find possible adjacent squares. These are indicated in the map by two rectangles, each enclosing two 1's. The upper right rectangle represents the area enclosed by $\overline{X}Y$. This is determined by observing that the two-square area is in row 0, corresponding to $\overline{X}$, and the last two columns, corresponding to Y. Similarly, the lower left rectangle represents the product term $X\overline{Y}$. (The second row represents X and the two left columns represent $\overline{Y}$.) The logical sum of these two product terms gives the simplified expression.

$$F = \overline{X}Y + X\overline{Y}$$ ■

There are cases where two squares in the map are considered to be adjacent even though they do not touch each other. In Figure 2-11, m_0 is adjacent to m_2 and m_4 is adjacent to m_6 because the minterms differ by one variable. This can be readily verified algebraically.

$$m_0 + m_2 = \overline{X}\overline{Y}\overline{Z} + \overline{X}Y\overline{Z} = \overline{X}\overline{Z}(\overline{Y} + Y) = \overline{X}\overline{Z}$$

$$m_4 + m_6 = X\overline{Y}\overline{Z} + XY\overline{Z} = X\overline{Z}(\overline{Y} + Y) = X\overline{Z}$$

Consequently, we must modify the definition of adjacent squares to include this and other similar cases. This is done by considering the map as being drawn on a surface where the right and left edges touch each other to form adjacent squares.

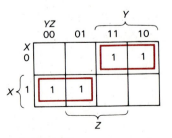

FIGURE 2-12
Map for Example 2-3; $F(X, Y, Z)$
$= \Sigma m(2, 3, 4, 5) = \overline{X}Y + X\overline{Y}$

Consider now any combination of four adjacent squares in the three-variable map. Any such combination represent the logical sum of four minterms and results in an expression of only one literal. As an example, the logical sum of the four adjacent minterms 0, 2, 4, and 6 reduces to a single literal term $\overline{Z}$.

$$m_0 + m_2 + m_4 + m_6 = \overline{X}\,\overline{Y}\,\overline{Z} + \overline{X}Y\overline{Z} + X\overline{Y}\,\overline{Z} + XY\overline{Z}$$

$$= \overline{X}\,\overline{Z}(\overline{Y} + Y) + X\overline{Z}(\overline{Y} + Y)$$

$$= \overline{X}\,\overline{Z} + X\overline{Z} = \overline{Z}(\overline{X} + X) = \overline{Z}$$

The number of adjacent squares that may be combined must always represent a number that is a power of two such as 1, 2, 4, and 8. As a larger number of adjacent squares are combined, we obtain a product term with fewer literals.

One square represents a minterm of three literals.

Two adjacent squares represent a product term of two literals.

Four adjacent squares represent a product term of one literal.

Eight adjacent squares encompasses the entire map and produces a function which is always equal to logic-1.

Example 2-4

Simplify the two Boolean functions

$$F_1(X, Y, Z) = \Sigma m(3, 4, 6, 7)$$

$$F_2(X, Y, Z) = \Sigma m(0, 2, 4, 5, 6)$$

The map for F_1 is shown in Figure 2-13(a). There are four squares marked with 1's, one for each minterm of the function. Two adjacent squares are combined in the third column to give a two-literal term YZ. The remaining two squares with 1's are also adjacent by the new definition and are shown in the diagram with their values enclosed in half rectangles. These two squares when combined, give the two-literal term $X\overline{Z}$. The simplified function becomes

$$F_1 = YZ + X\overline{Z}$$

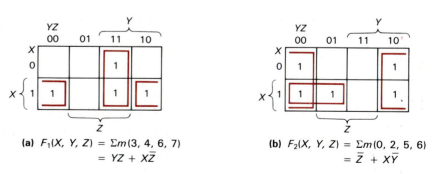

(a) $F_1(X, Y, Z) = \Sigma m(3, 4, 6, 7)$
$= YZ + X\overline{Z}$

(b) $F_2(X, Y, Z) = \Sigma m(0, 2, 5, 6)$
$= \overline{Z} + X\overline{Y}$

FIGURE 2-13
Maps for Example 2-4

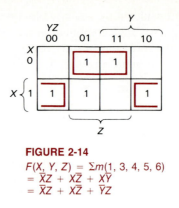

FIGURE 2-14
$F(X, Y, Z) = \Sigma m(1, 3, 4, 5, 6)$
$= \overline{X}Z + X\overline{Z} + X\overline{Y}$
$= \overline{X}Z + X\overline{Z} + \overline{Y}Z$

The map for F_2 is shown in Fig. 2-13(b). First we combine the four adjacent squares in the first and last columns to give the single literal term $\overline{Z}$. The remaining single square representing minterm 5 is combined with an adjacent square that is already being used once. This is not only permissible but rather desirable since the two adjacent squares give the two-literal term $X\overline{Y}$ while the single square represents the three-literal minterm $X\overline{Y}Z$. The simplified function is

$$F_2 = \overline{Z} + X\overline{Y}$$

There are occasions when there are two alternate ways of combining squares to produce equally simplified expressions. An example of this is demonstrated in the map of Figure 2-14. Minterms 1 and 3 are combined to give the term $\overline{X}Z$ and minterms 4 and 6 produce the term $X\overline{Z}$. However, there are two ways that the square of minterm 5 can be combined with another adjacent square to produce a third two-literal term. Combining it with minterm 4 gives the term $X\overline{Y}$. We could choose instead to combine it with minterm 1 to give the term $\overline{Y}Z$. Each of the two possible simplified expressions listed in Figure 2-14 has three terms of two literals each; so there are two possible simplified solutions for this function.

If a function is not expressed as a sum of minterms, we can use the map to obtain the minterms of the function and then simplify the function. It is necessary to have the algebraic expression in sum of products, from which each product term is plotted in the map. The minterms of the function are then read directly from the map. Consider the following Boolean function.

$$F = \overline{X}Z + \overline{X}Y + X\overline{Y}Z + YZ$$

Three product terms in the expression have two literals and are represented in a three-variable map by two squares each. The two squares corresponding to the first term, $\overline{X}Z$, are found in Figure 2-15 from the coincidence of $\overline{X}$ (first row) and Z (two middle columns) to give squares 001 and 011. Note that when marking 1's in the squares, it is possible to find a 1 already placed there from a preceding term. This happens with the second term $\overline{X}Y$ which has 1's in squares 011 and 010, but square 011 is common with the first term $\overline{X}Z$ so only one 1 is marked in it. Continuing in this fashion we find that the function has five minterms as indicated by the five 1's in the map of Figure 2-15. The minterms are read directly from the

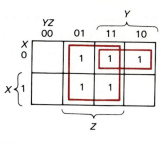

FIGURE 2-15
$F(X, Y, Z) = \Sigma m(1, 2, 3, 5, 7) =$
$Z + \overline{X}Y$

map to be 1, 2, 3, 5, and 7. The function as originally given has too many product terms. It can be simplified to only two terms.

$$F = Z + \overline{X}Y$$

Four-Variable Map

There are 16 minterms for four binary variables and therefore, a four-variable map consists of 16 squares as shown in Figure 2-16. The minterm assignment in each square is indicated in part (a) of the diagram. The map is redrawn in (b) to show the relationship of the four variables. The rows and columns are numbered in a special sequence so that only one bit of the binary number changes in value between any two adjacent squares. The minterms corresponding to each square can be obtained from the concatenation of the row number with the column number. For example, the numbers in the third row (11) and the second column (01), when concatenated, give the binary number 1101, the binary equivalent of 13. Thus, the square in the third row and second column represents minterm m_{13}. In addition, each variable is marked in the map to show the eight squares where it appears

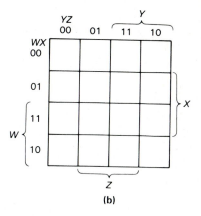

(a)

(b)

FIGURE 2-16
Four-Variable Map

uncomplemented. The other eight squares where no label is indicated correspond to the variable being complemented. Thus, W appears complemented in the first two rows and uncomplemented in the second two rows.

The map simplification of four-variable functions is similar to the method used to simplify three-variable functions. Adjacent squares are defined to be squares next to each other. In addition, the map is considered to lie on a surface with the top and bottom edges, as well as the right and left edges, touching each other to form adjacent squares. For example, m_0 and m_2 are two adjacent squares, as are m_3 and m_{11}. The combination of squares that can be taken during the simplification process in the four-variable map is as follows:

One square represents a minterm of four literals.

Two adjacent squares represent a product term of three literals.

Four adjacent squares represent a product term of two literals.

Eight adjacent squares represent a product term of one literal.

Sixteen squares produce a function which is always equal to logic-1.

No other combination of adjacent squares can be used. The following examples show the procedure for simplifying four-variable Boolean functions.

Example 2-5   Simplify the Boolean function

$$F(W, X, Y, Z) = \Sigma m(0, 1, 2, 4, 5, 6, 8, 9, 12, 13, 14)$$

The minterms of the function are marked with 1's in the map of Figure 2-17. Eight adjacent squares in the two left columns are combined to form the one literal term $\overline{Y}$. The remaining three 1's cannot be combined together to give a simplified term. They must be combined as two or four adjacent squares. The top two 1's on the right are combined with the top two 1's on the left to give the term $\overline{W}\overline{Z}$. Note again that it is permissible to take the same square more than once. We are now left with a square marked with 1 in the third row and fourth column (minterm 1100). Instead of taking this square alone which will give a term of four literals,

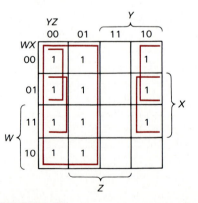

FIGURE 2-17
Map for Example 2-5; $F = \overline{Y} + \overline{W}\overline{Z} + X\overline{Z}$

we combine it with squares already used to form an area of four adjacent squares in the two middle rows and the two end columns, giving the term $X\overline{Z}$. The simplified expression is the logical sum of the three terms.

$$F = \overline{Y} + \overline{W}\overline{Z} + X\overline{Z}$$

■

Example 2-6

Simplify the Boolean function

$$F = \overline{A}\overline{B}\overline{C} + \overline{B}C\overline{D} + \overline{A}BC\overline{D} + A\overline{B}\overline{C}$$

This function has four variables A, B, C, and D. It is expressed in sum of products with three terms of three literals each and one term of four literals. The area in the map covered by this function is shown in Figure 2-18. Each term of three literals is represented in the map with two squares. $\overline{A}\overline{B}\overline{C}$ is represented in squares 0000 and 0001, $\overline{B}C\overline{D}$ in squares 0010 and 1010, and $A\overline{B}\overline{C}$ in squares 1000 1001. The term with four literals is minterm 0110. The function is simplified in the map by taking the 1's in the four corners to give the term $\overline{B}\overline{D}$. This is possible because these four squares are adjacent when the map is drawn on a surface with top and bottom or left and right edges touching one another. The two 1's in the top row are combined with the two 1's in the bottom row to give the term $\overline{B}\overline{C}$. The remaining 1 in square 0110 is combined with its adjacent square 0010 to give the term $\overline{A}C\overline{D}$. The simplified function is

$$F = \overline{B}\overline{D} + \overline{B}\overline{C} + \overline{A}C\overline{D}$$

■

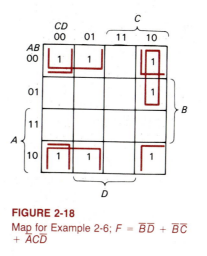

FIGURE 2-18
Map for Example 2-6; $F = \overline{B}\overline{D} + \overline{B}\overline{C} + \overline{A}C\overline{D}$

2-5   MAP MANIPULATION

When combining adjacent squares in a map, it is necessary to ensure that all the minterms of the function are included. At the same time it is necessary to minimize the number of terms in the simplified function by avoiding any redundant terms whose minterms are already covered by other terms. In this section we consider a manipulative procedure that facilitates the recognition of correct patterns in the map. Other topics to be covered are product of sums simplification and the simplification of incompletely specified functions. We will also show how the four variable map can be extended to cover five variable Boolean functions.

Essential Prime Implicants

The procedure for combining squares in the map may be made more systematic if we understand the meaning of the terms referred to as prime implicant and essential prime implicant. A prime implicant is a product term obtained by combining the maximum possible number of adjacent squares in the map. If a minterm in a square is covered by only one prime implicant, that prime implicant is said to be essential. In Figure 2-14, the terms $\overline{X}Z$ and $X\overline{Z}$ are essential prime implicants and the terms $X\overline{Y}$ and $\overline{Y}Z$ are non-essential prime implicants.

The prime implicants of a function can be obtained from the map by combining all possible maximum number of squares. This means that a single 1 on a map represents a prime implicant if it is not adjacent to any other 1's. Two adjacent 1's form a prime implicant provided they are not within a group of four adjacent squares. Four adjacent 1's form a prime implicant if they are not within a group of eight adjacent squares, and so on. The essential prime implicants are found by looking at each square marked with a 1 and checking the number of prime implicants that cover it. The prime implicant is essential if it is the only prime implicant that covers the minterm. The procedure for finding the simplified expression from the map requires that we first determine all the essential prime implicants. The simplified expression is obtained from the logical sum of all the essential prime implicants plus other prime implicants that may be needed to cover any remaining minterms not covered by the essential prime implicants. This procedure will be clarified by means of two examples.

Consider the map of Figure 2-19. There are three ways that we can combine four adjacent squares. The product terms obtained from these combinations are the prime implicants of the function. The terms $\overline{A}D$ and $B\overline{D}$ are essential prime implicants but $\overline{A}B$ is not essential. This is because minterms 1 and 3 can be covered

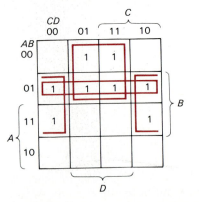

FIGURE 2-19
Prime Implicants $\overline{A}D$, $B\overline{D}$, and $\overline{A}B$

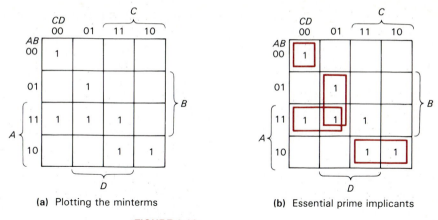

(a) Plotting the minterms

(b) Essential prime implicants

FIGURE 2-20
Simplification with Prime Implicants

only by the term $\overline{A}D$ and minterms 12 and 14 can be covered only by the term $B\overline{D}$. But minterms 4, 5, 6, and 7 are covered by two prime implicants so the term $\overline{A}B$ is not an essential prime implicant. In fact, once the essential prime implicants are taken, the third term is not needed in this case because all the minterms are already covered by the essential prime implicants. The simplified expression for the function of Figure 2-19 is

$$F = \overline{A}D + B\overline{D}$$

A second example is shown in Figure 2-20. The function plotted in part (a) has seven minterms. If we try to combine adjacent squares, we will find that there are six prime implicants. In order to obtain a minimum number of terms for the function, we must first determine the prime implicants that are essential. As shown in part (b) of the figure, the function has four essential prime implicants. Product term $\overline{A}\,\overline{B}\,\overline{C}\,\overline{D}$ is essential because it is the only prime implicant that covers minterm 0. Similarly, product terms $B\overline{C}D$, $AB\overline{C}$, and $A\overline{B}C$ are essential prime implicants because they are the only prime implicants that cover minterms 5, 12, and 10, respectively. Minterm 15 can be covered by two prime implicants. The simplified expression for the function consists of the logical sum of the four essential prime implicants and one prime implicant that covers minterm 15.

$$F = \overline{A}\,\overline{B}\,\overline{C}\,\overline{D} + B\overline{C}D + AB\overline{C} + A\overline{B}C + \begin{cases} ACD \\ \text{or} \\ ABD \end{cases}$$

The identification of essential prime implicants in the map augments the pattern of adjacent squares and shows the alternatives available for simplifying the Boolean function.

Product of Sums Simplification

The simplified Boolean functions derived from the map in all previous examples were expressed in sum of products. With minor modification, the product of sums form can be obtained.

The procedure for obtaining a simplified expression in product of sums follows from the basic properties of Boolean functions. The 1's placed in the squares of the map represent the minterms of the function. The minterms not included in the function belong to the complement of the function. From this we see that the complement of a function is represented in the map by the squares not marked by 1's. If we mark the empty squares with 0's and combine them into valid adjacent squares, we obtain a simplified expression of the complement of the function. We then take the complement of $\overline{F}$ to obtain the function F as a product of sums. This is done by taking the dual, and complementing each literal as described in Example 2-2.

Example 2-7

Simplify the following Boolean function in product of sums form.

$$F(A, B, C, D) = \Sigma m(0, 1, 2, 5, 8, 9, 10)$$

The 1's marked in the map of Figure 2-21 represent the minterms of the function. The squares marked with 0's represent the minterms not included in F and therefore denote the complement of F. Combining the squares marked with 0's we obtain the simplified complemented function

$$\overline{F} = AB + CD + B\overline{D}$$

Taking the dual and complementing each literal gives the complement of $\overline{F}$. This is F in product of sums.

$$F = (\overline{A} + \overline{B})(\overline{C} + \overline{D})(\overline{B} + D) \qquad \blacksquare$$

The previous example shows the procedure for obtaining the product of sums simplification when the function is originally expressed in sum of minterms. The procedure is also valid when the function is originally expressed in product of maxterms or product of sums. Remember that the maxterm numbers are the same as the minterm numbers of the complemented function; so 0's are entered in the

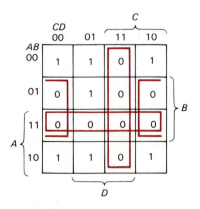

FIGURE 2-21
Map for Example 2-7;
$F = (\overline{A} + \overline{B})(\overline{C} + \overline{D})(\overline{B} + D)$

map for the maxterms or for the complement of the function. To enter a function expressed as a product of sums in the map, we must take the complement of the function and from it find the squares to be marked by 0's. For example, the function

$$F = (\overline{A} + \overline{B} + C)(B + D)$$

can be plotted in the map by first taking its complement

$$\overline{F} = AB\overline{C} + \overline{B}\overline{D}$$

and then marking 0's in the squares representing the minterms of $\overline{F}$. The remaining squares are marked with 1's. Then, combining the 1's gives the simplified expression in sum of products form. Combining the 0's and then complementing gives the simplified expression in product of sums. Thus, for any function plotted in the map we can derive the simplified function in either one of the two standard forms.

Don't Care Conditions

The list of minterms of a Boolean function specify the conditions under which the function is equal to 1. The function is assumed to be equal to 0 for the rest of the minterms. This assumption is not always valid since there are applications where the function is not specified for certain combinations of the variables. As an example, the four-bit binary code for the decimal digits has six combinations which are not used and consequently are considered as unspecified. Functions that have unspecified outputs for some input combinations are called incompletely specified functions. In most applications, we simply do not care what value is assumed by the function for the unspecified minterms. For this reason it is customary to call the unspecified minterms of a function don't care conditions. These don't care conditions can be used on a map to provide further simplification of the function.

It should be realized that a don't care minterm cannot be marked with a 1 on the map because it would require that the function always be a 1 for such combination. Likewise, putting a 0 on the square requires the function to be 0. To distinguish the don't care condition from 1's and 0's, a cross (X) is used. Thus, a cross inside a square in the map indicates that we do not care whether the value of 0 or 1 is assigned to F for the particular minterm.

When choosing adjacent squares to simplify the function in a map, the don't care minterms may be assumed to be either 1 or 0. When simplifying the function, we can choose to include each don't care minterm with either the 1's or the 0's depending on which combination gives the simplest expression. In addition, a don't care minterm need not be taken at all if it does not contribute to covering a larger number of squares. The choice depends entirely on the simplification that can be achieved.

To clarify the procedure for handling the don't care conditions, consider the following incompletely specified function that has three don't care minterms.

$$F(W, X, Y, Z) = \Sigma m(1, 3, 7, 11, 15)$$

$$d(W, X, Y, Z) = \Sigma m(0, 2, 5)$$

The minterms of F are the variable combinations that make the function equal to 1. The minterms of d are the don't care minterms that may be assigned either 0

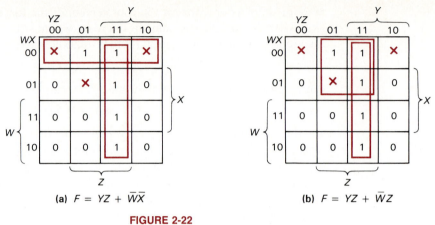

(a) $F = YZ + \overline{W}\overline{X}$ (b) $F = YZ + \overline{W}Z$

FIGURE 2-22
Example with Don't Care Conditions

or 1. The map simplification is shown in Figure 2-22. The minterms of F are marked by 1's, those of d are marked by crosses, and the remaining squares are filled with 0's. To get the simplified function in sum of products, we must include all the five 1's in the map, but we may or may not include any of the crosses, depending on the way the function is simplified. The term YZ covers the four minterms in the third column. The remaining minterm in square 0001 can be combined with square 0011 to give a three-literal term. However, by including one or two adjacent crosses we can combine four adjacent squares to give a two-literal term. In part (a) of the diagram, don't care minterms 0 and 2 are included with the 1's which results in the simplified function

$$F = YZ + \overline{W}\overline{X}$$

In part (b), don't care minterm 5 is included with the 1's and the simplified function now is

$$F = YZ + \overline{W}Z$$

The two expressions listed above represent two functions which are algebraically unequal. Both cover the specified minterms of the function but each covers different don't care minterms. As far as the incompletely specified function is concerned, both expressions are acceptable. The only difference is in the value of F for the unspecified minterms.

It is also possible to obtain a simplified product of sums expression for the function of Figure 2-22. In this case, the way to combine the 0's is to include don't care minterms 0 and 2 with the 0's to give a simplified complemented function

$$\overline{F} = \overline{Z} + W\overline{Y}$$

Taking the complement of $\overline{F}$ gives the simplified expression in product of sums form.

$$F = Z(\overline{W} + Y)$$

The above examples show that the don't care minterms in the map are initially considered as representing a choice of 1 or 0. The choice is made depending on the way we want to simplify the incompletely specified function. However, once the choice is made, the simplified function will have specific values for all the minterms of the function, including those that were initially unspecified.

Five-Variable Map

Maps for more than four variables are not as simple to use. A five-variable map needs 32 squares and a six-variable map needs 64 squares. When the number of variables becomes large, the number of squares becomes excessively large and the geometry for combining adjacent squares becomes more involved.

The five-variable map is shown in Figure 2-23. It consists of two four-variable maps with variables A, B, C, D, and E. Variable A distinguishes between the two maps as indicated on top of the diagram. The left-hand four-variable map represents the 16 squares where $A = 0$, and the other four-variable map represents the squares where $A = 1$. Minterms 0 through 15 belong with $A = 0$ and minterms 16 through 31 with $A = 1$. Each four-variable map retains the previously defined adjacency when taken separately. In addition, each square in the $A = 0$ map is adjacent to the corresponding square in the $A = 1$ map. For example, minterm 4 is adjacent to minterm 20 and minterm 15 to 31. The best way to visualize this new rule for adjacent squares is to consider the two half maps as being one on top of the other. Any two squares that fall one over the other are considered adjacent.

From inspection, and taking into account the new definition of adjacent squares, it is possible to show that any 2^k adjacent squares, for $k = 0, 1, 2, 3, 4$, in the five-variable map represents a product term of $5 - k$ literals. For example, four adjacent squares combine an area in the five-variable map that represents a product term of $5 - 2 = 3$ literals.

Following the procedure used for the five-variable map, it is possible to construct a six-variable map with four four-variable maps to obtain the required 64 squares. Maps with six or more variables need too many squares and are impractical to use. The alternative is to employ computer programs specifically written to facilitate the simplification of Boolean functions with a large number of variables.

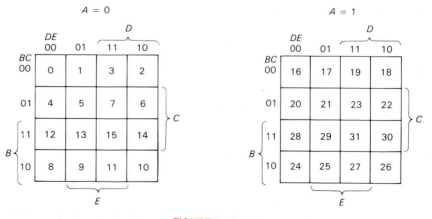

FIGURE 2-23
Five-Variable Map

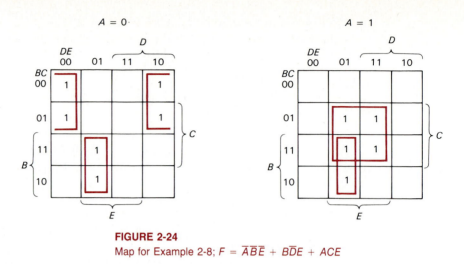

FIGURE 2-24
Map for Example 2-8; $F = \overline{A}B\overline{E} + B\overline{D}E + ACE$

Example 2-8   Simplify the Boolean function

$$F(A, B, C, D, E) = \Sigma m(0, 2, 4, 6, 9, 13, 21, 23, 25, 29, 31)$$

The five-variable map for this function is shown in Figure 2-24. There are six minterms from 0 to 15 that belong to the part of the map with $A = 0$. The other five minterms belong with $A = 1$. Four adjacent squares in the $A = 0$ map are combined to give the three literal term $\overline{A}B\overline{E}$. Note that it is necessary to include $\overline{A}$ with the term because all the squares are associated with $A = 0$. The two squares in column 01 and the last two rows are common to both parts of the map. Therefore, they constitute four adjacent squares and give the three-literal term $B\overline{D}E$. Variable A is not included here because the adjacent squares belong to both $A = 0$ and $A = 1$. The term ACE is obtained from the four adjacent squares that are entirely within the $A = 1$ map. The simplified function is the logical sum of the three terms.

$$F = \overline{A}B\overline{E} + B\overline{D}E + ACE$$

2-6   NAND AND NOR GATES

Since Boolean functions are expressed in terms of AND, OR, and complement operations, it is a straightforward procedure to implement a Boolean function with AND, OR, and inverter gates. The possibility of constructing gates with other logic operations is of practical interest. Factors to be taken into consideration when constructing other types of gates are the feasibility and economy of producing the gate with electronics components, the possibility of extending the gate to more than two inputs, and the ability of the gate to implement Boolean functions alone or in conjunction with other gates.

In addition to the AND, OR, and inverter gates, there are other logic gates which are available commercially and used extensively in the design of digital circuits. The graphic symbols and truth tables of eight logic gates are shown in Figure 2-25. The gates are shown with two binary input variables X and Y and one

Graphic symbols

Name	Distinctive shape	Rectangular shape	Algebraic equation	Truth table

AND — & — $F = XY$

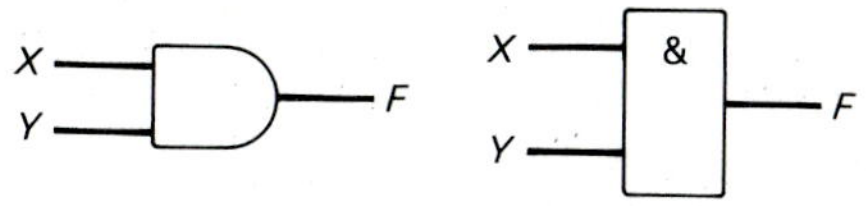

X	Y	F
0	0	0
0	1	0
1	0	0
1	1	1

OR — ≥1 — $F = X + Y$

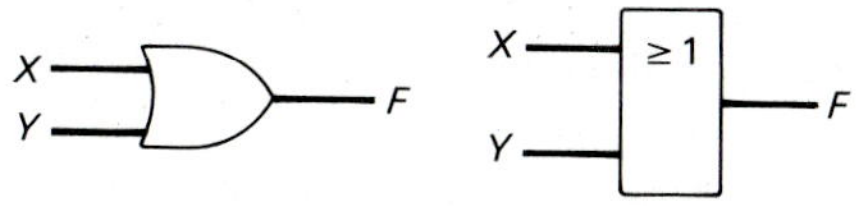

X	Y	F
0	0	0
0	1	1
1	0	1
1	1	1

Inverter — 1 — $F = \overline{X}$

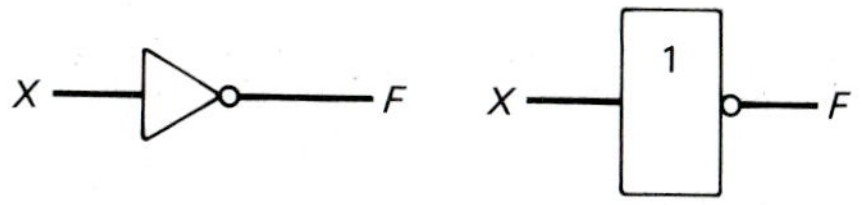

X	F
0	1
1	0

Buffer — 1 — $F = X$

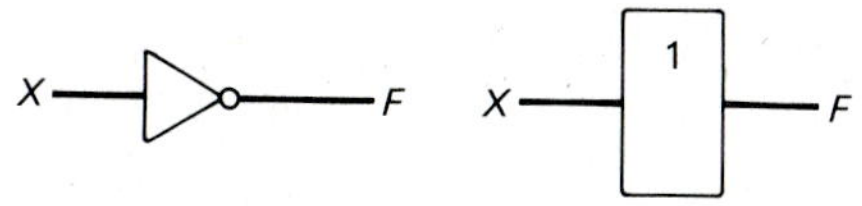

X	F
0	0
1	1

NAND — & — $F = \overline{X \cdot Y}$

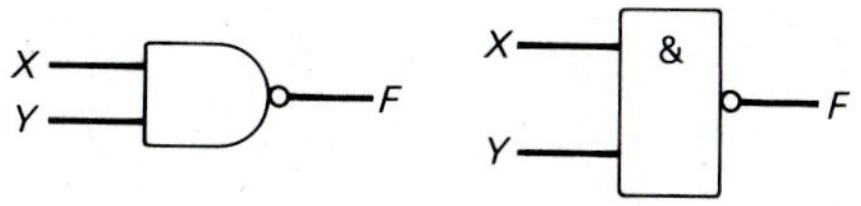

X	Y	F
0	0	1
0	1	1
1	0	1
1	1	0

NOR — ≥1 — $F = \overline{X + Y}$

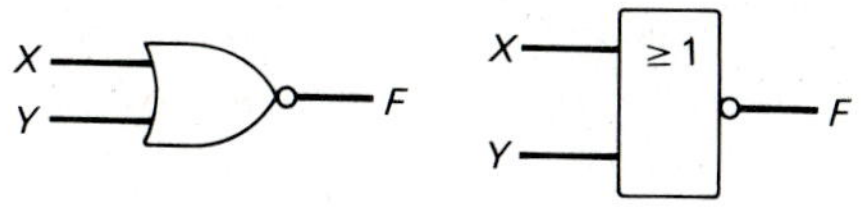

X	Y	F
0	0	1
0	1	0
1	0	0
1	1	0

Exclusive-OR (XOR) — =1 — $F = X\overline{Y} + \overline{X}Y = X \oplus Y$

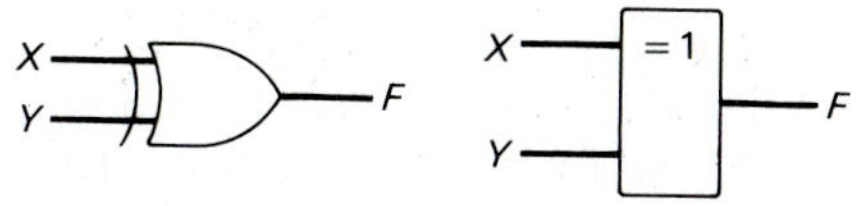

X	Y	F
0	0	0
0	1	1
1	0	1
1	1	0

Exclusive-NOR (XNOR) — =1 — $F = XY + \overline{X}\overline{Y} = \overline{X \oplus Y}$

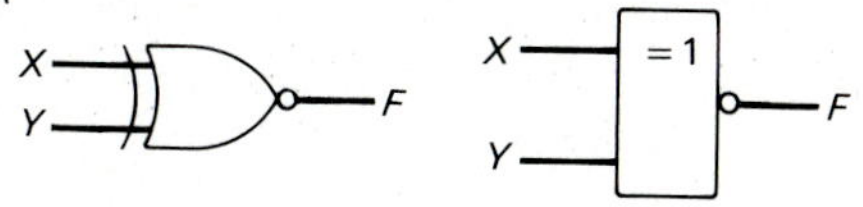

X	Y	F
0	0	1
0	1	0
1	0	0
1	1	1

FIGURE 2-25
Digital Logic Gates

output binary variable F. Two graphic symbols are drawn for each gate. The rectangular shape symbols are recommended by the Institute of Electrical and Electronics Engineers (IEEE) Standard Graphic Symbols for Logic Functions (IEEE Standard 91-1984). The distinctive shape symbols have been used in the past and are considered as alternative to the standard. The rectangular shape symbols are more convenient when used with computer graphics. In this book we will retain the distinctive shape symbols because of their extensive use in the technical literature.

The AND, OR, and inverter gates were defined previously. The inverter circuit inverts the logic sense of a binary signal to produce the complement operation. The small circle in the output of the graphic symbol of an inverter designates the logic complement. The triangle symbol by itself designates a buffer circuit. A buffer does not produce any particular logic operation, since the binary value of the output is equal to the binary value of the input. This circuit is used merely for power amplification of the electrical signal.

The NAND gate is the complement of the AND operation. Its name is an abbreviation of Not AND. The graphic symbol consists of an AND symbol followed by a small circle. The NOR gate (an abbreviation of Not OR) is the complement of the OR operation and is symbolized by an OR graphic symbol followed by a small circle. The NAND and NOR gates are extensively used as standard logic gates and are in fact far more popular than the AND and OR gates. This is because NAND and NOR gates are easily constructed with electronics circuits and because Boolean functions can be easily implemented with them.

The exclusive-OR (XOR) gate is similar to the OR gate but excludes the combination of both X and Y being equal to 1. The graphic symbol of the XOR gate is similar to the OR gate except for the additional curved line on the input side. The exclusive-NOR is the complement of the exclusive-OR, as indicated by the small circle on the output side of the graphic symbol. The exclusive-OR has the special symbol $\oplus$ to designate its operation.

In the rest of this section we will investigate the implementation of digital circuits with NAND and NOR gates. The XOR gate is discussed in the next section.

NAND Gate

The NAND gate is said to be a universal gate because any digital system can be implemented with it. To show that any Boolean function can be implemented with NAND gates, we need only to show that the logical operations of AND, OR, and complement can be obtained with NAND gates only. This is shown in Figure 2-26. The complement operation is obtained from a one-input NAND gate which behaves exactly like an inverter gate. The AND operation requires two NAND gates. The first produces the NAND operation and the second inverts the logical sense of the signal. The OR operation is achieved through a NAND gate with additional inverters in each input.

A convenient way to implement a Boolean function with NAND gates is to obtain the simplified Boolean function in terms of Boolean operators and then convert the function to NAND logic. The conversion of an algebraic expression

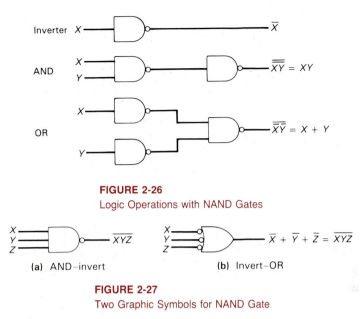

FIGURE 2-26
Logic Operations with NAND Gates

(a) AND–invert   (b) Invert–OR

FIGURE 2-27
Two Graphic Symbols for NAND Gate

from AND, OR, and complement to NAND can be done by simple circuit manipulation techniques that change AND-OR diagrams to NAND diagrams.

To facilitate the conversion to NAND logic, it is convenient to define an alternate graphic symbol for the gate. Two equivalent graphic symbols for the NAND gate are shown in Figure 2-27. The AND-invert symbol as defined previously, consists of an AND graphic symbol followed by a small circle. Instead, however, it is possible to represent a NAND gate by an OR graphic symbol which is preceded by a small circle in each input. The invert-OR symbol for the NAND gate follows DeMorgan's theorem and the convention that small circles denote complementation.

The two graphic symbols are useful in the analysis and design of NAND circuits. When both symbols are mixed in the same diagram, the circuit is said to be in *mixed notation*.

Two-Level Implementation

The implementation of Boolean functions with NAND gates requires that the function be in sum of products form. To see the relationship between a sum of product expression and its equivalent NAND implementation, consider the logic diagrams drawn in Figure 2-28. All three diagrams are equivalent and implement the function

$$F = AB + CD$$

The function is implemented in (a) with AND and OR gates. In (b) the AND gates are replaced by NAND gates and the OR gate is replaced by a NAND gate with an OR-invert graphic symbol. Remember that a small circle denotes complementation and two circles along the same line represent double complementation;

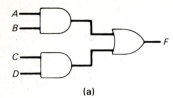

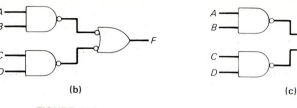

(a) (b) (c)

FIGURE 2-28
Three Ways to Implement $F = AB + CD$

so both can be removed. Removing the small circles in the gates of (b) produces the circuit of (a). Therefore, the two diagrams implement the same function and are equivalent.

In Figure 2-28(c), the output NAND gate is redrawn with the AND-invert graphic symbol. When drawing NAND logic diagrams, the circuit shown in either (b) or (c) is acceptable. The one in (b) is in mixed notation and represents a more direct relationship with the Boolean expression it implements. The NAND implementation in Figure 2-28(c) can be verified algebraically. The function it implements can be easily converted to a sum of products form by using DeMorgan's theorem.

$$F = \overline{\overline{AB} \cdot \overline{CD}} = AB + CD$$

Example 2-9

Implement the following Boolean function with NAND gates.

$$F(X, Y, Z) = \Sigma m(1, 2, 3, 4, 5, 7)$$

The first step is to simplify the function in sum of products form. This is done by means of the map of Figure 2-29(a) from which the simplified function is obtained.

$$F = X\overline{Y} + \overline{X}Y + Z$$

The two-level NAND implementation is shown in Figure 2-29(b) in mixed notation. Note that input Z must have a one-input NAND gate (inverter) to compensate for the small circle in the second level gate. An alternate way of drawing the logic diagram is shown in Figure 2-29(c). Here all the NAND gates are drawn with the same graphic symbol. The inverter with input Z has been removed but the input variable is complemented and denoted by $\overline{Z}$. ∎

The procedure described in the previous example indicates that a Boolean function can be implemented with two levels of NAND gates. The procedure for obtaining the logic diagram from a Boolean function is as follows:

1. Simplify the function and express it in sum of products.
2. Draw a NAND gate for each product term of the expression that has at least two literals. The inputs to each NAND gate are the literals of the term. This constitutes a group of first-level gates.
3. Draw a single gate using the AND-invert or the invert-OR graphic symbol in the second level, with inputs coming from outputs of first level gates.
4. A term with a single literal requires an inverter in the first level. However,

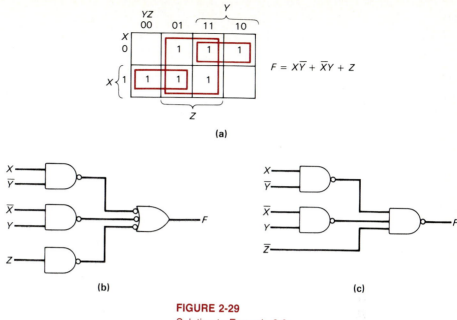

$$F = X\overline{Y} + \overline{X}Y + Z$$

(a)

(b)　　　　　　　　　　　　(c)

FIGURE 2-29
Solution to Example 2-9

if the single literal is complemented it can be connected directly to an input of the second level NAND gate.

Multilevel NAND Circuits

The standard form of expressing Boolean functions results in a two level implementation. There are occasions when the design of digital systems results in gating structures with three or more levels. The most common procedure in the design of multilevel circuits is to express the Boolean function in terms of AND, OR, and complement operations. The function can then be implemented directly with AND and OR gates. Then, if necessary, it can be converted into an all NAND circuit.

Consider for example the Boolean function.

$$F = A(CD + B) + B\overline{C}$$

Although it is possible to remove the parentheses and reduce the expression into a standard sum of products form, we choose to implement it as a multilevel circuit for illustration. The AND-OR implementation is shown in Figure 2-30(a). There are four levels of gating in the circuit. The first level has two AND gates. The second level has an OR gate followed by an AND gate in the third level and an OR gate in the fourth level. A logic diagram with a pattern of alternate levels of AND and OR gates can be easily converted into a NAND circuit by using the mixed notation. This is shown in Figure 2-30(b). The procedure is to change every AND gate to an AND-invert graphic symbol and every OR gate to an invert-OR graphic symbol. The NAND circuit performs the same logic as the AND-OR diagram as long as there are two small circles along the same line. The small circle associated with input B causes an extra complementation which must be compensated for by changing the input literal to $\overline{B}$.

The general procedure for converting a multilevel AND-OR diagram into an all NAND diagram using mixed notation is as follows:

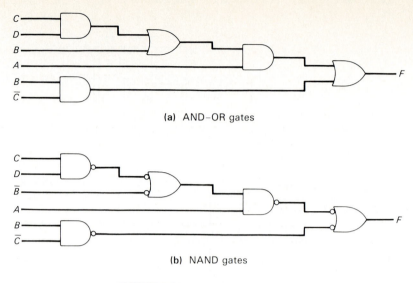

(a) AND–OR gates

(b) NAND gates

FIGURE 2-30
Implementing $F = A(CD + B) + B\overline{C}$

1. Convert all AND gates to NAND gates with AND-invert graphic symbols.
2. Convert all OR gates to NAND gates with invert-OR graphic symbols.
3. Check all the small circles in the diagram. For every small circle that is not counteracted by another small circle along the same line, insert an inverter (one-input NAND gate) or complement the input variable.

As another example, consider the multilevel Boolean function.

$$F = (A\overline{B} + \overline{A}B)(C + \overline{D})$$

The AND-OR implementation is shown in Figure 2-31(a) with three levels of gating.

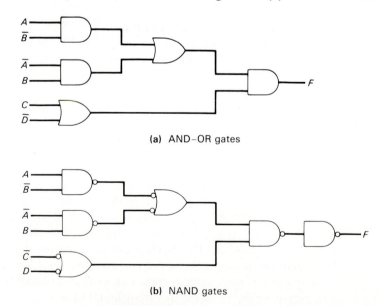

(a) AND–OR gates

(b) NAND gates

FIGURE 2-31
Implementing $F = (A\overline{B} + \overline{A}B)(C + \overline{D})$

The conversion into NAND with mixed notation is presented in part (b) of the diagram. The two additional small circles associated with inputs C and $\overline{D}$ cause these two literals to be complemented to $\overline{C}$ and D. The small circle in the output NAND gate complements the output value; so we need to insert an inverter gate at the output in order to complement the signal again and get the original value.

NOR gate

The NOR operation is the dual of the NAND operation. Therefore, all procedures and rules for NOR logic are the dual of the corresponding procedures and rules developed for NAND logic. The NOR gate is another universal gate that can be used to implement any Boolean function. The implementation of the AND, OR, and complement operations with NOR gates is shown in Figure 2-32. The complement operation is obtained from a one-input NOR gate. The OR operation requires two NOR gates and the AND operation is obtained with a NOR gate that has inverters in each input.

The two graphic symbols for the mixed notation are shown in Figure 2-33. The OR-invert symbol defines the NOR operation as an OR followed by a complement. The invert-AND symbol complements each input and then performs an AND operation. The two symbols designate the same NOR operation and are logically identical because of DeMorgan's theorem.

The two-level implementation with NOR gates requires that the function be simplified in product of sums form. Remember that the simplified product of sums expression is obtained from the map by combining the 0's and complementing. A product of sums expression is implemented with a first level of OR gates that produce the sum terms followed by a second level AND gate to produce the product.

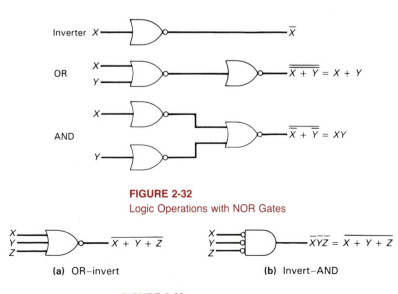

FIGURE 2-32
Logic Operations with NOR Gates

FIGURE 2-33
Two Graphic Symbols for NOR Gate

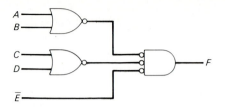

FIGURE 2-34
Implementing $F = (A + B)(C + D)E$
with NOR Gates

The transformation from the OR-AND diagram to a NOR diagram is achieved by changing the OR gates to NOR gates with OR-invert graphic symbols and the AND gate to a NOR gate with an invert-AND graphic symbol. A single literal term going into the second level gate must be complemented. Figure 2-34 shows the NOR implementation of a function expressed in product of sums.

$$F = (A + B)(C + D)E$$

The OR-AND pattern can be easily detected by the removal of the small circles along the same line. Variable E is complemented to compensate for the third small circle at the input of the second level gate.

The procedure for converting a multilevel AND-OR diagram to an all NOR diagram is similar to the one presented for NAND gates. For the NOR case we must convert each OR gate to an OR-invert symbol and each AND gate to an invert-AND symbol. Any small circle that is not compensated for by another small circle along the same line needs an inverter or the complementation of the input literal.

The transformation of the AND-OR diagram of Figure 2-31(a) into a NOR diagram is shown in Figure 2-35. The Boolean function for this circuit is:

$$F = (A\overline{B} + \overline{A}B)(C + \overline{D})$$

The equivalent AND-OR diagram can be recognized from the NOR diagram by removing all the small circles. Removing the small circles at the inputs requires that we complement the input literals.

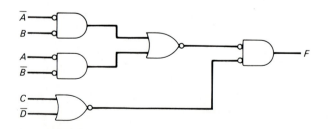

FIGURE 2-35
Implementing $F = (A\overline{B} + \overline{A}B)(C + \overline{D})$ with NOR Gates

2-7   EXCLUSIVE-OR-GATE

The exclusive-OR (XOR), denoted by $\oplus$, is a logical operation that performs the function

$$X \oplus Y = X\overline{Y} + \overline{X}Y$$

It is equal to 1 if only one variable is equal to 1 but not both. The exclusive-NOR, also known as the equivalence, is the complement of the exclusive-OR and is expressed by the function

$$\overline{X \oplus Y} = XY + \overline{X}\,\overline{Y}$$

It is equal to 1 if both X and Y are equal to 1 or if both are equal to 0. The two functions can be shown to be the complement of each other. This can be done by means of a truth table or by algebraic manipulation.

$$\overline{X \oplus Y} = \overline{X\overline{Y} + \overline{X}Y} = (\overline{X} + Y)(X + \overline{Y}) = XY + \overline{X}\,\overline{Y}$$

The following identities apply to the exlusive-OR operation:

$$X \oplus 0 = X \qquad\qquad X \oplus 1 = \overline{X}$$
$$X \oplus X = 0 \qquad\qquad X \oplus \overline{X} = 1$$
$$X \oplus \overline{Y} = \overline{X \oplus Y} \qquad \overline{X} \oplus Y = \overline{X \oplus Y}$$

Any of these identities can be proven by using a truth table or by replacing the $\oplus$ operation by its equivalent Boolean expression. It can also be shown that the exclusive-OR operation is both commutative and associative.

$$A \oplus B = B \oplus A$$

$$(A \oplus B) \oplus C = A \oplus (B \oplus C) = A \oplus B \oplus C$$

This means that the two inputs to an exclusive-OR gate can be interchanged without affecting the operation. It also means that we can evaluate a three-variable exclusive-OR operation in any order and for this reason, three or more variables can be expressed without parentheses. This would imply the possibility of using exclusive-OR gates with three or more inputs. However, multiple-input exclusive-OR gates are difficult to fabricate with hardware. In fact even a two-input function is usually constructed with other types of gates. A two-input exclusive-OR function is constructed with conventional gates using two inverters, two AND gates, and an OR gate. Figure 2-36 shows the implementation with four NAND gates. The mixed notation NAND diagram performs the following operation:

$$X(\overline{X} + \overline{Y}) + Y(\overline{X} + \overline{Y}) = X\overline{Y} + \overline{X}Y$$

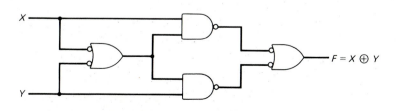

FIGURE 2-36
Exclusive-OR Constructed with NAND Gates

Transmission Gate

The exclusive-OR can be constructed by means of a special circuit called *transmission gate*. This type of gate is available with CMOS type electronic circuits (discussed in the next section). The operation of the transmission gate (TG) is shown in Figure 2-37. X is the input, Y is the output, and the two terminals C and $\overline{C}$ are control inputs. The circuit functions as an electronic switch. When $C = 1$ and $\overline{C} = 0$, there is a closed path between X and Y for the signal to pass. When $C = 0$ and $\overline{C} = 1$, the path disconnects and the circuit behaves like an open switch. Normally, the control inputs are connected through an inverter as shown in Fig. 2-37(c) so that C and $\overline{C}$ are the complement of each other.

An exclusive-OR gate can be constructed with two transmission gates and two inverters as shown in Figure 2-38. Input A controls the paths in the transmission gates and input B provides the output for Y. When input A is equal to 0, transmission gate TG1 is closed and output Y is equal to input B. When input A is equal to 1, TG2 is closed and output Y is equal to the complement of input B. This results in the exclusive-OR truth table as indicated in the table of Figure 2-38.

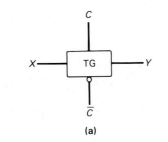

(a)

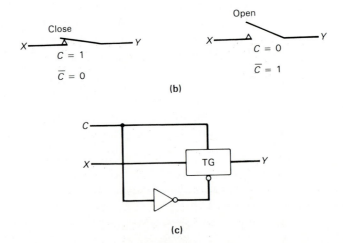

(c)

FIGURE 2-37
Transmission Gate (TG)

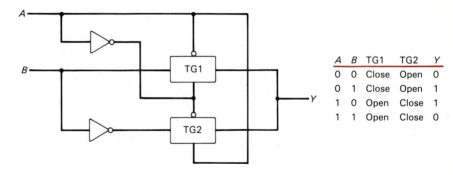

A	B	TG1	TG2	Y
0	0	Close	Open	0
0	1	Close	Open	1
1	0	Open	Close	1
1	1	Open	Close	0

FIGURE 2-38
Exclusive-OR Constructed with Transmission Gates

Odd Function

The exclusive-OR operation with three or more variables can be converted into an ordinary Boolean function by replacing the $\oplus$ symbol with its equivalent Boolean expression. In particular, the three-variable case can be converted to a Boolean expression as follows:

$$X \oplus Y \oplus Z = (X\overline{Y} + \overline{X}Y)\overline{Z} + (XY + \overline{X}\overline{Y})Z$$
$$= X\overline{Y}\overline{Z} + \overline{X}Y\overline{Z} + \overline{X}\overline{Y}Z + XYZ$$

The Boolean expression clearly indicates that the three-variable exclusive-OR function is equal to 1 if only one variable is equal to 1 or if all three variables are equal to 1. Whereas in the two-variable function only one variable need be equal to 1; with the three or more variables, an odd number variable must be equal to 1. As a consequence, the multiple-variable exclusive-OR operation is defined as an *odd function*.

The Boolean function derived from the three-variable exclusive-OR operation is expressed as the logical sum of four minterms whose binary numerical values are 001, 010, 100, and 111. Each of these binary numbers have an odd number of 1's. The other four minterms not included in the function are 000, 011, 101, and 110, and they have an even number of 1's. In general, an n-variable exclusive-OR function is an odd function defined as the logical sum of the $2^n/2$ minterms whose binary numerical values have an odd number of 1's.

The definition of an odd function can be clarified by plotting it in a map. Figure 2-39(a) shows the map for the three-variable exclusive-OR function. The four minterms of the function are a unit distance apart from each other. The odd function is identified from the four minterms whose binary values have an odd number of 1's. The four-variable case is shown in Fig. 2-39(b). The eight minterms marked with 1's in the map constitute the odd function. Note the characteristic pattern of the distance between the 1's in the map. It should be mentioned that the minterms not marked with 1's in the map have an even number of 1's and constitute the complement of the odd function. An odd function is implemented by means of two-input exclusive-OR gates as shown in Figure 2-40. The complement of an odd function is obtained by replacing the output gate with an exclusive-NOR gate.

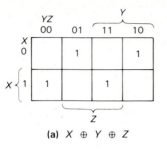

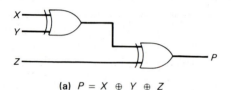

(a) $X \oplus Y \oplus Z$

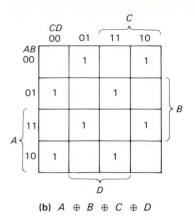

(b) $A \oplus B \oplus C \oplus D$

FIGURE 2-39
Maps for Multiple-Variable Exclusive-OR

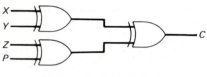

(a) $P = X \oplus Y \oplus Z$ **(b)** $C = X \oplus Y \oplus Z \oplus P$

FIGURE 2-40
Multiple-Input Exclusive-OR Functions

Parity Generation and Checking

Exclusive-OR functions are very useful in systems requiring error detection and correction codes. As discussed in Section 1-5, a parity bit is a scheme for detecting errors during transmission of binary information. A parity bit is an extra bit included with a binary message to make the number of 1's either odd or even. The message, including the parity bit, is transmitted and then checked at the receiving end for errors. An error is detected if the checked parity does not correspond with the one transmitted. The circuit that generates the parity bit in the transmitter is called a *parity generator*. The circuit that checks the parity in the receiver is called a *parity checker*.

As an example, consider a three bit message to be transmitted with an even parity bit. Table 2-8 shows the truth table for the parity generator. The three bits X, Y, and Z constitute the message and are the inputs to the circuit. The parity bit P is the output. For even parity, the bit P must be generated to make the total number of 1's even (including P). From the truth table we see that P constitutes an odd function because it is equal to 1 for those minterms whose numerical values have an odd number of 1's. Therefore, P can be expressed as a three-variable exclusive-OR function.

$$P = X \oplus Y \oplus Z$$

The logic diagram for the parity generator is shown in Figure 2-40(a).

TABLE 2-8
Even Parity Generator Truth Table

Three Bit Message			Parity Bit
X	Y	Z	P
0	0	0	0
0	0	1	1
0	1	0	1
0	1	1	0
1	0	0	1
1	0	1	0
1	1	0	0
1	1	1	1

The three bits in the message together with the parity bit are transmitted to their destination where they are applied to a parity-checker circuit to check for possible errors in the transmission. Since the information was transmitted with even parity, the four bits received must have an even number of 1's. An error occurs if the four bits received have an odd number of 1's, indicating that at least one bit has changed in value during transmission. The output of the parity checker, denoted by C, will be equal to 1 if an error occurs, that is, if the four bits received have an odd number of 1's. This is, by definition, an odd function and can be implemented with exclusive-OR gates.

$$C = X \oplus Y \oplus Z \oplus P$$

The logic diagram of the parity checker is shown in Figure 2-40(b).

It is obvious from the foregoing example that parity generation and checking circuits always have an output function that includes half of the minterms whose numerical values have either an odd or even number of 1's. As a consequence, they can be implemented with exclusive-OR gates. A function with an even number of 1's is the complement of an odd function. It is implemented with exclusive-OR gates except that the gate associated with the output must be an exclusive-NOR to provide the complementation.

2-8 INTEGRATED CIRCUITS

Digital circuits are constructed with integrated circuits. An integrated circuit (abbreviated IC) is a small silicon semiconductor crystal, called a *chip*, containing the electronic components for the digital gates. The various gates are interconnected inside the chip to form the required circuit. The chip is mounted in a ceramic or plastic container, and connections are welded to external pins to form the integrated circuit. The number of pins may range from 14 in a small IC package to 64 or more in a larger package. Each IC has a numeric designation printed on the surface of the package for identification. Each vendor publishes a data book or catalog that contains the exact description and all the necessary information about the ICs that it manufactures.

The size of the IC package is very small. For example, four AND gates are enclosed inside a 14-pin IC package with dimensions of $20 \times 8 \times 3$ millimeters. An entire microprocessor is enclosed within a 40-pin IC package with dimensions of $50 \times 15 \times 4$ millimeters.

Levels of Integration

As the technology of ICs has improved, the number of gates that can be put in a single silicon chip has increased considerably. The differentiation between those chips that have a few internal gates and those having hundreds or thousands of gates is made by a customary reference to a package as being either a small, medium, or large scale integration device.

Small scale integration (SSI) devices contain several independent gates in a single package. The inputs and outputs of the gates are connected directly to the pins in the package. The number of gates is usually less than ten and is limited by the number of pins available in the IC.

Medium scale integration (MSI) devices have a complexity of approximately 10 to 100 gates in a single package. They usually perform specific elementary digital functions, serving as decoders, adders, and registers. MSI digital functions are presented in Chapters 3 and 5.

Large scale integration (LSI) devices contain between 100 and a few thousand gates in a single package. They include digital systems such as processors, memory chips, and programmable modules. LSI logic systems are introduced in Chapters 6 and 8.

Very large scale integration (VLSI) devices contain thousands of gates within a single package. Examples are large memory arrays and complex microcomputer chips. Because of their small size and low cost, VLSI devices have revolutionized the computer system design technology, giving the designer the capabilities to create structures that previously were not economical.

Digital Logic Families

Digital integrated circuits are classified not only by their logical operation but also by the specific circuit technology to which they belong. The circuit technology is referred to as a digital logic family. Each logic family has its own basic electronic circuit upon which more complex digital circuits and functions are developed. The basic circuit in each technology is a NAND, a NOR, or an inverter gate. The electronic components used in the constructon of the basic circuit are usually used as the name of the technology. Many different logic families of integrated circuits have been introduced commercially. The following are the most popular.

TTL	Transistor-Transistor Logic
ECL	Emitter-Coupled Logic
MOS	Metal-Oxide Semiconductor
CMOS	Complementary Metal-Oxide Semiconductor

TTL is a widespread logic family that has been in operation for some time and is considered as standard. ECL has an advantage in systems requiring high speed operation. MOS is suitable for circuits that need high component density, and CMOS is preferable in systems requiring low power consumption.

The transistor-transistor logic family evolved from a previous technology that used diodes and transistors for the basic NAND gate. This technology was called DTL for diode-transistor logic. Later the diodes were replaced by transistors to improve the circuit operation and the name of the logic family was changed to TTL. This is the reason for mentioning the world transistor twice.

There are several variations of the TTL family beside the standard TTL, such as high-speed TTL, low-power TTL, Schottky TTL, low-power Schottky TTL, and advanced low-power Schottky TTL. The power supply voltage for TTL circuits is 5 volts, and the two logic levels are approximately 0 and 3.5 volts.

The emitter-coupled logic (ECL) family provides the highest speed digital circuits in integrated form. ECL is used in systems such as supercomputers and signal processors where high speed is essential. The transistors in ECL gates operate in a nonsaturated state, a condition that allows the achievement of propagation delays of 1 to 2 nanoseconds.

The metal-oxide semiconductor (MOS) is a unipolar transistor that depends upon the flow of only one type of carrier which may be electrons (n-channel) or holes (p-channel). This is in contrast to the bipolar transistor used in TTL and ECL gates, where both carriers exist during normal operation. A p-channel MOS is referred to as PMOS and an n-channel as NMOS. NMOS is the one that is commonly used in circuits with only one type of MOS transistor. Complementary MOS (CMOS) technology uses one PMOS and one NMOS transistor connected in a complementary fashion in all circuits. The most important advantages of MOS over bipolar transistors are the high packing density of circuits, a simpler processing technique during fabrication, and a more economical operation because of the low power consumption.

The characteristics of digital logic families are usually compared by analyzing the circuit of the basic gate in each family. The most important parameters that are evaluated and compared are as follows.

Fan-out specifies the number of standard loads that the output of a typical gate can drive without impairing its normal operation. A standard load is usually defined as the amount of current needed by an input of another similar gate of the same family.

Power-dissipation is the power consumed by the gate which must be available from the power supply.

Propagation delay is the average transition delay time for the signal to propagate from input to output when the binary signal changes in value. The operating speed is inversely proportional to the propagation delay.

Noise margin is the minimum external noise voltage that causes an undesirable change in the circuit output.

Positive and Negative Logic

The binary signal at the inputs and outputs of any gate have one of two values, except during transition. One signal value represents logic-1 and the other logic-0. Since two signal values are assigned to two logic values, there exist two different

FIGURE 2-41
Signal Assignment and Logic Polarity

assignments of signal level to logic value as shown in Figure 2-41. The higher signal level is designated by H and the lower signal level by L. Choosing the high level H to represent logic-1 defines a positive logic system. Choosing the low level L to represent logic-1 defines a negative logic system. The terms positive and negative are somewhat misleading since both signals may be positive or both may be negative. It is not the actual signal values that determine the type of logic, but rather the assignment of logic values to the relative amplitudes of the two signal levels.

Integrated circuit data sheets define digital gates not in terms of logic values but rather in terms of signal values such as H and L. It is up to the user to decide on a positive or negative logic assignment. Consider for example the TTL gate shown in Figure 2-42(b). The truth table for this gate as given in a data book is listed in Figure 2-42(a). This specifies the physical behavior of the gate where H is 3.5 volts and L is 0 volt. The truth table of Figure 2-42(c) assumes positive logic assignment with H = 1 and L = 0. This truth table is the same as the one for the AND operation. The graphic symbol for a positive logic AND gate is shown in Figure 2-42(d).

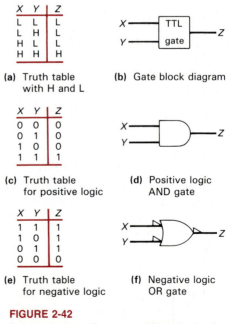

FIGURE 2-42
Demonstration of Positive and Negative Logic

Now consider the negative logic assignment for the same physical gate with L = 1 and H = 0. The result is the truth table of Figure 2-42(e). This table represents the OR operation even though the entries are reversed. The graphic symbol for the negative logic OR gate is shown in Figure 2-42(f). The small triangles in the inputs and output designate a *polarity indicator*. The presence of this polarity indicator along a terminal signifies that negative logic is assumed for the signal. Thus, the same physical gate can operate either as a positive logic AND gate or as a negative logic OR gate.

The conversion from positive logic to negative logic, and vice versa, is essentially an operation that changes 1's to 0's and 0's to 1's in both the inputs and the output of a gate. Since this operation produces the dual of a function, the change of all terminals from one polarity to the other results in taking the dual of the function. The result of this conversion is that all AND operations are converted to OR operations (or graphic symbols) and vice versa. In addition, one must not forget to include the polarity indicator triangle in the graphic symbols when negative logic is assumed. In this book we will not use negative logic gates but assume that all gates operate with a positive logic assignment.

REFERENCES

1. BOOLE, G., *An Investigation of the Laws of Thought*. New York: Dover, 1954.
2. KARNAUGH, M., "A MAP METHOD FOR SYNTHESIS OF COMBINATIONAL LOGIC CIRCUITS," *Transactions of AIEE, Communication and Electronics*, 72, Part I (Nov. 1953), 593–99.
3. MANO, M. M., *Digital Design*. Englewood Cliffs: Prentice-Hall, 1984.
4. ROTH, C. H., *Fundamentals of Logic Design*. 3rd ed. St. Paul: West, 1985.
5. FLETCHER, W. I., *An Engineering Approach to Digital Design*. Englewood Cliffs: Prentice-Hall, 1980.
6. ERCEGOVAC, M. D., AND LANG, T., *Digital Systems and Hardware/Firmware Algorithms*. New York: Wiley, 1985.
7. *The TTL Data Book for Design Engineers*. Dallas: Texas Instruments, 1983.
8. *High-Speed CMOS Logic Data Book*. Dallas: Texas Instruments, 1984.
9. *IEEE Standard Graphic Symbols for Logic Functions*. (ANSI/IEEE Std 91-1984.) New York: The Institute of Electrical and Electronics Engineers.

PROBLEMS

2-1 Demonstrate by means of truth tables the validity of the following identities:
(a) DeMorgan's theorem for three variables $\overline{XYZ} = \overline{X} + \overline{Y} + \overline{Z}$
(b) The second distributive law. $X + YZ = (X + Y)(X + Z)$
(c) $\overline{X}Y + \overline{Y}Z + X\overline{Z} = X\overline{Y} + Y\overline{Z} + \overline{X}Z$

2-2 Prove the identity of each of the following Boolean equations using algebraic manipulation.
(a) $\overline{X}\overline{Y} + XY + \overline{X}Y = \overline{X} + Y$
(b) $\overline{X}Y + X\overline{Y} + XY + \overline{X}\overline{Y} = 1$
(c) $\overline{X} + XY + X\overline{Z} + X\overline{Y}\overline{Z} = \overline{X} + Y + \overline{Z}$
(d) $X\overline{Y} + \overline{Y}\overline{Z} + \overline{X}Z + \overline{X}\overline{Z} = X\overline{Y} + \overline{X}Z$

2-3   Simplify the following Boolean expressions to a minimum number of literals.
(a) $XYZ + \overline{X}Y + XY\overline{Z}$
(b) $\overline{X}YZ + XZ$
(c) $(X + Y)(X + \overline{Y})$
(d) $XY + X(WZ + W\overline{Z})$
(e) $(X + \overline{Y} + X\overline{Y})(XY + \overline{X}Z + YZ)$ [Answer: $XY + \overline{X}\overline{Y}Z$]

2-4   Reduce the following Boolean expressions to the indicated number of literals.
(a) $\overline{A}\,\overline{C} + ABC + A\overline{C}$ To three literals
(b) $(\overline{CD} + A) + A + CD + AB$ To three literals
(c) $\overline{A}B(\overline{D} + \overline{C}D) + B(A + \overline{A}CD)$ To one literal
(d) $(\overline{A} + C)(\overline{A} + \overline{C})(A + B + \overline{C}D)$ To four literals

2-5   Using DeMorgan's theorem, express the following function

$$F = XY + \overline{X}\overline{Y} + \overline{Y}Z$$

(a) with only OR and complement operations.
(b) with only AND and complement operations.

2-6   Find the complement of the following expressions:
(a) $X\overline{Y} + \overline{X}Y$
(b) $(A\overline{B} + C)\overline{D} + E$
(c) $AB(\overline{C}D + C\overline{D}) + \overline{A}\,\overline{B}(\overline{C} + D)(C + \overline{D})$
(d) $(A + \overline{B} + C)(\overline{A} + \overline{C})(A + B)$

2-7   Obtain the truth table of the following functions and express each function in sum of minterms and product of maxterms.
(a) $(XY + Z)(Y + XZ)$
(b) $(\overline{A} + B)(\overline{B} + C)$
(c) $\overline{Y}Z + WX\overline{Y} + WX\overline{Z} + \overline{W}XZ$

2-8   For the Boolean functions E and F as given in the following truth table

X	Y	Z	E	F
0	0	0	1	0
0	0	1	1	0
0	1	0	1	1
0	1	1	0	1
1	0	0	0	0
1	0	1	0	0
1	1	0	0	1
1	1	1	0	1

(a) List the minterms and maxterms of each function.
(b) List the minterms of $\overline{E}$ and $\overline{F}$.
(c) Express E and F in sum of minterms in algebraic form.
(d) Simplify each function to an expression with a minimum number of literals.

2-9   Convert the following expressions into sum of products and product of sums.
(a) $(AB + C)(B + \overline{C}D)$
(b) $\overline{X} + X(X + \overline{Y})(Y + \overline{Z})$

2-10 Draw the logic diagram for the following Boolean expressions.

(a) $B\overline{C} + AB + ACD$
(b) $(A + B)(C + D)(\overline{A} + B + D)$
(c) $(AB + \overline{A}\,\overline{B})(CD + \overline{C}D)$

2-11 Simplify the following Boolean functions by means of a three-variable map.
(a) $F(X, Y, Z) = \Sigma m(2, 3, 6, 7)$
(b) $F(X, Y, Z) = \Sigma m(3, 5, 6, 7)$
(c) $F(A, B, C) = \Sigma m(0, 2, 3, 4, 6)$
(d) $F(A, B, C) = \Sigma m(1, 3, 5, 7)$

2-12 Simplify the following Boolean expressions using a map.
(a) $XY + Y\overline{Z} + \overline{X}\,\overline{Y}\overline{Z}$
(b) $\overline{A}\,\overline{B} + BC + \overline{A}B\overline{C}$

2-13 Simplify the following Boolean functions by means of a four-variable map.
(a) $F(A, B, C, D) = \Sigma m(3, 7, 11, 13, 14, 15)$
(b) $F(W, X, Y, Z) = \Sigma m(2, 3, 10, 11, 12, 13, 14, 15)$
(c) $F(A, B, C, D) = \Sigma m(0, 2, 4, 5, 6, 7, 8, 10, 13, 15)$

2-14 Simplify the following Boolean functions using a map.
(a) $F(W, X, Y, Z) = \Sigma m(1, 4, 5, 6, 12, 14, 15)$
(b) $F(A, B, C, D) = \Sigma m(0, 1, 2, 4, 5, 7, 11, 15)$

2-15 Simplify the following expressions by means of a four-variable map.
(a) $\overline{A}D + BD + \overline{B}C + A\overline{B}D$
(b) $\overline{X}Z + \overline{W}X\overline{Y} + W(\overline{X}Y + X\overline{Y})$
(c) $A\overline{B}C + \overline{B}\,\overline{C}\overline{D} + BCD + AC\overline{D} + \overline{A}\,\overline{B}C + \overline{A}B\overline{C}D$
(d) $ABC + CD + B\overline{C}D + \overline{B}C$

2-16 Find the minterms of the following expressions by first plotting each expression in a map.
(a) $XY + Y\overline{Z} + X\overline{Y}Z$
(b) $\overline{Y}Z + WX\overline{Y} + WX\overline{Z} + \overline{W}\overline{X}Z$
(c) $ABC + \overline{B}\,\overline{D} + \overline{A}BD$

2-17 Find all the prime implicants for the following Boolean functions and determine which are essential.
(a) $F(W, X, Y, Z) = \Sigma m(0, 2, 4, 5, 6, 7, 8, 10, 13, 15)$
(b) $F(A, B, C, D) = \Sigma m(0, 2, 3, 5, 7, 8, 10, 11, 14, 15)$
(c) $F(A, B, C, D) = \Sigma m(1, 3, 4, 5, 10, 11, 12, 13, 14, 15)$

2-18 Simplify the following Boolean functions in product of sums.
(a) $F(W, X, Y, Z) = \Sigma m(0, 2, 5, 6, 7, 8, 10)$
(b) $F(A, B, C, D) = \Pi M(1, 3, 5, 7, 13, 15)$

2-19 Simplify the following expressions in (1) sum of products and (2) products of sums.
(a) $A\overline{C} + \overline{B}D + \overline{A}CD + ABCD$
(b) $(\overline{A} + \overline{B} + \overline{D})(A + \overline{B} + \overline{C})(\overline{A} + B + \overline{D})(B + \overline{C} + \overline{D})$
(c) $(\overline{A} + \overline{B} + D)(\overline{A} + \overline{D})(A + B + \overline{D})(A + \overline{B} + C + D)$

2-20 Simplify the following Boolean function F together with the don't care conditions d.
(a) $F(X, Y, Z) = \Sigma m(0, 1, 2, 4, 5)$ $d(X, Y, Z) = \Sigma m(3, 6, 7)$
(b) $F(A, B, C, D) = \Sigma m(0, 6, 8, 13, 14)$ $d(A, B, C, D) = \Sigma m(2, 4, 10)$
(c) $F(A, B, C, D) = \Sigma m(1, 3, 5, 7, 9, 15)$ $d(A, B, C, D) = \Sigma m(4, 6, 12, 13)$

2-21 Simplify the following Boolean functions by means of a five-variable map.
(a) $F(A, B, C, D, E) = \Sigma m(0, 1, 4, 5, 16, 17, 21, 25, 29)$
(b) $\overline{A}BC\overline{E} + \overline{A}\,\overline{B}C\overline{D} + \overline{B}\overline{D}E + \overline{B}C\overline{D} + CD\overline{E} + BD\overline{E}$

2-22   Simplify the Boolean function F together with the don't care conditions d, in (1) sum of products and (2) product of sums.
(a) $F(W, X, Y, Z) = \Sigma m(0, 1, 2, 3, 7, 8, 10)$
    $d(W, X, Y, Z) = \Sigma m(5, 6, 11, 15)$
(b) $F(A, B, C, D) = \Sigma m(3, 4, 13, 15)$
    $d(A, B, C, D) = \Sigma m(1, 2, 5, 6, 8, 10, 12, 14)$

2-23   Simplify each of the following expressions and implement them with NAND gates.
(a) $A\overline{B} + ABD + AB\overline{D} + \overline{A}\,\overline{C}D + \overline{A}B\overline{C}$ (b) $BD + BC\overline{D} + A\overline{B}C\overline{D}$

2-24   Implement the following expression with two-input NAND gates.
$(\overline{AB} + \overline{A}\,\overline{B})(\overline{CD} + \overline{C}D)$

2-25   Draw the NAND logic diagram for each of the following expressions using a multiple level NAND circuit.
(a) $W(X + Y + Z) + XYZ$ (b) $(A\overline{B} + C\overline{D})E + BC(A + B)$

2-26   Simplify each of the following expressions and implement them with NOR gates.
(a) $A\overline{B} + C\overline{D} + \overline{A}CD$ (b) $\overline{A}B\overline{C}D + \overline{A}BC\overline{D} + A\overline{B}\overline{C}D + \overline{A}B\overline{C}D$

2-27   Repeat problems 2-23 and 2-25 using NOR gates.

2-28   Show that the dual of the exclusive-OR is also its complement.

2-29   Derive the circuits for a three-bit parity generator and four-bit parity checker using an odd parity bit.

2-30   Implement the following Boolean function:
$F = A\overline{B}C\overline{D} + \overline{A}BC\overline{D} + A\overline{B}\overline{C}D + \overline{A}B\overline{C}D$
with exclusive-OR and AND gates.

2-31   Construct an exclusive-NOR circuit with two inverters and two transmission gates.

2-32   TTL SSI come mostly in 14-pin packages. Two pins are reserved for power and the other pins are used for input and output terminals. Give the number of gates that can be enclosed in one package if it contains the following types of gates:
(a) Two-input exclusive-OR gates   (d) Five-input NOR gates
(b) Three-input AND gates   (e) Eight-input NAND gates
(c) Four-input NAND gates

2-33   Show that a positive logic NAND gate is a negative logic NOR gate and vice versa.

2-34   An integrated circuit logic family has AND gates with fan-out of 5 and buffer gates with fan-out of 10. Show how the output signal of a single AND gate can be applied to 50 other gate inputs using buffers.

3

COMBINATIONAL SYSTEMS

3-1 INTRODUCTION

Logic circuits for digital systems may be combinational or sequential. A combinational circuit consists of logic gates whose outputs at any time are determined directly from the values of the present inputs. A combinational circuit performs a specific information processing operation which can be specified logically by a set of Boolean expressions. Sequential circuits employ storage elements called flip-flops in addition to the logic gates. Their outputs are a function of the inputs and the state of the storage elements. The state of storage elements, in turn, is a function of previous inputs. As a consequence, the outputs of a sequential circuit depend not only on the present values of the inputs, but also on past inputs, and the circuit behavior must be specified by a time sequence of inputs and internal states. Sequential circuits are presented in the next chapter.

A combinational circuit consists of input variables, logic gates, and output variables. The logic gates accept signals from the inputs and generate signals at the outputs. This process transforms binary information from a given input data to a required output data. A block diagram of a combinational circuit is shown in Figure 3-1. The n input variables come from an externl source and the m output variables

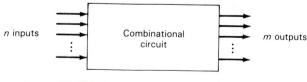

FIGURE 3–1
Block Diagram of Combinational Circuit

go to an external destination. Each input and output variable exists physically as a binary signal that represents the equivalent of logic-1 or logic-0.

For n input variables, there are 2^n possible binary combinations. For each binary combination of the input variables, there is one possible output binary value. Thus, a combinational circuit can be specified by a truth table that lists the output values for each combination of the input variables. A combinational circuit can also be described by m Boolean functions, one for each output variable. Each output Boolean function is expressed as a function of the n input variables.

In Chapter 1 we learned to recognize binary numbers and binary codes that represent discrete quantities of information. In Chapter 2 we introduced the various logic gates and learned how to simplify Boolean functions in order to achieve economical gate implementations. The purpose of this chapter is to use the knowledge acquired in the previous chapters and formulate various systematic analysis and design procedures of combinational circuits. The various examples introduced in this chapter provide some practice in dealing with such circuits.

There are several combinational circuits that are employed extensively in the design and construction of digital computers. These components are available in integrated circuits and are classified as MSI (medium scale integration) circuits. Some of these components are presented in this chapter with an explanation of their logical properties. The MSI functions presented in this chapter will provide a catalog of elementary digital components which are used extensively as basic building blocks in the design of digital computers and systems.

3-2   ANALYSIS PROCEDURE

The analysis of a combinational circuit consists of determining the function that the circuit implements. It starts with a given logic circuit diagram and culminates with a set of Boolean functions or a truth table together with a possible explanation of the circuit's operation. If the logic diagram to be analyzed is accompanied by a function name or a statement of what it is assumed to accomplish, then the analysis problem reduces to a verification of the stated function.

The first step in the analysis is to make sure that the given circuit is combinational and not sequential. The diagram of a combinational circuit has logic gates with no feedback or storage elements. A feedback path exists if there is a connection from the output of one gate to the input of a second gate that forms part of the input of the first gate. Feedback paths or storage elements in a digital circuit may result in a sequential circuit and must be analyzed according to procedures outlined in Chapter 4.

Once the logic diagram is verified to be a combinational circuit, one can proceed to obtain the output Boolean functions or the truth table. If the function of the circuit is under investigation, then it is necessary to interpret the operation of the circuit from the derived Boolean functions or truth table. The success of such investigation is enhanced if one has previous experience and familiarity with a wide variety of digital circuits. The ability to correlate a truth table with an information processing task is an art one acquires with experience.

Derivation of Boolean Functions

To obtain the output Boolean functions from a logic diagram proceed as follows:

1. Label all gate outputs that are a function of input variables with arbitrary symbols. Determine the Boolean functions for each gate.
2. Label the gates that are a function of input variables and previous labeled gates with different arbitrary symbols. Find the Boolean functions for these gates.
3. Repeat the process outlined in step 2 until the outputs of the circuit are obtained in terms of the input variables.

The analysis of the combinational circuit of Figure 3-2 will illustrate this procedure. We note that the circuit has four binary input variables A, B, C, and D, and two binary output variables F_1 and F_2. The outputs of the various gates are labeled with intermediate symbols. The outputs of gates that are a function of input variables only are T_1 and T_2. The Boolean functions for these two outputs are

$$T_1 = \overline{B}C$$

$$T_2 = \overline{A}B$$

Next we consider the outputs of gates that are a function of already defined symbols.

$$T_3 = A + T_1 = A + \overline{B}C$$

$$T_4 = T_2 \oplus D = (\overline{A}B) \oplus D = \overline{A}B\overline{D} + AD + \overline{B}D$$

$$T_5 = T_2 + D = \overline{A}B + D$$

The Boolean functions for the outputs are

$$F_2 = T_5 = \overline{A}B + D$$

$$F_1 = T_3 + T_4 = A + \overline{B}C + \overline{A}B\overline{D} + AD + \overline{B}D$$

$$= A + \overline{B}C + B\overline{D} + \overline{B}D$$

The last simplification for F_1 can be verified by algebraic manipulation or by means of a map.

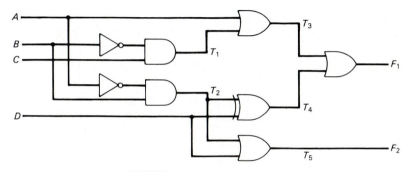

FIGURE 3–2
Logic Diagram for Analysis Example

Derivation of the Truth Table

The derivation of the truth table for a combinational circuit is a straightforward process once the output Boolean functions are known. To obtain the truth table from the logic diagram without going through the derivation of the Boolean functions proceed as follows:

1. Determine the number of input variables in the circuit. For n inputs, list the binary numbers from 0 to $2^n - 1$ in a table.
2. Label the outputs of selected gates with arbitrary symbols.
3. Obtain the truth table for the outputs of those gates that are a function of the input variables only.
4. Proceed to obtain the truth table for the outputs of those gates that are a function of previously defined values until the columns for all outputs are determined.

The process is illustrated by the combinational circuit for a binary adder in Figure 3-3. The problem here is to verify that the circuit forms the arithmetic sum of the three bits at input X, Y, and Z. The two outputs F_2 and F_1 range in value from binary 00 to 11 (decimal 3) depending on the number of 1's in the inputs. For example, when $XYZ = 101$, F_2F_1 must be equal to binary 10 to indicate that there are two 1's in the inputs.

Table 3-1 shows the procedure for deriving the truth table of the circuit. First, we form the eight binary combinations for the three input variables. The truth table for F_2 is determined from the values of inputs X, Y, and Z. F_2 is equal to 1 when $XY = 11$, or $XZ = 11$, or $YZ = 11$. Otherwise it is equal to 0. The truth table for $\overline{F_2}$ is the complement of F_2. The truth table for T_1 and T_2 are the AND and OR functions of the input variables, respectively. The binary values for T_3 are derived from ANDing T_2 and $\overline{F_2}$. Thus T_3 is equal to 1 when both T_2 and $\overline{F_2}$ are equal to 1 and to 0 otherwise. Finally, F_1 is equal to 1 for those combinations in which either T_1 or T_3 or both are equal to 1.

Inspection of the truth table reveals that $F_2F_1 = 00$, 01, 10, or 11, when the total number of 1's in the three inputs XYZ is either zero, one, two, or three,

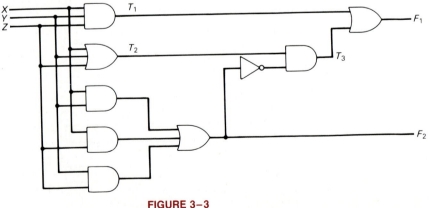

FIGURE 3–3
Logic Diagram for Binary Adder

TABLE 3-1
Truth Table for Binary Adder

X	Y	Z	F_2	$\overline{F_2}$	T_1	T_2	T_3	F_1
0	0	0	0	1	0	0	0	0
0	0	1	0	1	0	1	1	1
0	1	0	0	1	0	1	1	1
0	1	1	1	0	0	1	0	0
1	0	0	0	1	0	1	1	1
1	0	1	1	0	0	1	0	0
1	1	0	1	0	0	1	0	0
1	1	1	1	0	1	1	0	1

respectively. This verifies the operation of the circuit as a binary adder. The design of a binary adder with a different gate structure is presented in Section 3-4.

3-3 DESIGN PROCEDURE

The design of combinational circuits starts from the specification of the problem and culminates in a logic circuit diagram or a set of Boolean functions from which the logic diagram can be obtained. The procedure involves the following steps:

1. From the specifications of the circuit, determine the required number of inputs and outputs and assign a letter symbol to each.
2. Derive the truth table that defines the required relationship between inputs and outputs.
3. Obtain the simplified Boolean functions for each output as a function of the input variables.
4. Draw the logic diagram.

A truth table for a combinational circuit consists of input columns and output columns. The input columns are obtrained from the 2^n binary numbers for the n input variables. The binary values for the outputs are determined from the stated specifications. The output functions specified in the truth table give the exact definition of the combinational circuit. It is important that the verbal specifications be interpreted correctly in the truth table. Word specifications are very often incomplete and any wrong interpretation may result in an incorrect truth table.

The output binary functions listed in the truth table are simplified by any available method such as algebraic manipulation, the map method, or by means of computer generated simplification programs. Usually there is a variety of simplified expressions from which to choose. In a particular application, certain criteria will serve as a guide in the process of choosing an implementation. A practical design must consider such constraints as the minimum number of gates, minimum number of inputs to a gate, minimum propagation time of the signal through the gates, minimum number of interconnections, limitations of the driving capability of each gate, and various other criteria that must be taken into consideration when designing with integrated circuits. Since the importance of each constraint is dictated by the particular application, it is difficult to make a general statement about what constitutes an acceptable implementation. In most cases the simplification begins by satisfying an elementary objective, such as producing the simplified Boolean functions in a standard form, and then meets other performance criteria. The following examples illustrate the outlined procedure.

Example 3-1

Design a combinational circuit with three inputs and one output. The output must be logic-1 when the binary value of the inputs is less than three and logic-0 otherwise. Use only NAND gates.

The design of the circuit is undertaken in Figure 3-4. We designate the inputs with the letter symbols X, Y, Z, and the output with F. The truth table is listed

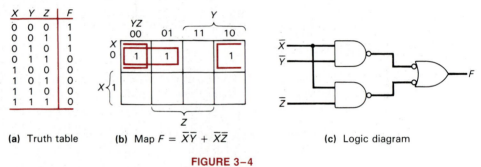

X	Y	Z	F
0	0	0	1
0	0	1	1
0	1	0	1
0	1	1	0
1	0	0	0
1	0	1	0
1	1	0	0
1	1	1	0

(a) Truth table   (b) Map $F = \bar{X}\bar{Y} + \bar{X}\bar{Z}$ (c) Logic diagram

FIGURE 3–4
Solution to Example 3–1

in part (a). $F = 1$ when the binary inputs are 0, 1, or 2; otherwise $F = 0$. The simplified output Boolean function is derived from the map in part (b). The NAND logic diagram is drawn in part (c) with mixed symbolic notation (see Section 2-6).

Code Converter

When a combinational circuit has two or more outputs, each output must be expressed separately as a function of all the input variables. An example of a multiple output circuit is a code converter. A code converter is a circuit that translates information from one binary code to another. The inputs of the circuit provide the bit combination of the elements as specified by the first code and the outputs generate the corresponding bit combination of the second code. The combinational circuit performs the transformation from one code to the other. The design of a code converter will be illustrated by means of an example that converts the binary coded decimal (BCD) to the excess-3 code for the decimal digits.

Since both codes use four bits to represent each decimal digit, there must be four input variables and four output variables. Designate the inputs by A, B, C, D and the outputs by W, X, Y, Z. The truth table relating the input and output variables is shown in Table 3-2. The bit combinations for the inputs and their

TABLE 3-2
Truth Table for Code Converter Example

Decimal Digit	Input BCD				Output Excess-3			
	A	B	C	D	W	X	Y	Z
0	0	0	0	0	0	0	1	1
1	0	0	0	1	0	1	0	0
2	0	0	1	0	0	1	0	1
3	0	0	1	1	0	1	1	0
4	0	1	0	0	0	1	1	1
5	0	1	0	1	1	0	0	0
6	0	1	1	0	1	0	0	1
7	0	1	1	1	1	0	1	0
8	1	0	0	0	1	0	1	1
9	1	0	0	1	1	1	0	0

corresponding outputs are obtained directly from Table 1-5. Note that four binary variables may have 16 bit combinations, but only 10 are listed in the truth table. The six input bit combinations 1010 through 1111 are not listed under the input columns. These combinations have no meaning in the BCD code, and we can assume that they will never occur. Since they will never occur, it does not matter what binary values we assign to the outputs and therefore, we can treat them as don't care conditions.

The maps in Figure 3-5 are plotted to obtain the simplified Boolean functions for the outputs. Each one of the four maps represent one of the outputs of the circuit as a function of the four inputs. The 1's in the map are obtained directly from the truth table by going over the output columns one at a time. For example, the column under output W has 1's for minterms 5, 6, 7, 8, and 9. Therefore, the map for W must have five 1's in the squares that correspond to these minterms. The six don't care minterms 10 through 15 are each marked with an X in all the maps. The simplified functions in sum of products are listed under the map of each variable.

The two-level AND-OR logic diagram for the circuit can be obtained directly from the Boolean expressions derived from the maps. There are, however, various other possibilities for a logic diagram that implements the circuit. For example, expressions may be manipulated algebraically for the purpose of using common gates. The manipulation shown below illustrates the flexibility obtained with multiple output systems when implemented with three levels of gates.

$$W = A + BC + BD = A + B(C + D)$$

$$X = \overline{B}C + \overline{B}D + B\overline{C}\,\overline{D} = \overline{B}(C + D) + B\overline{C}\,\overline{D}$$

$$Y = CD + \overline{C}\,\overline{D} = \overline{C \oplus D}$$

$$Z = \overline{D}$$

The logic diagram that implements the above expressions is drawn in Figure 3-6.

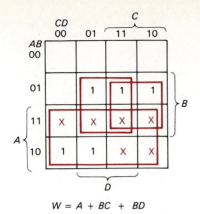

$$W = A + BC + BD$$

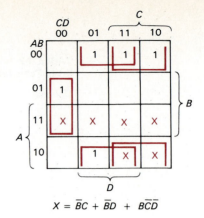

$$X = \overline{B}C + \overline{B}D + B\overline{C}\overline{D}$$

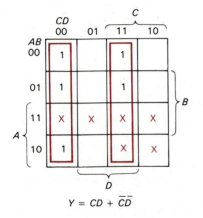

$$Y = CD + \overline{C}\overline{D}$$

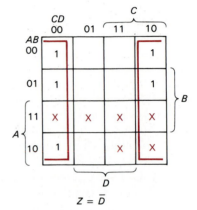

$$Z = \overline{D}$$

FIGURE 3–5
Maps for BCD to Excess-3 Code Converter

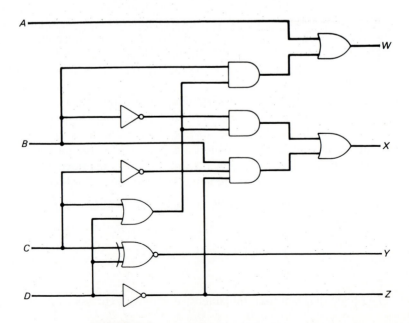

FIGURE 3–6
Logic Diagram of BCD to Excess-3 Code Converter

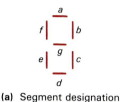

(a) Segment designation

(b) Numeric designation for display

FIGURE 3-7
Seven-Segment Display

BCD to Seven-Segment Decoder

Digital readout found in electronic calculators and digital watches use display devices such as light emitting diodes (LED) or liquid crystal display (LCD). Each digit of the display is formed from seven segments, each consisting of one LED or one crystal which can be illuminated by digital signals. A BCD to seven-segment decoder is a combinational circuit that accepts a decimal digit in BCD and generates the appropriate outputs for selection of segments that display the decimal digit. The seven outputs of the decoder (a, b, c, d, e, f, g) select the corresponding segments in the display as shown in Figure 3-7(a). The numeric designation chosen to represent the decimal digits is shown in Figure 3-7(b).

The BCD to seven-segment decoder has four inputs for the BCD digit and seven outputs for choosing the segments. The truth table of the combinational circuit is listed in Table 3-3. Each decimal digit illuminates the proper segments for the decimal display. For example, BCD 0011 corresponds to decimal 3 whose display needs segments a, b, c, d, and g. The truth table assumes that a logic-1 signal illuminates the segment and a logic-0 signal turns the segment off. Some seven-segment displays operate in a reverse fashion and are illuminated by a logic-0 signal.

The six binary combinations 1010 through 1111 have no meaning in BCD. In the previous example we assigned these combinations to don't care conditions. If we do the same here, the design will most likely produce some arbitrary and

TABLE 3-3
Truth Table for BCD to Seven-Segment Decoder

BCD Input				Seven-Segment Output						
A	*B*	*C*	*D*	*a*	*b*	*c*	*d*	*e*	*f*	*g*
0	0	0	0	1	1	1	1	1	1	0
0	0	0	1	0	1	1	0	0	0	0
0	0	1	0	1	1	0	1	1	0	1
0	0	1	1	1	1	1	1	0	0	1
0	1	0	0	0	1	1	0	0	1	1
0	1	0	1	1	0	1	1	0	1	1
0	1	1	0	1	0	1	1	1	1	1
0	1	1	1	1	1	1	0	0	0	0
1	0	0	0	1	1	1	1	1	1	1
1	0	0	1	1	1	1	1	0	1	1
All other inputs				0	0	0	0	0	0	0

meaningless display for the unused combinations. A better choice may be to turn off all the segments when any one of the unused input combinations occur. This can be accomplished by assigning all 0's to minterms 10 through 15.

The information from the truth table can be transferred into seven maps from which the simplified output functions can be derived. The plotting of the seven functions in maps is left for an exercise (see Problem 3-10). One possible way of simplifying the seven functions results in the following Boolean functions:

$$a = \overline{A}C + \overline{A}BD + \overline{B}\,\overline{C}\,\overline{D} + A\overline{B}\,\overline{C}$$

$$b = \overline{A}\,\overline{B} + \overline{A}\,\overline{C}\,\overline{D} + \overline{A}CD + A\overline{B}\,\overline{C}$$

$$c = \overline{A}B + \overline{A}D + \overline{B}\,\overline{C}\,\overline{D} + A\overline{B}\,\overline{C}$$

$$d = \overline{A}\,C\overline{D} + \overline{A}\,\overline{B}\,C + \overline{B}\,\overline{C}\,\overline{D} + A\overline{B}\,\overline{C} + \overline{A}B\overline{C}D$$

$$e = \overline{A}\,C\overline{D} + \overline{B}\,\overline{C}\,\overline{D}$$

$$f = \overline{A}B\overline{C} + \overline{A}\,\overline{C}\,\overline{D} + \overline{A}B\overline{D} + A\overline{B}\,\overline{C}$$

$$g = \overline{A}\,C\overline{D} + \overline{A}\,\overline{B}\,C + \overline{A}B\overline{C} + A\overline{B}\,\overline{C}$$

The implementation of the seven functions requires 14 AND gates and seven OR gates. There are a total of 27 product terms in all seven functions and it would seem that 27 AND gates will be needed. However, there are six common terms whose corresponding AND gates can share two or more outputs. For example, the term $\overline{B}\,\overline{C}\,\overline{D}$ occurs in a, c, d, and e. The output of the AND gate that implements this product term goes to the inputs of the OR gates in all four functions.

In general, the total number of gates can be reduced in a multiple-output combinational circuit by using common terms in the output functions. The maps of the output functions may help in finding the common terms by combining identical adjacent squares in two or more maps. Some of the common terms may not be prime implicants of the individual functions. The designer must use some ingenuity to combine squares in the maps in such a way as to create common terms.

The BCD to seven-segment decoder is called a decoder by most manufacturers of integrated circuits because it converts or decodes a binary code to a decimal digit. However, it is actually a code converter that converts a four-bit decimal code to a seven-bit code. The word *decoder* is usually reserved for another type of circuit that is presented in Section 3-5.

3-4 ARITHMETIC CIRCUITS

An arithmetic circuit is a combinational circuit that performs arithmetic operations such as addition, subtraction, multiplication, and division with binary numbers or with decimal numbers in a binary code. The most basic arithmetic operation is the addition of two binary digits. This simple addition consists of four possible elementary operations: $0 + 0 = 0$, $0 + 1 = 1$, $1 + 0 = 1$, and $1 + 1 = 10$. The first three operations produce a sum of one digit, but when both the augend and addend are equal to 1, the binary sum consists of two digits. When the addition results in an additional significant bit, the carry obtained from the addition of two

TABLE 3–4
Truth table of half adder

Inputs		Outputs	
X	Y	C	S
0	0	0	0
0	1	0	1
1	0	0	1
1	1	1	0

bits is added to the next higher order pair of significant bits. A combinational circuit that performs the addition of two bits is called a *half adder*. One that performs the addition of three bits (two significant bits and a previous carry) is called a *full adder*. The name of the circuits stem from the fact that two half adders are employed to implement a full adder. The full adder circuit is the basic arithmetic component from which all other arithmetic circuits are constructed.

Half Adder

A half adder is an arithmetic circuit that generates the sum of two binary digits. The circuit has two inputs and two outputs. The input variables are the augend and addend bits to be added and the output variables produce the sum and carry. We assign the symbols X and Y to the two inputs and S (sum) and C (carry) to the outputs. The truth table for the half adder is listed in Table 3–4. The C output is 1 only when both inputs are 1. The S output represents the least significant bit of the sum. The Boolean functions for the two outputs can be easily obtained from the truth table.

$$S = \overline{X}Y + X\overline{Y} = X \oplus Y$$

$$C = XY$$

The half adder can be implemented with one exclusive-OR and one AND gate as shown in Figure 3-8.

Full Adder

A full adder is a combinational circuit that forms the arithmetic sum of three input bits. It consists of three inputs and two outputs. Two of the input variables, denoted by X and Y, represent the two significant bits to be added. The third input, Z,

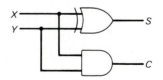

FIGURE 3–8
Logic Diagram of Half Adder

TABLE 3-5
Truth Table of Full Adder

Inputs			Outputs	
X	Y	Z	C	S
0	0	0	0	0
0	0	1	0	1
0	1	0	0	1
0	1	1	1	0
1	0	0	0	1
1	0	1	1	0
1	1	0	1	0
1	1	1	1	1

represents the carry from the previous lower significant position. Two outputs are necessary because the arithmetic sum of three bits ranges in value from zero to three, and binary two and three need two digits. Again, the two outputs are designated by the symbols S for sum and C for carry; the binary variable S gives the value of the least significant bit of the sum; and the binary variable C gives the output carry.

The truth table of the full adder is listed in Table 3-5. The values for the outputs are determined from the arithmetic sum of the three input bits. When all input bits are 0, the outputs are 0. The S output is equal to 1 when only one input is equal to 1 or when all three inputs are equal to 1. The C output has a carry of 1 if two or three inputs are equal to 1.

The maps for the two outputs of the full adder are shown in Figure 3-9. The simplified sum of product functions for the two outputs are

$$S = \overline{X}\overline{Y}Z + \overline{X}Y\overline{Z} + X\overline{Y}\overline{Z} + XYZ$$

$$C = XY + XZ + YZ$$

This implementation requires seven AND gates and two OR gates. However, the map for output S is recognized as an exclusive-OR function as discussed in Section 2-7. Furthermore, the C output function can be manipulated as shown in Figure

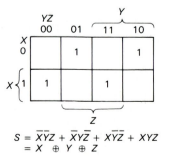

$$S = \overline{X}\overline{Y}Z + \overline{X}Y\overline{Z} + X\overline{Y}\overline{Z} + XYZ$$
$$= X \oplus Y \oplus Z$$

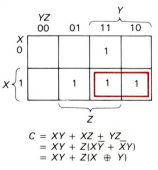

$$C = XY + XZ + YZ$$
$$= XY + Z(X\overline{Y} + \overline{X}Y)$$
$$= XY + Z(X \oplus Y)$$

FIGURE 3-9
Maps for Full Adder

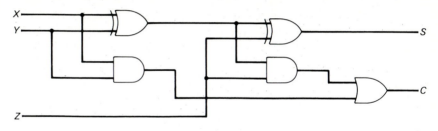

FIGURE 3–10
Logic Diagram of Full Adder

3-9 to include the exclusive-OR of X and Y. The Boolean functions for the full adder in terms of exclusive-OR operations can be expressed as follows:

$$S = X \oplus Y \oplus Z$$

$$C = XY + Z(X \oplus Y)$$

The logic diagram for this implementation is shown in Figure 3-10. It consists of two half adders and an OR gate.

Binary Parallel Adder

The sum of two n-bit binary numbers can be generated in serial or parallel fashion. The serial addition method uses only one full adder and a storage device to hold the output carry. Each pair of bits is transferred one at a time through the single full adder to produce a string of output bits for the sum. The stored output carry from one pair of bits is used as an input carry for the next pair of bits. The parallel method uses n full adders and all bits are applied simultaneously to produce the sum.

A binary parallel adder is a digital circuit that produces the arithmetic sum of two binary numbers in parallel. It consists of full adder circuits connected in cascade, with the output carry from one full adder connected to the input carry of the next full adder. Figure 3-11 shows the interconnection of four full adders (FA) to provide a 4-bit parallel adder. The augend bits of A and the added bits of B are designated by subscript numbers from right to left, with subscript 0 denoting the lowest order bit. The carries are connected in a chain through the full adders. The input carry to the parallel adder is C_0 and the output carry is C_4. An n-bit parallel adder

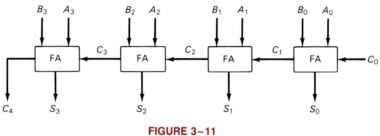

FIGURE 3–11
4-Bit Parallel Adder

requires n full adders with each output carry connected to the input carry of the next-higher-order full adder.

Consider the two binary numbers $A = 1011$ and $B = 0011$. Their sum $S = 1110$ is formed with a four-bit parallel adder as follows:

Input carry	0 1 1 0
Augend A	1 0 1 1
Addend B	0 0 1 1
Sum S	1 1 1 0
Output carry	0 0 1 1

The input carry in the least significant position is 0. Each full adder receives the corresponding bits of A and B and the input carry, and generates the sum bit for S and the output carry. The output carry in each position is transferred to the input carry of the next-higher-order position.

The 4-bit adder is a typical example of a digital component which is available in medium scale integration (MSI) packages. It can be used in many applications involving arithmetic operations. Observe that the design of this circuit by the usual method would require a truth table with 512 entries since there are nine inputs to the circuit. By using an iterative method of cascading an already known full adder circuit, it is possible to obtain a simple and straightforward implementation.

Binary Adder-Subtractor

The subtraction of binary numbers can be done most conveniently by means of complements as discussed in Section 1-4. Remember that the subtraction $A - B$ can be done by taking the 2's complement of B and adding it to A. The 2's complement can be obtained by taking the 1's complement and adding one to the least significant bit. The 1's complement can be implemented easily with inverter circuits and we can add one to the sum by making the input carry of the parallel adder equal to 1.

The circuit for subtracting $A - B$ consists of a parallel adder as shown in Figure 3-11 with inverters placed between each B terminal and the corresponding full adder input. The input carry C_0 must be equal to 1. The operation performed becomes A plus the 1's complement of B plus 1. This is equal to A plus the 2's complement of B. For unsigned numbers, this gives $A - B$ if $A \geq B$ or the 2's complement of $(B - A)$ if $A < B$. For signed numbers, the result is $A - B$ provided there is no overflow. (See Section 1-5).

The addition and subtraction operations can be combined into one circuit with one common binary adder. This is done by including an exclusive-OR gate with each full adder. A 4-bit adder-subtractor circuit is shown in Figure 3-12. Input S controls the operation. When $S = 0$ the circuit is an adder and when $S = 1$ the circuit becomes a subtractor. Each exclusive-OR gate receives input S and one of the inputs of B. When $S = 0$, we have $B \oplus 0 = B$. The full adders receive the value of B, the input carry is 0 and the circuit performs A plus B. When $S = 1$, we have $B \oplus 1 = \bar{B}$ and $C_0 = 1$. The circuit performs the operation A plus the 2's complement of B.

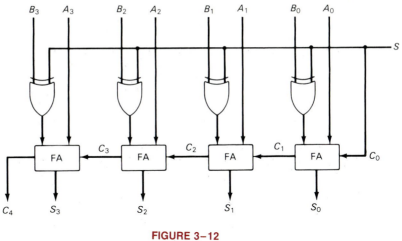

FIGURE 3–12
Adder-Subtractor Circuit

BCD Adder

Computers or calculators that perform arithmetic operations directly in the decimal number system represent decimal numbers in binary coded form. An adder for such a system must employ arithmetic circuits that accept coded decimal numbers and present results in the same code. For binary addition, it is sufficient to consider a pair of significant bits together with a previous carry. A decimal adder requires a minimum of nine inputs and five outputs since four bits are required to code each decimal digit and the circuit must have an input and output carry. There is a wide variety of possible decimal adder circuits, depending upon the code used to represent the decimal digits. Here we consider a decimal adder for the BCD code.

The rules for BCD addition were established in Section 1-6. First, the BCD digits are added as if they were two 4-bit binary numbers. When the binary sum is less than or equal to 1001 (decimal 9), the corresponding BCD digit sum is correct. However, when the binary sum is greater than 1001, we obtain a nonvalid BCD result. The addition of binary 0110 (decimal 6) to the binary sum converts it to the correct BCD representation and also produces an output carry as required.

Consider the addition of two decimal digits in BCD with an input carry. Since each digit does not exceed 9, the sum cannot be greater than $9 + 9 + 1 = 19$. The logic circuit that checks for the necessary BCD correction can be derived by detecting the occurrence of the binary numbers from 1010 through 10011 (decimal 10 through 19). It is obvious that a correction is needed when the binary sum has an output carry. This condition occurs when the sum is greater than or equal to 16. The other six combinations from 1010 through 1111 that need a correction have a 1 in the most significant position and a 1 in the second or third significant position.

A BCD adder that adds two BCD digits and produces a sum digit in BCD is shown in Figure 3-13. It has two 4-bit binary adders and a correction circuit. The two decimal digits together with an input carry are added in the first 4-bit binary adder to produce the binary sum. The condition for correction can be expressed by the following Boolean function.

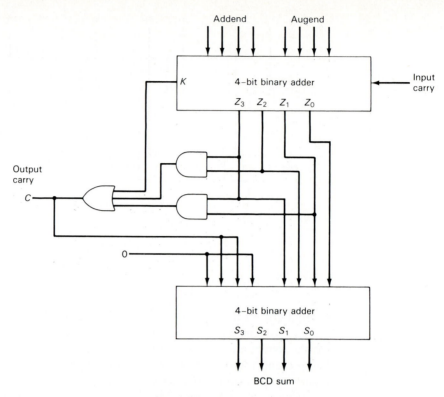

FIGURE 3–13
Block Diagram of BCD Adder

$$C = K + Z_1 Z_3 + Z_2 Z_3$$

C is the output carry from the BCD adder and K is the output carry from the first binary adder. The two terms with the Z variables detect the binary outputs from 1010 through 1111.

When the BCD carry is equal to 0, nothing is added to the binary sum. This condition occurs if the sum of the two digits plus input carry is less than or equal to binary 1001. When the output carry is equal to 1, binary 0110 is added to the binary sum through the second 4-bit adder. This condition occurs when the sum is greater than or equal to 1010. Any output carry from the second binary adder can be neglected.

A decimal parallel adder that adds two n decimal digits needs n BCD adders. The output carry from each BCD adder must be connected to the input carry of the adder in the next higher position.

Binary Multiplier

Multiplication of binary numbers is performed in the same way as with decimal numbers. The multiplicand is multiplied by each bit of the multiplier, starting from the least significant bit. Each such multiplication forms a partial product. Successive

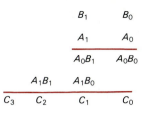

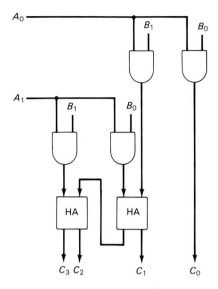

FIGURE 3–14
A 2-Bit by 2-Bit Binary Multiplier

partial products are shifted one position to the left. The final product is obtained from the sum of the partial products.

To see how a binary multiplier can be implemented with a combinational circuit, consider the multiplication of two 2-bit numbers as shown in Figure 3-14. The multiplicand bits are B_1 and B_0, the multiplier bits are A_1 and A_0 and the product is $C_3C_2C_1C_0$. The first partial product is formed by multiplying B_1B_0 by A_0. The multiplication of two bits such as A_0 and B_0 produces a 1 if both bits are 1; otherwise it produces a 0. This is identical to an AND operation. Therefore, the partial product can be implemented with AND gates as shown in the diagram. The second partial product is formed by multiplying B_1B_0 by A_1 and is shifted one position to the left. The two partial products are added with two half adder (HA) circuits. Usually there are more bits in the partial products and it will be necessary to use full adders to produce the sum of the partial products. Note that the least significant bit of the product does not have to go through an adder since it is formed by the output of the first AND gate.

A combinational circuit binary multiplier with more bits can be constructed in a similar fashion. A bit of the multiplier is ANDed with each bit of the multiplicand in as many levels as there are bits in the multiplier. The binary output in each level of AND gates is added in parallel with the partial product of the previous level to form a new partial product. The last level produces the product. For J multiplier bits and K multiplicand bits we need $J \times K$ AND gates and $(J - 1)$ K-bit adders to produce a product of $J + K$ bits.

As a second example, consider a multiplier circuit that multiplies a binary number of four bits by a number of three bits. Let the multiplicand be represented by $B_3B_2B_1B_0$ and the multiplier by $A_2A_1A_0$. Since $K = 4$ and $J = 3$, we need 12 AND gates and two 4-bit adders to produce a product of 7 bits. The logic diagram of the multiplier circuit is shown in Figure 3-15.

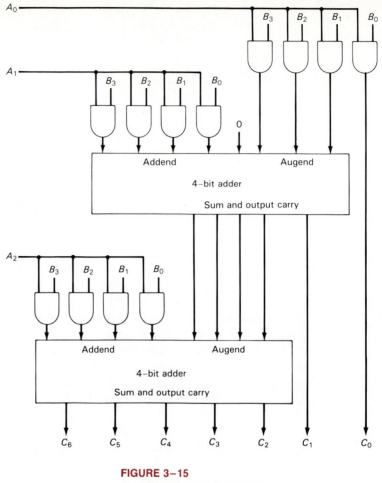

FIGURE 3-15
A 4-Bit by 3-Bit Binary Multiplier

3-5 DECODERS

Discrete quantities of information are represented in digital computers with binary codes. A binary code of n bits is capable of representing up to 2^n distinct elements of the coded information. A decoder is a combinational circuit that converts binary information from the n coded inputs to a maximum of 2^n unique outputs. If the n-bit coded information has unused bit combinations, the decoder may have fewer than 2^n outputs.

The decoders presented in this section are called n-to-m-line decoders where $m \leq 2^n$. Their purpose is to generate the 2^n (or fewer) minterms of n input variables. A decoder has n inputs and m outputs and is referred to as an $n \times m$ decoder.

The logic diagram of a 3-to-8-line decoder is shown in Figure 3-16. The three inputs are decoded into eight outputs, each output representing one of the minterms of the three input variables. The three inverters provide the complement of the

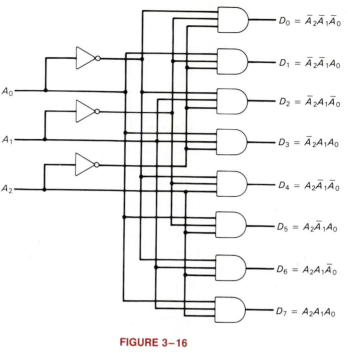

FIGURE 3–16
3-to-8-Line Decoder

inputs, and each one of the eight AND gates generates one of the minterms. A particular application of this decoder is a binary-to-octal conversion. The input variables represent a binary number and the outputs represent the eight digits in the octal number system. However, a 3-to-8-line decoder can be used for decoding any three-bit code to provide eight outputs, one for each element of the code.

The operation of the decoder may be clarified from the truth table listed in Table 3-6. For each possible input combination, there are seven outputs that are equal to 0 and only one that is equal to 1. The output variable equal to 1 represents the minterm equivalent of the binary number that is available in the input lines.

Some decoders are constructed with NAND instead of AND gates. Since a

TABLE 3-6
Truth Table for 3-to-8-Line Decoder

Inputs			Outputs							
A_2	A_1	A_0	D_7	D_6	D_5	D_4	D_3	D_2	D_1	D_0
0	0	0	0	0	0	0	0	0	0	1
0	0	1	0	0	0	0	0	0	1	0
0	1	0	0	0	0	0	0	1	0	0
0	1	1	0	0	0	0	1	0	0	0
1	0	0	0	0	0	1	0	0	0	0
1	0	1	0	0	1	0	0	0	0	0
1	1	0	0	1	0	0	0	0	0	0
1	1	1	1	0	0	0	0	0	0	0

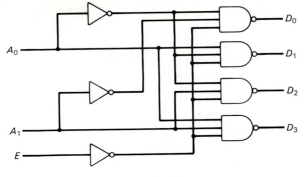

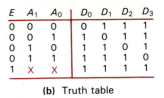

E	A_1	A_0	D_0	D_1	D_2	D_3
0	0	0	0	1	1	1
0	0	1	1	0	1	1
0	1	0	1	1	0	1
0	1	1	1	1	1	0
1	X	X	1	1	1	1

(b) Truth table

(a) Logic diagram

FIGURE 3–17

A 2-to-4-Line Decoder with Enable Input

NAND gate produces the AND operation with an inverted output, it becomes more economical to generate the decoder minterms in their complement form. Furthermore, most commercial decoders include one or more *enable* inputs to control the circuit operation. A 2-to-4-line decoder with an enable input constructed with NAND gates is shown in Figure 3-17. The circuit operates with complemented outputs and a complemented enable input E. The decoder is enabled when E is equal to 0. As indicated by the truth table, only one output can be equal to 0 at any given time, all other outputs are equal to 1. The output with a value of 0 represents the minterm selected by inputs A_1 and A_0. The circuit is disabled when E is equal to 1, regardless of the values of the other two inputs. When the circuit is disabled, none of the outputs are equal to 0 and none of the minterms are selected. In general, a decoder may operate with complemented or uncomplemented outputs. The enable input may be activated with a 0 or with a 1 signal. Some decoders have two or more enable inputs that must satisfy a given logic condition in order to enable the circuit.

Decoder Expansion

There are occasions when a certain size decoder is needed, but only smaller sizes are available. When this occurs, it is possible to combine two or more decoders with enable inputs to form a larger decoder. Thus, if a 6-to-64-line decoder is needed, it is possible to construct it with four 4-to-16-line decoders.

Figure 3-18 shows how decoders with enable inputs can be connected to form a larger decoder. Two 2-to-4-line decoders are combined to achieve a 3-to-8-line decoder. The two least significant bits of the input are connected to both decoders. The most significant bit is connected to the enable input of one decoder and through an inverter to the enable input of the other decoder. When $A_2 = 0$, the upper decoder is enabled and the other is disabled. The lower decoder outputs become inactive with all outputs at 0. The upper decoder generates the minterms D_0 through D_3 using the values of A_1 and A_0. When $A_2 = 1$, the enable conditions are reversed and minterms D_4 through D_7 are generated. Note that these decoders are enabled with a logic-1 signal.

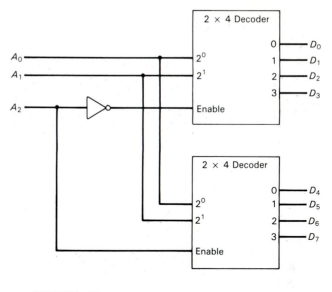

FIGURE 3–18
A 3 × 8 Decoder Constructed with Two 2 × 4 Decoders

The example demonstrates the usefulness of the enable input in decoders or any other combinational logic component. Enable inputs are a convenient feature for interconnecting two or more integrated circuits for the purpose of expanding the digital function into a similar function with more inputs and outputs.

Combinational Circuit Implementation

A decoder provides the 2^n minterms of n input variables. Since any Boolean function can be expressed as a sum of minterms, one can use a decoder to generate the minterms and an external OR gate to form their logical sum. In this way, any combinational circuit with n inputs and m outputs can be implemented with an n-to-2^n-line decoder and m OR gates.

The procedure for implementing a combinational circuit by means of a decoder and OR gates requires that the Boolean functions for the circuit be expressed as a sum of minterms. This form can be obtained from the truth table or by plotting each function in a map. A decoder is then chosen that generates all the minterms of the input variables. The inputs to each OR gate are selected from the decoder outputs according to the minterm list of each function.

Example 3-2   Implement a full adder circuit with a decoder and OR gates.

From the truth table of the full adder (Table 3-5) we obtain the functions for the combinational circuit in sum of minterms.

$$S(X, Y, Z) = \Sigma m(1, 2, 4, 7)$$

$$C(X, Y, Z) = \Sigma m(3, 5, 6, 7)$$

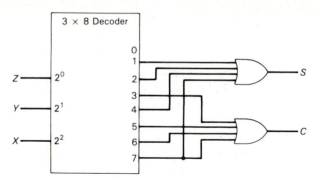

FIGURE 3–19
Implementing a Full Adder Using a Decoder

Since there are three inputs and a total of eight minterms, we need a 3-to-8-line decoder. The implementation is shown in Figure 3-19. The decoder generates the eight minterms for X, Y, Z. The OR gate for output S forms the logical sum of minterms 1, 2, 4, and 7. The OR gate for output C forms the logical sum of minterms 3, 5, 6, and 7.   ■

A function with a long list of minterms requires an OR gate with a large number of inputs. A function having a list of k minterms can be expressed in its complement form with $2^n - k$ minterms. If the number of minterms in a function F is greater than $2^n/2$ then its complement $\bar{F}$ can be expressed with fewer minterms. In such a case, it is advantageous to use a NOR gate instead of an OR gate. The OR portion of the gate produces the logical sum of the minterms of $\bar{F}$. The output of the NOR gate complements this sum and generates the normal output F.

If NAND gates are used for the decoder, as in Figure 3-17, the external gates must be NAND gates instead of OR gates. This is because a two level NAND gate circuit implements a sum of minterms function and is equivalent to a two level AND-OR circuit (see Section 2-6).

The decoder method can be used to implement any combinational circuit. However, its implementation must be compared with all other possible implementations to determine the best solution. In some cases this method may provide the best solution, especially if the combinational circuit has many outputs and each output function is expressed with a small number of minterms.

3-6   ENCODERS

An encoder is a digital function that performs the inverse operation of a decoder. An encoder has 2^n (or less) input lines and n output lines. The output lines generate the binary code corresponding to the input value. An example of an encoder is the octal-to-binary encoder whose truth table is given in Table 3-7. It has eight inputs, one for each of the octal digits, and three outputs that generate the corresponding binary number. It is assumed that only one input has a value of 1 at any given time; otherwise the circuit has no meaning.

TABLE 3-7
Truth Table for Octal-to-Binary Encoder

Inputs								Outputs		
D_7	D_6	D_5	D_4	D_3	D_2	D_1	D_0	A_2	A_1	A_0
0	0	0	0	0	0	0	1	0	0	0
0	0	0	0	0	0	1	0	0	0	1
0	0	0	0	0	1	0	0	0	1	0
0	0	0	0	1	0	0	0	0	1	1
0	0	0	1	0	0	0	0	1	0	0
0	0	1	0	0	0	0	0	1	0	1
0	1	0	0	0	0	0	0	1	1	0
1	0	0	0	0	0	0	0	1	1	1

The encoder can be implemented with OR gates using inputs determined directly from the truth table. Output $A_0 = 1$ if the input octal digit is 1 or 3 or 5 or 7. Similar conditions apply for the other two outputs. These conditions can be expressed by the following output Boolean functions:

$$A_0 = D_1 + D_3 + D_5 + D_7$$

$$A_1 = D_2 + D_3 + D_6 + D_7$$

$$A_2 = D_4 + D_5 + D_6 + D_7$$

The encoder can be implemented with three OR gates.

The encoder defined in Table 3-7 has the limitation that only one input can be active at any given time. If two inputs are active simultaneously, the output produces an undefined combination. For example, if D_3 and D_6 are 1 simultaneously, the output of the encoder will be 111 because all the three outputs are equal to 1. This does not represent a binary 3 nor a binary 6. To resolve this ambiguity, encoder circuits must establish an input priority to ensure that only one input is encoded. If we establish a higher priority for inputs with higher subscript numbers and if both D_3 and D_6 are 1 at the same time, the output will be 110 because D_6 has higher priority than D_3.

Another ambiguity, in the octal-to-binary encoder is that an output of all 0's is generated when all the inputs are 0, but this output is the same as when D_0 is equal to 1. This discrepancy can be resolved by providing one more output to indicate that at least one input is equal to 1.

Priority Encoder

A priority encoder is a combinational circuit that implements the priority function. The operation of the priority encoder is such that if two or more inputs are equal to 1 at the same time, the input having the highest priority will take precedence. The truth table of a four-input priority encoder is given in Table 3-8. The X's designate don't care conditions. Input D_3 has the highest priority; so regardless of the values of the other inputs, when this input is 1, the output for A_1A_0 is 11 (binary 3). D_2 has the next priority level. The output is 10 if $D_2 = 1$ provided that $D_3 =$

TABLE 3-8
Truth Table of Priority Encoder

Inputs				Outputs		
D_3	D_2	D_1	D_0	A_1	A_0	V
0	0	0	0	0	0	0
0	0	0	1	0	0	1
0	0	1	X	0	1	1
0	1	X	X	1	0	1
1	X	X	X	1	1	1

0, regardless of the values of the other two lower-priority inputs. The output for D_1 is generated only if higher-priority inputs are 0, and so on down the priority levels. The valid output designated by V is set to 1 only when one or more of the inputs are equal to 1. If all inputs are 0, V is equal to 0, and the other two outputs of the circuit are not used.

The maps for simplifying outputs A_1 and A_0 are shown in Figure 3-20. The minterms for the two functions are derived from Table 3-8. Although the table has only five rows, when each don't care is replaced first by 0 and then by 1, we obtain all 16 possible input combinations. For example, the third row in the table with 001X represents minterms 0010 and 0011 since X can be assigned either 0 or 1. The simplified functions obtained from the maps are listed under each map. The condition for output V is an OR function of all the input variables. The priority encoder is implemented in Figure 3-21 according to the following Boolean functions:

$$A_0 = D_3 + D_1\overline{D}_2$$

$$A_1 = D_2 + D_3$$

$$V = D_0 + D_1 + D_2 + D_3$$

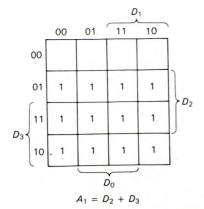

$$A_1 = D_2 + D_3$$

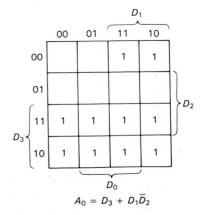

$$A_0 = D_3 + D_1\overline{D}_2$$

FIGURE 3–20
Maps for Priority Encoder

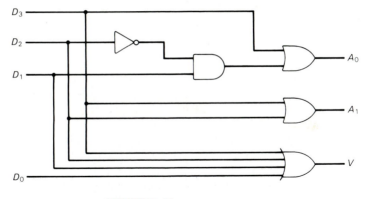

FIGURE 3–21
Logic Diagram of a 4-Input Priority Encoder

3-7   MULTIPLEXERS

A multiplexer is a combinational circuit that selects binary information from one of many input lines and directs it to a single output line. The selection of a particular input line is controlled by a set of selection variables. Normally, there are 2^n input lines and n selection variables whose bit combinations determine which input is selected.

A 4-to-1-line multiplexer is shown in Figure 3-22. Each of the four inputs D_0 through D_3 is applied to one input of an AND gate. Selection lines S_1 and S_0 are decoded to select a particular AND gate. The outputs of the AND gates are applied to a single OR gate to provide the 1-line ouput. To demonstrate the circuit op-

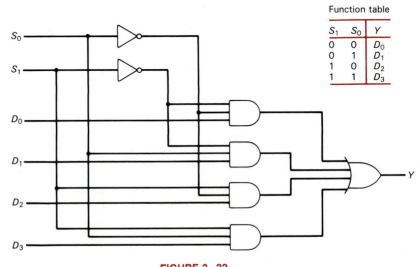

Function table

S_1	S_0	Y
0	0	D_0
0	1	D_1
1	0	D_2
1	1	D_3

FIGURE 3–22
4-to-1-Line Multiplexer

eration, consider the case when $S_1 S_0 = 10$. The AND gate associated with input D_2 has two of its inputs equal to 1 and the third input connected to D_2. The other three AND gates have at least one input equal to 0, which makes their outputs equal to 0. The OR gate output is now equal to the value of D_2, providing a path from the selected input to the output. The function table in the figure lists the input that provides the path to the output for each combination of the binary selection variables. A multiplexer is also called a *data selector* since it selects one of many inputs and steers the binary information to the output line.

The AND gates and inverters in the multiplexer resemble a decoder circuit, and indeed, they decode the input selection lines. In general, a 2^n-to-1-line mutliplexer is constructed from an n-to-2^n decoder by adding 2^n input lines to it, one from each data input. The size of the multiplexer is specified by the number 2^n of its data input lines and the single output line. It is then implied that it also contains n selection lines. The multiplexer is often abbreviated as MUX.

A multiplexer can be constructed with transmission gates. The transmission gate is available only with CMOS type integrated circuits, and its operation is explained in conjunction with Figure 2-37. A 4-to-1-line multiplexer implemented with transmission gates (TG) is shown in Figure 3-23. The TG circuit provides a transmission path between the horizontal input and output lines when the two vertical control inputs have the value of 1 in the uncircled terminal and 0 in the circled terminal.

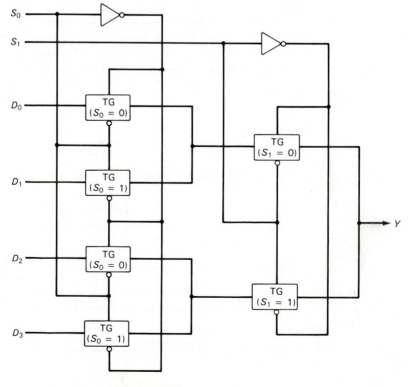

FIGURE 3–23
Multiplexer with Transmission Gates (TG)

With an opposite polarity in the control inputs, the path disconnects, and the circuit behaves like an open switch. The two selection inputs S_1 and S_0 control the transmission path in the TG circuits. Inside each box is marked the condition for the circuit to be closed. Thus, if $S_0 = 0$ and $S_1 = 0$ there is a closed path from input D_0 to output Y and the other three inputs are disconnected by one of the other TG circuits.

As in decoders, multiplexers may have an enable input to control the operation of the unit. When the enable input is in the inactive state, the outputs are disabled, and when it is in the active state, the circuit functions as a normal multiplexer. The enable input is useful for expanding two or more multiplexers into a multiplexer with a larger number of inputs.

In some cases, two or more multiplexers are enclosed within a single integrated circuit package. The selection and the enable inputs in multiple-unit construction are usually common to all multiplexers. As an illustration, a quadruple 2-to-1-line multiplexer is shown in Figure 3-24. The circuit has four multiplexers, each capable

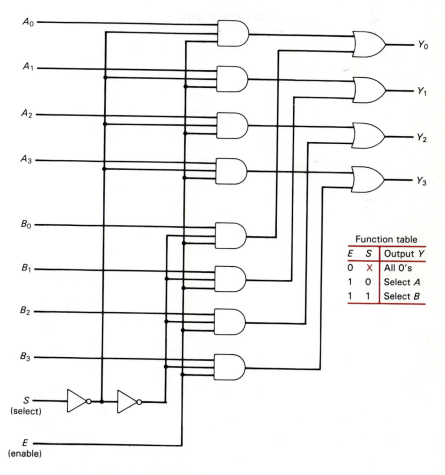

Function table

E	S	Output Y
0	X	All 0's
1	0	Select A
1	1	Select B

FIGURE 3-24
Quadruple 2-to-1-Line Multiplexer

of selecting one of two input lines. Output Y_0 can be selected to come from either input A_0 or B_0. Similarly, output Y_1 may have the value of A_1 or B_1, and so on. Input selection line S selects one of the lines in each of the four multiplexers. The enable input E must be active for normal operation. Although the circuit contains four multiplexers, we can also think of it as a circuit that selects one of two 4-bit data lines. As shown in the function table, the unit is enabled when $E = 1$. Then, if $S = 0$, the four A inputs have a path to the four outputs. On the other hand, if $S = 1$, the four B inputs are applied to the outputs. The outputs have all 0's when $E = 0$, regardless of the values of S.

Boolean Function Implementation

It was shown in Section 3-5 that a decoder can be used to implement a Boolean function by employing an external OR gate. A reference to the logic diagram of a multiplexer reveals that it is essentially a decoder that includes the OR gate within the unit. The minterms of a function are generated in a multiplexer by the circuit associated with the selection inputs. The individual minterms can be selected by the data inputs. This provides a method of implementing a Boolean function of n variables with a multiplexer that has n selection inputs and 2^n data inputs, one for each minterm.

We will now show a more efficient method for implementing a Boolean function of n variables with a multiplexer that has $n - 1$ selection inputs. The first $n - 1$ variables of the function are connected to the selection inputs of the multiplexer. The remaining single variable of the function is used for the data inputs. If the single variable is denoted by Z, the data inputs of the multiplexer will be either $Z, \overline{Z}, 1$, or 0. To demonstrate this procedure, consider the Boolean function of three variables

$$F(X, Y, Z) = \Sigma\, m(1, 2, 6, 7)$$

The function can be implemented with a 4-to-1-line multiplexer as shown in Figure 3-25. The two variables X and Y are applied to the selection lines in that order;

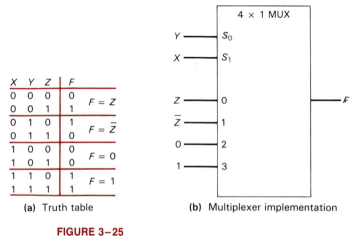

X	Y	Z	F	
0	0	0	0	$F = Z$
0	0	1	1	
0	1	0	1	$F = \overline{Z}$
0	1	1	0	
1	0	0	0	$F = 0$
1	0	1	0	
1	1	0	1	$F = 1$
1	1	1	1	

(a) Truth table

(b) Multiplexer implementation

FIGURE 3–25
Implementing a Boolean Function with a Multiplexer

X is connected to the S_1 input and Y to the S_0 input. The values for the data input lines are determined from the truth table of the function. When $XY = 00$, output F is equal to Z because $F = 0$ when $Z = 0$ and $F = 1$ when $Z = 1$. This requires that variable Z be applied to data input 0. The operation of the multiplexer is such that when $XY = 00$, data input 0 has a path to the output which makes F equal to Z. In a similar fashion we can determine the required input to lines 1, 2, and 3 from the value of F when $XY = 01, 10$, and 11, respectively. This particular example shows all four possibilities that can be obtained for the data inputs.

The general procedure for implementing any Boolean function of n variables with a multiplexer with $n - 1$ selection inputs and 2^{n-1} data inputs follows from the above example. The Boolean function is first listed in a truth table. The first $n - 1$ variables listed in the table are applied to the selection inputs of the multiplexer. For each combination of the selection variables, we evaluate the output as a function of the last variable. This can be 0, 1, the variable, or the complement of the variable. These values are then applied to the data inputs in the proper order. As a second example, consider the implementation of the following Boolean function:

$$F(A, B, C, D) = \Sigma\, m(1, 3, 4, 11, 12, 13, 14, 15)$$

This is implemented with a multiplexer with three selection inputs as shown in Figure 3-26. Note that the first variable A must be connected to selection input S_2 so that A, B, C correspond to selection inputs S_2, S_1, and S_0, respectively. The values for the data inputs are determined from the truth table listed in the figure. The corresponding data line number is determined from the binary combination of ABC. For example, when $ABC = 101$, the table shows that $F = D$; so input variable D is applied to data input 5. The binary constants 0 and 1 correspond to two signal values. If TTL type integrated circuits are used, then logic-0 corresponds to signal ground and logic-1 is equivalent to a five-volt signal.

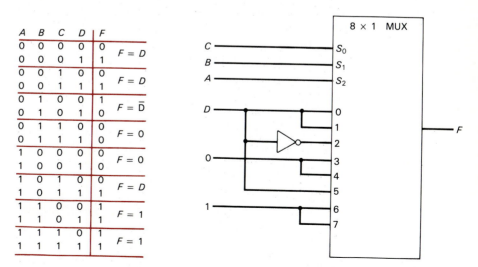

A	B	C	D	F
0	0	0	0	0
0	0	0	1	1
0	0	1	0	0
0	0	1	1	1
0	1	0	0	1
0	1	0	1	0
0	1	1	0	0
0	1	1	1	0
1	0	0	0	0
1	0	0	1	0
1	0	1	0	0
1	0	1	1	1
1	1	0	0	1
1	1	0	1	1
1	1	1	0	1
1	1	1	1	1

$F = D$
$F = D$
$F = \bar{D}$
$F = 0$
$F = 0$
$F = D$
$F = 1$
$F = 1$

FIGURE 3-26
Implementing a 4-Input Function with a Multiplexer

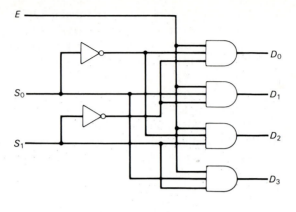

FIGURE 3–27
1-to-4-Line Demultiplexer

Demultiplexer

A demultiplexer is a digital function that performs the inverse operation of a multiplexer. A demultiplexer receives information from a single line and transmits it to one of 2^n possible output lines. The selection of the specific output is controlled by the bit combination of n selection lines. A 1-to-4-line demultiplexer is shown in Figure 3-27. The data input E has a path to all four outputs, but the input information is directed to only one of the outputs as specified by the two selection lines S_1 and S_0. For example, if $S_1 S_0 = 10$, output D_2 will be the same as the input value of E, while all other outputs remain inactive at logic-0.

A careful inspection of the demultiplexer circuit will show that it is identical to a 2-to-4-line decoder with enable input. For the decoder, the data inputs are S_1 and S_0 and the enable is input E. For the demultiplexer, input E provides the data while the other inputs accept the selection variables. Although the two circuits have different applications, their logic diagrams are exactly the same. For this reason, a decoder with enable input is referred to as a *decoder/demultiplexer*.

3-8 STANDARD GRAPHIC SYMBOLS

Often used digital components such as adders, decoders, and multiplexers are available commercially in integrated circuits and are classified as MSI functions. Standard graphic symbols have been developed for these and other components so that the user can recognize each function from the unique graphic symbol assigned to it. This standard, known as ANSI/IEEE Std. 91-1984, has been approved by industry, government, and professional organizations and is consistent with international standards.

The standard uses a rectangular shape outline to represent each particular logic function. Within the outline there is a general qualifying symbol denoting the logical operation performed by the unit. For example, the general qualifying symbol for a multiplexer is MUX. The size of the outline is arbitrary and can be either a square or rectangular shape with arbitrary length-width ratio. Input lines are placed on the left and output lines are placed on the right. If the direction of signal flow is reversed, it must be indicated by arrows. The rectangular shape symbols for the digital gates were introduced in Figure 2-25.

An example of a standard graphic symbol is the 4-bit parallel adder shown in Figure 3-28. The qualifying symbol for an adder is the Greek letter Σ. The preferred letters for the arithmetic operands are P and Q. The bit-grouping symbols in the two types of inputs and the sum output are the decimal equivalent of the weights of the bits to the power of 2. Thus, the input labeled 3 corresponds to the value of $2^3 = 8$. The input carry is designated by CI and the output carry by CO.

Before introducing the graphic symbols of other components, it is necessary to review some terminology. As mentioned in Section 2-8, a positive logic system defines the more positive of two signal levels (designated by H) as logic-1 and the more negative signal level (designated by L) as logic-0. Negative logic assumes the opposite assignment. A third alternative is to employ a mixed-logic convention where the signals are considered entirely in terms of their H and L values. At any point in the circuit, the user is allowed to define the logic polarity by assigning logic-1 to either the H or L signal. The mixed-logic notation uses a small right-angle triangle graphic symbol to designate a negative logic polarity at any input or output terminal. (See Figure 2-42f.)

Integrated circuit manufacturers specify the operation of integrated circuits in terms of H and L signals. When an input or output is considered in terms of positive logic, it is defined as *active-high*. When it is considered in terms of negative logic, it is assumed to be *active-low*. Active-low inputs or outputs are recognized by the presence of the small triangle polarity indicator graphic symbol. When positive logic is used exclusively throughout the entire system, the small triangle polarity symbol is equivalent to the small circle that designates a negation. In this book we assume positive logic throughout, and we will employ the small circle when drawing logic diagrams. When an input or output line does not include the small circle, we will define it to be active if it is logic-1. A line that includes the small circle symbol

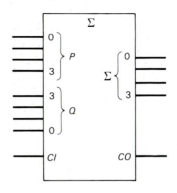

FIGURE 3–28

Standard Graphic Symbol for a 4-Bit Parallel Adder

will be considered active if it is in the logic-0 state. However, we will use the small triangle polarity symbol to indicate active-low assignment in all drawings that represent standard diagrams. This will conform with integrated circuit data books where the polarity symbol is usually employed. The easiest way to understand what has been said is to realize that the small triangle polarity symbol is equivalent to the small circle negation symbol when positive logic is used.

Standard Graphic Symbol for Decoder

The graphic symbol for the decoder is shown in Figure 3-29. In (a) we have a 3-to-8-line decoder with an enable input designated by *EN*. Inputs are on the left and outputs on the right. The identifying symbol X/Y indicates that the circuit converts from code X to code Y. The inputs are assigned binary weights 1, 2, and 4 equivalent to 2^0, 2^1 and 2^2. The outputs are assigned numbers from 0 to 7. The sum of the weights of the inputs determine the output that is active. Thus, if the two input lines with weights 1 and 4 are activated, the total weight is $1 + 4 = 5$ and output 5 is activated. Of course the *EN* input must be activated for any output to be active. The two letter symbol *EN* is reserved to identify an input that enables outputs. If the input labeled *EN* is active, all outputs are active or inactive according to the input conditions that affect them. If the *EN* input is inactive, then all outputs are inactive.

A 2-to-4-line decoder with an active-low enable input and active-low outputs is shown in Figure 3-29(b). The circuit is enabled if the enable input is active. This means that the enable signal must be at a low-level state as indicated by the polarity symbol. If the circuit is not enabled, all outputs are inactive and in the high-level state. When the circuit is enabled, the input weights determine which output will be active. The polarity symbols in the outputs indicate that the selected output will be at a low level. For positive logic assignment, the inputs and outputs are as specified in the truth table of Figure 3-17(b).

The decoder is a special case of a more general component referred to as a *coder*. A coder is a device that receives an input binary code on a number of inputs

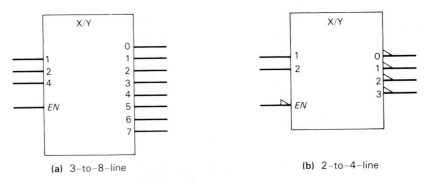

(a) 3–to–8–line   (b) 2–to–4–line

FIGURE 3–29
Standard Graphic Symbol for a Decoder

and produces a different binary code on a number of outputs. Instead of using the qualifying symbol X/Y, the coder can be specified by the code name. For example, the 3-to-8-line decoder of Figure 3-29(a) can be symbolized with the name BIN/ OCT since the circuit converts a 3-bit binary code into an 8 output octal value. When the digital component represented by the outline is also a commercial integrated circuit, it is customary to write the IC pin number along each input and output line.

Standard Graphic Symbol for the Multiplexer

Before showing the graphic symbol of a multiplexer, it is necessary to define a notation called *AND dependency*. The letter *G* followed by a number is reserved for specifying AND dependency. Any input or output in a block diagram which is labeled with the number associated with *G* is considered to be ANDed with it. For example, if one input in the block diagram has the label *G*1 and another input is labeled with the number 1, then the two inputs labeled *G*1 and 1 are considered to be ANDed together internally.

An example of AND dependency is shown in Figure 3-30. In (a) we have a portion of a graphic symbol with two AND dependency labels *G*1 and *G*2. There are two inputs labeled with the number 1 and one input labeled with the number 2. The equivalent interpretation is shown in part (b) of the figure. Note that the AND gates are drawn with the ampersand (&) inside a rectangular shape outline to conform with the standard shapes. Input *X* labeled *G*1 is considered to be ANDed with inputs *A* and *B* which are labeled with a 1. Similarly, input *Y* is ANDed with input *C* to conform with the dependency between *G*2 and 2.

The AND dependency is sometimes represented by a shorthand notation like G_7^0. This symbol stands for eight AND dependency symbols from 0 to 7 as follows:

$$G0, G1, G2, G3, G4, G5, G6, G7$$

At any given time, only one out of the eight AND gates can be active. The active

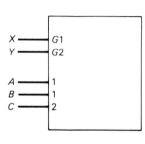

(a) Block with *G*1 and *G*2

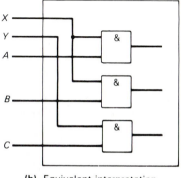

(b) Equivalent interpretation

FIGURE 3–30
Example of a G (AND) Dependency

AND gate is determined from the inputs associated with the G symbol. These inputs are marked with weights equal to the powers of 2. For the eight AND gates listed above, the weights are 0, 1, and 2, corresponding to the numbers 2^0, 2^1, and 2^2, respectively. The AND gate that is active at any given time is determined from the sum of the weights of the active inputs. Thus, if inputs 0 and 2 are active, the AND gate that is active has the number $2^0 + 2^2 = 5$. This makes $G5$ active and the other seven AND gates inactive.

The standard graphic symbol for the multiplexer is shown in Figure 3-31. The label MUX identifies the device as a multiplexer. The symbols inside the block are part of the standard notation, but the symbols marked outside are user defined symbols. In order to understand the standard notation, we use the same external variables here as in the logic diagrams of the multiplexers in Section 3-7.

The diagram of Figure 3-31 (a) represents an 8-to-1-line multiplexer with enable (EN) input. The AND dependency is marked with G_7^0 and is associated with the inputs enclosed in brackets. These inputs have weights of 0, 1, and 2. They are actually what we have called the selection inputs. The eight data inputs are marked with numbers from 0 to 7. The net weight of the active inputs associated with the G symbol specify the number in the data input that is active. For example, if selection inputs $S_2 S_1 S_0 = 110$, then inputs 1 and 2 associated with G are active. This gives a numerical value for the AND dependency of $2^2 + 2^1 = 6$, which makes $G6$ active. Since $G6$ is ANDed with data input number 6, it makes this input active. Thus the output will be equal to data input D_6 provided that the enable input is active.

The diagram of Figure 3-31(b) represents the quadruple 2-to-1-line multiplexer whose logic diagram is shown in Figure 3-24. The enable and selection inputs are common to all four multiplexers. This is indicated in the standard notation by the indented box at the top of the diagram which represents a *common control block*. The inputs to a common control block control all lower sections of the diagram.

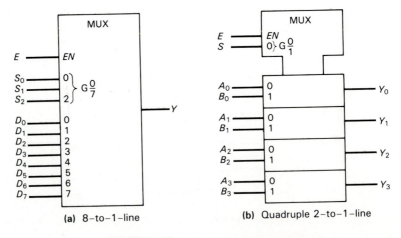

(a) 8-to-1-line   **(b)** Quadruple 2-to-1-line

FIGURE 3-31
Standard Graphic Symbols for Multiplexers

The common enable input *EN* is active when in the high level state. The AND dependency G_1^0 represents two AND gates *G0* and *G1*. When $S = 0$, *G0* is active and the inputs marked with 0 are active. When $S = 1$, *G1* is active and the inputs marked with 1 are active. The active inputs are applied to the corresponding outputs if *EN* is active.

Dependency Notation

The most important aspect of the standard logic symbols is the dependency notation. Dependency notation is used to provide the means of denoting the relationship between different inputs or outputs without actually showing all the elements and interconnections between them. We have already defined the *G* (AND) dependency in connection with the symbol for the multiplexer. The ANSI/IEEE standard defines ten other types of dependencies. Each dependency is denoted by a letter symbol (except *EN*). The letter appears at the input or output and is followed by a number. Each input or output affected by that dependency is labeled with that same number.

The eleven dependencies and their corresponding letter designation are as follows:

G	—	Denotes an AND (gate) relationship
EN	—	Specifies an enable action
C	—	Identifies a control dependency
S	—	Specifies a setting action
R	—	Specifies a resetting action
M	—	Identifies a mode dependency
A	—	Identifies an address dependency
Z	—	Indicates an internal interconnection
X	—	Indicates a controlled transmission.
V	—	Denotes an OR relationship
N	—	Denotes a negate (exclusive-OR) relationship

The *G* and *EN* dependencies were introduced in this section. The control dependency *C* is used to identify a clock input in a sequential element and to indicate which input is controlled by it. The set *S* and reset *R* dependencies are used to specify internal logic states of an SR flip-flop. The *C*, *S*, and *R* dependencies are explained in Section 4-3 in conjunction with the flip-flop circuit. The mode *M* dependency is used to identify inputs that select the mode of operation of the unit. The mode dependency is presented in Chapter 5 in conjunction with registers and counters. The address *A* dependency is used to identify the address input of a memory. It is introduced in Chapter 6 in conjunction with the memory unit.

The *Z* dependency is used to indicate interconnections inside the unit. It signifies the existence of internal logic connections between inputs, outputs, internal inputs and internal outputs, in any combination. The *X* dependency is used to indicate the controlled transmission path in a transmission gate similar to the one shown in Figure 2-37.

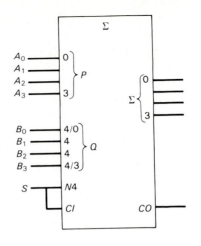

FIGURE 3–32
Graphic Symbol for an Adder-Subtractor

The V and N dependencies are used to denote the Boolean relationships of OR and exclusive-OR similar to the G that denotes the Boolean AND. An example of a graphic symbol that uses the N dependency is shown in Figure 3-32. This is the symbol for the adder-subtractor circuit from Figure 3-12. The arithmetic operands are P and Q as in the adder. Input S is labeled with $N4$ and the four Q inputs have the numerical label 4. The dependency notation here implies the existence of the exclusive-OR relationship between the S input and each of the B inputs. This means that when $S = 0$, operand Q is equal to the B inputs, but when $S = 1$, the four inputs are negated by an exclusive-OR gate and Q becomes the 1's complement of B.

Qualifying Symbols for Inputs and Outputs

In addition to the dependency notation, the ANSI/IEEE standard graphic symbols for logic functions provide a list of qualifying symbols associated with inputs, outputs, and other connections. They include the polarity and negation symbols, symbols for internal connections, symbols for inside the outline, and symbols for nonlogic connections. The entire list of symbols is too numerous to be included here. Some of the most common used symbols are shown in Figure 3-33.

The active-low input or output is the polarity indicator. As mentioned previously, it is equivalent to the logic negation when positive logic is assumed. The *EN* input is similar to the *EN* dependency except that it does not need to be followed by a number. If there is no number following it, the simple *EN* input has the effect of enabling all the outputs when it is active.

The dynamic input is associated with the clock input in flip-flop circuits. It indicates that the input is active on a transition from a low to high level signal. This is explained in more detail in Section 4-3. The three-state output has a third external high-impedance state which has no logic significance. This is explained in Section 7-4 in conjunction with the construction of a common bus system.

Symbol	Description

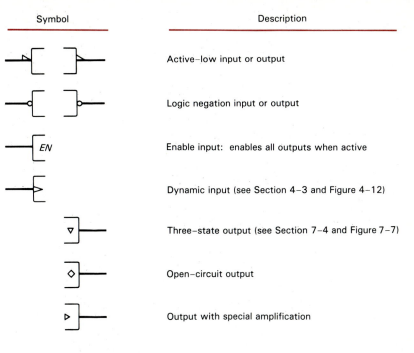

Active–low input or output

Logic negation input or output

EN Enable input: enables all outputs when active

Dynamic input (see Section 4–3 and Figure 4–12)

Three–state output (see Section 7–4 and Figure 7–7)

Open–circuit output

Output with special amplification

FIGURE 3–33
Qualifying Symbols Associated with Inputs and Outputs

The open-circuit output is also referred to as an open-collector or open-drain output. One of the two possible logic states of this type of output corresponds to an external high-impedance condition. An externally connected resistor is sometimes required in order to produce the proper logic level. The diamond shape symbol may have a bar on top for high-type or on the bottom for low-type. The high or low type specifies the logic level when the output is not in the high-impedance state. For example, TTL type integrated circuits have a special output called open-collector output. These outputs are recognized by a diamond shape symbol with a bar under it. When used as part of a distribution function, two or more open-collector outputs connected to a common resistor perform a positive-logic AND function or a negative-logic OR function.

The output with special amplification is used in outputs of gates that provide special driving capabilities. Such gates are employed in components like clock drivers or bus oriented transmitters.

REFERENCES

1. PEATMAN, J. B. *Digital Hardware Design.* New York: McGraw-Hill, 1980
2. BLAKESLEE, T. R. *Digital Design with Standard MSI and LSI.* 2nd ed. New York: Wiley, 1979.
3. MANO, M. M. *Digital Design.* Englewood Cliffs: Prentice-Hall, 1984.

4. SANDIGE, R. S. *Digital Concepts Using Standard Integrated Circuits*. New York: McGraw-Hill, 1978.

5. *IEEE Standard Graphic Symbols for Logic Functions*. (ANSI/IEEE Std. 91-1984.) New York: The Institute of Electrical and Electronics Engineers.

6. KAMPEL, I. *A Practical Introduction to the New Logic Symbols*. Boston: Butterworths, 1985.

7. *The TTL Data Book*. Vol. 2. Dallas: Texas Instruments, 1985.

8. *High-Speed CMOS Logic Data Book*. Dallas: Texas Instruments, 1984.

PROBLEMS

3-1 Determine the Boolean functions for outputs J and K as a function of the four inputs in the circuit of Figure P3-1.

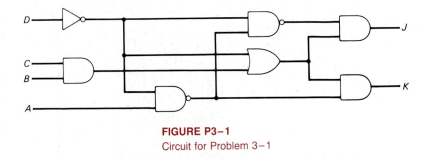

FIGURE P3–1
Circuit for Problem 3–1

3-2 Obtain the truth table for the circuit shown in Figure P3-2. Draw an equivalent circuit for F with fewer NAND gates.

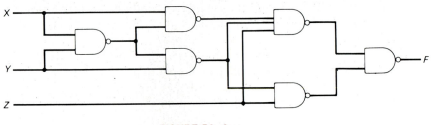

FIGURE P3–2
Circuit for Problem 3–2

3-3 Verify that the circuit of Figure P3-3 generates the exclusive-NOR function.

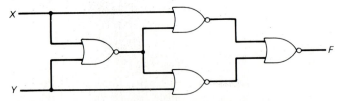

FIGURE P3–3
Circuit for Problem 3–3

3-4 A majority function is generated in a combinational circuit when the output is equal to 1 if the input variables have more 1's than 0's. The output is 0 otherwise. Design a 3-input majority function.

3-5 Design a combinational circuit that detects an error in the representation of a decimal digit in BCD. In other words, obtain a logic diagram whose output is equal to 1 when the inputs contain any one of the six unused bit combinations in the BCD code.

3-6 Design a combinational circuit that accepts a three-bit number and generates an output binary number equal to the square of the input number.

3-7 Design a combinational circuit whose input is a four-bit number and whose output is the 2's complement of the input number.

3-8 Design a combinational circuit that converts a decimal digit from the 8 4-2-1 code to BCD (see Table 1-5).

3-9 Design a combinational circuit that converts a decimal digit from the 2 4 2 1 code to the 8 4-2-1 code (see Table 1-5).

3-10 (a) Plot the seven maps for each of the outputs for the BCD to seven-segment decoder specified in Table 3-3.
(b) Simplify the seven output functions in sum of products and determine the total number of gates that will be needed to implement the decoder.
(c) Verify that the seven output functions listed in the text give a valid simplification. Compare the number of gates with the circuit obtained in part (b).

3-11 Draw the logic diagram of the BCD to seven-segment decoder from the Boolean functions listed in Section 3-3 of the text. Use only 21 NAND gates. Assume that both the complemented and uncomplemented inputs are available.

3-12 Design a combinational circuit that forms the binary sum of two 2-bit numbers A_1A_0 and B_1B_0. Do not use half adders or full adders. Design the circuit starting with a truth table.

3-13 The logic diagram of the first stage of a 4-bit adder as implemented in integrated circuit type 74283 is shown in Figure P3-13. Verify that the circuit implements a full adder.

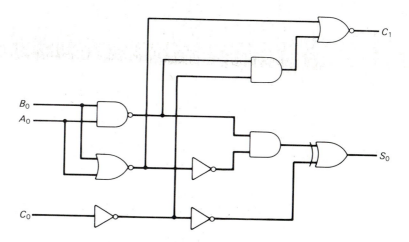

FIGURE P3–13
Circuit for Problem 3–13

3-14 Construct a BCD to excess-3 code converter with a 4-bit adder. Remember that the excess-3 code digit is obtained by adding three to the corresponding BCD digit. What must be done to change the circuit to an excess-3 to BCD code converter?

3-15 The adder-subtractor circuit of Figure 3-12 has the following values for input select S and data inputs A and B. In each case, determine the values of the outputs S_3, S_2, S_1, S_0, and C_4.

	S	A	B
(a)	0	0111	0110
(b)	0	1000	1001
(c)	1	1100	1000
(d)	1	0101	1010
(e)	1	0000	0001

3-16 How many don't care input combinations are there in a BCD adder?

3-17 Design a combinational circuit that generates the 9's complement of a BCD digit.

3-18 Construct a BCD adder-subtractor using the BCD adder from Figure 3-13 and the 9's complementer of Problem 3-17. Use block diagrams for both components showing only inputs and outputs.

3-19 It is necessary to design a decimal adder for two digits represented in the excess-3 code. Show that the correction after adding the two digits with a 4-bit binary adder is as follows:
(a) The output carry is equal to the carry from the binary adder.
(b) If the output carry = 1, then add 0011.
(c) If the output carry = 0, then add 1101.
Construct the decimal adder with two 4-bit adders and an inverter.

3-20 Design a binary multiplier that multiplies two 4-bit numbers. Use AND gates and binary adders.

3-21 Design a combinational circuit that compares two 4-bit numbers A and B to check if they are equal. The circuit has one output X, so that $X = 1$ if $A = B$ and $X = 0$ if A is not equal to B.

3-22 Design a BCD-to-decimal decoder using the unused combinations of the BCD code as don't care conditions.

3-23 Construct a 5-to-32-line decoder with four 3-to-8-line decoders with enable input and one 2-to-4-line decoder. Use standard graphic diagrams.

3-24 A combinational circuit is defined by the following three Boolean functions. Design the circuit with a decoder and external gates.

$$F_1 = \overline{X}\overline{Y} + XY\overline{Z}$$

$$F_2 = \overline{X} + Y$$

$$F_3 = XY + \overline{X}\overline{Y}$$

3-25 A combinational circuit is specified by the following three Boolean functions. Implement the circuit with a decoder constructed with NAND gates (similar to Figure 3-17) and external NAND gates.

$$F_1(A, B, C) = \Sigma\, m(0, 5, 7)$$

$$F_2(A, B, C) = \Sigma\, m(2, 3, 4)$$

$$F_3(A, B, C) = \Sigma\, m(1, 6, 7)$$

3-26 Draw the logic diagram of a 2-to-4-line decoder with only NOR gates. Include an enable input.

3-27 Design a 4-input priority encoder with inputs and outputs as in Table 3-8 but with input D_0 having the highest priority.

3-28 Derive the truth table of an octal-to-binary priority encoder.

3-29 Construct an 8-to-1-line multiplexer with enable input using transmission gates.

3-30 Construct a 16-to-1-line mutliplexer with two 8-to-1-line multiplexers and one 2-to-1-line multiplexer. Use standard block diagram symbols.

3-31 Implement a full adder with a dual 4-to-1-line multiplexer.

3-32 Implement the following Boolean function with a multiplexer.

$$F(A, B, C, D) = \Sigma\, m(0, 3, 5, 6, 8, 9, 14, 15)$$

3-33 Implement the Boolean function defined in the truth table of Figure 3-26 with a 4-to-1-line multiplexer and external gates. Connect inputs A and B to the selection lines. The input requirements for the four data lines will be a function of variables C and D. These values are obtained by expressing F as a function of C and D for each of the four cases when $AB = 00$, 01, 10, and 11. These functions may have to be implemented with external gates.

3-34 Rearrange the truth table for the circuit of Figure 3-17 and verify that it can function as a demultiplexer.

3-35 Draw the graphic symbol for a BCD-to-decimal decoder with enable input. This is similar to Figure 3-29 but with four data inputs and ten outputs.

3-36 Draw the graphic symbol for a binary-to-octal decoder with three enable inputs, $E1$, $E2$, and $E3$. The circuit is enabled if $E1 = 1$, $E2 = 0$, and $E3 = 0$ (assuming positive logic). The qualifying symbol name for the decoder is BIN/OCT. The enable symbol EN is placed at the output of an AND gate with inputs $E1$, $E2$, and $E3$. The rectangular shape AND gate symbol is placed within the rectangular shape outline of the decoder. (This is the same as TTL type integrated circuit 74138.)

3-37 Draw the graphic symbol diagram of a dual 4-to-1-line multiplexer with separate enable inputs and common selection inputs. (This is the same as TTL type integrated circuit 74153.)

3-38 Define in your own words:
(a) Positive and negative logic. (d) Common control block.
(b) Active-high and active-low. (e) Dependency notation.
(c) Polarity indicator.

3-39 Show an example of a graphic symbol that has the three Boolean dependencies G, V, and N. Draw the equivalent interpretation.

4

SEQUENTIAL LOGIC

4-1 INTRODUCTION

The digital circuits considered thus far have been combinational where the outputs at any point in time are entirely dependent upon the inputs that are presented at that time. Although every digital system is likely to have a combinational circuit, most systems encountered in practice also include storage elements, which requires that the system be described in terms of sequential circuits.

A block diagram of a sequential circuit is shown in Figure 4-1. It consists of a combinational circuit and storage elements that together form a feedback system. The storage elements are devices capable of storing binary information within them. The binary information stored at any given time defines the *state* of the sequential circuit. The sequential circuit receives binary information from external inputs. These inputs, together with the present state of the storage elements, determine the binary value of the outputs. They also determine the condition for changing the state of the storage elements. The block diagram demonstrates that the outputs

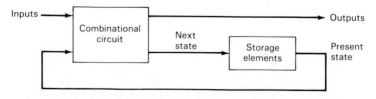

FIGURE 4-1
Block Diagram of a Sequential Circuit.

in a sequential circuit are a function not only of external inputs but also of the present state of the storage elements. The next state of the storage elements is also a function of the inputs and the present state. Thus, a sequential circuit is specified by a time sequence of inputs, outputs, and internal states.

There are two main types of sequential circuits, and their classification depends on the timing of the signals. A *synchronous sequential circuit* is a system whose behavior can be defined from the knowledge of its signals at discrete instants of time. The behavior of an *asynchronous sequential circuit* depends upon the order in which the inputs change, and the state of the circuit can be affected at any instant of time. The storage elements commonly used in asynchronous sequential circuits are time-delay devices. The storage capability of a time-delay device is due to the fact that it takes a finite time for the signal to propagate through the device. In practice, the internal propagation delay of logic gates is of sufficient duration to produce the needed delay so that actual delay units may not be necessary. In gate type asynchronous systems, the storage elements consist of logic gates where propagation delay provides the required storage. Thus, an asynchronous sequential circuit may be regarded as a combinational circuit with feedback. Because of the feedback among logic gates, the system may operate in an unpredictable manner and sometimes may even become unstable. The various problems encountered in asynchronous systems impose many difficulties on the designer, and for this reason they are very seldom used.

A synchronous sequential circuit employs signals that affect the storage elements only at discrete instants of time. Synchronization is achieved by a timing device called a *clock generator* that produces a periodic train of *clock pulses*. The clock pulses are distributed throughout the system in such a way that storage elements are affected only upon the arrival of each pulse. In practice, the clock pulses are applied with other signals that specify the required change in the storage elements. The outputs of storage elements change only when clock pulses are present. Synchronous sequential circuits that use clock pulses in the input of storage elements are called *clocked sequential circuits*. Clocked sequential circuits are the type most frequently encountered in practice. They seldom manifest instability problems and their timing is easily broken down into independent discrete steps, each of which can be considered separately.

The storage elements employed in clocked sequential circuits are called *flip-flops*. A flip-flop is a binary storage device capable of storing one bit of information. Normally, a sequential circuit will use many flip-flops to store as many bits as necessary. The block diagram of a synchronous clocked sequential circuit is shown in Figure 4-2. The outputs can come from either the combinational circuit or from the flip-flops. The flip-flops receive their inputs from the combinational circuit and also from a train of pulses that occur at fixed intervals of time as shown in the timing diagram. The next state of the flip-flops can change only during a clock pulse transition. When a clock pulse is not active, the feedback loop is broken because the flip-flop outputs cannot change even if the outputs of the combinational circuit change in value. Thus, the transition from one state to the other occurs only at predetermined time intervals dictated by the clock pulses.

A flip-flop circuit has two outputs, one for the normal value and one for the complemented value of the bit that is stored in it. Binary information can enter a

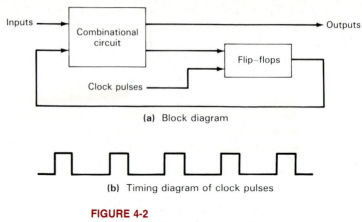

(a) Block diagram

(b) Timing diagram of clock pulses

FIGURE 4-2
Synchronous Clocked Sequential Circuit

flip-flop in a variety of ways, a fact which gives rise to different types of flip-flops. This chapter presents the types of flip-flops available and examines their operation and logical properties. It then proceeds to develop methods and procedures for the analysis and design of synchronous clocked sequential circuits.

4-2   LATCHES

A flip-flop circuit can maintain a binary state indefinitely (as long as power is delivered to the circuit), until directed by an input signal to switch states. The major differences among the various types of flip-flops are in the number of inputs they possess and the manner in which the inputs affect the binary state. The most basic types of flip-flops operate with signal levels and are referred to as *latches*. The latches introduced here are the basic circuits from which all flip-flops are constructed. Although latches can be useful for storing binary information, they are not practical for use in synchronous sequential circuits. The types of flip-flops employed in sequential circuits are presented in the next section.

SR Latch

The SR latch is a circuit with two cross-coupled NOR gates or two cross-coupled NAND gates. It has two inputs labeled S for set and R for reset. The SR latch constructed with two cross-coupled NOR gates is shown in Figure 4-3. The latch has two useful states. When output $Q = 1$ and $\overline{Q} = 0$, it is said to be in the set state. When $Q = 0$ and $\overline{Q} = 1$, it is in the reset state. Output Q and $\overline{Q}$ are normally the complements of each other. An undefined state occurs when both outputs are equal to 0. This occurs when both inputs are equal to 1 at the same time.

Under normal conditions, both inputs of the latch remain at 0 unless the state has to be changed. The application of a momentary 1 to the S input causes the latch to go to the set state. The S input must go back to 0 before any other changes can occur. As shown in the function table, there are two input conditions that cause the circuit to be in the set state. The first condition is the action that must

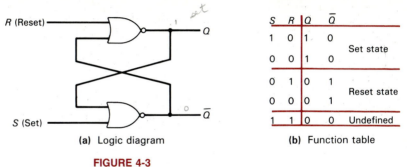

S	R	Q	$\bar{Q}$	
1	0	1	0	Set state
0	0	1	0	
0	1	0	1	Reset state
0	0	0	1	
1	1	0	0	Undefined

(a) Logic diagram   (b) Function table

FIGURE 4-3
SR Latch with NOR Gates

be taken by input S to bring the circuit to the set state. Removing the active input from S leaves the circuit in the same state. After both inputs return to 0 it is possible to shift to the reset state by momentarily applying a 1 to the R input. We can then remove the 1 from R and the circuit remains in the reset state. Thus, when both inputs S and R are equal to 0, the latch can be in either the set or the reset state, depending on which input was a 1 just prior to the change.

If a 1 is applied to both the S and R inputs of the latch, both outputs go to 0. This produces an undefined state because it results in an unpredictable next state when both inputs return to 0. It also violates the requirement that outputs Q and $\bar{Q}$ be the complement of each other. In normal operation this condition is avoided by making sure that 1's are not applied to both inputs simultaneously.

The SR latch with two cross-coupled NAND gates is shown in Figure 4-4. It operates with both inputs normally at 1 unless the state of the latch has to be changed. The application of a momentary 0 to the S input causes output Q to go to 1, putting the latch in the set state. When the S input goes back to 1, the circuit remains in the set state. After both inputs go back to 1, we are allowed to change the state of the latch by placing a 0 in the R input. This causes the circuit to go to the reset state and stay there even after both inputs return to 1. The condition that is undefined for the NAND latch is when both inputs are equal to 0 at the same time.

Comparing the NAND with the NOR latch we note that the input signals for the NAND require the complement values of those used for the NOR latch. Because the NAND latch requires a 0 signal to change its state, it is sometimes

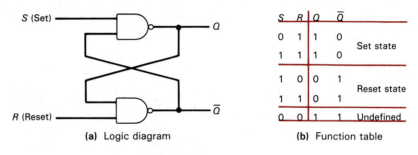

S	R	Q	$\bar{Q}$	
0	1	1	0	Set state
1	1	1	0	
1	0	0	1	Reset state
1	1	0	1	
0	0	1	1	Undefined

(a) Logic diagram   (b) Function table

FIGURE 4-4
SR Latch with NAND Gates

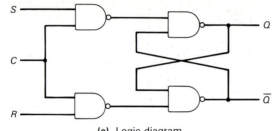

C	S	R	Next state of Q
0	X	X	No change
1	0	0	No change
1	0	1	$Q = 0$; Reset state
1	1	0	$Q = 1$; Set state
1	1	1	Indeterminate

(a) Logic diagram   (b) Function table

FIGURE 4-5
SR Latch with Control Input

referred to as an $\overline{S}$-$\overline{R}$ latch. The bar above the letters designates the fact that the inputs must be in their complement form to activate the circuit.

The operation of the basic SR latch can be improved by providing an additional control input that determines when the state of the latch can be changed. An SR latch with a control input is shown in Figure 4-5. It consists of the basic SR latch and two additional NAND gates. The control input C acts as an enable signal for the other two inputs. The output of the NAND gates stays at the logic-1 level as long as the control input remains at 0. This is the quiescent condition for the SR latch. When the control input goes to 1, information from the S or R input is allowed to reach the SR latch. The set state is reached with $S = 1$, $R = 0$, and $C = 1$. To change to the reset state, the inputs must be $S = 0$, $R = 1$, and $C = 1$. In either case, when C returns to 0, the circuit remains in its current state. When the control input disables the circuit by applying a 0 to C, the state of the output does not change, regardless of the values of S and R. Moreover, when $C = 1$ and both the S and R inputs are equal to 0, the state of the circuit does not change. These conditions are listed in the function table accompanying the diagram.

An indeterminate condition occurs when all three inputs are equal to 1. This condition places 0's in both inputs of the basic SR latch which places it in the undefined state. When the control input goes back to 0, we cannot positively determine the next state as it depends on whether the S or R input goes to 0 first. This indeterminate condition makes the circuit of Figure 4-5 difficult to manage, and it is seldom used in practice. Nevertheless, it is an important circuit because all other latches and flip-flops are constructed from it. It should be mentioned that sometimes the SR latch with control input is referred to as an SR (or RS) flip-flop. However, to qualify as a flip-flop, the circuit must fulfill the requirements that are mentioned in the next section.

D Latch

One way to eliminate the undesirable condition of the indeterminate state in the SR latch is to insure that inputs S and R are never equal to 1 at the same time. This is done in the D latch shown in Figure 4-6. This latch has only two inputs, D (data) and C (control). The D input goes directly to the S input, and its complement is applied to the R input. As long as the control input is at 0, the cross-coupled SR latch has both inputs at the 1 level and the circuit cannot change state regardless

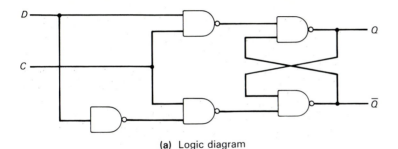

C	D	Next state of Q
0	X	No change
1	0	Q = 0; Reset state
1	1	Q = 1; Set state

(a) Logic diagram   (b) Function table

FIGURE 4-6
D Latch

of the value of D. The D input is sampled when $C = 1$. If D is 1, the Q output goes to 1 placing the circuit in the set state. If D is 0, output Q goes to 0 and the circuit switches to the reset state.

The D latch receives the designation from its ability to hold *data* in its internal storage. It is suited for use as a temporary storage for binary information between a unit and its environment. The binary information present at the data input of the D latch is transferred to the Q output when the control input is enabled. The output follows the data input as long as the enable remains active. When the control input is disabled, the binary information that was present at the data input at the time the transition occurred is retained at the Q output until the control input is enabled again.

The D latch can be constructed with transmission gates as shown in Figure 4-7. (The transmission gate is defined in Figure 2-37.) The C input controls two transmission gates TG. When $C = 1$, the TG connected to input D has a closed path and the one connected to output Q has an open path. This produces an equivalent circuit from input D through two inverters to output Q. Thus the output follows the data input as long as C remains active. When C switches to 0, the first TG disconnects input D from the circuit and the second TG produces a closed path between the two inverters at the output. Thus the value that was present at input D at the time that C went from 1 to 0 is retained at the Q output.

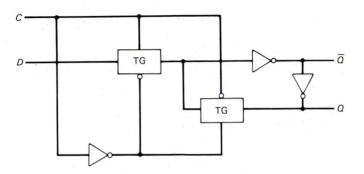

FIGURE 4-7
D Latch with Transmission Gates

4-3   FLIP-FLOPS

The state of a latch of flip-flop is switched by a momentary change in the control input. The momentary change is called a *trigger* and the transition it causes is said to trigger the flip-flop. The D latch with clock pulses in its control input is essentially a flip-flop that is triggered every time the pulse goes to the logic-1 level. As long as the pulse input remains in the active level, any changes in the data input will change the state of the latch.

As seen from the block diagram of Figure 4-2, a sequential circuit has a feedback path from the outputs of the flip-flops to the combination circuit. As a consequence, the data inputs of the flip-flops are derived in part from the outputs of the same and other flip-flops. When latches are used for the storage elements, a serious difficulty arises. The state transitions of the latches start as soon as the pulse changes to the logic-1 level. The new state of a latch may appear at the output while the pulse is still active. This output is connected to the inputs of the latches through a combinational circuit. If the inputs that are applied to the latches keep changing while the clock pulse is still in the logic-1 level, the latches will start responding to new values, and a new output state may occur. This results in an unpredictable situation since the state of latches may keep changing for as long as the clock pulse stays in the active level. Because of this unreliable operation, the output of a latch cannot be applied to the input of the same or another latch when all the latches are triggered by a common clock pulse source.

Flip-flop circuits are constructed in such a way as to make them operate properly when they are part of a sequential circuit that employs one common clock pulse generator. There are two ways that a latch can be modified to form a reliable flip-flop. One way is to employ two latches in a special configuration that isolates the output of the flip-flop from being affected while its input is changing. This type of circuit is called a *master-slave* flip-flop. Another way is to produce a flip-flop that triggers only during a signal *transition* from 0 to 1 (or from 1 to 0) and is disabled during the clock pulse duration. This type of circuit is called an *edge-triggered* flip-flop. We will now proceed to show the implementation of both types of flip-flops.

Master-Slave Flip-Flop

The master-slave flip-flop consists of two latches and an inverter. A D-type master-slave flip-flop is shown in Figure 4-8. The first D latch is called the master and the second, the slave. When the clock pulse input C is 0, the output of the inverter is

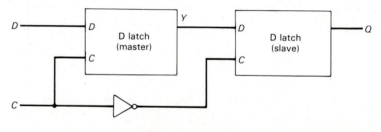

FIGURE 4-8
Master-Slave D Flip-Flop

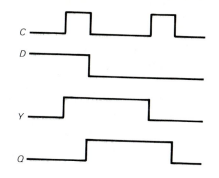

FIGURE 4-9

Timing Relationship with a Master-Slave
Flip-Flop

1. The slave latch is enabled and its output Q is equal to the master output Y. The master latch is disabled because $C = 0$. When the input pulse changes to the logic-1 level, the data in the external D input is transferred to the master. The slave, however, is disabled as long as the pulse remains in the 1 level because its C input is equal to 0. Any changes in the external D input changes the master output Y but cannot affect the slave output Q. When the pulse returns to 0, the master is disabled and is isolated from the D input. At the same time the slave is enabled, and the value of Y is transferred to the output of the flip-flop at Q.

The timing relationships shown in Figure 4-9 illustrate the sequence of events that occur in the D-type master-slave flip-flop. Assume that initially the flip-flop is in the reset state prior to the occurrence of a pulse; so $Y = 0$ and $Q = 0$. The data input D is equal to 1 and the next clock pulse should change the flip-flop to the set state with $Q = 1$. After the pulse transition from 0 to 1, the master latch is set and changes Y to 1. The slave latch is not affected because its C input is 0. Since the master is an internal circuit, its change of state is not noticed in the output Q. Even though the input may be changing, the output of the flip-flop remains in its previous state. When the pulse returns to 0, the information from the master is allowed to pass through to the slave, making the external output $Q = 1$. The external input D can change at the same time that the pulse goes through its negative transition. This is because once the C input reaches 0, the master is disabled and its data input has no effect until the next clock pulse. The timing diagram of Figure 4-9 continues with a second clock pulse that finds the external D input at 0. The circuit changes to 0 by first switching the master and then the slave output.

If we replace the master D latch in Figure 4-8 with an SR latch with control input, we will obtain a master-slave SR flip-flop. Remember that the SR flip-flop has the undesirable condition of producing an indeterminate next state when inputs S and R both equal 1 (see function table of Figure 4-5) and so is seldom used in practice.

A modified version of the SR flip-flop that eliminates the undesirable condition is the JK flip-flop. In this type of flip-flop, the condition that both inputs are equal to 1 causes the output to complement its value. The master-slave JK flip-flop is shown in Figure 4-10. The master is an SR latch with the control input receiving

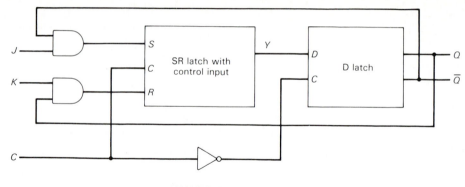

FIGURE 4-10
Master-Slave JK Flip-Flop

the clock pulses. The slave is a D latch that operates with the complement of the clock pulse. The J input behaves like the S input to set the flip-flop. The K input is similar to the R input for resetting the flip-flop. The only difference between the SR and JK flip-flops is their response to the condition when both inputs are equal to 1. As can be verified from the diagram, this condition complements the outputs in the JK flip-flop. This is because of the feedback connection from the outputs to the inputs. When $Q = 1$ and $K = 1$ the R input is equal to 1. The S input is 0, even if $J = 1$, because $\overline{Q}$, being the complement of Q, must be 0. The next clock pulse will reset the flip-flop and change the Q output to 0. Similarly, if we start with $Q = 0$, the clock pulse will set the flip-flop and change output Q to 1. In either case, the condition of $J = 1$ and $K = 1$ causes the outputs of the flip-flop to complement in response to a clock pulse.

Now consider a sequential system containing many master-slave flip-flops, with the outputs of some flip-flops going to inputs of other flip-flops. Assume that the clock pulses to all flip-flops are synchronized and occur at the same time. At the beginning of each clock pulse, some of the masters change state, but all the slaves remain in the previous state. That means that the outputs of the flip-flops are still in the present state while the internal masters have changed to the next state. After the clock pulse returns to 0, some of the outputs change state, but none of the new states have an effect on any of the masters until the next pulse. Thus the states of flip-flops in a synchronous system can change simultaneously during the same clock pulse, even though outputs of flip-flops are connected to inputs of the same or other flip-flops. This is possible because the new state appears at the outputs only after the clock pulse has returned to 0.

For reliable sequential circuit operation, all signals must propagate from the outputs of flip-flops, through the combinational circuit, and back to inputs of master-slave flip-flops, while the clock pulse remains in the logic-0 level. Any changes that occur at the inputs of flip-flops after the pulse goes to the logic-1 level are not recognized by the outputs. In most applications, the clock pulse width is very narrow compared to the clock period which makes the low level duration of the clock stay on longer. Since the master triggers on the positive transition of the pulse and the slave on the negative transition, the master-slave is classified as a *pulse-triggered* flip-flop.

Edge-Triggered Flip-Flop

An *edge-triggered* flip-flop ignores the pulse while it is at a constant level but triggers only during the *transition* of the clock signal. Some edge-triggered flip-flops trigger on the positive edge (0 to 1 transition) and others trigger on the negative edge (1 to 0 transition).

The logic diagram of a D-type positive-edge-triggered flip-flop is shown in Figure 4-11. It consists of three SR latches. Two latches respond to the external D (data) and C (clock) inputs. The third latch provides the outputs for the flip-flop. The S and R inputs of the output latch are maintained at logic-1 level when $C = 0$. This causes the output to remain in its present state. Input D may be equal to 0 or 1. If $D = 0$ when C becomes 1, R changes to 0. This causes the flip-flop to go to the reset state making $Q = 0$. If now, while $C = 1$, there is a change in the D input, terminal R remains at 0. Thus, the flip-flop is locked out and is unresponsive to further changes in the D input until the clock returns to 0 and another positive transition occurs. Similarly, if $D = 1$ when C goes from 0 to 1, S changes to 0. This causes the circuit to go to the set state making $Q = 1$. Any change in D while $C = 1$ does not affect the output.

In summary, when the input clock in the positive-edge-triggered flip-flop makes a positive transition, the value of D is transferred to Q. A negative transition from 1 to 0 does not affect the output; nor is it affected when C is in either the steady logic-1 level or the logic-0 level. Hence this type of flip-flop responds to the transition from 0 to 1 and nothing else.

The timing of the response of a flip-flop to input data and clock must be taken into consideration when using edge-triggered flip-flops. There is a minimum time called *setup time* in which the D input must be maintained at a constant value prior to the occurrence of the clock transition. Similarly, there is a definite time called the *hold time* that the D input must not change after the application of the positive transition of the pulse. The *propagation delay time* of the flip-flop is defined as the

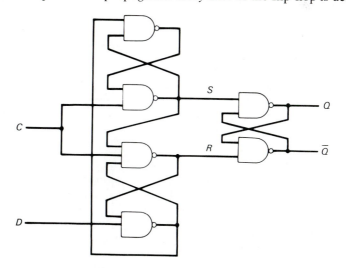

FIGURE 4-11
D-Type Positive-Edge-Triggered Flip-Flop

time interval between the trigger edge and the stabilization of the output to the new state. These and other parameters are specified in integrated circuit data books.

Standard Graphic Symbols

The standard graphic symbols for the different kinds of flip-flops are shown in Figure 4-12. A flip-flop or latch is designated by a rectangular shape block with inputs on the left and outputs on the right. One output designates the normal state of the flip-flop, and the other with a small circle designates the complement output. The graphic symbol for the D latch or D flip-flop has inputs *D* and *C* indicated inside the block. The graphic symbol for the JK flip-flop has inputs *J*, *K*, and *C* inside. The D latch has no other symbols besides the *D* and *C* inputs. The master-slave is considered to be a pulse-triggered flip-flop and is indicated as such with an upside down L symbol in front of the outputs. This is to show that the output signal changes on the falling edge of the pulse. The edge-triggered flip-flop has an arrowhead shape symbol in front of the letter *C* to designate a *dynamic input*. The dynamic indicator symbol denotes the fact that the flip-flop responds to the positive-edge transitions of the input clock pulses. A small circle outside the block along the dynamic indicator designates a negative-edge transition for triggering the circuit.

When using different types of flip-flops in the same sequential circuit, one must ensure that all flip-flop outputs change at the same time, whether they respond on the positive or negative transition of the pulse. Those flip-flops that behave opposite

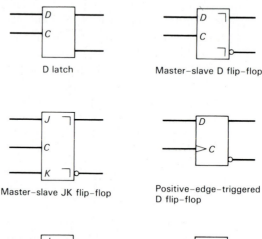
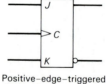
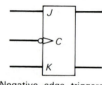

FIGURE 4-12
Standard Graphic Symbols for Latch and Flip-Flops

from the adopted polarity transition can be changed by the addition of inverters in their clock inputs. A preferred procedure is to provide both positive and negative pulses in the master clock generator. Apply the positive pulses to pulse-triggered (master-slave) and negative-edge-triggered flip-flops and negative pulses to the positive-edge-triggered flip-flops. In this way all flip-flop outputs will change at the same time.

In this book we will assume that all flip-flops are of the positive-edge-triggered type. This will provide a uniform graphic symbol and consistent timing diagrams.

Characteristic Tables

A characteristic table defines the logical properties of a flip-flop by describing its operation in tabular form. The characteristic tables of four types of flip-flops are presented in Table 4-1. They define the next state as a function of the inputs and present state. $Q(t)$ refers to the present state prior to the application of a pulse. $Q(t + 1)$ is the next state one clock period later. Note that the pulse input at C is not listed in the characteristic table but is implied to occur between time t and $t + 1$.

The characteristic table for the JK flip-flop shows that the next state is equal to the present state when inputs J and K are both equal to 0. This can be expressed as $Q(t + 1) = Q(t)$ indicating that the clock pulse produces no change of state. When $K = 1$ and $J = 0$, the next clock pulse resets the flip-flop with $Q(t + 1) = 0$. With $J = 1$ and $K = 0$, the flip-flop sets with $Q(t + 1) = 1$. When both J and K are equal to 1, the next state changes to the complement of the present state which can be expressed as $Q(t + 1) = \overline{Q}(t)$.

The SR flip-flop is similar to the JK when S is replaced by J and R by K except for the indeterminate case. The question mark for the next state when S and R are both equal to 1 indicates an unpredictable next state. The SR flip-flop is important only for historical reasons. Its graphic symbol is similar to the JK with the inputs marked with S and R instead of J and K.

The next state of a D flip-flop is dependent only on the D input and is independent of the present state. This can be expressed as $Q(t + 1) = D(t)$. Note that

TABLE 4-1
Flip-Flop Characteristic Tables

(a) JK Flip-Flop				(b) SR Flip-Flop			
J	**K**	**Q(t+1)**	**Operation**	**S**	**R**	**Q(t+1)**	**Operation**
0	0	$Q(t)$	No change	0	0	$Q(t)$	No change
0	1	0	Reset	0	1	0	Reset
1	0	1	Set	1	0	1	Set
1	1	$\overline{Q}(t)$	Complement	1	1	?	Indeterminate

(c) D Flip-Flop			(d) T Flop-Flop		
D	**Q(t+1)**	**Operation**	**T**	**Q(t+1)**	**Operation**
0	0	Reset	0	$Q(t)$	No change
1	1	Set	1	$\overline{Q}(t)$	Complement

the D flip-flop does not have a no change condition. This condition can be accomplished either by disabling the clock pulses in the C input or by leaving the clock pulses and connecting the output back into the D input when the state of the flip-flop must remain the same.

The T (toggle) flip-flop listed in Table 4-1 is obtained from a JK flip-flop when inputs J and K are tied together. The graphic symbol for the T flip-flop is the same as the JK except that the J and K inputs are connected externally to provide a single input marked T. The characteristic table has only two conditions. When $T = 0$ ($J = K = 0$) a clock pulse does not change the state. When $T = 1$ ($J = K = 1$) a clock pulse complements the state of the flip-flop. Like the SR, the T flip-flop is important only for historical reasons and is readily obtained from the JK when needed.

Direct Inputs

Flip-flops available in integrated circuit packages provide special inputs for setting and resetting the flip-flop asynchronously. These inputs are usually called direct set and direct reset. They affect the output on the negative (or positive) *level* of the signal without the need of a clock. When power is turned on in a digital system, the states of its flip-flops can be anything. The direct inputs are useful for bringing all flip-flops in a digital system to an initial state prior to their clocked operation.

The graphic symbol of the JK flip-flop with direct set and reset is shown in Figure 4-13. The notation $C1$, $1J$, and $1K$ are examples of control dependency. An input labeled Cn, where n is any number, is a control input that controls all the other inputs starting with the number n. In this case, $C1$ controls inputs $1J$ and $1K$. S and R have no 1 in front of the letter, and therefore, they are not controlled by the clock at $C1$. The S and R inputs have a small circle along the input line to indicate that they are active when in the logic-0 level.

The function table specifies the circuit operation. The first three entries in the table specify the operation of the direct inputs S and R. These inputs behave like a NAND SR latch (see Figure 4-4) and are independent of the clock and the J and K inputs. The last four entries in the function table specify the clock operation when both the S and R inputs are inactive and in the logic-1 level. The clock at C is shown with an upward arrow to indicate that the flip-flop is a positive-edge-triggered type. The J and K inputs respond to the clock in the usual manner.

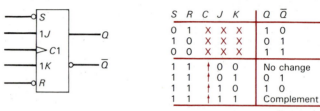

S	R	C	J	K	Q	$\bar{Q}$
0	1	X	X	X	1	0
1	0	X	X	X	0	1
0	0	X	X	X	1	1
1	1	↑	0	0	No change	
1	1	↑	0	1	0	1
1	1	↑	1	0	1	0
1	1	↑	1	1	Complement	

(a) Graphic symbol   (b) Function table

FIGURE 4-13
JK Flip-Flop with Direct Set and Reset

4-4   ANALYSIS PROCEDURE

The behavior of a sequential circuit is determined from the inputs, the outputs, and the state of its flip-flops. The outputs and the next state are both a function of the inputs and the present state. The analysis of a sequential circuit consists of obtaining a suitable description that demonstrates the time sequence of inputs, outputs, and flip-flop states.

A logic diagram is recognized as a sequential circuit if it includes flip-flops. The flip-flops may be of any type and the logic diagram may or may not include a combinational circuit. In this section, we introduce an algebraic representation for specifying the logic diagram of a sequential circuit. We then present a state table and state diagram that describe the behavior of the sequential circuit. Specific examples will be used throughout the discussion to illustrate the various procedures.

Input Equations

The logic diagram of a sequential circuit consists of flip-flops and combinational gates. The knowledge of the type of flip-flops used and a list of Boolean functions for the combinational circuit provide all the information needed to draw the logic diagram of the sequential circuit. The part of the combinational circuit that generates the signals for the inputs of flip-flops can be described by a set of Boolean functions called *input equations*. We will adopt the convention of using the flip-flop input symbol to denote the input equation variable and a subscript to designate the name of the flip-flop. As an example, consider the following flip-flop input equations.

$$J_A = XB + \overline{Y}C$$

$$K_A = Y\overline{B} + C$$

J_A and K_A are two Boolean variables. The J and K symbols are the inputs of a JK flip-flop. The subscript letter A is the symbolic name of the flip-flop output. The implementation of the two input equations is shown in the logic diagram of Figure 4-14. The JK flip-flop has been assigned an output symbol letter A. It has two inputs J and K and an input clock C. The combinational circuit drawn in the diagram is the implementation of the algebraic expression given by the input equations.

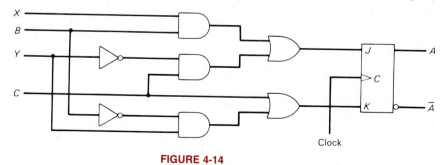

FIGURE 4-14
Implementing Input Equations

The outputs of the combinational circuit, denoted by J_A and K_A, are then applied to the J and K inputs of flip-flop A.

From this example we see that a flip-flop input equation is a Boolean expression for a combinational circuit. The subscripted symbol is a variable name for the output of the combinational circuit. This output is always connected to the input of a flip-flop, thus the name input equation.

The flip-flop input equations constitute a convenient algebraic expression for specifying the logic diagram of a sequential circuit. They imply the type of flip-flop from the letter symbol, and they fully specify the combinational circuit that drives the flip-flops. Time is not included explicitly in these equations but is implied from the clock at the C input of the flip-flop.

An example of a sequential circuit is shown in Figure 4-15. The circuit consists of two D-type flip-flops, an input X and an output Y. It can be specified by the following equations:

$$D_A = AX + BX$$

$$D_B = \overline{A}X$$

$$Y = (A + B)\overline{X}$$

The first two are the input equations for the flip-flops and the third equation specifies the output Y. Note that the input equations use the symbol D which is the same as the input symbol of the flip-flops. The subscripts A and B designate the output names given to the two flip-flops.

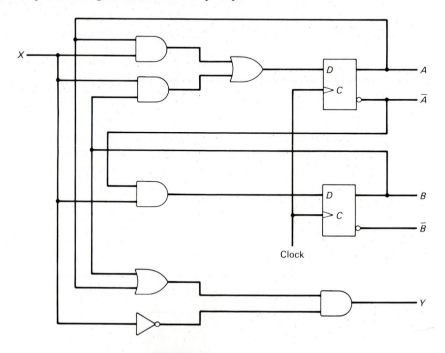

FIGURE 4-15
Example of a Sequential Circuit

TABLE 4-2
State Table for Circuit of Figure 4-15

Present state		Input	Next state		Output
A	B	X	A	B	Y
0	0	0	0	0	0
0	0	1	0	1	0
0	1	0	0	0	1
0	1	1	1	1	0
1	0	0	0	0	1
1	0	1	1	0	0
1	1	0	0	0	1
1	1	1	1	0	0

State Table

The time sequence of inputs, outputs, and flip-flop states can be enumerated in a *state table*. The state table for the circuit of Figure 4-15 is shown in Table 4-2. The table consists of four sections labeled *present state, input, next state,* and *output.* The present state section shows the states of flip-flops A and B at any given time t. The input section gives a value of X for each possible present state. The next state section shows the states of the flip-flops one clock period later at time $t + 1$. The output section gives the value of Y for each present state.

The derivation of a state table consists of first listing all possible binary combinations of present state and inputs. In this case we have eight binary combinations from 000 to 111. The next state values are then determined from the logic diagram or from the input equations. For a D flip-flip we have the relationship $A(t + 1) = D_A(t)$. This means that the next state of flip-flop A is equal to the present value of its input D (see Table 4-1). The value of the D input is specified in the input equation as a function of the present state of A and B and input X. Therefore, the next state of flip-flop A must satisfy the equation

$$A(t + 1) = D_A = AX + BX$$

The next state section in the state table under column A has three 1's where the present state and input value satisfy the conditions $AX = 11$ or $BX = 11$. Similarly, the next state of flip-flop B is derived from the input equation

$$B(t + 1) = D_B = \overline{A}X$$

and is equal to 1 when the present state of A is 0 and input X is equal to 1. The output column is derived from the output equation

$$Y = A\overline{X} + B\overline{X}$$

The state table of any sequential circuit with D-type flip-flops is obtained by the procedure outlined in the above example. In general, a sequential circuit with m flip-flops and n inputs needs 2^{m+n} rows in the state table. The binary numbers from 0 through $2^{m+n} - 1$ are listed under the present state and input columns. The next state section has m columns, one for each flip-flop. The binary values

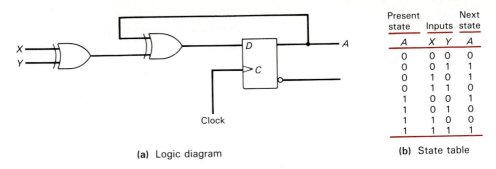

(a) Logic diagram

Present state	Inputs		Next state
A	X	Y	A
0	0	0	0
0	0	1	1
0	1	0	1
0	1	1	0
1	0	0	1
1	0	1	0
1	1	0	0
1	1	1	1

(b) State table

FIGURE 4-16
Logic Diagram and State Table for $D_A = A \oplus X \oplus Y$

for the next state are derived directly from the D flip-flop input equations. The output section has many columns as there are output variables. Its binary value is derived from the circuit or from the Boolean function in the same manner as in a truth table.

The external outputs of a sequential circuit may come from logic gates or from outputs of flip-flops. The output section in the state table is necessary only if there are outputs from logic gates. Any external output taken directly from flip-flops are already listed in the present state columns of the state table. Therefore, the output section of the state table is excluded if there are no external outputs from gates.

As an example, suppose we want to obtain the logic diagram and state table of a sequential circuit that is specified by the input equation

$$D_A = A \oplus X \oplus Y$$

The D_A symbol implies a D-type flip-flop with output designated by the letter A. The X and Y variables are taken as inputs. The logic diagram and state table are shown in Figure 4-16. The state table has one column for the present state and two columns for the inputs. There are no external outputs. The next state column is derived from the input equation that specifies an odd function (see Section 2-7).

Analysis with JK Flip-Flops

So far we have considered the state table for sequential circuits that employ D-type flip-flops in which case the next state values are obtained directly from the input equations. For circuits with other types of flip-flops such as JK, the next-state values are obtained by following a two-step procedure:

1. Obtain the binary values of each flip-flop input equation in terms of the present state and input variables.

2. Use the corresponding flip-flop characteristic from Table 4-1 to determine the next state.

To illustrate this procedure, consider the sequential circuit with two JK flip-flops A and B and one input X specified by the following input equations:

TABLE 4-3
State Table for Circuit with JK Flip-Flops

state		Input	Next state		Flip-Flop inputs			
A	B	X	A	B	J_A	K_A	J_B	K_B
0	0	0	0	1	0	0	1	0
0	0	1	0	0	0	0	0	1
0	1	0	1	1	1	1	1	0
0	1	1	1	0	1	0	0	1
1	0	0	1	1	0	0	1	1
1	0	1	1	0	0	0	0	0
1	1	0	0	0	1	1	1	1
1	1	1	1	1	1	0	0	0

$$J_A = B \qquad K_A = B\overline{X}$$
$$J_B = \overline{X} \qquad K_B = A\overline{X} + \overline{A}X$$

The state table is shown in Table 4-3. The binary values listed under the columns labeled flip-flop inputs are not part of the state table. They are needed for the purpose of evaluating the next state as specified in step 1 of the procedure listed above. These binary values are obtained directly from the four input equations in a manner similar to that for obtaining a truth table from an algebraic expression. The next state of each flip-flop is evaluated from the corresponding J and K inputs and the characteristic table of the JK flip-flop listed in Table 4-1. There are four cases to consider. When $J = 1$ and $K = 0$, the next state is 1. When $J = 0$ and $K = 1$, the next state is 0. When $J = K = 0$, there is no change of state and the next state value is the same as the present state. When $J = K = 1$, the next state bit is the complement of the present state bit. Examples of the last two cases occur in the table when the present state and input (ABX) is 100. J_A and K_A are both equal to 0 and the present state of A is 1. Therefore, the next state of A remains the same and is equal to 1. In the same row of the table, J_B and K_B are both equal to 1. Since the present state of B is 0, the next state of B is complemented and changes to 1.

State Diagram

The information available in a state table may be represented graphically in a form of a state diagram. In this type of diagram, a state is represented by a circle, and the transition between states is indicated by directed lines connecting the circles. Examples of state diagrams are shown in Figure 4-17. The diagram in (a) is for the sequential circuit of Figure 4-15 and the state table of Table 4-2. The state diagram provides the same information as the state table and is obtained directly from it. The binary number inside each circle identifies the state of the flip-flops. The directed lines are labeled with two binary numbers separated by a slash. The input value during the present state is labeled first and the number after the slash gives the output during the present state. For example, the directed line from state

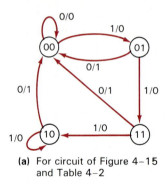

(a) For circuit of Figure 4−15 and Table 4−2

(b) For circuit of Figure 4−16

FIGURE 4-17
State Diagrams

00 to 01 is labeled 1/0, meaning that when the sequential circuit is in the present state 00 and the input is 1, the output is 0. After the next clock transition, the circuit goes to the next state, 01. The same clock transition may change the input value. If the input changes to 0 then the output becomes 1, but if the input remains at 1 the output stays at 0. This information is obtained from the state diagram along the two directed lines emanating from the circle with state 01. A directed line connecting a circle with itself indicates that no change of state occurs.

The state diagram of Figure 4-17(b) is for the sequential circuit of Figure 4-16. Here we have only one flip-flop with two states. There are two binary inputs and no outputs. The slash is not included when there are no outputs and only the inputs are indicated along the directed lines. There are two input conditions for each state transition in the diagram and they are separated by a comma. Normally, when there are two input variables, each state will have four directed lines coming out of the corresponding circle, one for each binary combination of the input values.

There is no difference between a state table and a state diagram except in the manner of representation. The state table is easier to derive from a given logic diagram and input equations. The state diagram follows directly from the state table. The state diagram gives a pictorial view of state transitions and is the form suitable for human interpretation of the circuit operation. For example, the state diagram of Fig. 4-17(a) clearly shows that, starting at state 00, the output is 0 as long as the input stays at 1. The first 0 input after a string of 1's gives an output of 1 and sends the circuit back to the initial state of 00. The state diagram of Figure 4-17(b) shows that the circuit stays at a given state as long as the two inputs have the same value (00 or 11). There is a state transition only when the two inputs are different (01 or 10).

4-5 DESIGN WITH D FLIP-FLOPS

The design of clocked sequential circuits starts from a set of specifications and culminates in a logic diagram or a list of Boolean functions from which the logic diagram can be obtained. In contrast to a combinational circuit, which is fully specified by a truth table, a sequential circuit requires a state table for its specification. The first step in the design of sequential circuit is to obtain a state table or an equivalent representation such as a state diagram.

A synchronous sequential circuit is made up of flip-flops and combinational gates. The design of the circuit consists of choosing the flip-flops and finding a combinational circuit structure which, together with the flip-flops, produces a circuit that fulfills the stated specifications. The number of flip-flops is determined from the number of states in the circuit realizing that n flip-flops can represent up to 2^n binary states. The combinational circuit is derived from the state table by evaluating the flip-flop input equations and output functions. In fact, once the type and number of flip-flops are determined, the design process involves a transformation from a sequential circuit problem into a combinational circuit problem. In this way the techniques of combinational circuit design can be applied.

Design Procedure

This section presents a procedure for the design of sequential circuits with D-type flip-flops. The design with JK or any other type of flip-flop is covered in the next section. The design procedure is carried out by going through the following steps:

1. Obtain the state table from the problem statement or from the state diagram.
2. Derive the flip-flop input equations from the next state conditions in the state table.
3. Derive the output functions if there are output conditions in the state table.
4. Simplify the input equations and output functions.
5. Draw the logic diagram with D flip-flops and combinational gates as specified by the input equations and output functions.

The design procedure will be illustrated by means of the following example. We wish to design a clocked sequential circuit that operates according to the state diagram shown in Figure 4-18. The state diagram specifies four states, one input,

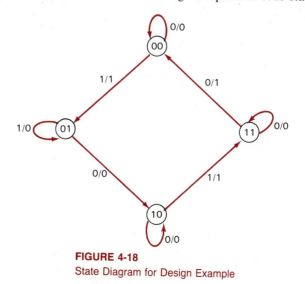

FIGURE 4-18
State Diagram for Design Example

TABLE 4-4
State Table for Design Example

Present state		Input	Next state		Output
A	B	X	A	B	Y
0	0	0	0	0	0
0	0	1	0	1	1
0	1	0	1	0	0
0	1	1	0	1	0
1	0	0	1	0	0
1	0	1	1	1	1
1	1	0	1	1	0
1	1	1	0	0	0

and one output. Two D flip-flops are needed to represent the four states. Label the flip-flop outputs with the letters A and B, the input with X and the output with Y.

The state table of the circuit is listed in Table 4-4. It is derived directly from the state diagram. The flip-flop input equations are obtained from the next state values. The output function is given by the binary values of Y. The three Boolean equations for the combinational gates can be expressed as a sum of minterms of the present state variables A and B and the input variable X.

$$A(t + 1) = D_A(A, B, X) = \Sigma \, m(2, 4, 5, 6)$$

$$B(t + 1) = D_B(A, B, X) = \Sigma \, m(1, 3, 5, 6)$$

$$Y(A, B, X) \quad = \Sigma \, m(1, 5)$$

The Boolean functions are simplified by means of the maps plotted in Figure 4-19. The simplified functions are

$$D_A = A\overline{B} + B\overline{X}$$

$$D_B = \overline{A}X + \overline{B}X + AB\overline{X}$$

$$Y = \overline{B}X$$

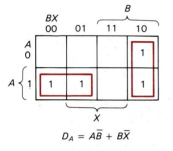

$$D_A = A\overline{B} + B\overline{X}$$

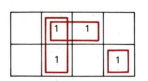

$$D_B = \overline{A}X + \overline{B}X + AB\overline{X}$$

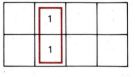

$$Y = \overline{B}X$$

FIGURE 4-19
Maps for Input Equations and Output Y

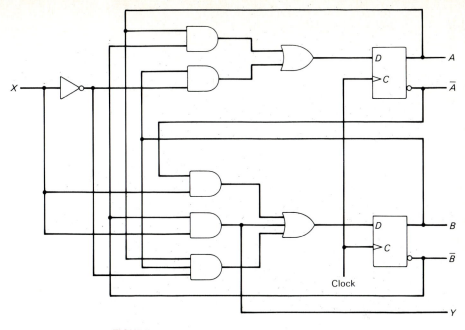

FIGURE 4-20
Logic Diagram for Sequential Circuit with D Flip-Flops

The logic diagram of the sequential circuit is shown in Figure 4-20.

Design with Unused States

A circuit with n flip-flops would have 2^n binary states. There are occasions when a sequential circuit uses less than this maximum possible number of states. States that are not used in specifying the sequential circuit are not listed in the state table. When simplifying the input equations, the unused states can be treated as don't care conditions.

Consider the state table listed in Table 4-5. The table defines three flip-flops A, B, and C, and one input X. There is no output column which means that the flip-

TABLE 4-5
State Table for Second Design Example

Present state			Input	Next state		
A	B	C	X	A	B	C
0	0	1	0	0	0	1
0	0	1	1	0	1	0
0	1	0	0	0	1	1
0	1	0	1	1	0	0
0	1	1	0	0	0	1
0	1	1	1	1	0	0
1	0	0	0	1	0	1
1	0	0	1	1	0	0
1	0	1	0	0	0	1
1	0	1	1	1	0	0

141

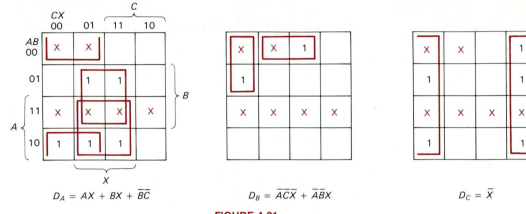

$$D_A = AX + BX + \overline{B}\overline{C}$$

$$D_B = \overline{A}\overline{C}\overline{X} + \overline{A}\overline{B}X$$

$$D_C = \overline{X}$$

FIGURE 4-21
Maps for Simplifying Input Equations

flops serve as outputs of the circuit. With three flip-flops it is possible to specify eight states, but the state table lists only five states. There are three unused states that are not included in the table. These are binary states 000, 110, and 111. When an input of 0 or 1 is included with the unused present state values we obtain six unused combinations for the present state and input columns. These are 0000, 0001, 1100, 1101, 1110, and 1111. These six combinations are not listed in the state table and may be treated as don't care minterms.

The three input equations for the D flip-flops are derived from the next state values and simplified in the maps of Figure 4-21. Each map has six don't care minterms in the squares corresponding to binary 0, 1, 12, 13, 14, and 15. The simplified equations are

$$D_A = AX + BX + \overline{B}\overline{C}$$

$$D_B = \overline{A}\overline{C}X + \overline{A}\overline{B}X$$

$$D_C = \overline{X}$$

The logic diagram can be obtained directly from the input equations and will not be drawn here.

One factor neglected up to this point in the design is the initial state of a sequential circuit. Since one does not know in what state the flip-flops will settle when the power in a digital system is first turned on, it is customary to provide a *master reset* switch to initialize the states of all flip-flops in the system. Typically, the master reset signal is applied to all flip-flops in their asynchronous inputs (see Figure 4-13) before the clocked operations start. In most cases, flip-flops are reset to 0, but some may be set to 1, depending on the initial state desired.

There are occasions where the circuit is not reset to any particular initial state and may end up being in an unused state. On other occasions, an undesirable noise signal may send the circuit to an unused state. In both of these cases it is necessary to ensure that the circuit eventually goes into one of the valid states so it can resume normal operation. Otherwise, if the sequential circuit circulates among unused states, there will be no way to bring it back to its intended sequence of state transitions. Although one can assume that this undesirable condition is not supposed to occur, a careful designer must ensure that if it occurs, the circuit will resume its proper operations after a few clock pulses.

It was stated previously that unused states in a sequential circuit can be treated as don't care conditions. Once the circuit is designed, the n flip-flops in the system can be in any one of 2^n possible states. If some of these states were taken as don't care conditions, the circuit must be investigated to determine the effect of these unused states. The next state from an unused state can be determined from the analysis of the circuit. In any case, it is always wise to analyze a circuit obtained from a design to ensure that no mistakes were made during the design process.

As an illustration, we will analyze the sequential circuit obtained from the previous design to determine the effect of the unused states. The analysis of the circuit may be done by the method outlined in the previous section. The maps of the input equations may also be of help. We need to start from the logic diagram or from the input equations specifying the logic diagram and derive the state table, including all eight states that the three flip-flops can maintain. If the derived state table matches the information from Table 4-5, then we know that the design is correct. In addition, we must determine the next states from the unused states 000, 110, and 111.

The maps of Figure 4-21 can help in finding the next state from each of the unused states. Take for example the unused state 000. If the circuit exhibits a noise signal and goes erroneously to state 000, an input $X = 0$ will transfer the circuit to some next state and an input $X = 1$ will transfer it to another (or the same) next state. We first investigate minterm $ABCX = 0000$ in the three maps (present state 000 and input 0). We note that this minterm is taken with the 1's of the function in all three cases. This means that the outputs of all three D flip-flops will go to 1 during the next clock transition making the next state 111. Minterm $ABCX = 0001$ (present state 000 and input 1) is included with the 1's in D_A and D_B and with the 0's in D_C. Therefore, the next state in this case will be 110. The effect of the other two unused states can be derived in a similar fashion from minterms 1100 through 1111.

The result of the analysis is shown in the state diagram of Figure 4-22. The

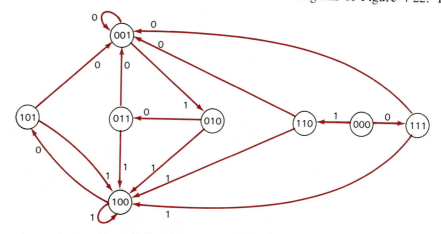

FIGURE 4-22

State Diagram for Circuit with Unused States

circuit operates as intended as long as it stays within the states 001, 010, 011, 100, and 101. If the circuit is forced to one of the unused states 000, 110, or 111 because of an external disturbance, it eventually goes to one of the valid states within one or two clock periods. Thus the circuit is said to be *self-correcting*, since it eventually goes to a valid state from which it continues to operate as required.

An undesirable situation occurs if the circuit, when in an unused state, circulates and stays among unused states for all possible input combinations. It is important to analyze the circuit to see that this does not happen. If it does, the circuit must be redesigned by specifying valid next states from unused present states in order to ensure that the circuit returns to its normal operation among the valid states.

4-6   DESIGN WITH JK FLIP-FLOPS

The design of a sequential circuit with flip-flops other than the D type is complicated by the fact that the input equations for the circuit must be derived indirectly from the state table. When D-type flip-flops are employed, the input equations are obtained directly from the next state. This is not the case for the JK and other types of flip-flops. In order to determine the input equations for these flip-flops it is necessary to derive a functional relationship between the state table and the input equations.

Flip-Flop Excitation Table

The flip-flop characteristic tables presented in Table 4-1 provide the value of the next state when the inputs and present state are known. These tables are useful for the analysis of sequential circuits and for defining the operation of the flip-flops. During the design process we usually know the transition from present state to next state and wish to find the flip-flop input conditions that will cause the required transition. For this reason, we need a table that lists the required inputs for a given change of state. Such a table is called an *excitation table*.

Table 4-6 presents the excitation tables for four different types of flip-flops. Each table has a column for the present state $Q(t)$, the next state $Q(t + 1)$, and a column for each input to show how the required transition is achieved. There are four possible transitions from present state to next state. The required input conditions for each of the four transitions are derived from the information available in the characteristic table. The symbol X in the table represents a don't care condition which means that it does not matter whether the input is 0 or 1.

The excitation table for the JK flip-flop can be derived from the knowledge of how the flip-flop operates. Consider the first entry in the table. The transition from a present state of 0 to a next state of 0 can be accomplished in two ways. If $J = 0$ and $K = 0$, there is no change of state and the flip-flop stays at 0. If $J = 0$ and $K = 1$, the flip-flop resets to 0. This dictates that J must be equal to 0 but K can be either 0 or 1 and in either case we obtain the required transition. This is indicated in the first row of the table by a 0 under J and a don't care symbol under K. The transformation from a present state of 0 to a next state of 1 can also be done in two ways. Letting $J = 1$ and $K = 0$ sets the flip-flop to 1. Letting $J = 1$ and

TABLE 4-6
Flip-Flop Excitation Tables

(a) JK Flip-Flop			
$Q(t)$	$Q(t + 1)$	J	K
0	0	0	X
0	1	1	X
1	0	X	1
1	1	X	0

(b) SR Flip-Flop			
$Q(t)$	$Q(t + 1)$	S	R
0	0	0	X
0	1	1	0
1	0	0	1
1	1	X	0

(c) D Flip-Flop		
$Q(t)$	$Q(t + 1)$	D
0	0	0
0	1	1
1	0	0
1	1	1

(d) T Flip-Flop		
$Q(t)$	$Q(t + 1)$	T
0	0	0
0	1	1
1	0	1
1	1	0

$K = 1$ complements the flip-flop from 0 to 1. For this case it is necessary that J be equal to 1, but it does not matter if K is 0 or 1; in either case we get the proper transition. This information is listed in the second row of the table. In a similar manner, it is possible to derive the rest of the entries in the excitation tables for the JK flip-flop and the other three flip-flops.

The excitation tables for the T and D flip-flops have no don't care conditions and can be specified with an excitation function. The excitation table for the D flip-flop shows that the next state is always equal to the D input and is independent of the present state. This can be represented algebraically with an excitation function.

$$D = Q(t + 1)$$

Therefore, the values for input D can be taken directly from the values in the next state column, as was done in the previous section.

The excitation table for the T flip-flop shows that the T input is equal to the exclusive-OR of the present state and the next state. This can be expressed by the following excitation function:

$$T = Q(t) \oplus Q(t + 1)$$

Design Procedure

The design procedure for sequential circuits with JK flip-flops is the same as with D flip-flops except that the input equations must be evaluated from the present state to next state transition derived from the excitation table. To illustrate the procedure we will design the sequential circuit specified by Table 4-7. This is the same as Table 4-4 but without the output section. In addition to having columns for the present state, input, and next state, as in a conventional state table, the table also shows the flip-flop input conditions from which we obtain the input equations. The flip-flop inputs in the table are derived from the state table in

TABLE 4-7
State Table with JK Flip-Flop Inputs

Present state		Input	Next state		Flip-Flop inputs			
A	*B*	*X*	*A*	*B*	J_A	K_A	J_B	K_B
0	0	0	0	0	0	X	0	X
0	0	1	0	1	0	X	1	X
0	1	0	1	0	1	X	X	1
0	1	1	0	1	0	X	X	0
1	0	0	1	0	X	0	0	X
1	0	1	1	1	X	0	1	X
1	1	0	1	1	X	0	X	0
1	1	1	0	0	X	1	X	1

conjunction with the excitation table for the JK flip-flop. For example, in the first row of Table 4-7 we have a transition for flip-flop *A* from 0 in the present state to 0 in the next state. In Table 4-6 for the JK flip-flop we find that a transition of states from 0 to 0 requires that input *J* be 0 and input *K* be a don't-care. So 0 and X are entered in the first row under J_A and K_A. Since the first row also shows a transition for flip-flop *B* from 0 in the present state to 0 in the next state, 0 and X are inserted in the first row under J_B and K_B. The second row of the table shows a transition for flip-flop *B* from 0 in the present state to 1 in the next state. From the excitation table we find that a transition from 0 to 1 requires that *J* be 1 and *K* be a don't care, so 1 and X are copied in the second row under J_B and K_B. This process is continued for each row in the table and for each flip-flop, with the input conditions from the excitation table copied into the proper row of the particular flip-flop being considered.

The flip-flop inputs in Table 4-7 specify the truth table for the input equations as a function of present state *A* and *B* and input *X*. The input equations are simplified in the maps of Figure 4-23. The next state values are not used during the simplification since the input equations are a function of the present state and input only. Note the advantage of using JK type flip-flops when designing sequential circuits. The fact that there are so many don't care entries indicates that the combinational circuit for the input equations is likely to be simpler because don't care minterms usually help in obtaining simpler expressions. If there are unused states in the state table, there will be additional don't care conditions in the map.

The four input equations for the two JK flip-flops are listed under the maps of Figure 4-23. The logic diagram of the sequential circuit is drawn in Figure 4-24.

As a final example, consider the design of a sequential circuit with T flip-flops. Using the state table portion of Table 4-7, we obtain the binary values for the T flip-flop inputs from the excitation functions for *A* and *B*.

$$T_A = A(t) \oplus A(t + 1)$$

$$T_B = B(t) \oplus B(t + 1)$$

Going over the present state and next state values for *A* and *B* in the state table we determine the binary values for T_A and T_B in the following manner. For each

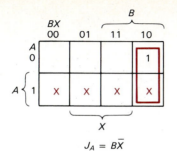

$$J_A = B\bar{X}$$

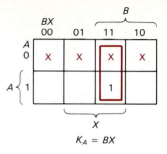

$$K_A = BX$$

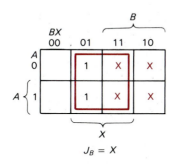

$$J_B = X$$

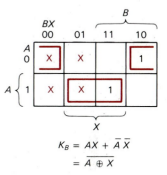

$$K_B = AX + \bar{A}\,\bar{X}$$
$$= \overline{A \oplus X}$$

FIGURE 4-23
Maps for *J* and *K* Input Equations

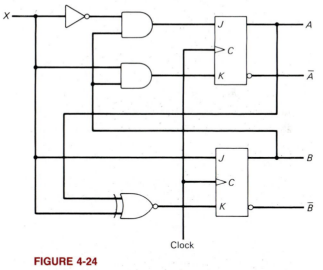

Clock

FIGURE 4-24
Logic Diagram for Sequential Circuit with JK Flip-Flops

present to next state transition from 0 to 1 or from 1 to 0, we place a 1 in the corresponding *T* input. For each case where there is no change (from 0 to 0 or from 1 to 1), we place a 0 in the corresponding *T* input. The input equations can be obtained from the minterms that produce a 1 in the flip-flop input columns. These are

$$T_A(A,\ B,\ X) = \Sigma m(2,7) = ABX + \bar{A}B\bar{X}$$

$$T_B(A,\ B,\ X) = \Sigma m(1,\ 2,\ 5,\ 7) = ABX + \bar{A}B\bar{X} + \bar{B}X$$

147

The algebraic expressions are the simplified input equations from which one can draw the gates of the sequential circuit. The circuit consists of two T flip-flops, three AND gates, two OR gates, and an inverter. Remember that a T flip-flop can be constructed from a JK flip-flop with inputs J and K tied together to form a single input T.

REFERENCES

1. Mano, M. M. *Digital Design*. Englewood Cliffs: Prentice-Hall, 1984.
2. Peatman, J. B. *Digital Hardware Design*. New York: McGraw-Hill, 1980.
3. Kohavi, Z. *Switching and Automata Theory*. 2nd ed. New York: McGraw-Hill, 1978.
4. Hill, F. J., and Peterson, G. R. *Introduction to Switching Theory and Logical Design*. 3rd ed. New York: Wiley, 1981.
5. Givone, D. D. *Introduction to Switching Circuit Theory*. New York: McGraw-Hill, 1970.
6. Roth, C. H. *Fundamentals of Logic Design*. 3rd ed. New York: West, 1985.
7. Booth, T. L. *Introduction to Computer Engineering*. 3rd ed. New York: Wiley, 1984.

PROBLEMS

4-1   The D latch shown in Figure 4-6 can be constructed with only four NAND gates. This can be done by removing the inverter and connecting the output of the upper NAND gate to the input of the lower gate. Show that the modified circuit is the same as the original circuit by deriving the Boolean functions to the R input of the SR latch in each circuit.

4-2   Obtain the logic diagram of a D latch using NOR gates only.

4-3   Draw the logic diagram of a D-type master-slave flip-flop using transmission gates and inverters.

4-4   Draw the logic diagram of a JK-type master-slave flip-flop using nine NAND gates.

4-5   Draw the timing diagram similar to Figure 4-9 for a JK-type master-slave flip-flop during four clock pulses. Show the timing signals of C, J, K, Y, and Q. Assume that initially the output Q is equal to 1. With the first pulse $J = 0$ and $K = 1$. Then for successive pulses J goes to 1, followed by K going to 0, and then J going back to 0. Assume that each input changes after the negative edge of the pulse.

4-6   Repeat problem 4-5 using a positive-edge-triggered JK flip-flop. Show the timing diagrams for C, J, K, and Q.

4-7   A set-dominant flip-flop has a set and reset inputs. It differs from a conventional SR flip-flop in that when both S and R are equal to 1 the flip-flop is set. Obtain the characteristic table of the set-dominant flip-flop.

4-8   A JN flip-flop has two inputs J and N. Input J behaves like the J input of a JK flip-flop and input N behaves like the complement of the K input of a JK flip-flop (that is $N = \overline{K}$).
(a) Obtain the characteristic table of the flip-flop.
(b) Show that by connecting the two inputs together one obtains a D-type flip-flop.

4-9   Draw the graphic symbol of the following flip-flops.

(a) Negative-edge-triggered D flip-flop.

(b) Master-slave SR flip-flop.

(c) Positive-edge-triggered T flip-flop.

4-10 A sequential circuit with two D-type flip-flops A and B, two inputs X and Y, and one output Z is specified by the following input equations:

$$D_A = \overline{X}Y + XA \qquad D_B = \overline{X}B + XA \qquad Z = B$$

(a) Draw the logic diagram of the circuit.

(b) Derive the state table.

(c) Derive the state diagram.

4-11 A sequential circuit has three D flip-flops A, B, and C, and one input X. It is described by the following input equations:

$$D_A = (B\overline{C} + \overline{B}C)X + (BC + \overline{B}\overline{C})\overline{X}$$

$$D_B = A$$

$$D_C = B$$

(a) Derive the state table for the circuit.

(b) Draw two state diagrams; one for $X = 0$ and the other for $X = 1$.

4-12 A sequential circuit has one flip-flop Q, two inputs X and Y and one output S. It consists of a full adder circuit connected to a D flip-flop as shown in Figure P4-12. Derive the state table and state diagram of the sequential circuit.

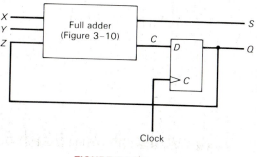

FIGURE P4-12

Circuit for Problem 4-12

4-13 Starting from state 00 in the state diagram of Figure 4-17(a), determine the state transitions and output sequence that will be generated when an input sequence of 010110111011110 is applied.

4-14 Draw the state diagram of the sequential circuit specified by the state table in Table 4-3.

4-15 Draw the logic diagram of a sequential circuit with two JK flip-flops and one input. The circuit is specified by the input equations associated with the flip-flop inputs in Table 4-3.

4-16 A sequential circuit has two JK flip-flops, one input X, and one output Y. The logic diagram of the circuit is shown in Figure P4-16. Derive the state table and state diagram of the circuit.

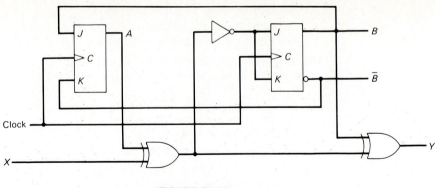

FIGURE P4-16
Circuit for Problem 4-16

4-17 A sequential circuit has two JK flip-flops A and B, two inputs X and Y, and one output Z. The flip-flop input equations and output function are as follows:

$$J_A = BX + \overline{B}\,\overline{Y} \qquad K_A = \overline{B}X\overline{Y} \qquad Z = AXY + B\overline{X}\,\overline{Y}$$

$$J_B = \overline{A}X \qquad K_B = A + X\overline{Y}$$

(a) Draw the logic diagram of the circuit.
(b) Derive the state table and state diagram.

4-18 Design a sequential circuit with two D flip-flops A and B and one input X. When $X = 0$, the state of the circuit remains the same. When $X = 1$, the circuit goes through the state transitions from 00 to 01 to 11 to 10 back to 00, and repeat.

4-19 A sequential circuit has three flip-flops A, B, C, one input X, and one output Y. The state diagram is shown in Figure P4-19. Design the circuit with D flip-flops. Analyze the circuit to ensure that it is self-correcting.

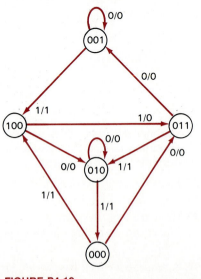

FIGURE P4-19
State Diagram for Problems 4-19 and 4-24

4-20 Convert a D-type flip-flop into a JK flip-flop using external gates. The gates can be derived by means of sequential circuit design procedure starting from a state table with the D flip-flop output as the present and next state and with J and K as inputs.

4-21 Derive the characteristic functions for the JK, D, and T type flip-flops. The characteristic function is an algebraic function that expresses the next state $Q(t + 1)$ as a function of the present state $Q(t)$ and the input(s) of the flip-flop.

4-22 Derive an excitation table for the JN flip-flop defined in Problem 4-8.

4-23 Derive the excitation table of the set-dominant flip-flop defined in Problem 4-7.

4-24 Design a sequential circuit for the state diagram given in Figure P4-19 using JK flip-flops. Analyze the circuit to make sure that it is self-correcting.

4-25 Design a sequential circuit with two JK flip-flops A and B and two inputs E and X. If $E = 0$, the circuit remains in the same state regardless of the value of X. When $E = 1$ and $X = 1$, the circuit goes through the state transitions from 00 to 01 to 10 to 11 back to 00, and repeats, When $E = 1$ and $X = 0$, the circuit goes through the state transitions from 00 to 11 to 10 to 01 back to 00, and repeats.

4-26 Design the sequential circuit specified by the state table of Table 4-7 using SR flip-flops.

4-27 Using the state table part of Table 4-7 (remove the flip-flop input list for J and K), derive a new list of binary values for the inputs of two T flip-flops T_A and T_B. Verify the corresponding input equations listed in Section 4-6 and draw the logic diagram of the circuit with T flip-flops.

5

REGISTERS
AND COUNTERS

5-1 INTRODUCTION

A clocked sequential circuit consists of a group of flip-flops and combinational gates connected to form a feedback path. The flip-flops are essential because, in their absence, the circuit reduces to a purely combinational circuit (provided there is no feedback among the gates). A circuit with flip-flops is considered a sequential circuit even in the absence of combinational gates. Circuits that include flip-flops are usually classified by the function they perform rather than by the name sequential circuit. Two such circuits are known as registers and counters.

A register is a group of flip-flops. Each flip-flop is capable of storing one bit of information. An n-bit register has a group of n flip-flops and is capable of storing any binary information of n bits. In addition to the flip-flops, a register may have combinational gates that perform certain data processing tasks. In its broadest definition, a register consists of a group of flip-flops and gates that effect their transition. The flip-flops hold the binary information and the gates control when and how new information is transferred into the register.

A counter is essentially a register that goes through a predetermined sequence of states upon the application of clock pulses. The gates in the counter are connected in such a way as to produce the prescribed sequence of binary states. Although counters are a special type of register, it is common to differentiate them by giving them a special name.

Registers and counters are available in integrated circuits and are classified as MSI functions. They also form part of complex VLSI chips. They are extensively used in the design of digital systems in general and digital computers in particular. Registers are useful for storing and manipulating binary information. Counters are employed in circuits that generate timing signals to sequence and control the operations in a digital system. Knowledge of the operation of these two components is indispensable for the understanding of the organization and design of digital computers.

5-2   REGISTERS

Various types of registers are available commercially. The simplest register is one that consists of only flip-flops without any external gates. Figure 5-1(a) shows such a register constructed with four D-type flip-flops. The common clock input triggers all flip-flops on the rising edge of each pulse and the binary data available at the four inputs are transferred into the 4-bit register. The four outputs can be sampled at any time to obtain the binary information stored in the register. The *clear* input goes to the R inputs of all four flip-flops. When this input goes to 0, all flip-flops are reset asynchronously. The clear input is useful for clearing the register to all 0's prior to its clocked operation. The R inputs must be maintained at logic-1 during normal clocked operation. The symbol $C1$ for the clock and $1D$ for the input indicates that the clock enables the D input but not the R input (see Figure 4-13).

The transfer of new information into a register is referred to as *loading* the register. If all the bits of the register are loaded simultaneously with a common clock pulse, we say that the loading is done in parallel. A clock transition applied to the C inputs of the register of Figure 5-1(a) will load all four inputs in parallel. In this configuration, the clock must be inhibited from the circuit if the content of the register must be left unchanged.

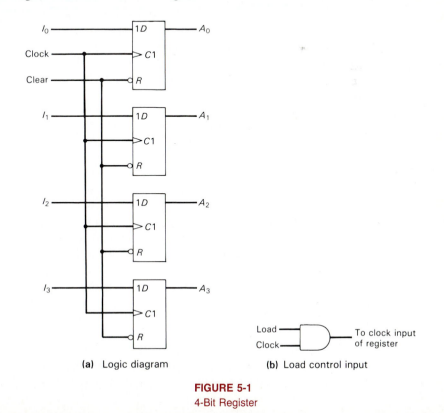

(a) Logic diagram   (b) Load control input

FIGURE 5-1
4-Bit Register

Most digital systems have a master clock generator that supplies a continuous train of clock pulses. The clock pulses are applied to all flip-flops and registers in the system. The master clock acts like a pump that supplies a constant beat to all parts of the system. A separate control signal must be used to decide which specific clock pulse will have an effect on a particular register. The clock pulses must be removed from the register when its content must not be changed. This can be done with a *load control* input ANDed with the clock as shown in Figure 5-1(b). The output of the AND gate is applied to the C inputs of the register. When the load control signal is 0, the output of the AND gate is 0, the clock is inhibited from the C inputs, and the content of the register remains the same. When the load control signal is 1, the clock pulses pass through the AND gate to the C terminals and new information can be transferred into the register with the next positive transition of the clock.

Register with Parallel Load

Inserting an AND gate in the path of clock pulses means that logic is performed with clock pulses. The insertion of logic gates produces uneven propagation delays between the master clock and the inputs of flip-flops. To fully synchronize the system, we must ensure that all clock pulses arrive simultaneously throughout the system so that all flip-flops trigger at the same time. However, performing logic with clock pulses inserts variable delays and may cause the system to go out of synchronism. For this reason, it is advisable to control the operation of the register with the D inputs instead of removing the clock from the C inputs of the flip-flops.

A 4-bit register with a load control input that is directed through gates and into the D inputs is shown in Figure 5-2. The C inputs receive clock pulses at all times. The buffer gate in the clock input reduces the power requirement from the clock generator. Less power is required when the clock is connected to only one input gate than would be needed by four inputs if the buffer was not used.

The load input in the register determines the action to be taken with each clock pulse. When the load input is 1, the data in the four inputs are transferred into the register with the next positive transition of a clock pulse. When the load input is 0, the data inputs are inhibited and the D inputs of the flip-flops are connected to their outputs. The feedback connection from output to input is necessary because the D flip-flop does not have a no change condition. With each clock pulse, the D input determines the next state of the output. To leave the output unchanged, it is necessary to make the D input equal to the present value of the output.

Note that the clock pulses are applied to the C inputs at all times. The load input determines whether the next pulse will accept new information or leave the information in the register intact. The transfer of information from inputs to register is done simultaneously with all four bits during a single pulse transition.

Standard Graphic Symbols

The standard graphic symbols for logic functions were introduced in Section 3-8. The standard graphic symbol for a register is equivalent to the symbol used for a group of flip-flops with common clock input. Figure 5-3(a) shows the standard

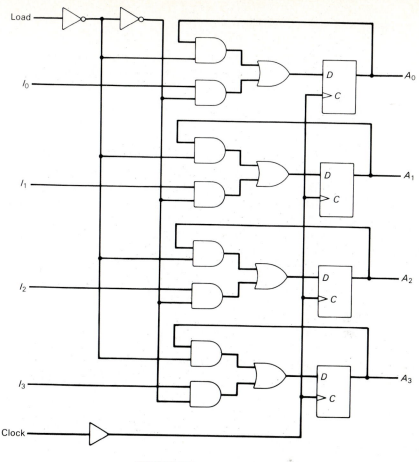

FIGURE 5-2
4-Bit Register with Parallel Load

block diagram symbol for a group of four D-type flip-flops with common clock and clear inputs. The clock input $C1$ and the clear input R appear in the upper block referred to as a common control block. The inputs to a common control block are considered as inputs to each of the elements in the lower sections of the diagram.

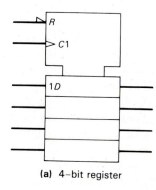

(a) 4–bit register

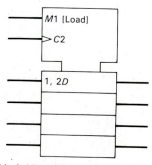

(b) 4–bit register with parallel load

FIGURE 5-3
Standard Graphic Symbols for Registers

The notation $C1$ is a control dependency that controls all the $1D$ inputs. Thus, the $1D$ input in each flip-flop is triggered by the common $C1$ input signal. The common R input resets all flip-flops. The $1D$ symbol is used only once in the upper section instead of repeating it in each section.

The small right-angle triangle along the R input is a polarity indicator. It signifies that the input is active-low. When positive logic assignment is used, the low signal is equivalent to logic-0 and therefore, a small complementing circle can be used instead. However, we will show the polarity symbol for active-low when drawing standard block diagram graphic symbols. This will conform with integrated circuit data books where the polarity symbol is usually employed.

The standard block diagram symbol for a register with parallel load is shown in Figure 5-3(b). The common control block shows input $M1$ for the load and $C2$ for the clock. The letter M is used to indicate a *mode* dependency. The symbol [LOAD] is optional. Each flip-flop section has the notation $1,2D$ at the input. The 1 refers to $M1$, the 2 refers to $C2$, and D is the input type of the flip-flop. The symbol $1,2D$ designates the fact that the D input is triggered with clock $C2$ provided that the load input $M1$ is active. Note that the symbol $1,2D$ is written only once in the top section and is assumed to be repeated in the lower sections.

The convention used in the dependency notation dictates that the number following C determines which input is affected by it. In Figure 5-3(a), we chose $C1$ and $1D$. In Figure 5-3(b), the identifying number 1 was chosen for the mode dependency M and the number 2 for the control dependency C. The D input is affected by both, and we place both identifying numbers in front of the D symbol. We could have chosen $M2$ and $C1$ instead, and it does not make a difference in this case.

5-3   SHIFT REGISTERS

A register capable of shifting its binary information in one or both directions is called a *shift register*. The logical configuration of a shift register consists of a chain of flip-flops in cascade, with the output of one flip-flop connected to the input of the next flip-flop. All flip-flops receive common clock pulses which initiate the shift from one stage to the next.

The simplest possible shift register is one that uses only flip-flops, as shown in Figure 5-4(a). The output of a given flip-flop is connected to the D input of the flip-flop at its right. The clock is common to all flip-flops. The *serial input* determines what goes into the leftmost position during the shift. The *serial output* is taken from the output of the rightmost flip-flop.

The standard graphic symbol for a shift register is shown in Figure 5-4(b). The qualifying symbol for a shift register is SRG followed by a number that designates the number of stages. Thus SRG4 denotes a 4-bit shift register. The serial input is applied to $1D$ and the common clock to $C1$. The arrow following the symbol $C1$ designates the fact that each clock transition shifts the register one position from left to right. The register shifts its contents with every clock pulse during the positive edge transition. This is indicated by the dynamic indicator symbol in front of $C1$.

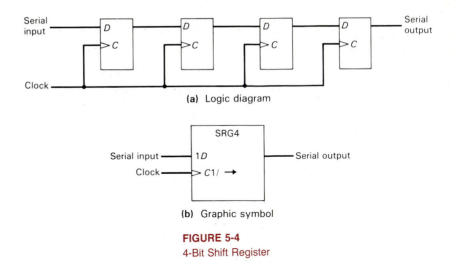

(a) Logic diagram

(b) Graphic symbol

FIGURE 5-4
4-Bit Shift Register

Sometimes it is necessary to control the shift so that it occurs only with certain pulses but not with others. This can be done by inhibiting the clock from the input of the register when we do not want it to shift. It will be shown later that the shift operation can be controlled through the D inputs of the flip-flops rather than through the clock input. If however, the shift register in Figure 5-4 is used, the shift can be controlled by connecting the clock through an AND gate with an input that controls the shift.

Serial Transfer

A digital system is said to operate in a serial mode when information is transferred and manipulated one bit at a time. Information is transferred one bit at a time by shifting the bits out of one register and into a second register. This is in contrast to parallel transfer where all the bits of the register are transferred at the same time.

The serial transfer of information from register A to register B is done with shift registers as shown in the diagram of Figure 5-5(a). The serial output of register A is connected to the serial input of register B. The serial input of register A is shown to receive 0's while its data are transferred to register B. It is also possible for register A to receive other binary information or, if we want to maintain the data in register A, we can connect its serial output to its serial input so that the information is shifted back into the register. The initial content of register B is shifted out through its serial output and is lost unless it is transferred to a third shift register. The shift control input determines when and how many times the registers are shifted. This is done with an AND gate that allows the clock pulses to pass only when the shift control is active.

We assume that each shift register has four stages. The control unit that supervises the transfer must be designed to enable the shift registers, through the shift control signal, for a fixed time of four clock pulses. This is shown in the timing

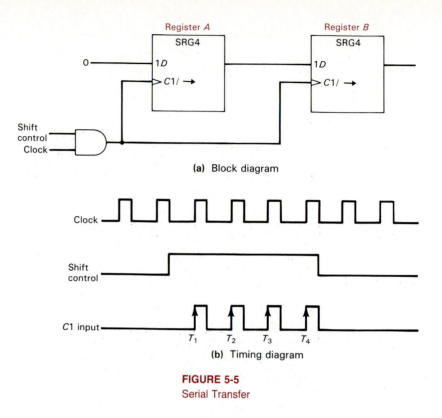

(a) Block diagram

(b) Timing diagram

FIGURE 5-5
Serial Transfer

diagram of Figure 5-5(b). The shift control signal is synchronized with the clock and changes value after the negative transition of a pulse. The next four pulses find the shift control in the active state so that the output of the AND gate connected to the C inputs of the registers produces four pulses T_1, T_2, T_3, and T_4. Each positive transition of these pulses causes a shift in both registers. After the fourth pulse, the shift control changes back to 0 during the negative transition of the clock, and the shift registers are disabled.

Assume that the binary content of register A before the shift is 1011, and that of register B is 0010. The serial transfer from A to B occurs in four steps as shown in Table 5-1. With the first pulse T_1, the rightmost bit of A is shifted into the leftmost bit of B, the leftmost bit of A receives a 0 from the serial input and, at the same time, all other bits of A and B are shifted one position to the right. The next three pulses perform identical operations, shifting the bits of A into B one at a time while transferring 0's to A. After the fourth shift, the shift control goes to 0 and the shifts stop. Register B contains 1011 which is the previous value of A. Register A contains all 0's.

The difference between serial and parallel modes of operation should be apparent from this example. In the parallel mode, information is available from all bits of a register and all bits can be transferred simultaneously during one clock pulse. In the serial mode, the registers have a single serial input and a single serial output. The information is transferred one bit at a time while the registers are shifted in the same direction.

TABLE 5-1
Serial Transfer Example

Timing pulse	Shift register A				Shift register B			
Initial value	1	0	1	1	0	0	1	0
After T_1	0	1	0	1	1	0	0	1
After T_2	0	0	1	0	1	1	0	0
After T_3	0	0	0	1	0	1	1	0
After T_4	0	0	0	0	1	0	1	1

Serial Addition

Operations in digital computers are usually done in parallel because it is a faster mode of operation. Serial operations are slower but have the advantage of requiring less equipment. To demonstrate the serial mode of operation, we will show the operation of a serial adder. The parallel counterpart was presented in Section 3-4.

The two binary numbers to be added serially are stored in two shift registers. Bits are added one pair at a time through a single full adder (FA) circuit as shown in Figure 5-6. The carry out of the full adder is transferred into a D flip-flop. The output of this carry flip-flop is then used as the input carry for the next pair of significant bits. The sum bit in the S output of the full adder could be transferred into a third shift register, but we have chosen to transfer the sum bits into register A as the contents of the register are shifted out. The serial input of register B can receive a new binary number as its contents are shifted out during the addition.

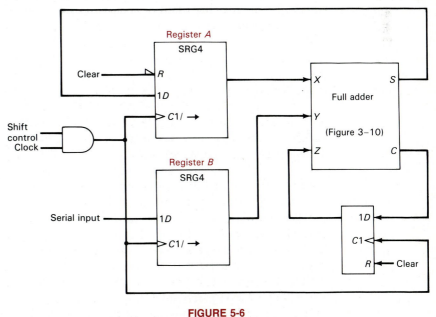

FIGURE 5-6
Serial Addition

The operation of the serial adder is as follows. Register A holds the augend, register B holds the addend, and the carry flip-flop is reset to 0. The serial output of A and B provide a pair of significant bits for the full adder at X and Y. The output of the carry flip-flop provides the input carry at Z. The shift control enables the clock for both registers and the flip-flop. Each clock pulse shifts both registers once to the right, transfers the sum bit from S into the leftmost flip-flop of A, and transfers the output carry into the carry flip-flop. The shift control enables the registers for as many clock pulses as there are bits in the registers (four pulses in this example). For each pulse, a new sum bit is transferred to A, a new carry is transferred to the flip-flop, and both registers are shifted once to the right. This process continues until the shift control is disabled. Thus, the addition is accomplished by passing each pair of bits and the previous carry through a single full adder circuit and transferring the sum, one bit at a time, into register A.

Initially we could clear register A to 0 and then add the first number from B. While B is shifted through the full adder, we can transfer a second number to it through its serial input. The second number can be added to the contents of register A while a third number is transferred serially into register B. This may be repeated to form the addition of two, three, or more numbers and accumulate their sum in register A.

Comparing the serial adder with the parallel adder described in Section 3-4, we note the following differences. The parallel adder must use a register with parallel load whereas the serial adder uses shift registers. The number of full adder circuits in the parallel adder is equal to the number of bits in the binary number, whereas the serial adder requires only one full adder and a carry flip-flop. Excluding the registers, the parallel adder is a combinational circuit, whereas the serial adder is a sequential circuit because it includes the carry flip-flop. This is typical of serial operations because the result of each bit-time operation may depend not only on the present bits but also on previous results which must be stored in temporary flip-flops.

5-4   SHIFT REGISTER WITH PARALLEL LOAD

If there is access to all the flip-flop outputs of a shift register, information entered serially by shifting can be taken out in parallel from the outputs of all flip-flops. If a parallel load capability is added to a shift register, then data entered in parallel can be taken out in serial fashion by shifting out the data in the register. Thus a shift register with parallel load can be used for converting incoming parallel data to serial transfer and vice versa.

The logic diagram of a 4-bit shift register with parallel load is shown in Figure 5-7. There are two control inputs, one for the shift and the other for the load. Each stage of the register consists of a D flip-flop, an OR gate, and three AND gates. The first AND gate enables the shift operation. The second AND gate enables the input data. The third AND gate restores the contents of the register when no operation is required.

The operation of the register is recorded in the function entries of Table 5-2. When both the shift and load control inputs are 0, the third AND gate in each

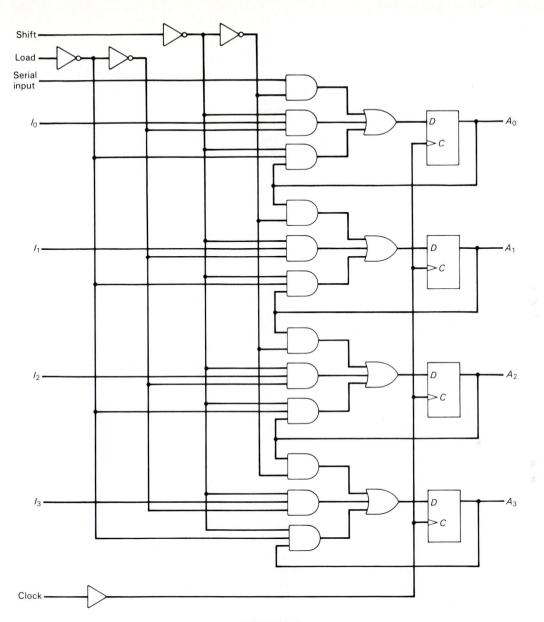

FIGURE 5-7
Shift Register with Parallel Load

TABLE 5-2
Function Table for the Register of Figure 5-7

Shift	Load	Operation
0	0	No change
0	1	Load parallel data
1	X	Shift down from A_0 to A_3

stage is enabled and the output of each flip-flop is applied to its D input. A positive transition of the clock restores the contents of the register and no change in output occurs. When the shift input is 0 and the load input is 1, the second AND gate in each stage is enabled and the input data is applied to the corresponding D input of the flip-flop. The next positive clock transition transfers the input data into the register. When the shift input is equal to 1, the first AND gate in each stage is enabled and the other two are disabled. Since the load input is disabled by the second AND gate, we mark it with a don't care entry in the table. The shift operation causes the data from the serial input to be transferred to flip-flop A_0, the output of A_0 to be transferred to flip-flop A_1, and so on down the flip-flop stages. The next positive transition of the clock shifts the contents of the register downward with the serial input going to the first stage. Note that because of the way the circuit is drawn, the shifting occurs in the downward direction. If we rotate the page a quarter turn counterclockwise, the register will be shifting from left to right.

Shift registers are often used to interface digital systems situated remotely from each other. For example, suppose it is necessary to transmit an n-bit quantity between two points. If the distance is far it will be expensive to use n lines to transmit the n bits in parallel. It may be more economical to use a single line and transmit the information serially, one bit at a time. The transmitter accepts the n-bit data in parallel into a shift register and then transmits the data serially along the common line. The receiver accepts the data serially into a shift register. When all n bits are accumulated they can be taken from the outputs of the register in parallel. Thus the transmitter performs a parallel-to-serial conversion of data and the receiver does a serial-to-parallel conversion.

Bidirectional Shift Register

A register capable of shifting in one direction only is called a *unidirectional shift register*. A register that can shift in both directions is called a *bidirectional shift register*. It is possible to modify the circuit of Figure 5-7 by adding a fourth AND gate in each stage for shifting the data in the upward direction. An investigation of the resultant circuit will reveal that the four AND gates together with the OR gate in each stage constitute a multiplexer with the selection inputs controlling the operation of the register.

One stage of a bidirectional shift register with parallel load is shown in Figure 5-8. Each stage consists of a D flip-flop and a 4-to-1-line multiplexer. The two selection inputs S_1 and S_0 select one of the multiplexer inputs for the D flip-flop. The selection lines control the mode of operation of the register according to the function table of Table 5-3. When the mode control $S_1S_0 = 00$, input 0 of the multiplexer is selected. This condition forms a path from the output of each flip-flop into the input of the same flip-flop. The next clock transition transfers into each flip-flop the binary value it held previously, and no change of state occurs. When $S_1S_0 = 01$, the terminal marked 1 in the multiplexer has a path to the D input of each flip-flop. This causes a shift-down operation, the serial input is

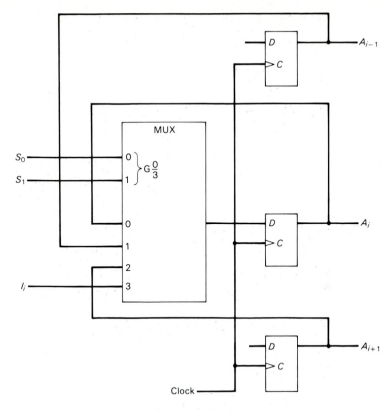

FIGURE 5-8
One Typical Stage of a Bidirectional Shift Register with Parallel Load

transferred into the first stage, and the contents of each stage A_{i-1} are transferred into stage A_i. When $S_1S_0 = 10$ a shift-up operation results in another serial input going into the last stage, and stage A_{i+1} being transferred into stage A_i. Finally, when $S_1S_0 = 11$, the binary information on each parallel input line is transferred into the corresponding flip-flop, resulting in a parallel load operation.

TABLE 5-3
Function Table for the Register of Figure 5-8

Mode control		Register
S_1	S_0	Operation
0	0	No change
0	1	Shift down
1	0	Shift up
1	1	Parallel load

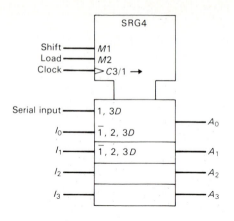

FIGURE 5-9
Graphic Symbol for Shift Register
with Parallel Load

Standard Graphic Symbols

The standard graphic symbol for a shift register was presented in Figure 5-4(b). If we include a parallel load with the register, it is necessary to modify the diagram to show the common control signals and the input parallel data. Figure 5-9 shows the graphic symbol for the unidirectional shift register with parallel load whose detail diagram is shown in Figure 5-7. The common control block has the qualifying symbol SRG4 which stands for a 4-bit shift register. It has three dependency symbols. $M1$ and $M2$ are mode dependencies for the shift and load operations. The control dependency $C3$ is for the clock input. The symbol $/1 \rightarrow$ following $C3$ indicates that the register shifts to the right or in the downward direction when $M1$ is active.

The four blocks below the common block represent the four flip-flops. Flip-flop A_0 has two inputs. The serial input has a label $1,3D$. This means that the D input of the flip-flop is active when $M1$ (shift) is active and $C3$ goes through a positive clock transition. The other input of A_0 and the inputs of the other blocks are for the parallel data. This is denoted by the label $\overline{1},2,3D$. The bar over the 1 specifies that $M1$ must be inactive, the 2 is for $M2$ (load), and 3 is for the clock $C3$. If both $M1$ and $M2$ are inactive (both equal to 0) there is no active input and therefore, the outputs are not affected by the clock transition. Note that the parallel load input is labeled only in the first and second block. This is the convention of the standard. When there are identical blocks under the control of a common block, the inputs must be labeled in the topmost block, although they may be labeled in all the blocks if desired.

Figure 5-10 shows the graphic symbol for the bidirectional shift register with parallel load. The common control block shows an R input for resetting all flip-flops to 0 asynchronously. The mode select consists of two inputs and the mode dependency M may take a binary number from 0 to 3. This is indicated by the symbol $M\frac{0}{3}$ which stands for $M0, M1, M2, M3$, and is similar to the notation for the G dependency in multiplexers. The symbol associated with the clock is:

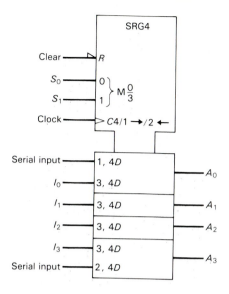

FIGURE 5-10

Graphic Symbol for Bidirectional Shift Register
with Parallel Load

$$C4 \; /1\rightarrow \; /2\leftarrow$$

$C4$ is the control dependency for the clock. The $/1\rightarrow$ symbol indicates that the register shifts right (down in this case) when the mode is $M1$ ($S_1S_0 = 01$). The $/2\leftarrow$ symbol indicates that the register shifts left (up in this case) when the mode is $M2$ ($S_1S_0 = 10$). The right and left directions are obtained when the page is turned 90 degrees counterclockwise.

The blocks below the common block represent the four flip-flops. The first flip-flop has a serial input for shift down denoted by $1,4D$ (mode $M1$, clock $C4$, input D). The last flip-flop has a serial input for shift up denoted by $2,4D$ (mode $M2$, clock $C4$, input D). All four flip-flops have a parallel input denoted by the label $3,4D$ (mode $M3$, clock $C4$, input D). Thus $M3$ ($S_1S_0 = 11$) is for parallel load. The remaining mode $M0$ ($S_1S_0 = 00$) has no effect on the outputs because it is not included in the input labels.

5-5 RIPPLE COUNTERS

A register that goes through a prescribed sequence of states upon the application of input pulses is called a *counter*. The input pulses may be clock pulses or they may originate from some external source and they may occur at a fixed interval of time or at random. The sequence of states may follow the binary number sequence or any other sequence of states. A counter that follows the binary number sequence is called a *binary counter*. An n-bit binary counter consists of n flip-flops and can count in binary from 0 through $2^n - 1$.

Counters are available in two categories, ripple counters and synchronous counters. In a ripple counter, the flip-flop output transition serves as a source for triggering other flip-flops. In other words, the C input of some or all flip-flops are triggered not by the common clock pulses but rather by the transition that occurs in other flip-flop outputs. In a synchronous counter, the C inputs of all flip-flops receive the common clock pulse and the change of state is determined from the present state of the counter. Synchronous counters are presented in the next two sections. Here we present the binary ripple counter and explain its operation.

Binary Ripple Counter

The logic diagram of a 4-bit binary ripple counter is shown in Figure 5-11. The counter is constructed with complementing flip-flops of the JK type. The output of each flip-flop is connected to the C input of the next flip-flop in sequence. The flip-flop holding the least significant bit receives the incoming count pulses. The J and K inputs of all the flip-flops are connected to a permanent logic-1. This makes

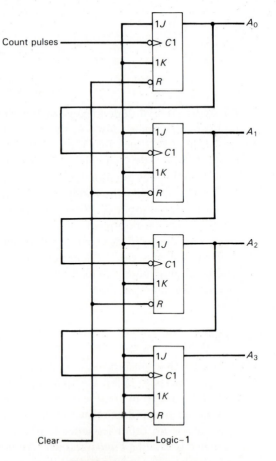

FIGURE 5-11
4-Bit Binary Ripple Counter

TABLE 5-4
Count Sequence of Binary Counter

Up Count Sequence				Down Count Sequence			
A_3	A_2	A_1	A_0	A_3	A_2	A_1	A_0
0	0	0	0	1	1	1	1
0	0	0	1	1	1	1	0
0	0	1	0	1	1	0	1
0	0	1	1	1	1	0	0
0	1	0	0	1	0	1	1
0	1	0	1	1	0	1	0
0	1	1	0	1	0	0	1
0	1	1	1	1	0	0	0
1	0	0	0	0	1	1	1
1	0	0	1	0	1	1	0
1	0	1	0	0	1	0	1
1	0	1	1	0	1	0	0
1	1	0	0	0	0	1	1
1	1	0	1	0	0	1	0
1	1	1	0	0	0	0	1
1	1	1	1	0	0	0	0

each flip-flop complement if the signal in its C input goes through a negative transition. The small circle in front of the dynamic indicator symbol next to the $C1$ label indicates that the flip-flops respond to the negative edge transition of the input. The negative transition occurs when the output of the previous flip-flop, to which C is connected, goes from 1 to 0. A 0-level signal in the R inputs clears the register to 0 asynchronously. The R label does not have a 1 in front of it which indicates that its input is independent of the input at $C1$.

To understand the operation of a binary counter, refer to its count sequence given on the left side of Table 5-4. The count starts with binary 0 and increments by one with each count pulse input. After the count of 15, the counter goes back to 0 to repeat the count. The least significant bit (A_0) is complemented with each count pulse input. Every time that A_0 goes from 1 to 0, it complements A_1. Every time that A_1 goes from 1 to 0, it complements A_2. Every time that A_2 goes from 1 to 0, it complements A_3, and so on for any higher-order bits in the ripple counter. For example, consider the transition from count 0011 to 0100. A_0 is complemented with the count pulse. Since A_0 goes from 1 to 0, it triggers A_1 and complements it. As a result, A_1 goes from 1 to 0 which complements A_2 changing it from 0 to 1. A_2 does not trigger A_3 because A_2 produces a positive transition and the flip-flop responds only to negative transitions. Thus the count from 0011 to 0100 is achieved by changing the bits one at a time from 0011 to 0010 ($A_0 = 0$) then to 0000 ($A_1 = 0$) and finally to 0100 ($A_2 = 1$). The flip-flops change one at a time in succession and the signal propagates through the counter in a ripple fashion from one stage to the next.

The standard graphic symbol for a 4-bit binary ripple counter is shown in Figure 5-12. The qualifying symbol for the ripple counter is RCTR. The designation DIV 16 stands for divide by 16. This is the cycle length of the counter as it repeatedly

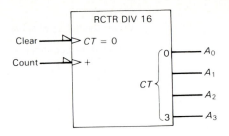

FIGURE 5-12
Graphic Symbol for the Binary
Ripple Counter

cycles over 16 counts from 0 to 15. Since the count input does not go to the C inputs of all stages, it has no $C1$ label, and the symbol + is used instead to indicate a count-up operation. The dynamic symbol next to the + together with the polarity symbol along the input line signify that the count is affected with a negative-edge transition of the input signal. The symbol CT designates the *content* of the counter. An active-low (logic-0) signal in the clear input changes the content of the counter to 0. The bit-grouping from 0 to 3 in the output represent values for the weights to the power of 2. Thus 0 represents the value 2^0 and 3 represents the value 2^3.

Binary Down-Counter

A binary counter with a normal binary count is considered as an up-counter. A binary counter with a reverse count is called a down-counter. In a down-counter, the binary count is decremented by one with every input count pulse. The count of a 4-bit down counter starts from binary 15 and continues to binary 14, 13, 12, down to 0 and back to 15. The count sequence for the binary down-counter is listed in Table 5-4.

There are various ways that a binary down-counter can be constructed. As can be seen from Table 5-4, the down-count is the complement of the up-count. Therefore, one way of achieving a down-counter is to use the circuit from Figure 5-11 but take the outputs from the complement outputs of the flip-flops.

Two other possible constructions can be obtained. From an investigation of the down-count sequence in the table, we find that the least significant bit is complemented after each count, and other bits are complemented if their previous least significant bits go from 0 to 1. (Recall that in the up-count the previous bit must go from 1 to 0 to complement the next bit.) The circuit of Figure 5-11 can be modified in one of two ways to change it to a down-counter. In the first case, we connect the complement output of each flip-flop to the C input of the next flip-flop in sequence. When the normal output of a flip-flop goes from 0 to 1 as required, the complement output goes from 1 to 0 producing the negative-edge transition for complementing the next stage. In the second case, we leave the circuit of Figure 5-11 as is except that we use flip-flops that trigger on the positive-edge transition. This means that the small circle in front of the dynamic indicator next to the $C1$ label must be removed from the diagram. When a flip-flop output goes from 0 to 1 it produces a positive-edge transition and the next flip-flop will be complemented.

The standard graphic symbol for a binary down-counter is the same as in Figure 5-12 except that the $-$ symbol is used to indicate a count-down operation. A counter that can count both up and down must have a mode input to select between the two operations.

BCD Ripple Counter

A decimal counter follows a sequence of 10 states instead of the 16 states of a binary counter. The particular states are dictated by the binary code that represents the decimal digit. The binary coded decimal (BCD) uses binary numbers 0000 through 1001 to represent the coded decimal digits from 0 to 9. Thus a BCD counter follows the binary count from 0 to 9 but instead of continuing with the count of 10 as in a binary counter, the BCD counter goes from 9 to 0 and then repeats the count.

The binary ripple counter of Figure 5-12 can be operated as a BCD counter by making the external connections as shown in Figure 5-13. Outputs A_1 and A_3 are connected to the inputs of a NAND gate. The output of the NAND gate is connected to the clear input of the counter. When both A_1 and A_3 are equal to 1, the output of the NAND gate becomes 0 (a low-level signal) and all four outputs clear to 0 irrespective of the count input. The counter starts from 0000, and every count input increments it by 1 until it reaches the count of 1001. The next count changes the output to 1010, making A_1 and A_3 equal to 1. This momentary output cannot be sustained, because the four flip-flops clear to 0, with the result that the output goes immediately to 0000. Thus the input pulse after the count of 1001 changes the output to 0000, producing a BCD count.

The BCD counter of Figure 5-13 is a *decade counter*, since it counts through one decade from 0 to 9. To count in decimal from 0 to 99 we need two decades, from 0 to 999 we need three decades, and so on. Multiple decade counters can be constructed by connecting BCD counters in cascade, one for each decade. The input to the second, third, and all succeeding decades comes from output A_3 of the previous decade. When the count in a given decade goes from 1001 to 0000, A_3 goes from 1 to 0, producing a negative transition for triggering the next higher

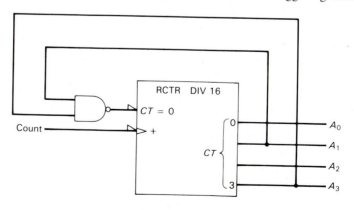

FIGURE 5-13
BCD Ripple Counter

order decade. For instance, the count after 399 will be 400, which in BCD goes from 0011 1001 1001 to 0100 0000 0000.

5-6   SYNCHRONOUS BINARY COUNTERS

Synchronous counters are different from ripple counters in that clock pulses are applied to the inputs of all flip-flops. The common clock triggers all flip-flops simultaneously rather than one at a time, as happens in a ripple counter. The decision whether the flip-flop is complemented or not is determined by the J and K data inputs. If J and K are both equal to 0, the flip-flop does not change state even in the presence of a pulse. If J and K are both equal to 1, the flip-flop complements after the clock transition.

Design of Binary Counter

The design procedure for a synchronous counter is the same as with any other synchronous sequential circuit. A counter may operate without an external input except for the clock pulses. The output of the counter is taken from the outputs of the flip-flops without any additional outputs from gates. In the absence of inputs and outputs, the state table of a counter will consist of columns for the present state and next state only.

The state table of a 4-bit binary counter is listed in Table 5-5. The present state shows the 16 states from 0000 to 1111. The next state is equal to the present state value plus one. When the circuit reaches the state 1111 it goes to the next state, 0000, which causes the counter to repeat its cycle.

TABLE 5-5
State Table and Flip-Flop Inputs for Binary Counter

Present state				Next state				Flip-Flop inputs							
A_3	A_2	A_1	A_0	A_3	A_2	A_1	A_0	J_{A3}	K_{A3}	J_{A2}	K_{A2}	J_{A1}	K_{A1}	J_{A0}	K_{A0}
0	0	0	0	0	0	0	1	0	X	0	X	0	X	1	X
0	0	0	1	0	0	1	0	0	X	0	X	1	X	X	1
0	0	1	0	0	0	1	1	0	X	0	X	X	0	1	X
0	0	1	1	0	1	0	0	0	X	1	X	X	1	X	1
0	1	0	0	0	1	0	1	0	X	X	0	0	X	1	X
0	1	0	1	0	1	1	0	0	X	X	0	1	X	X	1
0	1	1	0	0	1	1	1	0	X	X	0	X	0	1	X
0	1	1	1	1	0	0	0	1	X	X	1	X	1	X	1
1	0	0	0	1	0	0	1	X	0	0	X	0	X	1	X
1	0	0	1	1	0	1	0	X	0	0	X	1	X	X	1
1	0	1	0	1	0	1	1	X	0	0	X	X	0	1	X
1	0	1	1	1	1	0	0	X	0	1	X	X	1	X	1
1	1	0	0	1	1	0	1	X	0	X	0	0	X	1	X
1	1	0	1	1	1	1	0	X	0	X	0	1	X	X	1
1	1	1	0	1	1	1	1	X	0	X	0	X	0	1	X
1	1	1	1	0	0	0	0	X	1	X	1	X	1	X	1

Binary counters are most efficiently constructed with complementing T or JK flip-flops. They also can be designed with D-type flip-flops. We will design a counter with JK flip-flops first and then will repeat the design with D flip-flops.

The procedure for designing a sequential circuit with JK flip-flops was presented in Section 4-6. This procedure is used here to obtain the circuit of the binary counter. First we obtain the flip-flop inputs for each J and K and list them in Table 5-5. This is done by using the excitation conditions given in Table 4-6. We then simplify the input equations by means of maps as shown in Figure 5-14. The maps for the least significant flip-flop are not drawn. These two maps contain only 1's and don't care terms which makes both J_{A0} and K_{A0} equal to 1. Note that the input

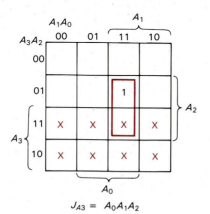

$$J_{A3} = A_0 A_1 A_2$$

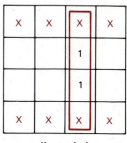

$$K_{A3} = A_0 A_1 A_2$$

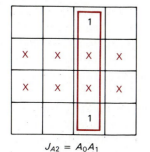

$$J_{A2} = A_0 A_1$$

$$K_{A2} = A_0 A_1$$

$$J_{A1} = A_0$$

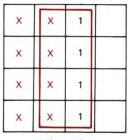

$$K_{A1} = A_0$$

FIGURE 5-14
Maps for Input Equations of a Binary Counter

equations for J and K are the same for each flip-flop. This indicates that T flip-flops could be used instead of JK.

In many applications it is necessary to control the operation of the counter with a *count enable* input. If we designate such an input with the variable E, the input equations for the binary counter can be expressed as follows:

$$J_{A0} = K_{A0} = E$$

$$J_{A1} = K_{A1} = A_0 E$$

$$J_{A2} = K_{A2} = A_0 A_1 E$$

$$J_{A3} = K_{A3} = A_0 A_1 A_2 E$$

When $E = 0$, all J and K inputs are equal to 0 and the flip-flops remain in the same state even in the presence of clock pulses. When $E = 1$, the first input equation becomes $J_{A0} = K_{A0} = 1$ and the other input equations reduce to the equations derived in the maps of Figure 5-14.

The flip-flop in the least significant position of a synchronous binary counter is complemented with every clock pulse transition. A flip-flop in any other position is complemented with a clock pulse transition if all least significant bits are equal to 1. In an n-bit binary counter, the input equation for flip-flop A_i at any stage of i for $i = 1, 2, 3, \ldots n$ is

$$J_{Ai} = K_{Ai} = A_0 A_1 A_2 \ldots A_{i-1} E$$

Synchronous binary counters have a regular pattern as can be seen from the 4-bit binary counter shown in Figure 5-15. The C inputs of all flip-flops receive the common clock pulses. The first stage A_0 is complemented when the counter is enabled with input E being a 1. The other J and K inputs are equal to 1 if all previous least significant stages are equal to 1 and the count is enabled. The chain of AND gates generates the required logic for the J and K inputs. The output carry can be used to extend the counter to more stages with each stage having an additional flip-flop and an AND gate.

Note that the flip-flops trigger on the positive-edge transition of the clock. The polarity of the clock is not essential here as it was with the ripple counter. The synchronous counter can be triggered either with the positive or the negative edge of the clock transition.

Counter with D Flip-Flops

A binary counter can be designed with D flip-flops by following the design procedure outlined in Section 4-5. The input equations for the D flip-flops are obtained directly from the next state values in Table 5-5. The input equations can be expressed in sum of minterms as a function of the present state.

$$D_{A0}(A_3, A_2, A_1, A_0) = \Sigma\, m(0, 2, 4, 6, 8, 10, 12, 14)$$

$$D_{A1}(A_3, A_2, A_1, A_0) = \Sigma\, m(1, 2, 5, 6, 9, 10, 13, 14)$$

$$D_{A2}(A_3, A_2, A_1, A_0) = \Sigma\, m(3, 4, 5, 6, 11, 12, 13, 14)$$

$$D_{A3}(A_3, A_2, A_1, A_0) = \Sigma\, m(7, 8, 9, 10, 11, 12, 13, 14)$$

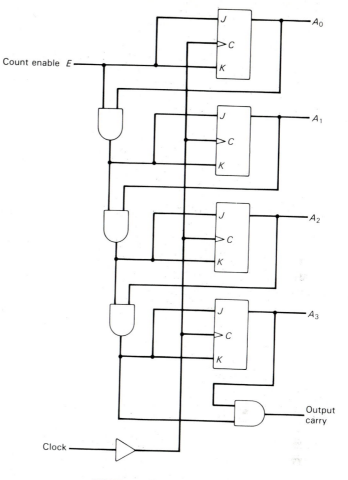

FIGURE 5-15
4-Bit Synchronous Binary Counter

Simplifying the four functions with maps and adding a count enable input E we obtain the following input equations for the counter (see Problem 5-20).

$$D_{A0} = A_0 \oplus E$$

$$D_{A1} = A_1 \oplus (A_0 E)$$

$$D_{A2} = A_2 \oplus (A_0 A_1 E)$$

$$D_{A3} = A_3 \oplus (A_0 A_1 A_2 E)$$

The input equation for any flip-flop A_i in state i can be expressed as:

$$D_{Ai} = A_i \oplus (A_0 A_1 A_2 \ldots A_{i-1} E)$$

The logic diagram of a 4-bit binary counter with D flip-flop is shown in Figure 5-16. Note that the circuit has the same chain of AND gates for the carry as before. The only difference between the circuit of Figure 5-16 and the counter with JK

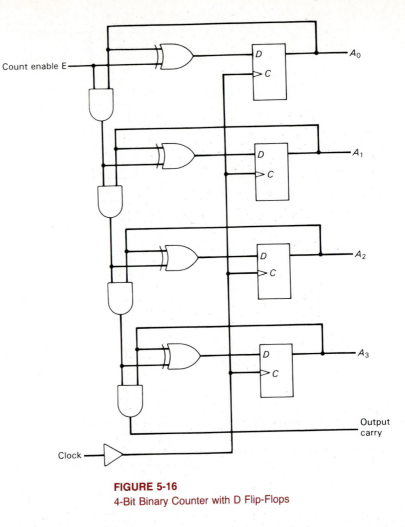

FIGURE 5-16
4-Bit Binary Counter with D Flip-Flops

flip-flops shown in Figure 5-15 is the exclusive-OR gate in each flip-flop input. This indicates that the D flip-flop together with the exclusive-OR gate correspond to a T-type flip-flop. One input of the exclusive-OR gate comes from the output of the D flip-flop and the other input of the gate is equivalent to an input for a T-type flip-flop. (See Problem 5-21.)

Up-Down Binary Counter

A synchronous count-down binary counter goes through the binary states in reverse order from 1111 to 0000 and back to 1111 to repeat the count. It is possible to design a count-down counter in the usual manner, but the result is predictable from inspection of the binary count-down. The bit in the least significant position is complemented with each count pulse. A bit in any other position is complemented if all lower significant bits are equal to 0. For example, the next state after the present state of 0100 is 0011. The least significant bit is always complemented. The second significant bit is complemented because the first bit is 0. The third significant bit is complemented because the first two bits are equal to 0. But the fourth bit does not change because all lower significant bits are not equal to 0.

The logic diagram of a synchronous count-down binary counter is similar to the circuit of the binary up-counter except that the inputs to the AND gates must come from the complement outputs of the flip-flops. The two operations can be combined to form a counter that can count both up and down, which is referred to as an up-down binary counter. The up-down counter needs a mode input to select between the two operations. Designate the mode select input by S with $S = 1$ for up-count and $S = 0$ for down-count. Let variable E be a count enable input with $E = 1$ for normal up or down counting and $E = 0$ for disabling both counts. If we use T-type flip-flops (that is $T = J = K$), a 4-bit up-down binary counter can be described by the following input equations:

$$T_{A0} = E$$

$$T_{A1} = A_0SE + \overline{A}_0\overline{S}E$$

$$T_{A2} = A_0A_1SE + \overline{A}_0\overline{A}_1\overline{S}E$$

$$T_{A3} = A_0A_1A_2SE + \overline{A}_0\overline{A}_1\overline{A}_2\overline{S}E$$

The output carries for the next stage are

$$C_{\text{up}} = A_0A_1A_2A_3SE \qquad \text{For count up}$$

$$C_{\text{dn}} = \overline{A}_0\overline{A}_1\overline{A}_2\overline{A}_3\overline{S}E \qquad \text{For count down}$$

The output carries supply the input for complementing the next flip-flop if the counter is extended to a fifth stage.

The logic diagram of the circuit can be easily obtained from the input equations but is not drawn here. However, the standard graphic symbol for the 4-bit up-down counter is shown in Figure 5-17. The qualifying symbol for a synchronous

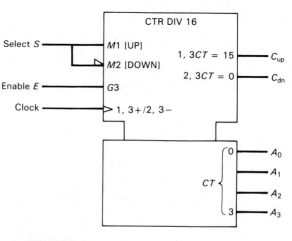

FIGURE 5-17
Graphic Symbol for a 4-Bit Up-Down Binary Counter

counter is CTR. The label DIV 16 designates a cycle length of 16 as in the binary count. There is a single select input S that is split into the two modes $M1$ and $M2$ to show the mode of operation. When input S is high, $M1$ is active and the counter counts up. When input S is low, $M2$ is active and the counter counts down. $M2$ is recognized as active-low from the polarity indicator along its input line. Note that the convention in this symbology is to recognize that a *single* input exists but this is a way of assigning to it two possible modes of operation. The count enable input uses the G dependency with the number 3. The label associated with the clock is

$$>1,3 + /2,3 -$$

The arrowhead shape symbol is the dynamic indicator signifying a positive-edge triggering. The plus ($+$) and the 1,3 associated with it indicate that $M1$ and $G3$ must be active to effect the count-up operation ($S = 1$ and $E = 1$). The count-down operation is symbolized by a minus ($-$) and is affected when $M2$ and $G3$ are active ($S = 0$ and $E = 1$). The output carry for the count up is active when $M1$ and $G3$ are active and the content of the counter is equal to 15 (binary 1111). The output carry for the count down is active when $M2$ and $G3$ are active and the contents of the counter is 0000. These conditions conform with the equations for the carries that were developed previously.

Binary Counter with Parallel Load

Counters employed in digital systems quite often require a parallel load capability for transferring an initial binary number prior to the count operation. Figure 5-18 shows the logic diagram of a register that has a parallel load capability and can also operate as a counter. The input load control when equal to 1 disables the count operation and causes a transfer of data from the four parallel inputs into the four flip-flops. If the load input is 0 and the count input is 1, the circuit operates as a binary counter. The output carry becomes a 1 if all four flip-flops are equal to 1 while the count input is enabled. This is the condition for complementing the flip-flop that contains the next significant bit. This output is useful for expanding the counter to more stages.

The operation of the circuit is summarized in Table 5-6. With the load and count inputs both at 0, the outputs do not change even when pulses are applied to the C terminals. If the load input is maintained at logic-0, the count input controls the operation of the counter and the outputs change to the next binary count for each positive transition of the clock. The input data is loaded into the flip-flops when the load control input is equal to 1 regardless of the value of the count input because the count input is inhibited when the load input is active.

TABLE 5-6
Function Table for the Register of Figure 5-18

Load	Count	Operation
0	0	No change
0	1	Count next binary state
1	X	Load inputs

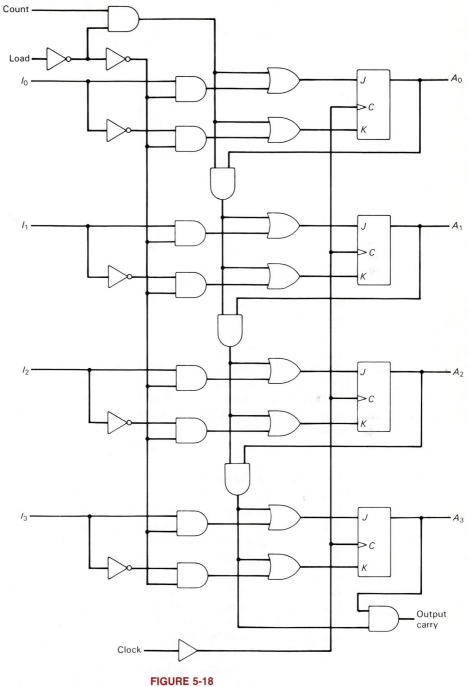

FIGURE 5-18
4-Bit Binary Counter with Parallel Load

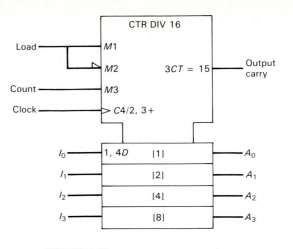

FIGURE 5-19
Graphic Symbol for a 4-Bit Binary Counter
with Parallel Load

Counters with parallel load are very useful in the design of digital computers. In subsequent chapters we will refer to them as registers with load and increment operations. The *increment* operation adds one to the contents of a register. By enabling the count input during one clock period, the content of the register can be incremented by one.

The standard graphic symbol for the 4-bit counter with parallel load is shown in Figure 5-19. The single load input is split into two modes labeled $M1$ and $M2$. When the load input is high, $M1$ is active, and when the load input is low, $M2$ is active, as indicated by the polarity symbol. The condition for counting is designated by the label associated with the clock input.

$$>C4/2,3 +$$

This means that the circuit counts up ($+$ symbol) when $M2$ and $M3$ are active (load $= 0$, and count $= 1$) and the clock in $C4$ goes through a positive transition. The parallel inputs have the label $1,4D$ meaning that the D inputs are active when $M1$ is active (load $= 1$) and the clock goes through a positive transition. The output carry is designated by the label

$$3CT = 15$$

This is interpreted to mean that the output carry is active (equal to 1) if $M3$ is active (count $= 1$) and the content (CT) of the counter is 15 (binary 1111).

The binary counter with parallel load can be converted into a synchronous BCD counter (without load input) by connecting to it an external AND gate as shown in Figure 5-20. The counter starts with an all 0's output; and the count input is active at all times. As long as the output of the AND gate is 0, $M2$ is active and each clock pulse transition increments the counter by one. When the output reaches the count of 1001, both A_0 and A_3 become 1, making the output of the AND gate equal to 1. This condition makes $M1$ active and $M2$ inactive; so on the next clock transition, the register does not count but is loaded from its four inputs. Since all

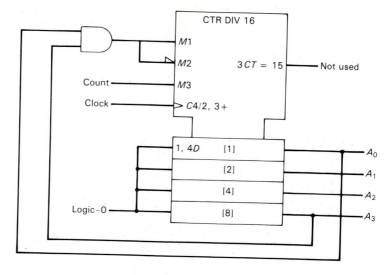

FIGURE 5-20
Synchronous BCD Counter

four inputs are connected to logic-0, an all 0's value is loaded into the register following the count of 1001. Thus the circuit counts from 0000 through 1001 and back to 0000, as is required for a BCD counter.

5-7   OTHER SYNCHRONOUS COUNTERS

Counters can be designed to generate any desired number of state sequence. A divide-by-N counter (also known as a modulo-N counter) is a counter that goes through a repeated sequence of N states. The sequence may follow the binary count or may be any other arbitrary sequence. In any case, the design of the counter follows the procedure presented in Chapter 4 for the design of synchronous sequential circuits. To demonstrate the procedure, we will present the design of two counters: One is a BCD counter and the other has an arbitrary sequence of states.

BCD Counter

A BCD counter can be obtained from a binary counter with parallel load as was shown in the previous section. It is also possible to design a BCD counter using individual flip-flops and gates. Assuming T-type flip-flops for the counter, we derive the state table and input conditions as shown in Table 5-7. The T input in each case is equal to 1 if the flip-flop is complemented during the transition from present state to next state. The T input is equal to 0 if the next state is the same as the present state. An output Y is included in the table. This output is equal to 1 when the present state is 1001. In this way, Y can enable the count of the next decade while its own decade switches from 1001 to 0000.

The flip-flop input equations are obtained from the flip-flop inputs listed in the table and can be simplified by means of maps. The unused states for minterms

TABLE 5-7
State Table and Flip-Flop Inputs for BCD Counter

Present state				Next state				Output	Flip-Flop inputs			
A_8	A_4	A_2	A_1	A_8	A_4	A_2	A_1	Y	T_{A8}	T_{A4}	T_{A2}	T_{A1}
0	0	0	0	0	0	0	1	0	0	0	0	1
0	0	0	1	0	0	1	0	0	0	0	1	1
0	0	1	0	0	0	1	1	0	0	0	0	1
0	0	1	1	0	1	0	0	0	0	1	1	1
0	1	0	0	0	1	0	1	0	0	0	0	1
0	1	0	1	0	1	1	0	0	0	0	1	1
0	1	1	0	0	1	1	1	0	0	0	0	1
0	1	1	1	1	0	0	0	0	1	1	1	1
1	0	0	0	1	0	0	1	0	0	0	0	1
1	0	0	1	0	0	0	0	1	1	0	0	1

1010 through 1111 are taken as don't care conditions. The simplified input equations for the BCD counter are

$$T_{A1} = 1$$

$$T_{A2} = A_1\overline{A}_8$$

$$T_{A4} = A_1A_2$$

$$T_{A8} = A_1A_8 + A_1A_2A_4$$

$$Y = A_1A_8$$

The circuit can be drawn with four T flip-flops, five AND gates and one OR gate. Synchronous BCD counters can be cascaded to form counters for decimal numbers of any length. The cascading is done by connecting output Y to the T inputs of the next-higher-order decade.

Arbitrary Count Sequence

We wish to design a counter that has a repeated sequence of six states as listed in Table 5-8. In this sequence, flip-flops B and C repeat the binary count 00, 01, 10, while flip-flop A alternates between 0 and 1 every three counts. The count sequence for the counter is not straight binary and two states, 011 and 111, are not included in the count. The choice of JK-type flip-flops results in the flip-flop input conditions listed in the table. Inputs K_B and K_C have only 1's and X's in their columns; so these inputs are always equal to 1. The other flip-flop input equations can be simplified using minterms 3 and 7 as don't care conditions. The simplified functions are

$$J_A = B \qquad K_A = B$$

$$J_B = C \qquad K_B = 1$$

$$J_C = \overline{B} \qquad K_C = 1$$

TABLE 5-8
State Table and Flip-Flop Inputs for Counter

Present state			Next state			Flip-Flop inputs					
A	B	C	A	B	C	J_A	K_A	J_B	K_B	J_C	K_C
0	0	0	0	0	1	0	X	0	X	1	X
0	0	1	0	1	0	0	X	1	X	X	1
0	1	0	1	0	0	1	X	X	1	0	X
1	0	0	1	0	1	X	0	0	X	1	X
1	0	1	1	1	0	X	0	1	X	X	1
1	1	0	0	0	0	X	1	X	1	0	X

The logic diagram of the counter is shown in Figure 5-21(a). Since there are two unused states, we analyze the circuit to determine their effect. The state diagram so obtained is drawn in Figure 5-21(b). If the circuit ever goes to one of the unused states, the next count pulse transfers it to one of the valid states and continues to count correctly. Thus the counter is self-correcting. A self-correcting counter is one that can start from any state and eventually reach the normal count sequence even if it starts from an unused state.

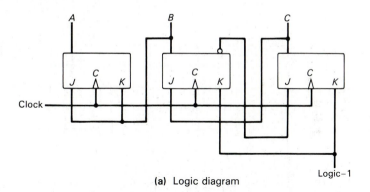

(a) Logic diagram

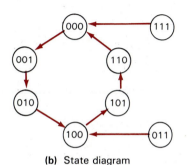

(b) State diagram

FIGURE 5-21
Counter with Arbitrary Count

Timing Sequence

The sequence of operations in a digital system is specified by a control unit. The control unit that supervises the operations in a digital system may contain special timing signals that determine the time sequence in which the operations are executed. The timing signals can be generated by means of a counter and a decoder as shown in Figure 5-22. The 2-bit binary counter goes through four distinct states. The decoder receives the output of the counter and decodes the four states into four distinct timing signals.

The timing diagram of Figure 5-22(b) shows the waveforms of the counter and decoder outputs. Each decoder output becomes active on the positive transition of the clock and stays active during one clock period. At any given time, only one

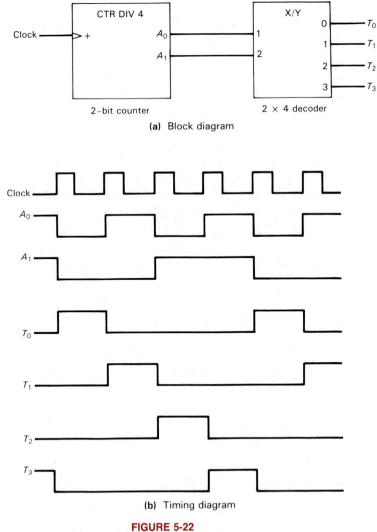

(a) Block diagram

(b) Timing diagram

FIGURE 5-22
Generation of Timing Signals

timing signal is active while the others remain inactive. The period of each timing signal is one fourth of the clock period.

The timing signals, when enabled by the clock pulses, will provide a multiple-phase clock. For example, if T_0 is ANDed with the clock, the output of the AND gate will generate clock pulses at one-fourth the frequency of the master clock. The other three decoder outputs, if ANDed with the clock, will also generate clock pulses at one-fourth frequency of the master clock but will be displaced from each other by one period. Multiple-phase clocks are useful for triggering registers with different clocks so that operations can occur at different time periods.

To generate 2^n timing signals, we need an n-bit binary counter connected to an n-to-2^n-line decoder. For example, 16 timing signals can be generated with a 4-bit binary counter and a 4-to-16-line decoder. The 16 timing signals so obtained are mutually exclusive. Only one timing signal is active at any given clock period while the other 15 signals are maintained at logic-0.

REFERENCES

1. PEATMAN, J. B. *Digital Hardware Design.* New York: McGraw-Hill, 1980.
2. BLAKESLEE, T. R. *Digital Design with Standard MSI and LSI.* 2nd ed. New York: Wiley, 1979.
3. HILL, F. J., AND PETERSON, G. R. *Digital Logic and Microprocessors.* New York: Wiley, 1984.
4. FLETCHER, W. I. *An Engineering Approach to Digital Design.* Englewood Cliffs: Prentice-Hall, 1979.
5. *IEEE Standard Graphic Symbols for Logic Functions.* (ANSI/IEEE Std 91-1984.) New York: The Institute of Electrical and Electronics Engineers.
6. KAMPEL, I. *A Practical Introduction to the New Logic Symbols.* Boston: Butterworths, 1985.
7. MANN, F. A. *Overview of IEEE Standard 91-1984.* Dallas: Texas Instruments, 1984.
8. *The TTL Data Book.* Vol 1. Dallas: Texas Instruments, 1984.

PROBLEMS

5-1 Change the AND gate in Figure 5-1(b) into a NAND gate. Explain the operation of the NAND gate for controlling the input data into the register. Draw a timing diagram showing the relationship between the two inputs and the output of the gate.

5-2 What is the purpose of the buffer gate in the clock input of the register of Figure 5-2?

5-3 Explain the purpose of the common control block when used with the standard graphic symbology.

5-4 What are the graphic symbols for (a) a polarity indicator and (b) a dynamic indicator. What do these two indicators signify?

5-5 Draw the graphic symbol of a 4-bit register with parallel load using the label $C1$ for the clock and $M2$ for the load input.

5-6 The content of a 4-bit register is initially 1101. The register is shifted six times to the right with the serial input being 101101. What is the content of the register after each shift?

5-7   What is the difference between serial and parallel transfer? Explain how to convert serial data to parallel and parallel data to serial. What type of register is needed?

5-8   The serial adder of Figure 5-6 uses two 4-bit registers. Register A holds the binary number 0101 and register B holds 0111. The carry flip-flop is initially reset to 0. List the binary values in register A and the carry flip-flop after each shift.

5-9   What changes are needed in Figure 5-6 to convert it to a serial subtractor that subtracts the content of register B from the content of register A? Explain how it is possible to detect if $A < B$. What will be the result of the subtraction if $A < B$?

5-10   Modify the register of Figure 5-7 so it will operate according to the following function table:

Shift	Load	Register operation
0	0	No change
0	1	Load parallel data
1	0	Shift down
1	1	Clear register to 0

5-11   Draw the logic diagram of a 4-bit register with mode selection inputs S_1 and S_0. The register is to be operated according to the following function table:

S_1	S_0	Register operation
0	0	No change
0	1	Complement output
1	0	Clear register to 0
1	1	Load parallel data

5-12   Draw the four stages of the bidirectional shift register with parallel load shown in Figure 5-8.

5-13   Explain all the symbols used in the standard graphic diagram of Figure 5-10.

5-14   Using external connections and the shift register from Figure 5-9, construct a bidirectional shift register (without parallel load). This can be done by connecting the outputs into the inputs in the proper order and using the load input to control the shift left operation.

5-15   (a) A ring counter is a shift register, as in Figure 5-4, with the serial output connected to the serial input. Starting from an initial state of 1000, list the sequence of states of the four flip-flops after each shift.

(b) A switch-tail ring counter uses the complement of the serial output for the serial input. Starting from an initial state of 0000, list the sequence of states after each shift until the register returns to 0000.

5-16   A flip-flop has a 10 nanosecond delay between the time its C input goes from 1 to 0 and the time the output is complemented. What is the maximum delay in a 10-bit binary ripple counter that uses these flip flops? What is the maximum frequency the counter can operate reliably?

5-17   How many flip-flops will be complemented in a 10-bit binary ripple counter to reach the next count after
(a)   1001100111.   (b)   0011111111.

5-18 Using the 4-bit binary ripple counter of Figure 5-12 and a NAND gate, construct a counter that counts from 0000 through 1011. Repeat for a count from 0000 through 0101.

5-19 Draw the logic diagram of a 4-bit ripple binary down-counter using
(a) Flip-flops that trigger on the positive transition of the clock.
(b) Flip-flops that trigger on the negative transition of the clock.

5-20 Starting from the state table of Table 5-5, obtain the simplified input equations for the synchronous binary counter with D flip-flops. Include a count enable input E.

5-21 Using sequential circuit design procedure, convert a D-type flip-flop to a T-type flip-flop. Show that what is needed is an exclusive-OR gate.

5-22 Draw the logic diagram of a 4-bit synchronous up-down binary counter with an enable input E and a mode input S. Use JK flip-flops.

5-23 Draw the graphic symbol of a 4-bit up-down binary counter shown in Figure 5-17 but remove the active-low line labeled $M2$. (Remember that S has only one input.) Modify the label associated with the clock to confirm to this change but leave the operation of the circuit the same. (You will need to use a bar over the 1 as in Figure 5-9.)

5-24 Repeat Problem 5-18 but use the synchronous binary counter of Figure 5-19.

5-25 Using two circuits of the type shown in Figure 5-19, construct a binary counter that counts from 0 through binary 64.

5-26 Verify the flip-flop input equations of the synchronous BCD counter specified in Table 5-7. Draw the logic diagram of the BCD counter and include a count enable input.

5-27 Design a synchronous BCD counter with JK flip-flops.

5-28 Design a binary counter with the following repeated binary sequence. Use JK-type flip-flops.
(a) 0, 1, 2.   (b) 0, 1, 2, 3, 4, 5, 6.

5-29 Design a counter with the following repeated binary sequence: 0, 1, 3, 7, 6, 4. Use T-type flip-flops.

5-30 Design a counter with the following repeated binary sequence: 0, 1, 2, 4, 6. Use D-type flip-flops.

5-31 Add four 2-input AND gates to the circuit of Figure 5-22(a). One input in each gate is connected to one output of the decoder. The other input in each gate is connected to the clock. Label the outputs of the AND gates P_0, P_1, P_2, and P_3. Show the timing diagram of the modified circuit.

5-32 Show the circuit and the timing diagram for generating six repeated timing signals T_0 through T_5.

MEMORY AND PROGRAMMABLE LOGIC

6-1 INTRODUCTION

A digital computer consists of three major units: the central processing unit, the memory unit, and the input-output unit. The memory unit is a device to which binary information is transferred for storage and from which information is available when needed for processing. When data processing takes place, information from the memory is first transferred to selected registers in the central processing unit. Intermediate and final results obtained in the central processing unit are transferred back to memory. Binary information received from an input device is first stored in memory and information transferred to an output device is taken from memory. A memory unit is a collection of binary cells which is capable of storing a large quantity of binary information.

There are two types of memories that communicate directly with the central processing unit: *random-access memory* (RAM) and *read-only memory* (ROM). Random-access memory can accept new information for storage to be available later for use. The process of storing new information in memory is referred to as a memory *write* operation. The process of transferring the stored information out of memory is referred to as a memory *read* operation. Random-access memory can perform both the write and read operations. Read-only memory can perform only the read operation. This means that suitable binary information is already stored inside the memory which can be retrieved or read at any time. However, the existing information cannot be altered because read-only memory can only read; it cannot write.

(a) Conventional symbol

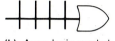
(b) Array logic symbol

FIGURE 6-1
Conventional and Array Logic Diagrams for OR Gate

Read-only memory is a *programmable logic device*. The binary information that is stored within a programmable logic device must be specified in some fashion and then embedded with the hardware. This process is referred to as *programming* the unit. The world programming here refers to a hardware procedure that specifies the bits that are inserted into the hardware configuration of the device.

Read-only memory (ROM) is one example of a programmable logic device (PLD). Other such units are the programmable logic array (PLA) and the programmable array logic (PAL). A programmable logic device is an integrated circuit with internal logic gates that are connected through electronic fuses. In the original state of the device, all the fuses are intact. Programming the device involves blowing those fuses along the paths that must be removed in order to obtain the particular configuration of the desired logic function. In this chapter we introduce the three programmable logic devices and establish procedures for their use in the design of digital systems.

A typical programmable logic device may have hundreds of gates interconnected through hundreds of internal fuses. In order to show the internal logic diagram in a concise form, it is necessary to employ a special gate symbology applicable to array logic. Figure 6-1 shows the conventional and array symbols for a multiple input OR gate. Instead of having multiple input lines to the gate, we draw a single line to the gate. The input lines are drawn perpendicular to this line and are connected to the gate through internal fuses. In a similar fashion, we can draw the array logic for an AND gate. This type of graphical representation for the inputs of gates will be used throughout this chapter when drawing array logic diagrams.

6-2 RANDOM-ACCESS MEMORY (RAM)

A memory unit is a collection of storage cells together with associated circuits needed to transfer information in and out of the device. Memory cells can be accessed for information transfer to or from any desired random location and hence the name *random-access memory*.

A memory unit stores binary information in groups of bits called *words*. A word in memory is an entity of bits that move in and out of storage as a unit. A memory word is a group of 1's and 0's and may represent a number, an instruction, one or more alphanumeric characters, or any other binary coded information. A group of eight bits is called a *byte*. Most computer memories use words that are multiples of 8 bits in length. Thus, a 16-bit word contains two bytes, and a 32-bit word is made up of four bytes. The capacity of a memory unit is usually stated as the total number of bytes that it can store.

The communication between a memory and its environment is achieved through data input and output lines, address selection lines, and control lines that specify

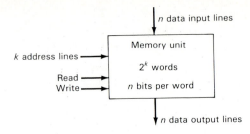

FIGURE 6-2
Block Diagram of Memory Unit

the direction of transfer. A block diagram of the memory unit is shown in Figure 6-2. The n data input lines provide the information to be stored in memory and the n data output lines supply the information coming out of memory. The k address lines specify the particular word chosen among the many available. The two control inputs specify the direction of transfer desired: The write input causes binary data to be transferred into the memory; and the read input causes binary data to be transferred out of memory.

The memory unit is specified by the number of words it contains and the number of bits in each word. The address lines select one particular word. Each word in memory is assigned an identification number called an address. Addresses range from 0 to $2^k - 1$, where k is the number of address lines. The selection of a specific word inside the memory is done by applying the k-bit binary address to the address lines. A decoder inside the memory accepts this address and opens the paths needed to select the word specified. Computer memories may range from 1024 words, requiring an address of 10 bits, to 2^{32} words, requiring 32 address bits. It is customary to refer to the number of words (or bytes) in a memory with one of the letters K (kilo), M (mega), or G (giga). K is equal to 2^{10}, M is equal to 2^{20}, and G is equal to 2^{30}. Thus, $64K = 2^{16}$, $2M = 2^{21}$, and $4G = 2^{32}$.

Consider, for example, the memory unit with a capacity of 1K words of 16 bits each. Since $1K = 1024 = 2^{10}$ and 16 bits constitute two bytes, we can say that the memory can accommodate 2048 or 2K bytes. Figure 6-3 shows the possible content of the first three and the last three words of this memory. Each word contains 16 bits which can be divided into two bytes. The words are recognized by their decimal addresses from 0 to 1023. An equivalent binary address consists of 10 bits. The first address is specified using ten 0's, and the last address is specified with ten 1's. This is because 1023 in binary is equal to 1111111111. A word in memory is selected by its binary address. When a word is read or written, the memory operates on all 16 bits as a single unit.

The $1K \times 16$ memory of Figure 6-3 has 10 bits in the address and 16 bits in each word. If we have a $64K \times 10$ memory it is necessary to include 16 bits in the address and each word will consist of 10 bits. The number of address bits needed in a memory is dependent on the total number of words that can be stored in the memory and is independent of the number of bits in each word. The number of bits in the address is determined from the relationship $2^k = m$, where m is the total number of words and k is the number of address bits.

Memory address

Binary	Decimal	Memory content
0000000000	0	1011010101011100
0000000001	1	1010101110001001
0000000010	2	0000110101000110
.	.	.
.	.	.
.	.	.
.	.	.
.	.	.
1111111101	1021	1001110100010101
1111111110	1022	0000110100011110
1111111111	1023	1101111000100100

FIGURE 6-3
Contents of a 1024 $\times$ 16 Memory

Write and Read Operations

The two operations that a random-access memory can perform are the write and read operations. The write signal specifies a transfer-in operation and the read signal specifies a transfer-out operation. On accepting one of these control signals, the internal circuits inside the memory provide the desired function. The steps that must be taken for the purpose of transferring a new word to be stored into memory are as follows:

1. Transfer the binary address of the desired word to the address lines.
2. Transfer the data bits that must be stored in memory to the data input lines.
3. Activate the *write* input.

The memory unit will then take the bits from the input data lines and store them in the word specified by the address lines.

The steps that must be taken for the purpose of transferring a stored word out of memory are as follows:

1. Transfer the binary address of the desired word to the address lines.
2. Activate the *read* input.

The memory unit will then take the bits from the word that has been selected through the address and apply them to the output data lines. The content of the selected word does not change after reading.

Commercial memory components available in integrated circuit chips sometimes provide the two control inputs for reading and writing in a somewhat different configuration. Instead of having separate read and write inputs to control the two operations, some integrated circuits provide two control inputs: one input selects the unit and the other determines the operation. The memory operations that result from these control inputs are shown in Table 6-1.

The memory select (sometimes called chip select) is used to enable the particular memory chip in a multichip implementation of a large memory. When the memory

TABLE 6-1
Control Inputs to Memory Chip

Memory select	Read/write	Memory operation
0	X	None
1	0	Write to selected word
1	1	Read from selected word

select is inactive, the memory chip is not selected and no operation can be performed. When the memory select input is active, the read/write input determines the operation to be performed.

Standard Graphic Symbol

The standard graphic symbol for the RAM is shown in Figure 6-4. The numbers 16×4 that follow the qualifying symbol RAM designate the number of words in the memory and the number of bits per word. The common control block is shown with four address lines and two control inputs. Each bit of the word is shown in a separate section with an input and output data line. The address dependency A is used to identify the address inputs of the memory. Data inputs and outputs affected by the address are labeled with the letter A. The bit grouping from 0 through 3 provide the binary address that ranges from $A0$ through $A15$.

The operation of the memory is specified by means of the dependency notation (see Section 3-8). The RAM graphic symbol uses four dependencies: A (address), G (AND), EN (enable), and C (control). Input $G1$ is to be considered ANDed with $1EN$ and $1C2$ because $G1$ has a 1 after the letter G and the other two each has a 1 in their label. The EN dependency is used to identify an enable input that controls the data outputs. The dependency $C2$ controls the inputs as indicated by the $2D$ label. Thus, for a write operation we have the $G1 - 1C2$ dependency, the

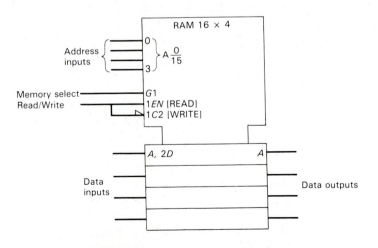

FIGURE 6-4
Standard Graphic Symbol for a 16×4 RAM

$C2 - 2D$ dependency, and the $An - A$ dependency, where n is the binary address in the four address inputs. For a read operation we have the $G1 - 1EN$ dependency and the $An - A$ dependency for the outputs. The interpretation of these dependencies results in the operation of the memory as listed in Table 6-1.

Timing Waveforms

The operation of the memory unit is controlled by an external device such as a central processing unit (CPU). The CPU is usually synchronized with its own clock pulses. The memory, however, does not employ internal clock pulses and its read and write operations are specified by the two control inputs. The *access time* of a memory is the time required to select a word and either read or write it. The CPU must provide the memory control signals in such a way as to synchronize its internal clocked operations with the read and write operations of the memory. This means that the access time of the memory must be within a time period equal to a fixed number of CPU clock pulse periods.

Assume, as an example, that a CPU operates with a clock frequency of 5 MHz, giving a period for one clock pulse of 200 nsec (1 nsec $= 10^{-9}$ seconds). Suppose now that the CPU communicates with a memory with access time that does not exceed 500 nsec. That means that the write cycle terminates the storage of the selected word within a 500 nsec interval, and that the read cycle provides the output data of the selected word within 500 nsec or less. Since the period of the CPU pulse is 200 nsec, it will be necessary to devote at least two and a half (possibly three) clock pulses to each memory request.

The memory cycle timing shown in Figure 6-5 is for a CPU with a 5 MHz clock and a memory with 500 nsec maximum access time. The write cycle in part (a) shows three 200 nsec pulses $T1$, $T2$, and $T3$. For a write operation, the CPU must provide the address and input data to the memory. This is done at the beginning of the $T1$ pulse. The two lines that cross each other in the address and data waveforms designate a possible change in value of the multiple lines. The memory select and the read/write signals must be activated after the signals in the address lines are stable to avoid destroying data in other memory words. The memory select signal switches to the high level and the read/write signal switches to the low level to indicate a write operation. The two control signals must stay active for at least 500 nsec. The address and data signals must remain stable for a short time after the control signals are deactivated. At the completion of the third clock pulse, the memory write operation is completed and the CPU can access the memory again with the next $T1$ pulse.

The read cycle shown in Figure 6-5(b) has an address for the memory which is provided by the CPU. The memory select and the read/write signals must be in their high level for a read operation. The memory places the data of the word selected by the address into the output data lines within a 500 nsec interval (or less) from the time that the memory select is activated. The CPU can transfer the data into one of its internal registers during the negative transition of the $T3$ pulse. The next $T1$ pulse is available for another memory request. Pulse $T1$ is also available for an internal CPU operation that uses the previous memory data word.

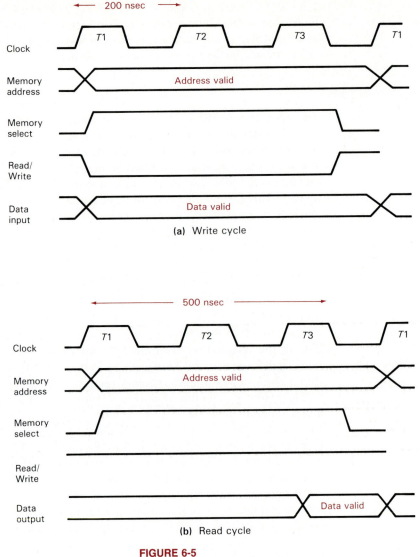

(a) Write cycle

(b) Read cycle

FIGURE 6-5
Memory Cycle Timing Waveforms

Types of Memories

The mode of access of a memory system is determined by the type of components used. In a random-access memory, the word locations may be thought of as being separated in space, with each word occupying one particular location. In a sequential-access memory, the information stored in some medium is not immediately accessible but is available only at certain intervals of time. A magnetic tape unit is of this type. Each memory location passes the read and write heads in turn, but information is read out only when the requested word has been reached. In a random-access memory, the access time is always the same regardless of the particular location of the word. In a sequential-access memory, the time it takes to access a word depends on the position of the word with respect to the reading head position and therefore, the access time is variable.

Integrated circuit RAM units are available in two possible operating modes, *static* and *dynamic*. The static RAM consists essentially of internal flip-flops that store the binary information. The stored information remains valid as long as power is applied to the unit. The dynamic RAM stores the binary information in the form of electric charges that are applied to capacitors. The capacitors are provided inside the chip by MOS transistors. The stored charge on the capacitors tends to discharge with time and the capacitors must be periodically recharged by *refreshing* the dynamic memory. Refreshing is done by cycling through the words every few milliseconds to restore the decaying charge. Dynamic RAM offers reduced power consumption and larger storage capacity in a single memory chip, but static RAM is easier to use and has shorter read and write cycles.

Memory units that lose stored information when power is turned off are said to be *volatile*. Integrated circuit RAMs, both static and dynamic, are of this category since the binary cells need external power to maintain the stored information. In contrast, a nonvolatile memory, such as magnetic disk, retains its stored information after removal of power. This is because the data stored on magnetic components is manifested by the direction of magnetization, which is retained after power is turned off. Another nonvolatile memory is the ROM discussed in Section 6-5.

A nonvolatile property is desirable in digital computers to store programs that are needed while the computer is in operation. Programs and data that cannot be altered are stored in ROM. Other large programs are maintained on magnetic disks. When power is turned on, the computer can use the programs from ROM. The other programs residing on the disks can be transferred into the computer RAM as needed. Before turning the power off, the user transfers the binary information from the computer RAM into a disk if this information must be retained.

6-3   MEMORY DECODING

In addition to the storage components in a memory unit, there is a need for decoding circuits to select the memory word specified by the input address. In this section we present the internal construction of a random-access memory and demonstrate the operation of the decoder. To be able to include the entire memory in one diagram, the memory unit presented here has a small capacity of 16 bits arranged in 4 words of 4 bits each. We then present a two-dimensional coincident decoding arrangement to show a more efficient decoding scheme which is sometimes used in large memories.

In addition to internal decoders, a memory unit may also need external decoders. This happens when integrated-circuit RAM chips are connected in a multichip memory configuration. The use of an external decoder to provide a large capacity memory will be demonstrated by means of an example.

Internal Construction

The internal construction of a random-access memory of m words and n bits per word consists of $m \times n$ binary storage cells and associated decoding circuits for selecting individual words. The binary storage cell is the basic building block of a memory unit. The equivalent logic of a binary cell that stores one bit of information is shown in Figure 6-6. Although the cell is shown to include gates and a flip-flop, internally it is constructed with two transistors having multiple inputs. A binary storage cell must be very small so that as many cells as possible can be packed into the small area available in the integrated circuit chip. The binary cell stores one bit in its internal flip-flop. The select input enables the cell for reading or writing and the read/write input determines the cell operation when it is selected. A 1 in the read/write input provides the read operation by forming a path from the flip-flop to the output terminal. A 0 in the read/write input provides the write operation by forming a path from the input terminal to the flip-flop. Note that the flip-flop operates without a clock and is similar to an SR latch.

The logical construction of a small RAM is shown in Figure 6-7. It consists of four words of four bits each and has a total of 16 binary cells. Each block labeled BC represents a binary cell with its three inputs and one output as specified in Figure 6-6(b). A memory with four words needs two address lines. The two address inputs go through a 2×4 decoder to select one of the four words. The decoder is enabled with the memory select input. When the memory select is 0, all outputs of the decoder are 0 and none of the memory words are selected. With the memory select at 1, one of the four words is selected, dictated by the value in the two address lines. Once a word has been selected, the read/write input determines the operation. During the read operation, the four bits of the selected word go through OR gates to the output terminals. (Note that the OR gates are drawn according to the array logic established in Figure 6-1.) During the write operation, the data available in the input lines are transferred into the four binary cells of the selected word. The binary cells that are not selected are disabled and their previous binary values remain unchanged. When the memory select input that goes into the decoder

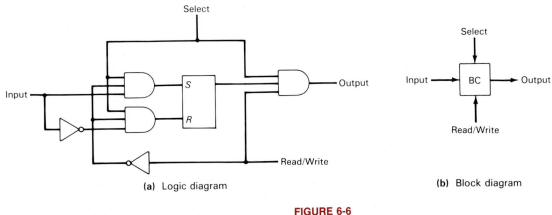

(a) Logic diagram

(b) Block diagram

FIGURE 6-6

Memory Cell

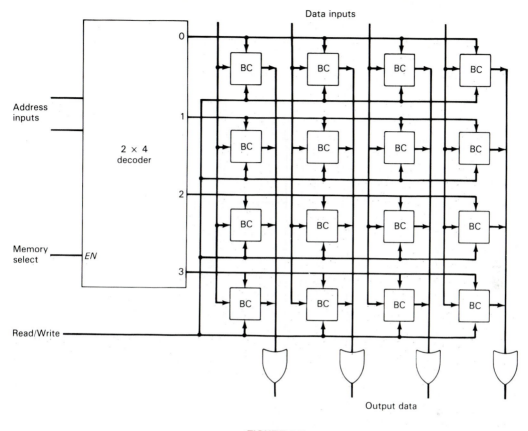

FIGURE 6-7
Diagram of a 4 × 4 RAM

is equal to 0, none of the words are selected and the contents of all cells remain unchanged regardless of the value of the read/write input.

Commercial random-access memories may have a capacity of thousands of words and each word may range from 1 to 64 bits. The logical construction of a large capacity memory would be a direct extension of the configuration shown here. A memory with 2^k words of n bits per word requires k address lines that go into a $k \times 2^k$ decoder. Each one of the decoder outputs selects one word of n bits for reading or writing.

Coincident Decoding

A decoder with k inputs and 2^k outputs requires 2^k AND gates with k inputs per gate. The total number of gates and the number of inputs per gate can be reduced by employing two decoders with a coincident selection scheme. In this configuration, two $k/2$-input decoders are used instead of one k-input decoder. One decoder performs the horizontal X-selection and the other the vertical Y-selection in a two-dimensional matrix selection scheme.

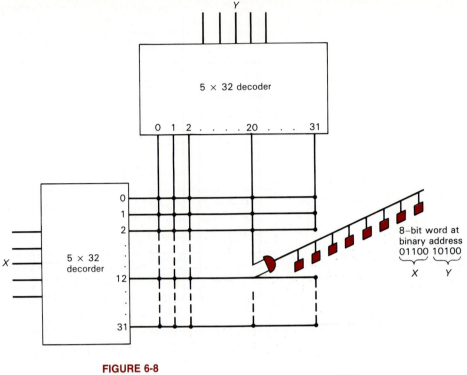

FIGURE 6-8
Two Dimensional Decoding Structure for a 1K × 8 RAM

The coincident selection pattern is demonstrated in Figure 6-8 for a 1K × 8 memory. Instead of using a single 10 × 1024 decoder, we use two 5 × 32 decoders. With the single decoder we would need 1024 AND gates with 10 inputs in each. With two decoders we only need 64 AND gates with five inputs in each. The five most significant bits of the address go to input X and the five least significant bits go to input Y. Each word of eight bits within the memory array is selected by the coincidence of one X line and one Y line. Thus, each word in memory is selected by the coincidence between one of 32 horizontal lines and one of 32 vertical lines for a total of 1024 words. As an example, consider the word with the address 404. The 10-bit binary equivalent of 404 is 01100 10100. This makes X = 01100 (binary 12) and Y = 10100 (binary 20). The 8-bit word that is selected lies in the X decoder output number 12 and the Y decoder output number 20. All eight bits of the word are selected simultaneously for reading or writing.

Array of RAM Chips

Integrated circuit RAM chips are available in a variety of sizes. If the memory unit needed for an application is larger than the capacity of one chip, it is necessary to combine a number of chips in an array to form the required memory size. The capacity of the memory depends on two parameters: the number of words and the number of bits per word. An increase in the number of words requires that we increase the address length. Every bit added to the length of the address doubles

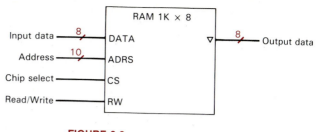

FIGURE 6-9
Block Diagram of a 1K × 8 RAM Chip

the number of words in memory. The increase in the number of bits per word requires that we increase the length of the data input and output lines, but the address length remains the same.

To demonstrate with an example, let us first introduce a typical RAM chip as shown in Figure 6-9. The capacity of the RAM is 1024 words of 8 bits each. It requires a 10-bit address and 8 input and output lines. These are shown in the block diagram by a single line and a number indicating the total number of inputs or outputs. The CS (chip select) input selects the particular RAM chip and the RW (read/write) input specifies the read or write operation when the chip is selected. The triangle symbol shown with the outputs is the standard graphic symbol for a *three-state* output. A three-state output may be in one of three possible states: a signal equivalent to binary 0, a signal equivalent to binary 1, or a high-impedance state. The high-impedance state behaves like an open circuit: it does not carry any signal and does not have a logic significance. The CS input of the RAM controls the behavior of the data output lines. When $CS = 0$, the chip is not selected and all its data outputs are in the high-impedance state. With $CS = 1$ and $RW = 1$, the data output lines carry the eight bits of the selected word.

Suppose that we want to increase the number of words in the memory by using two or more RAM chips. Since every bit added to the address doubles the binary number that can be formed, it is natural to increase the number of words in factors of two. For example, two RAM chips will double the number of words and add one bit to the composite address. Four RAM chips multiply the number of words by four and add two bits to the composite address.

Consider the possibility of constructing a 4K × 8 RAM with four 1K × 8 RAM chips. This is shown in Figure 6-10. The 8 input data lines go to all the chips. The three-state outputs can be connected together to form the common 8 output data lines. This type of output connection is possible only with three-state outputs. This is because only one chip select input will be active at any time while the other three chips will be disabled. The 8 outputs of the selected chip will contain 1's and 0's, and the other three will be in a high-impedance state with no logic significance to disturb the output binary signals of the selected chip.

The 4K word memory requires a 12-bit address. The 10 least significant bits of the address are applied to the address inputs of all four chips. The other two most significant bits are applied to a 2 × 4 decoder. The four outputs of the decoder are applied to the CS inputs of each chip. The memory is disabled when the enable input of the decoder is equal to 0. This causes all four outputs of the decoder to

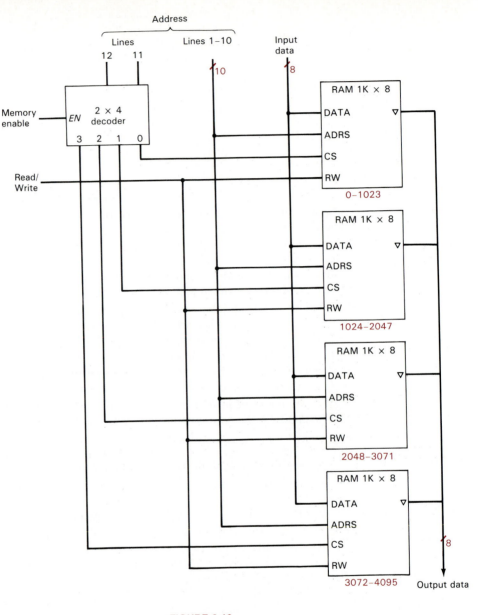

FIGURE 6-10
Block Diagram of 4K × 8 RAM

be in the 0 state and none of the chips are selected. When the decoder is enabled, address bits 12 and 11 determine the particular chip that is selected. If bits 12 and 11 are equal to 00, the first RAM chip is selected. The remaining ten address bits select a word within the chip in the range from 0 to 1023. The next 1024 words are selected from the second RAM chip with a 12-bit address that starts with 01 and follows by the ten bits from the common address lines. The address range for each chip is listed in decimal under its block diagram in Figure 6-10.

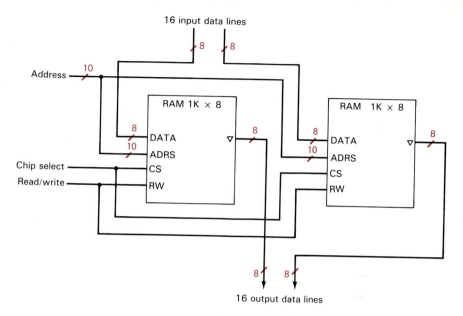

FIGURE 6-11
Block Diagram of 1K × 16 RAM

It is also possible to combine two chips to form a composite memory containing the same number of words but with twice as many bits in each word. Figure 6-11 shows the interconnection of two 1K × 8 chips to form a 1K × 16 memory. The 16 input and output data lines are split between the two chips. Both receive the same 10-bit address and the common *CS* and *RW* control inputs.

The two techniques just described may be combined to assemble an array of identical chips into a large capacity memory. The composite memory will have a number of bits per word that is a multiple of that for one chip. The total number of words will increase in factors of two times the word capacity of one chip. An external decoder is needed to select the individual chips from the additional address bits of the composite memory.

To reduce the number of pins in the package, many RAM integrated circuits provide common terminals for the input data and output data. The common terminals are said to be *bidirectional* which means that for the read operation they act as outputs and for the write operation they act as inputs. Bidirectional lines are constructed with three-state buffers and are discussed further in Section 7-4.

6-4 ERROR DETECTION AND CORRECTION

The complexity level of a memory array may cause occasional errors in storing and retrieving the binary information. The reliability of a memory unit may be improved by employing error-detecting and correcting codes. The most common error-detection scheme is the parity bit. (See Section 2-7.) A parity bit is generated and stored along with the data word in memory. The parity of the word is checked after reading it from memory. The data word is accepted if the parity sense is correct.

If the parity checked results in an inversion, an error is detected but it cannot be corrected.

An error-correcting code generates multiple check bits that are stored with the data word in memory. Each check bit is a parity over a group of bits in the data word. When the word is read back from memory, the associated parity bits are also read and compared with a new set of check bits generated from the read data. If the check bits compare, it signifies that no error has occurred. If the check bits do not compare with the stored parity, they generate a unique pattern called a *syndrome* that can be used to identify the bit in error. A single error occurs when a bit changes in value from 1 to 0 or from 0 to 1 during the write or read operation. If the specific bit in error is identified, then the error can be corrected by complementing the erroneous bit.

Hamming Code

One of the most common error-correcting codes used in random-access memories was devised by R. W. Hamming. In the Hamming code, k parity bits are added to an n-bit data word, forming a new word of $n + k$ bits. The bit positions are numbered in sequence from 1 to $n + k$. Those positions numbered as a power of 2 are reserved for the parity bits. The remaining bits are the data bits. The code can be used with words of any length. Before giving the general characteristics of the code, we will illustrate its operation with a data word of eight bits.

Consider for example the 8-bit data word 11000100. We include 4 parity bits with the 8-bit word and arrange the 12 bits as follows:

Bit position	1	2	3	4	5	6	7	8	9	10	11	12
	P_1	P_2	1	P_4	1	0	0	P_8	0	1	0	0

The four parity bits P_1 through P_8 are in positions 1, 2, 4, and 8. The eight bits of the data word are in the remaining positions. Each parity bit is calculated as follows:

$$P_1 = \text{XOR of bits } (3, 5, 7, 9, 11) = 1 \oplus 1 \oplus 0 \oplus 0 \oplus 0 = 0$$

$$P_2 = \text{XOR of bits } (3, 6, 7, 10, 11) = 1 \oplus 0 \oplus 0 \oplus 1 \oplus 0 = 0$$

$$P_4 = \text{XOR of bits } (5, 6, 7, 12) = 1 \oplus 0 \oplus 0 \oplus 0 = 1$$

$$P_8 = \text{XOR of bits } (9, 10, 11, 12) = 0 \oplus 1 \oplus 0 \oplus 0 = 1$$

Remember that the exclusive-OR operation performs the odd function. It is equal to 1 for an odd number of 1's in the variables and to 0 for an even number of 1's. Thus, each parity bit is set so that the total number of 1's in the checked positions, including the parity bit, is always even.

The 8-bit data word is stored in memory with the 4 parity bits as a 12-bit composite word. Substituting the four P bits in their proper positions, we obtain the 12-bit composite word stored in memory.

Bit position	1	2	3	4	5	6	7	8	9	10	11	12
	0	0	1	1	1	0	0	1	0	1	0	0

When the 12 bits are read from memory they are checked again for possible errors. The parity is checked over the same combination of bits including the parity bit. The four check bits are evaluated as follows:

$$C_1 = \text{XOR of bits } (1, 3, 5, 7, 9, 11)$$

$$C_2 = \text{XOR of bits } (2, 3, 6, 7, 10, 11)$$

$$C_4 = \text{XOR of bits } (4, 5, 6, 7, 12)$$

$$C_8 = \text{XOR of bits } (8, 9, 10, 11, 12)$$

A 0 check bit designates a even parity over the checked bits and a 1 designates an odd parity. Since the bits were stored with even parity, the result $C = C_8 C_4 C_2 C_1$ = 0000 indicates that no error has occurred. However, if $C \neq 0$, the 4-bit binary number formed by the check bits gives the position of the erroneous bit. For example, consider the following three cases:

Bit Position	1	2	3	4	5	6	7	8	9	10	11	12	
	0	0	1	1	1	0	0	1	0	1	0	0	No error
	1	0	1	1	1	0	0	1	0	1	0	0	Error in bit 1
	0	0	1	1	0	0	0	1	0	1	0	0	Error in bit 5

In the first case, there is no error in the 12-bit word. In the second case there is an error in bit position number 1 because it changed from 0 to 1. The third case shows an error in bit position 5 with a change from 1 to 0. Evaluating the XOR of the corresponding bits we determine the four check bits to be as follows:

	C_8	C_4	C_2	C_1
No error	0	0	0	0
Error in bit 1	0	0	0	1
Error in bit 5	0	1	0	1

Thus, for no error we have $C = 0000$; with an error in bit 1 we obtain $C = 0001$; and with an error in bit 5 we get $C = 0101$. The binary number of C, when it is not equal to 0000, gives the position of the bit in error. The error can be corrected by complementing the corresponding bit. Note that an error can occur in the data word or in one of the parity bits.

The Hamming code can be used for data words of any length. In general, for k check bits and n data bits, the total number of bits $(n + k)$ that can be accommodated in a coded word is $2^k - 1$. In other words, the relationship $n + k = 2^k - 1$ must hold. This gives $n = 2^k - 1 - k$ (or less) as the number of bits for the data word. For example, when $k = 3$, the total number of bits in the coded word is $n + k = 2^3 - 1 = 7$, giving $n = 7 - 3 = 4$. For $k = 4$, we have $n + k = 15$, giving $n = 11$. The data word may be less than 11 bits but must have at least 5 bits; otherwise, only three check bits will be needed. This justifies the use of 4 check bits for the 8 data bits in the previous example.

The grouping of bits for parity generation and checking can be determined from a list of the binary numbers from 0 through $2^k - 1$. (Table 1-2 gives such a list).

The least significant bit is a 1 in the binary numbers 1, 3, 5, 7, and so on. The second significant bit is a 1 in the binary numbers 2, 3, 6, 7, and so on. Comparing these numbers with the bit positions used in generating and checking parity bits in the Hamming code, we note the relationship between the bit groupings in the code and the position of the 1-bits in the binary count sequence. Note that each group of bits starts with a number that is a power of 2, for example, 1, 2, 4, 8, 16, and so forth. These numbers are also the position number for the parity bits.

The Hamming code can detect and correct only a single error. Multiple errors are not detected. By adding another parity bit to the coded word, the Hamming code can be used to correct a single error and detect double errors. If we include this additional parity bit, the previous 12-bit coded word becomes $001110010100P_{13}$ where P_{13} is evaluated from the exclusive-OR of the other 12 bits. This produces the 13-bit word 0011100101001 (even parity). When the 13-bit word is read from memory, the check bits are evaluated and also the parity P over the entire 13 bits. If $P = 0$, the parity is correct (even parity), but if $P = 1$, the parity over the 13 bits is incorrect (odd parity). The following four cases can occur:

If $C = 0$ and $P = 0$ No error occurred

If $C \neq 0$ and $P = 1$ A single error occurred which can be corrected.

If $C \neq 0$ and $P = 0$ A double error occurred which is detected but cannot be corrected.

If $C = 0$ and $P = 1$ An error occurred in the P_{13} bit.

Note that this scheme cannot detect more than two errors.

Integrated circuits are available commercially that use a modified Hamming code to generate and check parity bits for a single-error-correction double-error-detection scheme. One that uses an 8-bit data word and a 5-bit check word is IC type 74637. Other integrated circuits are available for data words of 16 and 32 bits. These circuits can be used in conjunction with a memory unit to correct a single error or detect double errors during the write or read operations.

6-5   READ-ONLY MEMORY (ROM)

A read-only memory (ROM) is essentially a memory device in which permanent binary information is stored. The binary information must be specified by the designer and is then embedded in the unit to form the required interconnection pattern. ROMs come with special internal electronic fuses that can be "programmed" for a specific configuration. Once the pattern is established, it stays within the unit even when power is turned off and on again.

A block diagram of a ROM is shown in Figure 6-12. It consists of k inputs and n outputs. The inputs provide the address for the memory and the outputs give

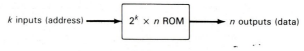

FIGURE 6-12
ROM Block Diagram

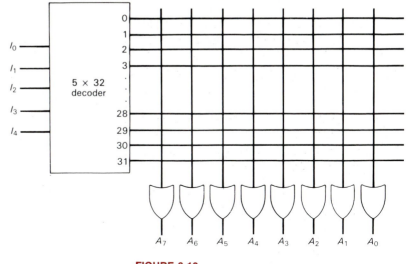

FIGURE 6-13
Internal Logic of a 32 × 8 ROM

the data bits of the stored word which is selected by the address. The number of words in a ROM is determined from the fact that k address input lines are needed to specify 2^k words. Note that the ROM does not have data inputs because it does not have a write operation. Integrated circuit ROM chips have one or more enable inputs and come with three-state outputs to facilitate the construction of large arrays of read-only memories.

Consider for example a 32 × 8 ROM. The unit consists of 32 words of 8 bits each. There are 5 input lines that form the binary numbers from 0 through 31 for the address. Figure 6-13 shows the internal logic construction of the ROM. The five inputs are decoded into 32 distinct outputs by means of a 5 × 32 decoder. Each output of the decoder represents a memory address. The 32 outputs of the decoder are connected through fuses to each of the eight OR gates. The diagram shows the array logic convention used in complex circuits (see Figure 6-1). Each OR gate must be considered as having 32 inputs. Each output of the decoder is connected through a fuse to one of the inputs of each OR gate. Since each OR gate has 32 internal fuses and there are 8 OR gates, the ROM contains 32 × 8 = 256 internal fuselinks. In general, a $2^k \times n$ ROM will have an internal $k \times 2^k$ decoder and n OR gates. Each OR gate has 2^k inputs which are connected through fuses to each of the outputs of the decoder.

The internal binary storage of a ROM is specified by a truth table that shows the word content in each address. For example, the content of a 32 × 8 ROM may be specified with a truth table similar to the one shown in Table 6-2. The truth table shows the five inputs under which are listed all 32 addresses. Each input specifies the address of a word of 8 bits whose value is listed under the output columns. Table 6-2 shows only the first four and the last four words in the ROM. The complete table must include the list of all 32 words.

The hardware procedure that programs the ROM results in blowing internal fuses according to a given truth table. For example, programming the ROM ac-

TABLE 6-2
ROM Truth Table (Partial)

Inputs					Outputs							
I_4	I_3	I_2	I_1	I_0	A_7	A_6	A_5	A_4	A_3	A_2	A_1	A_0
0	0	0	0	0	1	0	1	1	0	1	1	0
0	0	0	0	1	0	0	0	1	1	1	0	1
0	0	0	1	0	1	1	0	0	0	1	0	1
0	0	0	1	1	1	0	1	1	0	0	1	0
⋮								⋮				
1	1	1	0	0	0	0	0	0	1	0	0	1
1	1	1	0	1	1	1	1	0	0	0	1	0
1	1	1	1	0	0	1	0	0	1	0	1	0
1	1	1	1	1	0	0	1	1	0	0	1	1

cording to the truth table given by Table 6-2 results in the configuration shown in Figure 6-14. Every 0 listed in the truth table specifies a fuse to be blown and every 1 listed specifies a path that is obtained by an intact fuse. As an example, the table specifies the 8-bit word 10110010 for permanent storage at input address 00011. The four 0's in the word are programmed by blowing the fuses between output 3 of the decoder and the inputs of the OR gates associated with outputs A_6, A_3, A_2, and A_0. The four 1's in the word are marked in the diagram with a cross to designate an intact fuse. When the input of the ROM is 00011, all the outputs of the decoder are 0 except output 3 which is at logic-1. The signal equivalent to logic-1 at decoder output 3 propagates through the fuses and the OR gates to outputs A_7, A_5, A_4,

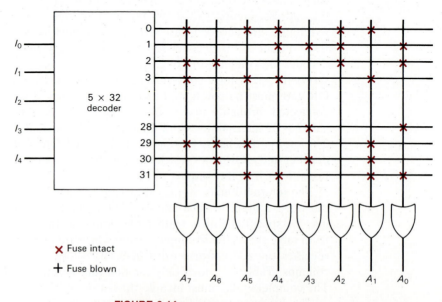

FIGURE 6-14
Programming the ROM According to Table 6-2

and A_1. The other four outputs remain at 0. The result is that the stored word 10110010 is applied to the eight data outputs.

Types of ROMs

The required paths in a ROM may be programmed in three different ways. The first is called *mask programming* and is done by the semiconductor company during the last fabrication process of the unit. The procedure for fabricating a ROM requires that the customer fill out the truth table he wishes the ROM to satisfy. The truth table may be submitted on a special form provided by the manufacturer or in a specified format on a computer output medium. The manufacturer makes the corresponding mask for the paths to produce the 1's and 0's according to the customer's truth table. This procedure is costly because the vendor charges the customer a special fee for custom masking the particular ROM. For this reason, mask programming is economical only if a large quantity of the same ROM configuration is to be ordered.

For small quantities, it is more economical to use a second type of ROM called a *programmable read-only memory* or PROM. When ordered, PROM units contain all the fuses intact giving all 1's in the bits of the stored words. The fuses in the PROM are blown by application of current pulses through the output terminals for each address. A blown fuse defines a binary 0 state and an intact fuse gives a binary 1 state. This allows the user to program the PROM in his own laboratory to achieve the desired relationship between input addresses and stored words. Special instruments called *PROM programmers* are available commercially to facilitate this procedure. In any case, all procedures for programming ROMs are hardware procedures even though the word programming is used. The hardware procedure for programming ROMs or PROMs is irreversible and, once programmed, the fixed pattern is permanent. Once a bit pattern has been established, the unit must be discarded if the bit pattern is to be changed.

A third type of ROM available is called *erasable PROM* or EPROM. The EPROM can be restructured to the initial value even though its fuses have been blown previously. When the EPROM is placed under a special ultraviolet light for a given period of time, the short wave radiation discharges the internal gates that serve as fuses. After erasure, the EPROM returns to its initial state and can be reprogrammed to a new set of words. Certain PROMs can be erased with electrical signals instead of ultraviolet light. These PROMs are called *electrically erasable PROM* or EEPROM.

Combinational Circuit Implementation

It was shown in Section 3-5 that a decoder generates the 2^k minterms of the k input variables. By inserting OR gates to sum the minterms of Boolean functions, we were able to generate any desired combinational circuit. The ROM is essentially a device that includes both the decoder and the OR gates within a single unit. By leaving intact the fuses of those minterms that are included in the function, the ROM outputs can be programmed to represent the Boolean functions of the output variables in a combinational circuit.

The internal operation of a ROM can be interpreted in two ways. The first interpretation is that of a memory unit that contains a fixed pattern of stored words. The second interpretation is of a unit that implements a combinational circuit. From this point of view, each output terminal is considered separately as the output of a Boolean function expressed as a sum of minterms. For example, the ROM of Figure 6-14 may be considered as a combinational circuit with eight outputs, each being a function of the five input variables. Output A_7 can be expressed as a sum of minterms as follows. (The three dots represent minterms 4 through 27 which are not specified in the figure.)

$$A_7(I_4, I_3, I_2, I_1, I_0) = \Sigma\, m(0, 2, 3, \ldots, 29)$$

An intact fuse produces a minterm for the sum and a blown fuse removes the minterm from the sum.

ROMs are widely used to implement complex combinational circuits directly from their truth table. They are useful for converting from one alphanumeric code, such as ASCII, to another, like EBCDIC. They can generate complex arithmetic operations such as multiplication or division, and in general, they are used in applications requiring a large number of inputs and outputs.

In practice, when a combinational circuit is designed by means of a ROM, it is not necessary to design the logic or to show the internal gate connections of fuses inside the unit. All that the designer has to do is specify the particular ROM by its IC number and provide the ROM truth table. The truth table gives all the information for programming the ROM. No internal logic diagram is needed to accompany the truth table.

Example 6-1

Design a combinational circuit using a ROM. The circuit accepts a 3-bit number and generates an output binary number equal to the square of the input number.

The first step is to derive the truth table of the combinational circuit. In most cases this is all that is needed. In other cases, we can use a partial truth table for the ROM by utilizing certain properties in the output variables. Table 6-3 is the truth table for the combinational circuit. Three inputs and six outputs are needed to accommodate all possible binary numbers. We note that output B_0 is always

TABLE 6-3
Truth Table for Circuit of Example 6-1

Inputs			Outputs						Decimal
A_2	A_1	A_0	B_5	B_4	B_3	B_2	B_1	B_0	
0	0	0	0	0	0	0	0	0	0
0	0	1	0	0	0	0	0	1	1
0	1	0	0	0	0	1	0	0	4
0	1	1	0	0	1	0	0	1	9
1	0	0	0	1	0	0	0	0	16
1	0	1	0	1	1	0	0	1	25
1	1	0	1	0	0	1	0	0	36
1	1	1	1	1	0	0	0	1	49

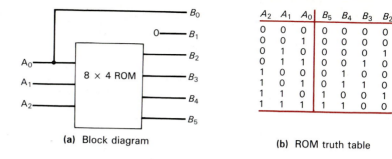

(a) Block diagram

A_2	A_1	A_0	B_5	B_4	B_3	B_2
0	0	0	0	0	0	0
0	0	1	0	0	0	0
0	1	0	0	0	0	1
0	1	1	0	0	1	0
1	0	0	0	1	0	0
1	0	1	0	1	1	0
1	1	0	1	0	0	1
1	1	1	1	1	0	0

(b) ROM truth table

FIGURE 6-15

ROM Implementation of Example 6-1

equal to input A_0; so there is no need to generate B_0 with a ROM. Moreover, output B_1 is always 0; so this output is a known constant. We actually need to generate only four outputs with the ROM; the other two are readily obtained. The minimum size ROM needed must have three inputs and four outputs. Three inputs specify eight words; so the ROM must be of size 8×4. The ROM implementation is shown in Figure 6-15. The three inputs specify eight words of four bits each. The truth table in Figure 6-15(b) specifies the information needed for programming the ROM. The block diagram of Figure 6-15(a) shows the required connections of the combinational circuit.

The previous example is too simple for actual implementation with a ROM. It is presented here for illustration purposes only. The design of complex combinational circuits with a ROM requires that we determine the number of inputs and outputs of the circuit. The size of ROM needed to implement the circuit is at least $2^k \times n$, where k is the number of inputs and n is the number of outputs. The truth table accompanying the ROM must list the 2^k binary addresses and provide the n-bit word for each address.

6-6   PROGRAMMABLE LOGIC DEVICE (PLD)

A programmable logic device (PLD) is an integrated circuit with an array of gates that are connected by programming fuses. The designer can specify the internal logic by means of a table or a list of Boolean functions. These specifications are then translated into a fuse pattern required to program the device. The gates in a PLD are divided into an AND array and an OR array to provide an AND-OR sum of products implementation. The initial state of a PLD has all the fuses intact. Programming the device involves the blowing of internal fuses to achieve a desired logic function.

There are three major types of PLDs and they differ in the placement of fuses in the AND-OR array. Figure 6-16 shows the fuse locations of the three PLDs. The programmable read-only memory (PROM) has a fixed AND array constructed as a decoder and programmable fuses for the output OR gates. The PROM implements Boolean functions in sum of minterms. The programmable array logic (PAL) has a fused programmable AND array and a fixed OR array. The AND

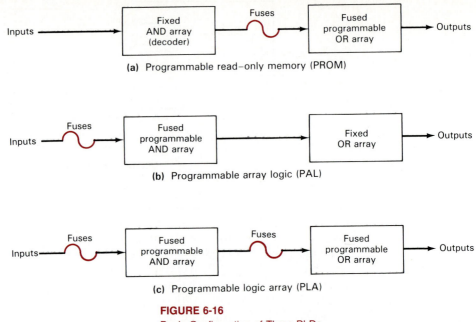

FIGURE 6-16
Basic Configuration of Three PLDs

gates are programmed to provide the product terms for the Boolean functions which are logically summed in each OR gate. The most flexible PLD is the programmable logic array (PLA) where both the AND and OR arrays can be programmed. The product terms in the AND array may be shared by any OR gate to provide the required sum of products implementation. The names PAL and PLA emerged from different vendors during the development of programmable logic devices. The implementation of combinational circuits with a PROM was demonstrated in the previous section. The design of combinational circuits with PLA and PAL is presented in the next two sections.

Some PLDs include flip-flops within the integrated circuit chip in addition to the AND and OR arrays. The result is a sequential circuit as shown in Figure 6-17. A PAL or a PLA may include a number of flip-flops connected by fuses to form the sequential circuit. The circuit outputs can be taken from the OR gates or from the outputs of the flip-flops. Additional programmable fuses are available to include the flip-flop variables in the product terms formed with the AND array. The flip-flops may be of the D or the JK type.

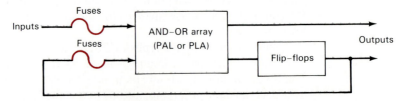

FIGURE 6-17
Sequential Programmable Logic Device

The advantage of using the PLD in the design of digital systems is that it can be programmed to incorporate a complex logic function within one integrated circuit. The use of programmable logic devices is an alternative to another design technology called VLSI (very large scale integration) design. VLSI design refers to the design of digital systems that contain thousands of gates within a single integrated circuit chip. The basic component used in VLSI design is the *gate array*. A gate array consists of a pattern of gates fabricated in an area of silicon which is repeated thousands of times until the entire chip is covered with identical gates. Arrays of one thousand to ten thousand gates can be fabricated within a single integrated-circuit chip depending on the technology used. The design with gate arrays requires that the designer specifies the layout of the chip and the way that the gates are routed and connected. The first few levels of fabrication process are common and independent of the final logic function. Additional fabrication levels are required to interconnect the gates in order to realize the desired function. This is usually done by means of computer aided design (CAD) methods. Both the gate array and the programmable logic device require extensive computer software tools to facilitate the design procedure.

6-7   PROGRAMMABLE LOGIC ARRAY (PLA)

The PLA is similar to the PROM in concept except that the PLA does not provide full decoding of the variables and does not generate all the minterms. The decoder is replaced by an array of AND gates that can be programmed to generate any product term of the input variables. The product terms are then connected to OR gates to provide the sum of products for the required Boolean functions.

The internal logic of a PLA with three inputs and two outputs is shown in Figure 6-18. Such a circuit is too small to be available commercially but is presented here to demonstrate the typical logic configuration of a PLA. The diagram uses the array logic graphic symbols for complex circuits. Each input goes through a buffer and an inverter shown in the diagram with a composite graphic symbol that has both the true and complement outputs. Each input and its complement are connected through fuses to the inputs of each AND gate as indicated by the intersections between the vertical and horizontal lines. The outputs of the AND gates are connected by fuses to the inputs of each OR gate. The output of the OR gate goes to an XOR gate where the other input can be programmed to receive a signal equal to either logic-1 or logic-0. The output is inverted when the XOR input is connected to 1 (since $X \oplus 1 = \overline{X}$). The output does not change when the XOR input is connected to 0 (since $X \oplus 0 = X$). The particular Boolean functions implemented in the PLA of Figure 6-18 are

$$F_1 = A\overline{B} + AC + \overline{A}B\overline{C}$$

$$\overline{F_2} = AC + BC$$

The product terms generated in each AND gate are listed along the output of the gate in the diagram. The product term is determined from the inputs with intact fuses. The output of an OR gate gives the logic sum of the selected product terms.

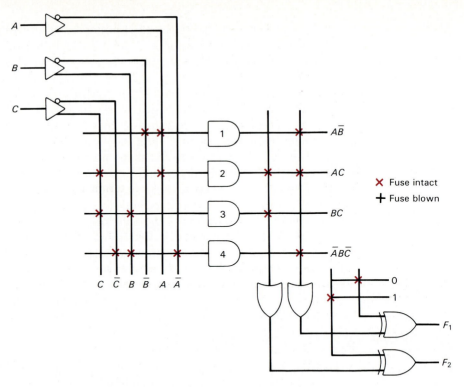

FIGURE 6-18
PLA with 3 Inputs, 4 Product Terms, and 2 Outputs

The output may be complemented or left in its true form depending on the fuses associated with the XOR gate.

The fuse map of a PLA can be specified in a tabular form. For example, the programming table that specifies the fusing of the PLA of Figure 6-18 is listed in Table 6-4. The PLA programming table consists of three sections. The first section lists the product terms numerically. The second section specifies the required paths between inputs and AND gates. The third section specifies the paths between the AND and OR gates. For each output variable we may have a T (for true) or C (for complement). The product terms listed on the left are not part of the table;

TABLE 6-4
PLA Programming Table

	Product term	Inputs			Outputs	
		A	B	C	(T) F_1	(C) F_2
$A\bar{B}$	1	1	0	—	1	—
AC	2	1	—	1	1	1
BC	3	—	1	1	—	1
$\bar{A}B\bar{C}$	4	0	1	0	1	—

they are included for reference only. For each product term, the inputs are marked with 1, 0, or — (dash). If a variable in the product term appears in its true form, the corresponding input variable is marked with a 1. If it appears complemented, the corresponding input variable is marked with a 0. If the variable is absent in the product term, it is marked with a dash.

The paths between the inputs and the AND gates are specified under the column heading *inputs* in the programming table. A 1 in the input column specifies an intact fuse from the input variable to the AND gate. A 0 in the input column specifies an intact fuse from the complement of the variable to the input of the AND gate. A dash specifies a blown fuse in both the input variable and its complement. It is assumed that an open terminal in the input of an AND gate behaves like a 1.

The paths between the AND and OR gates are specified under the column heading *outputs*. The output variables are marked with 1's for those product terms that are included in the function. Each product term that has a 1 in the output column requires a path from the output of the AND gate to the input of the OR gate. Those marked with a dash specify a blown fuse. It is assumed that an open terminal in the input of an OR gate behaves like a 0. Finally, a T (true) output dictates that the other input of the corresponding XOR gate be connected to 0, and a C (complement) specifies a connection to 1.

The size of a PLA is specified by the number of inputs, the number of product terms and the number of outputs. A typical integrated circuit PLA may have 16 inputs, 48 product terms, and 8 outputs. For n inputs, k product terms, and m outputs the internal logic of the PLA consists of n buffer-inverter gates, k AND gates, m OR gates, and m XOR gates. There are $2n \times k$ fuses between the inputs and the AND array; $k \times m$ fuses between the AND and OR arrays; and m fuses associated with the XOR gates.

When designing a digital system with a PLA, there is no need to show the internal connections of the unit as was done in Figure 6-18. All that is needed is a PLA programming table from which the PLA can be programmed to supply the required logic. As with a ROM, the PLA may be mask programmable or field programmable. With mask programming, the customer submits a PLA program table to the manufacturer. This table is used by the vendor to produce a custom-made PLA that has the required internal logic specified by the customer. A second type of PLA available is called a *field programmable logic array* or FPLA. The FPLA can be programmed by the user by means of certain recommended procedures. Commercial hardware programmer units are available for use in conjunction with FPLAs.

When implementing a combinational circuit with PLA, careful investigation must be undertaken in order to reduce the number of distinct product terms, since a PLA has a finite number of AND gates. This can be done by simplifying each Boolean function to a minimum number of terms. The number of literals in a term is not important since all the input variables are available anyway. Both the true and complement of the function should be simplified to see which one can be expressed with fewer product terms and which one provides product terms that are common to other functions.

Example 6-2   Implement the following two Boolean functions with a PLA.

$$F_1(A, B, C) = \Sigma\, m(0, 1, 2, 4)$$

$$F_2(A, B, C) = \Sigma\, m(0, 5, 6, 7)$$

The two functions are simplified in the maps of Figure 6-19. Both the true and complement of the functions are simplified in sum of products. The combination that gives a minimum number of product terms is

$$F_1 = \overline{AB + AC + BC}$$

$$F_2 = AB + AC + \overline{A}\,\overline{B}\,\overline{C}$$

This gives four distinct product terms: AB, AC, BC, and $\overline{A}\,\overline{B}\,\overline{C}$. The PLA programming table for this combination is shown in Figure 6-19. Note that output F_1 is the true output even though a C is marked over it in the table. This is because $\overline{F}_1$ is generated with an AND-OR circuit and is available at the output of the OR gate. The XOR gate complements the function to produce the true F_1 output.

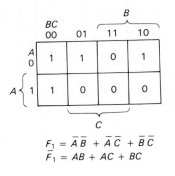

$$F_1 = \overline{A}\,\overline{B} + \overline{A}\,\overline{C} + \overline{B}\,\overline{C}$$
$$\overline{F}_1 = AB + AC + BC$$

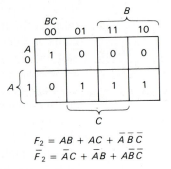

$$F_2 = AB + AC + \overline{A}\,\overline{B}\,\overline{C}$$
$$\overline{F}_2 = \overline{A}C + \overline{A}B + AB\overline{C}$$

PLA programming table

Product term	Inputs A B C	Outputs (C) F_1	Outputs (T) F_2
AB	1 1 1 −	1	1
AC	2 1 − 1	1	1
BC	3 − 1 1	1	−
$\overline{A}\,\overline{B}\,\overline{C}$	4 0 0 0	−	1

FIGURE 6-19
Solution to Example 6-2

The combinational circuit used in Example 6-2 is too simple for implementing with a PLA. It was presented here merely for demonstration purposes. A typical commercial PLA has over 10 inputs and 50 product terms. The simplification of Boolean functions with so many variables should be carried out by means of computer assisted simplification procedures. This is where computer software is of help in the design of complex digital systems. The computer aided design program must simplify each function and its complement to a minimum number of terms. The program then selects a minimum number of product terms that cover all functions in their true or complement form. The PLA programming table is then generated from which is obtained the required fuse map. The fuse map is applied to an FPLA programmer that goes through the hardware procedure of blowing the internal fuses in the integrated circuit.

6-8 PROGRAMMABLE ARRAY LOGIC (PAL)

The PAL is a programmable logic device with a fixed OR array and programmable AND array. Because only the AND gates are programmable, the PAL is easier to program but is not as flexible as the PLA. Figure 6-20 shows the logic configuration of a typical PAL. It has four inputs and four outputs. Each input has a buffer-inverter gate, and each output is generated by a fixed OR gate. There are four sections in the unit, each composed of a 3-wide AND-OR array. This is the term used to indicate that there are three programmable AND gates in each section. Each AND gate has 10 fused programmable inputs. This is shown in the diagram with 10 vertical lines intersecting each horizontal line. The horizontal line symbolizes the multiple input configuration of the AND gate. One of the outputs is connected to a buffer-inverter gate and then fed back into the inputs of the AND gates through fuses.

Commercial PAL devices contain more gates than the one shown in Figure 6-20. A typical PAL integrated circuit may have eight inputs, eight outputs, and eight sections each consisting of an 8-wide AND-OR array. The output terminals are sometimes bidirectional which means that they can be programmed as inputs instead of outputs if desired. Some PAL units incorporate D-type flip-flops in the outputs. The outputs of the flip-flops are fed back through a buffer-inverter gate into the AND programmed array. This provides a capability for implementing sequential circuits.

When designing with a PAL, the Boolean functions must be simplified to fit into each section. Unlike the PLA, a product term cannot be shared among two or more OR gates. Therefore, each function can be simplified by itself without regard to common product terms. The number of product terms in each section is fixed, and if the number of terms in the function is too large, it may be necessary to use two sections to implement one Boolean function.

As an example of using a PAL in the design of a combinational circuit, consider the following Boolean functions given in sum of minterms.

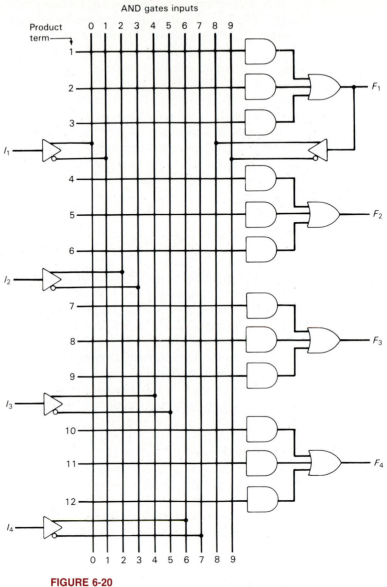

FIGURE 6-20
PAL with 4 Inputs, 4 Outputs, and 3-Wide AND-OR Structure

$$W(A, B, C, D) = \Sigma\, m(2, 12, 13)$$

$$X(A, B, C, D) = \Sigma\, m(7, 8, 9, 10, 11, 12, 13, 14, 15)$$

$$Y(A, B, C, D) = \Sigma\, m(0, 2, 3, 4, 5, 6, 7, 8, 10, 11, 15)$$

$$Z(A, B, C, D) = \Sigma\, m(1, 2, 8, 12, 13)$$

TABLE 6-5
PAL Programming Table

Product term	A	B	C	D	W	Outputs	
1	1	1	0	—	—	$W =$	$AB\overline{C}$
2	0	0	1	0	—		$+\ \overline{A}\,\overline{B}C\overline{D}$
3	—	—	—	—	—		
4	1	—	—	—	—	$X =$	A
5	—	1	1	1	—		$+\ BCD$
6	—	—	—	—	—		
7	0	1	—	—	—	$Y =$	$\overline{A}B$
8	—	—	1	1	—		$+\ CD$
9	—	0	—	0	—		$+\ \overline{B}\,\overline{D}$
10	—	—	—	—	1	$Z =$	W
11	1	—	0	0	—		$+\ A\overline{C}\,\overline{D}$
12	0	0	0	1	—		$+\ \overline{A}\,\overline{B}\,\overline{C}D$

Simplifying the four functions to a minimum number of terms results in the following Boolean functions:

$$W = AB\overline{C} + \overline{A}\,\overline{B}C\overline{D}$$

$$X = A\ +\ BCD$$

$$Y = \overline{A}B\ +\ CD\ +\ \overline{B}\,\overline{D}$$

$$Z = AB\overline{C} + \overline{A}\,\overline{B}C\overline{D}\ + A\overline{C}\,\overline{D}\ +\ \overline{A}\,\overline{B}\,\overline{C}D$$

$$= W + A\overline{C}\,\overline{D} + \overline{A}\,\overline{B}\,\overline{C}D$$

Note that the function for Z has four product terms. The logical sum of two of these terms is equal to W. By using W it is possible to reduce the number of terms for Z from four to three.

The PAL programming table is similar to the one used for the PLA except that only the inputs of the AND gates need to be programmed. Table 6-5 lists the PAL programming table for the four Boolean functions. The table is divided into four sections with three product terms in each to conform with the PAL of Figure 6-20. The first two sections need only two product terms to implement the Boolean function. The last section for output Z needs four product terms. Using the output from W we can reduce the function to three terms.

The fuse map for the PAL as specified in the programming table is shown in Figure 6-21. For each 1 or 0 in the table we mark the corresponding intersection in the diagram with the symbol for an intact fuse. For each dash we mark the diagram with blown fuses in both the true and complement inputs. If the AND gate is not used, we leave all its input fuses intact. Since the corresponding input receives both the true and complement of each input variable, we have $A \cdot \overline{A} = 0$ and the output of the AND gate is always 0.

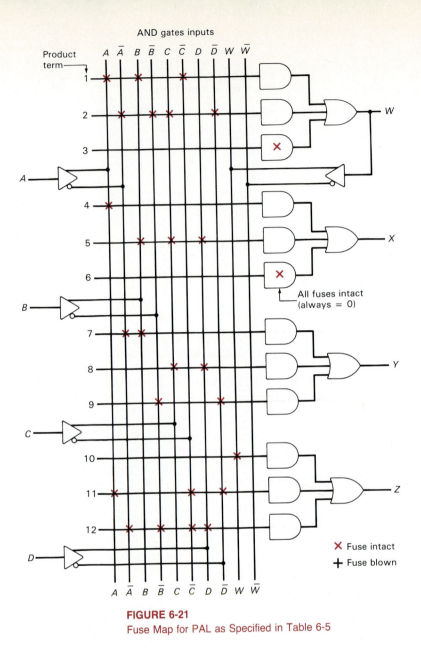

FIGURE 6-21
Fuse Map for PAL as Specified in Table 6-5

As with all PLDs, the design with PALs is facilitated by using computer aided design techniques. The blowing of internal fuses is a hardware procedure done with the help of special electronic instruments.

REFERENCES

1. PEATMAN J. B. *Digital Hardware Design*. New York: McGraw-Hill, 1980.
2. BLAKESLEE, T. R. *Digital Design with Standard MSI and LSI*. 2nd ed. New York: Wiley, 1979.

3. *The TTL Data Book*. Vol 4. Dallas: Texas Instruments, 1984

4. KITSON, B., ED. *Programmable Array Logic Handbook*. Sunnyvale, CA: Advanced Micro Devices, 1983.

5. HAMMING, R. W. "Error Detecting and Error Correcting Codes." *Bell System Tech. Jour.*, 29 (1950): 147–160.

6. LIN, S., AND COSTELLO, D. J., JR. *Error Control Coding*. Englewood Cliffs: Prentice-Hall, 1983.

PROBLEMS

6-1 The following memory units are specified by the number of words times the number of bits per word. How many address lines and input-output data lines are needed in each case?
(a) 2K × 16; (b) 64K × 8; (c) 16M × 32; (d) 96K × 12.

6-2 Give the number of bytes stored in the memories listed in Problem 6-1 (a), (b), and (c).

6-3 Word number 535 in the memory shown in Figure 6-3 contains the binary equivalent of 2209. List the 10-bit address and the 16-bit memory content of the word.

6-4 Draw the standard graphic symbol of a 256 × 1 RAM. Include the symbol for three-state output.

6-5 Show the memory cycle timing waveforms for the write and read operations. Assume a CPU clock of 2.5 MHz and a memory cycle time of 600 nsec.

6-6 Draw the standard graphic diagram of the 4 × 4 RAM of Figure 6-7 including three-state outputs. Construct an 8 × 8 memory using four 4 × 4 RAM units.

6-7 A 16K × 4 memory uses coincident decoding by splitting the internal decoder into *X*-selection and *Y*-selection.
(a) What is the size of each decoder and how many AND gates are required for decoding the address?
(b) Determine the *X* and *Y* selection lines that are enabled when the input address is the binary equivalent of 6,000.

6-8 (a) How many 128 × 8 RAM chips are needed to provide a memory capacity of 2048 bytes?
(b) How many lines of the address must be used to access 2048 bytes? How many of these lines are connected to the address inputs of all chips?
(c) How many lines must be decoded for the chip select inputs? Specify the size of the decoder.

6-9 A computer uses RAM chips of 1024 × 1 capacity.
(a) How many chips are needed and how should their address lines be connected to provide a memory capacity of 1024 bytes?
(b) How many chips are needed to provide a memory capacity of 16K bytes? Explain in words how the chips are to be connected.

6-10 An integrated circuit RAM chip has a capacity of 1024 words of 8 bits each (1K × 8).
(a) How many address and data lines are there in the chip?
(b) How many chips are needed to construct a 16K × 16 RAM?
(c) How many address and data lines are there in the 16K × 16 RAM?
(d) What size of decoder is needed to construct the 16K × 16 memory from the 1K × 8 chips? What are the inputs to the decoder and where are its outputs connected?

6-11 Given the 8-bit data word 01011011, generate the 13-bit composite word for the Hamming code that corrects single errors and detects double errors.

6-12 Given the 11-bit data word 11001001010, generate the 15-bit Hamming code word.

6-13 A 12-bit Hamming code word containing 8 bits of data and 4 parity bits is read from memory. What was the original 8-bit data word that was written into memory if the 12-bit word read out is
(a) 000011101010   (b) 101110000110   (c) 101111110100

6-14 How many parity check bits must be included with the data word to achieve single error correction and double error detection when the data word contains (a) 16 bits; (b) 32 bits; (c) 48 bits.

6-15 It is necessary to formulate the Hamming code for 4 data bits D_3, D_5, D_6, and D_7, together with three parity bits P_1, P_2, and P_4.
(a) Evaluate the 7-bit composite code word for the data word 0010.
(b) Evaluate the three check bits C_4, C_2, and C_1, assuming no error.
(c) Assume an error in bit D_5 during writing into memory. Show how the error in the bit is detected and corrected.
(d) Add a parity bit P_8 to include a double error detection in the code. Assume that errors occurred in bits P_2 and D_5. Show how the double error is detected.

6-16 Given a 32 × 8 ROM chip with an enable input, show the external connections necessary to construct a 128 × 8 ROM with four chips and a decoder.

6-17 A ROM chip of 4096 × 8 bits has two chip select inputs and operates from a 5-volt power supply. How many pins are needed for the integrated circuit package? Draw a block diagram and label all input and output terminals in the ROM.

6-18 The 32 × 6 ROM together with the 2^0 line as shown in Figure P6-18 converts a 6-bit binary number to its corresponding 2-digit BCD number. For example, binary 100001 converts to BCD 011 0011 (decimal 33). Specify the truth table for the ROM.

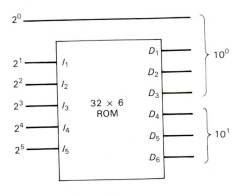

FIGURE P6-18
Binary-to-Decimal ROM Converter

6-19 Specify the size of a ROM (number of words and number of bits per word) that will accommodate the truth table for the following combinational circuit components.
(a) A binary multiplier that multiplies two 4-bit numbers.
(b) A 4-bit adder-subtractor (see Figure 3-12).
(c) A quadruple 2-to-1-line multiplexer with common select and enable inputs (see Figure 3-24).
(d) A BCD to seven segment decoder with an enable input.

6-20 Tabulate the truth table for an 8×4 ROM that implements the following four Boolean functions.

$$A(X, Y, Z) = \Sigma\, m(1, 2, 4, 6)$$

$$B(X, Y, Z) = \Sigma\, m(0, 1, 6, 7)$$

$$C(X, Y, Z) = \Sigma\, m(2, 6)$$

$$D(X, Y, Z) = \Sigma\, m(1, 2, 3, 5, 7)$$

6-21 Obtain the PLA programming table for the four Boolean functions listed in Problem 6-20. Minimize the number of product terms.

6-22 Derive the PLA programming table for the combinational circuit that squares a 3-bit number. Minimize the number of product terms. (See Figure 6-15 for the equivalent ROM implementations.)

6-23 List the PLA programming table for the BCD to excess-3 code converter whose Boolean functions are simplified in Figure 3-5.

6-24 Repeat Problem 6-23 using a PAL.

6-25 The following is a truth table of a 3-input, 4-output combinational circuit. Obtain the PAL programming table for the circuit and mark the fuses to be blown in a PAL diagram similar to the one shown in Figure 6-20.

Inputs			Outputs			
X	Y	Z	A	B	C	D
0	0	0	0	1	0	0
0	0	1	1	1	1	1
0	1	0	1	0	1	1
0	1	1	0	1	0	1
1	0	0	1	0	1	0
1	0	1	0	0	0	1
1	1	0	1	1	1	0
1	1	1	0	1	1	1

6-26 Modify the PAL diagram in Figure 6-20 by including three clocked D-type flip-flops between the OR gates and outputs F_2, F_3, and F_4. The diagram should conform with the block diagram of a sequential circuit as shown in Figure 6-17. This will require three additional buffer-inverter gates and six vertical lines for the flip-flop outputs to be connected to the AND array through programmable fuses. Using the modified PAL diagram, show the fuse map that will implement a 3-bit binary counter with a carry output in F_1.

7
REGISTER TRANSFER AND COMPUTER OPERATIONS

7-1 INTRODUCTION

A digital system is a sequential logic system constructed with flip-flops and gates. It was shown in Chapter 4 that sequential circuits can be specified by means of state tables. To specify a large digital system with state tables is very difficult, if not impossible, because the number of states would be prohibitively large. To overcome this difficulty, digital systems are designed using a modular approach. The system is partitioned into modular subsystems, each of which performs some functional task. The modules are constructed from such digital devices as registers, counters, decoders, multiplexers, arithmetic elements, and control logic. The various modules are interconnected by common data and control paths to form the digital computer system.

Digital modules are best defined by the registers they contain and the operations that are performed on the binary information stored in them. Examples of register operations are shift, count, clear, and load. In this configuration, the registers are assumed to be the basic components of the digital system and the information flow and processing tasks among the data stored in the registers are referred to as *register transfer* operations. The register transfer operations of digital systems are specified by the following three basic components:

1. The set of registers in the system and their function.
2. The operations that are performed with the information stored in the registers.
3. The control that supervises the sequence of operations in the system.

A *register*, as defined in the register transfer notation, is a group of flip-flops that stores binary information and has the capability of performing one or more elementary operations. A register can load new information or shift the information to the right or the left. A counter is considered to be a register that performs the increment-by-one operation. A flip-flop standing alone is considered as a 1-bit register that can be set, cleared, or complemented. In fact, the flip-flops and associated gates of any sequential circuit are called a register by this method of designation.

The operations performed on the information stored in registers are called *microoperations*. A microoperation is an elementary operation that can be performed in parallel on a string of bits during one clock-pulse period. The result of the operation may replace the previous binary information in a register or may be transferred to another register. The digital functions introduced in Chapter 5 are registers that implement microoperations. A counter with parallel load is capable of performing the microoperations increment and load. A bidirectional shift register is capable of performing the shift right and shift left microoperations.

The control that initiates the sequence of operations consists of timing signals that sequence the operations in a prescribed manner. Certain conditions which depend on results of previous operations may determine the sequence of future operations. The outputs of the control logic are binary variables that initiate the various microoperations in the registers.

This chapter introduces the components of the register transfer with a symbolic notation for representing registers and specifying the operations on the contents of the registers. The register transfer method uses a set of expressions and statements that resemble the statements used in programming languages. This notation provides the necessary tools for specifying the prescribed set of interconnections among various digital functions.

Instead of having individual registers performing the microoperations directly, computer systems employ a number of storage registers in conjunction with a common operational unit called an *arithmetic logic unit*, abbreviated ALU. To perform a microoperation, the contents of specified registers are placed in the inputs of the common ALU. The ALU performs an operation and the result of the operation is then transferred to a destination register. The ALU is a combinational circuit so that the entire register transfer operation from the source registers through the ALU and into the destination register can be performed during one clock pulse period. The shift microoperations are often performed in a separate unit. The shift unit is usually shown separately, but sometimes this unit is considered to be part of the overall arithmetic and logic unit.

A group of registers connected to a common ALU is called a *processor unit*. The processor unit is that part of a digital computer that implements the data processing operations in the system. The processor unit, when combined with a control unit that supervises the sequence of operations, is called the *central processing unit* abbreviated CPU. The second part of this chapter is concerned with the organization and design of the processor unit. The design of a particular arithmetic logic unit is undertaken to show the design process involved in implementing a complex digital circuit. The next chapter deals with the organization and design of the control unit. Chapter 10 demonstrates the detailed design of a central processing unit.

7-2 REGISTER TRANSFER

The registers in a digital system are designated by capital letters (sometimes followed by numerals) that denote the function of the register. For example, the register that holds an address for the memory unit is usually called the memory address register and is designated by the name AR. Other designations for registers are PC, IR, $R1$, and $R2$. The individual flip-flops in an n-bit register are numbered in sequence from 0 through n-1, starting from 0 in the rightmost position and increasing toward the left. Figure 7-1 shows the representation of registers in block diagram form. The most common way to represent a register is by a rectangular box with the name of the register inside as in Figure 7-1(a). The individual bits can be distinguished as in (b). The numbering of bits in a 16-bit register can be marked on top of the box as shown in (c). A 16-bit register is partitioned into two parts in (d). Bits 0 through 7 are assigned the symbol L (for low byte) and bits 8 through 15 are assigned the symbol H (for high byte). The name of the 16-bit register is PC. The symbol $PC(0\text{-}7)$ or $PC(L)$ refers to the low-order byte and $PC(8\text{-}15)$ or $PC(H)$ to the high order byte.

Information transfer from one register to another is designated in symbolic form by means of a replacement operator. The statement

$$R2 \leftarrow R1$$

denotes a transfer of the contents of register $R1$ into register $R2$. It designates a replacement of the contents of $R2$ by the contents of $R1$. By definition, the contents of the source register $R1$ do not change after the transfer.

A statement that specifies a register transfer implies that circuits are available from the outputs of the source register to the inputs of the destination register and that the destination register has a parallel load capability. Normally, we do not want the transfer to occur with every clock pulse, but only under a predetermined condition. A conditional statement is symbolized with an *if-then* statement

$$\text{If } (T_1 = 1) \text{ then } (R2 \leftarrow R1)$$

where T_1 is a timing signal generated in the control section. It is sometimes convenient to separate the control variables from the register transfer operation by

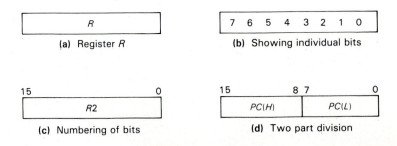

(a) Register R

(b) Showing individual bits

(c) Numbering of bits

(d) Two part division

FIGURE 7-1
Block Diagram of a Register

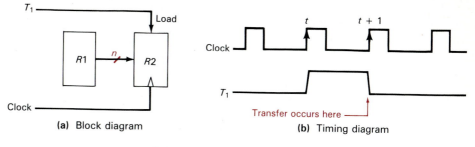

(a) Block diagram

(b) Timing diagram

FIGURE 7-2
Transfer from $R1$ to $R2$ when $T_1 = 1$

specifying a *control function*. A control function is a Boolean variable that can be equal to 1 or 0. The control function is included in the statement as follows:

$$T_1: R2 \leftarrow R1$$

The control condition is terminated with a colon. It symbolizes the requirement that the transfer operation be executed by the hardware only if $T_1 = 1$.

Every statement written in a register transfer notation implies a hardware construction for implementing the transfer. Figure 7-2 shows the block diagram that depicts the transfer from $R1$ to $R2$. The n outputs of register $R1$ are connected to the n inputs of register $R2$. The letter n will be used to indicate any number of bits for the register. It will be replaced by an actual number when the length of the register is known. Register $R2$ has a load control input which is activated by the timing variable T_1. It is assumed that the timing variable is synchronized with the same clock as the one applied to the register. As shown in the timing diagram, T_1 is activated by the rising edge of a clock pulse at time t. The next positive transition of the clock at time $t + 1$ finds $T_1 = 1$ and the inputs of $R2$ are loaded into the register in parallel. T_1 may go back to 0 at time $t + 1$ while timing variable T_2 becomes a 1 (see Figure 5-22).

Note that the clock is not included as a variable in the register transfer statements. It is assumed that all transfers occur during a clock edge transition. Even though the control condition such as T_1 becomes active at time t, the actual transfer does not occur until the register is triggered by the next positive transition of the clock.

The basic symbols of the register transfer notation are listed in Table 7-1. Registers are denoted by capital letters, and numerals may follow the letters. Parentheses are used to denote a part of a register by specifying the range of bits or by

TABLE 7-1
Basic Symbols for Register Transfers

Symbol	Description	Examples
Letters (and numerals)	Denotes a register	AR, $R2$
Parentheses ( )	Denotes a part of a register	$R2(0-7)$, $R2(L)$
Arrow ←	Denotes transfer of information	$R2 \leftarrow R1$
Comma ,	Separates two microoperations	$R2 \leftarrow R1$, $R1 \leftarrow R2$
Square brackets [ ]	Specify an address for memory	$DR \leftarrow M[AR]$

giving a symbol name to a portion of a register. The arrow denotes a transfer of information and the direction of transfer. A comma is used to separate two or more operations that are executed at the same time. The statement

$$T_3: R2 \leftarrow R1, R1 \leftarrow R2$$

denotes an operation that exchanges the contents of two registers during one common clock pulse provided $T_3 = 1$. This simultaneous operation is possible with registers that have edge-triggered flip-flops.

The square brackets are used in conjunction with memory transfer. The letter M designates a memory word, and the register enclosed inside the square brackets provides the address of the word in memory. This is explained in more detail in Section 7-4.

Multiplexer Selection

There are occasions when a register receives information from two different sources at different times. Consider the following conditional statement:

If $(T_1 = 1)$ then $(R0 \leftarrow R1)$ else if $(T_2 = 1)$ then $(R0 \leftarrow R2)$

The contents of register $R1$ are to be transferred to register $R0$ when timing variable T_1 occurs; otherwise, the contents of register $R2$ are transferred to $R0$ when T_2 occurs. The conditional statement may be broken into two parts using control functions.

$$T_1: R0 \leftarrow R1$$

$$\overline{T}_1 T_2: R0 \leftarrow R2$$

This specifies a hardware connection from two registers, $R1$ and $R2$, to one common destination register $R0$. This type of operation requires a multiplexer to select between the two source registers according to the values of the timing variables.

The block diagram of the circuit that implements the above two statements using 4-bit registers is shown in Figure 7-3(a). The quadruple 2×1 multiplexer selects between the two source registers. When $T_1 = 1$ register $R1$ is selected and when $T_1 = 0$, register $R2$ is selected by the multiplexer. Thus, when $T_1 = 1$, $R1$ is loaded into $R0$ irrespective of the value of T_2. When $T_2 = 1$ and $T_1 = 0$, $R2$ is loaded into $R0$. When both T_1 and T_2 are equal to 0, the multiplexer selects $R2$ for the inputs of $R0$ but the inputs are not loaded into the register because the load control input is equal to 0.

The detail logic diagram of the hardware implementation is shown in Figure 7-3(b). The diagram uses standard graphic symbols as presented in previous chapters. The graphic symbol for the registers is taken from Figure 5-3(b) and for the multiplexer from Figure 3-31(b). The enable input EN in the multiplexer is activated with the same condition as the load input of the destination register.

It is important to be able to relate the information given in a block diagram with the detail wiring connections in the corresponding logic diagram. In subsequent discussions we will present other block diagrams for various digital systems. In order to save space, the detailed logic diagram may be omitted. However, it should

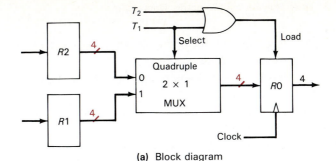

(a) Block diagram

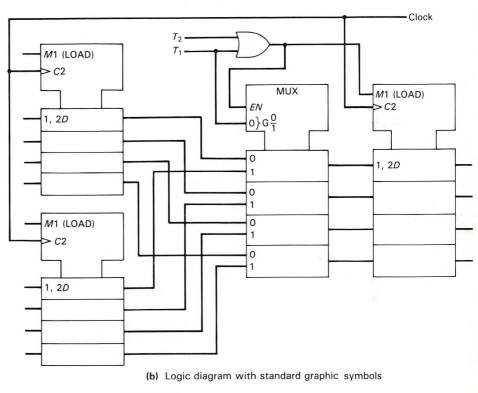

(b) Logic diagram with standard graphic symbols

FIGURE 7-3
Use of Multiplexers to Select Between Two Registers

be a straightforward procedure to obtain the logic diagram with detail wiring from the information given in the block diagram.

7-3 MICROOPERATIONS

A microoperation is an elementary operation performed with the data stored in registers. The type of microoperations most often encountered in digital computers are classified into four categories:

1. Register transfer microoperations transfer binary information from one register to another.

2. Arithmetic microoperations perform arithmetic operations on numbers stored in registers.

3. Logic microoperations perform bit manipulation operations on non-numeric data stored in registers.

4. Shift microoperations perform shift operations on contents of registers.

The register transfer microoperation was introduced in the previous section. This type of microoperation does not change the information content when the binary information moves from the source register to the destination register. The other three types of microoperations change the information content during the transfer. Among all possible operations that can exist in digital systems, there is a basic set from which all other operations can be obtained. In this section we define a set of basic microoperations, their symbolic notation, and the digital hardware that implements them.

Arithmetic Microoperations

The basic arithmetic microoperations are addition, subtraction, increment, decrement, and shift. Arithmetic shifts are explained later in conjunction with the shift microoperations. The arithmetic microoperation defined by the following statement:

$$R0 \leftarrow R1 + R2$$

specifies an *add* microoperation. It states that the contents of register $R1$ are to be added to the contents of register $R2$ and the sum transferred to register $R0$. To implement this statement with hardware we need three registers and the digital component that performs the addition operation, such as a parallel adder. The other basic arithmetic microoperations are listed in Table 7-2. Subtraction is most often implemented through complementation and addition. Instead of using the minus operator, we can specify the subtraction by the following statement:

$$R0 \leftarrow R1 + \overline{R2} + 1$$

$\overline{R2}$ is the symbol for the 1's complement of $R2$. Adding 1 to the 1's complement produces the 2's complement. Adding the contents of $R1$ to the 2's complement of $R2$ is equivalent to $R1 - R2$.

The increment and decrement microoperations are symbolized by a plus-one and minus-one operation, respectively. These microoperations are implemented with a combinational circuit or with a binary up-down counter.

The arithmetic operations multiply and divide are not listed in Table 7-2. The multiplication operation can be represented by the symbol * and the division be a /. These two operations are valid arithmetic operations but are not included in the basic set of microoperations. The only place where these operations can be considered as microoperations is in a digital system where they are implemented by means of a combinational circuit. In such a case, the signals that perform these operations propagate through gates, and the result of the operation can be trans-

TABLE 7-2
Arithmetic Microoperations

Symbolic designation	Description
$R0 \leftarrow R1 + R2$	Contents of $R1$ plus $R2$ transferred to $R0$
$R0 \leftarrow R1 - R2$	Contents of $R1$ minus $R2$ transferred to $R0$
$R2 \leftarrow \overline{R2}$	Complement the contents of $R2$ (1's complement)
$R2 \leftarrow \overline{R2} + 1$	2's complement the contents of $R2$
$R0 \leftarrow R1 + \overline{R2} + 1$	$R1$ plus the 2's complement of $R2$ (subtraction)
$R1 \leftarrow R1 + 1$	Increment the contents of $R1$ (count up)
$R1 \leftarrow R1 - 1$	Decrement the contents of $R1$ (count down)

ferred into a destination register by a clock pulse as soon as the output signal propagates through the combinational circuit. In many computers, the multiplication operation is implemented with a sequence of add and shift microoperations. Division is implemented with a sequence of subtract and shift microoperations. To specify the hardware in such a case requires a list of statements that use the basic microoperations of add, subtract, and shift.

There is a direct relationship between the statements written in a register transfer notation and the registers and digital functions that are required for their implementation. To illustrate with an example, consider the following two statements:

$$\overline{X}T_1: R1 \leftarrow R1 + R2$$

$$XT_1: R1 \leftarrow R1 + \overline{R2} + 1$$

Timing variable T_1 initiates an operation to add or subtract. If, at the same time, control variable X is equal to 0 then $\overline{X}T_1 = 1$ and the contents of $R2$ are added to the contents of $R1$. If $X = 1$, then $XT_1 = 1$ and the contents of $R2$ are subtracted from $R1$. Note that the two control functions are Boolean functions and reduce to 0 when $T_1 = 0$, a condition that inhibits the execution of either operation.

The implementation of the two statements is shown in block diagram form in Figure 7-4. An n-bit adder-subtractor (similar to the one shown in Figure 3-12)

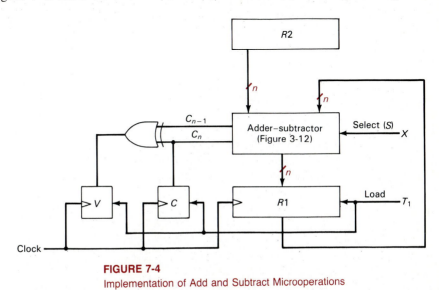

FIGURE 7-4
Implementation of Add and Subtract Microoperations

receives its input data from registers $R1$ and $R2$. The sum or difference is applied to the inputs of $R1$. The select input S in the adder-subtractor selects the operation in the circuit. When $S = 0$, the two inputs are added and when $S = 1$, $R2$ is subtracted from $R1$. Applying the control variable X to the select input provides the required operation. The output of the adder-subtractor is loaded into $R1$ if $\overline{X}T_1 = 1$ or if $XT_1 = 1$. This can be simplified to only T_1 since

$$\overline{X}T_1 + XT_1 = (\overline{X} + X)T_1 = T_1$$

Thus, control variable X selects the operation and timing variable T_1 loads the result into $R1$. The output carry C_n is transferred to flip-flop C. The function of flip-flop V is to detect for overflow as explained below.

Overflow

When two numbers of n digits each are added and the sum occupies $n + 1$ digits, we say that an overflow occurred. This is true for binary or decimal numbers whether signed or unsigned. When the addition is performed with paper and pencil, an overflow is not a problem, since there is no limit to the width of the page to write down the sum. An overflow is a problem in digital computers because the length of registers is finite. A result that contains $n + 1$ bits cannot be accommodated in a register with a standard length of n bits. For this reason, many computers detect the occurrence of an overflow, and when it occurs, a corresponding flip-flop is set which can then be checked by the user.

The detection of an overflow after the addition of two binary numbers depends on whether the numbers are considered to be signed or unsigned. When two unsigned numbers are added, an overflow is detected from the end carry out of the most significant position. In the case of signed numbers, the leftmost bit always represents the sign and negative numbers are in 2's complement form. When two signed numbers are added, the sign bit is treated as part of the number and the end carry does not indicate an overflow (see Section 1-5).

An overflow cannot occur after an addition if one number is positive and the other is negative, since adding a positive number to a negative number produces a result which is smaller than the larger of the two original numbers. An overflow may occur if the two numbers added are both positive or both negative. To see how this can happen, consider the following example. Two signed binary numbers, $+70$ and $+80$, are stored in two 8-bit registers. The range of numbers that each register can accommodate is from binary $+127$ to binary -128. Since the sum of the two numbers is $+150$, it exceeds the capacity of the 8-bit register. This is true if the numbers are both positive or both negative. The two additions in binary are shown below together with the last two carries.

carries: 0 1		carries: 1 0	
$+70$	0 1000110	-70	1 0111010
$+80$	0 1010000	-80	1 0110000
$+150$	1 0010110	-150	0 1101010

Note that the 8-bit result that should have been positive has a negative sign bit and the 8-bit result that should have been negative has a positive sign bit. If, however, the carry out of the sign bit position is taken as the sign bit of the result, then the 9-bit answer so obtained will be correct. Since the answer cannot be accommodated within 8 bits, we say that an overflow occurred.

An overflow condition can be detected by observing the carry *into* the sign bit position and the carry *out* of the sign bit position. If these two carries are not equal, an overflow condition is produced. This is indicated in the examples where the two carries are explicitly shown. If the two carries are applied to an exclusive-OR gate, an overflow will be detected when the output of the gate is equal to 1.

The addition and subtraction of two binary numbers with digital hardware is shown in Figure 7-4. If the numbers are considered unsigned, then the C bit detects a carry after addition or a borrow after subtraction. If the numbers are considered to be signed, then the V bit detects an overflow. If $V = 0$ after an addition or subtraction, it indicates that no overflow occurred and the answer in $R1$ is correct. If $V = 1$, then the result of the operation contains $n + 1$ bits. Only n bits of the number are in $R1$. The $(n + 1)$th bit is the sign bit and has been shifted out of position into the carry bit C.

Logic Microoperations

Logic microoperations are useful for manipulating the bits stored in a register. These operations consider each bit in the register separately and treat it as a binary variable. The symbols for the four basic logic microoperations are shown in Table 7-3. The complement microoperation is the same as the 1's complement and uses a bar on top of the register name. The symbol $\wedge$ is used to denote the AND microoperation and the symbol $\vee$ to denote the OR microoperation. By using these special symbols it is possible to differentiate between the add microoperation symbolized by a $+$ and the OR microoperation. Although the $+$ symbol has two meanings, it will be possible to distinguish between them by noting where the symbol occurs. When this symbol occurs in a microoperation, it denotes an addition operation. When it occurs in a control or Boolean function, it denotes an OR operation. The OR microoperation will always use the $\vee$ symbol. For example, in the statement

$$T_1 + T_2: R1 \leftarrow R2 + R3, R4 \leftarrow R5 \vee R6$$

the $+$ between T_1 and T_2 is an OR operation between two variables in a control (Boolean) function. The $+$ between $R2$ and $R3$ specifies an add microoperation. The OR microoperation is designated by the symbol $\vee$ between registers $R5$ and $R6$.

TABLE 7-3
Logic Microoperations

Symbolic designation	Description
$R \leftarrow \bar{R}$	Complements all bits of register R
$R0 \leftarrow R1 \wedge R2$	Logic AND microoperation (clears bits)
$R0 \leftarrow R1 \vee R2$	Logic OR microoperation (sets bits)
$R0 \leftarrow R1 \oplus R2$	Logic XOR microoperation (complements bits)

The logic microoperations can be easily implemented with a group of gates. The complement of a register of n bits is obtained with n inverter gates. The AND microoperation is obtained from a group of AND gates, each of which receives a pair of bits from two source registers. The outputs of the gates are applied to the inputs of the destination register. The OR and Exclusive-OR microoperations require a similar arrangement of gates.

The logic microoperations can change bit values, clear a group of bits, or insert new bit values in a register. The following examples show how the bits of register $R1$ are manipulated by logic microoperations with a logic operand in $R2$.

The AND microoperation is used for clearing to 0 a bit or a selected group of bits in a register. The Boolean relationships $X \cdot 0 = 0$ and $X \cdot 1 = X$ dictate that a binary variable X when ANDed with 0 produces a 0 but when ANDed with 1 it does not change the value of X. A given bit or a group of bits in a register can be cleared to 0 if ANDed with 0. Consider the following example.

$$10101101\ 10101011 \qquad R1$$

$$00000000\ 11111111 \qquad R2$$

$$00000000\ 10101011 \qquad R1 \leftarrow R1 \wedge R2$$

The 16-bit logic operand in $R2$ has 0's in the high order byte and 1's in the low order byte. By ANDing this with the contents of $R1$, it is possible to clear to 0's the high order byte of $R1$ and leave the bits in the low order byte unchanged. Thus, the AND operation can be used to selectively clear bits of a register. This operation is sometimes referred to as *masking out* the bits because it masks or deletes all 1's from a selected portion of a register.

The OR microoperation is used to set a bit or a group of bits in a register. The Boolean relationships $X + 1 = 1$ and $X + 0 = X$ dictate that the binary variable X when ORed with 1 produces a 1 but when ORed with 0 it does not change the value of X. A given bit or a group of bits in a register can be set to 1 if ORed with 1. Consider the following example.

$$10101101\ 10101011 \qquad R1$$

$$11111111\ 00000000 \qquad R2$$

$$11111111\ 10101011 \qquad R1 \leftarrow R1 \vee R2$$

The high order byte of $R1$ is set to all 1's by ORing it with all 1's in the $R2$ operand. The low order byte remains unchanged because it is ORed with 0's.

The XOR (exclusive-OR) microoperation is used to complement a bit or a group of bits in a register. The Boolean relationships $X \oplus 1 = \overline{X}$ and $X \oplus 0 = X$ dictate that when the binary variable X is XORed with 1 it is complemented but when XORed with 0 it remains unchanged. By XORing a bit or a group of bits in a register with 1, it is possible to complement the selected bits. Consider the example

$$10101101\ 10101011 \qquad R1$$

$$11111111\ 00000000 \qquad R2$$

$$01010010\ 10101011 \qquad R1 \leftarrow R1 \oplus R2$$

TABLE 7-4
Shift Microoperations

Symbolic designation	Description
$R \leftarrow$ shl R	Shift left register R
$R \leftarrow$ shr R	Shift right register R
$R \leftarrow$ rol R	Rotate left register R
$R \leftarrow$ ror R	Rotate right register R
$R \leftarrow$ asl R	Arithmetic shift left R
$R \leftarrow$ asr R	Arithmetic shift right R

The high order byte in $R1$ is complemented after the XOR operation with the operand in $R2$.

Shift Microoperations

Shift microoperations are used for serial transfer of data. They are also used in arithmetic, logic and control operations. The contents of a register can be shifted to the left or the right. There are no standard symbols for the shift microoperations. Here we will adopt the symbols *shl* and *shr* for shift left and shift right operations. For example

$$R1 \leftarrow \text{shl } R1, \; R2 \leftarrow \text{shr } R2$$

are two microoperations that specify a 1-bit shift to the left of register $R1$ and a 1-bit shift to the right of register $R2$. The register symbol must be the same on both sides of the arrow as in the increment operation.

While the bits of a register are shifted, the end bit position receives information from the serial input. The end position is the rightmost bit of the register during a shift left operation and the leftmost bit of the register during a shift right operation. The bit transferred to the end position through the serial input is assumed to be 0 during a logical shift, which is symbolized by shl or shr. In a *rotate* operation, the serial output is connected to the serial input and the bits of the register rotate without any loss of information. The symbol used for the rotate is shown in Table 7-4.

An arithmetic shift is a microoperation that shifts a signed binary number to the left or right. An arithmetic shift left multiplies a signed binary number by 2. An arithmetic shift right divides the number by 2. Arithmetic shifts must leave the sign bit unchanged because the sign of the number remains the same when it is multiplied or divided by 2.

The leftmost bit in a register holds the sign bit, and the remaining bits hold the number. Figure 7-5 shows a typical register of n bits. Bit R_{n-1} in the leftmost position holds the sign bit. R_0 is the least significant bit and R_{n-2} is the most

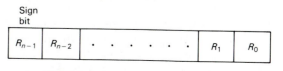

FIGURE 7-5
Defining Register R for Arithmetic Shifts

significant bit of the number. It is assumed that negative numbers have a 1 in the sign bit and are in 2's complement form.

The arithmetic shift right leaves the sign bit unchanged and shifts the number (including the sign bit) to the right. Thus, R_{n-1} remains the same, R_{n-2} receives the bit from R_{n-1} and so on for the other bits in the register. The bit in R_0 is lost.

The arithmetic shift left inserts a 0 into R_0, and shifts all other bits to the left. The initial bit of R_{n-1} is lost and replaced by the bit from R_{n-2}. A sign reversal occurs if the bit in R_{n-1} changes in value after the shift. This happens if the multiplication by 2 causes an overflow. An overflow occurs after an arithmetic shift left if R_{n-1} is not equal to R_{n-2} *before* the shift. An overflow flip-flop V_s can be used to detect an arithmetic shift overflow.

$$V_s = R_{n-1} \oplus R_{n-2}$$

If $V_s = 0$, there is no overflow, but if $V_s = 1$, there is an overflow and a sign reversal after the shift. V_s must be transferred into the overflow flip-flop with the same clock pulse that shifts the register.

7-4   BUS TRANSFER

A typical digital computer has many registers and paths must be provided to transfer information from one register to another. The number of wires will be excessive if separate lines and multiplexers are used between each register and all other registers in the system. A more efficient scheme for transferring information between registers in a multiple register configuration is a *bus* system. A bus structure consists of a set of common lines, one for each bit of a register, through which binary information is transferred one at a time. Control signals select which register will be the source and which will be the destination during each register transfer.

One way of constructing a common bus system is with multiplexers and a decoder. The multiplexers select one source register whose binary information is then placed on the bus. The decoder selects one destination register to accept the information from the bus. The construction of a bus system for four registers is shown in Figure 7-6. Each register has n bits numbered from 0 through n-1. The bits in the same significant position in each register are applied to a 4-to-1-line multiplexer to form one line of the bus. Only three multiplexers are shown in the diagram. The complete circuit must have n multiplexers numbered 0 to n-1. The n lines formed by the common bus system are routed to the n inputs of each register. The transfer of information from the bus into one destination register is accomplished by activating the load control input of the selected register. The particular load input is selected from the outputs of the decoder.

The MUX select inputs determine which register will place its contents on the bus. The MUX select inputs can be either 00, 01, 10, or 11, which select register $R0$, $R1$, $R2$, or $R3$, respectively. The destination select inputs to the decoder determine the register that receives the information from the bus. The destination select inputs can be either 00, 01, 10, or 11, and they select the destination register $R0$, $R1$, $R2$, or $R3$, respectively.

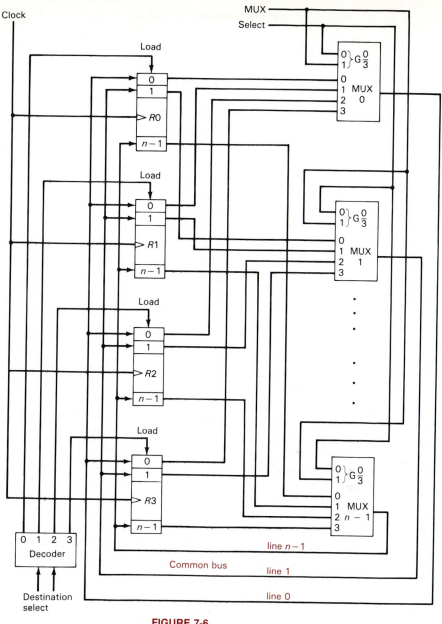

FIGURE 7-6
Bus System for Four Registers

To illustrate with a particular example, consider the transfer given by the following statement:

$$R2 \leftarrow R0$$

The control variables that enable this transfer must select register $R0$ as the source for the bus and register $R2$ as the destination. The multiplexer select inputs must be binary 00. This causes bit 0 of $R0$ to be applied to line 0 of the bus through

MUX 0. At the same time bit 1 of $R0$ is applied to line 1 of the bus through MUX 1. This repeats for all other bus lines up to line n-1 which receives bit n-1 of $R0$ through MUX n-1. Thus, the n-bit value of $R0$ is placed on the common bus lines when the MUX select is 00. The destination select inputs must be binary 10. This activates output 2 of the decoder which in turn activates the load input of $R2$. With the next clock transition, the contents of $R0$, being on the bus, are loaded into register $R2$ to complete the transfer.

Three-State Bus Buffers

A bus system can be constructed with three-state gates instead of multiplexers. A three-state gate is a digital circuit that exhibits three states. Two of the states are signals equivalent to logic-1 and logic-0 as in a conventional gate. The third state is a *high-impedance* state. The high-impedance state behaves like an open circuit which means that the output is disconnected and does not have a logic significance. Three-state gates may perform any conventional logic such as AND or NAND. However, the one most commonly used in the design of a bus system is the buffer gate.

The graphic symbol of a three-state buffer gate is shown in Figure 7-7. It is distinguished from a normal buffer by its small triangle symbol in front of the output terminal. The circuit has a normal input and a control input that determines the output state. When the control input is equal to 1, the output is enabled and the gate behaves like any conventional buffer, with the output equal to the normal input. When the control input is 0, the output is disabled and the gate goes to a high-impedance state, regardless of the value in the normal input. The high-impedance state of a three-state gate provides a special feature not available in other gates. Because of this feature, a large number of three-state gate outputs can be connected with wires to form a common bus line without endangering loading effects.

The construction of a bus system with three-state buffers is demonstrated in Figure 7-8. The outputs of four buffers are connected together to form a single bus line. (This type of connection cannot be done with gates that do not have three-state outputs.) The control inputs to the buffers determine which one of the four normal inputs will communicate with the bus line. No more than one buffer may be in the active state at any given time. The connected buffers must be controlled so that only one three-state buffer has access to the bus line while all other buffers are maintained in a high-impedance state.

One way to ensure that no more than one control input is active at any given time is to use a decoder as shown in the diagram. When the enable input of the decoder is 0, all of its four outputs are 0, and the bus line is in a high-impedance

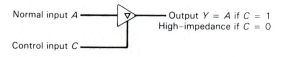

FIGURE 7-7
Graphic Symbol for a Three-State Buffer

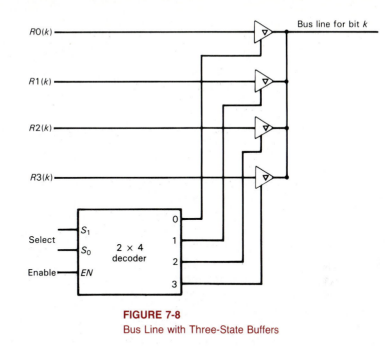

FIGURE 7-8
Bus Line with Three-State Buffers

state because all four buffers are disabled. When the enable input is active, one of the three-state buffers will be active depending on the binary value in the select inputs of the decoder. Careful investigation will reveal that Figure 7-8 represents another way of constructing a 4×1 multiplexer. The diagram shows the inputs marked with a register name and the bit value in parenthesis. Thus, $R0(k)$ designates bit k in register $R0$. The circuit of Figure 7-8 can replace the multiplexer in Figure 7-6 that produces the bus line for bit k. To construct a common bus for four n-bit registers with three-state buffers requires n groups of four buffers each to produce the outputs for the n-bit bus. Only one decoder is necessary to select between the four registers.

There are occasions where it is necessary to employ a bidirectional bus system that can transfer information in both directions. A bidirectional bus allows the binary information to flow in either of two directions. A bidirectional bus can be constructed with three-state buffers to control the direction of information flow in the bus. One line of a bidirectional bus is shown in Figure 7-9. The bus control has two selection lines S_{in} for input transfer and S_{out} for output transfer. These selection lines control two three-state buffers connected back to back. When $S_{in} = 1$ and $S_{out} = 0$, the bottom buffer is enabled and the top buffer is disabled by going to a high-impedance state. This forms a path for input data coming from the bus to pass through the bottom buffer and into the input of a flip-flop register. When $S_{out} = 1$ and $S_{in} = 0$, the top buffer is enabled and the bottom buffer goes to a high-impedance state. This forms a path for output data coming from a register in the system to pass through the upper buffer and out to the bus line. The bus line can be disabled by making both control signals 0. This puts both buffers in a high-impedance state, which prevents any input or output transfer of information

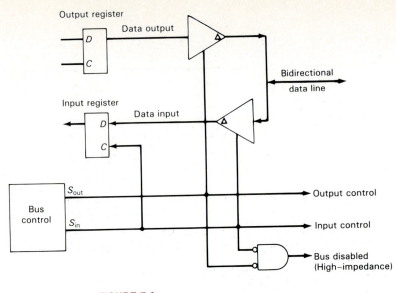

FIGURE 7-9
Bidirectional Bus Line with Three-State Buffers

through the bus line. This condition will exist when an external source is using the common bus to communicate with some other external destination. The two selection lines can be used to inform the external modules connected to the bus of the state which the bidirectional bus is at any given time.

Memory Transfer

The operation of a memory unit was described in Section 6-2. The transfer of information from a memory word to the outside environment is called a read operation. The transfer of new information into a memory word is called a write operation. A memory word will be symbolized by the letter M. The particular memory word among the many available is selected by the memory address during the transfer. It is necessary to specify the address of M when writing memory transfer operations. This will be done by enclosing the address in square brackets following the letter M.

Consider a memory unit that receives the address from a register called address register symbolized by AR. The data is transferred to another register called data register symbolized by DR. The read operation can be stated as follows:

$$\text{Read: } DR \leftarrow M[AR]$$

This causes a transfer of information into DR from the selected memory word specified by the address in AR.

The write operation is a transfer from DR to the selected memory word M. This can be stated symbolically as follows:

$$\text{Write: } M[AR] \leftarrow DR$$

This causes a transfer of information from DR into the memory word selected by the address in AR.

In some systems, the memory unit receives address and data from many registers connected to common buses. Consider the case depicted in Figure 7-10. The address for the memory comes from an address bus. Four registers are connected to this bus and any one may supply an address. The memory data is connected to a bidirectional data bus. The contents of the selected memory word during a read operation can go to any one of four registers which are selected by a decoder. The data word for the memory during a write operation comes from one of four registers selected by the data bus. The direction of information flow in the data bus is determined from the bus control inputs. For a read operation, the path is from memory to a data register. For a write operation the path is from a data register to memory. Each bidirectional line is controlled by a pair of three-state buffers as indicated in Figure 7-9.

A memory transfer statement in a multiple register system must specify the address register and the data register used. For example, the transfer of information from data register $D2$ to a memory word selected by the address in register $A1$ is symbolized by the statement

$$M[A1] \leftarrow D2$$

This is a write operation with $A1$ supplying the address. The statement does not specify the buses explicitly. Nevertheless, it implies the required selection inputs for the address bus to be 01 (for $A1$) and the register select for write inputs to be 10 (for $D2$). The bus control activates the write and output control signals.

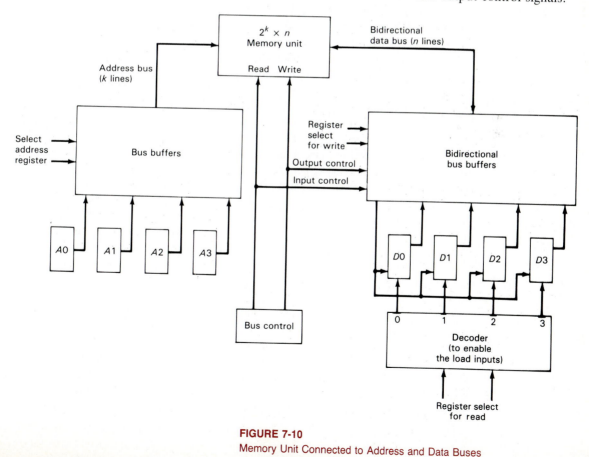

FIGURE 7-10
Memory Unit Connected to Address and Data Buses

The read operation in a memory with buses can be specified in a similar manner. The statement

$$D0 \leftarrow M[A3]$$

symbolizes a read operation from a memory word whose address is given by register $A3$. The information coming out of memory is transferred to data register $D0$. Again, this statement implies the required selection inputs for the address bus to be 11 (for $A3$) and the inputs to the decoder to be 00 (for $D0$) while the bus control activates the read and input control signals.

7-5   PROCESSOR UNIT

The processor unit is a central component in a digital computer system. It consists of a number of registers and the digital circuits that implement various microoperations. The processor part of the computer is sometimes referred to as the *data path* because it forms the paths for the operations among the registers. The various paths are said to be controlled by means of gates that form the required path for each particular operation. In a typical processor unit, the data paths are formed by means of buses and other common lines. The control gates that formulate the given path are essentially multiplexers and decoders whose selection lines specify the required path. The processing of information is done by one common circuit referred to as the arithmetic logic unit, abbreviated ALU.

When a large number of registers are included in a processor unit, it is most efficient to connect them through common buses. The registers communicate with each other not only for direct data transfer, but also while performing various microoperations. A bus organization with four registers and an ALU is shown in Figure 7-11. Each register is connected to two sets of multiplexers to form input buses A and B. The selection inputs in each set of multiplexers select one register for the corresponding bus. The A and B buses are applied to the inputs of a common arithmetic logic unit. The select inputs of the ALU determine the particular operation that is performed. The shift operations are implemented in the shifter. The output data from the ALU may be shifted to the right or to the left, or may go through the shifter without a change, depending on the shift select input. The result of the operation is placed on the output bus which in turn is connected to the inputs of all registers. The destination register that receives the result from the output bus is selected by a decoder. The decoder activates one register load input to provide the transfer path between the data in the output bus and the destination register.

The output bus has additional terminals for transferring data from the processor unit to an external device. External data can enter the processor unit through the input data terminals in one of the multiplexers.

It is sometimes convenient to supplement the ALU with a number of status bits. The status bits are useful for checking certain relationships between the values of A and B after an ALU operation. Four status bits are shown in Figure 7-11. The carry C and the overflow V are explained in conjunction with Figure 7-4. The zero

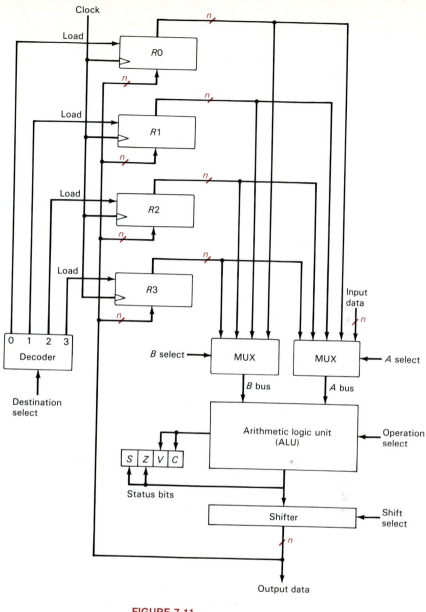

FIGURE 7-11
Block Diagram of a Processor Unit

status bit Z is set to 1 if the output of the ALU contains all 0's, and cleared to 0 otherwise. Thus, $Z = 1$ if the result of an operation is zero, and $Z = 0$ if the result is nonzero. The sign status bit S is set to the value of the sign bit of the result. The sign bit is always the leftmost bit out of the ALU.

A typical processor unit will have more than four registers. Computers with 16 or more registers are quite common. The construction of a bus system with a large number of registers requires larger multiplexers and ALU, otherwise, it is similar to the organization depicted in Figure 7-11.

The control unit that supervises the bus system in the processor must direct the information flow through the buses, the ALU, and the shifter by selecting the various components in the unit. For example, to perform the microoperation

$$R1 \leftarrow R2 + R3$$

the control unit must provide binary selection variables to the following selection inputs:

1. MUX A selector: to place the contents of $R2$ onto bus A.
2. MUX B selector: to place the contents of $R3$ onto bus B.
3. ALU operation selector: to provide the arithmetic operation $A + B$.
4. Shift selector: to provide a direct transfer from the outputs of the ALU onto the output bus (no shift).
5. Decoder destination selector: to load the contents of the output bus into $R1$.

The five sets of selection variables must be generated simultaneously and must be available in the corresponding terminals at the beginning of a clock pulse period. The binary data from the two source registers must propagate through the multiplexers, the ALU, the shifter, and into the inputs of the destination register, all during one clock pulse period. Then, when the next clock edge transition arrives, the binary information on the output bus is loaded into the destination register. To achieve a fast response time, the ALU is constructed with fast circuits and the shifter is implemented with combinational gates.

The operation of the multiplexers, the buses, and the destination decoder was presented in the previous section. The design of an ALU and shifter is undertaken in the next two sections. The control of the processor unit through its selection inputs is demonstrated in Section 7-8.

7-6 ARITHMETIC LOGIC UNIT (ALU)

An arithmetic logic unit (ALU) is a combinational circuit that performs a set of basic arithmetic and logic microoperations. The ALU has a number of selection lines used to select a particular operation in the unit. The selection lines are decoded within the ALU so that k selection variables can specify up to 2^k distinct operations.

Figure 7-12 shows the block diagram of a typical 4-bit ALU. The four data inputs from A are combined with the four data inputs from B to generate an operation at the F outputs. The mode select input S_2 distinguishes between arithmetic and logic operations. The two function select inputs S_1 and S_0 specify the particular arithmetic or logic operation to be generated. With three selection lines, it is possible to specify four arithmetic operations with S_2 in one state and four logic operations with S_2 in the other state. The input and output carries have meaning only during an arithmetic operation. The input carry C_{in} is quite often used as a fourth selection variable for arithmetic operations. In this way, it is possible to double the number of arithmetic operations from four to eight.

The design of a typical ALU will be carried out in three stages. First, the design of the arithmetic section will be undertaken. Second, the design of the logic section

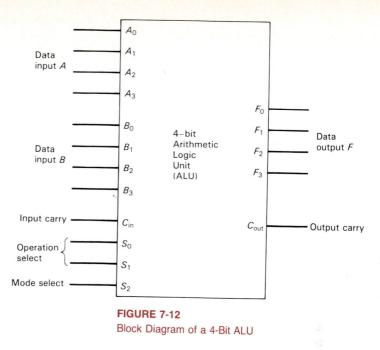

FIGURE 7-12

Block Diagram of a 4-Bit ALU

will be presented. The two sections will then be combined to form the arithmetic logic unit.

Arithmetic Circuit

The basic component of an arithmetic circuit is the parallel adder. A parallel adder is constructed with a number of full-adder circuits connected in cascade (see Figure 3-11). By controlling the data inputs to the parallel adder, it is possible to obtain different types of arithmetic operations. The block diagram of Figure 7-13 demonstrates a possible configuration where one set of inputs to the parallel adder is controlled by two selection lines S_1 and S_0. There are n bits in the arithmetic circuit with two inputs, A and B, and one output F. The n inputs from B go through a combinational circuit to the Y inputs of the parallel adder. The input carry C_{in} goes to the carry input of the full-adder circuit in the least significant bit position. The output carry C_{out} is from the full adder in the most significant position. The output of the parallel adder is calculated from the following arithmetic sum

$$F = A + Y + C_{in}$$

where A is the n-bit binary number at the X inputs and Y is the n-bit binary number at the Y inputs of the parallel adder. C_{in} is the input carry which can be equal to 0 or 1. Note that the symbol $+$ in the above equation denotes an arithmetic plus.

By controlling the value of Y with the two selection inputs S_1 and S_0, it is possible to obtain a variety of arithmetic operations. This is shown in Table 7-5. If the inputs from B are ignored and we insert all 0's into the Y inputs, the output sum becomes $F = A + 0 + C_{in}$. This gives $F = A$ when $C_{in} = 0$ and $F = A + 1$ when $C_{in} = 1$. In the first case we have a direct transfer from input A to output F. In the second case, the value of A is incremented by 1. For a straight arithmetic addition, it is necessary to transfer the B inputs into the Y inputs of the parallel

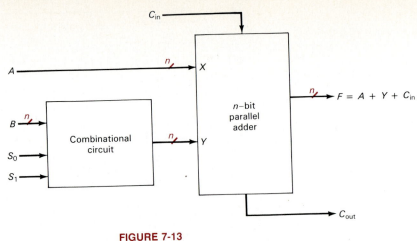

FIGURE 7-13
Block Diagram of an Arithmetic Circuit

adder. This gives $F = A + B$ when $C_{in} = 0$. Arithmetic subtraction is achieved when Y is made the complement of B to obtain $F = A + \bar{B} + 1$ when $C_{in} = 1$. This gives A plus the 2's complement of B which is equivalent to subtraction. Inserting all 1's into the inputs of Y produces the decrement operation $F = A - 1$ when $C_{in} = 0$. This is because a number with all 1's is equal to the 2's complement of 1. For example, the 2's complement of binary 0001 is 1111. Adding a number A to the 2's complement of 1 produces $F = A + $ 2's complement of $1 = A - 1$.

The combinational circuit in Figure 7-13 can be implemented with n multiplexers. The data inputs to each multiplexer in stage i for $i = 0, 1, 2, \ldots, n-1$ are: $0, B_i$, $\bar{B}_i$, and 1, corresponding to selection values $S_1 S_0$: 00, 01, 10, and 11, respectively. Thus the arithmetic circuit can be constructed with n multiplexers and n full adders.

The number of gates in the combinational circuit can be reduced if, instead of using multiplexers, we go through the logic design of one stage of the combinational circuit. This can be done as shown in Figure 7-14. The truth table for one typical stage i for the combinational circuit is listed in Figure 7-14(a). The inputs are S_1, S_0, B_i, and the output is Y_i. Following the requirements specified in Table 7-5, we let $Y_i = 0$ when $S_1 S_0 = 00$, and similarly assign the other three values of Y_i for each of the combinations of the selection variables. Output Y_i is simplified in the map in Figure 7-14(b).

$$Y_i = B_i S_0 + \bar{B}_i S_1$$

S_1 and S_0 are common to all n stages. Each stage i is associated with input B_i and output Y_i for $i = 0, 1, 2, \ldots, n-1$.

The logic diagram of a 4-bit arithmetic circuit is shown in Figure 7-15. The four

TABLE 7-5
Arithmetic Circuit Function Table

Select		Input	$F = A + Y + C_{in}$	
S_1	S_0	Y	$C_{in} = 0$	$C_{in} = 1$
0	0	all 0's	$F = A$ (transfer)	$F = A + 1$ (increment)
0	1	B	$F = A + B$ (add)	$F = A + B + 1$
1	0	$\bar{B}$	$F = A + \bar{B}$	$F = A + \bar{B} + 1$ (subtract)
1	1	all 1's	$F = A - 1$ (decrement)	$F = A$ (transfer)

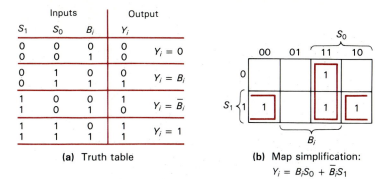

Inputs			Output	
S_1	S_0	B_i	Y_i	
0	0	0	0	$Y_i = 0$
0	0	1	0	
0	1	0	0	$Y_i = B_i$
0	1	1	1	
1	0	0	1	$Y_i = \overline{B_i}$
1	0	1	0	
1	1	0	1	$Y_i = 1$
1	1	1	1	

(a) Truth table

(b) Map simplification:
$$Y_i = B_i S_0 + \overline{B_i} S_1$$

FIGURE 7-14
Combinational Circuit for One Stage of Arithmetic Circuit

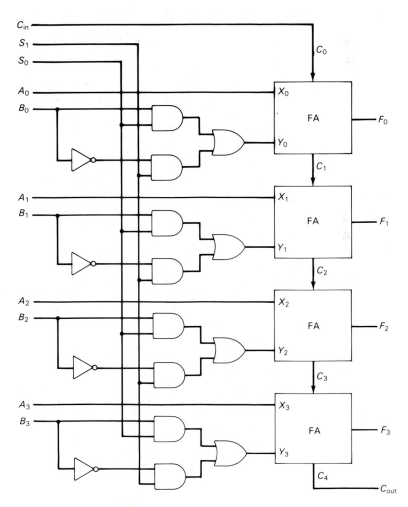

FIGURE 7-15
Logic Diagram of a 4-Bit Arithmetic Circuit

full-adder (FA) circuits constitute the parallel adder. The carry into the first stage is the input carry C_{in}. All other carries are connected internally from one stage to the next. The selection variables are S_1, S_0, and C_{in}. Variables S_1 and S_0 control all Y inputs of the full adders according to the Boolean function derived in Figure 7-14(b). C_{in} adds 1 to the sum when it is equal to 1. The eight arithmetic operations of the circuit as a function of S_1, S_0, and C_{in} are listed in Table 7-5.

Logic Circuit

The logic microoperations manipulate the bits of the operands by treating each bit in a register as a binary variable. There are four basic logic operations from which all others can be derived. They are the AND, OR, XOR (exclusive-OR), and complement.

Figure 7-16(a) shows one stage of the logic circuit. It consists of four gates and a multiplexer. Each of the four logic operations is generated through a gate that performs the required logic. The outputs of the gates are applied to a multiplexer with two selection variables S_1 and S_0. These selection variables choose one of the data inputs of the multiplexer and direct its value to the output. The diagram shows one typical stage with subscript i. For a logic circuit with n bits, the diagram must be repeated n times for $i = 0, 1, 2, \ldots, n-1$. The selection variables are applied to all stages. The function table in Figure 7-16(b) lists the logic operations obtained for each combination of the selection variables.

Arithmetic Logic Unit

The logic circuit can be combined with the arithmetic circuit to produce an arithmetic logic unit. Selection variables S_1 and S_0 can be common to both circuits provided we use a third selection variable to differentiate between the two. The configuration of one stage of the ALU is illustrated in Figure 7-17. The outputs of the arithmetic and logic circuits in each stage are applied to a 2×1 multiplexer

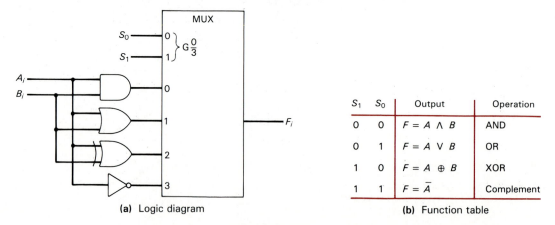

	(a) Logic diagram			S_1	S_0	Output	Operation

(a) Logic diagram

S_1	S_0	Output	Operation
0	0	$F = A \wedge B$	AND
0	1	$F = A \vee B$	OR
1	0	$F = A \oplus B$	XOR
1	1	$F = \overline{A}$	Complement

(b) Function table

FIGURE 7-16
One Stage of a Logic Circuit

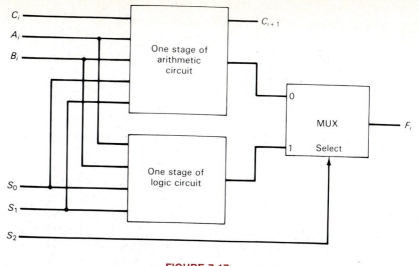

FIGURE 7-17
One Stage of ALU

with selection variable S_2. When $S_2 = 0$, the arithmetic output is selected, and when $S_2 = 1$, the logic output is selected. Note that the diagram shows just one typical stage of the ALU. The circuit of Figure 7-17 must be repeated n times for an n-bit ALU. The output carry C_{i+1} of a given arithmetic stage must be connected to the input carry C_i of the next stage in sequence. The input carry to the first stage is the input carry C_{in} which provides a selection variable for the arithmetic operations.

The ALU specified in Figure 7-17 provides eight arithmetic and four logic operations. Each operation is selected through the variables S_2, S_1, S_0, and C_{in}. The input carry C_{in} is used for selecting an arithmetic operation only.

Table 7-6 lists the 12 operations of the ALU. The first 8 are arithmetic operations and are selected with $S_2 = 0$. The next 4 are logic operations and are selected with $S_2 = 1$. The input carry has no effect during the logic operations and is marked with a 0 for convenience.

TABLE 7-6
Function Table for ALU

Operation Select				Operation	Function
S_2	S_1	S_0	C_{in}		
0	0	0	0	$F = A$	Transfer A
0	0	0	1	$F = A + 1$	Increment A
0	0	1	0	$F = A + B$	Addition
0	0	1	1	$F = A + B + 1$	Add with carry
0	1	0	0	$F = A + \overline{B}$	A plus 1's complement of B
0	1	0	1	$F = A + \overline{B} + 1$	Subtraction
0	1	1	0	$F = A - 1$	Decrement A
0	1	1	1	$F = A$	Transfer A
1	0	0	0	$F = A \wedge B$	AND
1	0	1	0	$F = A \vee B$	OR
1	1	0	0	$F = A \oplus B$	XOR
1	1	1	0	$F = \overline{A}$	Complement A

245

7-7   SHIFTER UNIT

The shifter attached to the bus system transfers the output of the ALU onto the output bus. The shifter transfers the information by shifting it to the right or left. Provision must be made for a direct transfer with no shift from the ALU to the output bus. The shifter provides the shift operations commonly not available in the ALU.

An obvious choice for a shifter would be a bidirectional shift register with parallel load. Information from the ALU can be transferred to the register in parallel and then shifted to the right or left. In this type of configuration, a clock pulse is needed for loading the output of the ALU into the shift register, and another pulse is needed for the shift. These two pulses are in addition to the clock pulse required to transfer the information from the shift register to the selected destination register.

The transfer from a source register to a destination register through the ALU and shifter can be done with only one clock pulse when the ALU and shifter are implemented as combinational circuits. In a combinational circuit, the signals propagate through gates without the need of a clock pulse. Hence, the only clock needed in the processor bus system is for loading the data from the output bus into the selected destination register.

A combinational circuit shifter unit can be constructed with multiplexers as shown in Figure 7-18. The two selection variables H_1 and H_0 are applied to all four multiplexers to select the type of operation in the shifter. With $H_1 H_0 = 00$, no

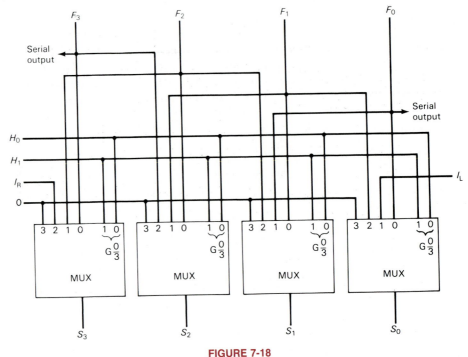

FIGURE 7-18
4-Bit Shifter

TABLE 7-7
Function Table for Shifter

H_1	H_0	Operation	Function
0	0	$S \leftarrow F$	Transfer F to S (no shift)
0	1	$S \leftarrow$ shl F	Shift left F into S
1	0	$S \leftarrow$ shr F	Shift right F into S
1	1	$S \leftarrow 0$	Transfer 0's into S

shift is executed and the inputs from F go directly to the shifter outputs in S. The next two values of the selection variables cause a shift left and a shift right operation. When $H_1H_0 = 11$, the multiplexers select the inputs attached to logic-0 and the S outputs are all equal to 0. Table 7-7 summarizes the operation of the shifter.

The diagram of Figure 7-18 shows only four stages of the shifter. The shifter, of course, must have n stages in a system with n parallel lines. Inputs I_R and I_L are the serial inputs for the shift right and shift left, respectively. Another selection variable may be employed to specify what goes into I_R and I_L during the shift. For example, a third selection variable, H_2, when in one state can select a 0 for the serial input during the shift. When H_2 is in the other state, the data can be rotated together with the value in the carry status bit. In this way, a carry produced during an ALU addition operation can be shifted to the right and into the most significant bit position of a register.

Barrel Shifter

In some processor applications the data must be shifted more than once during a single operation. A barrel shifter is a circuit that shifts the input data bits by a number of positions dictated by the binary value of a set of selection lines. The shift is a cyclic rotation which means that the input binary information is shifted in one direction and the bit coming from the most significant end of the shifter is brought back to the least significant position.

A 4-bit barrel shifter is shown in Figure 7-19. It consists of four multiplexers with two common selection lines S_1 and S_0. The selection variables determine the number of positions that the input data will be shifted to the left by rotation. When $S_1S_0 = 00$, no shift occurs and the inputs form a direct path to the outputs. When $S_1S_0 = 01$, the input binary information is rotated once with D_0 going to Y_1, D_1 $S_1S_0 = 01$, the input binary information is rotated once with D_0 going to Y_1, D_1 input is rotated by two positions, and when $S_1S_0 = 11$, the rotation is by three bit positions.

Table 7-8 gives the function table for the 4-bit barrel shifter. For each binary value of the selection variables, the table lists the inputs that go to the corresponding output. Thus, to rotate three positions, S_1S_0 must be equal to 11; and D_0 goes to Y_3, D_1 goes to Y_0, D_2 goes to Y_1, and D_3 goes to Y_2.

A barrel shifter with 2^n input and output lines requires 2^n multiplexers each having 2^n data inputs and n selection inputs. The number of rotation positions is dictated by the selection variables and can be from 0 (no shift) to $2^n - 1$ positions.

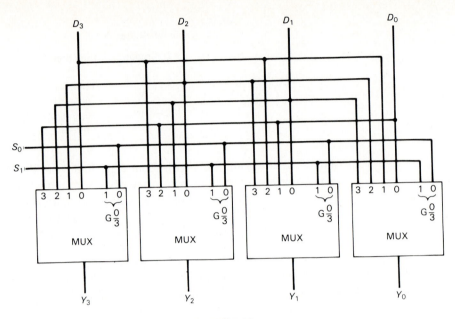

FIGURE 7-19
4-Bit Barrel Shifter

TABLE 7-8
Function Table for 4-Bit Barrel Shifter

Select		Output				Operation
S_1	S_0	Y_3	Y_2	Y_1	Y_0	
0	0	D_3	D_2	D_1	D_0	No shift
0	1	D_2	D_1	D_0	D_3	Rotate once
1	0	D_1	D_0	D_3	D_2	Rotate twice
1	1	D_0	D_3	D_2	D_1	Rotate three times

7-8   CONTROL WORD

The selection variables in a processor unit control the microoperations executed within the unit during any given clock pulse transition. The selection variables control the buses, the ALU, the shifter, and the destination register. We will now demonstrate by means of an example how the control variables select the micro-operations. The example defines a specific processor together with its selection variables. The choice of control variables for some typical microoperations will then be demonstrated.

A block diagram of a processor unit is shown in Figure 7-20. It has a register file of seven registers $R1$ through $R7$. The outputs of the seven registers go through two sets of multiplexers to select the inputs to the ALU. Input data from an external source (such as a memory unit) are selected by the same multiplexers. The output

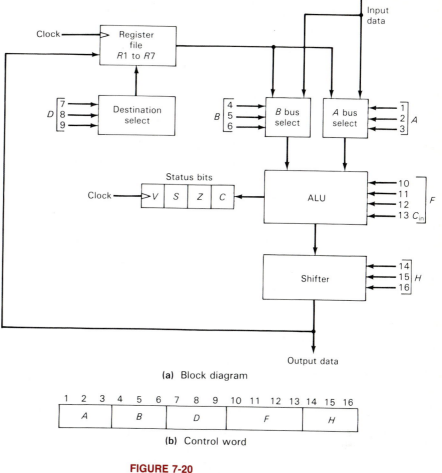

(a) Block diagram

(b) Control word

FIGURE 7-20
Processor Unit with Control Variables

of the ALU goes through a shifter and into the output bus. The output from the shifter can be transferred to any one of the registers and can also be directed to an external destination. The ALU provides the binary data for the four status bits: C (carry), Z (zero), S (sign), and V (overflow).

There are 16 binary selection inputs in the unit and their combined value specifies a *control word*. The 16-bit control word is defined in Figure 7-20(b). It consists of five parts called fields, with each field designated by a letter symbol. Four of the fields contain three bits each, and one field has four bits. The three bits of A select a source register for one input of the ALU. The three bits of B select a register for the second input of the ALU. The three bits of D select a destination register. The four bits of F select one of 12 operations in the ALU. The three bits of H select the type of shift in the shifter unit. The 16-bit control word, when applied to the selection inputs, specifies a particular microoperation.

TABLE 7-9
Encoding of Control Word for Processor Unit

Binary code	A	B	D	F with $C_{in} = 0$	F with $C_{in} = 1$	H
				Function of selection fields		
000	Input	Input	None	$F = A$	$F = A + 1$	No shift
001	R1	R1	R1	$F = A + B$	$F = A + B + 1$	SHL
010	R2	R2	R2	$F = A + \overline{B}$	$F = A - B$	SHR
011	R3	R3	R3	$F = A - 1$	$F = A$	Bus $= 0$
100	R4	R4	R4	$F = A \wedge B$	—	—
101	R5	R5	R5	$F = A \vee B$	—	ROL
110	R6	R6	R6	$F = A \oplus B$	—	ROR
111	R7	R7	R7	$F = \overline{A}$	—	—

The functions of all selection variables are specified in Table 7-9. The 3-bit binary code listed in the first column of the table specifies the binary code for each of the five fields. The register selected by fields A, B, and D is the one with the decimal number equivalent to the binary number in the code. When the A or B field is 000, the corresponding multiplexer selects the external input data. When D = 000, no destination register is selected but the contents of the output bus are available for the external outputs. The encoding of the F field is dependent on the value of the input carry C_{in}. The four bits in the F field for each operation are determined from the three bits in the corresponding first column of the table and the bit of C_{in}. The operations listed for the ALU are the same as the ones specified in Table 7-6.

The first four entries for the code in the H field specify the shift operations of Table 7-7. The H field has a third selection variable to distinguish between a logical shift and a shift by rotation. The SHL (shift left) and SHR (shift right) operations listed in the table are logical shifts, which means that 0 is applied to their corresponding serial inputs. When the third selection variable in the H field is equal to 1, it indicates a shift by rotation. This is designated in the table by the symbols ROL (rotate left) and ROR (rotate right). The ROL operation shifts the input data to the left and inserts the value of the serial output into the serial input. The same applies to the ROR operation except that the shift is to the right.

A control word of 16 bits is needed to specify a microoperation for the processor. The control word for a given microoperation can be derived from the selection variables. For example, the subtract microoperation given by the statement

$$R1 \leftarrow R2 - R3$$

specifies $R2$ for the A input of the ALU, $R3$ for the B input of the ALU, an ALU operation $F = A - B$, no shift for the shifter, and $R1$ for the destination register. Thus, the control word is specified by the five fields and the corresponding binary value for each field is obtained from the encoding listed in Table 7-9. The binary control word for the subtract microoperation is 0100110010101000 and is obtained as follows:

TABLE 7-10
Examples of Microoperations for the Processor

Microoperation	Symbolic designation					Control word				
	A	B	D	F	H	A	B	D	F	H
$R1 \leftarrow R2 - R3$	R2	R3	R1	$F = A - B$	No shift	010	011	001	0101	000
$R4 \leftarrow$ shr $(R5 + R6)$	R5	R6	R4	$F = A + B$	SHR	101	110	100	0010	010
$R7 \leftarrow R7 + 1$	R7	—	R7	$F = A + 1$	No shift	111	000	111	0001	000
$R1 \leftarrow R2$	R2	—	R1	$F = A$	No shift	010	000	001	0000	000
Output $\leftarrow R3$	R3	—	None	$F = A$	No shift	011	000	000	0000	000
$R4 \leftarrow$ rol $R4$	R4	—	R4	$F = A$	ROL	100	000	100	0000	101
$R5 \leftarrow 0$	—	—	R5	—	Bus $= 0$	000	000	101	0000	011

Field:	A	B	D	F	H
Symbol:	$R2$	$R3$	$R1$	$F = A - B$	No shift
Control word:	010	011	001	0101	000

The control word for this microoperation and few others are listed in Table 7-10.

The next example in the table is an add and shift microoperation given by the statement

$$R4 \leftarrow \text{shr } (R5 + R6)$$

It specifies an arithmetic addition for the ALU and a shift right operation for the shifter. The sum that is generated in the ALU is shifted to the right, dividing it by 2. The result of the operation is to produce the average value of the two unsigned binary numbers stored in registers $R5$ and $R6$ (provided there is no carry). From knowledge of the symbols in each field, the control word in binary is derived as shown in Table 7-10.

The increment and transfer microoperations do not use the B input of the ALU. For these cases, the B field is marked with a dash. For convenience, we assign 000 to any unused field when formulating the binary control word, although any other binary number may be used. To put the contents of a register into the output terminals, we place the contents of the register into the A input of the ALU, but none of the registers is selected to accept the data. The ALU operation $F = A$ places the information from the register into the output terminals. To shift or rotate the contents of a register without performing an operation in the ALU, we must specify an ALU operation $F = A$. This places the contents of the A input into the F output of the ALU without any change. To clear a register to 0, the output bus is made equal to all 0's with H = 011. The destination field D is made equal to the code for the register.

It is apparent from these examples that many other microoperations can be generated in the processor unit. The most efficient way to generate control words with a large number of bits is to store them in a memory unit. A memory unit that stores control words is referred to as a *control memory*. The output of the control memory is applied to the selection inputs of the processor. By reading consecutive control words from memory, it is possible to initiate the desired sequence of microoperations for the processor. This type of control organization, called *microprogramming*, is discussed in more detail in the next chapter.

REFERENCES

1. MANO, M. M. *Computer System Architecture*. Englewood Cliffs: Prentice-Hall, 1982.

2. BOOTH, T. L. *Introduction to Computer Engineering Hardware and Software Design*. 3rd ed. New York: Wiley, 1984.

3. DIETMEYER, D. L. *Logic Design of Digital Systems*. 2nd ed. Boston: Allyn & Bacon, 1978.

4. GOSLING, J. B. *Design of Arithmetic Units for Digital Computers*. New York: Springer-Verlag, 1980.

5. ERCEGOVAC, M., AND LANG, T. *Digital Systems and Hardware/Firmware Algorithms*. New York: Wiley, 1985.

6. KLINE, R. M. *Structured Digital Design*. Englewood Cliffs: Prentice-Hall, 1983.

PROBLEMS

7-1 Show the block diagram of the hardware that implements the following register transfer statement:

$$T_3: R2 \leftarrow R1, R1 \leftarrow R2$$

7-2 The outputs of four registers $R0$, $R1$, $R2$, and $R3$ are connected through multiplexers to the inputs of a fifth register $R5$. Each register is eight bits long. The required transfers are dictated by four timing variables T_0 through T_3 as follows:

$$T_0: R5 \leftarrow R0$$

$$T_1: R5 \leftarrow R1$$

$$T_2: R5 \leftarrow R2$$

$$T_3: R5 \leftarrow R3$$

The timing variables are mutually exclusive and only one variable can be equal to 1 at any given time while the other three are equal to 0. Draw a block diagram showing the hardware implementation of the register transfers. Include the connections necessary from the four timing variables to the selection lines of the multiplexers and to the load input of register $R5$.

7-3 Using two 4-bit registers $R1$ and $R2$, a quadruple 2-to-1-line multiplexer with enable, and four inverters, draw the circuit diagram that implements the following statements:

$T_1: R2 \leftarrow R1$	Transfer $R1$ to $R2$
$T_2: R2 \leftarrow \overline{R2}$	Complement $R2$
$T_3: R2 \leftarrow 0$	Clear $R2$ synchronous with the clock

The three timing variables T_1 through T_3 are mutually exclusive and only one variable can be equal to 1 at any given time. Use standard graphic diagrams as in Figure 5-3(b) for the registers and Figure 3-31(b) for the multiplexer.

7-4 Draw the block diagram for the hardware that implements the following statements:

$$XT_1 + YT_2: AR \leftarrow AR + BR$$

Where AR and BR are two n-bit registers, X and Y are control variables, and T_1 and T_2 are timing variables. Include the logic gates for the control function. (Remember that the symbol + designates an OR operation in a control or Boolean function, but it represents an arithmetic plus in a microoperation.)

7-5 Consider the following register transfer statements for the two 4-bit registers $R1$ and $R2$.

$$XT: R1 \leftarrow R1 + R2$$

$$\overline{X}T: R1 \leftarrow R2$$

When timing variable $T = 1$, the contents of $R2$ are added to the contents of $R1$ if $X = 1$, or the contents of $R2$ are transferred to $R1$ if $X = 0$. Draw a logic diagram showing the implementation of the two statements. Use standard graphic symbols for the 4-bit registers (Figure 5-3[b]), the 4-bit adder (Figure 3-28), and the multiplexer that selects the inputs to $R1$ (Figure 3-31[b]). In the diagram, show how the control variables X and T select the inputs to $R1$.

7-6 Using a 4-bit counter with parallel load as in Figure 5-19 and a 4-bit adder as in Figure 3-28, draw the logic diagram with standard graphic symbols that implements the following statements:

$$T_1: R1 \leftarrow R1 + R2 \qquad \text{Add } R2 \text{ to } R1$$

$$\overline{T}_1T_2: R1 \leftarrow R1 + 1 \qquad \text{Increment } R1$$

7-7 A digital system has three registers: AR, BR, and PR. Three flip-flops provide the control variables for the system: S is a flip-flop which is set by an external start signal to start the system operation; F and R are two flip-flops used for sequencing the microoperations when the system is in operation. A fourth flip-flop D is set by the system when the operation is completed. The operation of the digital system is described by the following register transfer statements:

$$S: PR \leftarrow 0, S \leftarrow 0, D \leftarrow 0, F \leftarrow 1$$

$$F: F \leftarrow 0, \text{ if } (AR = 0) \text{ then } (D \leftarrow 1) \text{ else } (R \leftarrow 1)$$

$$R: PR \leftarrow PR + BR, AR \leftarrow AR - 1, R \leftarrow 0, F \leftarrow 1$$

(a) Show that the digital system multiplies the contents of registers AR and BR and places the product in register PR.

(b) Draw a block diagram of the hardware implementation. Include a start input signal to set flip-flop S and a done output signal from flip-flop D.

7-8 Assume that registers $R1$ and $R2$ in Figure 7-4 hold two n-bit unsigned numbers. When the select input X is equal to 1, the adder-subtractor circuit performs the arithmetic operation $R1$ + 2's complement of $R2$. This sum and the output carry C_n are transferred into $R1$ and C when $T_1 = 1$ and the clock goes through a positive transition.

(a) Show that if $C = 1$, then the value transferred to $R1$ is equal to $R1 - R2$. But if $C = 0$, the value transferred to $R1$ is the 2's complement of $(R2 - R1)$. (See Section 1-4 and example 1-9 for the procedure of subtracting unsigned numbers with 2's complement.)

(b) Indicate how the value in the C bit can be used to detect a borrow after the subtraction of two unsigned numbers.

7-9 Convert the following decimal numbers to signed binary with eight bits each (including the sign). Perform the operation with the signed binary numbers and check the last

two carries. State whether the carries indicate an overflow. Remember that 8-bit numbers have a capacity range from $+127$ to -128.
(a) $(+65) + (+36)$ (c) $(-36) + (-90)$
(b) $(+65) - (-90)$ (d) $(-65) - (+90)$

7-10 Perform the logic AND, OR, and XOR with the two 8-bit numbers 10011100 and 10101010.

7-11 Given the 16-bit value 01011010 11000011. What operation must be performed
(a) to clear to 0 the last eight bits?
(b) to set to 1 the first eight bits?
(c) to complement the middle eight bits?

7-12 The following logic microoperation is performed with registers AR and BR.

$$AR \leftarrow AR \wedge \overline{BR} \qquad \text{Complement } BR \text{ and AND to } AR$$

Determine how the bits in AR are manipulated by the bits in BR.

7-13 Starting from the eight bits 10110010, show the values obtained after each of the shift microoperations listed in Table 7-4.

7-14 Show that the statement

$$R1 \leftarrow R1 + R1$$

is the same as the logical shift left of register $R1$.

7-15 (a) Represent the number -26 as an 8-bit signed number. Show how the number can be multiplied and divided by 2 by means of the arithmetic shift microoperation. Indicate if there is an overflow.
(b) Repeat with the equivalent binary number -94 and $+94$.

7-16 Let S_1 and S_0 be the selection variables for the multiplexer in the bus system of Figure 7-6 and D_1 and D_0 be the selection variables for the destination decoder.
(a) Determine the transfer that occurs when the control variables $S_1 S_0 D_1 D_0$ equal (1) 0001; (2) 0110; (3) 1111.
(b) Give the 4-bit selection for the following transfers: (1) $R0 \leftarrow R1$; (2) $R2 \leftarrow R1$; (3) $R3 \leftarrow R2$.

7-17 Draw a diagram of a bus system similar to the one shown in Figure 7-6 but use three-state buffers and a decoder instead of the multiplexers.

7-18 The following memory transfers are specified for the system of Figure 7-10.
(a) $D2 \leftarrow M[A3]$ (b) $M[A1] \leftarrow D0$
Specify the memory operation and determine the binary selection variables for the two bus buffers and the decoder.

7-19 A processor unit like the one in Figure 7-11 has 30 registers. How many selection lines are needed for each set of multiplexers and for the decoder?

7-20 Given an 8-bit ALU with outputs F_0 through F_7 and carries C_7 and C_8, show the logic circuit for setting the four status bits, C (carry), V (overflow), Z (zero), and S (sign).

7-21 Assume that the 4-bit ALU of Figure 7-12 is enclosed in one IC package. Show the connections among two such ICs to form an 8-bit ALU.

7-22 Design an arithmetic circuit with one selection variable S and two n-bit data inputs A and B. The circuit generates the following four arithmetic operations in conjunction with the input carry C_{in}. Draw the logic diagram for the first two stages.

S	$C_{in} = 0$	$C_{in} = 1$
0	$F = A + B$ (add)	$F = A + 1$ (increment)
1	$F = A - 1$ (decrement)	$F = A + \bar{B} + 1$ (subtract)

7-23 Show the logic diagram of a 4-bit arithmetic circuit that performs the operations specified in Table 7-5. Use four multiplexers and four full adders.

7-24 Design a four bit arithmetic circuit with two selection variables S_1 and S_0 that generates the following arithmetic operations. Draw the logic diagram of one typical stage.

S_1	S_0	$C_{in} = 0$	$C_{in} = 1$
0	0	$F = A + B$ (add)	$F = A + B + 1$
0	1	$F = A$ (transfer)	$F = A + 1$ (increment)
1	0	$F = \bar{B}$ (complement)	$F = \bar{B} + 1$ (negate)
1	1	$F = A + \bar{B}$	$F = A + \bar{B} + 1$ (subtract)

7-25 Design an arithmetic circuit with one selection variable S and two data inputs A and B. When $S = 0$, the circuit performs the addition operation $F = A + B$. When $S = 1$, the circuit performs the increment operation $F = A + 1$.

7-26 Input X_i and Y_i of each full-adder circuit in an arithmetic circuit has the digital logic specified by the following Boolean functions

$$X_i = A_i \qquad Y_i = \bar{B_i}S + B_i\bar{C}_{in}$$

where S is a selection variable, C_{in} is the input carry, and A_i and B_i are the input data in stage i.
(a) Draw the logic diagram of the 4-bit arithmetic circuit.
(b) Determine the four arithmetic operations performed when S and C_{in} are equal to 00, 01, 10, and 11.

7-27 Design a digital circuit that performs the four logic operations of exclusive-OR, exclusive-NOR, NOR and NAND. Use two selection variables. Show the logic diagram of one typical stage.

7-28 Add another multiplexer to the shifter of Figure 7-18 with two separate selection lines G_1 and G_0. This multiplexer is used to specify the serial input I_R during the shift right operation in the following manner:

G_1	G_0	Operation
0	0	Logical shift right ($I_R = 0$)
0	1	Rotate right ($I_R = F_0$)
1	0	Rotate right with carry ($I_R = C, C = F_0$)
1	1	Arithmetic shift right ($I_R = F_3$)

Show the connection of the multiplexer to the shifter.

7-29 The shift select H field as defined in Table 7-9 has three variables H_2, H_1, and H_0. The last two selection variables are used for the shifter as specified in Table 7-7. Design the circuit associated with selection variable H_2 that causes a rotation.

7-30 Obtain the function table of a 4-bit barrel shifter that rotates the bits to the right. (Table 7-8 assumes a rotation to the left.) Draw the circuit with four multiplexers.

7-31 Obtain the function table of an 8-bit barrel shifter that rotates the bits to the left.

7-32 Specify the control word that must be applied to the processor of Figure 7-20 to implement the following microoperations:

(a) $R2 \leftarrow R1 + 1$ (e) $R1 \leftarrow$ shl $R1$

(b) $R3 \leftarrow R4 + R5$ (f) $R2 \leftarrow$ ror $R2$

(c) $R6 \leftarrow \overline{R6}$ (g) $R5 \leftarrow R3 + R1$

(d) $R7 \leftarrow R7 - 1$ (h) $R6 \leftarrow R7$

7-33 Given the following 16-bit control word for the processor unit of Figure 7-20, determine the microoperation that is executed for each control word.

(a) 001 010 011 0101 000 (d) 000 001 000 1000 000

(b) 110 000 001 0000 001 (e) 111 000 011 0000 110

(c) 010 010 010 1100 000

CONTROL LOGIC DESIGN

8-1 INTRODUCTION

The binary information stored in a digital computer can be classified as either data or control information. Data are discrete elements of information that are manipulated to perform arithmetic, logic, shift, and other data processing tasks. These operations are implemented with digital components such as adders, decoders, multiplexers, counters, and shift registers. Control information provides command signals that supervise the various operations in the data section to accomplish the desired data processing tasks. The logic design of a digital system can be divided into two distinct parts. One part is concerned with the design of the digital circuits that perform the data processing operations. The other part is concerned with the design of the control circuit that supervises the operations and determines the sequence in which they are executed.

The timing for all registers in a synchronous digital system is controlled by a master clock generator. The clock pulses are applied to all flip-flops and registers in the system, including the flip-flops and registers in the control unit. The continuous clock pulses do not change the state of a register unless the register is enabled by a control signal. The binary variables that control the selection inputs of multiplexers and the load inputs of registers are generated in the control subsystem.

The relationship between the control logic and the data processor subsystems in a digital system is shown in Figure 8-1. The data processor part may be a general purpose processor unit with many registers and a common ALU, or it may consist of individual registers and associated digital circuits that perform various micro-

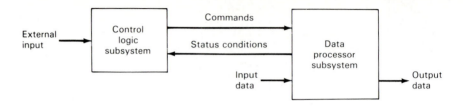

FIGURE 8-1
Control and Data Processor Interaction

operations. The control logic initiates properly sequenced command signals to the data processor. The control logic uses status conditions from the data processor to serve as decision variables for determining the sequence of the controlled operations.

The control logic that generates the signals for sequencing the operations in the data processor is essentially a sequential circuit with internal states that dictate the control commands for the system. At any given time, the state of the sequential control initiates a prescribed set of commands. Depending on status conditions and other external inputs, the sequential control goes to the next state to initiate other operations. The digital circuits that act as the control logic provide a time sequence of signals for initiating the microoperations in the data processor subsystem, and they also determine the next state of the control subsystem itself.

There are two major types of control organization: hardwired control and microprogrammed control. In the *hardwired* organization, the control logic is implemented with gates and flip-flops similar to a sequential circuit. It has the advantage that it can be optimized to produce a fast mode of operation. In the *microprogrammed* organization, the control information such as control functions or control words are stored as 1's and 0's in a special memory. A hardwired control, as the name implies, requires changes in the wiring among the various components if the design has to be modified or corrected. In the microprogrammed control, any required changes or modifications can be done merely by changing the contents of the memory.

In addition to providing the basic principles of both types of control organizations, this chapter presents specific examples that illustrate both methods. The microprogrammed organization is illustrated with an example that controls the operations of a general purpose processor unit. The various ways available for the design of a hardwired control are illustrated with an example of a binary multiplier. The last two sections in the chapter present the organization of a very simple computer and show how the computer can be designed by the hardwired method. The design of a computer central processing unit with a microprogrammed control organization is presented in Chapter 10.

8-2   MICROPROGRAMMED CONTROL

The purpose of the control unit in a digital system is to initiate a series of sequential steps of microoperations. During any given time, certain microoperations are to be initiated while others remain idle. The control variables at any given time can be represented by a string of 1's and 0's called a control word. As such, control words can be programmed to initiate the various components in the data processor subsystem in an organized manner. A control unit whose binary control variables are stored in a memory is called a *microprogrammed control unit*. Each word in control memory contains within it a *microinstruction*. The microinstruction specifies one or more microoperations for the system. A sequence of microinstructions constitutes the microprogram. Since alterations of the microprogram are not needed once the control unit is in operation, the control memory can be a read only memory (ROM). The use of a microprogram involves placing all control variables in words of ROM for use by the control unit through successive read operations. The content of the word in ROM at a given address specifies the microoperations for the data processor subsystem.

A more advanced development known as dynamic microprogramming permits a microprogram to be loaded initially from the computer console or from an auxiliary memory such as magnetic disk. Control units that use dynamic microprogramming employ a writable control memory. This type of memory can be used for writing (to change the microprogram) but is used mostly for reading. A memory which is part of a control unit, is referred to as a *control memory*.

The general configuration of a microprogrammed control unit is demonstrated in the block diagram of Figure 8-2. The control memory is assumed to be ROM, within which all control information is permanently stored. The control memory address register specifies the address of the microinstruction and the control data register holds the microinstruction read from memory. The microinstruction contains a control word that specifies one or more microoperations for the data processor. Once these operations are executed, the control must determine its next address. The location of the next microinstruction may be the next one in sequence, or it may be located somewhere else in the control memory. For this reason, it is necessary to use some bits of the present microinstruction to control the generation of the address of the next microinstruction. The next address may also be a function of external input conditions. While the microoperations are being executed, the next address is computed in the next address generator circuit and then transferred into the control address register to read the next microinstruction. Thus, a microinstruction contains bits for initiating microoperations in the data processor part and bits that determine the address sequence for the control memory itself.

The next address generator is sometimes called a microprogram *sequencer*, as it determines the address sequence that is read from control memory. The address of the next microinstruction can be specified in several ways depending on the sequencer inputs. Typical functions of a microprogram sequencer are incrementing the control address register by one, loading into the control address register an

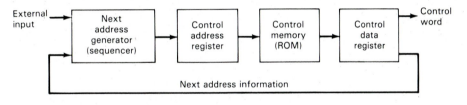

FIGURE 8-2
Microprogrammed Control Organization

address from control memory, transferring an external address, and loading an initial address to start the control operations.

The control data register holds the present microinstruction while the next address is computed and read from memory. The data register is sometimes called a *pipeline register*. It allows the microoperations specified by the control word to be executed simultaneously with the generation of the next microinstruction. This configuration requires a two phase clock, with one phase applied to the address register and the other to the data register.

The system can operate without the control data register by applying a single phase clock to the address register. The control word and next address information are taken directly from the control memory. It must be realized that a ROM operates as a combination circuit, with the address value as the input and the corresponding word as the output. The content of the specified word in ROM remains in the output wires as long as its address value remains in the address register. No read signal is needed, unlike random access memory. Each clock pulse will execute the microoperations specified by the control word and also transfer a new address to the control address register. In the example that follows we assume a single phase clock, and therefore, we do not use a control data register. In this way the address register is the only component in the control system that receives clock pulses. The other two components, the sequencer and the control memory, are combinational circuits and do not need a clock.

The main advantage of the microprogrammed control is the fact that, once the hardware configuration is established, there should be no need for further hardware or wiring changes. If we want to establish a different control sequence for the system, all we need to do is specify a different set of microinstructions for the control memory. The hardware configuration should not be changed for different operations; the only thing that must be changed is the microprogram residing in control memory.

8-3 CONTROL OF PROCESSOR UNIT

To show the general properties of the microprogram organization, we will demonstrate a configuration that includes the control of a processor unit. A general purpose processor unit was developed in Chapter 7 and shown in block diagram in Figure 7-20. It has seven registers $R1$ through $R7$, an ALU, a shifter, and four status bits $C, Z, S,$ and V. A microoperation is selected with a control word of 16 bits which is divided into 5 fields A, B, D, F, and H.

A microprogrammed unit for controlling the processor is shown in Figure 8-3. It has a control memory ROM with 64 words of 26 bits each, a control address register CAR, and two multiplexers MUX1 and MUX2. In order to select between 64 words of memory we need an address of 6 bits. To select among 8 multiplexer inputs we need 3 bits for MUX 2 select. One bit selects between an external address and the address field of the microinstruction with MUX1. Adding the 16 bits for the control word that selects a microoperation in the processor unit gives a total of 26 bits for the microinstruction. Thus, each microinstruction read from control

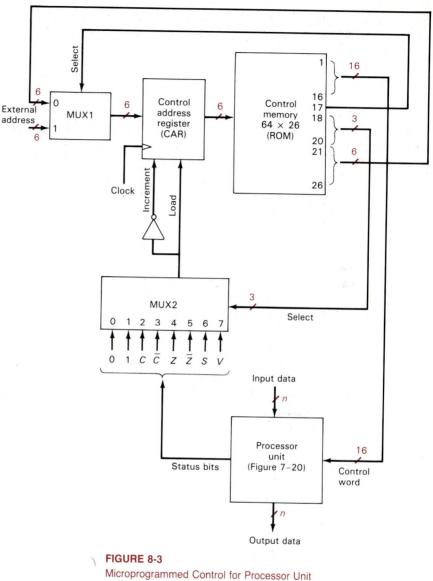

FIGURE 8-3

Microprogrammed Control for Processor Unit

memory contains the 16 bits of a control word for the processor and 10 bits for selecting the next address in the control address register, CAR.

The status bits from the processor unit are applied to the inputs of MUX2. If the selected input is equal to 1, then the load input of CAR is enabled, and the 6-bit address from MUX1 is loaded into CAR. If the selected input is equal to 0, CAR is incremented by one. Thus, bits 18, 19, and 20 of the present microinstruction select one of the inputs from MUX2 and the binary value of this input determines the operation performed on CAR.

Input 0 of MUX2 is connected to a binary constant which is always equal to 0. This input, when selected, generates a 0 output in MUX2 which enables the increment operation in CAR. Thus, when MUX2 select bits are equal to 000, CAR is incremented by one. Similarly, input 1 of MUX2 is always equal to 1; so when MUX2 select bits are equal to 001, the load input to CAR is enabled and a new address is loaded into the register. This causes an unconditional branch to the address given by bits 21 through 26 of the present microinstruction (provided bit 17 is equal to 0). Both the true and complement inputs of C and Z status bits are applied to MUX2 inputs. In this way, it is possible to specify a branch to a new address depending on whether $C = 1$ or $C = 0$. The other two status bits, S and V, have only the true value.

The input into CAR is a function of bit 17 of the microinstruction. If bit 17 is equal to 0, the address field of the microinstruction is loaded into CAR. If bit 17 is equal to 1, an external address is loaded into CAR. The external address is for the purpose of initiating a new sequence of microinstructions which can be specified by the external environment.

The operation of the control unit is as follows. At any given clock pulse transition, the control address register CAR receives a new address. The 26-bit microinstruction at this address is read from control memory. The control word of the microinstruction specifies a microoperation in the processor and MUX1 and MUX2 determine the next operation for CAR. The signals propagate through the combinational circuits such as ROM, ALU, shifter, and multiplexers but the actual microinstruction is not terminated until a clock pulse transition occurs. The next transition of the clock transfers the result of the microoperation into the destination register in the processor, updates the required status bits, and puts a new address into CAR. The new address in CAR specifies a microinstruction that is read from control memory and is executed with the next transition of the clock. This process repeats for each clock transition. Note that the same clock pulse transition that executes the microoperation in the processor unit also transfers the next address to CAR.

Encoding of Microinstructions

The 26 bits of the microinstruction are divided into eight fields. The number of bits in each field and the symbolic name assigned to each is shown in Table 8-1. In order to facilitate writing microprograms we will assign a symbolic name to each binary combination of each field. Fields A, B, and D specify registers $R1$ through $R7$ in the processor unit. Bit combination 000 in fields A and B specifies an input data symbolized by INP. The destination field D does not select a register when its binary code is 000 and we will symbolize that with NONE. The encoding of bits and the corresponding symbols for fields F, H, and MUX2 are specified in the next three tables. MUX1 select can be either 0 or 1. We designate 0 by the symbol INT (for internal address) and 1 by EXT (for external address). The 6-bit address field is designated by the decimal equivalent of the binary address.

The ALU operations are listed in Table 8-2. Each operation is recognized by the 4-bit binary code assigned to it and its corresponding three letter symbol. The table also specifies how the status bits are affected by each operation. When the bit is not affected by the operation we mark it with an N in the table. A Y indicates that the operation updates the corresponding bit according to the result of the

TABLE 8-1
Microinstruction Format

Bits	Field	Symbols	Function
1–3	A	INP, $R1 - R7$	Right input of ALU
4–6	B	INP, $R1 - R7$	Left input of ALU
7–9	D	NONE, $R1 - R7$	Destination register
10–13	F	See Table 8-2	ALU operation
14–16	H	See Table 8-3	Shifter operation
17	MUX1	INT, EXT	MUX1 select (INT = 0, EXT = 1)
18–20	MUX2	See Table 8-4	MUX2 select
21–26	ADRS	Address number	Address field

INP: input data to processor; NONE: none of the registers are selected; INT: internal address field of microinstruction; EXT: external address.

operation. The Z (zero) and S (sign) bits are affected by all the operations except TSF. The S bit after a logic operation is considered as the leftmost bit of the result. The add and subtract operations also update the C (carry) and V (overflow) bits. There are two transfer operations in the ALU. The one symbolized by TSF (code 0000) does not change the status bits. The other symbolized by TRC (code 0111) resets the C bit to 0 and updates the Z and S bits.

The shifter operations are listed in Table 8-3. The no shift operation is symbolized by NSH and the all zeros output is recognized by the symbol ZERO. The other six operations specify shifts and rotates either to the left or right. SHL and SHR receive 0 in their corresponding serial inputs. ROL and ROR rotate the bit from the serial output into the corresponding serial input. RLC and RRC insert the value of the status bit C into the serial input and transfer the serial output bit into the C flip-flop. Note that the rotate with carry operations affect the carry status bit.

The binary select input to MUX2 and a symbolic name for each combination are listed in Table 8-4. The binary code 000 chooses a 0 input for the multiplexer which causes CAR to be incremented. We designate this condition by NEXT,

TABLE 8-2
ALU Operations (F Field)

Binary code	Symbol	Status bits*				Function
		Z	S	C	V	
0000	TSF	N	N	N	N	Transfer A
0001	INC	Y	Y	N	N	Increment A by one
0010	ADD	Y	Y	Y	Y	Add $A + B$
0101	SUB	Y	Y	Y	Y	Subtract $A - B$
0110	DEC	Y	Y	N	N	Decrement A by one
0111	TRC	Y	Y	0	N	Transfer A and reset carry
1000	AND	Y	Y	N	N	A AND B
1010	OR	Y	Y	N	N	A OR B
1100	XOR	Y	Y	N	N	A exclusive-OR B
1110	COM	Y	Y	N	N	Complement A

*N = status bit not affected; Y = status bit affected by the operation; 0 = reset to 0.

TABLE 8-3
Shifter Operations (H field)

Binary code	Symbol	Function
000	NSH	No shift
001	SHL	Shift left with serial input = 0
010	SHR	Shift right with serial input = 0
011	ZERO	All zeros in output of shifter
100	RLC	Rotate left with carry
101	ROL	Rotate left
110	ROR	Rotate right
111	RRC	Rotate right with carry

TABLE 8-4
Select Input to MUX2

Binary code	Symbol	Function
000	NEXT	Go to next address by incrementing CAR
001	LAD	Load address into CAR (branch unconditionally)
010	LC	Load on carry (branch if $C = 1$)
011	LNC	Load on no carry (branch if $C = 0$)
100	LZ	Load on zero (branch if $Z = 1$)
101	LNZ	Load on non zero (branch if $Z = 0$)
110	LS	Load on sign (branch if $S = 1$)
111	LV	Load on overflow (branch if $V = 1$)

meaning that the next microinstruction in sequence will be chosen. The binary code 001 chooses a 1 input for the multiplexer which causes the loading of the input address into *CAR*. This is designated by the symbol LAD and is essentially an unconditional branch operation. The other six inputs to MUX2 cause a branching to the specified address depending on a given status bit condition or its complement.

Examples of Microinstructions

Before going through an actual microprogram for the control unit it will be instructive to show examples of a few typical microinstructions. Table 8-5 lists six examples of microinstructions in symbolic form and also gives the corresponding 26-bit binary equivalent. The *CAR* address is the address where the microinstruction is assumed to be stored in control memory. The symbols on top of the table are the eight fields of the microinstruction format.

The first example is for a microinstruction stored in address 36. The ALU operation in the F field specifies a logical AND which is performed with the contents of register *R*1 (field A) and register *R*2 (field B). The result of the operation is transferred into register *R*1 (field D). MUX2 select has the symbol NEXT meaning that *CAR* will be incremented by one. The address field and the MUX1 select do not contribute to the selection of the next address and therefore, these two fields

TABLE 8-5
Examples of Microinstructions (Not a Microprogram)

CAR address	Control Word					Select		Address field
	A	B	D	F	H	MUX1	MUX2	
36	R1	R2	R1	AND	NSH	—	NEXT	—
	001	010	001	1000	000	0	000	000000
40	R3	—	R3	DEC	NSH	INT	LAD	43
	011	000	011	0110	000	0	001	101011
45	—	—	NONE	TSF	NSH	—	NEXT	—
	000	000	000	0000	000	0	000	000000
52	—	—	R4	TSF	ZERO	INT	LS	37
	000	000	100	0000	011	0	110	100101
56	R5	—	R5	TSF	SHL	INT	LNC	62
	101	000	101	0000	001	0	011	111110
59	R6	R7	R2	ADD	NSH	EXT	LAD	—
	110	111	010	0010	000	1	001	000000

are marked with a dash. The microinstruction can be specified with the following register transfer statement:

$$R1 \leftarrow R1 \wedge R2, \ CAR \leftarrow CAR + 1$$

The binary values for the microinstruction are listed under the symbols in each field. These values are obtained from Tables 8-1 through 8-4. The fields marked with a dash are not used, and therefore, any binary number can be substituted for the dash. For convenience and consistency we will mark these places with 0's. The 26-bit word that must be stored in control memory at address 36 is 001 010 001 1000 000 0 000 000000.

The second microinstruction in Table 8-5 resides in address 40. The equivalent register transfer statement for this microinstruction is

$$R3 \leftarrow R3 - 1, \ CAR \leftarrow 43$$

It decrements $R3$ and branches to the microinstruction at address 43. The branching to address 43 is specified by the LAD and INT symbols in MUX2 and MUX1 fields.

The microinstruction at address 45 is an example where the control word specifies no operation for the processor. The TSF in the ALU field does not change the status bits. The NONE in the D field results in no change in the processor registers. The NSH in the H field does no shifting in the shifter. If we choose 0's for the unused fields, then the control word will consist of 16 0's. This will not produce any operation in the processor but the input data will be applied to the output data. A binary microinstruction with 26 0's produces no operation in the processor and increments CAR by one. This is equivalent to a no operation microinstruction.

The microinstruction at address 52 performs the following operations:

$$R4 \leftarrow 0, \text{ if } (S = 1) \text{ then } (CAR \leftarrow 37) \text{ else } (CAR \leftarrow CAR + 1)$$

The ZERO in the H field produces an all 0's in the shifter and this output is transferred into $R4$. The TSF operation is required to make sure that none of the status bits are affected. The symbol LS in MUX2 selects the S (sign) status bit from the processor. If $S = 1$, then the address field of the microinstruction, being the binary equivalent of 37 in this case, is loaded into CAR. If $S = 0$, CAR is incremented. This is the way that all branch conditions operate on CAR.

The microinstruction at address 56 performs the following operations

$$R5 \leftarrow \text{shl } R5, \text{ if } (C = 0) \text{ then } (CAR \leftarrow 62) \text{ else } (CAR \leftarrow CAR + 1)$$

and the one at address 59

$$R2 \leftarrow R6 + R7, \quad CAR \leftarrow \text{External address}$$

The external address is selected by MUX1 through the symbol EXT. The LAD for MUX2 enables the load input of CAR. The address field of the microinstruction is not used.

8-4   MICROPROGRAM EXAMPLES

We now demonstrate by means of two examples how to write microprograms for control memory. We will assume that an external address initiates a sequence of microinstructions in control memory. This sequence constitutes a microprogram *routine*. The external address supplies the first address where the microprogram routine resides in control memory. The routine is terminated with a microinstruction that loads a new external address to start executing a different routine. Thus, the control memory is divided into several routines and an external control determines which routine should be executed. The branch to the required routine is accomplished by the application of the corresponding external address.

Microprogram Example

The first microprogram example has no specific application but it shows how the status bits are used for conditional branch microinstructions. In this example we will write a microprogram starting from address 20 that subtracts the contents of register $R2$ from the contents of register $R1$ and places the difference in register will write a microprogram starting from address 20 that subtracts the contents of If $R1 = R2$ then $R4$ is increment by one. The contents of $R4$ are then applied to the output terminals of the processor and the microprogram routine terminates by branching to an external address. It is assumed that all binary numbers are unsigned. The operations to be performed can be summarized as follows:

1. $R3 \leftarrow R1 - R2$. This updates C and Z
2. If $R1 < R2$ (detected by $C = 0$) then $R4 \leftarrow R4 + R1$
   If $R > R2$ (detected by $C = 1$ and $Z = 0$) then $R4 \leftarrow R4 + R2$
   If $R1 = R2$ (detected by $Z = 1$) then $R4 \leftarrow R4 + 1$
3. Output $\leftarrow R4$ and branch to external address.

The condition for C after a subtraction of two unsigned binary numbers is presented in Section 1-4 and Example 1-9. The subtraction $R1 - R2$ is done by adding $R1$

TABLE 8-6
Register Transfer Statements for Example

Address	Microoperations and branch conditions
20	$R3 \leftarrow R1 - R2, CAR \leftarrow CAR + 1$
21	If $(C = 1)$ then $(CAR \leftarrow 23)$ else $(CAR \leftarrow CAR + 1)$
22	$R4 \leftarrow R4 + R1, CAR \leftarrow 26$
23	If $(Z = 0)$ then $(CAR \leftarrow 25)$ else $(CAR \leftarrow CAR + 1)$
24	$R4 \leftarrow R4 + 1, CAR \leftarrow 26$
25	$R4 \leftarrow R4 + R2, CAR \leftarrow CAR + 1$
26	Output $\leftarrow R4, CAR \leftarrow$ external address

to the 2's complement of $R2$. If $R1 \geq R2$ then $C = 1$, and if $R1 < R2$ then $C = 0$. To detect the condition $R1 > R2$ we must have $C = 1$, provided that $R1$ is not equal to $R2$, which is detected from $Z = 0$. When $R1 = R2$, the subtraction $R1 - R2$ is 0, and the Z bit is set to 1.

Before writing the symbolic microprogram it may be instructive to obtain the sequence of microoperations in terms of register transfer statements. This is shown in Table 8-6. At address 20 we place the microinstruction that subtracts $R2$ from $R1$. This operation updates the C and Z status bits. If $C = 1$ and $Z = 0$, we go to address 25 to add $R2$ to $R4$. If $C = 0$, we go to address 22 to add $R1$ to $R4$. If $Z = 1$ we go to address 24 to increment $R4$. After one of these operations is executed, the microprogram goes to address 26 to output the contents of $R4$ and branch to an external address.

The symbolic microprogram for the example is listed in Table 8-7. The transformation from the register transfer statements to the symbolic microprogram is a straightforward procedure. The microinstruction in address 21 specifies no operation for the processor and a branch condition depending on the value of C. Note that the value of C is determined from the result of the previous operation. Although the carry is available from the ALU during the subtraction operation in the previous microinstruction, it is not transferred into the status bit flip-flop until the next clock pulse. This same clock pulse also transfers the difference into $R3$ and increments CAR. Therefore, the value of C is not available in the status flip-flop until after CAR is incremented. The last microinstruction shows how the content of $R4$ is placed on the output terminals with the TSF and NSH operations. None of the

TABLE 8-7
Symbolic Microprogram for Example

CAR address	Control word					Select		Address field
	A	B	D	F	H	MUX1	MUX2	
20	$R1$	$R2$	$R3$	SUB	NSH	—	NEXT	—
21	—	—	NONE	TSF	NSH	INT	LC	23
22	$R4$	$R1$	$R4$	ADD	NSH	INT	LAD	26
23	—	—	NONE	TSF	NSH	INT	LNZ	25
24	$R4$	—	$R4$	INC	NSH	INT	LAD	26
25	$R4$	$R2$	$R4$	ADD	NSH	—	NEXT	—
26	$R4$	—	NONE	TSF	NSH	EXT	LAD	—

TABLE 8-8
Binary Microprogram for Example

ROM address	Memory content						
	A	B	D	F	H	MUX	ADRS
010100	001	010	011	0101	000	0 000	000000
010101	000	000	000	0000	000	0 010	010111
010110	100	001	100	0010	000	0 001	011010
010111	000	000	000	0000	000	0 101	011001
011000	100	000	100	0001	000	0 001	011010
011001	100	010	100	0010	000	0 000	000000
011010	100	000	000	0000	000	1 001	000000

processor registers receive this information although we could have transferred the data back to $R4$ without loss of information.

The binary microprogram is listed in Table 8-8. The binary values are obtained from the symbolic microinstructions and the corresponding binary codes given in Tables 8-1 through 8-4. When a ROM is used for the control memory, the binary microprogram provides the truth table for the hardware fabrication of the unit.

Counting the Number of 1's

The second microprogram example counts the number of 1's stored in register $R1$ and sets register $R2$ to that number. For example, if $R1 = 00110110$ the microprogram routine counts the four 1's in the register and sets $R2$ to the binary number 100. The numerical example assumes eight bits in $R1$ but the microprogram will count the number of 1's when the register has any other number of bits. The count is done by shifting each bit from $R1$ one at a time into the C status bit and incrementing $R2$ each time that C is equal to 1.

Although the microprogram can be derived directly from the statement of the problem, it may be instructive to construct a flowchart that shows the sequence of microoperations and decision paths. The flowchart for the microprogram routine is shown in Figure 8-4. We assume that the routine starts from address 8. Register $R2$ is initially reset to 0. The content of $R1$ is transferred through the ALU to update the Z bit and reset the carry bit C to 0. If $Z = 1$, it means that the content of $R1$ is zero which signifies that there are no 1's in the number. In that case, the microprogram routine terminates with $R2$ equal to 0. If the value of Z is equal to 0, it indicates that the content of $R1$ is not zero, and therefore, there are some 1's stored in it. $R1$ together with the carry are shifted by rotation as many times as necessary until a 1 is transferred into C. For every 1 detected in C, register $R2$ is incremented by one and the microprogram branches back to check if $R1$ is equal to 0. The program loop is repeated until all the 1's in $R1$ are counted. Note that the value of C is always 0 before the rotation with the content of $R1$.

The microprogram in symbolic form is listed in Table 8-9. The routine starts at address 8 by clearing $R2$ to 0. The microinstruction in address 9 uses the ALU operation TRC (transfer and reset carry) which transfers the contents of register $R1$ through the ALU, resets the carry to 0, and updates the Z and S bits (see Table 8-2). The microinstruction at address 10 checks the value of Z and if equal to 1,

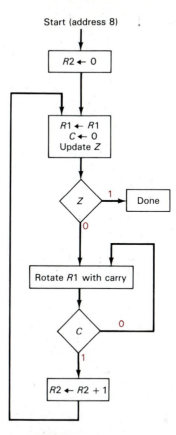

FIGURE 8-4
Flowchart for Counting the
Number of 1's

it indicates that $R1$ contains all 0's and the routine is terminated by accepting a new external address. If Z is not equal to 1, the microprogram continues with the microinstruction at address 11. The RRC (rotate right with carry) operation places the least significant bit of $R1$ into C and shifts $R1$ to the right. The value of C is checked in the microinstruction at address 12. If it is 0, control goes back to address 11 to rotate again until C becomes a 1. When $C = 1$, control goes to address 13

TABLE 8-9
Microprogram for Counting the Number of 1's

CAR address	Control word					Select		Address field
	A	B	D	F	H	MUX1	MUX2	
8	—	—	$R2$	TSF	ZERO	—	NEXT	—
9	$R1$	—	$R1$	TRC	NSH	—	NEXT	—
10	—	—	NONE	TSF	NSH	EXT	LZ	—
11	$R1$	—	$R1$	TSF	RRC	—	NEXT	—
12	—	—	NONE	TSF	NSH	INT	LNC	11
13	$R2$	—	$R2$	INC	NSH	INT	LAD	9

to increment $R2$ and then returns to address 9 to check the content of $R1$ for an all 0's quantity.

The reader familiar with assembly language programming will realize that writing microprograms is very similar to writing assembly language programs for a computer. The microprogram concept is a systematic procedure for designing the control unit of a digital system. Once the microinstruction format is established, the design is done by writing a microprogram, which is similar to writing a program for a computer. For this reason, the microprogram method is sometimes referred to as *firmware* to distinguish it from the purely hardware method (which is also called hardwired control) and the software concept which constitutes a purely programming method.

8-5   DESIGN EXAMPLE: BINARY MULTIPLIER

The microprogrammed control organization is extensively used in the design of digital computers. However, the microprogram method is too expensive for the design of small digital systems and is not fast enough for high speed computers. A second alternative to control design is the hardwired control method. The hardwired control is essentially a sequential circuit whose state at any given time determines the microoperations to be executed in the data processor subsystem.

We will demonstrate the procedure for designing hardwired control by means of two examples. The first example is a circuit that multiplies two unsigned binary numbers. The second example is concerned with the design of a simple digital computer. A combinational circuit multiplier that uses many adders and AND gates was developed in Section 3-4. Here we design a sequential multiplier that uses only one adder and a shift register. The data processor part of the multiplier is developed in this section. The design of the control subsystem is presented in the next section. The design of the hardwired control of the simple computer is presented in Sections 8-7 and 8-8.

Binary Multiplier

The multiplication of two binary numbers is done with paper and pencil by successive additions and shifting. This process is best illustrated with a numerical example. Let us multiply the two binary numbers 10111 and 10011.

23	10111	Multiplicand
19	10011	Multiplier
	10111	
	10111	
	00000	
	00000	
	10111	
437	110110101	Product

The process consists of looking at successive bits of the multiplier, least significant bit first. If the multiplier bit is a 1, the multiplicand is copied down; otherwise, 0's are copied down. The numbers copied down in successive lines are shifted one position to the left from the previous number. Finally, the numbers are added and their sum forms the product. Note that the product obtained from the multiplication of two binary numbers of n bits each can have up to $2n$ bits.

When the above procedure is implemented with digital hardware, it is convenient to change the process slightly. First, instead of providing digital circuits to store and add simultaneously as many binary numbers as there are 1's in the multiplier, it is convenient to provide circuits for the summation of only two binary numbers, and successively accumulate the partial products in a register. Second, instead of shifting the multiplicand to the left, the partial product is shifted to the right, which results in leaving the partial product and the multiplicand in the required relative positions. Third, when the corresponding bit in the multiplier is 0, there is no need to add all 0's to the partial product, since this will not alter its value.

Equipment Configuration

The register configuration for the binary multiplier is shown in Figure 8-5. The multiplicand is stored in register B, the multiplier is stored in register Q, and the partial product is formed in register A. A binary adder is employed for adding the content of register B to the content of register A. The C flip-flop stores the carry after the addition. The P counter is initially set to hold a binary number equal to the number of bits in the multiplier. The counter is decremented after the formation of each partial product. When the content of the counter reaches zero, the product is formed in the double register A and Q and the process stops.

The control logic stays in an initial state until the start signal S becomes a 1. The system then performs the multiplication. The sum of A and B forms the partial product which is transferred to A. The output carry from the addition, whether 0 or 1, is transferred to C. Both the partial product in A and the multiplier in Q are

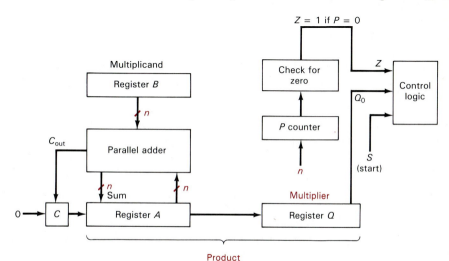

FIGURE 8-5

Block Diagram of a Binary Multiplier

shifted to the right. The least significant bit of A is shifted into the most significant position of Q; the carry from C is shifted into the most significant position of A; and 0 is shifted into C. After the shift right operation, one bit of the partial product is transferred into Q while the multiplier bits in Q are shifted one position to the right. In this manner, the least significant bit of register Q, designated by Q_0, always holds the bit of the multiplier that must be inspected next. The control logic receives this bit and also output Z from a circuit that checks P for zero. These two inputs are the status conditions from the data processor. The start input S is an external input. The outputs of the control logic initiate the required microoperations in the register.

Flowchart

A flowchart showing the sequence of operations in the binary multiplier is shown in Figure 8-6. Initially, the multiplicand is in B and the multiplier in Q. The multiplication process starts when S becomes 1. Register A and flip-flop C are reset to 0 and the sequence counter P is loaded with a binary number n, which is equal to the number of bits in the multiplier.

Next we enter a loop that keeps forming the partial products. The multiplier bit in Q_0 is checked, and if it is equal to 1, the multiplicand in B is added to the partial product in A. The carry from the addition is transferred to C. The partial product in A is left unchanged if $Q_0 = 0$. The P counter is decremented by one regardless of the value in Q_0. Registers A and Q are then shifted once to the right to obtain a new partial product. This shift operation is symbolized in the flowchart in compact form with the statement

$$AQ \leftarrow \text{shr } CAQ, \ C \leftarrow 0$$

CAQ is a composite register made up of flip-flop C and registers A and Q. If we use the individual register symbols, the shift operation can be described by the following microoperations:

$$A \leftarrow \text{shr } A, \ Q \leftarrow \text{shr } Q, \ A_{n-1} \leftarrow C, \ Q_{n-1} \leftarrow A_0, \ C \leftarrow 0$$

Both registers A and Q are shifted right. The leftmost bit of A, designated by A_{n-1}, receives the carry from C. The leftmost bit of Q, or Q_{n-1}, receives the bit from the rightmost position of A in A_0; and C is reset to 0. In essence, this is a long shift of the composite register CAQ with 0 inserted into the serial input which is at C.

The value in the P counter is checked after the formation of each partial product. If the content of P is not zero, status bit Z is equal to 0 and the process repeats to form a new partial product. The process stops when the P counter reaches 0 which causes control input Z to be 1. Note that the partial product formed in A is shifted into Q one bit at a time and eventually replaces the multiplier. The final product is available in A and Q, with A holding the most significant bits and Q the least significant bits of the product.

The previous numerical example is repeated in Table 8-10 to clarify the multiplication process. The procedure follows the steps outlined in the flowchart.

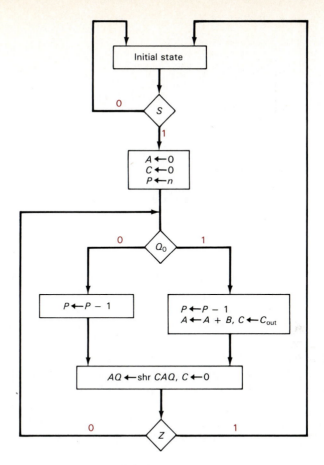

FIGURE 8-6
Flowchart for Binary Multiplier

TABLE 8-10
Numerical Example for Binary Multiplier

Multiplicand B = 10111

	C	A	Q	P
Multiplier in Q	0	00000	10011	101
$Q_0 = 1$; add B		<u>10111</u>		
First partial product	0	10111		100
Shift right CAQ	0	01011	11001	
$Q_0 = 1$; add B		<u>10111</u>		
Second partial product	1	00010		011
Shift right CAQ	0	10001	01100	
$Q_0 = 0$; shift right CAQ	0	01000	10110	010
$Q_0 = 0$; shift right CAQ	0	00100	01011	001
$Q_0 = 1$; add B		<u>10111</u>		
Fifth partial product	0	11011		000
Shift right CAQ	0	01101	10101	
Final product in AQ = 0110110101				

The type of registers needed for the data processor subsystem can be derived from the microoperations listed in the flowchart. Register A must be a shift register with parallel load to accept the sum from the adder and must have a synchronous clear capability to reset the register to 0. Register Q is a shift register. The counter P is a binary down counter with a facility to parallel load a binary constant. The C flip-flop must be designed to accept the input carry and have a synchronous reset capability. Registers B and Q will need a parallel load capability in order to receive the multiplicand and multiplier prior to starting the multiplication process.

8-6 HARDWIRED CONTROL FOR MULTIPLIER

The design of a hardwired control is a sequential circuit design problem. As such, it may be convenient to formulate the state diagram of the sequential control. A flowchart is very similar to a state diagram. The rectangular blocks that designate function boxes in the flowchart may be considered as states in a sequential circuit. The diamond shaped blocks that designate decision boxes in the flowchart determine the conditions for the next state transition in the state diagram. The microoperations that must be executed at a given state are specified within the function boxes. Although it is possible to formulate this relationship between a flowchart and a state diagram, the conversion from one form to the other is not unique. Consequently, different designers may produce different state diagrams for the same flowchart, and each may be a correct representation of the system.

We start the design by assigning an initial state T_0 to the sequential controller. We then determine the required transitions to other states T_1, T_2, T_3, and so on. For each state, we determine the microoperations that must be initiated by the control. This procedure produces the state diagram for the controller, together with a list of register transfer operations which are to be executed while the control circuit is in each state.

The control state diagram for the binary multiplier is shown in Figure 8-7(a). The information for the diagram is taken directly from the flowchart of Figure 8-6. The four states T_0 through T_3 are related to the rectangular function boxes in the flowchart. S and Z are taken from the diamond shaped decision boxes. The register transfer operations for each state as given in the flowchart are listed below the state diagram in Figure 8-7(b).

From the state diagram we see that the control stays in an initial state T_0 until S becomes 1. It then goes to state T_1 to initialize A, C, and P. Control then goes to state T_2. In this state, register P is decremented and the contents of B are added to A if $Q_0 = 1$; otherwise, A is left unchanged. The two register transfer statements associated with T_2 are

$$T_2: P \leftarrow P - 1$$

$$Q_0 T_2: A \leftarrow A + B, \; C \leftarrow C_{\text{out}}$$

The first statement is always executed when $T_2 = 1$. The second statement is executed during state T_2 provided that Q_0 is also equal to 1. Thus the status bit variable Q_0 is included with timing variable T_2 to form a control (or Boolean)

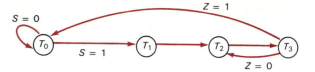

(a) State diagram

T_0: Initial state

T_1: $A \leftarrow 0$, $C \leftarrow 0$, $P \leftarrow n$

T_2: $P \leftarrow P - 1$

$L = Q_0 T_2$: $A \leftarrow A + B$, $C \leftarrow C_{out}$

T_3: $AQ \leftarrow$ shr CAQ, $C \leftarrow 0$

(b) Register transfer statements

FIGURE 8-7

Control State Diagram and List of Microoperations

function $Q_0 T_2$. Note that it is necessary to decrement P at state T_2 so that the decremented value can be checked at state T_3. Remember that all the operations are synchronized with the clock and are actually executed in response to a clock transition.

Control goes to T_3 after T_2. At state T_3, the composite register CAQ is shifted to the right and the contents of P are checked for zero. If $Z = 1$, the multiplication operation is terminated and control goes to the initial state T_0. If $Z = 0$, control goes to state T_2 to form a new partial product.

The block diagram of the control logic is shown in Figure 8-8. The inputs to the control logic are the external signal S and the two status conditions Z and Q_0. The outputs are T_0, T_1, T_2, T_3, and $L = Q_0 T_2$. The AND gate that generates variable L is shown separately although it is part of the control logic.

The outputs of the control circuit must be connected to the data processor subsystem to initiate the microoperations in the registers. Output T_1 must be connected to the load input of P and to the reset inputs of A and C. Output T_2 must be connected to the decrement input of P. Output L must be connected to the load input of A and C to receive the sum and output carry from the adder. Output T_3 must be connected to the shift control input of registers A and Q and to the reset input of C. Output T_0 has no effect on the data processor since it only indicates that the system is in an initial state.

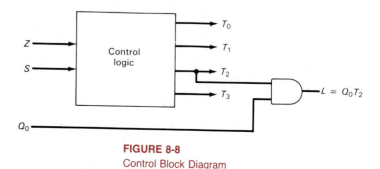

FIGURE 8-8

Control Block Diagram

275

Once the control sequence has been established, the sequential system that implements the control must be designed. Since the control is a sequential circuit, it can be designed by the sequential logic procedure as outlined in Chapter 4. However, in most cases this method is difficult to carry out because of the large number of states and inputs that a typical control circuit may have. As a consequence, it is necessary to use specialized methods for control logic design which may be considered as variations of the classical sequential logic method. We will now present two such design procedures.

Sequence Register and Decoder

The sequence register and decoder method, as the name implies, uses a register to sequence the control states and a decoder to provide an output for each state. A register with n flip-flops can have up to 2^n states and an n-to-2^n-line decoder will have up to 2^n outputs. An n-bit sequence register is essentially a circuit with n flip-flops together with the associated gates that effect their state transition.

The control state diagram for the binary multiplier has four states and two inputs. To implement it with a sequence register and decoder we need two flip-flops for the register and a 2-to-4-line decoder. Although this is a simple example, the procedure outlined below applies to more complicated situations as well.

The state table for the sequential control is shown in Table 8-11. It is derived directly from the state diagram of Figure 8-7(a). We designate the two flip-flops by G_1 and G_0 and assign the binary state 00, 01, 10, and 11, to T_0, T_1, T_2, and T_3, respectively. Note that the input columns have don't care entries whenever the input variable is not used. The outputs of the sequential circuit are designated by variables T_0 through T_3. The particular output variable that is equal to 1 at any given time is determined from the equivalent binary value of the present state. Thus, when the present state of the register is $G_1G_0 = 00$, output T_0 must be equal to 1 while the other three outputs remain at 0. Since the outputs are a function of only the present state, they can be generated with a decoder circuit having the two inputs G_1 and G_0 and the four outputs T_0 through T_3.

The sequential circuit can be designed from the state table by means of the classical procedure presented in Chapter 4. This example has a small number of states and inputs so we could use maps to simplify the Boolean functions. In most other control logic applications, the number of states and inputs is much larger. The application of the classical method requires an excessive amount of work to

TABLE 8-11
State Table for Control Circuit

Present state		Inputs		Next state		Outputs			
G_1	G_0	S	Z	G_1	G_0	T_0	T_1	T_2	T_3
0	0	0	X	0	0	1	0	0	0
0	0	1	X	0	1	1	0	0	0
0	1	X	X	1	0	0	1	0	0
1	0	X	X	1	1	0	0	1	0
1	1	X	0	1	0	0	0	0	1
1	1	X	1	0	0	0	0	0	1

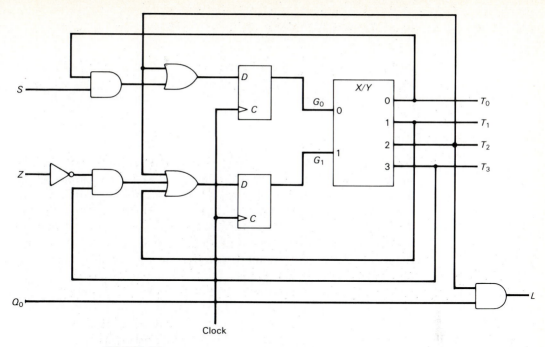

FIGURE 8-9
Logic Diagram of Control for Binary Multiplier Using a Sequence Register and Decoder

obtain the simplified input equations for the flip-flops. The design can be simplified if we take into consideration the fact that the decoder outputs are available for use in the design. Instead of using the flip-flop outputs as the present state conditions, we might as well use the outputs of the decoder to obtain this information. The outputs of the decoder are T_0 through T_3. These variables can be used to supply the present state conditions for the sequential circuit. Moreover, instead of using maps to simplify the flip-flop input equations, we can obtain them directly from the state table by inspection. Although this may not result in a minimal circuit, the possible waste of a few gates may be worth the time saved from the simplicity of the procedure. For example, from the next state conditions in the state table we find that the next state of G_1 is equal to 1 when the present state is T_1, or when the present state is T_2, or when the present state is T_3 provided that $Z = 0$. These conditions give the input equation for G_1.

$$D_{G1} = T_1 + T_2 + T_3\overline{Z}$$

Where D_{G1} is the D input of flip-flop G_1. Similarly, the input equation for flip-flop G_0 is

$$D_{G0} = T_0S + T_2$$

When deriving input equations by inspection from the state table, we cannot be sure that the Boolean functions have been simplified in the best possible way. For this reason, it is advisable to analyze the circuit to ensure that the derived equations do indeed produce the required state transitions as specified by the original state diagram.

The logic diagram of the control circuit is drawn in Figure 8-9. It consists of a register with two flip-flops G_1 and G_0 and a 2 × 4 decoder. The outputs of the decoder are used to obtain the next state of the circuit according to the Boolean input equations listed above. The outputs of the controller should be connected to the data processor part of the system to initiate the required microoperations.

One Flip-Flop per State

Another possible method of control logic design is to use one flip-flop per state in the sequential circuit. Only one flip-flop is set to 1 at any particular time; all others are reset to 0. The single bit is made to propagate from one flip-flop to the other under the control of decision logic. In such a configuration, each flip-flop represents a state that is activated only when the control bit is transferred to it.

It is obvious that this method uses a maximum number of flip-flops for the sequential circuit. For example, a sequential circuit with 12 states requires a minimum of four flip-flops in a conventional sequential circuit. With the one flip-flop per state method, the control circuit uses 12 flip-flops, one for each state. At first glance, it may seem that this method would increase system cost since more flip-flops are used. But the method offers some advantages which may not be apparent at first. One advantage of this method is the simplicity with which it can be designed. This type of controller can be designed by inspection from the state diagram that describes the control sequence. No state or excitation tables are needed if D-type flip-flops are employed. This offers a savings in design effort, an increase in operational simplicity, and a possible decrease in the total number of gates since a decoder is not needed.

We will demonstrate the design procedure by obtaining the control circuit specified by the state diagram of Figure 8-7(a). Since there are four states in the state diagram, we choose four D flip-flops and label their outputs T_0, T_1, T_2, and T_3. The input equations for setting each flip-flop to 1 is determined from the present state and the input conditions along the corresponding directed lines going into the state. For example, flip-flop T_0 is set to 1 with the next clock pulse transition if the circuit is in present state T_3 and input Z is equal to 1 or if the circuit is in present state T_0 and S is equal to 0. These conditions are specified by the flip-flop input equation

$$D_{T0} = T_0\overline{S} + T_3Z$$

where D_{T0} denotes the D input of flip-flop T_0. In fact, the condition for setting a flip-flop to 1 is obtained directly from the state diagram from the condition specified in the directed lines going into the corresponding flip-flop state ANDed with the previous flip-flop state. If there is more than one directed line going into a state, all conditions must be ORed. Using this procedure for the other three flip-flops we obtain the input equations

$$D_{T1} = T_0S$$

$$D_{T2} = T_1 + T_3\overline{Z}$$

$$D_{T3} = T_2$$

The logic diagram of the controller is shown in Figure 8-10. It consists of four D flip-flops T_0 through T_3 and the associated gates specified by the input equations

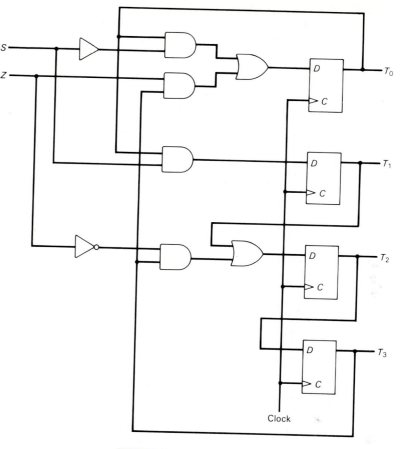

FIGURE 8-10
One Flip-Flop Per State Controller

listed above. The outputs of the flip-flops must be connected to the corresponding inputs in the registers of the data processor subsystem.

Initially flip-flop T_0 must be set to 1 and all other flip-flops must be reset to 0 so that the flip-flop representing the initial state is enabled. Once started, the one flip-flop per state controller will propagate from one state to the other in the proper manner. Only one flip-flop will be set to 1 with each clock pulse transition; all others are reset to 0 because their D inputs are maintained at 0.

Sometimes, the one flip-flop per state controller is implemented with a register that has a common asynchronous input for resetting all flip-flops initially to 0. In that case, it is possible to transfer the circuit into its initial state by modifying the input equation for T_0 as follows:

$$D_{T0} = T_0\overline{S} + T_3Z + \overline{T}_0\overline{T}_1\overline{T}_2\overline{T}_3$$

The third term in the equation sets flip-flop T_0 to 1 with the first clock pulse, just after all the flip-flops are reset to 0 asynchronously.

8-7   EXAMPLE OF A SIMPLE COMPUTER

In this and the next section we will introduce a simple digital computer and show how its operation can be defined by means of register transfer statements. We will then implement the computer by specifying the registers that are needed in the data processor subsystem and design the control subsystem by the hardwired method. The purpose here is to introduce the basic components of the digital computer and show another example of hardwired control. A more extensive study of the various concepts associated with digital computers will be covered in detail in the next chapter. The design of a more extensive digital computer is undertaken in Chapter 10.

Instruction Codes

A digital computer is a general purpose device capable of executing various operations and, in addition, can be instructed as to what specific operations it must perform. The user of a computer can control the process by means of a *program*. A program is a set of instructions that specifies the operations, operands, and the sequence in which processing is to occur. The data processing task may be altered by specifying a new program with different instructions or by specifying the same instructions with different data. Instruction codes, together with data, are stored in memory. The control reads each instruction from memory and places it in a control register. The control then interprets the instruction and proceeds to execute it by issuing a sequence of microoperations. Every computer has its own unique instruction set. The ability to store and execute instructions is the most important property of the general purpose computer.

An *instruction code* is a group of bits that instructs the computer to perform a specific operation. It is usually divided into parts, each having its own particular interpretation. The most basic part of an instruction code is its operation part. The *operation code* of an instruction is a group of bits that defines an operation, such as add, subtract, shift, or complement. The set of machine operations formulated for a computer depends on the processing it is intended to perform. The total number of operations obtained determines the set of machine operations.

The number of bits required for the operation code of an instruction is a function of the total number of operations used. It must consist of at least n bits for up to 2^n distinct operations. The designer assigns a bit combination (a code) to each operation. The control unit of the computer is designed to accept this bit configuration at the proper time in a sequence and to supply the proper commands to the data processor in order to execute the specified operation. As a specific example, consider a computer using 64 distinct operations, one of them an ADD operation. The operation code may consist of six bits, with a bit configuration 100110 assigned to the ADD operation. When the operation code 100110 is detected by the control unit, a command signal is applied to an adder circuit to add two binary numbers.

The operation part of an instruction code specifies the operation to be performed. The operation must be performed using data stored in computer registers or in memory. An instruction code, therefore, must specify not only the operation but also the registers or memory words where the operands are to be found. The operands may be specified in an instruction code in two ways. An operand is said to be specified explicitly if the instruction code contains special bits for its identification. For example, an instruction code may contain an operation part and a memory address specifying the location of the operand in memory. An operand is said to be specified explicitly if it is included as part of the definition of the operation. For example, an operation that complements a register implies the register in the operation part of the code.

Instruction Code Formats

The format of an instruction is usually depicted in a rectangular box symbolizing the bits of the instruction as they appear in memory words or in a control register. The bits of the instruction code are divided into groups that subdivide the instruction into parts called fields. Each field is assigned a task such as an operation code or a memory address. The various fields specify different functions for the instruction, and when shown together they constitute the instruction code format.

Consider, for example, the three instruction code formats depicted in Figure 8-11. The instruction format in (a) consists of an operation code which implies a register in the processor unit. It can be used to specify instructions such as "increment a processor register" or "complement a processor register." The register in this case is *implied* by the operation code. The instruction format in (b) has an operation code followed by an operand. This is called an *immediate operand* instruction because the operand follows immediately after the operation code. It can be used to specify instructions such as "add the operand to the present contents of a register" or "transfer the operand into a register" or it can specify any operation to be done between the given operand and a processor register. The instruction format specified in (c) gives the address of the operand in memory. In other words, the operation specified by the operation code is performed between a processor register and an operand which is stored in memory. The address of this operand is included as part of the instruction. This type of instruction is referred to as a *direct address* instruction.

The instruction formats shown in Figure 8-11 are three of many possible formats that can be formulated for a digital computer. They are presented here just as an example and should not be considered the only possibilities. In Chapter 9 we present and discuss other instructions and instruction code formats.

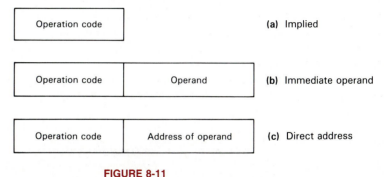

FIGURE 8-11
Three Possible Instruction Formats

Numerical Example

Assume that we have a memory unit with 8 bits per word and that an operation code contains 8 bits. The placement of the three instruction codes in memory in binary is shown in Figure 8-12. At address 25 we have an implied instruction that specifies an operation to increment register R. This operation can be symbolized by the statement

$$R \leftarrow R + 1$$

In memory address 35 and 36 we have an immediate operand instruction that occupies two 8-bit words. The first word at address 35 is the operation code for the instruction to transfer the operand to register R, symbolized by the statement

$$R \leftarrow \text{Operand}$$

The operand itself is stored immediately after the operation code at address 36.

In memory address 45 there is a direct address instruction that specifies the operation

$$R \leftarrow M[\text{address}]$$

The second word of the instruction at address 46 contains the address. Therefore, the operand to be transferred to register R is the one stored at this address. For the numerical example shown in the figure, we have the instruction symbolized by $R \leftarrow M[70]$. The symbol $M[70]$ signifies the contents of the memory word at address 70. Since this word contains the binary equivalent of 28, the result of the operation is the transfer of the 8-bit word 00011100 into register R.

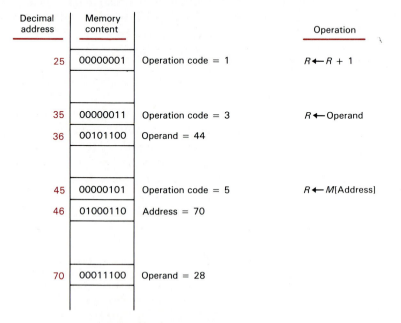

Decimal address	Memory content		Operation
25	00000001	Operation code = 1	$R \leftarrow R + 1$
35	00000011	Operation code = 3	$R \leftarrow \text{Operand}$
36	00101100	Operand = 44	
45	00000101	Operation code = 5	$R \leftarrow M[\text{Address}]$
46	01000110	Address = 70	
70	00011100	Operand = 28	

FIGURE 8-12
Memory Representation of Instructions

It must be realized that the placing of instructions in memory as shown in Figure 8-12 is only one of many possible alternatives. Only very small computers have 8-bit words. Large computers may have from 16 to 64 bits per word. In many computers, the entire instruction can be placed in one word, and in some, even two or more instructions can be placed in a single memory word.

At this point we must recognize the relationship between a computer *operation* and a hardware *microoperation*. An operation is specified by an instruction stored in computer memory. It is a binary code that tells the computer to perform a specific operation. The control unit in the computer retrieves the instruction from memory and interprets the operation code bits. It then issues a sequence of control functions to perform the required microoperations for the execution of the instruction.

Computer Block Diagram

The block diagram of a simple computer is shown in Figure 8-13. The computer consists of a memory unit, six registers, two decoders, and control logic gates. The memory has 256 words of 8 bits each, which is very small for a real computer, but sufficient for demonstrating the basic operations found in most computers. Instructions and data are stored in the memory, but all information processing is done in the registers. The six registers are listed in Table 8-12 together with a brief description of their function and the number of bits they contain.

The data register DR holds the contents of the memory word read from or written into memory. The address register AR holds the address of an operand

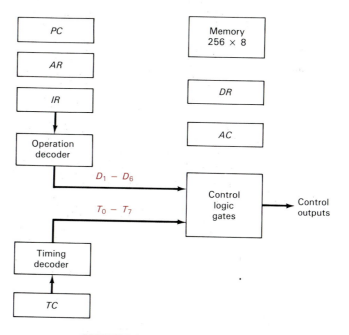

FIGURE 8-13

Block Diagram of a Simple Computer

TABLE 8-12
List of Registers for the Simple Computer

Register symbol	Number of bits	Register name	Function
DR	8	Data register	Holds contents of memory word
AR	8	Address register	Holds address of operand
AC	8	Accumulator	Processor register
IR	8	Instruction register	Holds operation code
PC	8	Program counter	Holds address of instruction
TC	3	Timing counter	Sequence register

when it has to be fetched from memory. The accumulator register is a general purpose register where the data processing is done. The instruction register IR receives the operation code of instructions. The decoder associated with this register supplies one output for each operation code encountered. Thus, decoder output $D_1 = 1$ if the operation code of the instruction is binary 1, output $D_2 = 1$ if the operation code is binary 2, and so on. The timing counter TC is also decoded to supply eight timing variables T_0 through T_7 (see Figure 5-22). The counter is incremented with every clock pulse, but it can be reset to 0 at any time to start a new sequence from T_0. The control logic gates receive the inputs from the decoders and generate the required control functions for the registers in the computer.

The program counter PC holds the current address of the instruction. The PC goes through a step-by-step counting sequence and causes the computer to read successive instructions previously stored in memory. To read an instruction, the content of PC is taken as the address for memory and a memory read cycle is initiated. The PC is then incremented by one; so it holds the next address in the sequence of instructions. An operation code read from memory into DR is transferred into IR. If the memory address part of the instruction is read into DR, this address is transferred into AR to access the operand.

Computer Instructions

Six instructions for the simple computer are listed in Table 8-13. We assume that there are eight bits in the operation code so it can be stored in one memory word. With eight bits it is possible to specify up to 256 operations. To simplify the presentation, we consider here only six operations. The symbolic names associated with the instructions are useful for listing programs in symbolic form instead of

TABLE 8-13
Six Instructions for the Simple Computer

Operation code	Symbolic name	Description	Function
00000001	INA	Increment AC	$AC \leftarrow AC + 1$
00000010	CMA	Complement AC	$AC \leftarrow \overline{AC}$
00000011	LDI OPRD	Load immediate operand	$AC \leftarrow OPRD$
00000100	ADI OPRD	Add immediate operand	$AC \leftarrow AC + OPRD$
00000101	LDA ADRS	Load to AC	$AC \leftarrow M[ADRS]$
00000110	STA ADRS	Store from AC	$M[ADRS] \leftarrow AC$

using binary codes. The first two instructions are implied instructions that increment and complement the accumulator register. The next two instructions are immediate type instructions. These instructions have two words, one for the operation code and the other for the immediate operand symbolized by OPRD. The OPRD following the symbol LDI stands for an actual operand that the programmer must specify. The instruction ADI OPRD adds the specified operand to the content of the accumulator.

The last two instructions in the table are direct address instructions. LDA is a symbol for the operation code and the ADRS following it stands for an address that the programmer must specify with this instruction. The load instruction transfers a memory operand into the accumulator register. The store instruction transfers the content of the accumulator into a memory word whose address is given by the instruction. The actual OPRD and ADRS values, together with their corresponding operation codes are stored in memory as shown in Figure 8-12.

To demonstrate how the instructions can be used to write a simple program, consider the arithmetic expression $83 - (52 + 25)$. The following program performs the computation and stores the result in memory at address 250. The subtraction is done by taking the 2's complement of $(52 + 25)$ and adding it to 83.

LDI 52	Load 52 into the AC
ADI 24	Add 25 to the AC
CMA	Complement AC
INA	Increment AC
ADI 83	Add 83 to the AC
STA 250	Store the contents of AC in $M[250]$

To store this program in memory it is necessary to convert all symbolic names to their corresponding 8-bit operation codes and convert the decimal numbers to binary.

8-8   DESIGN OF SIMPLE COMPUTER

We will now show the procedure for designing the simple computer defined in the previous section. The registers of the computer are defined in the block diagram of Figure 8-13. The instructions of the computer are listed in Table 8-13. A computer with only six instructions is not very useful. We must assume that it has many more instructions even though only six of them are considered here. A program written for the computer is stored in memory. This program consists of many instructions, but once in a while the instructions used will be one of the six listed. We first consider the internal operations needed to execute the instructions that are stored in memory.

Instruction Fetch Phase

The program counter PC is initialized so it holds the address of the first instruction of the program stored in memory. When a start switch is activated, the computer sequence follows a basic pattern. An operation code whose address is in PC is read from memory into DR. The operation code is then transferred from DR to IR and PC is incremented by one to prepare it for the address of the next word in memory. This sequence is called the *instruction fetch* phase, since it fetches the operation code from memory and places it in a control register. The timing variables T_0 and T_1 of the timing decoder are used as control functions for the fetch phase. This can be expressed with two register transfer statements as follows

$$T_0: DR \leftarrow M[PC]$$

$$T_1: IR \leftarrow DR, \; PC \leftarrow PC + 1$$

With timing variable T_0, the memory word specified by the address in PC is transferred into DR. This word is the operation code of an instruction. Timing variable T_1 transfers the operation code from DR into the instruction register IR and also increments PC by one. This prepares PC for the next read operation since it now contains the address of the next instruction word in memory. It is very important to realize that all the operations are synchronized with a common clock source. The same clock pulse transition that transfers the content of memory into DR when $T_0 = 1$, also triggers the timing counter TC and changes its contents from 000 to 001, which causes the timing decoder to go from T_0 to T_1.

The instruction fetch phase is common to all instructions. The microoperations and control functions that follow the instruction fetch are determined in the control section from the present operation code in IR. The output of IR is decoded by the operation decoder. This decoder has outputs D_1 through D_6, corresponding to the binary operation codes 00000001 through 00000110, assigned to the six instructions.

Execution of Instructions

During timing variable T_2, the operation code is in IR and only one output of the operation decoder is equal to 1. The control uses this output to determine the next microoperation in sequence. The INA (increment AC) instruction has an operation code 00000001 which makes decoder output $D_1 = 1$. The execution of this instruction can be specified by the following register transfer statement:

$$D_1T_2: AC \leftarrow AC + 1, \; TC \leftarrow 0$$

Thus, when $D_1 = 1$ at time T_2, the content of the AC is incremented by one and the timing counter TC is reset to 0. By resetting TC to 0, control goes back to timing variable T_0 to start the fetch phase and read the operation code of the next instruction in the program. Remember that PC is incremented during time T_1; so now it holds the address of the next instruction in sequence.

The LDI OPRD instruction has an operation code 00000011 which makes the output of the decoder $D_3 = 1$. The microoperations that execute this instruction are

$$D_3T_2: DR \leftarrow M[PC]$$

$$D_3T_3: AC \leftarrow DR, \; PC \leftarrow PC + 1, \; TC \leftarrow 0$$

The timing variable that follows the fetch phase when $D_3 = 1$ is T_2. At this time, the operand symbolized by OPRD is read from memory and placed in DR. Since the operand is in memory following the operation code, it is read from memory using the address in PC. The operand read into DR is then transferred to the AC. PC is incremented once again to prepare it for the address of the next instruction. In fact, PC is incremented every time a word that belongs to the program is read from memory. This prepares PC for reading the next word in sequence. Moreover, at the completion of an instruction execution, the control always resets TC to 0 in order to return to the fetch phase.

The LDA ADRS instruction has an operation code that makes $D_5 = 1$. The microoperations needed to execute this instruction are

$$D_5T_2: DR \leftarrow M[PC]$$

$$D_5T_3: AR \leftarrow DR, \ PC \leftarrow PC + 1$$

$$D_5T_4: DR \leftarrow M[AR]$$

$$D_5T_5: AC \leftarrow DR, \ TC \leftarrow 0$$

The address of the operand, symbolized by ADRS, resides in memory right after the operation code of the instruction. Since PC was incremented during the fetch phase, it now holds the address where ADRS is stored in memory. The value of ADRS is read from memory at time T_2. At time T_3, the address is transferred from DR to AR, and PC is incremented by one. Since ADRS specifies the address of the operand, a memory read during time T_4 causes the operand to be placed in DR. The operand from DR is transferred to AC and control goes back to the fetch phase.

The sequence of microoperations for the simple computer are listed in the flow-chart of Figure 8-14. The timing variables associated with the microoperations are indicated along the function boxes. The first two timing variables perform the fetch phase which reads the operation code into IR and decodes it. The microoperations that are executed during time T_2 depend on the operation code value in IR. This is indicated in the flowchart by six different paths that the control may take. Thus at time T_2 the AC is incremented if $D_1 = 1$, or the AC is complemented if $D_2 = 1$, or the operand is read from memory if D_3 or $D_4 = 1$, or the address part of the instruction is read from memory if D_5 or $D_6 = 1$. The particular microoperation executed at time T_2 is the one with the corresponding control function having a D variable equal to 1. The same can be said for the other timing variables.

The instruction ADI OPRD is executed similar to the way the LDI OPRD is executed except that the contents of DR is added to those of AC. The instruction STA ADRS is similar to the LDA ADRS except that the contents of AC are stored in memory.

A practical computer has many more instructions, and each instruction requires a fetch phase for reading its operation code from memory. The microoperations that execute the particular instruction are determined by the operation decoder output and sequenced by the timing variables. The list of control functions and microoperations for a practical computer would be much longer than the one shown in Figure 8-14. Obviously, the simple computer is not a practical device, but by using only six instructions, the basic function of a digital computer can be dem-

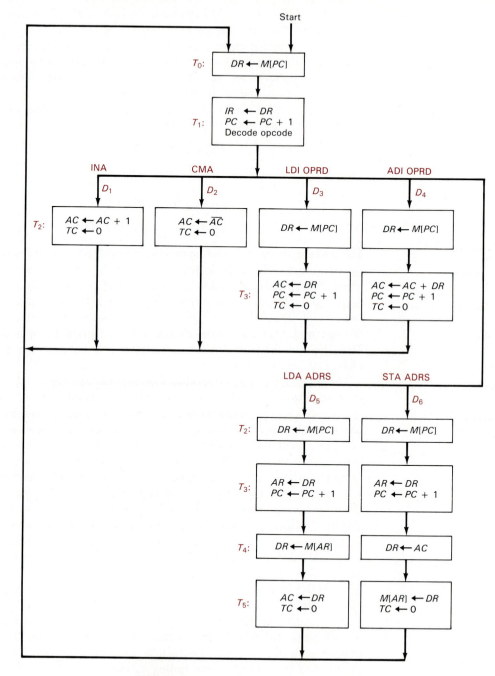

FIGURE 8-14
Microoperation Sequence for the Simple Computer

onstrated. The extension of this principle to a computer with more instructions and more processor registers should be apparent from this example.

Control Logic

It was shown that the register transfer notation is suitable for defining the operations specified by computer instructions and is a convenient method for specifying the sequence of internal operations in a digital computer. We will now show that the list of control functions and microoperations for a digital system is a convenient starting point for the design of the system. The list of microoperations specifies the type of registers and associated digital functions that must be incorporated into the data processing part of the system. The list of control functions specifies the logic gates required for the control unit. To demonstrate this procedure, we will go through the design of the simple computer based on the list of register transfer statements given in Figure 8-14.

The first step in the design is to scan the register transfer statements and retrieve all those statements that perform the same microoperation. For example, the microoperation $PC \leftarrow PC + 1$ is listed with timing variable T_1 and again with timing variable T_3 for the decoded instructions D_3, D_4, D_5, and D_6. The five conditions can be combined into one statement:

$$T_1 + (D_3 + D_4 + D_5 + D_6)T_3: PC \leftarrow PC + 1$$

Remember that a control function is a Boolean function. The symbol $+$ between the control variables denotes a Boolean OR operation and the absence of an operator denotes a Boolean AND operation. The above statement combines all the control conditions for incrementing PC. The hardware implementation of this statement is depicted in Figure 8-15. When the output of the combination circuit is equal to 1, the next clock pulse transition increments PC by one. Thus PC must be a binary counter and the increment input is used for enabling the count.

There are 12 different microoperations listed in Figure 8-14. For each distinct microoperation, we accumulate the associated control functions and OR them together. The result is shown in Table 8-14. The combined control functions obtained for each microoperation are equated to a binary variable C_i for $i = 1, 2, 3, \ldots, 12$. The 12 variables can be easily generated with OR and AND (or NAND) gates to constitute the control logic gates in the control unit of the computer.

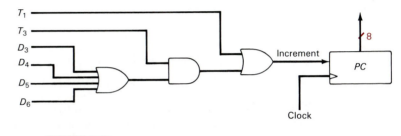

FIGURE 8-15
Implementation of $T_1 + (D_3 + D_4 + D_5 + D_6)T_3: PC \leftarrow PC + 1$

TABLE 8-14
Hardware Specification of Simple Computer

Control function	Microoperation
$C_1 = T_0 + (D_3 + D_4 + D_5 + D_6)T_2$:	$DR \leftarrow M[PC]$
$C_2 = T_1 + (D_3 + D_4 + D_5 + D_6)T_3$:	$PC \leftarrow PC + 1$
$C_3 = T_1$:	$IR \leftarrow DR$
$C_4 = D_1T_2$:	$AC \leftarrow AC + 1$
$C_5 = D_2T_2$:	$AC \leftarrow \overline{AC}$
$C_6 = D_3T_3 + D_5T_5$:	$AC \leftarrow DR$
$C_7 = D_4T_3$:	$AC \leftarrow AC + DR$
$C_8 = (D_5 + D_6)T_3$:	$AR \leftarrow DR$
$C_9 = D_6T_4$:	$DR \leftarrow AC$
$C_{10} = D_5T_4$:	$DR \leftarrow M[AR]$
$C_{11} = D_6T_5$:	$M[AR] \leftarrow DR$
$C_{12} = (D_1 + D_2)T_2 + (D_3 + D_4)T_3 + (D_5 + D_6)T_5$:	$TC \leftarrow 0$

Design of Computer

The design of the simple computer can be obtained from the information available in Table 8-14. The block diagram design is shown in Figure 8-16. It consists of the memory unit, six registers, two decoders, three multiplexers, an 8-bit adder, and control logic gates. The six registers are the ones listed in Table 8-12. The control logic gates receive their inputs from the two decoders and generate the 12 control functions C_1 through C_{12} according to the Boolean functions listed in Table 8-14. Any register that receives data from two sources needs a multiplexer to select between the two.

The control functions operate on the registers and memory to produce the required microoperations. For example, Table 8-14 shows that the control function C_1 must perform the microoperation $DR \leftarrow M[PC]$. This is a memory read operation with PC supplying the address and DR receiving the memory word. Therefore, C_1 selects the 8 bits from PC through MUX1, enables the read input of the memory, enables the load input of DR while MUX2 selects its inputs from the memory output data (because $C_9 = 0$).

The microoperations for the AC are determined from the following statements in Table 8-14.

$$C_4: AC \leftarrow AC + 1 \qquad \text{Increment } AC$$

$$C_5: AC \leftarrow \overline{AC} \qquad \text{Complement } AC$$

$$C_6: AC \leftarrow DR \qquad \text{Transfer } DR \text{ to } AC$$

$$C_7: AC \leftarrow AC + DR \qquad \text{Add } DR \text{ to } AC$$

The AC can be implemented with a counter that has the capability of complementing its contents and loading external data. The counter produces the increment microoperation and the load control enables the input data. When $C_6 = 1$, C_7 must be equal to 0, and MUX3 selects the outputs of DR to be loaded into the AC. When $C_7 = 1$, the outputs of the 8-bit adder are loaded into the AC. The

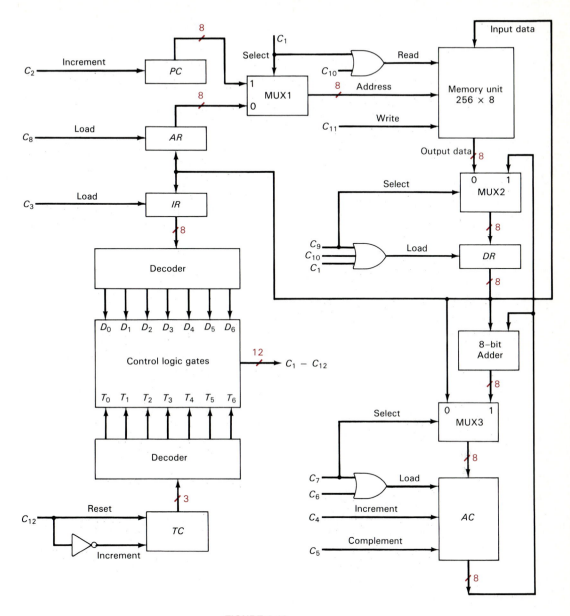

FIGURE 8-16
Hardware Design of the Simple Computer

timing counter TC is incremented with every clock pulse except when $C_{12} = 1$, which resets the counter to 0.

The other control functions enable the appropriate registers and select the proper paths through the multiplexers. Note that all six registers must be connected to a common clock pulse generator for a synchronous operation. The clock inputs have been omitted from the block diagram in order to simplify the drawing.

The registers and other digital functions specified in Figure 8-16 can be designed with integrated circuits. One can readily find commercial MSI circuits for all the registers, multiplexers, and decoders. The combinational circuit for the control logic gates can be constructed with individual gates. This part of the computer would be more efficiently implemented with a programmable logic device as explained in Chapter 6.

REFERENCES

1. MANO, M. M. *Computer System Architecture.* 2nd ed. Englewood Cliffs: Prentice-Hall, 1982.

2. ERCEGOVAC, M. D., AND LANG, T. *Digital Systems and Hardware/Firmware Algorithms.* New York: Wiley, 1985.

3. AGRAWALA, A. K., AND RAUSCHER, T. G. *Foundations of Microprogramming.* New York: Academic, 1976.

4. MYERS, G. J. *Digital System Design with LSI Bit-Slice Logic.* New York: Wiley, 1980.

5. ANDREWS, M. *Principles of Firmware Engineering in Microprogram Control.* Potomac, MD: Computer Science Press, 1980.

6. FLETCHER, W. I. *An Engineering Approach to Digital Design.* Englewood Cliffs: Prentice-Hall, 1980.

7. RHYNE, V. T. *Fundementals of Digital Systems Design.* Englewood Cliffs: Prentice-Hall, 1973.

8. CLARE, C. R. *Designing Logic Systems Using State Machines.* New York: McGraw-Hill, 1973.

9. HILL, F. J., AND PETERSON, G. R. *Digital Logic and Microprocessors.* New York: Wiley, 1984.

PROBLEMS

8-1 Define the following terms in your own words: (a) data processor subsystem; (b) control subsystem; (c) hardwired control; (d) microprogrammed control; (e) control memory; (f) control word; (g) microinstruction; (h) microprogram; (i) microoperation.

8-2 A microprogram control unit is similar to the one shown in Figure 8-3 with the following differences: (a) MUX1 has four inputs for *CAR*; (b) MUX2 has 15 input status bits; (c) the control memory has 1024 words. Formulate the microinstruction format and specify the number of bits in each field. What should be the size of the control memory?

8-3 A microinstruction stored in address 35 in the control memory of Figure 8-3 performs the operation

$$R1 \leftarrow R1 + R2, \ CAR \leftarrow CAR + 1$$

Give the microinstruction in symbolic form using the symbol LAD for MUX2.

8-4 Give a symbolic microinstruction that resets register *R4* to 0 and updates *Z* and *S* status bits without affecting the other two status bits. (Try an exclusive-OR operation.)

8-5 Give a symbolic microinstruction that resets register *R3* to 0 and resets the *C* status bit to 0. The other three status bits can be anything.

8-6   List the symbolic and binary microinstructions similar to Table 8-5 for the following register transfer statements.
(a) $R3 \leftarrow R1 - R2, CAR \leftarrow 17$
(b) $R5 \leftarrow \text{shr} (R4 + R5), CAR \leftarrow CAR + 1$
(c) If $(Z = 0)$ then $(CAR \leftarrow 21)$ else $(CAR \leftarrow CAR + 1)$
(d) $R6 \leftarrow R6, C \leftarrow 0, CAR \leftarrow CAR + 1$ (update Z and S)

8-7   Given the following binary microprogram starting from address 16 (similar to Table 8-8)
(a) List the corresponding symbolic microprogram as in Table 8-7.
(b) List the corresponding register transfer statements as in Table 8-6.

ROM address	Binary microprogram
010000	001 010 011 0101 000 0000 000000
010001	000 000 000 0000 000 0010 010011
010010	000 000 001 0000 001 0001 010011
010011	011 000 011 0001 000 0000 000000
010100	000 000 000 0000 000 1101 000000
010101	010 010 010 1100 000 0001 010000

8-8   Translate the microprogram of Table 8-9 to binary.

8-9   Write a microprogram to compute the average value of four unsigned binary numbers stored in registers $R1$, $R2$, $R3$, and $R4$. The average value is to be stored in register $R5$. The other two registers in the processor can be used for intermediate results. Care must be taken when an output carry occurs.

8-10   Write a microprogram (starting from address 1) that checks the sign of the binary number stored in register $R1$. If the number is positive, it is divided by two. If negative, it is multiplied by two. If an overflow occurs after the multiplication, $R1$ is reset to 0.

8-11   Write a microprogram that compares two unsigned binary numbers stored in registers $R1$ and $R2$. The register containing the smaller number is then reset to 0. If the two numbers are equal, both registers are reset to 0.

8-12   Write a microprogram to multiply two unsigned binary numbers. The multiplicand is in register $R1$, the multiplier is in register $R2$, and the product is formed in $R2$ (least significant half) and $R3$ (most significant half). Register $R4$ holds a binary number equal to the number of bits in the multiplier. Derive the algorithm in flowchart form and from it, write the microprogram.

8-13   List the contents of registers A, Q, P, and C (as in Table 8-10) during the process of multiplying the two unsigned binary numbers 11111 (multiplicand) and 10101 (multiplier).

8-14   Determine the time it takes to process the multiplication operation in the digital system described in Section 8-5. Assume that the Q register has n bits and the interval between two clock pulses is t seconds.

8-15   Prove that the multiplication of two n-bit numbers gives a product of no more than $2n$ bits. Show that this condition implies that no overflow can occur in the multiplier designed in Section 8-5.

8-16   The control state diagram of Figure 8-7(a) does not use variable Q_0 as a condition for state transition. Q_0 is used instead as part of a control function in the list of register transfers in Figure 8-7(b) and therefore, is omitted from the state table in Table 8-11.

Redesign the control for the binary multiplier so that Q_0 appears as a condition in the state diagram and as an input in the state table.

8-17 Consider the block diagram of the multiplier shown in Figure 8-6. Assume that the multiplier and multiplicand consist of 16 bits each.
   (a) How many bits can be expected in the product, and where is it placed?
   (b) How many bits are in the P counter and what is the binary number that must be loaded into it initially?
   (c) Design the combinational circuit that checks for zero in the P counter.

8-18 Design a digital system that multiplies two unsigned binary numbers by the repeated addition method. For example, to multiply 5×4, the digital system evaluates the product by adding the multiplicand four times: $5 + 5 + 5 + 5 = 20$. Let the multiplicand be in register BR, the multiplier in register AR, and the product in register PR. An adder circuit adds the contents of BR to PR. A zero detect circuit Z checks when AR becomes zero after each time that it is decremented. Design the control by the hardwired method.

8-19 Design a digital system with three 16-bit registers AR, BR, and CR to perform the following operations:
   (a) Transfer two 16-bit signed numbers to AR and BR after a start signal S is enabled.
   (b) If the number in AR is negative, divide the contents of AR by two and transfer the result to register CR.
   (c) If the number in AR is positive but non-zero, divide the contents of BR by two and transfer the result to register CR.
   (d) If the number in AR is zero, reset register CR to 0.

8-20 The state diagram of a control unit is shown in Figure P8-20. It has four states and two inputs Y and Z. Design the control by
   (a) the sequence register and decoder method and
   (b) the one flip-flop per state method.

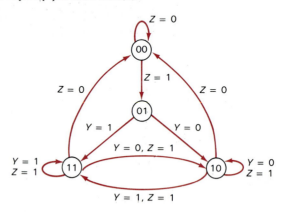

FIGURE P8-20
Control State Diagram for Problem 8-20

8-21 A digital computer has a memory unit with 24 bits per word. The instruction set consists of 150 different operations. There is only one type of instruction format with an operation code part and an address part. Each instruction is stored in one word of memory.
   (a) How many bits are needed for the operation code part?

(b) How many bits are left for the address part of the instruction?

(c) How many words are there in memory and what must be the memory size?

(d) What is the largest unsigned binary number that can be accommodated in one word of memory?

8-22 A signed binary number is stored in address 153 of the simple computer. Write a program that will multiply this number by -1.

8-23 Derive the control functions listed in Table 8-14 from the information available in the flowchart of Figure 8-14.

8-24 Specify an instruction format for the simple computer that performs the following operation:

$$AC \leftarrow AC + M[ADRS] \qquad \text{Add to } AC$$

List the sequence of microoperations for executing this instruction and include it in the flowchart of Figure 8-14.

8-25 Repeat Problem 8-24 for the following instruction:

$$M[ADRS] \leftarrow M[ADRS] + AC \qquad \text{Add to memory}$$

8-26 Assume that the memory of the simple computer in Figure 8-13 has 64K $\times$ 8 words. This will require a 16-bit address to specify an 8-bit word in memory.

(a) What should be the number of bits in each of the six registers of the computer?

(b) How many words of memory are now required to store the instruction LDA ADRS (see Table 8-13)?

(c) List the sequence of microoperations needed to execute this instruction.

8-27 Show the path that the data takes in the hardware of the simple computer of Figure 8-16 when the control function C_7 is enabled. Include the effect of the clock. Assume that $DR = 10101010$ and $AC = 01011111$. What happens to DR and AC after the clock pulse transition when $C_7 = 1$?

9
COMPUTER INSTRUCTIONS AND ADDRESSING MODES

9-1 INTRODUCTION

The physical and logical structure of computers is normally described in reference manuals provided with the computer system. Such manuals explain the internal construction of the computer including the processor registers available and their logical properties. They list all hardware implemented instructions, specify their binary code format, and provide a precise definition of each instruction. A computer will usually have a variety of instructions and instruction code formats. It is the function of the control unit within the computer to interpret each instruction code and provide the necessary control signals needed to process each instruction.

A few simple examples of instructions and instruction code formats are presented in Section 8-7. We will now expand this presentation by introducing the most common instructions found in commercial computers. We will also investigate the various instruction formats that may be encountered in a typical computer.

The format of an instruction is depicted in a rectangular box symbolizing the bits of the instruction code. The bits of the binary instruction are divided into groups called *fields*. The most common fields found in instruction formats are

1. An *operation code* field that specifies the operation to be performed.
2. An *address* field that designates either a memory address or a code for choosing a processor register.
3. A *mode* field that specifies the way the address field is to be interpreted.

Other special fields are sometimes employed under certain circumstances, as for example a field that gives the number of shifts in a shift type instruction or an operand field in an immediate type instruction.

The operation code field of an instruction is a group of bits that define various processor operations, such as add, subtract, complement, and shift. The most common operations available in computer instructions are enumerated and discussed in Sections 9-5 through 9-8. The bits that define the mode field of an instruction code specify a variety of alternatives for choosing the operands from the given address field. The various addressing modes that have been formulated for computers are presented in Section 9-3. The effect of including multiple address fields in an instruction is discussed in Section 9-2. Other topics covered in this chapter include stack organization and interrupt handling.

The various computer concepts introduced in this chapter are sometimes classified as being part of a broader field referred to as computer organization or computer architecture. They provide the necessary understanding of the internal organization and operation of digital computers. In the next chapter we use these topics to design a central processing unit (CPU).

9-2 ADDRESS FIELD

Operations specified by computer instructions are executed on some data stored in memory or in processor registers. Operands residing in memory are specified by their addresses. Operands residing in processor registers are specified by a register address. A register address is a binary code of n bits that specifies one of 2^n registers in the processor. Thus, a computer with 16 processor registers $R0$ through $R15$ will have in its instruction code a register address field of four bits. The binary code 0101, for example, will designate register $R5$.

Computers may have instructions of several different lengths containing varying number of addresses. The number of address fields in the instruction format of a computer depends upon the internal organization of its registers. Most instructions fall in one of three types of organization:

1. Single accumulator organization.
2. Multiple register organization.
3. Stack organization.

An example of an accumulator type organization is the simple computer presented in Section 8-7. All operations are performed with the implied accumulator register. The instruction format in this type of computer uses one memory address field. For example, the instruction that specifies an arithmetic addition has only one address field symbolized by X.

ADD X

ADD is the symbol for the operation code of the instruction and X gives the address of the operand in memory. This instruction results in the operation $AC \leftarrow AC + M[X]$. AC is the accumulator register and $M[X]$ symbolizes the memory word located at address X.

An example of a processor unit with multiple registers is presented in Section 7-5. The instruction format in this type of computer needs three registers. Thus, the instruction for the arithmetic addition may be written in symbolic form as

$$ADD \; R1, \; R2, \; R3$$

to denote the operation $R3 \leftarrow R1 + R2$. However, the number of register address fields in the instruction can be reduced from three to two if the destination register is the same as one of the source registers. Thus, the instruction

$$ADD \; R1, \; R2$$

will denote the operation $R2 \leftarrow R2 + R1$. Registers $R1$ and $R2$ are the source registers and $R2$ is also the destination register.

Computers with multiple processor registers employ the MOVE instruction to symbolize the transfer of data from one location to another. The instruction

$$MOVE \; R1, \; R2$$

denotes the transfer $R2 \leftarrow R1$. Transfer type instructions need two address fields to specify the source operand and the destination of transfer.

Multiple register type computers employ two or three address fields in the instruction format. Each address field may specify a processor register or a memory address. An instruction symbolized by

$$ADD \; X, \; R1$$

will specify the operation $R1 \leftarrow R1 + M[X]$. It has two address fields, one for register $R1$ and the other for the memory address X.

The stack organization will be presented in Section 9-4. Computers with stack organization have instructions that require one address field for transferring data to and from the stack. Operation type instructions such as ADD do not need an address field because the operation is performed directly with the operands in the stack.

To illustrate the influence of the number of address fields on computer programs, we will evaluate the arithmetic statement

$$X = (A + B)(C + D)$$

using one, two, or three address instructions.

We will use symbols ADD, SUB, MUL, and DIV for the four arithmetic operations. The LOAD and STORE symbols will be used for the operation codes that transfer data to and from the AC register and memory. The symbol MOVE designates the operation code for transferring data in a multiple register type processor. We will assume that the operands are in memory addresses symbolized by the letters A, B, C, and D. The result is to be stored in memory at a location whose address is X.

Three Address Instructions

Computers with three address instruction formats can use each address field to specify either a processor register or a memory address for an operand. The program in symbolic form that evaluates $X = (A + B)(C + D)$ is shown below, together with an equivalent register transfer statement for each instruction.

$$\begin{array}{lll}
\text{ADD} & \text{A, B, R1} & R1 \leftarrow M[A] + M[B] \\
\text{ADD} & \text{C, D, R2} & R2 \leftarrow M[C] + M[D] \\
\text{MUL} & \text{R1, R2, X} & M[X] \leftarrow R1 * R2
\end{array}$$

It is assumed that the computer has two processor registers, $R1$ and $R2$. The symbol $M[A]$ denotes the operand stored in memory at the address symbolized by A. The symbol $*$ designates multiplication.

The advantage of the three address format is that it results in short programs for evaluating arithmetic expressions. The disadvantage is that the binary coded instruction requires more bits to specify three addresses.

Two Address Instructions

Two address instructions are the most common in commercial computers. Here again each address field can specify either a processor register or a memory address. The program to evaluate $X = (A + B)(C + D)$ is as follows:

$$\begin{array}{lll}
\text{MOVE} & \text{A, R1} & R1 \leftarrow M[A] \\
\text{ADD} & \text{B, R1} & R1 \leftarrow R1 + M[B] \\
\text{MOVE} & \text{C, R2} & R2 \leftarrow M[C] \\
\text{ADD} & \text{D, R2} & R2 \leftarrow R2 + M[D] \\
\text{MUL} & \text{R2, R1} & R1 \leftarrow R1 * R2 \\
\text{MOVE} & \text{R1, X} & M[X] \leftarrow R1
\end{array}$$

The MOVE instruction moves or transfers the operands to and from memory and processor registers. The second operand listed in the symbolic instruction is assumed to be the destination where the result of the operation is transferred.

One Address Instructions

A computer with one address instructions uses an implied AC register. The program to evaluate the arithmetic statement is as follows:

$$\begin{array}{lll}
\text{LOAD} & \text{A} & AC \leftarrow M[A] \\
\text{ADD} & \text{B} & AC \leftarrow AC + M[B] \\
\text{STORE} & \text{T} & M[T] \leftarrow AC \\
\text{LOAD} & \text{C} & AC \leftarrow M[C] \\
\text{ADD} & \text{D} & AC \leftarrow AC + M[D] \\
\text{MUL} & \text{T} & AC \leftarrow AC * M[T] \\
\text{STORE} & \text{X} & M[X] \leftarrow AC
\end{array}$$

All operations are done between the AC register and a memory operand. The symbolic address T designates a temporary memory location required for storing the intermediate result.

The program for evaluating the arithmetic expression using a stack will be given in Section 9-4.

9-3   ADDRESSING MODES

The operation field of an instruction specifies the operation to be performed. This operation must be executed on some data stored in computer registers or memory words. The way the operands are chosen during program execution is dependent on the addressing mode of the instruction. The addressing mode specifies a rule for interpreting or modifying the address field of the instruction before the operand is actually referenced. Computers use addressing mode techniques for the purpose of accommodating one or both of the following provisions:

1. To give programming versatility to the user by providing such facilities as pointers to memory, counters for loop control, indexing of data, and program relocation.
2. To reduce the number of bits in the addressing field of the instruction.

The availability of the addressing modes gives the experienced programmer a flexibility for writing programs that are more efficient in the number of instructions and the execution time.

Basic Computer Cycle

In order to understand the various addressing modes to be presented in this section, it is imperative that we understand the basic operation cycle of the computer. The control unit of a computer is designed to execute each instruction in the program with a sequence of steps.

1. Fetch the instruction from memory into a control register.
2. Decode the instruction.
3. Locate the operands used by the instruction.
4. Fetch operands from memory (if necessary).
5. Execute the instruction in processor registers.
6. Store the results in the proper place.
7. Go back to step 1 to fetch the next instruction.

As explained in Section 8-8 there is one register in the computer called the program counter or *PC* that keeps track of the instructions in the program stored in memory. The *PC* holds the address of the instruction to be executed next and is incremented by one each time a word is read from the program in memory. The decoding done in step 2 is to determine the operation to be performed and the addressing mode of the instruction. The location of the operands in step 3 is determined from the addressing mode and the address field of the instruction. The computer then executes the instruction and returns to step 1 to fetch the next instruction in sequence.

In some computers the addressing mode of the instruction is specified using a distinct binary code. Other computers use a common binary code that designates both the operation and the addressing mode of the instruction. Instructions may be defined with a variety of addressing modes and sometimes, two or more addressing modes are combined in one instruction.

Operation code	Mode	Address

FIGURE 9-1
Instruction Format with Mode Field

An example of an instruction format with a distinct addressing mode field is shown in Figure 9-1. The operation code specifies the operation to be performed. The mode field is used to locate the operands needed for the operation. There may or may not be an address field in the instruction. If there is an address field, it may designate a memory address or a code for a processor register. Moreover, as discussed in the previous section, the instruction may have more than one address field. In that case, each address field is associated with its own particular addressing mode.

Implied Mode

Although most addressing modes modify the address field of the instruction, there is one mode that needs no address field at all. This is the implied mode. In this mode, the operand is specified implicitly in the definition of the operation code.

For example, the instruction "complement accumulator" is an implied mode instruction because the operand in the accumulator register is implied in the definition of the instruction. In fact, any instruction that uses an accumulator without a second operand is an implied mode instruction. Operation type instructions in a stack-organized computer are implied-mode instructions since the operands are implied to be on top of the stack.

Immediate Mode

In the immediate mode, the operand is specified in the instruction itself. In other words, an immediate mode instruction has an operand field rather than an address field. The operand field contains the actual operand to be used in conjunction with the operation specified in the instruction. Immediate-mode instructions are useful for initializing registers to a constant value.

Register and Register-Indirect Modes

It was mentioned previously that the address field of the instruction may specify either a memory address or a code for a processor register. When the address field specifies a processor register, the instruction is said to be in the register mode. In this mode, the operands are in registers that reside within the processor unit of the computer. The particular register is selected from a register address field in the instruction format. An n-bit field can specify any one of 2^n registers.

In the *register-indirect* mode the instruction specifies a register in the processor whose content gives the address of the operand in memory. In other words, the selected register contains the memory address of the operand rather than the operand itself. Before using a register-indirect mode instruction, the programmer must ensure that the memory address is placed in the processor register with a previous instruction. A reference to the register is then equivalent to specifying a memory address. The advantage of a register-indirect mode instruction is that the address field of the instruction uses fewer bits to select a register than would have been required to specify a memory address directly.

An *autoincrement* or *autodecrement* mode is similar to the register-indirect mode except that the register is incremented or decremented after (or before) its address value is used to access memory. When the address stored in the register refers to an array of data in memory, it is convenient to increment the register after each access to the array. This can be achieved by using a register-increment instruction. However, because it is such a common requirement, some computers incorporate a special mode that automatically increments the content of the register after the memory data is accessed.

Direct-Addressing Mode

In the direct addressing mode the address field of the instruction gives the address of the operand in memory in a computational type instruction. It is the branch address in a branch type instruction.

An example of a computational type instruction is shown in Figure 9-2. The instruction in memory consists of two words. The first word, at address 250, has the operation code for "load to *AC*" and a mode field specifying a direct address. The second word, at address 251, contains the address field symbolized by ADRS and is equal to 500. The *PC* holds the address of the instruction. The instruction is brought from memory into two control registers and *PC* is incremented twice. The execution of the instruction results in the operation

$$AC \leftarrow M[\text{ADRS}]$$

Since ADRS = 500 and $M[500] = 800$, the *AC* receives the number 800. After the instruction is executed, the *PC* holds the number 252, which is the address of the next instruction in the program.

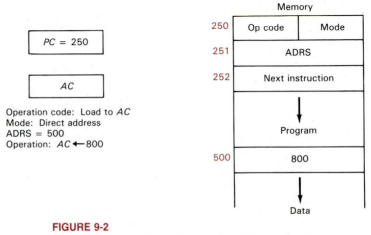

FIGURE 9-2
Example Demonstrating a Computational Type Instruction

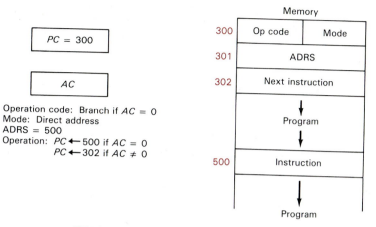

Memory

300	Op code	Mode
301	ADRS	
302	Next instruction	

PC = 300

AC

Operation code: Branch if $AC = 0$
Mode: Direct address
ADRS = 500
Operation: $PC \leftarrow 500$ if $AC = 0$
$ PC \leftarrow 302$ if $AC \neq 0$

500   Instruction

Program

FIGURE 9-3
Example Demonstrating a Branch Type Instruction

Next consider a branch type instruction as shown in Figure 9-3. If the contents of AC is equal to 0, control branches to ADRS; otherwise the program continues with the next instruction in sequence. When $AC = 0$, the branch to address 500 is accomplished by loading the value of the address field ADRS into the PC. Control then continues with the instruction at address 500. When $AC \neq 0$, no branch occurs; and the PC, which was incremented twice after reading the instruction, holds the address 302, the address of the next instruction in sequence.

The address field of an instruction is used by the control unit of the computer to obtain the operand from memory. Sometimes the value given in the address field is the address of the operand, but sometimes it is just an address from which the address of the operand is calculated. To differentiate among the various addressing modes it is necessary to distinguish between the address part of the instruction as given in the address field and the address used by the control when executing the instruction.

The *effective address* is defined to be the memory address obtained from the computation dictated by the addressing mode. The effective address is the address of the operand in a computational type instruction. It is the address where control branches, in response to a branch type instruction. In the direct-address mode, the effective address is equal to the address part of the instruction. In the register-indirect mode the effective address is the address stored in the selected register.

Indirect-Addressing Mode

In the indirect-addressing mode the address field of the instruction gives the address where the effective address is stored in memory. Control fetches the instruction from memory and uses the address part to access memory again to read the effective address.

Consider the instruction "load to AC" given in Figure 9-2. If the mode specifies an indirect address, the effective address is stored in $M[\text{ADRS}]$. Since ADRS = 500 and $M[\text{ADRS}] = 800$, the effective address is 800. This means that the operand that is loaded into the *AC* is the one found in memory at address 800 (not shown in the figure).

Relative-Addressing Mode

Some addressing modes require that the address field of the instruction be added to the content of a specified register in the CPU in order to evaluate the effective address. In the relative-addressing mode the effective address is calculated as follows

$$\text{Effective address} = \text{Address part of the instruction}$$

$$+ \text{ Contents of } PC$$

The address part of the instruction is considered as a signed number which can be either positive or negative. When this number is added to the contents of *PC*, the result produces an effective address whose position in memory is relative to the address of the next instruction in the program.

To clarify this with an example, let us assume that *PC* contains the number 250 and the address part of the instruction contains the number 500, as in Figure 9-2, with the mode field specifying a relative address. The instruction at location 250 is read from memory during the fetch phase and *PC* is incremented by one to 251. Since the instruction has a second word, control reads the address field into a control register and *PC* is incremented to 252. The effective address computation for the relative addressing mode is 252 + 500 = 752. The result is that the operand associated with the instruction is 752 locations relative to the location of the next instruction.

Relative addressing is often used in branch type instructions when the branch address is in the area surrounding the instruction word itself. It results in a shorter address field in the instruction format since the relative address can be specified with a smaller number of bits than the number of bits required to designate the entire memory address.

Indexed-Addressing Mode

In the indexed-addressing mode the content of an index register is added to the address part of the instruction to obtain the effective address. The index register is a special CPU register that contains an index value. The address field of the instruction defines the beginning address of a data array in memory. Each operand in the array is stored in memory relative to the beginning address. The distance between the beginning address and the address of the operand is the index value stored in the register. Any operand in the array can be accessed with the same instruction provided the index register contains the correct index value. The index register can be incremented to facilitate the access to consecutive operands.

Some computers dedicate one CPU register to function solely as an index register. This register is involved implicitly when an index mode instruction is used. In computers with many processor registers, any one of the CPU registers can be used as an index register. In such a case, the index register must be specified explicitly with a register field within the instruction format.

A variation of the index mode is the *base-register* mode. In this mode the content of a base register is added to the address part of the instruction to obtain the effective address. This is similar to indexed addressing except that the register is called a base register instead of index register. The difference between the two modes is in the way they are used rather than in the way they are computed. An index register is assumed to hold an index number which is relative to the address field of the instruction. A base register is assumed to hold a base address and the address field of the instruction gives a displacement relative to the base address.

Summary of Addressing Modes

In order to show the differences between the various modes, we will investigate the effect of the addressing mode on the instruction shown in Figure 9-4. The instruction in addresses 250 and 251 is "load to AC" with the address field ADRS (or an operand NBR) equal to 500. The PC has the number 250 for fetching this instruction. The content of a processor register $R1$ is 400 and the AC receives the operand after the instruction is executed. In the direct mode the effective address is 500 and the operand to be loaded into the AC is 800. In the immediate mode the operand 500 is loaded into the AC. In the indirect mode the effective address is 800 and the operand is 300. In the relative mode the effective address is 500 +

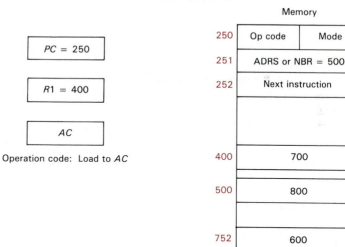

FIGURE 9-4

Numerical Example for Addressing Modes

TABLE 9-1
Symbolic Convention for Addressing Modes

Addressing mode	Symbolic convention	Register transfer	Refers to Figure 9-4	
			Effective address	Content of AC
Direct	LDA ADRS	$AC \leftarrow M[ADRS]$	500	800
Immediate	LDA #NBR	$AC \leftarrow NBR$	251	500
Indirect	LDA [ADRS]	$AC \leftarrow M[M[ADRS]]$	800	300
Relative	LDA $ADRS	$AC \leftarrow M[ADRS + PC]$	752	600
Index	LDA ADRS (R1)	$AC \leftarrow M[ADRS + R1]$	900	200
Register	LDA R1	$AC \leftarrow R1$	—	400
Register indirect	LDA (R1)	$AC \leftarrow M[R1]$	400	700

$252 = 752$ and the operand is 600. In the index mode the effective address is $500 + 400 = 900$ assuming that $R1$ is the index register. In the register mode the operand is in $R1$ and 400 is loaded into the AC. In the register indirect mode the effective address is the contents of $R1$ and the operand loaded into the AC is 700.

Table 9-1 lists the value of the effective address and the operand loaded into the AC for seven addressing modes. The table also shows the operation with a register transfer statement and the symbolic convention for each addressing mode. LDA is the symbol for the load-to-accumulator operation code. In the direct mode we use the symbol ADRS for the address part of the instruction. The # symbol precedes the operand NBR in the immediate mode. The symbol ADRS enclosed in square brackets symbolizes an indirect address. Some computers use the symbol @ to designate an indirect address. The symbol $ before the address makes the effective address relative to PC. An index mode instruction is recognized by the symbol of a register that is placed in parentheses after the address symbol. The register mode is indicated by giving the name of the processor register following LDA. In the register indirect mode the name of the register that holds the effective address is enclosed in parentheses.

9-4 STACK ORGANIZATION

A very useful feature included in many computers is a memory stack, also known as a last-in first-out (LIFO) list. A stack is a storage device that stores information in such a manner that the item stored last is the first item retrieved. The operation of a stack is sometimes compared to a stack of trays. The last tray placed on top of the stack is the first to be taken off.

The stack is useful for a variety of applications and its organization possesses special features that facilitate many data processing tasks. A stack is used in some electronic calculators and computers to facilitate the evaluation of arithmetic expressions. Its use in computers is mostly for handling of subroutines and interrupts as explained in Section 9-8.

A memory stack is essentially a portion of a memory unit accessed by an address that is always incremented or decremented after the memory access. The register that holds the address for the stack is called a *stack pointer* (*SP*) because its value always points at the top item of the stack. The two operations of a stack are insertion and deletion of items. The operation of insertion is called *push* and it can be thought of as the result of pushing a new item onto the top of the stack. The operation of deletion is called *pop* and it can be thought of as the result of removing one item so that the stack pops out. However, nothing is physically pushed or popped in a memory stack. These operations are simulated by decrementing or incrementing the stack pointer register.

Figure 9-5 shows a portion of a memory organized as a stack. The stack pointer register *SP* holds the binary address of the item that is currently on the top of the stack. Three items are presently stored in the stack, A, B, and C in consecutive addresses 103, 102, and 101, respectively. Item C is on top of the stack, so *SP* contains 101. To remove the top item, the stack is popped by reading the item at address 101 and incrementing *SP*. Item B is now on top of the stack since *SP* contains address 102. To insert a new item, the stack is pushed by first decrementing *SP* and then writing the new item on top of the stack. Note that item C has been read out but not physically removed. This does not matter as far as the stack operation is concerned, because when the stack is pushed, a new item is written on top of the stack regardless of what was there before.

We assume that the items in the stack communicate with a data register *DR*. A new item is inserted with the push operation as follows:

$$SP \leftarrow SP - 1$$

$$M[SP] \leftarrow DR$$

The stack pointer is decremented so it points at the address of the next word. A memory write microoperation inserts the word from *DR* onto the top of the stack. Note that *SP* holds the address of the top of the stack and that *M[SP]* denotes the memory word specified by the address presently in *SP*.

A new item is deleted with a pop operation as follows:

$$DR \leftarrow M[SP]$$

$$SP \leftarrow SP + 1$$

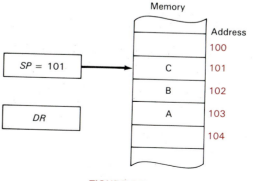

FIGURE 9-5
Memory Stack

The top item is read from the stack into DR. The stack pointer is then incremented to point at the next item in the stack.

The two microoperations needed for either the push or pop are access to memory through SP and updating SP. Which of the two microoperations is done first and whether SP is updated by incrementing or decrementing depends on the organization of the stack. In Figure 9-5 the stack grows by decreasing the memory address. The stack may be constructed to grow by increasing the memory address. In such a case, SP is incremented for the push operation and decremented for the pop operation. A stack may be constructed so that SP points at the next empty location above the top of the stack. In this case, the sequence of microoperations must be interchanged.

A stack pointer is loaded with an initial value. This initial value must be the bottom address of an assigned stack in memory. From then on, SP is automatically decremented or incremented with every push or pop operation. The advantage of a memory stack is that the processor can refer to it without having to specify an address, since the address is always available and automatically updated in the stack pointer.

Reverse Polish Notation (RPN)

A stack organization is very effective for evaluating arithmetic expressions. The common mathematical method of writing arithmetic expressions imposes difficulty when evaluated by a computer. Conventional arithmetic expressions are written in the *infix* notation, with each operator written between the operands. Consider the simple arithmetic expression

$$A * B + C * D$$

The operator $*$ denotes multiplication and is placed between the operands A and B and between C and D. The operator $+$ denoting addition is between the two products. To evaluate the arithmetic expression it is necessary to compute the product $A * B$, store this product, compute the product $C * D$, and then sum the two products. From this simple example we see that to evaluate arithmetic expressions in infix notation it is necessary to scan back and forth along the expression to determine the sequence of operations that must be performed.

The Polish mathematician Jan Lukasiewicz proposed that arithmetic expressions be written in *prefix* notation. This representation, referred to as *Polish notation* places the operator before the operands. *Postfix* notation, referred to as *reverse Polish notation*, places the operator after the operands. The following examples demonstrate the three representations.

$A + B$	Infix notation
$+ A B$	Prefix or Polish notation
$A B +$	Postfix or reverse Polish notation

Reverse Polish notation, also known as RPN, is a form suitable for stack manipulation. The expression

$$A * B + C * D$$

is written in RPN as

$$A \; B * C \; D * +$$

and is evaluated as follows. Scan the expression from left to right. When an operator is reached, perform the operation with the two operands to the left of the operator. Remove the two operands and the operator and replace them with the number obtained from the operation. Continue to scan the expression and repeat the procedure for every operator until there are no more operators.

For the above expression we find the operator $*$ after A and B. We perform the operation $A * B$ and replace A, B, and $*$ by the product to obtain

$$(A * B) \; C \; D * +$$

where $(A + B)$ is a single quantity obtained from the product. The next operator is a $*$ and its previous two operands are C and D; so we perform $C * D$ and obtain an expression with two operands and one operator:

$$(A * B) \; (C * D) \; +$$

The next operator is $+$ and the two operands on its left are the two products; so we add the two quantities to obtain the result.

The conversion from infix notation to reverse Polish notation must take into consideration the operational hierarchy adopted for infix notation. This hierarchy dictates that we first perform all arithmetic inside inner parentheses, then inside outer parentheses, then do multiplication and division, and finally, addition and subtraction. Consider the expression

$$(A + B) * [C * (D + E) + F]$$

To evaluate the expression we must first perform the arithmetic inside the parentheses and then evaluate the expression inside the square brackets. The multiplication of $C * (D + E)$ must be done prior to the addition of F. The last operation is the multiplication of the two terms between the parentheses and brackets. The expression can be converted to RPN by taking into consideration the operation hierarchy. The converted expression is

$$A \; B + D \; E + C * F + *$$

Proceeding from left to right, we first add A and B, then add D and E. At this point we are left with

$$(A + B) \; (D + E) \; C * F + *$$

Where $(A + B)$ and $(D + E)$ are each a single number obtained from the sum. The two operands for the next $*$ are C and $(D + E)$. These two numbers are multiplied and the product added to F. The final $*$ causes the multiplication of the last result with the number $(A + B)$. Note that all expressions in RPN are without parentheses.

The subtraction and division operations are not commutative, and the order of the operands is important. We define the RPN expression $A \; B \; -$ to mean $(A - B)$ and the expression $A \; B \; /$ to represent the division of $A \; / \; B$.

Stack Operations

Reverse Polish notation combined with a stack provides an efficient way to evaluate arithmetic expressions. This procedure is employed in some electronic calculators and also in some computers. The stack is particularly useful for handling long, complex problems involving chain calculations. It is based on the fact that any arithmetic expression can be expressed in parentheses-free Polish notation.

The procedure consists of first converting the arithmetic expression into its equivalent RPN. The operands are pushed onto the stack in the order that they appear. The initiation of an operation depends on whether we have a calculator or a computer. In a calculator, the operators are entered through the keyboard. In a computer they must be initiated by program instructions. The following operations are executed with the stack when an operation is specified: The two topmost operands in the stack are popped and used for the operation. The result of the operation is pushed into the stack, replacing the lower operand. By continuously pushing the operands onto the stack and performing the operations as defined above, the expression is evaluated in the proper order and the final result remains on top of the stack.

The following numerical example will clarify the procedure. Consider the arithmetic expression

$$(3 * 4) + (5 * 6)$$

In reverse Polish notation, it is expressed as

$$3\ 4 * 5\ 6 * +$$

Now consider the stack operations as shown in Figure 9-6. Each box represents one stack operation and the arrow always points to the top of the stack. Scanning the RPN expression from left to right, we encounter two operands. First the number 3 is pushed onto the stack, then the number 4. The next symbol is the multiplication operator *. This causes a multiplication of the two topmost numbers in the stack. The stack is popped twice for the operands and the product is pushed into the top of the stack in the lower position of the original operand. Next we encounter the two operands 5 and 6, and they are pushed onto the stack. The stack operation that results from the next * removes these two numbers and puts their product, 30, on the stack. The last operation causes an arithmetic addition of the two topmost numbers in the stack to produce the final result of 42.

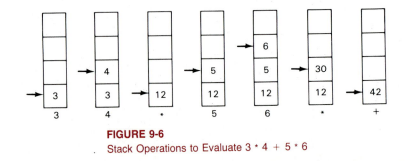

FIGURE 9-6
Stack Operations to Evaluate 3 * 4 + 5 * 6

Calculators that use RPN have an Enter key that functions as a push operation. When a number is keyed in following an Enter, the number is pushed onto the stack. When a number is keyed in following an operator, the calculator pushes the number on top of the stack and performs the operation with the two topmost numbers in the stack. Thus, the above expression is evaluated in an RPN calculator by using a sequence of keys as follows:

$$3 \text{ Enter } 4 * 5 \text{ Enter } 6 * +$$

Computer Stack

Most computers have a facility for a memory stack but only a few commercial computers have the appropriate instructions for evaluating arithmetic expressions with RPN. Such computers have a stack organized CPU with the top locations of the stack as registers. The rest of the stack is in memory. In this way, the operations that must be performed with the top two items of the stack are available in processor registers for manipulation with arithmetic circuits.

The PUSH and POP instructions require one address field to specify the source or destination operand. Operation type instructions for the stack such as ADD and MUL imply the two operands on top of the stack and do not require an address field in the instruction. The following program shows how the arithmetic statement

$$X = (A + B) * (C + D)$$

will be written for a computer stack (TOS stands for top of stack).

PUSH A	TOS ← A
PUSH B	TOS ← B
ADD	TOS ← (A + B)
PUSH C	TOS ← C
PUSH D	TOS ← D
ADD	TOS ← (C + D)
MUL	TOS ← (C + D) * (A + B)
POP X	M[X] ← TOS

9-5   DATA TRANSFER INSTRUCTIONS

Computers provide an extensive set of instructions to give the user the flexibility to carry out various computational tasks. The instruction set of different computers differ from each other mostly in the way the operands are determined from the address and mode fields. The actual operations available in the instruction set are not very different from one computer to another. It so happens that the binary code assignment in the operation code field is different in different computers, even for the same operation. It may also happen that the symbolic name given to instructions is different in different computers, even for the same instruction. Nevertheless, there is a set of basic operations that most computers include among their instructions. The basic set of instructions available in a typical computer is the subject that will be covered in the rest of this chapter.

Most computer instructions can be classified into three major categories:

1. Data transfer instructions.
2. Data manipulation instructions.
3. Program control instructions.

Data transfer instructions cause transfer of data from one location to another without changing the binary information content. Data manipulation instructions perform arithmetic, logic, and shift operations. Program control instructions provide decision making capabilities and change the path taken by the program when executed in the computer. In addition to the basic instruction set, a computer may have other instructions that provide special operations for particular applications.

In this section we present a list of some typical data transfer instructions. In the next section we present the various data manipulation instructions. Program control instructions are discussed in Section 9-8.

Common Data Transfer Instructions

Data transfer instructions move data from one place in the computer to another without changing the data content. The most common transfers are between memory and processor registers, between processor registers and input and output, and among the processor registers themselves. Table 9-2 gives a list of eight typical data transfer instructions used in many computers. Accompanying each instruction is a mnemonic symbol. This is the assembly language abbreviation recommended by an IEEE standard (reference 6). It must be realized that different computers may use different mnemonics for the same instruction name.

The load instruction has been used to designate a transfer from memory to a processor register, such as an accumulator. The store instruction designates a transfer from a processor register into a memory word. The move instruction has been used in computers with multiple processor registers to designate a transfer from one register to another. It has also been used for data transfer between registers and memory and between two memory words. The exchange instruction exchanges information between two registers or a register and a memory word. The push and

TABLE 9-2
Typical Data Transfer Instructions

Name	Mnemonic
Load	LD
Store	ST
Move	MOVE
Exchange	XCH
Push	PUSH
Pop	POP
Input	IN
Output	OUT

pop instructions transfer data between a memory stack and a processor register. The input and output instructions transfer data between processor registers and input and output devices.

Independent Versus Memory-Mapped I/O

The input and output (I/O) instructions are similar to the load and store instructions except that the transfer is from external registers instead of memory words. The computer is considered to have a certain number of input and output *ports* with one or more ports dedicated to communication with a specific input or output device. Each port is equivalent to an external register. The particular port is chosen by an address, similar to the way an address is used to select a word in memory. The input and output instructions include an address field in their format, for specifying the particular port selected for the transfer of input or output data.

There are two ways that the addresses are assigned for selecting both memory words and I/O ports. One method uses an independent I/O system and the other employs a memory-mapped configuration.

In the *independent I/O* system, the addresses assigned to memory and I/O ports are independent from each other. The computer has distinct input and output instructions with a separate address field that is interpreted by the control and used to select a particular I/O port. The independent I/O addressing method isolates memory and I/O selection so that the memory address range is not affected by the port address assignment. For this reason, this method is also referred to as an *isolated I/O* configuration.

The second alternative is to assign memory addresses to I/O ports. This configuration is referred to as *memory-mapped I/O*. There are no separate addresses for handling input and output transfers since I/O ports are treated as memory locations in one common address range. Each I/O port is regarded as a memory location, similar to a memory word. Computers that adopt the memory-mapped scheme have no distinct input or output instructions, because the same instructions are used for manipulating memory and for I/O data manipulation. For example, the load and store instructions used for memory transfer are also used for I/O transfer, provided that the address associated with the instruction is assigned to an I/O port and not to a memory word. The advantage of this scheme is that the same set of instructions can be used for reading and writing in memory and for the input and output of data.

9-6   DATA MANIPULATION INSTRUCTIONS

Data manipulation instructions perform operations on data and provide the computational capabilities for the computer. The data manipulation instructions in a typical computer are usually divided into three basic types:

1. Arithmetic instructions.
2. Logical and bit manipulation instructions.
3. Shift instructions.

A list of data manipulation instructions will look very much like the list of micro-operations given in Chapter 7. One must realize, however, that a microoperation is an elementary operation executed by the hardware of the computer. An instruction when executed in the computer must go through the instruction fetch phase to read the binary code from memory and the operands must be brought into processor registers according to the rules specified by the addressing mode. The last step is the execution of the instruction with one or more microoperations.

Arithmetic Instructions

The four basic arithmetic instructions are addition, subtraction, multiplication, and division. Most computers provide instructions for all four operations. Some small computers have only addition and subtraction instructions. The multiplication and division must then be generated by means of special programs. The four basic arithmetic operations are sufficient for formulating solutions to any numerical problem when used with numerical analysis methods.

A list of typical arithmetic instructions is given in Table 9-3. The increment instruction adds one to the value stored in a register or memory word. A common characteristic of the increment operation when executed in processor registers is that a binary number of all 1's when incremented produces a result of all 0's. The decrement instruction subtracts one from a value stored in a register or memory word. A number with all 0's when decremented, produces a number with all 1's.

The add, subtract, multiply, and divide instructions may be available for different types of data. The data type assumed to be in processor registers during the execution of these arithmetic operations is included in the definition of the operation code. An arithmetic instruction may specify unsigned or signed integers, binary or decimal numbers, or floating-point data. The arithmetic operations with binary and decimal integers was presented in Chapter 1. The floating-point representation is used for scientific calculations and is presented in the next section.

The number of bits in any register is finite and therefore the results of arithmetic operations are of finite precision. Most computers provide special instructions to facilitate double precision arithmetic. A carry flip-flop is used to store the carry from an operation. The instruction "add with carry" performs the addition with

TABLE 9-3
Typical Arithmetic Instructions

Name	Mnemonic
Increment	INC
Decrement	DEC
Add	ADD
Subtract	SUB
Multiply	MUL
Divide	DIV
Add with carry	ADDC
Subtract with borrow	SUBB
Subtract reverse	SUBR
Negate (2's complement)	NEG

two operands plus the value of the carry from the previous computation. Similarly, the "subtract with borrow" instruction subtracts two operands and a borrow which may have resulted from a previous operation. The reverse subtract instruction reverses the order of the operands and performs $B - A$ instead of $A - B$. The negate instruction performs the 2's complement of a signed number which is equivalent to multiplying it by -1.

Logical and Bit Manipulation Instructions

Logical instructions perform binary operations on strings of bits stored in registers or memory words. They are useful for manipulating individual bits or a group of bits that represent binary coded information. The logical instructions consider each bit of the operand separately and treat it as a Boolean variable. By proper application of the logical instructions, it is possible to change bit values, to clear a group of bits, or to insert new bit values into operands stored in registers or memory words.

Some typical logical and bit manipulation instructions are listed in Table 9-4. The clear instruction causes the specific operand to be replaced by 0's. The set instruction causes the operand to be replaced by 1's. The complement instruction inverts all the bits of the operand. The AND, OR, and XOR instructions produce the corresponding logical operations on individual bits of the operand. Although they perform Boolean operations, when used in computer instructions, the logical instructions should be considered as performing bit manipulation operations. There are three bit manipulation operations possible: A selected bit can be cleared to 0, set to 1, or be complemented. The three logical instructions are usually applied to do just that.

The AND instruction is used to clear to 0 a bit or a selected group of bits of an operand. For any Boolean variable X, the relationship $X \cdot 0 = 0$ and $X \cdot 1 = X$ dictates that a binary variable ANDed with a 0 produces a 0; but the variable does not change when ANDed with a 1. Therefore, the AND instruction is used to selectively clear bits of an operand by ANDing the operand with a string of bits that have 0's in the bit positions that must be cleared and 1's in the bit positions

TABLE 9-4
Typical Logical and Bit Manipulation Instructions

Name	Mnemonic
Clear	CLR
Set	SET
Complement	COM
AND	AND
OR	OR
Exclusive-OR	XOR
Clear carry	CLRC
Set carry	SETC
Complement carry	COMC

that remain the same. The AND instruction is also called a *mask* because it masks (by inserting 0's) a selected portion of an operand.

The OR instruction is used to set to 1 a bit or a selected group of bits of an operand. For any Boolean variable X, the relationships $X + 1 = 1$ and $X + 0 = X$ dictate that a binary variable ORed with a 1 produces a 1; but the variable does not change when ORed with a 0. Therefore, the OR instruction can be used to selectively set bits of an operand by ORing it with a string of bits with 1's in the bit positions that must be set to 1. The OR instruction is sometimes called a *bit set instruction*.

The XOR instruction is used to selectively complement bits of an operand. This is because of the Boolean relationships $X \oplus 1 = \overline{X}$ and $X \oplus 0 = X$. A binary variable is complemented when XORed with a 1 but does not change in value when XORed with 0. The XOR instruction is sometimes called a *bit complement instruction*.

A few other bit manipulation instructions are included in Table 9-4. Individual bits such as a carry can be cleared, set, or complemented with appropriate instructions. Other status bits or flag bits can be set or cleared by program instructions in a similar manner.

Shift Instructions

Instructions to shift the content of an operand are provided in several variations. Shifts are operations in which the bits of the operand are moved to the left or the right. The bit shifted in at the end of the word determines the type of shift used. Shift instructions may specify either logical shifts, arithmetic shifts, or rotate type operations. In any case the shift may be to the right or to the left.

Table 9-5 lists four types of shift instructions. The logical shift inserts 0 into the end bit position after the shift. The end position is the leftmost bit for shift right and the rightmost positions for shift left. Arithmetic shifts conform to the rules for shifting signed numbers. The arithmetic shift right instruction preserves the sign bit in the leftmost position. The sign bit is shifted to the right together with the rest of the number, but the sign bit itself remains unchanged. The arithmetic shift left instruction inserts 0 into the end bit in the rightmost position and is identical to the logical shift left instruction. For this reason many computers do not provide

TABLE 9-5
Typical Shift Instructions

Name	Mnemonic
Logical shift right	SHR
Logical shift left	SHL
Arithmetic shift right	SHRA
Arithmetic shift left	SHLA
Rotate right	ROR
Rotate left	ROL
Rotate right with carry	RORC
Rotate left with carry	ROLC

a distinct arithmetic shift left instruction when the logical shift left instruction is already available.

The rotate instructions produce a circular shift. Bits shifted out at one end of the word are not lost, as in a logical shift, but are rotated back into the other end. The rotate with carry instructions treats the carry bit as an extension of the register whose word is being rotated. Thus, a rotate left with carry instruction transfers the carry bit into the rightmost bit position of the register, transfers the leftmost bit of the register into the carry, and shifts the entire register to the left.

Some computers have a multiple field format for the shift instruction. One field contains the operation code and the others specify the type of shift and the number of positions that an operand is to be shifted. A possible instruction format of a shift instruction may include five fields as follows:

$$\text{OP} \quad \text{REG} \quad \text{TYPE} \quad \text{RL} \quad \text{COUNT}$$

Here OP is the operation code field for specifying a shift; REG is a register address that specifies the location of the operand. TYPE is a 2-bit field that specifies one of the four types of shifts (logical, arithmetic, rotate, and rotate with carry); RL is a 1-bit field that specifies whether a shift is to the right or the left; and COUNT is a k-bit field that specifies up to $2^k - 1$ shifts. With such a format, it is possible to specify the type of shift, the direction, and the number of shifts, all in one instruction.

9-7 FLOATING-POINT OPERATIONS

In many scientific calculations, the range of numbers is very large. The way to expand the range of numbers is to express them in floating-point notation. The floating-point number has two parts. The first part contains a *fraction* (sometimes called a *mantissa*) and the second part designates the position of the decimal point and is called the *exponent*. For example, the decimal number $+6132.789$ is represented in floating-point as

Fraction	Exponent
$+.6132789$	$+04$

The value of the exponent indicates that the actual position of the decimal point is four positions to the right of the indicated decimal point in the fraction. This representation is equivalent to the scientific notation $+.6132789 \times 10^{+4}$.

Decimal floating-point numbers are interpreted as representing a number in the form

$$F \times 10^E$$

where F is the fraction and E the exponent. Only the fraction and the exponent are physically represented in computer registers. The base 10 and the decimal point of the fraction are assumed and are not shown explicitly. A floating-point binary number is represented in a similar manner except that it uses a base 2 for the exponent. For example, the binary number $+1001.11$ is represented with an 8-bit fraction and 6-bit exponent as

Fraction	Exponent
01001110	000100

The fraction has a 0 in the leftmost position to denote a plus. The binary point of the fraction follows the sign bit but is not shown in the register. The exponent has the equivalent binary number $+4$. The floating-point number is equivalent to

$$F \times 2^E = +(.1001110)_2 \times 2^{+4}$$

A floating-point number is said to be *normalized* if the most significant digit of the fraction is nonzero. For example, the decimal fraction 0.350 is normalized but 0.0035 is not. Normalized numbers provide the maximum possible precision for the floating-point number. A zero cannot be normalized because it does not have a nonzero digit. It is usually represented in floating-point by all 0's in both the fraction and exponent.

Floating-point representation increases the range of numbers that can be accommodated in a given register. Consider a computer with 48-bit registers. Since one bit must be reserved for the sign, the range of signed integers will be $\pm(2^{47} - 1)$ which is approximately $\pm 10^{14}$. The 48 bits can be used to represent a floating-point number with 36 bits for the fraction and 12 bits for the exponent. The largest positive or negative number that can be accommodated is

$$\pm(1 - 2^{-35}) \times 2^{+2047}$$

This number is derived from a fraction that contains a sign bit and 35 1's, and an exponent with a sign bit and eleven 1's. The maximum exponent is $2^{11} - 1$ or 2047. The largest number that can be accommodated is approximately equivalent to decimal 10^{615}.

Arithmetic Operations

Arithmetic operations with floating-point numbers are more complicated than with integer numbers and their execution takes longer and requires more complex hardware. Adding and subtracting two numbers requires that the decimal points be aligned since the exponent parts must be equal before adding or subtracting the fractions. The alignment is done by shifting one fraction and adjusting its exponent until it is equal to the other exponent. Consider the sum of the following floating-point numbers.

$$.5372400 \times 10^2$$

$$+.1580000 \times 10^{-1}$$

It is necessary that the two exponents be equal before the fractions can be added. We can either shift the first number three positions to the left, or shift the second number three positions to the right. When the fractions are stored in registers, shifting to the left causes a loss of most significant digits. Shifting to the right causes a loss of least significant digits. The second method is preferable because it only reduces the precision while the first method may cause an error. The usual alignment procedure is to shift the fraction that has the smaller exponent to the right by a number of places equal to the difference between the exponents. After this is done, the fractions can be added.

$$.5372400 \times 10^2$$

$$+ \; .0001580 \times 10^2$$

$$.5373982 \times 10^2$$

When two normalized fractions are added, the sum may contain an overflow digit. An overflow can be corrected by shifting the sum once to the right and incrementing the exponent. When two numbers are subtracted, the result may contain most significant zeros in the fraction as shown in the following example:

$$.56780 \times 10^5$$

$$- \; .56430 \times 10^5$$

$$.00350 \times 10^5$$

A floating-point number that has a 0 in the most significant position is not normalized. To normalize the number, it is necessary to shift the fraction to the left and decrement the exponent until a nonzero digit appears in the first position. In the above example, it is necessary to shift left twice to obtain $.35000 \times 10^3$. In most computers, a normalization procedure is performed after each operation to ensure that all results are in normalized form.

Floating-point multiplication and division do not require an alignment of the fractions. The product can be formed by multiplying the two fractions and adding the exponents. Division is accomplished by dividing the fractions and subtracting the exponents.

In the examples shown we used decimal numbers to demonstrate the arithmetic operations of floating-point numbers. The same procedure applies to binary numbers with the exception that the base of the exponent is 2 instead of 10.

Biased Exponent

The fraction part of a floating-point number is usually in signed-magnitude representation. The exponent representation employed in most computers is known as a *biased representation*. The bias is an excess number which is added to the exponent so that internally all exponents become positive. As a consequence, the sign is removed from being a separate entity.

Consider for example the range of decimal exponents from -99 to $+99$. This is represented by two digits and a sign. If we use an excess 99 bias then the biased exponent e will be equal to $e = E + 99$, where E is the actual exponent. For $E = -99$, we have $e = -99 + 99 = 0$; and for $E = +99$, we have $e = 99 + 99 = 198$. In this way, the biased exponent is represented in a register as a positive number in the range from 000 to 198. Positive biased exponents have a range of numbers from 099 to 198. The subtraction of the bias 99 gives the positive values from 0 to $+99$. Negative biased exponents have a range from 098 to 000. The subtraction of 99 gives the negative values from -1 to -99.

The advantage of biased exponents is the fact that they contain only positive numbers. It is then simpler to compare their relative magnitude without being concerned with their signs. Another advantage is that the most negative exponent converts to a biased exponent with all 0's. The floating-point representation of zero is then a zero fraction and a zero biased exponent which is the smallest possible exponent.

Standard Operand Format

Arithmetic instructions that perform the operations with floating-point data use the suffix F. Thus, ADDF is an add instruction with floating-point numbers. There are two standard formats for representing a floating-point operand. The single precision data type consists of 32 bits and the double precision data type consists of 64 bits. When both types of data are available, the single precision instruction mnemonic uses an FS suffix and the double precision uses FL (for floating-point long).

The format of the IEEE standard (see reference 7) single precision floating-point operand is shown in Figure 9-7. It consists of 32 bits. The sign bit s designates the sign of the fraction. The biased exponent e contains 8 bits and uses an excess 127 number. The fraction f consists of 23 bits. The binary point is assumed to be immediately to the left of the most significant bit of the f field. In addition, an implied 1 bit is inserted to the left of the binary point which in effect expands the number to 24 bits representing a value from 1.0 to 2.0 (excluding 2). The component of the binary floating-point number that consists of a leading bit to the left of the implied binary point together with the fraction in the f field is called the *significand*. Some examples of f field values and the corresponding significands are shown below.

f Field	Significand	Decimal Equivalent
100 . . . 0	1.100 . . . 0	1.5
010 . . . 0	1.010 . . . 0	1.25
000 . . . 0	1.000 . . . 0	1.0

Even though the f field by itself may not be normalized, the significand is always normalized because it has a nonzero bit in the most significant position. Since normalized numbers must have a nonzero most significant bit, this 1 bit is not included explicitly in the format but must be inserted by the hardware during the arithmetic computations.

The exponent field uses an excess 127 bias value for normalized numbers. The range of valid exponents is from -126 (represented as 00000001) through $+127$ (represented as 11111110). The maximum (11111111) and minimum (00000000)

FIGURE 9-7
Standard Floating-Point Operand Format

TABLE 9-6
Evaluating Biased Exponents

| Exponent E in decimal | Biased exponent $e = E + 127$ | |
	Decimal	Binary
-126	$-126 + 127 = 1$	00000001
-001	$-001 + 127 = 126$	01111110
000	$000 + 127 = 127$	01111111
$+001$	$001 + 127 = 128$	10000000
$+126$	$126 + 127 = 253$	11111101
$+127$	$127 + 127 = 254$	11111110

values that the e field can take are reserved to indicate exceptional conditions. Table 9-6 shows some values of biased exponents and their actual values.

Normalized numbers are numbers that can be expressed as floating-point operands where the e field is neither all 0's nor all 1's. The value of the number is derived from the three fields in the format of Figure 9-7 using the following formula:

$$(-1)^s 2^{e-127} \times (1.f)$$

The most positive normalized number that can be obtained has a 0 for the sign bit for positive sign, a biased exponent equal to 254 and an f field with 23 1's. This gives an exponent $E = 254 - 127 = 127$. The significand is equal to $1 + 1 - 2^{-23} = 2 - 2^{-23}$. The maximum positive number that can be accommodated is

$$+ 2^{127} \times (2 - 2^{-23})$$

The least positive normalized number has a biased exponent equal to 00000001 and a fraction of all 0's. The exponent is $E = 1 - 127 = -126$ and the significand is equal to 1.0. The smallest positive number that can be accommodated is $+2^{-126}$. The corresponding negative numbers are the same except that the sign bit is negative.

As mentioned before, exponents with all 0's or all 1's (decimal 255) are reserved for special conditions:

1. When $e = 255$ and $f = 0$, the number represents plus or minus infinity. The sign is determined from the sign bit s.

2. When $e = 255$ and $f \neq 0$, the representation is considered to be *not a number* or NaN, regardless of the sign value. NaNs are used to signify invalid operations such as the multiplication of zero times infinity.

3. When $e = 0$ and $f = 0$, the number denotes plus or minus zero.

4. When $e = 0$, and $f \neq 0$, the number is said to be *denormalized*. This is the name given to numbers with a magnitude less than the minimum value that is represented in the normalized format.

9-8   PROGRAM CONTROL INSTRUCTIONS

The instructions of a program are stored in successive memory locations. When processed by the control, the instructions are read from consecutive memory locations and executed one by one. Each time an instruction is fetched from memory,

TABLE 9-7
Typical Program Control Instructions

Name	Mnemonic
Branch	BR
Jump	JMP
Skip next instruction	SKP
Call subroutine	CALL
Return from subroutine	RET
Compare (by subtraction)	CMP
Test (by ANDing)	TEST

the program counter *PC* is incremented so that it contains the address of the next instruction in sequence. After the execution of a data transfer or data manipulation instruction, control returns to the fetch phase and uses *PC* to fetch the next instruction in sequence. In contrast, a program control instruction, when executed, may change the address value in *PC* and cause the flow of control to be altered. The change in *PC* as a result of the execution of a program control instruction causes a break in the sequence of instruction execution. This is an important feature of digital computers since it provides control over the flow of program execution and a capability for branching to different program segments depending on previous computations.

Some typical program control instructions are listed in Table 9-7. The branch and jump instructions are used interchangeably to mean the same thing, although sometimes they are used to denote different addressing modes. The branch is usually a one address instruction. When executed, the branch instruction causes a transfer of the effective address into *PC*. Since *PC* contains the address of the instruction to be executed next, the next instruction will be fetched from the location specified by the effective address.

Branch and jump instructions may be conditional or unconditional. An unconditional branch instruction causes a branch to the specified effective address without any conditions. The conditional branch instruction specifies a condition for the branch such as a positive or negative result. If the condition is met, *PC* is loaded with the effective address and the next instruction is taken from this address. If the condition is not met, *PC* is not changed and the next instruction is taken from the next location in sequence.

The skip instruction does not need an address field. A conditional skip instruction will skip the next instruction if the condition is met. This is accomplished by incrementing *PC* during the execute phase in addition to its being incremented during the fetch phase. If the condition is not met, control proceeds to the next instruction in sequence, where the programmer inserts an unconditional branch instruction. Thus, a conditional skip instruction followed by an unconditional branch instruction causes a branch if the condition is not met, while a single conditional branch instruction causes a branch if the condition is met.

The call and return instructions are used in conjunction with subroutine programs. Their performance and implementation is discussed later in this section.

The compare and test instructions are not program control instructions because they do not change the program sequence directly. They are listed in Table 9-7 because of their application in setting conditions for subsequent conditional branch instructions. The compare instruction performs a subtraction between two operands, but the difference is not retained. However, the status bit conditions are updated as a result of the operation. Similarly, the test instruction performs the logical AND of two operands and updates certain status bits without retaining the result or changing the operands.

Conditional Branch Instructions

A conditional branch instruction is a branch instruction that may or may not cause a transfer of control depending on the state of the status bits in the processor. Each of these instructions tests different combination of status bits for a condition. If the condition is true, control is transferred to the effective address. If the condition is false, the program continues with the next instruction.

Table 9-8 gives a list of conditional branch instructions that depend directly on the status bits in the processor. Each instruction mnemonic is constructed with the letter B (for branch) and a letter for the name of the status bit. The letter N (for not) is included if the status bit is tested for a 0 condition. Thus BC is a branch if carry = 1, and BNC is branch if there is no carry (carry = 0).

The zero status bit is used to check if the result of an ALU operation is equal to zero or not. The carry bit is used to check the carry after addition or the borrow after subtraction of two operands in the ALU. It is also used in conjunction with the rotate instructions to check the bit shifted from the end position of a register into the carry position. The sign bit reflects the state of the leftmost bit of the output from the ALU. $S = 0$ denotes a positive sign and $S = 1$, a negative sign. Therefore, a branch on plus checks for a sign bit of 0, and a branch on minus checks for a sign bit of 1. It must be realized that these two conditional branch instructions can be used to check the value of the leftmost bit whether it represents a sign or not. The overflow bit is used in conjunction with arithmetic operations with signed numbers.

As stated previously, the compare instruction performs a subtraction of two operands, say $A - B$. The result of the operation is not transferred into a destination register, but the status bits are affected. The status bits provide information about the relative magnitude of A and B. Some computers provide special branch instructions that can be applied after the execution of a compare instruction. The specific conditions to be tested depend on whether the two numbers are considered to be unsigned or signed.

TABLE 9-8
Conditional Branch Instructions Relating to Status Bits

Branch condition	Mnemonic	Test condition
Branch if zero	BZ	$Z = 1$
Branch if no zero	BNZ	$Z = 0$
Branch if carry	BC	$C = 1$
Branch if no carry	BNC	$C = 0$
Branch if minus	BM	$S = 1$
Branch if plus	BP	$S = 0$
Branch if overflow	BV	$V = 1$
Branch if no overflow	BNV	$V = 0$

TABLE 9-9
Conditional Branch Instructions for Unsigned Numbers

Branch condition	Mnemonic	Condition	Status bits*
Branch if higher	BH	$A > B$	C or $Z = 0$
Branch if higher or equal	BHE	$A \geq B$	$C = 0$
Branch if lower	BL	$A < B$	$C = 1$
Branch if lower or equal	BLE	$A \leq B$	C or $Z = 1$
Branch if equal	BE	$A = B$	$Z = 1$
Branch if not equal	BNE	$A \neq B$	$Z = 0$

*Note that C here is a borrow bit

The relative magnitude of two unsigned binary numbers A and B can be determined by subtracting $A - B$ and checking the C and Z status bits. Most commercial computers consider the C status bit as a carry after addition and a borrow after subtraction. A borrow occurs when $A < B$ because the most significant position must borrow a bit to complete the subtraction. A borrow does not occur if $A \geq B$ because the difference $A - B$ is positive. The condition for borrow is the inverse of the condition for carry when the subtraction is done by taking the 2's complement of B. Computers that use the C status bit as a borrow after a subtraction, complement the output carry after adding the 2's complement of the subtrahend and call this bit a borrow.

The conditional branch instructions for unsigned numbers are listed in Table 9-9. It is assumed that a previous instruction updated status bits C and Z after a subtraction $A - B$. The words higher, lower, and equal are used to denote the relative magnitude between two unsigned numbers. The two numbers are equal if $A = B$. This is determined from the zero status bit Z which is equal to 1 because $A - B = 0$. A is lower than B and the borrow $C = 1$ when $A < B$. For A to be lower than or equal to B ($A \leq B$) we must have $C = 1$ or $Z = 1$. The relationship $A > B$ is the inverse of $A \leq B$ and is detected from the complement condition of the status bits. Similarly, $A \geq B$ is the inverse of $A < B$ and $A \neq B$ is the inverse of $A = B$.

The conditional branch instructions for signed numbers are listed in Table 9-10. Again it is assumed that a previous instruction updated the status bits S, V, and Z after a subtraction $A - B$. The words greater, less, and equal are used to denote the relative magnitude between two signed numbers. If $S = 0$, the sign of the difference is positive, and A must be greater than or equal to B, provided that $V = 0$ indicating that no overflow occurred. An overflow causes a sign reversal as discussed in Section 7-3. This means that if $S = 1$ and $V = 1$, there was a sign

TABLE 9-10
Conditional Branch Instructions for Signed Numbers

Branch condition	Mnemonic	Condition	Status bits
Branch if greater	BG	$A > B$	$(S \oplus V)$ or $Z = 0$
Branch if greater or equal	BGE	$A \geq B$	$S \oplus V = 0$
Branch if less	BL	$A < B$	$S \oplus V = 1$
Branch if less or equal	BLE	$A \leq B$	$(S \oplus V)$ or $Z = 1$

reversal and the result should have been positive, which makes A greater than or equal to B. Therefore, the condition $A \geq B$ is true if both S and V are equal to 0 or both are equal to 1. This is the complement of the exclusive-OR operation.

For A to be greater than but not equal to B ($A > B$), the result must be positive and nonzero. Since a zero result gives a positive sign, we must ensure that the Z bit is 0 to exclude the possibility of $A = B$. Note that the condition $(S \oplus V)$ or $Z = 0$ means that both the exclusive-OR operation and the Z bit must be equal to 0. The other two conditions in the table can be derived in a similar manner. The conditions BE (branch on equal) and BNE (branch on not equal) apply to signed numbers as well and can be determined from $Z = 1$ and $Z = 0$, respectively.

Subroutine Call and Return

A subroutine is a self contained sequence of instructions that performs a given computational task. During the execution of a program, a subroutine may be called to perform its function many times at various points in the program. Each time a subroutine is called, a branch is made to the beginning of the subroutine to start executing its set of instructions. After the subroutine has been executed, a branch is made again to return to the main program. A subroutine is also called a procedure.

The instruction that transfers control to a subroutine is known by different names. The most common names are call subroutine, call procedure, jump to subroutine, or branch to subroutine. The call subroutine instruction has a one address field. The instruction is executed by performing two operations. The address of the next instruction which is available in PC (called the return address) is stored in a temporary location and control is transferred to the beginning of the subroutine. The last instruction that must be inserted in every subroutine program is a *return* to the calling program. When this instruction is executed, the return address stored in the temporary location is transferred into PC. This results in a transfer of program control to the program that called the subroutine.

Different computers use different temporary locations for storing the return address. Some computers store it in a fixed location in memory, some store it in a processor register, and some store it in a memory stack. The advantage of using a stack for the return address is that when a succession of subroutines are called, the sequential return address can be pushed onto the stack. The return instruction causes the stack to pop, and the content of the top of the stack is then transferred to PC. In this way, the return is always to the program that last called the subroutine.

A subroutine call instruction is implemented with the following microoperations:

$$SP \leftarrow SP - 1 \qquad \text{Decrement the stack pointer}$$

$$M[SP] \leftarrow PC \qquad \text{Store return address in stack}$$

$$PC \leftarrow \text{Effective address} \qquad \text{Transfer control to subroutine}$$

The return instruction is implemented by popping the stack and transferring the return address to PC.

$$PC \leftarrow M[SP] \qquad \text{Transfer return address to PC}$$

$$SP \leftarrow SP + 1 \qquad \text{Increment stack pointer}$$

By using a subroutine stack, all return addresses are automatically stored by the hardware in the memory stack. The programmer does not have to be concerned or remember where to return after the subroutine is executed.

9-9   PROGRAM INTERRUPT

The concept of program interrupt is used to handle a variety of problems that arise out of normal program sequence. Program interrupt refers to the transfer of program control from a currently running program to another service program as a result of an externally or internally generated request. Control returns to the original program after the service program is executed.

The interrupt procedure is in principle similar to a subroutine call except for three variations.

1. The interrupt is initiated by an external or internal signal rather than from the executions of an instruction.

2. The address of the service program that processes the interrupt request is determined by a hardware procedure rather than from the address field of an instruction.

3. In response to an interrupt it is necessary to store all the information that defines the state of the computer rather than storing only the program counter.

After the computer has been interrupted and the corresponding service program has been executed, the computer must return to exactly the same state that it was before the interrupt occurred. Only if this happens will the interrupted program be able to resume exactly as if nothing has happened. The state of the computer at the end of an execution of an instruction is determined from the contents of the program counter and other processor registers and the values of various status bits. The collection of all status bits is sometimes called the *program status word* or PSW. The PSW is stored in a separate register and contains the status information that characterizes the state of the computer. Typically, it includes the status bits from the last ALU operation and it specifies what interrupts are allowed to occur and whether the computer is operating in a user or system mode. Many computers have a resident operating system that controls and supervises all other programs. When the computer is executing a program that is part of the operating system, the computer is placed in a system mode. Certain instructions are privileged and can be executed in the system mode only. The computer is in a user mode when executing user programs. The mode of the computer at any given time is determined from special status bits in the PSW.

Some computers store only the program counter when responding to an interrupt. The program that performs the data processing for servicing the interrupt must then include instructions to store all register contents and the PSW. Other computers store the program counter and all status and register contents in response to an interrupt. In some cases, there exist two sets of processor registers within the computer. In this way, when the program switches from the user to the system mode in response to an interrupt, it is not necessary to store the contents of processor registers because each computer mode employs its own set of registers.

The hardware procedure for processing interrupts is very similar to the execution of a subroutine instruction. The state of the processor is pushed onto a memory stack and the address of the first instruction of the interrupt service program is loaded into *PC*. The address of the service program is chosen by the hardware. Some computers assign one memory location for the beginning address of the service program. The service program must then determine the source of the interrupt and proceed to service it. Some computers assign a separate memory location for each possible interrupt source. Sometimes, the interrupt source hardware itself supplies the address of the service routine. In any case, the computer must possess some form of hardware procedure for selecting a branch address for servicing the interrupt through program instructions.

Most computers will not respond to an interrupt until the instruction that is in the process of being executed is completed. Then, just before going to fetch the next instruction, the control checks for any interrupt signals. If an interrupt has occurred, control goes to a hardware interrupt cycle. During this cycle, the contents of *PC* (and sometimes the state of the processor) is pushed onto the stack. The branch address for the particular interrupt is then transferred to *PC* and control goes to fetch the next instruction. The service program is then executed starting from the address available in *PC*. The last instruction in the service program is a return from the interrupt instruction. When this instruction is executed, the stack is popped to retrieve the return address which is then transferred to *PC*.

Types of Interrupts

There are three major types of interrupts that cause a break in the normal execution of a program. They are classified as

1. External interrupts.
2. Internal interrupts.
3. Software interrupts.

External interrupts come from input or output devices, from timing devices, from a circuit monitoring the power supply, or from any other external source. Conditions that cause external interrupts are an input or output device requests a transfer of data, an external device has completed transfer of data, time out of an event has occurred, or power failure is pending. Time out interrupt may result from a program that is in an endless loop and thus exceeds its time allocation. Power failure interrupt may have as its service program a few instructions that transfer the complete state of the processor into a nondestructive memory such as a disk in the few milliseconds before power ceases.

Internal interrupts arise from illegal or erroneous use of an instruction or data. Internal interrupts are also called *traps*. Examples of interrupts caused by internal conditions are register overflow, an attempt to divide by zero, an invalid operation code, memory stack overflow, and protection violation. These error conditions usually occur as a result of a premature termination of the instruction execution. The service programs that process the internal interrupts determine the corrective measure to be taken in each case.

External and internal interrupts are initiated by hardware conditions. A software interrupt is initiated by executing an instruction. A software interrupt is a special call instruction that behaves like an interrupt rather than a subroutine call. It can be used by the programmer to initiate an interrupt procedure at any desired point in the program. The most common use of the software interrupt is associated with a system call instruction. This instruction provides means for switching from a user mode to a system mode. Certain operations in the computer may be assigned to the operating system which always operates in the system mode. For example, a complex input or output procedure must be done in a system mode. A program written by a user must run in user mode. When an input or output transfer is required, the user program causes a software interrupt, which stores the old computer state and brings in a new state that belongs to the system mode. The calling program must pass information to the operating system in order to specify the particular task that is being requested.

Processing External Interrupts

External interrupts may have single or multiple interrupt input lines. If there are more interrupt sources than there are interrupt inputs in the computer, two or more sources are ORed to form a common line. An interrupt signal may originate at any time during program execution. To ensure that no information is lost, the computer acknowledges the interrupt only after the execution of the current instruction is completed and only if the state of the processor warrants it.

Figure 9-8 shows a possible external interrupt configuration. The diagram shows four sources ORed to a single interrupt input signal. The CPU has within it an enable interrupt flip-flop (*EIF*) that can be set or reset with two program instruc-

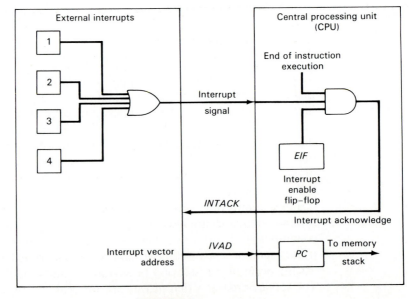

FIGURE 9-8
External Interrupt Configuration

tions. When *EIF* is reset, the interrupt signal is neglected. If *EIF* is set and the CPU is at the end of an instruction execution, the computer acknowledges the interrupt by enabling *INTACK* output. The interrupt source responds to *INTACK* by providing an interrupt vector address *IVAD* to the CPU. The program controlled *EIF* flip-flop allows the programmer to decide whether to use the interrupt facility or not. If an instruction to reset *EIF* has been inserted in the program, it means that the programmer does not want the program to be interrupted. An instruction to set *EIF* indicates that the interrupt facility will be active while the program is running.

The computer responds to an interrupt request signal if *EIF* = 1 and control has completed executing the present instruction. The microoperations that implement the interrupt cycle are as follows:

$SP \leftarrow SP - 1$	Decrement stack pointer
$M[SP] \leftarrow PC$	Store return address on top of stack
$EIF \leftarrow 0$	Reset enable interrupt flip-flop
$INTACK \leftarrow 1$	Enable interrupt acknowledge
$PC \leftarrow IVAD$	Transfer interrupt vector address to *PC*

Go to fetch phase

The return address available in *PC* is pushed onto the stack and *EIF* is reset to disable further interrupts. The program that services the interrupt can set *EIF* with an instruction whenever it is appropriate to enable other interrupts. The CPU assumes that the external source will provide an address in response to an acknowledge signal. This address is taken as the address of the first instruction of the program that services the interrupt. Obviously, a program must be written for that purpose and stored in memory.

The return from an interrupt is done with an instruction at the end of the service program similar to a return from a subroutine. The stack is popped and the return address is transferred to *PC*.

REFERENCES

1. MANO, M. M. *Computer System Architecture*. 2nd ed. Englewood Cliffs: Prentice-Hall, 1982.
2. TANENBAUM, A. S. *Structured Computer Organization*. 2nd ed. Englewood Cliffs: Prentice-Hall, 1984.
3. WAKERLY, J. F. *Microcomputer Architecture and Programming*. New York: Wiley, 1981.
4. LEWIN, M. H. *Logic Design and Computer Organization*. Reading, MA: Addison-Wesley, 1983.
5. HAYES, J. P. *Computer Architecture and Organization*. New York: McGraw-Hill, 1978.
6. *IEEE Standard for Microprocessor Assembly Language*. (IEEE Std 694-1985.) New York: The Institute of Electrical and Electronics Engineers.
7. *IEEE Standard for Binary Floating-Point Arithmetic*. (ANSI/IEEE Std 754-1985.) New York: The Institute of Electrical and Electronics Engineers.

PROBLEMS

9-1   Write a program to evaluate the arithmetic statement

$$X = (A + B * C) / (D + E * F - G * H)$$

(a) Use a general register computer with three address instructions.
(b) Use a general register computer with two address instructions.
(c) Use an accumulator type computer with one address instruction.

9-2   A two-word instruction is stored in memory at an address designated by the symbol W. The address field of the instruction (stored at $W + 1$) is designated by the symbol Y. The operand used during the execution of the instruction is stored at an address symbolized by Z. An index register contains the value X. State how Z is calculated from the other addresses if the addressing mode of the instruction is (a) direct; (b) indirect; (c) relative; (d) indexed.

9-3   A two-word relative mode branch type instruction is stored in memory at location 620 and 621 (decimal). The branch is made to an address equivalent to decimal 530. Let the address field of the instruction (stored at address 621) be designated by X.
(a) Determine the value of X in decimal.
(b) Determine the value of X in binary using 16 bits. (Note that the number is negative and must be in 2's complement. Why?)

9-4   How many times does the control unit refer to memory when it fetches and executes a two-word indirect addressing mode instruction if the instruction is (a) a computational type requiring an operand from memory; (b) a branch type.

9-5   What must be the address field of an indexed addressing mode instruction to make it the same as a register indirect mode instruction?

9-6   An instruction is stored at location 300 with its address field at location 301. The address field has the value 400. A processor register $R1$ contains the number 200. Evaluate the effective address if the addressing mode of the instruction is (a) direct; (b) immediate; (c) relative; (d) register indirect; (e) indexed with $R1$ as the index register.

9-7   Convert the following arithmetic expressions from infix to reverse Polish notation.
(a) $A + B + C + D$
(b) $A * B + A * (B * D + C * E)$
(c) $A * B / C + D$
(d) $A + B * [C * D + E * (F + G)]$

9-8   Convert the following arithmetic expressions from reverse Polish notation to infix notation.
(a) $A\ B\ C\ D\ E\ *\ /\ -\ +$
(b) $A B\ *\ C D\ *\ +\ E F\ *\ +$
(c) $A B\ +\ C\ *\ D\ +$
(d) $A B\ +\ C\ *\ D\ +\ E\ *\ F\ +\ G\ *\ H\ +$

9-9   Convert the following numerical arithmetic expression into reverse Polish notation and show the stack operations for evaluating the numerical result.

$$(3 + 4)\ [10\ (2 + 6) + 8]$$

9-10   A first-in first-out (FIFO) memory has a memory organization that stores information in such a manner that the item that is stored first is the first item that is retrieved. Show how a FIFO memory operates with three counters. A write counter WC holds the address for writing into memory. A read counter *RC* holds the address for reading from memory. An available storage counter *ASC* indicates the number of words stored in FIFO. *ASC* is incremented for every word stored and decremented for every item that is retrieved.

9-11 Write a program to evaluate the arithmetic statement given in Problem 9-1 using computer stack instructions.

9-12 A computer with independent I/O system has the following input and output instructions.

IN ADRS

OUT ADRS

Where ADRS is the address of an I/O register port. Give the equivalent instructions for a computer with memory-mapped I/O.

9-13 Assuming an 8-bit computer, show the multiple precision addition of the two 32-bit unsigned numbers listed below using the add with carry instruction. Each byte is expressed as a 2-digit hexadecimal number.

6E C3 56 7A + 13 55 6B 8F

9-14 Perform the logic AND, OR, and XOR with the two binary strings 10011100 and 10101010.

9-15 Given the 16-bit value 1001101011001101. What operation must be performed in order to
(a) clear the first 8 bits to 0
(b) set the last 8 bits to 1
(c) complement the middle 8 bits.

9-16 An 8-bit register contains the value 01111011 and the carry bit is equal to 1. Perform the eight shift operations given by the instructions listed in Table 9-5. Each time start from the initial value given above.

9-17 Show how the following two floating-point numbers are to be added to get a normalized result.

$$(-.13567 \times 10^{+3}) + (+.67430 \times 10^{-1})$$

9-18 A 36-bit floating-point number consists of 26 bits plus sign for the fraction and 8 bits plus sign for the exponent. What are the largest and smallest positive quantities for normalized numbers?

9-19 A 30-bit register holds a floating-point decimal number in BCD. The fraction occupies 21 bits for five decimal digits and a sign. The exponent occupies 9 bits for two decimal digits and a sign. What are the largest and smallest positive quantities for normalized decimal numbers?

9-20 A 4-bit exponent uses an excess 7 number for the bias. List all biased binary exponents from $+8$ through -7.

9-21 The IEEE standard double-precision floating-point operand format consists of 64 bits. The sign occupies one bit, the exponent has 11 bits, and the fraction occupies 52 bits. The exponent bias is 1023. There is an implied bit to the left of the binary point in the fraction. Infinity is represented with a biased exponent equal to 2047 and a fraction of 0.
(a) Give the formula for evaluating normalized numbers.

(b) List a few biased exponents in binary as is done in Table 9-6.

(c) Calculate the largest and smallest positive normalized numbers that can be accommodated.

9-22 Prove that if the equality $2^x = 10^y$ holds, then $y = 0.3x$. Using this relationship, calculate the largest and smallest normalized floating-point numbers in decimal that can be accommodated in the single precision IEEE format.

9-23 It is necessary to branch to ADRS if the bit in the least significant position of the operand in a 16-bit register is equal to 1. Show how this can be done with the TEST (Table 9-7) and BNZ (Table 9-8) instructions.

9-24 Consider the two 8-bit numbers $A = 01000001$ and $B = 10000100$.

(a) Give the decimal equivalent of each number assuming that (1) they are unsigned; and (2) they are signed.

(b) Add the two binary numbers and interpret the sum assuming that the numbers are (1) unsigned; and (2) signed.

(c) Determine the values of the C (carry), Z (zero), S (sign), and V (overflow) status bits after the addition.

(d) List the conditional branch instructions from Table 9-8 that will have a true condition.

9-25 The program in a computer compares two unsigned numbers A and B by performing a subtraction $A - B$ and updating the status bits. Let $A = 01000001$ and $B = 10000100$.

(a) Evaluate the difference and interpret the binary result.

(b) Determine the values of status bits C (borrow) and Z (zero).

(c) List the conditional branch instructions from Table 9-9 that will have a true condition.

9-26 The program in a computer compares two signed numbers A and B by performing the subtraction $A - B$ and updating the status bits. Let $A = 01000001$ and $B = 10000100$.

(a) Evaluate the difference and interpret the binary result.

(b) Determine the value of status bits S (sign), Z (zero), and V (overflow).

(c) List the conditional branch instructions from Table 9-10 that will have a true condition.

9-27 The content of the top of a memory stack is 5320. The content of the stack pointer SP is 3560. A two-word call subroutine instruction is located in memory at address 1120 followed by the address field of 6720 at location 1121. What are the contents of PC, SP and the top of the stack

(a) Before the call instruction is fetched from memory.

(b) After the call instruction is executed.

(c) After the return from subroutine.

9-28 What are the basic differences between a branch instruction, a call subroutine instruction, and program interrupt?

9-29 Give five examples of external interrupts and five examples of internal interrupts. What is the difference between a software interrupt and subroutine call?

9-30 A computer responds to an interrupt request signal by pushing onto the stack the contents of PC and the current PSW (program status word). It then reads a new PSW from memory from the location given by the interrupt vector address ($IVAD$). The first address of the service program is taken from memory at location $IVAD + 1$.

(a) List the sequence of microoperations for the interrupt cycle.

(b) List the sequence of microoperations for the return from interrupt instruction.

DESIGN
OF A CENTRAL
PROCESSING
UNIT (CPU)

10-1   INTRODUCTION

The central processing unit is the central component of a digital computer. Its purpose is to interpret instruction codes received from memory and perform arithmetic, logic, and control operations with data stored in internal registers, memory words, or I/O interface units. Externally, the CPU provides a bus system for transferring instructions, data, and control information to and from the modules connected to it.

A typical CPU is usually divided in two parts: the processor unit and the control unit. The processor unit consists of an arithmetic logic unit, a number of registers, and internal buses that provide the data paths for the transfer of information between the registers and the arithmetic logic unit. The control unit consists of a program counter, an instruction register, and timing and control logic. The control logic may be either hardwired or microprogrammed. If it is hardwired, registers, decoders, and a random set of gates are connected to provide the logic that determines the actions required to execute the various instructions. A microprogrammed control unit uses a control memory to store microinstructions and a sequencer to determine the order by which the microinstructions are read from control memory. The purpose of this chapter is to present a typical microprogrammed CPU and to show the detailed logic design of the unit including the microprogram.

The material in this chapter is presented mostly in the form of diagrams and tables. Background information from previous chapters is not repeated here. However, references are given to previous sections of the book where more detailed information can be found.

The design of the sample CPU is carried out in six parts in the following manner:

Section 10-2 shows the procedure for designing an arithmetic logic shift unit.

Section 10-3 presents the hardware of the processor unit.

Section 10-4 specifies a set of instruction formats for the CPU.

Section 10-5 specifies the microinstruction formats for the control memory.

Sections 10-6 through 10-8 show how to write the microprogram for the CPU.

Section 10-9 presents the hardware of the control unit.

The CPU can be designed from the hardware specifications given in Sections 10-3 and 10-9 and by loading the binary microprogram into control memory.

The position of the CPU among the other computer modules is shown in Figure 10-1. The memory unit stores the instructions, data, and other binary coded information needed by the processor. It is assumed that the access time of the memory is fast enough for the CPU to be able to read or write a word within one clock pulse period. Even though this restriction is not always applicable in a computer system, we assume it here in order to avoid complicating the design with a wait

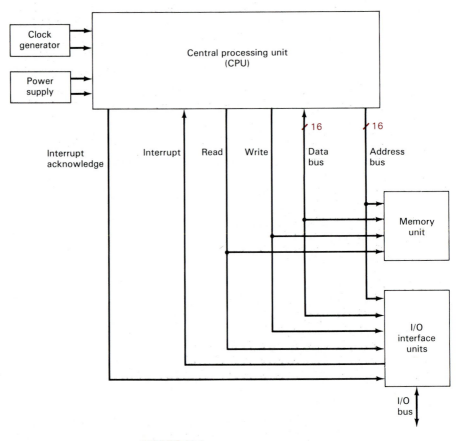

FIGURE 10-1
Block Diagram of the Sample Computer

period that stops the operations within the CPU until the memory cycle is completed.

The interface units provide a path for transferring information between the CPU and external input or output devices connected through the I/O bus. We assume a memory-mapped I/O method of addressing between the CPU and the registers in the interface units. By this method, there are no input or output instructions in the computer because the CPU can manipulate the data residing in interface registers with the same instructions that are used to manipulate memory locations. Each interface unit is organized as a set of registers that respond to the read or write signals in the normal address space of the 16-bit address. Typically, the bulk of the address space is assigned to memory words and a small segment is reserved for interface registers.

The communication between the CPU and external modules takes place via the address and data buses. The address bus consists of 16 lines and is unidirectional from the CPU to the other units. The data bus also consists of 16 lines but is bidirectional, allowing the information to flow in either direction. The read and write control lines from the CPU specify the direction of transfer in the data bus. The read signal informs the selected memory word or interface register to transfer data into the CPU. The write signal informs the selected unit that a data word is available for transfer from the CPU to the selected memory word or interface register.

Two other control lines are shown in Figure 10-1 for the interrupt and interrupt acknowledge signals. Their function is explained in conjunction with Figure 9-8. (The interrupt vector address IVAD shown in Figure 9-8 is transferred through the data bus.) Including the clock input and power supply lines, there are 40 external terminals in the CPU.

10-2 ARITHMETIC LOGIC SHIFT UNIT (ALSU)

The arithmetic logic shift unit (ALSU) is a combinational circuit that performs a number of arithmetic, logic, and shift microoperations. The control unit activates the microoperations when it executes the instructions in the program. The ALSU has a number of selection lines to select a particular operation in the unit. The selection variables are decoded by means of multiplexers so that k selection variables can specify up to 2^k distinct operations.

Figure 10-2 shows the general configuration of the ALSU. It is divided into four distinct subunits each of which is designed separately. There are 16 data lines for input A and another 16 data lines for input B. Each of the four subunits receives one or both sets of input data lines and produces a 16-bit output. In addition, all four subunits receive the two selection variables S_1 and S_0 and they respond to these two selection variables by generating one of four internal microoperations. The other two selection variables S_2 and S_3 are used to select one, and only one, of the four output functions from the subunits. This is then applied to the common 16-bit output F of the ALSU. Thus, an arithmetic operation is selected when $S_3 S_2 = 00$, a logic operation is selected when $S_3 S_2 = 01$, and a shift right or left operation is selected when $S_3 S_2 = 10$ or 11, respectively.

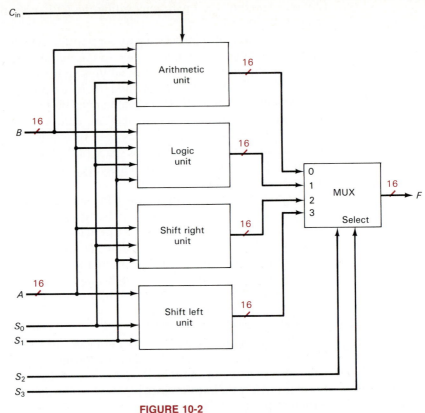

FIGURE 10-2
Arithmetic Logic Shift Unit (ALSU)

The detailed design of the arithmetic and logic units are described in Section 7-6. The input C_{in} acts as a third selection variable for the arithmetic unit to provide a total of eight arithmetic microoperations. The other three units each generate four microoperations. Thus there are a total of 20 microoperations in the ALSU. The list of the 20 microoperations is given in Table 10-1. Input C_{in} has a meaning only during an arithmetic operation. During logic operations it has no effect and can be assumed to be equal to 0. The first 12 operations are taken from Table 7-6 in Section 7-6. The last eight operations are for the two shift units whose internal construction is described here.

Shift Unit

The shift right unit is shown in Figure 10-3. The 16 inputs of A are designated A_0 through A_{15} and the 16 outputs of F as F_0 through F_{15}. The shift right operation is accomplished by connecting each input A_i to an output F_{i-1} for $i = 1, 2, 3, \ldots,$ 15. The rightmost bit in position A_0 is shifted out and stored in the carry flip-flop for future inspection if necessary. This is done only during the shift right operation when $S_3S_2 = 10$. The output bit from the left most position in F_{15} comes from the output of a multiplexer whose selection inputs S_1 and S_0 determine the type of

TABLE 10-1
ALSU Function Table

S_3	S_2	S_1	S_0	$C_{in} = 0$		$C_{in} = 1$	
0	0	0	0	$F = A$	Transfer	$F = A + 1$	Increment
0	0	0	1	$F = A + B$	Add	$F = A + B + 1$	Add plus 1
0	0	1	0	$F = A - B - 1$	Subtract minus 1	$F = A - B$	Subtract
0	0	1	1	$F = A - 1$	Decrement	$F = A$	Transfer
0	1	0	0	$F = A \wedge B$	AND		
0	1	0	1	$F = A \vee B$	OR		
0	1	1	0	$F = A \oplus B$	XOR		
0	1	1	1	$F = \overline{A}$	Complement		
1	0	0	0	$F =$ Logical shift right A			
1	0	0	1	$F =$ Rotate right A			
1	0	1	0	$F =$ Rotate right A with carry			
1	0	1	1	$F =$ Arithmetic shift right A			
1	1	0	0	$F =$ Logical shift left A			
1	1	0	1	$F =$ Rotate left A			
1	1	1	0	$F =$ Rotate left A with carry			
1	1	1	1	$F =$ Arithmetic shift left A			

shift. When the selection inputs are equal to 00, the type of operation is a logical shift right which inserts a 0 into F_{15}. A rotate right operation when the selection inputs are 01 requires that $F_{15} = A_0$. F_{15} receives the input carry when the operation is a rotate right with carry. The previous carry may come from either an arithmetic operation or from a previous shift operation. With selection inputs equal to 11 we have an arithmetic shift right operation which requires that the sign bit in the leftmost position remain unchanged so that $F_{15} = A_{15}$.

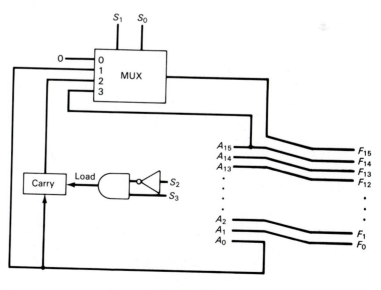

FIGURE 10-3
Shift Right Unit

The shift left unit is similar to Figure 10-3 except that the shift is to the left so that each input A_i is connected to an output F_{i+1}. Output F_0 receives a value from a 4×1 multiplexer with selection variables S_1 and S_0. The inputs of this multiplexer determine the type of shift much as the ones defined in Figure 10-3 did. Note that the arithmetic shift left operation is identical to the logical shift left with 0 insertion when the signed numbers are in 2's complement representation.

10-3   PROCESSOR UNIT

The block diagram of the processor unit is shown in Figure 10-4. It consists of a file of 14 registers, an ALSU, and three buses that provide the data path within the unit. Two sets of multiplexers select a register or the input data for the ALSU. A decoder selects a destination register by enabling its load input. All registers and the input and output data are 16 bits wide. The 17 bits of the control word that select a microoperation in the processor unit are divided into four fields: The A field specifies the input to the left side of the ALSU. The B field specifies the

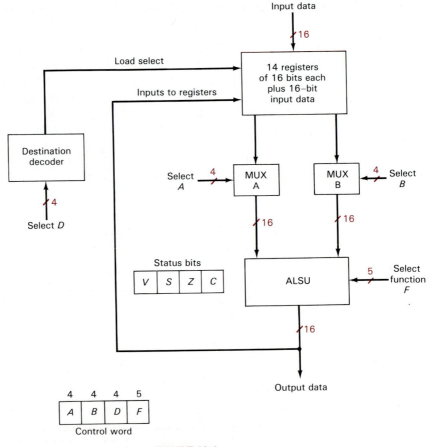

FIGURE 10-4
Processor Unit Hardware

input to the right side of the ALSU. The *D* field specifies the destination register. The *F* field designates the operation in the ALSU as given in Table 10-1. A detailed explanation of the processor unit is to be found in Sections 7-5 through 7-8.

The 14 registers in the processor unit are assigned special tasks by the CPU. The first eight registers, designated *R*0 through *R*7, are available to the user as general purpose registers that can be manipulated by program instructions. One register acts as a program counter and the other five registers are used by the control unit for storing temporary results. The status bits associated with the ALSU are symbolized by *C*, *Z*, *S*, and *V*. They are altered to reflect the results of the carry, zero, sign and overflow in the ALSU.

CPU Block Diagram

The position of the processor unit within the CPU is shown in Figure 10-5. The CPU consists of the processor unit, the control unit, four additional registers, and three-state buffers for two external buses. An address for memory or I/O interface is transferred to the address register *AR*. The data for a write operation is transferred to the data output register *DOR*. Information received after a read operation

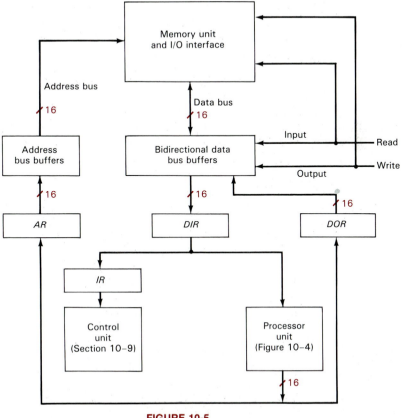

FIGURE 10-5
Block Diagram of CPU

is available in the data input register *DIR*. Instructions read during the fetch phase are transferred from *DIR* to the instruction register *IR*. The contents of *IR* determine the operations in the control unit. Data read from memory into *DIR* are applied to the data input lines in the processor unit and then manipulated in the ALSU. The construction of bus buffers for bidirectional transfer was covered in Section 7-4. The detailed construction of the control unit will be presented in Section 10-9.

The read and write signals are generated in the control unit by enabling corresponding flip-flops for one clock pulse period. It is assumed that the access time of the memory is sufficiently fast to be able to synchronize the operation of the memory with the clock pulses in the CPU. This means that the memory or interface responds to the read signal by placing the selected word in the data bus with enough time left to transfer it into the *DIR* prior to the next clock pulse from the one that enables the flip-flop read operation. In this way, the control can issue a read operation with one clock pulse and expect the data read from memory to be available in *DIR* at the next clock pulse. If we do not impose this requirement, the operations in the CPU must be delayed a number of clock pulses until the data word from memory is available in *DIR*. Note that this implies that the data input into *DIR* is not synchronized with the clock pulses in the CPU. *DIR* is actually a latch that follows the input data from the data bus as long as the input path is enabled in the bidirectional data bus by the read signal.

DIR is used only after a read operation to receive the data from the data bus. For a write operation, the data must be placed in *DOR* while the address is in *AR*. The write flip-flop when enabled by the control unit opens the output path through the bidirectional data bus buffers. The memory or interface stores the contents of the data bus in the word or interface register selected by the address bus within a time equal to one period of a CPU clock pulse.

Programmer Model

The computer as seen by the programmer and user is shown in Figure 10-6. Eight processor registers are used for manipulating data through program instructions. The last two registers are used as stack pointer and index register. The program counter can be changed by the programmer by means of branch type instructions. The status bits are affected by certain ALSU operations. The other parts of the computer of interest to the user are the ALSU, the memory unit, and the input and output addresses of external devices.

Even though the user and programmer can communicate with only 9 registers, there are actually 20 registers in the CPU. The other 11 registers are exclusively used by the control unit for internal operations.

CPU Registers

The 20 registers of the CPU can be divided into three groups. 14 registers are in the register file inside the processor unit. Three registers communicate with the data and address buses, and three registers are associated with the control unit. The following is a list of the 14 registers in the processor unit that communicate with the ALSU.

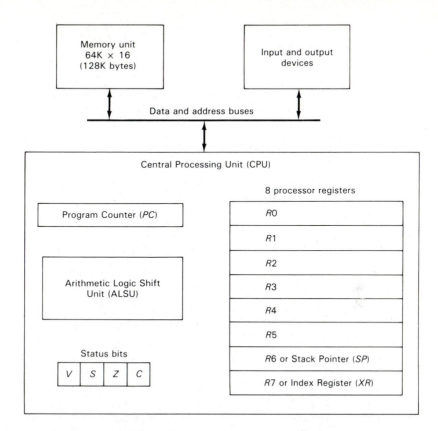

FIGURE 10-6
The Computer as Seen by the Programmer and the User

$R0$ through $R5$	Six general purpose registers
SP	Stack pointer
XR	Index register
PC	Program counter
SR	Source register
DR	Destination register
TR	Temporary register
ZR	Zero register (holds a constant 0)
NR	N = 16 register (holds a constant 16)

The last five registers are used by the control to store temporary results and necessary constants. The three registers that communicate with the address and data buses are

AR	Address register
DIR	Data input register
DOR	Data output register

The position of these registers is shown in Figure 10-5. The three registers associated with the control unit are

IR	Instruction register
CAR	Control address register
SBR	Subroutine register

CAR holds the address of the next microinstruction for control memory. *SBR* is used for storing the return address in conjunction with a subroutine call micro-instruction. These two registers are presented in Section 10-9 together with the hardware of the control unit.

10-4   INSTRUCTION FORMATS

The sequence of microoperations that are incorporated in a CPU is determined from the instructions that are defined for the computer. The instructions are stored in memory as part of a program and are presented to the control unit in a binary form. Each binary coded instruction contains a number of fields that provide the pertinent information needed by the control to execute the instruction in the CPU. The binary coded form of the instruction is defined by its instruction format. Different computers have different instruction formats; this is one aspect that gives each computer its special hardware characteristic.

The instruction format chosen for the sample CPU is shown in Figure 10-7. An instruction code consists of 16 bits divided into four general fields. The first field contains 2 bits that specify the instruction format type. There are 4 instruction types as indicated in the figure. The second field contains 6 bits that specify the operation code of the instruction. With 6 bits we can formulate 64 distinct operations independent of the instruction type. If we include the 2-bit type field with the operation code, it will be possible to define up to 256 instructions. The next 2 fields of the instruction format depend on the instruction type. They specify either a processor register or the addressing mode of a memory word or, as in types 2 and 3, they always contain eight zeros.

Type 0 instruction has two register fields in addition to the operation code field. It is used only in two or three operand type instructions such as move or add. It cannot be used for one operand type instruction such as increment or shift. The source register field and the destination register field each consists of three bits that specify one of the eight processor registers $R0$ through $R7$. Each register can be referred to directly or indirectly as specified by the indirect bit fields *SI* and *DI*. A direct reference means that the operand is in the register. An indirect register reference means that the register contains the address of the operand in memory. Note that the destination register is also the second source register in a three operand instruction. For example, an ADD operation adds the contents of the source register to the contents of the destination register and places the sum in the destination register. A two operand instruction, such as a MOVE, transfers the contents of the source register into the destination register.

Type 1 instruction format uses a register for one operand and a memory word for the second operand. It can be formulated for one or two operand instructions.

General format

2	6	4	4
Type	Operation code	Reg/Mode	Register

Type 0: Register-register. One-word instruction.

15 14	13 12 11 10 9 8	7	6 5 4	3	2 1 0
0 0	Operation code	SI	SRC	DI	DST

SRC —Source register
DST —Destination register
SI —Source indirect bit: =0 direct, =1 indirect
DI —Destination indirect bit: =0 direct, =1 indirect

Type 1: Memory-register. Two-word instruction (except for SD = 11).

15 14	13 12 11 10 9 8	7 6	5 4	3	2 1 0
0 1	Operation code	SD	MOD	I	REG
W					

W   —Memory word for address or immediate operand
REG —Register field
I   —Register indirect bit: =0 direct, =1 indirect
MOD —Addressing mode for memory word W
  00 —Direct address mode
  01 —Immediate mode (only as a source)
  10 —Relative to PC mode
  11 —Index mode
SD   —Source/destination and number of operands
  00 —2 operands. Source: memory word. Destination: register
  01 —2 operands. Source: register. Destination: memory word
  10 —1 operand specified by memory word W and MOD field
  11 —1 operand specified by REG and I fields (W not used)

Type 2: Branch type. Two-word instruction.

15 14	13 12 11 10 9 8	7	6	5	4	3	2	1	0
1 0	Operation code	0	0	0	0	0	0	0	0
W (Branch address)									

Type 3: Implied mode. One-word instruction.

15 14	13 12 11 10 9 8	7	6	5	4	3	2	1	0
1 1	Operation code	0	0	0	0	0	0	0	0

FIGURE 10-7
Instruction Formats for the Sample CPU

With one exception, type 1 instructions consist of two words. The second word is designated by W and follows the word of the instruction code. The register and indirect fields are similar to the corresponding fields in type 0. The MOD field specifies four addressing modes. In the direct address mode, the second word W contains the effective address defined as the address of the operand in memory. In the immediate mode, the value in W is the operand. In the relative mode, the value in W is added to the content of the program counter PC to obtain the effective address. In the index mode, the value in W is added to the content of the index register XR to obtain the effective address. The various addressing modes are discussed in more detail in Section 9-3.

The SD field specifies the source, the destination, as well as the number of operands in the instruction. When the first bit in the SD field is equal to 0, it specifies a two operand instruction, and when equal to 1, it specifies a one operand instruction. The second bit in the SD field specifies the source and destination operands. With $SD = 00$, the source operand is evaluated from the memory word W and the mode field MOD. The destination operand is determined from the REG and I fields. With $SD = 01$, the source and destination operand assignments are reversed. A one operand instruction, such as increment or shift, may have the operand either in a register or in memory. If in memory, the operand may be accessed through the addressing mode using W or the register indirect mode. Note that there are certain combinations in type 1 format that are not allowed. The immediate mode can be used only as a memory word source because it makes no sense to use it as a destination. Also when the SD field is 11, it specifies a one operand instruction residing in a register or in memory by means of a register indirect. This case does not use the memory word W and therefore, the instruction consists of only one word, and the MOD field is not used.

Type 2 format is dedicated exclusively to branch type instructions. The branch may be conditional or unconditional. The branch address W follows the instruction code. It is possible to modify this format to include a relative mode branch type instruction (see Problem 10-26). In this case, bits 0 through 7 are used for an offset number in the range of $+127$ through -128 to provide the relative address that must be added to PC when evaluating the effective address (instead of the second word W).

Type 3 format specifies an implied mode instruction such as set carry, return from interrupt, or no-operation. Bits 0 through 7 are not used and they are always equal to 0.

Computer Instructions

The complete design of the CPU must include a list of all the instructions for the computer together with the formats to which they belong. A complete list of instructions will be prohibitively long for our purpose here. However, a possible list of instructions that may be formulated can be found in Sections 9-5, 9-6, and 9-8. These three sections contain eight tables that list a set of instructions commonly found in computers.

In order to show the relationship between the instructions and their formats, we list some typical instructions in Table 10-2. Each instruction is assigned a sym-

TABLE 10-2
Some Typical Instructions and Their Codes

Symbolic name	6-bit op-code	4-Digit hexadecimal code				Operation
		Type 0	Type 1	Type 2	Type 3	
ADD	001001	09xx	49xx	—	—	Addition
SUB	001010	0Axx	4Axx	—	—	Subtraction
MOVE	001011	0Bxx	4Bxx	—	—	Move data
INR	010011	—	53xx	—	—	Increment
DCR	010100	—	54xx	—	—	Decrement
PUSH	011110	—	5Exx	—	—	Push stack
BR	100001	—	—	A100	—	Branch
BRC	100010	—	—	A200	—	Branch on carry
CALL	100111	—	—	A700	—	Call subroutine
RET	110001	—	—	—	F100	Return from subroutine

bolic name to be used by the programmer and a 6-bit binary code that is to be decoded by the control unit. The operation performed by the instruction determines the type of format to which it belongs. If an instruction has two or three operands, it can be formulated for both type 0 and type 1 formats. If it has one operand, it must be formulated using a type 1 format. Branch and call instructions are assigned to type 2 formats, and instructions that do not use an operand or an address field are assigned to format 3.

Each instruction contains 16 bits which is equivalent to 4 hexadecimal digits. The 4-digit hexadecimal codes assigned to the ten instructions in Table 10-2 are controlled by the format type to which they belong. The 6-bit code of the instruction together with the 2-bit type constitute an 8-bit code which can be specified with two hexadecimal digits. For example the ADD instruction has a 6-bit operation code 001001. The first eight bits of the ADD type 0 instruction are 00001001 which is equivalent to hexadecimal 09. The corresponding ADD instruction for type 1 is binary 01001001, equivalent to hexadecimal 49. The two small x's in type 0 and 1 formats are digit values to be determined from the last eight bits of the instruction which specify the mode and the registers used.

In order to clarify the use of type 0 and 1 formats, it will be instructive to show by example all the possible combinations that can be formulated for a typical instruction. The four ADD instructions that can be formulated with type 0 format are listed in Table 10-3. It is assumed that the source register is $R5$ and the des-

TABLE 10-3
Example of Type 0 Instruction

Hex code	SI	DI	Op-code	Operands	Operation
0952	0	0	ADD	R5, R2	$R2 \leftarrow R2 + R5$
095A	0	1	ADD	R5, (R2)	$M[R2] \leftarrow M[R2] + R5$
09D2	1	0	ADD	(R5), R2	$R2 \leftarrow R2 + M[R5]$
09DA	1	1	ADD	(R5), (R2)	$M[R2] \leftarrow M[R2] + M[R5]$

TABLE 10-4
Example of Type 1 Instruction with Two Operands

Hex code	SD	MOD	Mode	Op-code	Operands	Operation
4902	00	00	Direct	ADD	W, R2	$R2 \leftarrow R2 + M[W]$
4912	00	01	Immediate	ADD	#W, R2	$R2 \leftarrow R2 + W$
4922	00	10	Relative	ADD	$W, R2	$R2 \leftarrow R2 + M[PC + W]$
4932	00	11	Index	ADD	W(XR), R2	$R2 \leftarrow R2 + M[XR + W]$
4942	01	00	Direct	ADD	R2, W	$M[W] \leftarrow M[W] + R2$
4962	01	10	Relative	ADD	R2, $W	$M[PC + W] \leftarrow M[PC + W] + R2$
4972	01	11	Index	ADD	R2, W(XR)	$M[XR + W] \leftarrow M[XR + W] + R2$

tination register is $R2$. There are four possible ways that the two indirect bits SI and DI can be combined, resulting in the four instructions listed in the table. The notation used for the addressing modes conforms with the notation introduced in Table 9-1.

Table 10-4 lists all the addressing modes that can be formulated for the type 1 ADD instruction. We assume a REG field 0010 corresponding to register $R2$. The third hexadecimal digit in the instruction code desginates the value in SD and MOD fields. When $SD = 00$, the destination operand is in register $R2$ and the MOD field specifies four ways to obtain the source operand from the second word W. When $SD = 01$, the source operand is in register $R2$ and the MOD field specifies three ways to obtain the destination operand. As mentioned previously, the immediate mode can be used only as a source operand and can be listed only with $SD = 00$.

Table 10-4 shows seven different ways to formulate a type 1 ADD instruction. This instruction can be used also with a register indirect mode by making the last hexadecimal digit equal to A instead of 2. This gives a total of 14 combinations that we can formulate a type 1 ADD instruction. Including the four instructions from Table 10-3, we have a total of 18 ways that we can formulate any 2 operand instruction.

Table 10-5 lists all the addressing modes that can be formulated for the type 1 INR (increment) instruction. The first two digits of the hexadecimal operation code for INR are 53 as listed in Table 10-2. The next digit of the instruction reflects the values of SD and MOD. The last digit is made arbitrarily equal to 0 when the register field is not used; it is equal to 2 when register $R2$ is used directly, and equal to hexadecimal A when register $R2$ is used indirectly. The last two entries in the table represent a one operand instruction that needs only a register; so the

TABLE 10-5
Example of Type 1 Instruction with One Operand

Hex code	SD	MOD	Mode	Op-code	Operand	Operation
5380	10	00	Direct	INR	W	$M[W] \leftarrow M[W] + 1$
53A0	10	10	Relative	INR	$W	$M[PC + W] \leftarrow M[PC + W] + 1$
53B0	10	11	Index	INR	W(XR)	$M[XR + W] \leftarrow M[XR + W] + 1$
53C2	11	XX	Register	INR	R2	$R2 \leftarrow R2 + 1$
53CA	11	XX	Reg indirect	INR	(R2)	$M[R2] \leftarrow M[R2] + 1$

MOD field is not used and the second word *W* is not needed. Table 10-5 shows five different ways that we can formulate a one operand type 1 instruction.

Type 2 and 3 instructions have only one possible combination. Some examples are

BR W	Branch to *W*
CALL W	Call subroutine starting from address *W*
RET	Return from subroutine

Type 2 instructions require an address field given by the memory word *W*. Type 3 instructions are one word instructions.

10-5 MICROINSTRUCTION FORMATS

The sequence of microoperations in the CPU is controlled by means of a microprogram stored in control memory. The microprogram consists of microinstructions that control the data paths and operations in the CPU. An example of a microprogram that controls the processor unit of a CPU was presented in Section 8-3. The microprogram to be presented here controls not only the microoperations in the processor unit but also all other data paths in the CPU. It is also capable of decoding computer instructions and obtaining the operands according to the specified addressing code.

The two microinstruction formats chosen for the control memory of the sample CPU are shown in Figure 10-8(a). Each format consists of 23 bits and is divided into six fields. Each field is identified with a symbolic name and the number of bits in each field is indicated on top of the symbolic name. The first field designated *CS* (Control Sequence) is used to distinguish between the two formats. When the 2-bit *CS* field is equal to 00, 01, or 10, it designates a microoperation type A format. When *CS* is equal to 11, it designates a jump or call type B format. The diagram also shows the convention for writing microinstructions in symbolic form. The actual symbols that can be assigned to each field are defined in detail in Tables 10-6 through 10-10.

Figure 10-8(b) lists all the binary codes and their corresponding symbolic names which are assigned to each field of the microinstruction. The five tables present a summary of all the components of the microinstruction and provide a reference for writing microprograms. When writing microprograms in symbolic form we will use special symbols for each binary value of the encoded fields. In this way, it will be possible to write microprograms with symbolic names instead of using the actual binary values for each field. Figures 10-8(a) and 10-8(b) and Table 10-6 are placed together for quick reference. The function of each field will be explained in greater detail in the discussion that follows.

CS and *BR* Fields

The *CS* field is common to both microinstruction formats. It determines not only the format type but also the way the next microinstruction is selected from control memory. Table 10-6 lists the four ways that the 2-bit *CS* field makes this selection.

TABLE 10-6
Control Sequence and Branch Assignment

Binary code			
CS	**BR**	**Symbol**	**Operation**
00	—	NEXT	Use next address by incrementing CAR
01	—	RET	Return from subroutine
10	—	MAP	Map operation code into CAR
11	0	JUMP	Jump to AD if ST bit is satisfied
11	1	CALL	Call subroutine if ST bit is satisfied

Type A: Microoperation format.

2	4	4	4	5	4
CS	AS	BS	DS	FC	MS

CS —Control sequence (must be 00, 01, or 10 for type A)
AS —Select register for A bus input to ALSU
BS —Select register for B bus input to ALSU
DS —Select register for D bus destination from ALSU
FC —Function control selection for the ALSU
MS —Miscellaneous microoperations.

Symbolic microinstruction convention:

CS	AS BS DS	FC	MS
Table 10-6	Table 10-7	Table 10-8	Table 10-9

Type B: Jump or Call format.

2	1	1	4	11	4
CS	BR	PS	ST	AD	MS

CS —Control sequence (must be 11 for type B format)
BR —Branch type: 0 for Jump, 1 for Call
PS —Polarity select: 0 for False, 1 for True
ST —Select status bit for test multiplexer
AD —11-bit address for control memory
MS —Miscellaneous microoperation (same as type A)

Symbolic microinstruction convention:

CS BR	PS	ST	AD	MS
Table 10-6	T or F	Table 10-10	Symbolic address	Table 10-9

FIGURE 10-8(a)
Microinstruction Formats for Control Memory

Selection of ALSU Buses

Binary code	Symbols			Register selected
	AS	**BS**	**DS**	
0000	R0	R0	R0	Processor Register 0
0001	R1	R1	R1	Processor Register 1
0010	R2	R2	R2	Processor Register 2
0011	R3	R3	R3	Processor Register 3
0100	R4	R4	R4	Processor Register 4
0101	R5	R5	R5	Processor Register 5
0110	SP	SP	SP	Stack Pointer
0111	XR	XR	XR	Index Register
1000	PC	PC	PC	Program Counter
1001	SR	SR	SR	Source Register
1010	DR	DR	DR	Destination Register
1011	TR	TR	TR	Temporary register
1100	ZR	ZR	AR	See Table 10-7
1101	DIR	DIR	DOR	See Table 10-7
1110	R(D)	R(D)	R(D)	Register selected by $IR(0-2)$
1111	R(S)	NR	NONE	See Table 10-7

ALSU Function Control

FC Code	Symbol	Microoperation
00000	TSF	$F = A$
00001	INC	$F = A + 1$
00010	ADD	$F = A + B$
00011	ADP	$F = A + B + 1$
00100	SBM	$F = A - B - 1$
00101	SUB	$F = A - B$
00110	DEC	$F = A - 1$
01000	AND	$F = A \wedge B$
01010	OR	$F = A \vee B$
01100	XOR	$F = A \oplus B$
01110	COM	$F = \overline{A}$
10000	SHR	$F = $ Logical shift right A
10010	ROR	$F = $ Rotate right A
10100	RRC	$F = $ Rotate right A with carry
10110	ASR	$F = $ Arithmetic shift right A
11000	SHL	$F = $ Logical shift left A
11010	ROL	$F = $ Rotate left A
11100	RLC	$F = $ Rotate left A with carry
11110	ASL	$F = $ Arithmetic shift left A

Status Bits for Test Multiplexer

ST code	Symbol	Name
0000	U	Always = 1 for unconditional transfer
0001	C	Carry status bit
0010	Z	Zero status bit
0011	IR3	Instruction register bit 3
0100	IR4	Instruction register bit 4
0101	IR5	Instruction register bit 5
0110	IR6	Instruction register bit 6
0111	IR7	Instruction register bit 7
1000	S	Sign status bit
1001	V	Overflow status bit
1010	EIF	Enable Interrupt flip-flop
1011	INTS	Interrupt input signal

Miscellaneous Microoperations

MS code	Symbol	Operation
0000	—	No operation
0001	READ	Enable READ flip-flop
0010	WRITE	Enable WRITE flip-flop
0011	LIR	Load IR from DIR
0100	SCF	Set carry status flip-flop
0101	RCF	Reset carry status flip-flop
0110	EST	Enable to update the four status bits
0111	ECB	Enable to update the C status bit
1000	ESZ	Enable to update the S and Z status bits
1001	SEIF	Set enable interrupt flip-flop
1010	REIF	Reset enable interrupt flip-flop
1011	IACK	Generate interrupt acknowledge

FIGURE 10-8(b)
Symbols and Binary Codes for Microinstruction Fields

The 1-bit *BR* (branch) field comes into play when *CS* = 11. It determines the type of branch chosen for the type B microinstruction format. For *CS* = 11 and *BR* = 0 we use the symbol JUMP to designate a conditional branch dependent on the value of the selected status bit in the *ST* field. The address for the jump is specified in the 11-bit *AD* field. When *BR* = 1, the microinstruction specifies a conditional CALL subroutine. (The jump and call microinstructions are similar to the branch and call instructions discussed in Section 9-8). The symbol NEXT is used when the microprogram chooses the next microinstruction in sequence. The symbol RET designates a return from subroutine condition.

When *CS* = 10, the control unit performs a mapping from the bits of the operation code into an address for control memory. The MAP condition provides a decoding of the binary instruction. For example, suppose that the type 0 ADD instruction has an 8-bit operation 00001001 (see Table 10-3). The binary instruction is in the instruction register *IR* after it is fetched from memory. Suppose that we place the microprogram routine that executes this instruction in control memory starting from address 23. The hardware decoding requires that a mapping or transformation be carried out from the binary operation code 00001001 into an 11-bit address 00000010111 for control memory. This mapping must be done for each instruction in order to obtain the corresponding address of its microprogram routine. The binary mapping can be specified in a table that gives the relationships between each 8-bit operation code and its corresponding 11-bit address for control memory. The truth table can be implemented with hardware using a programmable logic device (see Section 6-6).

Figure 10-9 shows a block diagram that may clarify the way that the *CS* and *BR* fields select the address of the next microinstruction. The control memory consists of 23 bits, but here we show only the 2-bit *CS* field, the 1-bit *BR* field, and the 11-bit *AD* (address) field. The control address register *CAR* supplies the address

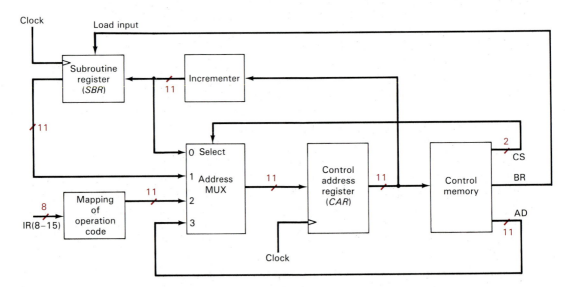

FIGURE 10-9
Selection of Next Address for Control Memory Using the CS and BR Fields

for control memory. The incrementer is a combinational circuit that adds one to the present value of CAR. The subroutine register SBR stores the return address when the microprogram calls a subroutine. For simplicity, we use here a single register for storing the return address instead of using a register stack.

While the present microinstruction is at the output terminals of the control memory, an address multiplexer selects the address for the next microinstruction. This address is loaded into CAR with the next clock pulse transition. The CS field is applied to the selection inputs of the address multiplexer. If $CS = 00$, CAR is incremented by one to proceed with the next microinstruction in sequence. A call subroutine microinstruction has $CS = 11$ and $BR = 1$. This causes the return address $CAR + 1$ to be loaded into the subroutine register SBR and the address in the AD field to be loaded into CAR. The return from subroutine condition transfers the content of SBR into CAR. An external address is transferred by mapping the operation code bits of the instruction in the instruction register $IR(8\text{-}15)$ into an 11-bit address for CAR. A jump microinstruction branches to the address in AD without loading the subroutine register. The jump and call microinstructions shown in Figure 10-9 are unconditional. The conditional jump and call depend on the values of the ST and PS fields, as will be explained subsequently.

Figure 10-9 is a simplified version of the microprogram sequencer that is part of the control hardware. A more detailed block diagram of the sequencer can be found in Figure 10-18.

AS, BS and DS Fields

As mentioned previously, when the CS field is equal to 00, 01, or 10, the other fields of the microinstruction are taken from type A format. Fields AS, BS, and DS specify source and destination registers for the ALSU buses, and the FC field specifies the ALSU operation. The binary code and corresponding symbols for the ALSU buses are shown in Table 10-7. The AS field selects a source register for the A input of the ALSU. BS selects a second source register for input B of the ALSU, and DS selects a destination register. There are 17 registers in the processor unit that are controlled by the microprogram. The first eight registers $R0$ through $R7$ are general purpose registers, with $R6$ acting as the stack pointer SP and $R7$ as the index register XR. The other nine registers are the program counter PC, three control registers labeled SR, DR, and TR, two registers ZR and NR that hold the binary constants zero and 16, and three registers, AR, DIR, and DOR, that communicate with the memory.

Certain restrictions apply to some registers. ZR and NR provide constants for the ALSU and can operate only as a source and never as a destination. Therefore, they are not included in the destination select field DS. The three registers that communicate with the memory are also restricted in their use. The data input register DIR can have only a source operand and is included in the AS and BS fields but not in the DS field. The address register AR and the data output register DOR can function only as destination registers since they receive the address and data from the processor. These two registers are assigned to the DS field only.

In addition to a direct selection of the 17 registers, the microinstruction can select registers that are specified directly in the computer instruction. Remember

TABLE 10-7
Selection of ALSU Buses

Binary code	Symbols			Register selected
	AS	**BS**	**DS**	
0000	R0	R0	R0	Processor register 0
0001	R1	R1	R1	Processor register 1
0010	R2	R2	R2	Processor register 2
0011	R3	R3	R3	Processor register 3
0100	R4	R4	R4	Processor register 4
0101	R5	R5	R5	Processor register 5
0110	SP	SP	SP	Stack pointer
0111	XR	XR	XR	Index register
1000	PC	PC	PC	Program counter
1001	SR	SR	SR	Source register
1010	DR	DR	DR	Destination register
1011	TR	TR	TR	Temporary register
1100	ZR	ZR	AR	See note below
1101	DIR	DIR	DOR	See note below
1110	R(D)	R(D)	R(D)	Register selected by IR(0-2)
1111	R(S)	NR	NONE	See note below

ZR—Holds 0's in all 16 bits and cannot be changed.

NR—Holds a constant (N = 16) and cannot be changed

R(S)—Register selected by the binary code in the source field in IR(4-6) as defined in Figure 10-7.

NONE—When DS = 1111 none of the registers is selected to receive the output from the ALSU.

AR, DIR, and DOR are registers that interface with the address and data buses (see Figure 10-5).

that registers $R0$ through $R7$ in the processor unit are available as general purpose registers and can be chosen by means of program instructions. Looking back at the instruction formats in Figure 10-7, we note that these registers are specified as a source in bits 4-6 and as destination in bits 0-2. These bits are part of the binary instruction that resides in the instruction register IR after the instruction is read from memory. When we assign to the AS field binary 1111, the hardware of the control unit will select a register for the A bus from the decoded value of the 3-bit code in IR(4-6). When writing symbolic microprograms, we designate this condition by the symbol $R(S)$ meaning that the register chosen is given by the 3-bit code in the source field of the instruction. For example, if the 3-bit code in IR(4-6) is equal to 011 and the AS field of the microinstruction is 1111 (the binary value for the symbol $R(S)$), the control will provide a path from register $R3$ in the processor into the A bus of the ALSU.

Similarly, we use the symbol $R(D)$ to designate a register chosen by the destination field of the instruction in IR(0-2). Note that $R(D)$ can be chosen for all three fields, but $R(S)$ is only available with the AS field.

When the DS field is specified with the symbol NONE, it is substituted with the binary value 1111. When this condition exists, none of the registers are selected to receive the data from the ALSU. This is equivalent to a "no operation" in the processor unit.

FC Field

Table 10-8 lists the microoperations that can be specified with the ALSU function control field *FC*. These operations are the same as the ones listed in Table 10-1. Each operation is assigned a symbolic name to be used when writing microprograms. The last bit in the 5-bit code for *FC* is the value of the input carry C_{in}. The input carry controls the arithmetic operations but has no effect on the logic and shift operations. The last bit of the binary code is chosen to be 0 for the logic and shift operations.

Table 10-8 gives a list of the status bits that have significance for each operation. All four status bits are important after an arithmetic operation of add and subtract. The other arithmetic and logic operations need only the sign and zero bits because they do not produce a carry or overflow. (The increment operation produces a carry at the same time that the number goes back to zero.) All shift operations affect the carry status bit. The arithmetic shift left operation may produce an overflow if the sign bit of the number changes after the shift. The status bits are affected after an arithmetic or logic operation only if they are enabled by a special code in the MS field. However, the carry bit is always updated with a shift operation as indicated in Figure 10-3. It will be assumed that the overflow bit will be automatically updated with an arithmetic shift left operation.

MS Field

Table 10-9 gives the list of the microoperations that can be generated with the 4-bit *MS* field. Note that this field is available in both microinstruction formats. When used with type A format, the *MS* field specifies a microoperation that can be generated simultaneously with the microoperation specified for the ALSU.

TABLE 10-8
ALSU Function Control

FC code	Symbol	Microoperation	Name	Status bits
00000	TSF	$F = A$	Transfer A	$S\ Z$
00001	INC	$F = A + 1$	Increment A	$S\ Z$
00010	ADD	$F = A + B$	Add	$S\ Z\ C\ V$
00011	ADP	$F = A + B + 1$	Add plus 1	$S\ Z\ C\ V$
00100	SBM	$F = A - B - 1$	Subtract minus 1	$S\ Z\ C\ V$
00101	SUB	$F = A - B$	Subtract	$S\ Z\ C\ V$
00110	DEC	$F = A - 1$	Decrement A	$S\ Z$
01000	AND	$F = A \wedge B$	AND	$S\ Z$
01010	OR	$F = A \vee B$	OR	$S\ Z$
01100	XOR	$F = A \oplus B$	Exclusive-OR	$S\ Z$
01110	COM	$F = \overline{A}$	Complement A	$S\ Z$
10000	SHR	$F = $ Logical shift right A		C
10010	ROR	$F = $ Rotate right A		C
10100	RRC	$F = $ Rotate right A with carry		C
10110	ASR	$F = $ Arithmetic shift right A		C
11000	SHL	$F = $ Logical shift left A		C
11010	ROL	$F = $ Rotate left A		C
11100	RLC	$F = $ Rotate left A with carry		C
11110	ASL	$F = $ Arithmetic shift left A		$C\ V$

TABLE 10-9
Miscellaneous Microoperations

MS code	Symbol	Operation
0000	—	No operation
0001	READ	Enable READ flip-flop
0010	WRITE	Enable WRITE flip-flop
0011	LIR	Load *IR* from *DIR*
0100	SCF	Set carry status flip-flop
0101	RCF	Reset carry status flip-flop
0110	EST	Enable to update the four status bits
0111	ECB	Enable to update the *C* status bit
1000	ESZ	Enable to update the *S* and *Z* status bits
1001	SEIF	Set enable interrupt flip-flop
1010	REIF	Reset enable interrupt flip-flop
1011	IACK	Generate interrupt acknowledge (Figure 10-1)

The operation symbolized by the READ symbol sets a flip-flop to 1. The output of this flip-flop provides the read signal for the memory unit. Thus, when the *MS* field in the microinstruction is equal to 0001, the next clock pulse sets the READ flip-flop and a read cycle is initiated. If the next microinstruction does not have 0001 in the *MS* field, the READ flip-flop is reset to 0 and the memory read cycle terminates. Similarly, the WRITE operation produces a memory write cycle when the corresponding WRITE flip-flop is set and then reset.

The operation symbolized by LIR is needed during the fetch phase. The instruction read from memory into the data input register *DIR* is transferred to the instruction register *IR* to be decoded by the control. The symbols SCF and RCF cause the setting or resetting of the carry status bit. This is useful when it is required to initialize the carry prior to a shift.

The *MS* field includes special conditions that enable the status bits in the processor to update them only when necessary. A microinstruction that specifies an arithmetic operation in the ALSU can update all the status bits by including the EST code in the *MS* field. If no status bits have to be updated, we must ensure that none of the three *MS* codes equivalent to EST, ECB, or ESZ is used. ECB updates only the carry bit and ESZ updates the sign and zero bits. The status bit conditions listed in Table 10-8 are given only as a suggestion. It is up to the designer who writes the microprogram to decide which status bits are to be updated after each instruction.

Other operations that are specified with the *MS* field include the setting and resetting of the EIF (enable interrupt flip-flop) and the generation of an interrupt acknowledge signal to an external device.

ST and *PS* Fields

The jump or call microinstruction in type B format is used for branching to a microinstruction out of sequence depending on a status bit condition. The status bits available for testing are listed in Table 10-10. The symbol *U* is used for the

TABLE 10-10
Status Bits For Test Multiplexer

ST code	Symbol	Name
0000	U	Always $= 1$ for unconditional transfer
0001	C	Carry status bit
0010	Z	Zero status bit
0011	IR3	Instruction register bit 3
0100	IR4	Instruction register bit 4
0101	IR5	Instruction register bit 5
0110	IR6	Instruction register bit 6
0111	IR7	Instruction register bit 7
1000	S	Sign status bit
1001	V	Overflow status bit
1010	EIF	Enable interrupt flip-flop
1011	INTS	Interrupt input signal

ST code 0000. This code, when applied to the select inputs of a multiplexer, makes the output of the multiplexer always equal to 1. The symbols *C*, *Z*, *S*, and *V* are for testing the status bits in the processor. Five bits from the instruction register *IR* are available for inspection by the microprogram. These bits specify the addressing modes of the instruction. Two status bits associated with the interrupt cycle are available for detection. The output of the EIF flip-flop indicates whether interrupts are allowed or prohibited. The interrupt input signal from external devices is checked by the control to find out if any interrupts are pending (see Figure 9-8).

The 1-bit field *PS* is associated with the *ST* field to determine the polarity of the tested bit. We can either test the true or false value of the status bit by letting *PS* be equal to 1 (symbolized by T) or to 0 (symbolized by F), respectively. If the tested bit polarity is satisfied, control branches to the address specified by the 11-bit *AD* field; otherwise, control continues with the next microinstruction in sequence. For example, a jump on carry, if true, will branch to *AD* if $C = 1$ but will continue with the next microinstruction if $C = 0$. A call on carry, if false, will branch to the subroutine at the address given by the *AD* field if $C = 0$ but will continue with next microinstruction if $C = 1$. An unconditional branch is achieved by specifying T for the *PS* field and U for the *ST* field. This condition will always be true because the status bit chosen with *ST* code of 0000 is always equal to 1.

10-6   EXAMPLES OF MICROINSTRUCTIONS

Before starting to write the microprogram for the CPU, it will be instructive to give a few examples of typical microinstructions. Table 10-11 lists nine examples of microinstructions in symbolic form. The symbols on top of the table are the six fields of type A format and the six fields of type B format. An entry in the label column is terminated with a colon and represents a symbolic address. The comments column explains the function of the microinstruction with register transfer statements and in words when appropriate.

TABLE 10-11
Examples of Symbolic Microinstructions

Label	CS CSBR	AS	BS PS	DS ST	FC AD	MS MS	Comments
1.	NEXT	SR	DR	DOR	ADD	EST	$DOR \leftarrow SR + DR$, enable status bits
2.	NEXT	DIR	XR	AR	ADD	—	$AR \leftarrow DIR + XR$
3. START:	NEXT	R(S)	—	SR	TSF	—	$SR \leftarrow R(S)$
4.	NEXT	PC	—	AR	TSF	READ	$AR \leftarrow PC$, set READ flip-flop
5.	RET	DIR	—	SR	TSF	SCF	$SR \leftarrow DIR$, set carry, return from subroutine
6.	MAP	—	—	NONE	—	—	Map operation code
7.		CALL	T	IR3	DEST	—	Call subroutine DEST if $IR3 = 1$
8.		JUMP	T	U	START	WRITE	Set WRITE flip-flop, jump to START
9. DEST:		JUMP	F	EIF	FETCH	—	Jump to FETCH if EIF $= 0$

The first six examples in the table have the symbols NEXT, RET, or MAP in the *CS* field. These are the symbols used with the type A microinstruction format. The CALL and JUMP symbols are used with the type B format. They are placed under the common symbol *CSBR* since they belong to both the *CS* and *BR* fields. Thus, a microinstruction is recognized as being of type A format if it has a symbolic entry under the *CS* field. The other symbols of the microinstruction belong to fields *AS*, *BS*, *DS*, *FC*, and *MS*. The type B microinstruction is recognized from the symbol JUMP or CALL under the combined *CSBR* fields. The other fields are *PS*, *ST*, *AD*, and *MS*.

The first microinstruction in the table specifies an ADD microoperation in the ALSU and an EST (enable status bits) condition in the *MS* field. This updates all four status bits *C*, *Z*, *S*, and *V* according to the sum produced in the output of the ALSU. The second microinstruction performs an addition in the ALSU but the status bits are not affected because the *MS* field is marked with a dash signifying a no operation condition.

The third microinstruction has the symbol START in the label column. This is a symbolic address that must also be present in the address field of a jump or call microinstruction as shown in example 8. The microinstruction transfers the content of *R(S)* (which is the processor register whose binary code is given by the source field of the instruction) into the control source register *SR*. The *BS* field is not used in this case and is marked with a dash. This is because the TSF (transfer) operation acts with the A bus data of the ALSU and neglects any value in the B bus.

The fourth example in the table shows a microinstruction that initiates a memory read cycle. This is done by transferring the address into the address register *AR* and setting the READ flip-flop to 1. The word read from memory at the address given by *AR* is assumed to be available in the data input register *DIR* for use with the next microinstruction in sequence.

The fifth and sixth microinstructions in the table show how to use the RET and MAP conditions for type A format. The other fields of the microinstruction may specify a microoperation for the ALSU or the *MS* field. If the *DS* field has the symbol NONE, then no operation is performed in the processor unit. The *MS* field performs no operation if it is marked with a dash.

The JUMP and CALL symbols are used with type B format. Example seven shows a call subroutine microinstruction that branches to the address symbolized by DEST if $IR3 = 1$. Example eight is an unconditional jump microinstruction that also sets the WRITE flip-flop to initiate a memory write cycle. Example nine shows a jump microinstruction that branches to the address symbolized by FETCH if the selected status bit is false, that is if $EIF = 0$. Note that the nine examples in Table 10-11 do not constitute a meaningful microprogram. Each microinstruction is independent of all others and is shown here only as an example for writing symbolic microinstructions.

Binary Microinstructions

Symbolic microinstructions are convenient when writing microprograms in a way that people can read and understand. But this is not the way that the microprogram is stored in control memory. The symbolic microinstructions must be translated to binary, either by means of a computer program called a microassembler or by the user if the microprogram is simple. The conversion from a symbolic microinstruction to its binary equivalent can be done using the encoding information listed in Figure 10-8(b).

Consider for example the first microinstruction in Table 10-11. It can be converted to binary as follows:

CS	AS	BS	DS	FC	MS
NEXT	SR	DR	DOR	ADD	EST
00	1001	1010	1101	00010	0110

The first line lists the symbolic names of the six fields of format A. The next line gives the corresponding symbols used in the microinstruction. From Figure 10-8(b) we extract the binary equivalent of each field to obtain the 23 bits of the binary microinstruction.

The microinstruction in example 6 in Table 10-11 is converted to binary in a similar fashion.

CS	AS	BS	DS	FC	MS
MAP	—	—	NONE	—	—
10	0000	0000	1111	00000	0000

The dashes in the *AS, BS,* and *FC* fields are assigned 0's, although any other binary value can be used since the information in these fields has no significance when none of the registers are affected. The dash in the *MS* field must be converted into 0000 to indicate a "no operation."

The microoperation in example 8 of Table 10-11 has a type B format. The symbolic address START must be assigned an 11-bit binary address value. Assuming that START is equivalent to address 3, we form the binary microinstruction as follows:

CSBR	PS	ST	AD	MS
JUMP	T	U	START	WRITE
110	1	0000	00000000011	0010

The T in the *PS* field converts to 1 and the START symbol converts to an 11-bit address equivalent to binary 3. The total number of bits in the microinstruction is 23.

10-7   MICROPROGRAM FOR COMPUTER CYCLE

We are now ready to start writing the microprogram for the CPU. This will be done in parts by writing the microprogram for the fetch phase, the interrupt phase, and for the execution of some typical instructions. Microprograms for some other instructions will be left as exercises. The basic computer cycle that fetches and executes each instruction is explained in Section 9-3.

The first microprogram example to be developed will be introduced in three different forms. First, the general procedure will be shown in flowchart form using register transfer notation. From this we will write the microprogram in symbolic form showing the values for each field of the microinstruction. The last step is to translate the symbolic microprogram to binary. The ultimate form of a micropro-gram is always the binary content that must be stored in control memory. For convenience, people use symbolic representation to formulate the logical sequence of microinstructions and then use a computer program to translate the micropro-gram to binary.

It is assumed that a user program is stored in main memory starting at some known address. When the system is reset, the program counter *PC* is loaded with the beginning address of this program and the control memory address register *CAR* is cleared to 0. The first microinstruction of the fetch phase will be stored at address 0 in control memory.

The flowchart of Figure 10-10 shows the three phases of the computer cycle. The first box lists the microinstructions for fetching an instruction from memory and placing it in the instruction register *IR*. The address from *PC* is transferred to *AR* and the signal from the READ flip-flop causes the memory to place the instruction into the data bus from which it is transferred into *DIR*. The instruction in *DIR* is then transferred into *IR*, and *PC* is incremented by one. The micro-instructions for the execute phase depend on the operation code found in *IR*(8-15). The 8-bit operation code is mapped into an address for *CAR*. This address points to the beginning of the microroutine that executes the instruction whose binary code is presently available in *IR*.

After the instruction is executed, the microprogram checks for a possible external interrupt. The computer cycle then repeats the fetch-execute-interrupt phases con-tinuously. We will now demonstrate one complete computer cycle by choosing a specific instruction and including the microprogram for the interrupt phase.

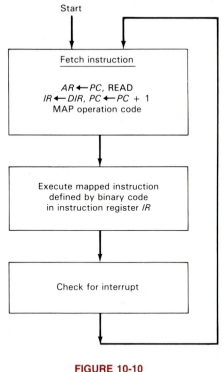

FIGURE 10-10
Computer Cycle

Type 0 ADD Instruction

Assume that the instruction transferred to *IR* at the end of the fetch phase is a type 0 ADD instruction. In order to follow the microprogram for this instruction it is necessary to review the type 0 format from Figure 10-7 and the four addressing modes listed in Table 10-3. The instruction code format is repeated in Figure 10-11 to provide a more convenient reference. The operation code in IR(8-15) is used to map into the 11-bit control memory address where the microprogram routine for this instruction resides. The selected source register is identified by the symbol $R(S)$ and the selected destination register is symbolized by $R(D)$. Bit 7 in *IR* is the source indirect bit and bit 3 is the destination indirect bit. When both these bits are equal to 0, the instruction specifies the microoperation

$$R(D) \leftarrow R(D) + R(S)$$

If an indirect bit is equal to 1, the operand must be retrieved from memory.

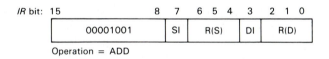

FIGURE 10-11
Type 0 ADD Instruction Format

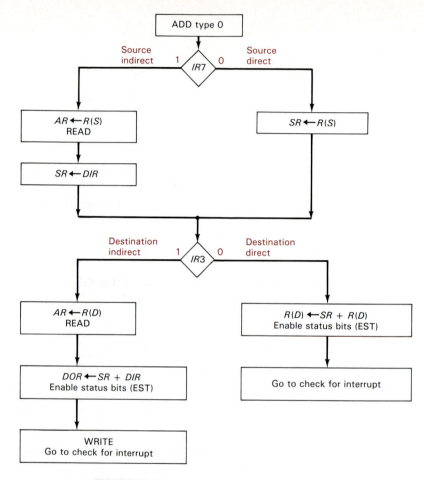

FIGURE 10-12

Microprogram Flowchart for Type 0 ADD Instruction

The sequence of microinstructions that execute the type 0 ADD instruction is shown in flowchart form in Figure 10-12. If $IR7 = 0$, the source operand is temporarily stored in control source register SR. If $IR7 = 1$, then the register specified by $R(S)$ contains the address of the operand in memory. This address is transferred to the address register AR and a read cycle is initiated. The memory places the operand in DIR from which it is then transferred to SR.

The second part of the flowchart checks the bit in $IR3$. If it is equal to 0, then SR is added to $R(D)$ and the sum transferred back to $R(D)$. If $IR3 = 1$, $R(D)$ has the address of the destination operand. The operand is first read from memory into DIR. Its contents are added to the contents of SR and the sum is transferred into the data output register DOR. A memory write cycle stores the contents of DOR into the memory word given by the address in AR. Remember that AR has the address that was originally in $R(D)$ which is the address of memory where the sum must be placed. After the instruction is executed, control branches to the interrupt phase.

Interrupt Phase

The flowchart for the interrupt microprogram is shown in Figure 10-13. EIF (enable interrupt flip-flop) is an internal flip-flop that can be set or reset by program instructions or by the hardware. Only when this flip-flop is set to 1 will an interrupt signal be acknowledged by the CPU. The interrupt signal is detected from the presence of the status bit symbolized by INTS. If both EIF and INTS are equal to 1, the microprogram goes through an interrupt routine; otherwise it goes back to fetch the next instruction. The external interrupt procedure is explained in Section 9-9 in conjunction with Figure 9-8.

The interrupt routine consists of pushing the return address from *PC* onto the stack and resetting EIF to 0 to disable further interrupts (EIF can be set later by the program). The interrupt acknowledge *INTACK* signal is sent to the external device from which the device responds by placing an interrupt vector address on the data bus. The content of the data bus in *DIR* is transferred into *PC*. Control then goes to the fetch phase to start the interrupt service program at the vector address.

It was mentioned in Section 9-9 that the current contents of the status bits must be stored in the stack after an interrupt request. This can be done with an instruction in the interrupt service program (see Problem 10-27).

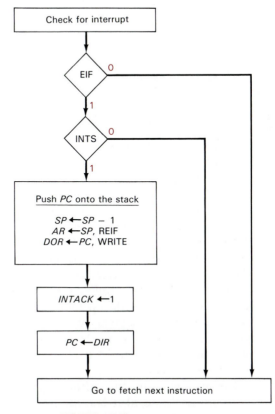

FIGURE 10-13
Flowchart for Interrupt Microprogram

TABLE 10-12
Symbolic Microprogram For One Computer Cycle

Label	CS CSBR	AS CSBR	BS PS	DS ST	FC AD	MS MS	Comments
Fetch instruction:							
FETCH:	NEXT	PC	—	AR	TSF	READ	$AR \leftarrow PC$, Read
	NEXT	PC	—	PC	INC	LIR	$PC \leftarrow PC + 1$, $IR \leftarrow$ DIR
	MAP	—	—	NONE	—	—	Map operation code
Type 0 ADD instruction:							
ADDT0:	NEXT	R(S)	—	SR	TSF	—	$SR \leftarrow R(S)$
		CALL	T	IR7	REGSRC	—	Call REGSRC if $IR7 = 1$
		JUMP	T	IR3	DESADD	—	Go to DESADD if $IR3 = 1$
	NEXT	SR	R(D)	R(D)	ADD	EST	$R(D) \leftarrow SR + R(D)$, EST
		JUMP	T	U	INTRPT	—	Go to INTRPT
DESADD:	NEXT	R(D)	—	AR	TSF	READ	$AR \leftarrow R(D)$, Read
	NEXT	SR	DIR	DOR	ADD	EST	$DOR \leftarrow SR + DIR$, EST
		JUMP	T	U	INTRPT	WRITE	Write, go to INTRPT
REGSRC:	NEXT	R(S)	—	AR	TSF	READ	$AR \leftarrow R(S)$, Read
	RET	DIR	—	SR	TSF	—	$SR \leftarrow DIR$, Return
Check for interrupt:							
INTRPT:		JUMP	F	EIF	FETCH	—	Go to FETCH if $EIF = 0$
		JUMP	F	INTS	FETCH	—	Go to FETCH if $INTS = 0$
	NEXT	SP	—	SP	DEC	—	$SP \leftarrow SP - 1$
	NEXT	SP	—	AR	TSF	REIF	$AR \leftarrow SP$, reset EIF
	NEXT	PC	—	DOR	TSF	WRITE	$DOR \leftarrow PC$, Write
	NEXT	—	—	NONE	—	IACK	Interrupt acknowledge
	NEXT	DIR	—	PC	TSF	—	$PC \leftarrow DIR$
		JUMP	T	U	FETCH	—	Go to FETCH

Symbolic Microprogram

The symbolic microprogram for one computer cycle is listed in Table 10-12. The FETCH and INTRPT routines are common to all cycles, but the instruction that is executed depends on the operation code that is mapped into the control memory. Here we assume a mapping of the type 0 ADD instruction. The microprogram uses a subroutine symbolized by REGSRC to show how a subroutine is formulated and terminated with a RET control sequence. A dash in a column indicates that the field is not used.

The microprogram for the fetch phase follows the sequence dictated by the flowcharts of Figure 10-10 and consists of three microoperations. The type 0 ADD microroutine ADDT0 follows the flowchart of Figure 10-12. The source operand is transferred into *SR* in the first microinstruction assuming that $IR7 = 0$. If $IR7 = 1$, the microprogram goes to subroutine REGSRC to read the operand from memory and place it in *SR*. *IR3* is then checked in the third microinstruction, and if equal to 1, the microprogram jumps to DESADD. The two operands are added and the four status bits *C, Z, S,* and *V* are updated according to the result obtain in the sum. The microprogram then jumps to the interrupt routine.

The INTRPT routine follows the sequence of operations shown in the flowchart of Figure 10-13. If either EIF or INTS is equal to 0, the microprogram jumps back to FETCH to read and execute the next instruction in the program. If both are equal to 1, the microprogram stores the return address from *PC* onto the stack and places the vector address into *PC*. The computer cycle terminates by jumping back to the fetch phase.

Binary Microprogram

The binary form of the microprogram is listed in Table 10-13. It is assumed that the fetch phase starts from address 0 and the interrupt phase starts from address 64. The microroutine for each instruction will reside in a different part of control memory as specified by the address that is mapped into *CAR*. Here we assume that the routine for the type 0 ADD instruction starts from address 16. The binary codes for the various fields are obtained from Figure 10-8(b). A dash in the symbolic microprogram is converted to all 0's. The binary values of each symbolic address

TABLE 10-13
Binary Microprogram

Address	CS / CS	AS / BR PS	BS / ST	DS FC / AD	MS / MS	
0 (FETCH)	00	1000	0000	1100 00000	0001	
1	00	1000	0000	1000 00001	0011	
2	10	0000	0000	1111 00000	0000	
16 (ADDT0)	00	1111	0000	1001 00000	0000	
17	11	1 1	0111	00000011000	0000	(REGSRC = 24)
18	11	0 1	0011	00000010101	0000	(DESADD = 21)
19	00	1001	1110	1110 00010	0110	
20	11	0 1	0000	00001000000	0000	(INTRPT = 64)
21 (DESADD)	00	1110	0000	1100 00000	0001	
22	00	1001	1101	1101 00010	0110	
23	11	0 1	0000	00001000000	0010	(INTRPT = 64)
24 (REGSRC)	00	1111	0000	1100 00000	0001	
25	01	1101	0000	1001 00000	0000	
64 (INTRPT)	11	0 0	1010	00000000000	0000	(FETCH = 0)
65	11	0 0	1011	00000000000	0000	(FETCH = 0)
66	00	0110	0000	0110 00110	0000	
67	00	0110	0000	1100 00000	1010	
68	00	1000	0000	1101 00000	0010	
69	00	0000	0000	1111 00000	1011	
70	00	1101	0000	1000 00000	0000	
71	11	0 1	0000	00000000000	0000	(FETCH = 0)

is determined from its position in the label column. The total number of bits in each binary microinstruction is 23.

10-8 MICROPROGRAM ROUTINES

The complete design of the CPU requires that we formulate a set of instructions for the computer and write the microprogram routines for each instruction in the set. A possible set of instructions for the computer was developed in Chapter 9. The microprogram for the entire CPU will not be carried out here because it will take too much space. However, we will show examples of microprogram routines for the execution of some instructions with different format types. These examples will provide enough information for writing other microprogram routines for additional instructions.

Type 1 ADD Instruction

In order to write the microprogram that executes a type 1 ADD instruction it is necessary to review the type 1 format from Figure 10-7. This format is repeated in Figure 10-14 to provide a more convenient reference. The operation code is in IR bits 8 through 15. The register specified by the register field in bits 0, 1, and 2 is denoted by $R(D)$. $IR3$ specifies a direct or indirect mode for the register. $IR4$ and $IR5$ constitute the MOD field that specifies four addressing modes in conjunction with the address field of the instruction in the second word W. $IR7$ in the SD field is equal to 0 for a two operand instruction and is equal to 1 for a one operand instruction; and $IR6$ specifies the source and destination operands. In addition, it may be advisable to refer to Table 10-4 for a list of seven possible ways that a type 1 ADD instruction can be formulated with bit I in $IR3$ equal to 0.

Figure 10-15 shows a flowchart for the microprogram routine that executes the type 1 ADD instruction. Bit $IR7$ must be equal to 0 for this two operand instruction; so we can save time by not checking it unless we want to check for format errors. The flowchart uses two subroutines whose microprograms are shown in flowchart form in Figures 10-16 and 10-17.

The microprogram starts by checking the bit in $IR6$. When $IR6$ is 0, the SD field is 00 since $IR7$ is assumed to be 0. This specifies a source operand in memory and a destination operand that is determined from the register field. The source operand is retrieved from memory into source register SR by means of the subroutine MEMSRC. The microprogram then jumps to the third microinstruction of the ADDT0 routine in Table 10-12 to complete the execution of the instruction.

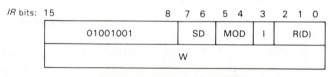

FIGURE 10-14
Type 1 ADD Instruction Format

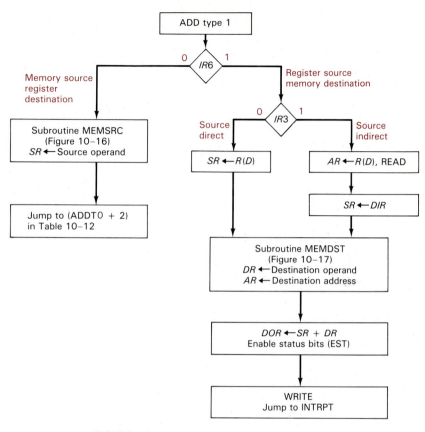

FIGURE 10-15
Microprogram Flowchart for Type 1 ADD Instruction

If $IR6 = 1$, then $SD = 01$. The source operand is evaluated from the register field and the destination operand is in memory. The indirect bit in $IR3$ determines if the register has the operand or the address of the operand. In either case, the source operand is transferred to SR. The microprogram then calls subroutine MEMDST to fetch the destination operand from memory and place it in the destination register DR. The address of the operand is available in AR. The two operands are added and stored in memory. The microprogram jumps to the interrupt routine to check for interrupts.

Subroutine MEMSRC shown in Figure 10-16 reads the source operand from memory and places it in the source register SR. The address in PC is transferred to AR in order to read the memory word W and place it in DIR. PC is then incremented by one. Bits $IR5$ and $IR4$ of the MOD field are checked to determine the addressing mode of the instruction. In the immediate mode, the operand W which is now in DIR is transferred into SR. In the other three modes, DIR holds the address field of the instruction. The effective address is computed and then transferred to AR to read the operand. The subroutine exits with the source operand in SR.

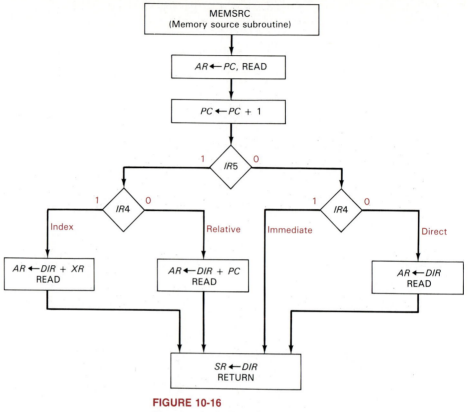

FIGURE 10-16
Flowchart for MEMSRC Subroutine

Figure 10-17 shows the flowchart for subroutine MEMDST. It reads the destination operand from memory and places it in the destination register *DR*. The immediate mode is not used as a destination, and if the instruction uses it by mistake, the microprogram treats it as a direct mode. The subroutine returns with the address of the destination in register *AR*.

The symbolic microprogram can be obtained from the three flowcharts. It will not be listed here but will be left as an exercise in the Problems section.

Type 1 Increment Instruction

The increment instruction must be of type 1 format with $IR7 = 1$ because it is a one operand instruction. Table 10-5 lists the five possible ways that this instruction can be formulated with the various addressing modes. The instruction format is as shown in Figure 10-14 except that the binary operation code is 01010011.

The symbolic microprogram routine for the increment instruction is listed in Table 10-14. If the bit in *IR6* is equal to 0, the *SD* field is equal to 10, indicating that the operand is in memory. Subroutine MEMDST from Figure 10-17 is called to place the operand in the destination register *DR* and the address of the operand

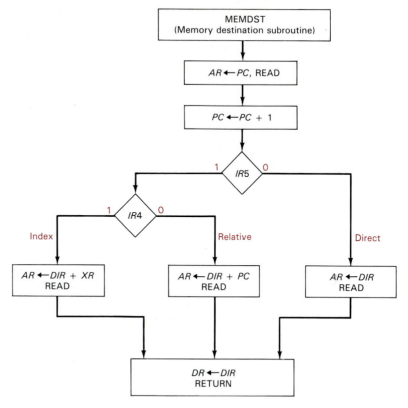

FIGURE 10-17
Flowchart for MEMDST Subroutine

TABLE 10-14
Microprogram for Type 1 Increment Instruction

Label	CS	AS CSBR	BS PS	DS ST	FC AD	MS MS	Comments
INR:		JUMP	T	IR6	REGINR	—	Reg operand if $IR6 = 1$
		CALL	T	U	MEMDST	—	Subroutine Figure 10-17
	NEXT	DR	—	DOR	INC	ESZ	$DOR \leftarrow DR + 1$, enable S, Z
		JUMP	T	U	INTRPT	WRITE	Store in memory
REGINR:		JUMP	T	IR3	INDINR	—	Indirect if $IR3 = 1$
	NEXT	R(D)	—	R(D)	INC	ESZ	$R(D) \leftarrow R(D) + 1$
		JUMP	T	U	INTRPT	—	Go to INTRPT
INDINR:	NEXT	R(D)	—	AR	TSF	READ	$AR \leftarrow R(D)$, Read
	NEXT	DIR	—	DOR	INC	ESZ	$DOR \leftarrow DIR + 1$
		JUMP	T	U	INTRPT	WRITE	Store in memory

in the address register *AR*. The number in *DR* is incremented and placed in *DOR*. The operand in *DOR* is then written into memory at the address given by *AR* and the microprogram jumps to check for interrupt.

If the bit in *IR*6 is equal to 1, then the *SD* field is equal to 11 and the operand is evaluated from the register field *R*(*D*). This is done in the microprogram beginning from the microinstruction at the symbolic address REGINR. If *IR*3 = 0, the operand in *R*(*D*) is incremented. If *IR*3 = 1, the instruction specifies a register-indirect mode and the microprogram jumps to INDINR. The operand is read from memory into *DIR*. It is then incremented and placed in *DOR*. The last microinstruction writes the operand in memory and jumps to check for interrupt. Note that the status bits *S* and *Z* are updated with this instruction.

Type 2 and 3 Instructions

Examples of symbolic microprogram routines for type 2 and 3 instructions are presented in Table 10-15. The branch unconditional instruction is executed with the BRNCH microroutine. The address field *W* is read from memory by using the address from *PC*. The value of *W* which is read into *DIR* is then transferred to *PC* in the second microinstruction.

The branch on carry instruction branches to the address in *W* if the carry bit is equal to 1. The microprogram routine BRC checks the status bit *C*, and if it is equal to 1, the microprogram jumps to BRNCH to execute the branch. If *C* is equal to 0, *PC* must be incremented by one in order to skip the second word of the instruction since it is not used. This prepares the *PC* for the address of the next instruction in the program.

The return from subroutine instruction pops the stack and transfers the contents of the top of the stack to *PC*. This is done by the routine RET. The stack pointer

TABLE 10-15
Microprogram Examples for Type 2 and 3 Instructions

Label	CS	AS CSBR	BS PS	DS ST	FC AD	MS MS	Comments
Branch unconditional microprogram (type 2 instruction):							
BRNCH:	NEXT	PC	—	AR	TSF	READ	*AR* ← *PC*, Read *W*
	NEXT	DIR	—	PC	TSF	—	*PC* ← *DIR*
	JUMP	T	U	INTRPT	—		Go to INTRPT
Branch on carry microprogram (type 2 instruction):							
BRC:		JUMP	T	C	BRNCH	—	If *C* = 1, go to BRNCH
	NEXT	PC	—	PC	INC	—	*PC* ← *PC* + 1
	JUMP	T	U	INTRPT	—		Go to INTRPT
Return from subroutine (type 3 instruction):							
RET:	NEXT	SP	—	AR	TSF	READ	*AR* ← *SP*, Read
	NEXT	DIR	—	PC	TSF	—	*PC* ← *DIR*
	NEXT	SP	—	SP	INC	—	*SP* ← *SP* + 1
	JUMP	T	U	INTRPT	—		Go to INTRPT

SP provides the address for the stack. The item on top of the stack is read from memory and placed in *DIR*. The content of *DIR* is transferred into *PC* and *SP* is incremented by one.

A careful study of the examples given in this section and the previous one should be helpful for writing microroutines for other instructions. The problems at the end of the chapter provide additional examples for writing microprogram routines.

10-9 CONTROL UNIT

The hardware of the control unit consists of the control memory that stores the microprogram, the address sequencing logic that chooses the next microinstruction address, and decoders and multiplexers that select the various components of the microoperation. The part of the control unit that determines the address of the next microinstruction is called the microprogram sequencer. In addition to the sequencer, the control must incorporate the hardware for decoding certain fields of the microinstruction.

Microprogram Sequencer

The block diagram of the microprogram sequencer together with the control memory are shown in Figure 10-18. The control memory has 2048 words of 23 bits each and requires an address of 11 bits. There are two multiplexers in the circuit. The address multiplexer selects an address from one of four sources and routes it into the control address register *CAR*. The new address loaded into *CAR* is then supplied to the control memory for reading the next microinstruction. The status multiplexer tests the value of a selected status bit and the result of the test is applied to an address selection logic circuit. The output of *CAR* is incremented and applied to one of the multiplexer inputs and to the subroutine register *SBR*. The other three inputs to the address multiplexer come from the address field *AD* of the present microinstruction, from the output of *SBR*, and from a mapping of the operation code in *IR*.

The mapping PLD is a programmable logic device (see Section 6-6) with eight inputs and 11 outputs. It maps or transforms the 8-bit operation code from its value in $IR(8\text{-}15)$ to an 11-bit control memory address. The value of the address is determined from the microprogram routine that executes the instruction. For example, if the 8-bit operation code for the type 0 ADD instruction is 00001001 as chosen in Table 10-2, and the microprogram routine that implements this instruction starts from address 16 as shown in Table 10-13, the mapping PLD transforms the 8-bit operation code 00001001 to an 11-bit address 00000010000.

The incrementer circuit in the sequencer is not a counter with flip-flops but rather a combinational circuit constructed with gates. The circuit can be designed with 11 half adder circuits (see Figure 3-8) connected in cascaded stages. The output carry from one stage is applied to the input of the next higher order stage. The input carry in the first least significant stage must be equal to 1 to provide the increment by one operation.

The *ST* field of the microinstruction selects one of the status bits from the inputs of the status multiplexer. The polarity of the selected bit is determined from the

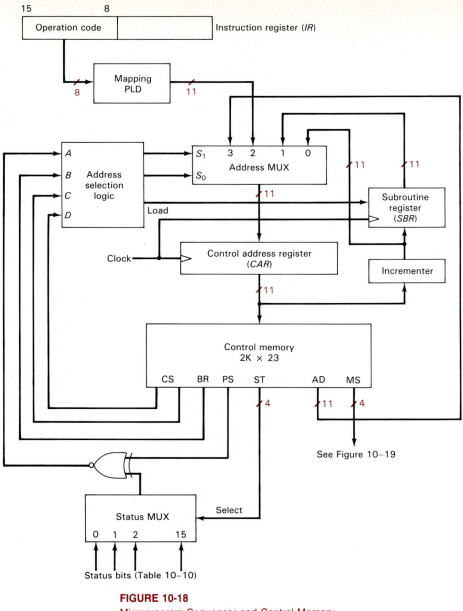

FIGURE 10-18
Microprogram Sequencer and Control Memory

bit value of the *PS* field. The exclusive-NOR gate produces an output of 1 if both of its inputs are equal to 1 or if both of its inputs are equal to 0. Thus the output of the gate is equal to 1 if the *PS* field bit is equal to the value of the selected status bit.

The address selection logic in the sequencer has four inputs and three outputs. The truth table for this circuit is shown in Table 10-16. Inputs *D* and *C* are identical to the bit values of the *CS* field and input *B* is equal to the bit value of the *BR* field. Input *A* receives the status of the selected bit from the status multiplexer. The values for S_1 and S_0 are determined from the required path in the address multiplexer. When *CS* is equal to 00, 01, or 10, inputs *D* and *C* go directly to

TABLE 10-16
Truth Table for Address Selection Logic

CS	BR	D C B A	S_1	S_0	Load	Address MUX selection	
00	—	0 0 X X	0	0	0	Increment CAR	(NEXT)
01	—	0 1 X X	0	1	0	Subroutine register	(RET)
10	—	1 0 X X	1	0	0	Mapping of op-code	(MAP)
11	0	1 1 0 0	0	0	0	Increment CAR	
11	0	1 1 0 1	1	1	0	AD field	(JUMP)
11	1	1 1 1 0	0	0	0	Increment CAR	
11	1	1 1 1 1	1	1	1	AD field, load SBR	(CALL)

outputs S_1 and S_0 and the other inputs of the address selection logic have no effect on the address multiplexer. When CS is equal to 11, the selected input to the address multiplexer depends on inputs B and A. When input A is equal to 0, it means that the selected bit in the status multiplexer does not have the required polarity. In this case, CAR is incremented by one. If input A is equal to 1, both S_1 and S_0 must be equal to 1 in order to transfer the address field AD through the address multiplexer. If input B is also equal to 1, it signifies a call subroutine microinstruction, and the load input to the subroutine register SBR is activated.

The truth table from Table 10-16 can be used to obtain the simplified Boolean functions for the address selection logic circuit. Using maps for the two functions we obtain the following simplified Boolean equations:

$$S_1 = ACD + \overline{C}D$$

$$S_0 = ACD + C\overline{D}$$

$$\text{Load} = ABCD$$

The combinational circuit has a common gate for the product term ACD. S_1 and S_0 can be implemented with three AND gates, two OR gates, and two inverters. The condition for storing the return address in SBR is generated by the load signal with an AND gate with inputs A, B, C, and D.

Decoding of Type A Microinstruction

The microprogram sequencer of Figure 10-18 implements the hardware necessary for the common field CS and the other fields of the type B microinstruction. The common field MS must be decoded separately and the other fields of type A microinstruction format need decoding circuits before they are applied to the buses in the processor unit.

Figure 10-19 shows the additional circuits necessary for interpreting the type A microinstruction. The CS and MS fields are common to both formats. The FC field is connected directly to the selection inputs of the ALSU to provide the specified operation. The AS, BS and DS fields designate the register to be applied to the CPU buses. The code assignment for the registers is given in Table 10-7. The DS field can choose any one of 14 destination registers. When $DS = 1110$, we use the

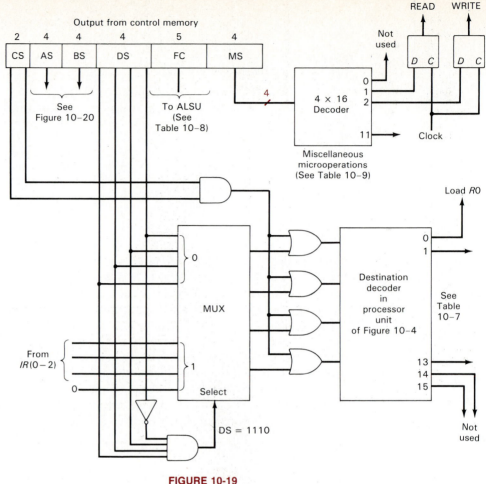

FIGURE 10-19
Decoding of a Type A Microinstruction

symbol $R(D)$ to designate a processor register $R0$ through $R7$ as specified by the 3-bit code in $IR(0\text{-}2)$. When $DS = 1111$, none of the registers are selected.

The multiplexer in Figure 10-19 implements the $R(D)$ symbolic designation. When DS is not equal to 1110, the multiplexer forms a path from its 0 inputs to the outputs. This transfers the 4-bit code from DS into the destination decoder in the processor unit. When $DS = 1110$, the multiplexer forms a path from its 1 inputs and transfers the bits from $IR(0\text{-}2)$ with a 0 in the fourth bit.

When the CS field is equal to binary 11 it designates a branch type B microinstruction. An ALSU operation must be inhibited when the CS field is equal to 11. This is done by forcing four 1's into the destination decoder in the processor unit. Output 15 of the decoder is not connected to any register load input and, therefore, none of the registers receives the output of the ALSU when the CS field is equal to 11.

The decoder for the MS field can provide up to 15 independent microoperations but only 11 microoperations are used and they are listed in Table 10-9. Output 0 of the decoder is not connected anywhere and provides a "no operation" condition. Outputs 1 and 2 of the decoder go to the D inputs of the READ and WRITE flip-flops. These flip-flops are set to 1 when their D input is equal to 1 while a clock pulse transition occurs. The outputs of the flip-flops generate the corresponding read and write signals for the memory unit and also control the bidirectional bus buffers in the data bus of the CPU (see Figure 10-5). When the D input of a flip-flop is equal to 0, the next clock transition resets the output to 0.

The two fields AS and BS that select registers for the input buses of the ALSU go through multiplexers as shown in Figure 10-20. The multiplexer associated with

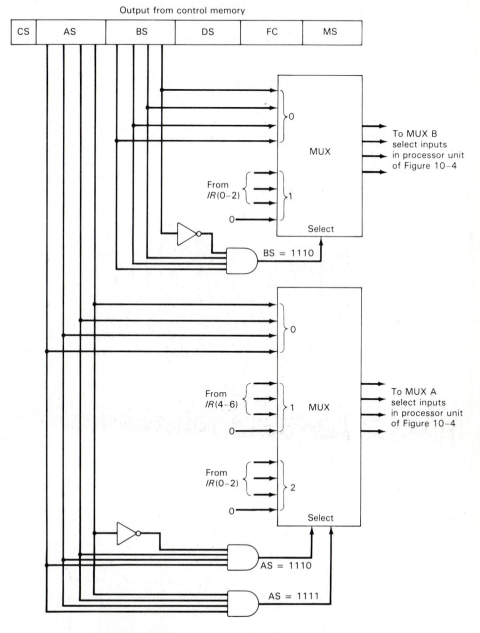

FIGURE 10-20

Selection of Registers in MUX A and MUX B of Processor Unit

BS implements the *R(D)* symbolic designation in a manner similar to the *DS* field. The output of this multiplexer is applied to the selection inputs of MUX B in the processor unit that selects the register for the *B* input of the ALSU. The multiplexer for *AS* implements the symbolic designations of *R(D)* and *R(S)* as defined in Table 10-7. The select inputs of the multiplexer are equal to 00 when the *AS* field is not equal to 1110 or 1111. This transfers the code from *AS* to the multiplexer output. The select inputs are equal to 01 when *AS* = 1111. This implements the *R(S)* condition by transferring the code from the source field in *IR*(4-6) into the select inputs of MUX A in the processor. The selection inputs are equal to 10 if *AS* = 1110. This implements the *R(D)* condition by transferring the code from the destination register in *IR*(0-2) into the select inputs of MUX A.

The control unit is synchronized with the same clock pulses that are applied also to the processor unit. Every clock pulse produces the following operations when applicable:

1. A microoperation is executed in the processor unit if *CS* is not equal to 11;
2. The microoperation specified in the *MS* field (if any) is executed;
3. The next microinstruction address is transferred into *CAR* and the corresponding microinstruction is read from control memory after a given time delay;
4. The return address is transferred into the subroutine register if a call instruction is satisfied.

All these operations occur simultaneously with the same common clock pulse transition. This is repeated for each clock pulse and each microinstruction that is read from control memory.

REFERENCES

1. MANO, M. M., *Computer System Architecture*. 2nd ed. Englewood Cliffs: Prentice-Hall, 1982.
2. TANENBAUM A. S. *Structured Computer Organization*. 2nd ed. Englewood Cliffs: Prentice-Hall, 1984.
3. LEWIN, M. H. *Logic Design and Computer Organization*. Reading, MA: Addison-Wesley, 1983.
4. HAMACHER, V. C., VRANESIC, Z. G., AND ZAKY S. G. *Computer Organization*, 2nd ed. New York: McGraw-Hill, 1984.
5. PROSSER, F. AND WINKEL, D. *The Art Digital Design*. 2nd ed. Englewood Cliffs: Prentice-Hall, 1987.

PROBLEMS

10-1 Draw the diagram of the shift left unit similar to Figure 10-3.

10-2 A bidirectional bus line with three-state buffers is shown in Figure 7-9. Using this figure as a reference, show the construction of one line of the bidirectional data bus buffer in the CPU block diagram of Figure 10-5.

10-3 Interpret the following hexadecimal instructions using Figure 10-7 and Table 10-2 as reference. Express each instruction in symbolic form and in register transfer notation.
(a) 4A4B; (b) 0BC9; (c) 5E80; (d) 4B25

10-4 For each of the following symbolic instructions, specify the operation in register transfer notation and give the corresponding hexadecimal code (see Table 10-2 and Figure 10-7).
(a) SUB (R3), R5
(b) MOVE R3, (R0)
(c) MOVE #W, (R1)
(d) PUSH W(X)

10-5 Evaluate the 4-digit hexadecimal code of the instruction that executes the following operations (use Table 10-2 and Figure 10-7).
(a) $R5 \leftarrow M[R2]$
(b) $M[W] \leftarrow R3$
(c) $XR \leftarrow XR - 1$
(d) $PC \leftarrow M[SP], SP \leftarrow SP + 1$

10-6 Repeat Table 10-4 using a register indirect mode with $R2$ as the selected register.

10-7 Each set of microoperations listed below can be specified with one microinstruction. Choose the symbolic name and binary value from Figure 10-8(b) for the fields of the microinstruction.
(a) $DR \leftarrow R(D), CAR \leftarrow CAR + 1$
(b) $R0 \leftarrow R0 - 1, DIR \leftarrow M[AR], CAR \leftarrow CAR + 1$
(c) $TR \leftarrow ZR + NR, M[AR] \leftarrow DOR, CAR \leftarrow SBR$

10-8 Convert each of the following 6-digit hexadecimal number to a 23-bit number. Let the binary number obtained from the conversion be a microinstruction as defined in Figure 10-8. Interpret the microinstruction and explain its operation.
(a) 1C1400;   (b) 620000;   (c) 334A26.

10-9 Table 10-7 lists a total of 17 registers in the three fields AS, BS, and DS.
(a) Identify the 14 registers inside the processor unit and the three registers that communicate with memory.
(b) Identify the nine registers that can be changed by program instructions.
(c) Identify three registers used by the control for temporary storage.
(d) Give examples where registers ZR and NR can be used. Why is it that these two registers are not listed under the DS field?
(e) What is the meaning of the symbols $R(S)$, $R(D)$, and NONE?

10-10 The NR register defined in Table 10-7 holds a constant for use in microprogram loops. Give the microinstruction that will transfer the content of NR to the temporary register TR for possible manipulation.

10-11 Modify the shift left circuit of Problem 10-1 by including the logic for updating the overflow status bit V during an arithmetic shift left microoperation.

10-12 The carry flip-flop in the status register is updated from the following four sources:
(a) From A_0 during a right shift (Figure 10-3).
(b) From A_{15} during a left shift (Problem 10-1).
(c) From the output carry C_{out} in the arithmetic unit when signals EST or ECB (Table 10-9) are enabled in the MS field.
(d) From the SCF and RCF microoperations in the MS field.

Design the gate logic for the input of the carry flip-flop using a JK type flip-flop.

10-13 Convert each of the nine symbolic microinstructions listed in Table 10-11 into a 23-bit binary equivalent. Assume that DEST = 9, START = 3, and FETCH = 0.

10-14 Determine the time it takes to fetch and execute a type 0 ADD instruction by going through the microprogram in Table 10-12. Assume that EIF = 1 but that there is no external interrupt. Assume that each microinstruction takes t nanoseconds. Evaluate the time for each of the four possible combinations of $IR(7)$ and $IR(3)$.

10-15 Write the symbolic microprogram for the type 1 ADD instruction from the information given in the flowchart of Figure 10-15.

10-16 Translate the microprogram listed in Table 10-14 into binary. Assume that the INR routine starts from address 32 and that INTRPT is at 64.

10-17 Draw a flowchart for the INR microroutine whose symbolic microprogram is listed in Table 10-14.

10-18 Write a microprogram for a type 0 MOVE instruction.

10-19 Write a microprogram for a type 1 MOVE instruction.

10-20 Write a microprogram for the PUSH stack instruction. Use the type 1 format with one operand. Note that all four modes are possible with the memory operand.

10-21 Write a microprogram for the type 1 NEGATE instruction. This instruction forms the 2's complement of the operand.

10-22 Write a microprogram for a type 2 CALL subroutine instruction.

10-23 Write a microprogram for the following type 2 instruction:

CALL subroutine if positive and non-zero

Assume that the S and Z status bits have been updated by a previous subtract instruction.

10-24 Write a microprogram for the logical shift right instruction. Use the type 1 instruction format (Figure 10-7) with two interpretations. When $IR(7) = 1$, the instruction has one operand and produces a single shift. When $IR(7) = 0$, then the REG and I fields of the instruction specify the operand to be shifted and W gives the number of times to shift. In the single shift case, the microprogram checks the SD and MOD fields to determine the operand. In the multiple shifts case, the SD and MOD fields are not used.

10-25 Write a microprogram for type 0 unsigned MULTIPLY instruction. The source and destination fields of the instruction specify the multiplier and multiplicand. The double length product is always left in registers $R0$ and $R1$.

10-26 Modify the type 2 instruction format of Figure 10-7 to include a relative mode branch instruction. This is done by using bit 13 of the instruction code to distinguish between the two addressing modes. If bit 13 is equal to 0, the interpretation remains the same as is shown in Figure 10-7, with W being the branch address. If bit 13 is equal to 1, bits 8-12 of the instruction specify the operation code and bits 0-7 contain a signed number in the range of $+127$ to -128 for the relative address. The second word W is not used in the relative mode because the branch address is computed by adding the contents of PC to the address field in $IR(0-7)$ with sign extension. The sign extension produces a 16-bit number with nine leading 0's if the sign bit $IR(7) = 0$ or a 16-bit number with nine leading 1's if the sign bit $IR(7) = 1$.

(a) Show any hardware addition that is needed in the CPU of Figure 10-5 to allow the 16-bit signed number with sign extension to enter the processor unit. (Try a multiplexer with IR and DIR as inputs going into the processor bus).

(b) What additions must be included in Table 10-9 and Table 10-10?

(c) Rewrite the two branch microprograms of Table 10-15 taking into account this new modification of the type 2 format.

10-27 The hardware of the processor unit as defined in Section 10-3 does not have a data path from the status bits to the memory unit. This path is necessary in order to push the status bits onto the stack after an interrupt or a call to subroutine. Similarly, a path must be provided to restore the status bits upon return from interrupt or subroutine. Modify the hardware of the CPU and write the microprogram routines for the instructions "push status bits" and "pop status bits." (One way that the hardware may be modified is to include two additional microoperations in Table 10-9 that transfer the status bits to and from the temporary register TR.)

10-28 Design the incrementer circuit shown in Figure 10-16 using 11 half adder circuits.

10-29 Derive the simplified Boolean functions for the address select logic from the truth table listed in Table 10-16.

10-30 Change the equivalence gate in Figure 10-16 to an exclusive-OR gate. Make any corrections in the entries of Table 10-16 to conform with this change and redesign the address selection logic.

10-31 Why is it that the processor unit must be disabled when the two bits of the CS field of the microinstruction are both equal to 1? Indicate how the hardware of the control unit fulfills this requirement.

INPUT–OUTPUT AND COMMUNICATION

11-1 INTRODUCTION

The input and output subsection of a computer provides an efficient mode of communication between the central processing unit (CPU) and the outside environment. Programs and data must be entered into computer memory for processing and results obtained from computations must be recorded or displayed for the user. Among the input and output devices that are commonly found in computer systems are keyboards, display terminals, printers, and magnetic disks. Other input and output devices encountered are magnetic tape drives, digital plotters, optical readers, analog-to-digital converters, and various data acquisition equipment. Computers can be used to control various processes such as machine tooling, assembly line procedures, and industrial control.

The input and output facility of a computer is a function of its intended application. The difference between a small and large system is partially dependent on the amount of hardware the computer has available for communicating with other devices and the number of devices connected to the system. Since each device behaves differently, it would be prohibitive to dwell on the detailed interconnections needed between the computer and each device. However, there are certain techniques and procedures that are common to most devices.

In this chapter we present some of the common characteristics found in the input-output subsystem of computers. The various techniques available for transferring data either in parallel, using many conducting paths, or serially, through communication lines, are presented. A description of the different types of transfer modes is given, starting from a simple example of program control transfer to a configuration of systems with multiple processors.

11-2 INPUT–OUTPUT INTERFACE

Devices that are in direct control of the processing unit are said to be connected on-line. These devices transfer binary information into and out of the memory unit upon command from the CPU. Input or output devices attached to the computer on-line are called *peripherals*.

Peripherals connected to a computer need special communication links for interfacing them with the central processing unit. The purpose of the communication link is to resolve the differences that exist between the central computer and each peripheral. The major differences are

1. Peripherals are electromechanical devices and their manner of operation is different from the operation of the CPU and memory which are electronic devices. Therefore, a conversion of signal values may be required.
2. The data transfer rate of peripherals is usually slower than the transfer rate of the CPU. Consequently, a synchronization mechanism may be needed.
3. Data codes and formats in peripherals differ from the word format in the CPU and memory.
4. The operating modes of peripherals differ from each other and each must be controlled in a way that does not disturb the operation of other peripherals connected to the CPU.

To resolve these differences, computer systems include special hardware components between the CPU and peripherals to supervise and synchronize all input and output transfers. These components are called *interface* units because they interface between the processor bus and the peripheral device. In addition, each device has its own controller to supervise the operations of the particular mechanism of that peripheral. For example, the controller in a printer attached to a computer controls the paper motion, the print timing, and the selection of printing characters.

I/O Bus and Interface Units

A typical communication link between the CPU and several peripherals is shown in Figure 11-1. Each peripheral has associated with it an interface unit. The common bus from the CPU is attached to all peripheral interfaces. To communicate with a particular device, the CPU places a device address on the address bus. Each interface attached to the common bus contains an address decoder which monitors the address lines. When the interface detects its own address, it activates the path between the bus lines and the device that it controls. All peripherals with addresses that do not correspond to the address in the bus are disabled by their interface. At the same time that the address is made available in the address bus, the CPU provides a function code in the control lines. The selected interface responds to the function code and proceeds to execute it. If data has to be transferred, the interface communicates with both the device and the CPU data bus to synchronize the transfer.

The four I/O devices shown in Figure 11-1 are employed in practically any general purpose digital computer. The keyboard is an input device used for entering data

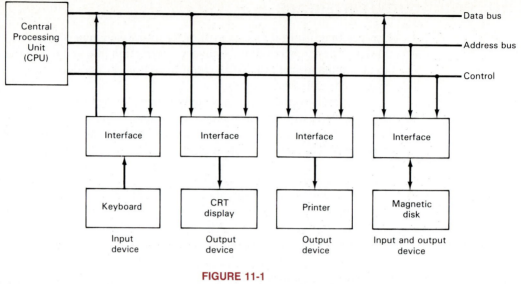

FIGURE 11-1
Connection of I/O Devices to CPU

into the computer. When the user depresses a key, the interface produces a binary code corresponding to the particular alphanumeric character in the keyboard. The most often used code is ASCII (American Standard Code for Information Interchange: see Table 1-6).

The CRT (cathode ray tube) display is often used as an output device for graphics or text entered from the keyboard and stored in computer memory. The CRT used in computer displays are the same type as in television sets. The graphics or text is displayed by positioning an electron beam in the tube and illuminating the surface at the proper time.

The printer is a useful output device for producing hard copy. Some printers print only one character at a time across a line. For faster printing, a high-speed line printer that can print an entire line at once is employed.

Magnetic disks are used for bulk storage of programs and data. The disk has a high-speed rotational surface which is coated with magnetic material. Access is achieved by moving a read/write mechanism to a track in the magnetized surface. When necessary, blocks of data are transferred to and from the disk and computer memory.

In addition to communicating with the I/O devices, the CPU of a computer must also communicate with the memory unit through an address and data bus. There are three ways that external computer buses communicate with memory and I/O. One method uses common data, address, and control buses for both memory and I/O. This configuration is referred to as memory-mapped I/O. The common address space is shared between the interface units and memory words, with each having a distinct address. Computers that adopt the memory-mapped scheme read and write from interface units as if they were assigned memory addresses.

The second alternative is to share a common address bus and data bus but use different control lines for memory and I/O. Such computers have separate read and write lines for memory and I/O. To read or write from memory, the CPU activates the memory read or memory write control. To input or output from an interface, the CPU activates the read I/O or write I/O control. In this way, the address assigned to memory and I/O interface units are independent from each other and are distinguished by separate control lines. This method is referred to as the isolated I/O configuration.

The third alternative is to have two independent sets of data, address, and control buses. This is possible in computers that include an I/O processor in the system in addition to the CPU. The memory communicates with both the CPU and I/O processor through a common memory bus. The I/O processor also communicates with the input and output devices through separate address, data, and control lines. The purpose of the I/O processor is to provide an independent pathway for the transfer of information between external devices and internal memory. The I/O processor is sometimes called a data channel.

Example of I/O Interface

A typical I/O interface unit is shown in block diagram form in Figure 11-2. It consists of two data registers called *ports*, a control register, a status register, a bidirectional data bus, and timing and control circuits. The function of the interface is to translate the signals between the CPU buses and the I/O device and to provide the needed hardware to satisfy the two sets of timing constraints.

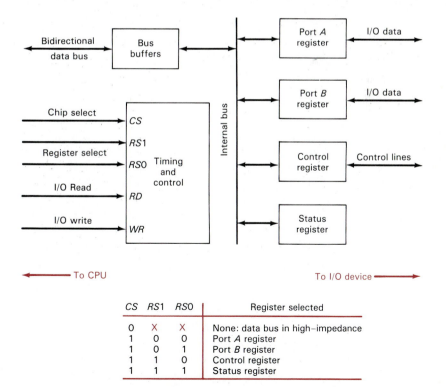

CS	RS1	RS0	Register selected
0	X	X	None: data bus in high–impedance
1	0	0	Port A register
1	0	1	Port B register
1	1	0	Control register
1	1	1	Status register

FIGURE 11-2
Example of I/O Interface Unit

The I/O data from the device can be transferred into either port *A* or port *B*. The interface may operate with an output device or with an input device or with a device that requires both input and output. If the interface is connected to a printer, it will only output data; and if it services a card reader, it will only input data. A magnetic tape unit transfers data in both directions but not at the same time; so the interface can use only one set of I/O bidirectional data lines.

The control register receives control information from the CPU. By loading appropriate bits into the control register, the interface and device can be placed in a variety of operating modes. For example, port *A* may be defined as an input port only. A magnetic tape unit may be instructed to rewind the tape or to start the tape moving in the forward direction. The bits in the status register are used for status conditions and for recording errors that may occur during the data transfer. For example, a status bit may indicate that port *A* has received a new data item from the device. Another bit in the status register may indicate that a parity error has occurred during the transfer.

The interface registers communicate with the CPU through the bidirectional data bus. The address bus selects the interface unit through the chip select input and the two register select inputs. A circuit must be provided externally (usually a decoder or a gate) to detect the address assigned to the interface registers. This circuit enables the chip select (*CS*) input when the interface is selected by the address bus. The two register select inputs *RS*1 and *RS*0 are usually connected to the two least significant lines of the address bus. These two inputs select one of the four registers in the interface as specified in the table accompanying the diagram. The content of the selected register is transferred into the CPU via the data bus when the I/O read signal is enabled. The CPU transfers binary information into the selected register via the data bus when the I/O write input is enabled.

Handshaking

The control lines out of the interface may be used for a variety of applications depending on the type of I/O device used. One important application of these lines is to control the timing of data transfer between the I/O device and the interface. Two units, such as an interface and the controller of the I/O device to which it is attached, are designed with different control and clock generators and are said to be asynchronous to each other. Asynchronous data transfer between two independent units requires that control signals be transmitted between the communicating units to indicate the time at which data is being transmitted. One method commonly used is to accompany each data item being transferred with a control signal that indicates the presence of data in the bus. The unit receiving the data item responds with another control signal to acknowledge receipt of the data. This kind of arrangement between two independent units is referred to as *handshaking*.

The basic principle of the two-wire handshaking procedure of data transfer is as follows. One control line is in the same direction as the data flow in the bus from the source to the destination. It is used by the source unit to inform the destination unit that there is valid data on the bus. The other control line is in the other direction from the destination to the source. It is used by the destination unit to acknowledge the acceptance of data. In this way, each unit informs the other unit of its status and the result is an orderly transfer through the bus.

Figure 11-3 shows the data transfer procedure. The I/O data bus carries binary information from the source unit to the destination unit. Here we assume that the interface is the source and the I/O device is the destination, but the same procedure applies if the transfer is in the other direction. Typically, the bus has multiple data lines to transfer a given number of bits at a time. The two handshaking lines are *data ready*, generated by the source unit, and *acknowledge*, generated by the destination unit. The timing diagram shows the exchange of signals between the two units. The initial state is when both the *data ready* and *acknowledge* are disabled

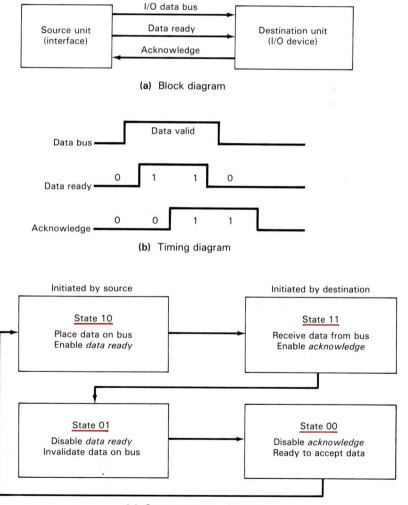

(a) Block diagram

(b) Timing diagram

(c) State sequence of events

FIGURE 11-3
Asynchronous Transfer Using Handshaking

and in the 00 state. The subsequent states are 10, 11, and 01. The state sequence shown in part (c) of the figure lists the events that occur as the transfer goes through the four states. The source unit initiates the transfer by placing the data on the bus and enabling its *data ready* signal. The *acknowledge* signal is activated by the destination unit after it receives the data from the bus. The source unit disables its *data ready* signal in response to the destination's *acknowledge*. The destination unit then disables its *acknowledge* signal and the system goes to the initial state. The source does not send the next data item unless the destination unit shows its readiness to accept new data by disabling its *acknowledge* line.

The handshaking scheme provides a high degree of flexibility and reliability because the successful completion of a data transfer relies on active participation by both units. If one unit is faulty, the data transfer will not be completed. Such an error can be detected by means of a *timeout* mechanism, which produces an alarm condition if the data transfer is not completed within a predetermined time interval. The timeout is implemented by means of an internal clock that starts counting time when the unit enables one of its handshaking control signals. If the return handshake signal does not respond within a given time period, the unit assumes that an error occurred. The timeout signal can be used to interrupt the CPU and execute a service routine that takes appropriate error recovery action.

11-3 SERIAL COMMUNICATION

The transfer of data between two units may be performed in parallel or serial. In parallel data transfer, each bit of the message has its own path and the total message is transmitted at the same time. This means that an *n*-bit message is transmitted in parallel through *n* separate conductor paths. In serial data transmission, each bit in the message is sent in sequence, one at a time. This method requires the use of one pair of conductors or one conductor and a common ground. Parallel transmission is faster but requires many wires. It is used for short distances and where speed is important. Serial transmission is slower but less expensive since it requires only one pair of conductors.

The way that computers and terminals remote from each other are connected is via telephone lines and other public and private communication facilities. Since telephone lines were originally designed for voice communication and computers communicate in terms of digital signals, some form of conversion may be needed. The converters are called *data sets*, *acoustic couplers*, or *modems* (from modulator-demodulator). A modem converts digital signals into audio tones to be transmitted over telephone lines and also converts audio tones from the line to digital signals for computer use. Various modulation schemes as well as different grades of communication media and transmission speeds are used.

Serial data can be transmitted between two points in three different modes: simplex, half-duplex, or full-duplex. A *simplex* line carries information in one direction only. This mode is seldom used in data communication because the receiver cannot communicate with the transmitter to indicate the occurrence of errors. Examples of simplex transmission are radio and television broadcasting.

A *half-duplex* transmission system is one that is capable of transmitting in both directions, but data can be transmitted in only one direction at a time. A pair of wires is needed for this mode. A common situation is for one modem to act as the transmitter and the other as the receiver. When transmission in one direction is completed, the roles of the modems are reversed to enable transmission in the opposite direction. The time required to switch a half-duplex line from one direction to the other is called the turnaround time.

A *full-duplex* transmission can send and receive data in both directions simultaneously. This can be achieved by means of a four-wire link, with a different pair of wires dedicated to each direction of transmission. Alternatively, a two-wire circuit can support full-duplex communication if the frequency spectrum is subdivided into two nonoverlapping frequency bands to create separate receive and transmit channels in the same physical pair of wires.

Serial transmission of data can be synchronous or asynchronous. In synchronous transmission, the two units share a common clock frequency rate, and bits are transmitted continuously at the adopted rate. In long distant serial transmission, the transmitter and receiver units are each driven by a separate clock of the same frequency. Synchronization signals are transmitted periodically between the two units to keep their clock frequencies in step with each other. In asynchronous transmission, binary information is sent only when it is available and the line remains idle when there is no information to be transmitted. This is in contrast to synchronous transmission where bits must be transmitted continuously to keep the clock frequencies in both units synchronized.

Asynchronous Transmission

One of the most common applications of serial transmission is for communication with a keyboard and serial printer. Each character consists of an alphanumeric code of eight bits with additional bits inserted at both ends of the character code. In the serial asynchronous data transmission technique, each character consists of three parts: the start bit, the character bits, and the stop bits. The convention is for the transmitter to rest at the 1-state when no characters are transmitted. The first bit, called the start bit, is always 0 and is used to indicate the beginning of a character. An example of this format is shown in Figure 11-4.

A transmitted character can be detected by the receiver from knowledge of the transmission rules. When a character is not being sent, the line is kept in the 1-state. The initiation of a character transmission is detected from the start bit, which is always 0. The character bits always follow the start bit. After the last bit of the

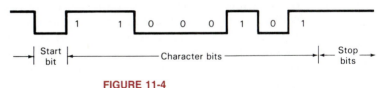

FIGURE 11-4
Format of Asynchronous Serial Transfer

character is transmitted, a stop bit is detected when the line returns to the 1-state for at least one bit time. Using these rules, the receiver can detect the start bit when the line goes from 1 to 0. A clock in the receiver examines the line at proper bit times. The receiver knows the transfer rate of the bits and the number of character bits to accept. After the character bits are transmitted, one or two stop bits are sent. The stop bits are always in the 1-state and frame the end of character to signify the idle or wait state.

At the end of the character, the line is held at the 1-state for a period of at least 1 or 2 bit times so that both the transmitter and receiver can resynchronize. The length of time that the line stays in this state depends on the amount of time required for the equipment to resynchronize. Some older electromechanical terminals use two stop bits but newer terminals use one stop bit. The line remains in the 1-state until another character is transmitted. The stop time insures that a new character will not follow for 1 or 2 bit times.

As an illustration, consider the serial transmission of a terminal with a transfer rate of 10 characters per second. Each transmitted character consists of a start bit, 8 information bits, and 2 stop bits, for a total of 11 bits. Ten characters per second means that each character takes 0.1 second for transfer. Since there are 11 bits to be transmitted, it follows that the bit time is 9.09 msec. The *baud* rate is defined as the rate at which serial information is transmitted and is equivalent to the data transfer in bits per second. Ten characters per second with an 11-bit format has a transfer rate of 110 baud.

The terminal has a keyboard and a printer. Every time a key is depressed, the terminal sends 11 bits serially along a wire. To print a character in the printer, an 11-bit message must be received along another wire. The terminal interface consists of a transmitter and a receiver. The transmitter accepts an 8-bit character from the computer and proceeds to send a serial 11-bit message to the printer line. The receiver accepts a serial 11-bit message from the keyboard line and forwards the 8-bit character code into the computer. Integrated circuits are available which are specifically designed to provide the interface between computer and similar interactive terminals.

Synchronous Transmission

Synchronous transmission does not use start-stop bits to frame characters. The modems used in synchronous transmission have internal clocks that are set to the frequency at which bits are being transmitted. For proper operation, it is required that the clock of the transmitter and receiver modems remain synchronized at all times. The communication line, however, carries only the data bits, from which the clock information must be extracted. Frequency synchronization is achieved by the receiving modem, from the signal transitions that occur in the received data. Any frequency shift that may occur between the transmitter and receiver clocks is continuously adjusted by maintaining the receiver clock at the frequency of the incoming bit stream. In this way, the same rate is maintained in both the transmitter and receiver.

Contrary to asynchronous transmission, where each character can be sent separately with its own start and stop bits, synchronous transmission must send a continuous message in order to maintain synchronism. The message consists of a group of bits that form a block of data. The entire block is transmitted with special control bits at the beginning and the end, in order to frame the entire block into one unit of information.

The communication lines, modems, and other equipment used in the transmission of information between two or more stations is called a *data link*. The orderly transfer of information in the data link is accomplished by means of a *protocol*. A data link protocol is a set of rules that are followed by interconnecting computers and terminals to ensure the orderly transfer of information. The purpose of the data link proctocol is to establish a connection between two stations, to identify the sender and receiver, to ensure that all messages are passed correctly without errors, and to handle all control functions involved in a sequence of data transfer. Protocols are divided into two major categories according to the message framing technique used. These are character-oriented protocol and bit-oriented protocol.

Character-Oriented Protocol

The character-oriented protocol is based on the binary code of a character set. The code most commonly used is ASCII. It is a 7-bit code with an eighth bit for parity check. The code has 128 characters, of which 95 are graphic characters and 33 are control characters. The list of ASCII characters can be found in Table 1-6. The control characters are used for the purpose of routing data, arranging the text in the desired format, and for the layout of the printed page. The characters that control the transmission are called *communication control* characters. These characters are listed in Table 11-1. Each character code has seven bits plus an even parity bit. It is referred to by a three-letter symbol. The role of each character in the control of data transmission is stated briefly in the function column of the table.

The SYN character serves as synchronizing agent between the transmitter and receiver. The 8-bit code 10010110 has the property that, upon circular shifting, it does not repeat itself until after a full 8-bit cycle. When the transmitter starts sending characters, it sends a few SYN characters first and then sends the actual message. The initial continuous string of bits accepted by the receiver is checked for a SYN character. In other words, with each clock period, the receiver checks

TABLE 11-1
ASCII Communication Control Characters

Code	Symbol	Meaning	Function
10010110	SYN	Synchronous idle	Establishes synchronism
10000001	SOH	Start of heading	Heading of block message
10000010	STX	Start of text	Precedes block of text
00000011	ETX	End of text	Terminates block of text
10000100	EOT	End of transmission	Concludes transmission
00000110	ACK	Acknowledge	Affirmative acknowledge
10010101	NAK	Negative acknowledge	Negative acknowledge
00000101	ENQ	Inquiry	Inquire if terminal is on
00010111	ETB	End of transmission block	End of block of data
10010000	DLE	Data link escape	Special control character

| SYN | SYN | SOH | Heading | STX | Text | ETX | BCC |

FIGURE 11-5

Typical Message Format for Character-Oriented Protocol

the last eight bits received. If they do not match the bits of the SYN character, the receiver accepts the next bit, rejects the previous high-order bit, and again checks the last eight bits received for a SYN character. This is repeated after each clock period and bit received until a SYN character is recognized. Once a SYN character is detected, the receiver has framed an 8-bit character. From here on, the receiver counts every eight bits and accepts them as the next character. Usually, the receiver checks two consecutive SYN characters to remove any doubt that the first one did not occur as a result of a noise signal on the line. Moreover, when the transmitter is idle and does not have any message characters to send, it sends a continuous string of SYN characters. The receiver recognizes these characters as a condition for synchronizing the line and goes into a synchronous idle state. In this state, the two units maintain bit and character synchronism even though no meaningful information is communicated.

Messages are transmitted through the data link with an established format consisting of a heading field, a text field, and an error checking field. A typical message format for the character-oriented protocol is shown in Figure 11-5. The two SYN characters assure proper synchronization at the start of the message. Following the SYN characters is the heading, which starts with an SOH (start of heading) character. The heading consists of an address and control information. The STX (start of text) character terminates the heading and signifies the beginning of text transmission. The text portion of the message is variable in length and may contain any ASCII characters except the communication control characters. The text field is terminated with the ETX (end of text) character. The last field is a block check character (BCC) used for error checking. It is usually either a longitudinal redundancy check (LRC) or a cyclic redundancy check (CRC). The LRC is an 8-bit parity over all the characters of the message in the frame. It is the accumulation of the exclusive-OR of all transmitted characters. The CRC is a polynomial code obtained from the message bits by passing them through a feedback shift register containing a number of exclusive-OR gates. This type of code is suitable for detecting burst errors occurring in the communication channel.

Bit-Oriented Protocol

The character-oriented protocol was originally developed to communicate with keyboard, printer, and display devices that use alphanumeric characters exclusively. As the data communication field expanded, it became necessary to transmit binary information that is not ASCII text. This happens, for example, when two remote computers send binary programs to each other over a communication channel. An arbitrary bit pattern in the text field becomes a problem in the character-oriented method. This is because any 8-bit pattern that corresponds to one of the communication control characters will be interpreted erroneously by the receiver.

Flag 01111110	Address 8 bits	Control 8 bits	Information Any number of bits	Frame check 16 bits	Flag 01111110

FIGURE 11-6
Frame Format for Bit-Oriented Protocol

The protocol that has been mostly used to solve this problem is the bit-oriented protocol.

The bit-oriented protocol is independent of any particular code. It allows the transmission of a serial bit stream of any length without the implication of character boundaries. Messages are organized in a specific format within a frame. In addition to the information field, a frame contains address, control, and error checking fields. The frame boundaries are determined from a special 8-bit number called a flag.

The frame format of the bit-oriented protocol is shown in Figure 11-6. A frame starts with the 8-bit flag 01111110 followed by an address and control sequence. The information field is not restricted in format or content and can be of any length. The frame check field is a CRC (cyclic redundancy check) sequence used for detecting errors in transmission. The ending flag indicates to the receiver station that the 16 bits just received are the CRC bits. The ending flag can be followed by another frame or a sequence of flags or a sequence of consecutive 1's. When two frames follow each other, the intervening flag is simultaneously the ending flag of the first frame and the beginning flag of the next frame. If no information is exchanged, the transmitter sends a series of flags to keep the line in the active state. The line is said to be in the idle state with the occurrence of 15 or more consecutive 1's. Frames with certain control messages are sent without information fields. A frame must have a minimum of 32 bits between two flags to accommodate the address, control, and the frame check fields. The maximum length depends on the condition of the communication channel and its ability to transmit long messages error-free.

To prevent a flag from occurring in the middle of a frame, the bit-oriented protocol uses a method called *zero insertion*. This requires that a 0 be inserted by the transmitting station after any succession of five consecutive 1's. The receiver always removes a 0 that follows a succession of five 1's. In this way, the bit pattern 01111110 is transmitted as 011111010 when it does not signify a flag. The received sequence is restored to its original value by the removal of the 0 following the five 1's. As a consequence, no pattern 01111110 is ever transmitted between the beginning and ending flags.

11-4 MODES OF TRANSFER

Binary information received from an external device is usually stored in memory for later processing. Information transferred from the central computer into an external device originates in the memory unit. The CPU merely executes the I/O instructions and may accept the data temporarily, but the ultimate source or destination is the memory unit. Data transfer between the central computer and I/O devices may be handled in a variety of modes. Some modes use the CPU as an intermediate path; others transfer the data directly to and from the memory unit. Data transfer to and from peripherals may be handled in one of four possible modes:

1. Data transfer under program control.
2. Interrupt initiated data transfer.
3. Direct memory access (DMA) transfer.
4. Transfer through an I/O processor (IOP).

Program controlled operations are the result of I/O instructions written in the computer program. Each data item transfer is initiated by an instruction in the program. Usually, the transfer is to and from a CPU register and peripheral. Other instructions are needed to transfer the data to and from the CPU and memory. Transferring data under program control requires constant monitoring of the peripheral by the CPU. Once a data transfer is initiated, the CPU is required to monitor the interface to see when a transfer can again be made. It is up to the programmed instructions executed in the CPU to keep close tabs on everything that is taking place in the interface unit and the external device.

In the program controlled transfer, the CPU stays in a program loop until the I/O unit indicates that it is ready for data transfer. This is a time consuming process since it keeps the processor busy needlessly. It can be avoided by using an interrupt facility and special commands to inform the interface to issue an interrupt request signal when the data are available from the device. The CPU can proceed to execute another program. The interface, meanwhile, keeps monitoring the device. When the interface determines that the device is ready for data transfer, it generates an interrupt request to the computer. Upon detecting the external interrupt signal, the CPU momentarily stops the task it is processing, branches to a service program to process the data transfer, and then returns to the task it was originally performing.

Transfer of data under program control is through the I/O bus and between the CPU and a peripheral. In direct memory access (DMA), the interface transfers data into and out of the memory unit through the memory bus. The CPU initiates the transfer by supplying the interface with the starting address and the number of words needed to be transferred, and then proceeds to execute other tasks. When the transfer is made, the interface requests memory cycles through the memory bus. When the request is granted by the memory controller, the interface transfers the data directly into memory. The CPU merely delays its operation to allow the direct memory I/O transfer. Since peripheral speed is usually slower than processor speed, I/O memory transfers are infrequent compared to processor access to memory. DMA transfer is discussed in more detail in Section 11-6.

Many computers combine the interface logic with the requirements for direct memory access into one unit and call it an I/O processor (IOP). The IOP can handle many peripherals through a DMA and interrupt facility. In such a system, the computer is divided into three separate modules: the memory unit, the CPU, and the IOP. I/O processors are presented in Section 11-7.

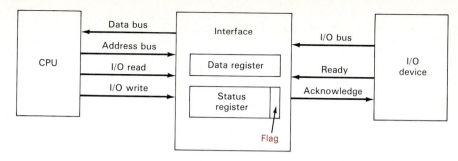

FIGURE 11-7
Data Transfer from Device to CPU

Example of Program Control Transfer

A simple example of data transfer from an I/O device through an interface into the CPU is shown in Figure 11-7. The device transfers bytes of data one at a time as they are available. When a byte of data is available, the device places it in the I/O bus and enables the ready line. The interface accepts the byte into its data register and enables the acknowledge line. The interface sets a bit in the status register which we will refer to as a *flag*. The device can now disable the ready line but it will not transfer another byte until the acknowledge line is disabled by the interface. This is according to the handshaking procedure established in Section 11-2.

Under program control, the CPU must check the flag to determine if there is a new byte in the interface data register. This is done by reading the status register into a CPU register and checking the value of the flag bit. If the flag is equal to 1, the CPU reads the data from the data register. The flag bit is then cleared to 0 either by the CPU or the interface, depending on how the interface circuits are designed. Once the flag is cleared, the interface disables the acknowledge line and the device can transfer the next data byte.

A flowchart of the program that must be written for the transfer is shown in Figure 11-8. The flowchart assumes that the device is sending a sequence of bytes which must be stored in memory. The program continually examines the status of the interface until the flag is set to 1. Each byte is brought into the CPU and transferred to memory until all of the data have been transferred.

The program control data transfer is used only in small computers or in systems that are dedicated to monitor a device continuously. The difference in information transfer rate between the CPU and the I/O device makes this type of transfer inefficient. To see why this is inefficient, consider a typical computer that can execute the instructions to read the status register and check the flag in 1 μsec. Assume that the input device transfers its data at an average rate of 100 bytes per second. This is equivalent to one byte every 10,000 μsec. This means that the CPU will check the flag 10,000 times between each transfer. The CPU is wasting time while checking the flag instead of doing some other useful processing task.

Interrupt Initiated Transfer

An alternative to the CPU constantly monitoring the flag is to let the interface inform the computer when it is ready to transfer data. This mode of transfer uses the interrupt facility. While the CPU is running a program, it does not check the

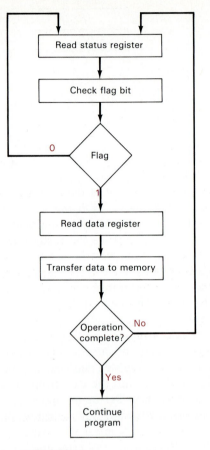

FIGURE 11-8
Flowchart for CPU Program to Input
Data

flag. However, when the flag is set, the computer is momentarily interrupted from proceeding with the current program and is informed of the fact that the flag has been set. The CPU deviates from what it is doing to take care of the input or output transfer. After the transfer is completed, the computer returns to the previous program to continue what it was doing before the interrupt.

The CPU responds to the interrupt signal by storing the return address from the program counter into a memory stack and then control branches to a service routine that processes the required I/O transfer. The way that the processor chooses the branch address of the service routine varies from one unit to another. In principle, there are two methods for accomplishing this. One is called *vectored interrupt* and the other *nonvectored interrupt*. In a nonvectored interrupt, the branch address is assigned to a fixed location in memory. In a vectored interrupt, the source that interrupts supplies the branch information to the computer. This information is called the *vector address*. In some computers the vector address is the first address of the service routine. In other computers, the vector address is an address that points to a location in memory where the first address of the service routine is stored. The vectored interrupt procedure is presented in Section 9-9 in conjunction with Figure 9-8.

11-5 PRIORITY INTERRUPT

A typical computer has a number of I/O devices attached to it with each device being able to originate an interrupt request. The first task of the interrupt system is to identify the source of the interrupt. There is also the possibility that several sources will request service simultaneously. In this case, the system must also decide which device to service first.

A priority interrupt is a system that establishes a priority over the various sources to determine which condition is to be serviced first when two or more requests arrive simultaneously. The system may also determine which conditions are permitted to interrupt the computer while another interrupt is being serviced. Higher priority interrupt levels are assigned to requests which, if delayed or interrupted, could have serious consequences. Devices with high speed transfers such as magnetic disks are given high priority and slow devices such as keyboards receive the lowest priority. When two devices interrupt the computer at the same time, the computer services the device with the higher priority first.

Establishing the priority of simultaneous interrupts can be done by software or hardware. A polling procedure is used to identify the highest priority source by software means. In this method, there is one common branch address for all interrupts. The program that takes care of interrupts begins at the branch address and polls the interrupt sources in sequence. The order in which they are tested determines the priority of each interrupt. The highest priority source is tested first and if its interrupt signal is on, control branches to a service routine for this source. Otherwise, the next lower priority source is tested, and so on. Thus, the initial service routine for all interrupts consists of a program that tests the interrupt sources in sequence and branches to one of many possible service routines. The particular service routine reached belongs to the highest priority device among all devices that interrupted the computer. The disadvantage of the software method is that if there are many interrupts, the time required to poll them can exceed the time available to service the I/O device. In this situation, a hardware priority interrupt unit can be used to speed up the operation.

A hardware priority interrupt unit functions as an overall manager in an interrupt system environment. It accepts interrupt requests from many sources, determines which of the incoming requests has the highest priority, and issues an interrupt request to the computer based on this determination. To speed up the operation, each interrupt source has its own interrupt vector address to access directly its own service routine. Thus, no polling is required because all the decisions are established by the hardware priority interrupt unit. The hardware priority function can be established either by a serial or parallel connection of interrupt lines. The serial connection is also known as the daisy chain method.

Daisy Chain Priority

The daisy chain method of establishing priority consists of a serial connection of all devices that request an interrupt. The device with the highest priority is placed in the first position, followed by lower priority devices in descending priority order to the lowest priority device, which is placed last in the chain. This method of connection between three devices and the CPU is shown in Figure 11-9. The interrupt request line is common to all devices and forms a wired logic connection. If any device has its interrupt signal in the low-level state, the interrupt line goes to the low-level state and enables the interrupt input in the CPU. When no interrupts are pending, the interrupt line stays in the high-level state and no interrupts are recognized by the CPU. This is equivalent to a negative-logic OR operation. The CPU responds to an interrupt request by enabling the interrupt acknowledge line. This signal is received by device 1 at its *PI* (priority in) input. The acknowledge signal passes on to the next device through the *PO* (priority out) output only if device 1 is not requesting an interrupt. If device 1 has a pending interrupt, it blocks the acknowledge signal from the next device by placing a 0 in the *PO* output. It then proceeds to insert its own interrupt vector address (*VAD*) into the data bus for the CPU to use during the interrupt cycle.

A device with a 0 in its *PI* input generates a 0 in its *PO* output to inform the next-lower-priority device that the acknowledge signal has been blocked. A device that is requesting an interrupt and has a 1 in its *PI* input will intercept the acknowledge signal by placing a 0 in its *PO* output. If the device does not have pending interrupts, it transmits the acknowledge signal to the next device by placing a 1 in its *PO* output. Thus, the device with *PI* = 1 and *PO* = 0 is the one with the highest priority that is requesting an interrupt and this device places its *VAD* on the data bus. The daisy chain arrangement gives the highest priority to the device that receives the interrupt acknowledge signal from the CPU. The farther the device is from the first position, the lower is its priority.

Figure 11-10 shows the internal logic that must be included within each device when connected in the daisy chain scheme. The device sets its RF flip-flop when it wants to interrupt the CPU. The output of the RF flip-flop goes through an

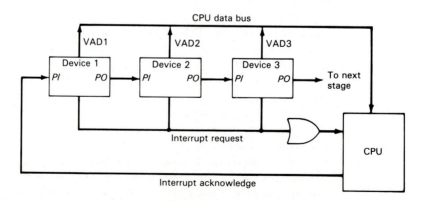

FIGURE 11-9
Daisy Chain Priority Interrupt

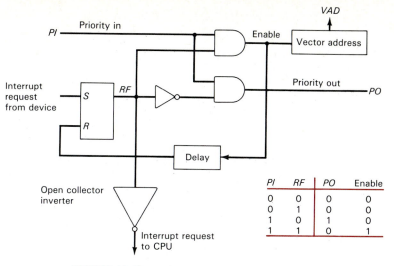

PI	RF	PO	Enable
0	0	0	0
0	1	0	0
1	0	1	0
1	1	0	1

FIGURE 11-10
One Stage of the Daisy Chain Priority Arrangement

open-collector inverter, a circuit that provides the wired logic for the common interrupt line. If $PI = 0$, both PO and the enable line to VAD are equal to 0, irrespective of the value of RF. If $PI = 1$ and $RF = 0$, then $PO = 1$ and the vector address is disabled. This condition passes the acknowledge signal to the next device through PO. The device is active when $PI = 1$ and $RF = 1$. This condition places a 0 in PO and enables the vector address for the data bus. It is assumed that each device has its own distinct vector address. The RF flip-flop is reset after a sufficient delay to ensure that the CPU has received the vector address.

Parallel Priority Hardware

The parallel priority interrupt method uses a register with bits set separately by the interrupt signal from each device. Priority is established according to the position of the bits in the register. In addition to the interrupt register the circuit may include a mask register to control the status of each interrupt request. The mask register can be programmed to disable lower priority interrupts while a higher priority device is being serviced. It can also provide a facility that allows a high priority device to interrupt the CPU while a lower priority device is being serviced.

The priority logic for a system of four interrupt sources is shown in Figure 11-11. It consists of an interrupt register with individual bits set by external conditions and cleared by program instructions. Interrupt input 3 has the highest priority and input 0 has the lowest priority. The mask register has the same number of bits as the interrupt register. By means of program instructions, it is possible to set or reset any bit in the mask register. Each interrupt bit and its corresponding mask bit are applied to an AND gate to produce the four inputs to a priority encoder. In this way, an interrupt is recognized only if its corresponding mask bit is set to 1 by the program. The priority encoder generates two bits of the vector address which is transferred to the CPU via the data bus. Output V of the encoder is set to 1 if an interrupt that is not masked has occurred. This provides the interrupt signal for the CPU.

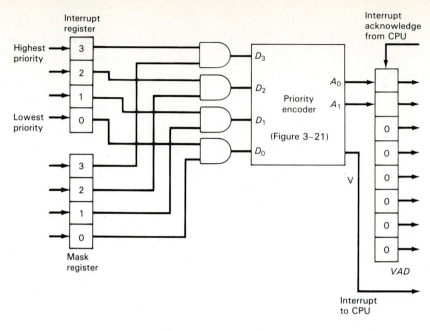

FIGURE 11-11
Priority Interrupt Hardware

The priority encoder is a circuit that implements the priority function. The logic of the priority encoder is such that, if two or more inputs occur at the same time, the input having the highest priority takes precedence. The circuit of a four-input priority encoder can be found in Section 3-6 and its truth table is listed in Table 3-8. Input D_3 has the highest priority, and so regardless of the values of other inputs, when this input is 1, the output is $A_1 A_0 = 11$. D_2 has the next priority level. The output is 10 if $D_2 = 1$ provided that $D_3 = 0$, regardless of the values of the other two lower priority inputs. The output is 01 when $D_1 = 1$ provided the two higher priority inputs are equal to 0; and so on down the priority levels. The interrupt output labeled V is equal to 1 when one or more inputs are equal to 1. If all inputs are 0, V is 0 and the other two outputs of the encoder are not used. This is because the vector address is not transferred to the CPU when $V = 0$.

The output of the priority encoder is used to form part of the vector address for the interrupt source. The other bits of the vector address can be assigned any values. For example, the vector address can be formed by appending six zeros to the outputs of the encoder. With this choice the interrupt vector for the four I/O devices are assigned the 8-bit binary numbers equivalent to decimal 0, 1, 2, and 3.

11-6 DIRECT MEMORY ACCESS (DMA)

The transfer of data between a fast storage device such as magnetic disk and memory is often limited by the speed of the CPU. Removing the CPU from the path and letting the peripheral device manage the memory buses directly would improve the speed of transfer. This transfer technique is called direct memory access (DMA). During DMA transfer, the CPU is idle and has no control of the memory buses.

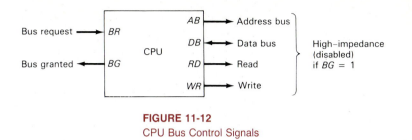

FIGURE 11-12
CPU Bus Control Signals

A DMA controller takes over the buses to manage the transfer directly between the I/O device and memory.

The CPU may be placed in an idle state in a variety of ways. One common method extensively used in microprocessors is to disable the buses through special control signals. Figure 11-12 shows two control signals in a CPU that facilitate the DMA transfer. The *bus request* (*BR*) input is used by the DMA controller to request from the CPU to relinquish control of the buses. When this input is active, the CPU terminates the execution of its present instruction and places the address bus, the data bus, and the read and write lines into a high-impedance state. After this is done, the CPU activates the *bus granted* (*BG*) output to inform the external DMA that it can take control of the buses. As long as the *BG* line is active, the CPU is idle and the buses are disabled. When the bus request input is disabled by the DMA, the CPU returns to its normal operation, disables the bus granted output, and takes control of the buses.

When the bus granted line is enabled, the external DMA controller takes control of the bus system to communicate directly with the memory. The transfer can be made for an entire block of memory words, suspending the CPU operation until the entire block is transferred. This is referred to as *burst transfer*. The transfer can be made one word at a time between CPU instruction executions. Such transfer is called *single cycle* or *cycle stealing*. The CPU merely delays its operation for one memory cycle to allow the direct memory I/O transfer to steal one memory cycle.

DMA Controller

The DMA controller needs the usual circuits of an interface to communicate with the CPU and I/O device. In addition, it needs an address register, a word count register, and a set of address lines. The address register and address lines are used for direct communication with the memory. The word count register specifies the number of words that must be transferred. The data transfer may be done directly between the device and memory under control of the DMA.

Figure 11-13 shows the block diagram of a typical DMA controller. The unit communicates with the CPU via the data bus and control lines. The registers in the DMA are selected by the CPU through the address bus by enabling the *DS* (DMA select) and *RS* (register select) inputs. The *RD* (read) and *WR* (write) inputs are bidirectional. When the *BG* (bus granted) input is 0, the CPU can communicate with the DMA registers through the data bus to read from or write to the DMA registers. When *BG* = 1, the CPU has relinquished the buses and the DMA can communicate directly with the memory by specifying an address in the address bus

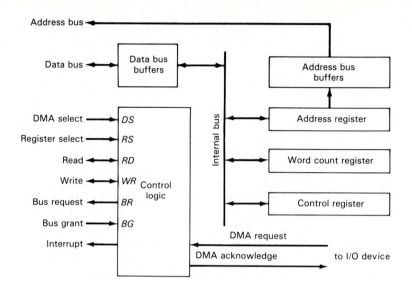

FIGURE 11-13
Block Diagram of a DMA Controller

and activating the *RD* or *WR* control. The DMA communicates with the external peripheral through the request and acknowledge lines by using a prescribed handshaking procedure.

The DMA controller has three registers: an address register, a word count register, and a control register. The address register contains an address to specify the desired location in memory. The address bits go through bus buffers into the address bus. The address register is incremented after each word is transferred to memory. The word count register holds the number of words to be transferred. This register is decremented by one after each word transfer and internally tested for zero. The control register specifies the mode of transfer. All registers in the DMA appear to the CPU as I/O interface registers. Thus, the CPU can read from or write to the DMA registers under program control via the data bus.

The DMA is first initialized by the CPU. After that, the DMA starts and continues to transfer data between memory and peripheral unit until an entire block is transferred. The initialization process is essentially a program consisting of I/O instructions that include the address for selecting particular DMA registers. The CPU initializes the DMA by sending the following information through the data bus:

1. The starting address of the memory block where data are available (for read) or where data are to be stored (for write)
2. The word count, which is the number of words in the memory block.
3. Control to specify the mode of transfer such as read or write.
4. A control to start the DMA transfer.

The starting address is stored in the address register. The word count is stored in the word count register, and the control information in the control register. Once the DMA is initialized, the microprocessor stops communicating with the DMA unless it receives an interrupt signal or if it wants to check how many words have been transferred.

DMA Transfer

The position of the DMA controller among the other components in a computer system is illustrated in Figure 11-14. The CPU communicates with the DMA through the address and data buses as with any interface unit. The DMA has its own address which activates the *DS* and *RS* lines. The CPU initializes the DMA through the data bus. Once the DMA receives the start control bit, it can start the transfer between the peripheral device and the memory.

When the peripheral device sends a DMA request, the DMA controller activates the *BR* line, informing the CPU to relinquish the buses. The CPU responds with its *BG* line, informing the DMA that its buses are disabled. The DMA then puts the current value of its address register onto the address bus, initiates the *RD* or *WR* signal, and sends a DMA acknowledge to the peripheral device.

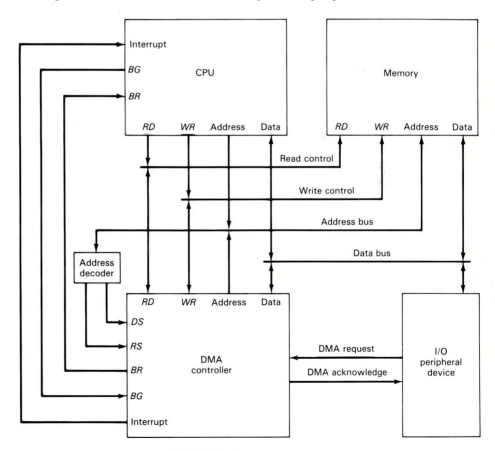

FIGURE 11-14
DMA Transfer in a Computer System

When the peripheral device receives a DMA acknowledge, it puts a word in the data bus (for write) or receives a word from the data bus (for read). Thus, the DMA controls the read or write operations and supplies the address for the memory. The peripheral unit can then communicate with memory through the data bus for direct transfer between the two units while the CPU is momentarily disabled.

For each word that is transferred, the DMA increments its address register and decrements its word count register. If the word count does not reach zero, the DMA checks the request line coming from the peripheral. For a high speed device, the line will be activated as soon as the previous transfer is completed. A second transfer is then initiated, and the process continues until the entire block is transferred. If the peripheral speed is slower, the DMA request line may come somewhat later. In this case, the DMA disables the bus request line so the CPU can continue to execute its program. When the peripheral requests a transfer, the DMA requests the buses again.

If the word count reaches zero, the DMA stops any further transfer and removes its bus request. It also informs the CPU of the termination by means of an interrupt. When the CPU responds to the interrupt, it reads the content of the word count register. The zero value of this register indicates that all the words were successfully transferred. The CPU can read this register at any time, as well check the number of words already transferred.

A DMA controller may have more than one channel. In this case, each channel has a request and acknowledge pair of control signals that are connected to separate peripheral devices. Each channel also has its own address register and word count register within the DMA controller. A priority among the channels may be established so that channels with high priority are serviced before channels with lower priority.

DMA transfer is very useful in many applications. It is used for fast transfer of information between magnetic disks and memory. It is also useful for updating the display in an interactive terminal. Typically, an image of the screen display of the terminal is kept in memory which can be updated under program control. The contents of the memory can be transferred to the screen periodically by means of DMA transfer.

11-7   MULTIPLE PROCESSOR SYSTEMS

Instead of having each interface communicate with the CPU, a computer may incorporate one or more external processors and assign them the task of communicating directly with all I/O devices. An input-ouput processor (IOP) may be classified as a processor with direct memory access capability that communicates with I/O devices. In this configuration, the computer system can be divided into a memory unit, and a number of processors comprised of the CPU and one or more IOPs. Each IOP takes care of input and output tasks, relieving the CPU of the housekeeping chores involved in I/O transfers. A processor that communicates with remote terminals over telephone and other communication media in a serial fashion is called a data communication processor (DCP).

A multiple processor system is an interconnection of two or more processors sharing a common memory and input-output equipment. The term processor includes CPU, IOP, DCP, and any other type of processor that the system may have. A multiple processor system may have multiple CPUs in addition to other processors.

Although large scale computers include two or more CPUs in their overall system configuration, it is the emergence of the microprocessor, or a CPU on a chip, that has been the major motivation for multiple processor systems. The fact that microprocessors take very little physical space and are very inexpensive brings about the feasibility of interconnecting a large number of microprocessors into a composite system. Very large scale integration circuit technology has reduced the cost of computer components to such a low level that the concept of applying multiple processors to meet system performance requirements has become an attractive design possibility.

The benefits derived from multiple processor organization is an improved system performance. It is achieved through partitioning an overall function into a number of tasks that each processor can handle individually. System tasks may be allocated to special purpose processors whose design is optimized to perform certain types of processing efficiently. An example is a computer system where one processor performs the computations for an industrial process control while others monitor and control the various parameters, such as temperature and flow rate. Another example is a computer where one processor performs high speed floating-point arithmetic computations and another takes care of routine data processing tasks. Performance also can be improved if a program can be decomposed into parallel executable tasks. The system function can be distributed among parallel concurrently-executing processors operating in parallel to reduce the overall execution time.

Multiprocessing improves the reliability of the system so that a failure or error in one part has a limited effect on the rest of the system. If a fault causes one processor to fail, a second processor can be assigned to perform the functions of the disabled processor. The system as a whole can continue to operate correctly with, perhaps, some loss in efficiency.

Input-Output Processor (IOP)

The IOP is similar to a CPU except that it is designed to handle the details of I/O processing. Unlike the DMA controller that must be set up entirely by the CPU, the IOP can fetch and execute its own instructions. IOP instructions are specifically designed to facilitate I/O transfers. In addition, the IOP can perform other processing tasks such as arithmetic, logic, branching, and code translation.

The block diagram of a computer with two processors is shown in Figure 11-15. The memory unit occupies a central position and can communicate with each processor by means of direct memory access. The CPU is responsible for processing data needed in the solution of computational tasks. The IOP provides a path for transfer of data between various peripheral devices and the memory unit. The CPU is usually assigned the task of initiating the I/O program. From then on, the IOP

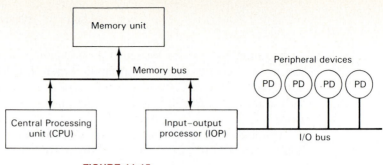

FIGURE 11-15
Block Diagram of a Computer with I/O Processor

operates independent of the CPU and continues to transfer data from external devices and memory.

The data formats of peripheral devices differ from memory and CPU data formats. The IOP must structure data words from many different sources. For example, it may be necessary to take four bytes from an input device and pack them into one 32-bit word before the transfer to memory. Data are gathered in the IOP at the device rate and bit capacity while the CPU is executing its own program. After the input data is assembled into a memory word, it is transferred from IOP directly into memory by stealing one memory cycle from the CPU. Similarly, an output word transferred from memory to the IOP is directed from the IOP to the output device at the device rate and bit capacity.

The communication between the IOP and the devices attached to it is similar to the program control method of transfer. Communication with the memory is similar to the direct memory access method. The way by which the CPU and IOP communicate depends on the level of sophistication included in the system. In very large scale computers, each processor is independent of all others and any one processor can initiate an operation. In most computer systems, the CPU is the master, while the IOP is a slave processor. The CPU is assigned the task of initiating all operations but I/O instructions are executed in the IOP. CPU instructions provide operations to start an I/O transfer and also to test I/O status conditions needed for making decisions on various I/O activities. The IOP, in turn, typically asks for CPU attention by means of an interrupt. It also responds to CPU requests by placing a status word in a prescribed location in memory to be examined later by a CPU program. When an I/O operation is desired, the CPU informs the IOP where to find the I/O program and then leaves the transfer details to the IOP.

Instructions that are read from memory by an IOP are sometimes called *commands*, to distinguish them from instructions that are read by the CPU. An instruction and a command have similar functions. Commands are prepared by experienced programmers and are stored in memory. The command words constitute the program for the IOP. The CPU informs the IOP where to find the commands in memory when it is time to execute the I/O program.

The communication between CPU and IOP may take different forms depending on the particular computer considered. In most cases, the memory unit acts as a message center where each processor leaves information for the other. To appreciate the operation of a typical IOP, we will illustrate, by a specific example, the method by which the CPU and IOP communicate. This is a simplified example that omits many operating details in order to provide an overview of basic concepts.

The sequence of operations may be carried out as shown in the flowchart of Figure 11-16. The CPU sends an instruction to test the IOP path. The IOP responds by inserting a status word in memory for the CPU to check. The bits of the status word indicate the condition of the IOP and I/O device, such as IOP overload condition, device busy with another transfer, or device ready for I/O transfer. The CPU refers to the status word in memory to decide what to do next. If all is in order, the CPU sends the instruction to start I/O transfer. The memory address received with this instruction tells the IOP where to find its program.

The CPU can now continue with another program while the IOP is busy with the I/O program. Both programs refer to memory by means of DMA transfer. When the IOP terminates the execution of its program, it sends an interrupt request

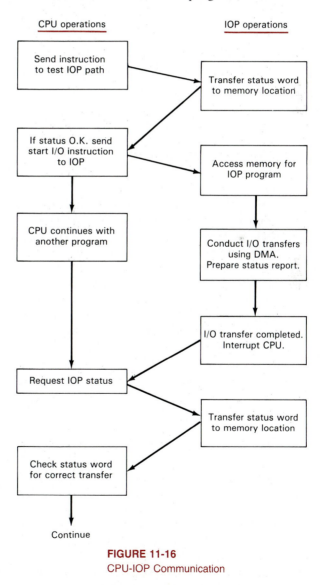

FIGURE 11-16
CPU-IOP Communication

to the CPU. The CPU responds to the interrupt by issuing an instruction to read the status from the IOP. The IOP responds by placing the contents of its status report into a specified memory location. The status word indicates whether the transfer has been completed or if any errors occurred during the transfer. From inspection of the bits in the status word, the CPU determines if the I/O operation was completed satisfactorily, without errors.

The IOP takes care of all data transfers between several I/O units and memory while the CPU is processing another program. The IOP and CPU compete for the use of memory so the number of devices that can be in operation is limited by the access time of the memory. It is not possible to saturate the memory by I/O devices in most systems, as the speed of most devices is much slower than the CPU. However, some very fast units, such as magnetic disks, can use an appreciable number of the available memory cycles. In that case, the speed of the CPU may deteriorate because it will often have to wait for the IOP to conduct memory transfers.

Interconnection Between Processors

The components that form a multiple processor system are CPUs, IOPs connected to input and output devices, and a memory unit that may be partitioned into a number of separate modules. The interconnection between the components can have different physical configurations depending on the number of transfer paths that are available between the processors and memory.

One possible configuration employs a common bus system with all the processors connected through a common path to memory. A time-shared common bus for four processors is shown in Figure 11-17. Only one processor can communicate with the memory at any given time. Transfer operations are conducted by the processor that is in control of the bus at the time. Any other processor wishing to initiate a transfer must first determine the availability status of the bus, and only after the bus becomes available can the processor address the memory to initiate the transfer. The system may exhibit memory access conflicts since one common bus is shared by all processors. Memory contentions must be resolved with a bus controller that establishes priorities among the requesting processors.

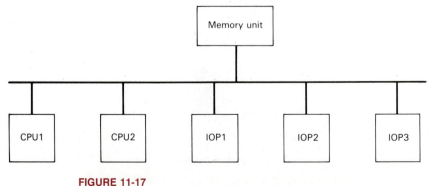

FIGURE 11-17
Time Shared Common Bus Multiple Processor Organization

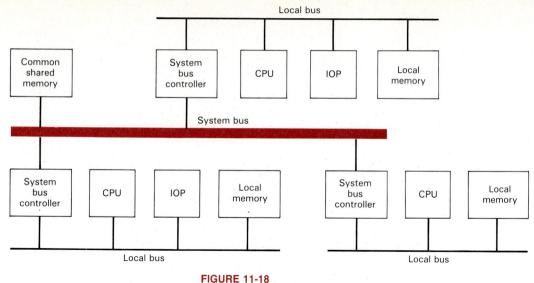

FIGURE 11-18
Dual-Bus Structure for Multiple Processors

A single common bus is restricted to one transfer at a time. This means that when one processor is communicating with the memory, all other processors are either busy with internal operations or must be idle waiting for the bus. The processors in the system can be kept busy more often through the implementation of a dual-bus structure as depicted in Figure 11-18. Here we have a number of local buses, each connected to its own local memory and to one or more processors. Each local bus may be connected to a CPU, an IOP, or any combination of processors. A system bus controller links each local bus to a common system bus. The memory connected to the common system bus is shared by all processors. If an IOP is connected directly to a system bus. The I/O devices attached to it may be made available to all processors. Only one processor can communicate with the shared memory and other common resources through the system bus at any given time. The other processors are kept busy communicating with their local memory and I/O devices.

Although the system shown in Figure 11-18 qualifies as a multiple processor system it can be classified more correctly as a multiple computer system. This is because a CPU, IOP, and memory, when connected together with a local bus, constitute a computer system in their own right. This type of multiple processor organization is the one most commonly employed in the design of multiple microprocessor systems.

Interprocessor Communication

The various processors in a multiple processor system must be provided with a facility for communicating with each other. The most common procedure is to set aside a portion of memory which is accessible to all processors. The primary use of the common memory is to act as a message center similar to a mailbox, where each processor can leave messages for other processors and pick up messages intended for it.

The sending processor structures a request, a message, or a procedure, and places it in the memory mailbox. Status bits residing in common memory are generally used to indicate the condition of the mailbox, whether it contains meaningful information and for which processor intended. The receiving processor can check the mailbox periodically to determine if there are valid messages for it. The response time of this procedure can be time consuming, since a processor will recognize a request only when it performs the polling of messages. A more efficient procedure is for the sending processor to alert the receiving processor directly by means of an interrupt signal. This can be accomplished through a software initiated interprocessor interrupt. It is done by an instruction in the program of one processor which when executed, produces an external interrupt condition in a second processor. This alerts the interrupted processor of the fact that a new message was inserted by the interrupting processor.

In addition to shared memory, a multiple processor system may have other shared resources. For example, a magnetic disk storage unit connected to an IOP may be available to all CPUs. This provides a facility for sharing of system programs stored in the disk. A communication path between two CPUs also can be established through a link between two IOPs associated with two different CPUs. This type of link allows each CPU to treat the other as an I/O device so that messages can be transferred through the I/O path.

Each processor in a multiple processor system must request access to common memory and other shared resources through a common bus system. If no other processor is currently using the common bus, the requesting processor may be granted access immediately. However, the requesting processor must wait if another processor is currently using the system bus. Furthermore, other processors may request the system bus at the same time. Arbitration must be performed to resolve this multiple contention for the shared resources. Arbitration procedures service all processor requests on the basis of established priority. The bus arbitration technique bears a strong resemblance to the interrupt priority logic discussed in Section 11-5.

A multiple processor system is considered to be a *tightly coupled* system. This is characteristic of a system that has all its major components (such as CPU, IOP, and I/O devices) in close proximity. Computers that are interconnected with each other by means of remote communication lines form a *computer network*. The computers in the network may be close to each other or in geographically remote locations. Synchronous serial transfer is employed to send messages between the computers. Data and control are transmitted in packets and each packet follows a prescribed communication protocol. The distinction that is made between a tightly coupled computer system and a computer network is that the former uses shared memory to communicate between the processors. The computers in a network communicate with each other in a serial fashion through a communication medium.

REFERENCES

1. MANO, M. M. *Computer System Architecture*. 2nd ed. Englewood Cliffs: Prentice-Hall, 1982.

2. LIPPIATT, A. G. AND WRIGHT, G. L. *The Architecture of Small Computer Systems*. 2nd ed. Englewood Cliffs: Prentice-Hall, 1985.

3. LIU, Y. C. AND GIBSON, G. A. *Microcomputer Systems: The 8086/8088 Family*. 2nd ed. Englewood Cliffs: Prentice-Hall, 1986.

4. HAMACHER, V. C., VRANESIC, Z. G. AND ZAKY, S. G. *Computer Organization*. 2nd ed. New York: McGraw-Hill, 1984.

5. HWANG, K. AND BRIGGS, F. A. *Computer Architecture and Parallel Processing*. New York: McGraw-Hill, 1984.

PROBLEMS

11-1 The addresses assigned to the four registers of the I/O interface of Figure 11-2 are equal to the binary equivalent of 12, 13, 14, and 15. Show the external circuit that must be connected between an 8-bit I/O address from the CPU and the CS, $RS0$, and $RS1$ inputs of the interface.

11-2 Six interface units of the type shown in Figure 11-2 are connected to a CPU that uses an I/O address of eight bits. Each one of the six chip select (CS) inputs is connected to a different address line. Thus, the high-order address line is connected to the CS input of the first interface unit and the sixth address line is connected to the CS input of the sixth interface unit. The two low-order address lines are connected to the $RS1$ and $RS0$ of all six interface units. Determine the 8-bit address of each register in each interface. (Total of 24 addresses.)

11-3 Derive a timing diagram and a sequence of events flow chart (as in Figure 11-3) for a transfer from the I/O device into the interface unit assuming that the interface initiates the transfer with a *request* handshake line. The other handshake is a *data ready* line from the device to the interface.

11-4 A commercial interface unit uses different names for the handshake lines associated with the transfer of data from the I/O device into the interface unit. The interface input handshake line is labeled STB (strobe), and the interface output handshake line is labeled IBF (input buffer full). A low-level signal on STB loads data from the I/O bus into the interface data register. A high-level signal on IBF indicates that the data item has been accepted by the interface. IBF goes low after an I/O read signal from the CPU when it reads the contents of the data register.
(a) Draw a block diagram showing the CPU, the interface, and the I/O device along with the pertinent interconnections between the three units.
(b) Draw a timing diagram for the handshaking transfer.
(c) Obtain a sequence of events flowchart for the transfer from the device to the interface and from the interface to the CPU.

11-5 How many characters per second can be transmitted over a 1200-baud line in each of the following modes? (Assume a character code of eight bits.)
(a) Synchronous serial transmission.
(b) Asynchronous serial transmission with two stop bits.
(c) Asynchronous serial transmission with one stop bit.

11-6 The address of a terminal connected to a data communication processor consists of two letters of the alphabet or a letter followed by one of the 10 numerals. How many different addresses can be formulated?

11-7 Sketch the timing diagram of the eleven bits (similar to Figure 11-4) that are transmitted over an asynchronous serial communication line when the ASCII letter C is transmitted with even parity.

11-8 What is the difference between synchronous and asynchronous serial transfer of information?

11-9 What is the minimum number of bits that a frame must have in the bit-oriented protocol?

11-10 Show how the zero insertion works in the bit-oriented protocol when a zero followed by the 10 bits that represent the binary equivalent of 1023 is transmitted.

11-11 Show the block diagram (similar to Figure 11-7) for the data transfer from the CPU to the interface and then to the I/O device. Determine a procedure for setting and clearing the flag bit.

11-12 Using the configuration established in Problem 11-11, obtain a flowchart (similar to Figure 11-8) for the CPU program to output data.

11-13 What is the basic advantage of using interrupt initiated data transfer over transfer under program control without an interrupt?

11-14 What happens in the daisy chain priority interrupt shown in Figure 11-9 when device 1 requests an interrupt after device 2 has sent an interrupt request to the CPU but before the CPU responds with the interrupt acknowledge?

11-15 Consider a computer without priority interrupt hardware. Any one of many sources can interrupt the computer and any interrupt request results in storing the return address and branching to a common interrupt routine. Explain how a priority can be established in the interrupt service program.

11-16 What should be done in Figure 11-11 to make the four *VAD* values equal to the binary equivalent of 76, 77, 78, and 79?

11-17 Design a parallel priority interrupt hardware for a system with eight interrupt sources.

11-18 (a) Obtain the truth table of an 8 × 3 priority encoder.
(b) The three outputs x, y, z, from the priority encoder are used to provide an 8-bit vector address in the form 101xyz00. List the eight addresses starting from the one with the highest priority.

11-19 Why are the read and write control lines in a DMA controller bidirectional? Under what condition and for what purpose are they used as inputs? Under what condition and for what purpose are they used as outputs?

11-20 It is necessary to transfer 256 words from a magnetic disk to a memory section starting from address 1230. The transfer is by means of the DMA as shown in Figure 11-14.
(a) Give the initial values that the CPU must transfer to the DMA controller.
(b) Give the step-by-step account of the actions taken during the input of the first two words.

11-21 What is the purpose of the system bus controller in Figure 11-18? Explain how the system can be designed to distinguish between references to local memory and references to commonly shared memory.

MEMORY MANAGEMENT

12-1 MEMORY HIERARCHY

The memory unit is an essential component in any digital computer since it is needed for storing programs and data. A very small computer with a limited application may be able to fulfill its intended task without the need of additional storage capacity. Most general purpose computers would run more efficiently if they are equipped with additional storage beyond the capacity of the main memory. There is just not enough space in one memory unit to accommodate all the programs used in a typical computer. Moreover, most computer installations accumulate and continue to accumulate large amounts of information. Not all accumulated information is needed by the processor at the same time. Therefore, it is more economical to use low cost storage devices to serve as backup for storing the information that is not currently used by the CPU. The memory unit that communicates directly with the CPU is called the *main memory*. Devices that provide backup storage are called *auxiliary memory*. The most common auxiliary memory devices used in computer systems are magnetic disks and magnetic tapes. Only programs and data currently needed by the processor reside in main memory. All other binary information is stored in auxiliary memory and transferred to main memory on a demand basis.

The total memory capacity of a computer can be visualized as being a hierarchy of components. The memory hierarchy system consists of all storage devices employed in a computer system from the slow but high capacity auxiliary memory to a relatively faster main memory, to an even smaller and faster cache memory accessible to the high speed processing logic. Figure 12-1 illustrates the components in a typical memory hierarchy. At the bottom of the hierarchy are the relatively slow magnetic tapes used to store removable files. Next are the magnetic disks used as backup storage. The main memory occupies a central position by being able to communicate directly with the CPU and with auxiliary memory devices through an I/O processor. When programs not residing in main memory are needed by the CPU, they are brought in from auxiliary memory. Programs not currently needed in main memory are transferred into auxiliary memory to provide space for currently used programs and data.

A special very high speed memory is sometimes used to increase the speed of processing by making current programs and data available to the CPU at a rapid rate. The cache memory included in Figure 12-1 is employed in computer systems to compensate for the speed differential between main memory access time and processor logic. Processor logic is usually faster than main memory access time with the result that processing speed is mostly limited by the speed of main memory. A technique used to compensate for the mismatch in operating speeds is to employ an extremely fast, small memory between the CPU and main memory with an access time close to processor logic propagation delays. This type of memory is called a *cache* memory. It is used to store segments of programs, currently being executed in the CPU, and temporary data, frequently needed in the calculations. By making programs and data available at a rapid rate, it is possible to increase the performance rate of the processor. The organization of cache memories is presented in Section 12-4.

In a computer system where the demand for service is high, it is customary to run all programs in one of two modes: a *batch mode* or *time-sharing mode*. In the batch mode, the programs are prepared off-line without the direct use of the computer. An operator loads all programs into the computer where they are executed one at a time. The operator retrieves the printed output and returns it to the user. What makes the batch mode efficient is the fact that programs can be fed into the computer as fast as they can be processed. In this way it is ensured that the computer is busy processing information most of the time.

In the time-sharing mode, many users communicate with the computer via remote interactive terminals. Because of slow human response compared to computer speed, the computer can respond to multiple users at the same time. This is accomplished by having many programs reside in memory while the system allocates a time-slice to each program for execution in the CPU.

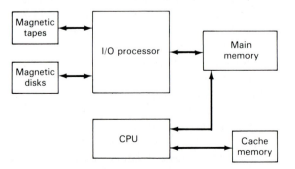

FIGURE 12-1
Memory Hierarchy in a Computer System

A major concept common to both batch and time-sharing modes is their use of *multiprogramming*. Multiprogramming refers to the existence of many programs in different parts of main memory at the same time. Thus, it is possible to keep all parts of the computer busy by working with several programs in sequence. For example, suppose a program is being executed in the CPU and an I/O transfer is required. The CPU initiates the I/O processor to start executing the transfer. This leaves the CPU free to execute another program. In a multiprogramming system, when one program is waiting for input or output transfer, there is another program ready to use the CPU.

With multiprogramming, the need arises for running partial programs, for varying the amount of main memory in use by a given program, and for moving programs around the memory hierarchy. Computer programs are sometimes too long to be accommodated in the total space available in main memory. Moreover, a computer system uses many programs and all the programs cannot reside in main memory at all times. A program with its data normally resides in auxiliary memory. When the program or a segment of the program is to be executed, it is transferred to main memory to be executed by the CPU. Thus, one may think of auxiliary memory as containing the totality of information stored in a computer system. It is the task of the operating system to maintain in main memory a portion of this information that is currently active. The part of the computer system that supervises the flow of information between auxiliary memory and main memory is called the *memory management system*. The hardware for a memory management system is presented in Section 12-5.

Other topics covered in this chapter are pipeline processing and associative memory. Pipeline processing is a technique for speeding the operations in a computer system. The associative memory is a content addressable type memory that is often used as part of a memory management system.

12-2 PIPELINE PROCESSING

Pipeline is a technique of decomposing a sequential process into suboperations with each subprocess being executed in a special dedicated segment that operates concurrently with all other segments. A pipeline can be visualized as a collection of processing segments through which binary information flows. Each segment performs partial processing dictated by the way the task is partitioned. The result obtained from the computation in each segment is transferred to the next segment in the pipeline. The final result is obtained after the data have passed through all segments. The name pipeline implies a flow of information analogous to an industrial assembly line. It is characteristic of pipelines that several computations can be in progress in distinct segments at the same time. The overlapping of computations is made possible by associating a register with each segment in the pipeline. The registers provide isolation between segments so that all can operate on separate data simultaneously.

The pipeline organization will be demonstrated by means of a simple example. Suppose that we want to perform the combined multiply and add operations with a stream of numbers.

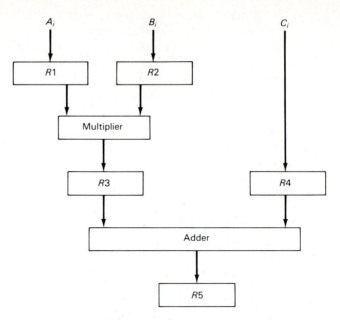

FIGURE 12-2
Example of Pipeline Processing

$$A_i * B_i + C_i \quad \text{for } i = 1,2,3, \ldots, 7$$

Each suboperation is to be implemented in a segment within a pipeline. Each segment has one or two registers and a combinational circuit as shown in Figure 12-2. $R1$ through $R5$ are registers that receive new data with every clock pulse. The multiplier and adder are combinational circuits (see Section 3-4). The suboperations performed in each segment of the pipeline are as follows:

$R1 \leftarrow A_i, R2 \leftarrow B_i$	Input A_i and B_i
$R3 \leftarrow R1 * R2, R4 \leftarrow C_i$	Multiply and input C_i
$R5 \leftarrow R3 + R4$	Add C_i to product

The five registers are loaded with new data every clock pulse. The effect of each clock pulse is shown in Table 12-1. It takes three clock pulses to fill up the pipe and retrieve the first output from $R5$. From there on, each clock pulse produces a new output and moves the data one step down the pipeline. This happens as long as new input data flow into the system. When no more input data are available, the clock pulses must continue until the last output emerges out of the pipeline.

Note that a pipeline processor performs simultaneous operations in each segment. No matter how many segments there are in the system, once the pipeline is full, it takes only one clock pulse to obtain an output, regardless of how many steps are required to execute the entire process. If the time it takes to process the suboperation in each segment is an interval t, and if there are k segments, then each complete computation is executed in $k \times t$ intervals. However, since successive

TABLE 12-1
Content of Registers in Pipeline Example

Pulse number	Segment 1		Segment 2		Segment 3
	R1	R2	R3	R4	R5
1	A_1	B_1	—	—	—
2	A_2	B_2	$A_1 * B_1$	C_1	—
3	A_3	B_3	$A_2 * B_2$	C_2	$A_1 * B_1 + C_1$
4	A_4	B_4	$A_3 * B_3$	C_3	$A_2 * B_2 + C_2$
5	A_5	B_5	$A_4 * B_4$	C_4	$A_3 * B_3 + C_3$
6	A_6	B_6	$A_5 * B_5$	C_5	$A_4 * B_4 + C_4$
7	A_7	B_7	$A_6 * B_6$	C_6	$A_5 * B_5 + C_5$
8	—	—	$A_7 * B_7$	C_7	$A_6 * B_6 + C_6$
9	—	—	—	—	$A_7 * B_7 + C_7$

operations are overlapped in the pipeline, the results are always delivered at every t interval after a setup time of $k \times t$ that it takes to fill up the pipeline.

Any operation that can be decomposed into a sequence of suboperations of about the same complexity can be implemented by a pipeline processor. The procedure is efficient only in those applications where the same computation must be repeated on a stream of input data. Pipeline data processing has been applied mostly to floating-point arithmetic operations.

Instruction Pipeline

Pipeline processing can occur not only in the data stream but in the instruction stream as well. An instruction pipeline reads consecutive instructions from memory while previous instructions are being executed in other segments. This causes the instruction fetch and execute phases to overlap and perform simultaneous operations. The only digression associated with such a scheme is that one of the instructions may cause a branch out of sequence. In that case, the pipeline must be emptied and all the instructions that have been read from memory after the branch instruction must be discarded.

An instruction pipeline can be implemented by means of a first-in first-out (FIFO) buffer. This is a type of unit that forms a queue rather than a stack. Whenever the execute phase is not using memory, the control increments the program counter and uses its address value to read consecutive instructions from memory. The instructions are inserted into the FIFO buffer so that they can be executed on a first-in first-out basis. Thus, an instruction stream can be placed in a queue, to wait for decoding and execution by the processor.

The instruction stream queuing mechanism provides an efficient way for reducing the average access time to memory for reading instructions. Whenever there is space in the FIFO buffer, the CPU executes an instruction fetch phase. The buffer acts as a queue from which control extracts instructions for execution. If the CPU executes an instruction that transfers control of a location out of normal sequence, the buffer is reset and the pipeline is declared empty. Control then fetches the instruction from the branch address and begins to refill the buffer from the new

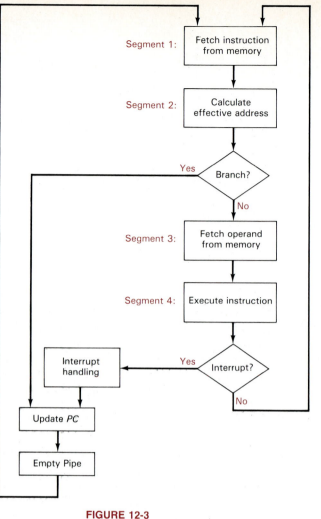

FIGURE 12-3
Four-segment CPU Pipeline

location. Often, branch instructions form a small fraction of the total number of instructions executed, so efficiency can be increased by this kind of instruction pipeline.

The instruction pipeline can be extended to include other phases in the CPU cycle. As an example, Figure 12-3 shows how the instruction cycle in the CPU can be processed with a four-segment pipeline. While an instruction is being executed in the processor, the next instruction in sequence is busy fetching an operand from memory. The effective address may be calculated in a separate arithmetic circuit for the third instruction and, whenever the memory is available, the fourth and all subsequent instructions can be fetched and placed in a FIFO instruction queue. Thus, up to four suboperations in the instruction cycle can overlap and up to four different instructions can be in process at the same time.

Once in a while, an instruction in the sequence may be a program control type that causes a branch out of normal sequence. In that case, the pending operations in the last two segments are completed and all information stored in the instruction buffer is deleted. The pipeline then restarts from the new address stored in the program counter. Similarly, an interrupt request, when acknowledged, will cause the pipeline to empty and start again from a new address value.

There are certain difficulties that will prevent the CPU pipeline from operating at its maximum rate. Different segments may take different times to operate on the incoming information. Some segments are skipped for certain operations. For example, a register mode instruction does not need an effective address calculation. Two or more segments may require memory access at the same time, causing one segment to wait until another is finished with the memory. Memory access conflicts are sometimes resolved by using a memory unit with multiple modules and storing the programs and data in separate modules. In this way, an instruction word and a data word can be read simultaneously from two different modules.

12-3   ASSOCIATIVE MEMORY

Many data processing applications require the search of items in a table stored in memory. The established way to search items in a table is to store all items where they can be addressed in sequence. The search procedure is a strategy for choosing a sequence of addresses, reading the content of memory at each address, and comparing the information read with the item being searched until a match occurs. The number of accesses to memory depends on the location of the item and the efficiency of the search algorithm. Many search algorithms have been developed to minimize the number of accesses while searching for an item in a random access memory.

The time required to find an item stored in memory can be reduced considerably if stored data can be identified for access by the content of the data itself rather than by an address. A memory unit accessed by content is called an *associative memory* or *content addressable memory*. This type of memory is accessed simultaneously and in parallel on the basis of data content. The memory is capable of finding an empty unused location to store a word. When a word is to be read from an associative memory, the content of the word, or part of the word, is specified. The memory locates the word that matches the specified content and marks it for reading.

Because of its organization, the associative memory is uniquely suited to do parallel searches by data association. Moreover, searches can be done on an entire word or on a specified field within a word. An associative memory is more expensive than a random access memory because each cell must have storage capability as well as logic circuits for matching its content with an external argument. For this reason, associative memories are used in applications where the search time is very critical and must be very short.

Hardware Organization

The block diagram of an associative memory is shown in Figure 12-4. It consists of a memory array and logic for m words of n bits per word. The argument register A has n bits, one for each bit of a word. The match register has m bits, one for

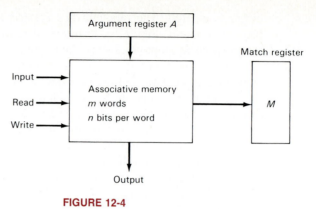

FIGURE 12-4
Block Diagram of Associative Memory

each word in memory. Each word is compared in parallel with the content of the argument register. The words that match the bits of the argument register set a corresponding bit in the match register. Reading is accomplished by a sequential access to memory for those words that have corresponding bits in the match register that have been set.

The internal organization of a typical binary cell consists of an elementary SR latch for storing the bit and the circuits for reading and writing as depicted in Figure 6-6 in Section 6-3. Additional circuits are needed for matching each word with the content of the argument register A. The match logic for each word can be derived from the comparison algorithm for two binary numbers. Let the bits of a word be designated by F_1, F_2, F_3, up to F_n, where n is the number of bits in the word. The content of the word will be equal to the argument in A if $A_i = F_i$ for $i = 1, 2, 3,$ ..., n. Two bits are equal if both are equal to 1 or if both are equal to 0. The equality of two bits can be expressed by the exclusive-NOR function

$$X_i = A_i F_i + \overline{A_i}\overline{F_i} = \overline{A_i \oplus F_i}$$

where $X_i = 1$ if the pair of bits in position i are equal and $X_i = 0$ if the two bits are not equal.

For a word to be equal to the argument in A we must have all X_i variables equal to 1. This is the condition for setting the corresponding match bit M_j to 1. The Boolean function for this condition is

$$M_j = X_1 X_2 X_3 \ldots X_n$$

and constitute an AND operation of all pairs of matched bits in word j.

The circuit for matching two words of four bits in an associative memory is shown in Figure 12-5. A_1 through A_4 are the bits from the argument register that must be compared. Each bit of A is compared with the corresponding bit of the memory in the same significant position. BC stands for binary cell and the comparison is done with an exclusive-NOR gate. The outputs of all exclusive-NOR gates belonging to the same word go to the inputs of a common AND gate to generate the match signal M_j for $j = 1, 2, 3, \ldots m$, where m is the number of words in the memory.

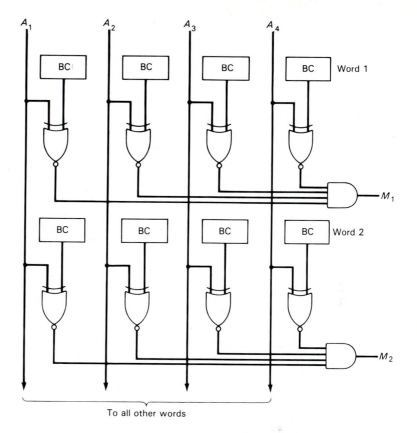

FIGURE 12-5
Match Logic for Two Words of Associative Memory

Read and Write Operations

If more than one word in the associative memory matches the argument value, all the matched words will have 1's in the corresponding bit position of the match register. It is then necessary to scan the bits of the match register one at a time. The matched words are read in sequence by applying a read signal to each word whose corresponding M bit is a 1.

In most applications, including applications in memory management hardware, the associative memory stores a table with no two identical items. In this case, only one word may match the argument value. By connecting output M_j directly to the read line of the same word (instead of the M register), the content of the matched word will be presented automatically at the outputs of the memory. Furthermore, if words having zero content are excluded, then an all zero output will indicate that no match occurred and that the searched item is not stored in memory.

An associative memory must have a write capability for storing the information to be searched. Since unwanted words have to be deleted and new words inserted one at a time, there is a need for a special register to distinguish between active and inactive words. This register, sometimes called a *tag register*, must have as many bits as there are words in memory. For every active word stored in memory, the corresponding bit in the tag register is set to 1. A word is deleted from memory by resetting its tag bit to 0. Words are stored in memory by scanning the tag register until the first 0 bit is encountered. This gives the first available inactive word and a position for writing a new word. After the new word is stored in memory it is made active by setting its tag bit to 1. An unwanted word when deleted from memory can be cleared to all 0's if this value is used to specify an empty location.

12-4   CACHE MEMORY

Analysis of a large number of typical programs has shown that references to memory at any given interval of time tends to be confined within a few localized areas in memory. This phenomenon is known as the *locality of reference*. The reason for this property may be understood considering that a typical computer program flows in a sequential fashion with program loops and subroutines encountered frequently. When a program loop is executed, the CPU repeatedly refers to the set of instructions in memory that constitute the loop. Every time a given subroutine is called, its set of instructions are fetched from memory. Thus loops and subroutines tend to localize the references to memory for fetching instructions. To a lesser degree, memory references to data also tend to be localized. Table lookup procedures repeatedly refer to a portion of memory where the table of items is stored. Iterative procedures refer to common memory locations and arrays of numbers confined within a local portion of memory. The result of all these observations is the locality of reference property which states that over a given interval of time, the addresses generated by a typical program refer to a few localized areas of memory repeatedly while the remaining of memory is accessed relatively infrequently.

If the active portion of the program and data are placed in a fast, small memory, the average memory access time can be reduced, thus reducing the total execution time of the program. As noted earlier, such a fast, small memory is referred to as a cache memory. It is placed between the CPU and main memory as illustrated in Fig. 12-1. The cache memory access time is less than the access time of main memory by a factor of 5 to 10. The cache is the fastest component in the memory hierarchy and approaches the speed of CPU components.

The basic operation of the cache is as follows. When the CPU needs to access memory, the cache is examined. If the word is found in the cache, it is read from the fast memory. If the word addressed by the CPU is not found in the cache, the main memory is accessed to read the word. A block of words containing the one just accessed is then transferred from main memory to cache memory. The block size may vary from one word (the one just accessed) to about 16 words adjacent to the one just accessed. In this manner, some data are transferred to cache so that future references to memory may find the required word in the fast cache.

The performance of cache memory is frequently measured in terms of a quantity called *hit ratio*. When the CPU refers to memory and finds the word in cache, it is said to produce a *hit*. If the word is not found in cache, then it is in main memory and it counts as a *miss*. The ratio of the number of hits divided by the total CPU references to memory (hits plus misses) is the hit ratio. The hit ratio is measured

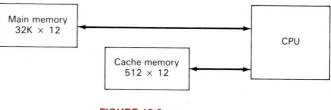

FIGURE 12-6
Example of Cache Memory

experimentally by running representative programs in the computer and measuring the number of hits and misses during a given interval of time. Hit ratios of 0.9 and higher have been reported. This high ratio verifies the validity of the locality of reference property.

The basic characteristic of cache memory is its fast access time. Therefore, very little time is wasted when searching for words in cache. The transformation of data from main memory to cache memory is referred to as a *mapping* process. Three types of mapping procedures are of practical interest in considering the organization of cache memory.

1. Associative mapping.
2. Direct mapping.
3. Set-associative mapping.

To help in the discussion of these three mapping procedures, we will use a specific example of a memory organization shown in Figure 12-6. The main memory can store 32K words of 12 bits each. The cache is capable of storing 512 of these words at any given time. For every word stored in cache, there is a duplicate copy in main memory. The CPU communicates with both memories. It first sends a 15-bit address to cache. If there is a hit, the CPU accepts the 12-bit data word from cache. If there is a miss, the CPU reads the word from main memory and the word is then transferred to cache.

Associative Mapping

The fastest and the most flexible cache organization uses an associative memory. This organization is illustrated in Fig. 12-7. The associative memory stores both the address and content (data) of the memory word. This permits any location in cache to store any word from main memory . The diagram shows three words stored in cache. The address value of 15 bits is shown as a 5-digit octal number and its corresponding 12-bit data word is shown as a 4-digit octal number. A CPU address of 15 bits is placed in the argument register and the associative memory is searched for a matching address. If the address is found, the corresponding 12-bit data is read and sent to the CPU. If no match occurs, the main memory is accessed for the word. The address-data pair is then transferred to the associative cache memory. If the cache is full, an address-data pair must be displaced to make room for a pair that is needed but is not presently in the cache. The decision concerning what pair to replace is determined from the replacement algorithm that

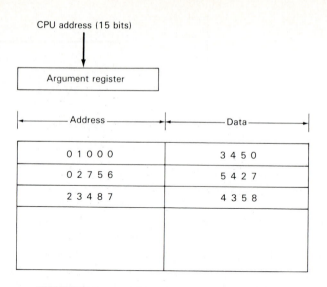

CPU address (15 bits)

Argument register

|—————— Address ——————|—————— Data ——————|

Address	Data
0 1 0 0 0	3 4 5 0
0 2 7 5 6	5 4 2 7
2 3 4 8 7	4 3 5 8

FIGURE 12-7
Associative Mapping Cache (All Numbers are in Octal)

the designer chooses for the cache. A simple procedure is to replace the words in cache in round-robin order whenever a new word is requested from main memory. This constitutes a first-in first-out (FIFO) replacement policy.

Direct Mapping

Associative memories are expensive compared to random-access memories because of the added logic associated with each cell. The possibility of using a random-access memory for the cache is investigated in Figure 12-8. The CPU address of 15 bits is divided into two fields. The nine low-order bits constitute the *index* field and the remaining six bits form the *tag* field. The figure shows that main memory needs an address that includes both the tag and the index bits. The number of bits in the index field is equal to the number of address bits required to access the cache memory.

In the general case, there are 2^k words in cache memory and 2^n in main memory. The n-bit memory address is divided into two fields: k bits for the index field and $n - k$ bits for the tag field. The direct mapping cache organization uses the n-bit address to access the main memory and the k-bit index to access cache. The internal organization of the words in cache memory is as shown in Figure 12-9(b). Each word in cache consists of the data word and its associated tag. When a new word is first brought into the cache, the tag bits are stored alongside the data bits. When the CPU generates a memory request, the index field is used for the address to access the cache. The tag field of the CPU address is compared with the tag field in the word read from cache. If the two tags match, there is a hit and the desired data word is in cache. If there is no match, there is a miss and the required word is read from main memory. It is then stored in the cache together with the new tag, replacing the previous value.

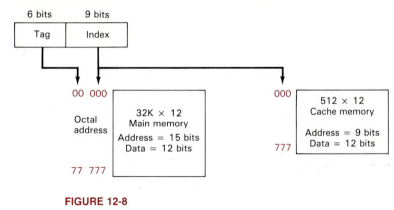

FIGURE 12-8
Addressing Relationships Between Main Memory and Cache

The disadvantage of direct mapping is that the hit ratio may drop considerably if two or more words with addresses having the same index but different tags are accessed repeatedly. However, this possibility is minimized by the fact that such words are relatively far apart in the address range (multiples of 512 locations in this example).

To see how the direct mapping scheme operates, consider the numerical example shown in Figure 12-9. The word at address zero is presently stored in cache (index = 000, tag = 00, data = 1220). Suppose that the CPU now wants to access the word at address 02000. The index address is 000, so it is used to access the cache. The two tags are then compared. The cache tag is 00 but the address tag is 02, which does not produce a match. Therefore, the main memory is accessed and the data word 5670 is transferred to the CPU. The cache word at index address 000 is then replaced with a tag of 02 and data of 5670.

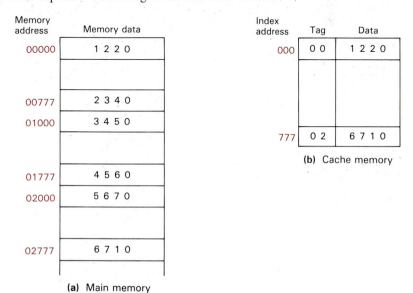

FIGURE 12-9
Direct Mapping Cache Organization

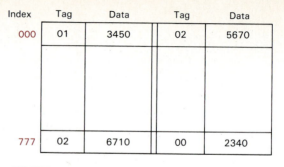

Index	Tag	Data	Tag	Data
000	01	3450	02	5670
777	02	6710	00	2340

FIGURE 12-10
Set Associative Mapping Cache with Set Size of Two

Set-Associative Mapping

It was mentioned previously that the disadvantage of direct mapping is that two words with the same index but with different tag values cannot reside in cache at the same time. A third type of cache organization, called set-associative mapping, is an improvement over the direct mapping organization in that each word of cache can store two or more words of memory under the same index address. Each data word is stored together with its tag, and the number of tag-data items in one word of cache is said to form a set. An example of a set-associative cache organization for a set size of two is shown in Figure 12-10. Each index address refers to two data words and their associated tags. Each tag requires six bits and each data word has 12 bits, so the word length is $2(6 + 12) = 36$ bits. An index address of nine bits can accommodate 512 words. Thus, the size of cache memory is 512×36. It can accommodate 1024 words of main memory since each word of cache contains two data words. In general, a set-associative cache of set size k will accommodate k words of main memory in each word of cache.

The octal numbers listed in Figure 12-10 refer to the main memory contents illustrated in Figure 12-9(a). The words stored at addresses 01000 and 02000 of main memory are stored in cache memory at index address 000. Similarly, the words at addresses 02777 and 00777 are stored in cache at index address 777. When the CPU generates a memory request, the index value of the address is used to access the cache. The tag field of the CPU address is then compared with both tags in the cache to determine if a match occurs. The comparison logic is done by an associative search of the tags in the set similar to an associative memory search, hence the name set-associative. The hit ratio will improve as the set size increases because more words with the same index but different tags can reside in cache. An increase in the set size increases the number of bits in the words of cache and requires more complex comparison logic.

12-5 VIRTUAL MEMORY MANAGEMENT

In a memory hierarchy system, programs and data are first stored in auxiliary memory. Portions of a program or data are brought into main memory as they are needed by the CPU. *Virtual memory* is a concept used in some computer systems that permits the user to construct his program as though he had a large memory space, equal to the total of auxiliary memory. Each address that is referenced by the CPU goes through an address mapping from the so-called virtual or logical address to a physical address in main memory. Virtual memory is used to give the programmer the illusion that he has a very large memory at his disposal, even though the computer may have a relatively small main memory. A virtual memory system provides a mechanism for translating program generated addresses into corresponding main memory locations. This is done dynamically, while programs are being executed in the CPU. The translation or mapping is handled automatically by the hardware by means of mapping tables.

In a multiprogramming environment where many programs reside in memory, it becomes necessary to move programs and data around in memory, to vary the amount of memory in use by a given program, and to prevent a program from changing other programs. The demands on computer memory brought about by multiprogramming have created the need for a memory management system. A memory management system is a collection of hardware and software procedures for managing the various programs residing in memory. The memory management software is part of an overall operating system available in the computer. Here we are concerned with the hardware unit associated with the memory management system.

Address Space and Memory Space

The address used by a program is called a virtual or *logical address*, and the set of such addresses is referred to as the *address space*. An address in main memory is called a location or *physical address*. The set of such locations is called the *memory space*. The address space is the set of addresses generated by the operating system for programs as they reference instructions and data. The memory space consists of the actual memory locations directly addressable for processing. In most computers the address and memory spaces are identical. The address space is allowed to be larger than the memory space in computers with virtual memory.

As an illustration, consider a computer with main memory capacity of 64K words. Sixteen bits are needed to specify a physical address in memory since 64K $= 2^{16}$. Suppose that the computer has available auxiliary memory for storing $2^{20} = 1024$K words. The auxiliary memory has a capacity of storing information equivalent to 16 memories since 64K $\times$ 16 $=$ 1024K.

The address mapping from address space to physical space can be simplified if the addresses are divided into groups of fixed size. The logical memory is broken down into groups of equal size called *pages*. The term *block* or *page frame* refers to groups of equal size in physical memory. For example, if a page or block consists of 1K words then, using the previous example, address space is divided into 1024 pages and main memory is divided into 64 blocks. Although both a page and a block are split into groups of 1K words, a page refers to the organization of address space, while a block refers to the organization of memory space. The programs are also considered to be split into pages. Portions of programs are moved from auxiliary memory to main memory in records equal to the size of a page.

Memory management systems divide programs and data into logical parts called *segments*. A segment may be generated by the programmer or by the operating system. Examples of segments are subroutines, arrays of data, tables of items, or users' programs.

Dynamic Address Translation

In many applications, the logical address space uses variable length segments. The length of each segment is allowed to grow or contract according to the needs of the program being executed. One way of specifying the length of a segment is by associating with it a number of equal size pages. To see how this is done, consider the logical address shown in Figure 12-11. The logical address is partitioned into three fields. The segment field specifies a segment number. The page field specifies the page within the segment, and the offset field gives the specific word within the page. A page field of k bits can specify up to 2^k pages and a segment field of m bits can specify up to 2^m segments. Each segment may be associated with just one page or with as many as 2^k pages. The length of a segment may vary according to the number of pages that are assigned to it.

A numerical example may clarify the assignment of a logical address. Consider a logical address of 20 bits with 4 bits assigned to the segment field, 8 bits to the page field, and the remaining 8 bits to the offset field. The 4-bit segment can specify 16 different segments. The 8-bit page number can specify up to 256 pages, and the 8-bit offset implies a page size of 256 words. This configuration allows each segment to have any number of pages up to 256. The smallest possible segment will have one page of 256 words. The largest possible segment will have 256 pages for a total of $256 \times 256 = 64K$ words.

The mapping of the logical address into a physical address is done by means of two tables, as shown in Figure 12-11. The segment number of the logical address specifies an address for the segment table. The entry in the segment table is a pointer address for a page table base. The page table base is added to the page

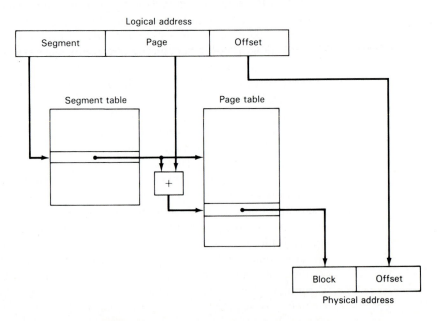

FIGURE 12-11
Address Translation in a Memory Management System

number given in the logical address. The sum produces a pointer address to an entry in the page table. The value in the page table provides the block number in physical memory. The concatenation of the block number with the offset produces the final physical mapped address.

The two mapping tables may be stored in two separate small memories or in main memory. In either case, a memory reference from the CPU will require three accesses to memory: one from the segment table, one from the page table, and one from main memory. This will slow the system significantly, compared to a conventional system that requires only one reference to memory. To avoid this speed penalty, a fast associative memory is used to hold the most recently referenced table entries. (This memory is sometimes called a translation lookaside buffer abbreviated TLB.) The first time a given block is referenced, its value together with the corresponding segment and page numbers are entered into the associative memory. Thus, the mapping process is first attempted by associative search with the given segment and page numbers. If it succeeds, the mapping delay is only that of the associative memory. If no match occurs, the slower table mapping procedure is used and the result transformed into the associative memory for future reference.

REFERENCES

1. MANO, M. M. *Computer System Architecture.* 2nd ed. Englewood Cliffs: Prentice-Hall, 1982.

2. HANLON, A. G. "Content-Addressable and Associative Memory Systems: A Survey." *IEEE Trans. on Electronic Computers.* EC-15 (Aug. 1966): 509–521.

3. BELL, J., CASASENT, D., AND BELL, C. G. "An Investigation of Alternative Cache Organizations." *IEEE Trans. on Computers.* C-23(Apr. 1974): 346–351.

4. DENNING, P. J. "Virtual Memory." *Computing Surveys.* (Sept. 1970): 153–187.

5. HAMACHER, V. C., VRANESIC, Z. G., AND ZAKY, S. G. *Computer Organization.* 2nd ed. New York: McGraw-Hill, 1984.

6. TANENBAUM, A. S. *Structure Computer Organization.* 2nd ed. Englewood Cliffs: Prentice-Hall, 1984

PROBLEMS

12-1 Explain the need for auxiliary memory devices. How are they different from main memory and from other peripheral devices?

12-2 Explain the need for memory hierarchy. What is the main reason for not having a large enough main memory for storing all the available information in a computer system?

12-3 Define multiprogramming and explain the function of a memory management unit in computers that use the multiprogramming organization.

12-4 In certain scientific computations it is necessary to perform the arithmetic operation $(A_i + B_i)(C_i + D_i)$ with a stream of numbers. Specify a pipeline configuration to carry out this task. List the contents of all registers in the pipeline for $i = 1$ through 6.

12-5 Obtain the complement function for the match logic of one word in an associative memory. In other words, show that the complement of M_j is obtained from the logical sum of exclusive-OR functions. Draw the logic diagram for $\overline{M}_j$ and terminate it with an inverter to obtain M_j.

12-6 Obtain the Boolean function for the match logic of one word in an associative memory taking into consideration a tag bit that indicates whether the word is active or inactive.

12-7 A digital computer has a memory unit of 64K $\times$ 16 and a cache memory of 1K words. The cache uses direct mapping.
(a) How many bits are there in the tag and index fields of the address?
(b) How many bits are there in each word of the cache, and how are they divided into functions?

12-8 A set-associative mapping cache has a set size of 2. The cache can accommodate a total of 2048 words from main memory. The main memory size is 128K $\times$ 32.
(a) Formulate all pertinent information required to construct the cache memory.
(b) What is the size of the cache memory?

12-9 The access time of a cache memory is 100 nsec and that of main memory 1000 nsec. The hit ratio is 0.9. What is the average access time of the system?

12-10 An address space is specified by 24 bits and the corresponding memory space by 16 bits.
(a) How many words are there in the address space?
(b) How many words in the memory space?
(c) If a page consists of 2K words, how many pages and blocks are there in the system?

12-11 The logical address space in a computer system consists of 128 segments. Each segment can have up to 32 pages of 4K words in each. Physical memory consists of 4K blocks of 4K words in each. Formulate the logical and physical address formats.

12-12 Give the binary number of the logical address formulated in Problem 12-11 for segment 36 and word number 2000 in page 15.

INDEX